onald's Pool on the *Fantasy.* You can see
ıe AquaDuck waterslide and Mickey's Pool
ı the background. (Photo: Laurel Stewart)

The *Magic*'s Twist 'n' Spout waterslide
(Photo: Len Testa)

ːhe *Fantasy*'s dedicated teen pool at
'ibe youth club (Photo: Erin Foster)

The *Fantasy*'s AquaLab splash area
(Photo: Ricky Brigante)

ıuests on the *Dream* and *Fantasy* can play
ıoofy-themed minigolf on Deck 13.
ᵓhoto: Laurel Stewart)

The decor gets spooky on Halloween cruises.
(Photo: Erin Foster)

he *Fantasy*'s adult pool at night
Photo: Laurel Stewart)

The *Magic*'s Quiet Cove Pool at night
(Photo: Laurel Stewart)

On Marvel Days at Sea, you might find Black Panther roaming around the ship. (Photo: Peter Couture)

Star Wars cruises have special guests from all parts of the universe. (Photo: Jon Norberg)

Vibe is the ships' teen hangout. This is the *Dream*'s version. (Photo: Erin Foster)

There's a quiet room just for napping at It's a Small World Nursery. (Photo: Erin Foster)

Monsters Academy, the *Monsters, Inc.*–themed play area in the Oceaneer Club on the *Dream* and the *Fantasy* (Photo: Laurel Stewart)

All four ships' Oceaneer Clubs feature Andy's Room, a Toy Story–themed play area. (Photo: Laurel Stewart)

The Walt Disney Theatre hosts major events and stage shows. (Photo: Jon Norberg)

Disney characters greet guests during every cruise. (Photo: Erin Foster)

'he brunch buffet at Palo includes a dessert able that shouldn't be missed. Photo: Erin Foster)

Cabanas buffet, found on all four ships, is a great place for breakfast and lunch. (Photo: Laurel Stewart)

'iana's Place on the *Wonder* serves Southern-style cuisine with Louisiana Creole flair. Photo: Laurel Stewart)

Big-city vistas unfold behind the bar at Skyline Lounge on the *Dream.* (Photo: Laurel Stewart)

Rapunzel's Royal Table is the newest estaurant on the *Magic*. (Photo: Scott Sanders/)isneyCruiseLineBlog.com)

Adult-beverage tastings are available on all DCL sailings. (Photo: Erin Foster)

'he *Fantasy*'s Enchanted Garden has lush atmosphere. (Photo: Laurel Stewart)

All four ships have Animator's Palate, where you experience the joy of Disney animation while you eat. (Photo: Erin Foster)

All four ships have fitness centers equipped with a wide range of cardio and weight machines. (Photo: Erin Foster)

Senses Spa offers a variety of massage options for singles and couples. (Photo: Erin Foster)

Deluxe Oceanview Stateroom with Verandah on the *Dream* (Photo: Scott Sanders/ DisneyCruiseLineBlog.com)

With their large portholes, Oceanview staterooms can feel just as airy as Verandah rooms—often at a much lower cost. (Photo: Erin Foster)

Many family staterooms include hidden bunk beds for children. (Photo: Erin Foster)

Your stateroom attendant will leave surprise visitors in your cabin each evening. (Photos: Erin Foster)

Castaway Cay's Pelican Plunge is a floating platform of fun.
(Photo: Scott Smith)

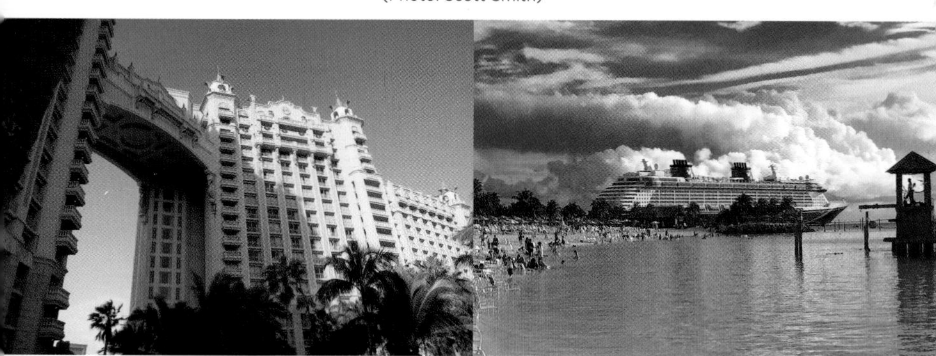

Nassau's Atlantis resort is the site of many Bahamian port adventures. (Photo: Erin Foster)

Cruisers enjoy the still waters of Castaway Cay's protected bay with the *Dream* in the distance. (Photo: Laurel Stewart)

Cabana guests at Castaway Cay enjoy their own dedicated beach area.
(Photo: Laurel Stewart)

Castaway Cay mixes expert theming, like that at Conched Out bar, with the natural beauty of the Caribbean. (Photo: Laurel Stewart)

The *Magic* docks at Akershus, Norway. (Photo: Erin Foster)

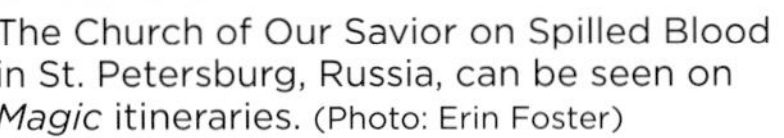

The Church of Our Savior on Spilled Blood in St. Petersburg, Russia, can be seen on *Magic* itineraries. (Photo: Erin Foster)

Canadian Coastline cruises visit charming fishing villages. (Photo: Erin Foster)

Mush! Dogsledding in Alaska (Photo: Erin Foster)

On this Adventures by Disney (AbD) Rhine River cruise, you can canoe through the center of a lovely French village. (Photo: Erin Foster)

Monte Carlo is an easy stop on many Mediterranean cruises. (Photo: Erin Foster)

AmaWaterways' *AmaViola* river-cruise ship is used by AbD. (Photo: Erin Foster)

An AbD river cruise tours Danube country. (Photo: Erin Foster)

THE *unofficial* GUIDE® to Disney Cruise Line

2019

COME CHECK US OUT!

Supplement your valuable guidebook with tips, news, and deals by visiting our websites:

theunofficialguides.com
touringplans.com

Sign up for the Unofficial Guide newsletter for even more travel tips and special offers.

Join the conversation on social media:

@theUGSeries

theUnofficialGuides

theUGSeries

theUGSeries

#theUGseries

Other Unofficial Guides

The Disneyland Story: The Unofficial Guide to the Evolution of Walt Disney's Dream

Universal vs. Disney: The Unofficial Guide to American Theme Parks' Greatest Rivalry

The Unofficial Guide Color Companion to Walt Disney World

The Unofficial Guide to Disneyland

The Unofficial Guide to Las Vegas

The Unofficial Guide to Mall of America

The Unofficial Guide to Universal Orlando

The Unofficial Guide to Walt Disney World

The Unofficial Guide to Washington, DC

THE *unofficial* GUIDE® TO Disney Cruise Line

2019

ERIN FOSTER with
LEN TESTA and RITCHEY HALPHEN

Please note that prices fluctuate and information changes owing to many factors that influence the travel industry. We therefore suggest that you write or call ahead for confirmation when making your travel plans. Every effort has been made to ensure the accuracy of information throughout this book, and the contents of this publication are believed to be correct at the time of printing. Nevertheless, the publishers cannot accept responsibility for errors or omissions, for changes in details given in this guide, or for the consequences of any reliance on the information provided by the same. Assessments of attractions, restaurants, and the like are subjective and may not reflect the publisher's opinion or readers' experiences. We welcome ideas, comments, and suggestions from readers for future editions.

The Unofficial Guides
An imprint of AdventureKEEN
2204 First Ave. S., Ste. 102
Birmingham, AL 35233
theunofficialguides.com, facebook.com/theunofficialguides, twitter.com/theugseries

Managing editor: Ritchey Halphen
Editor: Lisa C. Bailey
Cover and color-insert design: Scott McGrew
Text design: Vertigo Design, with updates by Annie Long
Maps and illustrations: Steve Jones
Proofreaders: Laura Franck, Susan Roberts McWilliams
Indexer: Sylvia Coates

Cover photo: The *Disney Dream* readies for a day at Castaway Cay, Disney Cruise Line's private island in the Bahamas. Photo © Erin Foster

For information on our other products and services or to obtain technical support, please contact us from within the United States at 888-604-4537 or by fax at 205-326-1012.

AdventureKEEN also publishes its books in a variety of electronic formats. Some content that appears in print may not be available in electronic formats.

ISBN-13: 978-1-62809-091-8; eISBN: 978-1-62809-092-5

Distributed by Publishers Group West

Manufactured in the United States of America

5 4 3 2 1

CONTENTS

LIST *of* MAPS *and* DIAGRAMS

ABOUT *the* AUTHORS

ERIN FOSTER researched and responded to more than 11,000 guest questions as a charter member of the official Disney Parks Moms Panel. Erin has visited Disneyland; Disneyland Paris; Disney Vacation Club properties in Hilton Head, South Carolina, and Hawaii; Hong Kong Disneyland; and Walt Disney World. She has also traveled on Disney Cruise Line voyages throughout the world and taken Adventures by Disney (AbD) journeys on four continents, including AbD ocean-cruise supplements and river cruises. When Erin isn't traveling, you can find her attending Broadway and off-Broadway shows with her husband and three young-adult daughters.

LEN TESTA is the coauthor of the Unofficial Guides series, covering Walt Disney World and Disneyland, Las Vegas, Universal Orlando, and Washington, DC. While Len has published works in travel, computer science, and endocrinology, it's widely acknowledged that he's just the pretty face for a group of people way more talented than he is (and "pretty face" is a stretch at best). Len sends love to his daughter, Hannah.

RITCHEY HALPHEN is an editor at AdventureKEEN, publisher of the Unofficial Guides. His only cruise so far has been on Norwegian Cruise Line's late lamented SS *Norway,* originally the French Line's SS *France*. A Disney cruise is on his bucket list—for research purposes, of course.

ACKNOWLEDGMENTS

MANY THANKS TO MY HUSBAND, JEFF, and daughters, Josie, Louisa, and Charlie, for always reminding me to take photos of the stateroom before we settle in. Additional thanks to the team at TouringPlans.com for their unfailing support and kindness. And I am always grateful to the women and men of the Disney Parks Moms Panel for sharing their all-encompassing knowledge of all things Disney. Special thanks to Kirsten Etmanski of Pure Magic Vacations for her detailed understanding of the booking nuances of Disney Cruise Line and Adventures by Disney, and to Scott Sanders of the Disney Cruise Line Blog for sharing his expertise on all things DCL.

This edition is dedicated to the memory of Emma Couture, an extraordinary Disney fan and an extraordinary person. *—Erin Foster*

IT TOOK A LIFEBOAT FULL OF PEOPLE to produce this book and its companion web content. David Davies created our website for Disney Cruise Line (DCL) information, wrote the Fare Tracker tool, and lent an expert eye to the proofreading of the text. Thanks also to Emily and Isabelle Sanders for testing the waterslides with us.

DCL kids' club research was carried out by Alex Duncan, "Captain" Kieran Duncan, Jacklyn Scirica, and Hannah Testa. Kelsey and Kathy Lubetich bravely navigated the waters and lumberjacks of Alaska for that coverage. Thanks also to Tammy Whiting of Storybook Destinations, Beci Mahnken and Stephanie Hudson of Mouse Fan Travel, and Sue Pisaturo and Lynne Amodeo of Small World Vacations for their help in determining cruise-pricing trends. Much respect to Matt Hochberg of RoyalCaribbeanBlog.com for his comparison of DCL and Royal Caribbean. *—Len Testa*

THANKS TO THE CREW who helped this book come together: my good buddy Lisa Bailey, who edited this edition for the third year in a row; Annie Long, our indefatigable typesetter; Steve Jones, who produced the maps and diagrams; Scott McGrew, who designed the cover and the color insert; and Sylvia Coates, who prepared the index. *—Ritchey Halphen*

INTRODUCTION

ABOUT *This* GUIDE

WHY "UNOFFICIAL"?

THE MATERIAL HEREIN originated with the authors and has not been reviewed, edited, or approved by the Walt Disney Company, Inc., or Disney Cruise Line (DCL). To the contrary, we represent and serve you, the consumer: if a ship serves mediocre food or has subpar entertainment, we say so. Through our independence, we hope that we can make selecting a cruise efficient and economical and help make your cruise experience on-target and fun.

Toward that end, our *unofficial* guide offers the following:

- Our recommendations for which ship to choose for your first cruise
- How to find the perfect itinerary, including specific cruises and dates
- When to book your cruise to get the cheapest fares
- What to pack, including travel documents for you and your children
- Color photos from throughout the ships, along with diagrams of the decks and staterooms
- Unbiased reviews of onboard restaurants, live entertainment, and nightlife
- The best family activities, including children's clubs, family games, outdoor sports, and more
- Where and when to meet Disney characters on board
- Full coverage of Disney's private island, Castaway Cay, along with ports and shore excursions
- Tips on how to choose the best stateroom for your needs
- Comparisons of Disney Cruise Line vacations to Royal Caribbean cruise vacations, Walt Disney World vacations, and Adventures by Disney river-cruise vacations

DISNEY CRUISE LINE: *An Overview*

IN 1998 THE WALT DISNEY COMPANY LAUNCHED—literally—its own cruise line with the 2,400-passenger **Disney Magic.** An almost identical ship, the **Disney Wonder,** entered service in 1999. Two larger ships, the **Disney Dream** and the **Disney Fantasy,** joined the fleet in 2011 and 2012, respectively.

unofficial **TIP**
Because DCL ships' decor and entertainment are based almost entirely on Disney films and characters, we don't recommend a Disney cruise to anyone who isn't at least mildly fond of Mickey and the gang.

In starting a cruise line, Disney put together a team of respected industry veterans, dozens of the world's best-known ship designers, and its own unrivaled creative talent. Together, they created the DCL ships, recognizing that even the smallest detail would be critical to the line's success.

The result? They succeeded, starting with the ships' appearance: simultaneously classic and innovative. Exteriors are traditional, reminiscent of the great ocean liners of the past, but even here you'll find a Disney twist or two. Inside, the ships feature up-to-the-minute technology and are brimming with novel ideas for dining, entertainment, and cabin design. Even Disney's exclusive cruise terminal at Port Canaveral, Florida, is part of the overall strategy, aiming to make even embarking and disembarking enjoyable.

For Port Canaveral and Miami cruises, Disney's private Bahamian island, **Castaway Cay,** was chosen to avoid the hassle of tendering. As for dining, Disney practically reinvented the concept for cruises when it introduced rotational dining (see Part Seven), where each evening you not only dine in a different restaurant with a different motif, but your waiters and dining companions also move with you.

DISNEY CRUISE LINE SHIPS IN A NUTSHELL

	Disney Magic	*Disney Wonder*	*Disney Dream*	*Disney Fantasy*
YEAR LAUNCHED	1998	1999	2011	2012
CAPACITY				
PASSENGERS (maximum)	2,713	2,713	4,000	4,000
CREW	950	950	1,458	1,458
TOTAL CAPACITY	3,663	3,663	5,458	5,458
PASSENGER DECKS	11	11	14	14
STATEROOMS				
INSIDE	256	256	150	150
OCEANVIEW	362	362	199	199
OUTSIDE VERANDAH	259	259	901	901
TOTAL STATEROOMS	877	877	1,250	1,250
THEME	Art Deco	Art Nouveau	Art Deco	Art Nouveau

The foundation of DCL's business is built on Bahamian and Caribbean cruises out of Port Canaveral, about 90 minutes from Walt Disney World, and Miami. Disney also offers Alaskan, Canadian, European, and Pacific cruises, as well as repositioning cruises. Other departure ports include Barcelona, Spain; Copenhagen, Denmark; Dover, England; Galveston, Texas; New Orleans; New York City; San Diego; San Juan, Puerto Rico; and Vancouver, Canada.

Bahamian cruises originating in Port Canaveral and Miami make at least one port call at Castaway Cay. DCL's Alaskan and European itineraries are well conceived and interesting; by comparison, its Bahamian and Caribbean itineraries are unimaginative and prosaic, but they're still good for first-time cruisers.

ON DECK: NEW SHIPS

DISNEY CRUISE LINE IS EXPANDING. Three as-yet-unnamed vessels, anticipated to launch in 2021, 2022, and 2023, are being constructed by Meyer Werft—the same shipyard that built the *Dream* and the *Fantasy*—and are expected to be slightly larger than the *Dream*-class ships, with about the same number of staterooms, indicating possibly larger staterooms or expanded entertainment areas. Here are the few specifics that we know at press time:

The ships will run on liquefied natural gas (LNG), the most environmentally friendly option available. The ships' hull numbers are **s.705** for Ship 5, which will debut in 2021; **s.718** for Ship 6, which will debut in 2022; and **s.706** for Ship 7, which will debut in 2023.

Disney is working with Port Canaveral to create terminal and dock space for two of the new LNG-powered ships. This indicates that Disney expects at least three of the eventual seven-ship fleet to be based at Port Canaveral at least part of the year, with the other ships' home ports located outside central Florida. (One rumor, reported by the *Miami Herald* in late 2018, has at least one of the *Dream*-class ships sailing from a year-round home port in Miami beginning in 2023.)

Disney is also negotiating with the Bahamian government to develop part of the 700-acre **Lighthouse Beach,** on the island of Eleuthera about 132 miles southeast of Disney's Castaway Cay. Besides providing a second exclusive stop in the Bahamas, Lighthouse Beach is up to 50 feet above sea level, which gives Disney a long-term hedge against rising oceans due to climate change. (In comparison, Castaway Cay is only about 6 feet above sea level—the approximate height by which pessimistic climate models predict oceans will have risen by the time Disney's 99-year lease on the island expires at the end of the century.)

Beyond all of this, details are scarce, but hey, it's fun to speculate: What will the new ships be named? Will they offer more suites, similar to other cruise lines? Will DCL venture into sailing in the Asian or Australian markets? How will the ships be decorated? How will the dining and entertainment offerings differ from those of the existing fleet?

The introduction of new ships also raises questions about the current Disney ships, particularly the *Magic* and *Wonder.* These first members of the fleet are now 20 years old—an age at which cruise ships tend to be retired, repurposed, or sold to a smaller line. Are the new ships a sign that drastic changes are ahead for the *Magic* and *Wonder*? Will they become less popular with other, newer Disney options? Will they be substantially rethemed at some point?

The list of questions is endless, but real answers likely won't be coming until early 2020, when sales will likely begin for sailings during the first half of 2021.

IS DISNEY CRUISE LINE RIGHT FOR ME?

MANY TRAVELERS, particularly adults traveling without children, may wonder if they'll enjoy a Disney Cruise Line vacation. It's a legitimate concern: Disney charges a premium for its voyages, particularly in the Caribbean, banking on brand loyalty and its reputation for high-quality family experiences.

Obviously, we're fans. We (Erin and Len) have more than 30 Disney cruises between us, and we keep booking more. But we do concede that there are many other fine options for cruise vacations—some of which may fit your needs and tastes better than DCL.

- If you're looking for the *ne plus ultra* in cruise-ship technology, choose **Royal Caribbean.** Its megaships are marvels.
- If you're looking for a sedate cruise experience, with relatively few children and younger families, choose **Holland America.**
- If you're looking for an all-out luxury experience, choose **Viking** or another European river-cruise company.
- If you wanna rock-and-roll all night and party every day, choose **Carnival.**
- If you're looking for that sweet spot between family-friendly and upscale, choose **Celebrity.**
- If you're accustomed to your valet carrying your steamer trunk for you, choose **Cunard.**
- If you're looking for Disney service on a smaller, more intimate scale, choose an **Adventures by Disney** river cruise. See Part 13, page 401, for details.

Disney offers great service, has some of the most attractive ships sailing, and goes out of its way to make sure everyone has a great time. While other cruise lines may be better in some areas, DCL gets among the most consistently strong marks across all categories.

DCL'S TARGET MARKET

DISNEY CRUISES ARE TAILORED to families who are new to cruising. But like the theme parks, the cruise line is a Disney product for kids of all ages. Each ship has at least one alternative restaurant, swimming pool, and nightclub just for adults.

Initially, cruise experts questioned whether Disney could fill its ships when kids are in school, but Disney determined that if 1%–2% of the estimated 40 million annual visitors to its resorts and parks bought a Disney cruise vacation, the ships would sell out. Disney was right, and after nearly 20 years of success, no one is questioning them.

COMPETITORS AND PRICES

DCL USES ITS REPUTATION for high quality, service, and entertainment to dispel novices' doubts about cruise vacations. Disney's main competitor is **Royal Caribbean International,** which offers Caribbean, Mediterranean, and Alaskan cruises similar to Disney's, with most of the same departure and destination ports. The two cruise lines often

A ROYAL CARIBBEAN FAN SPEAKS OUT

INSPIRED BY SEEING the lovely Barbi Benton on a rerun of *Fantasy Island,* we asked our good friend MATT HOCHBERG from RoyalCaribbeanBlog.com to weigh in on the differences between DCL and Royal Caribbean. A lifelong Disney fan who has run Disney-related podcasts and websites for more than a decade, Matt has an in-depth perspective on both cruise lines.

EVEN DISNEY CRUISE LINE FANS AGREE that Royal Caribbean offers a great family vacation at a fraction of Disney's prices. But beyond that, Royal Caribbean became my family's preferred cruise choice for a few simple reasons: more ships, more destinations, more latest-and-greatest cruising innovations, and more dining choices.

Where DCL has just 4 ships in its fleet (with 3 more to come after 2021), Royal Caribbean has 24, with another 5 currently under construction. More ships mean more destinations to visit and more ports to choose from. So while Royal and Disney both sail to the Caribbean, Alaska, Northern Europe, and the Mediterranean, only Royal goes to Australia, China, and other destinations. What's more, Royal offers many cruises to these places, not just one per year.

Royal also pushes the envelope in terms of what guests can do on board—surfing lessons, bumper cars, rock walls, zip lines, and ice skating—while the DCL ships don't.

Families often think of DCL as a no-brainer because of its programming for children, but Royal Caribbean's kids' offerings are getting steadily better. Each new ship has more space dedicated to children and more programming options than the one before. Adventure Ocean, Royal Caribbean's youth program, provides supervised games, events, and activities throughout the day and evening. Of course, there are all the fun onboard activities listed earlier for kids to enjoy, in addition to enhanced kids-only facilities and programming on select Royal Caribbean ships.

When it comes to theme parks, there's definitely a quality difference between Disney and the competition. But when it comes to cruising, I think Disney and Royal Caribbean are much more similar than they are different. If you find the idea of a Disney cruise appealing, you should also consider Royal Caribbean. I think they're equally engaging—and Royal Caribbean is a far better value.

have ships departing within days—sometimes hours—of each other, headed mostly to the same places.

Beyond staterooms, you'll find everything from bars and lounges to small art galleries, expansive spas, dedicated shopping areas, and specialty restaurants on both cruise lines. Here's how those offerings, plus pre- and postcruise services, compare between DCL and Royal Caribbean's newer ships, such as *Allure of the Seas, Oasis of the Seas,* and *Quantum of the Seas.*

AREA YOUTH CLUBS

WHO'S BETTER: Disney The kids and teens we've interviewed, including our own, prefer Disney's youth clubs by a wide margin. During our observations, DCL staff ensured that every child new to the club was introduced to the existing members, and the staff actively participated in planning and keeping organized a continuous set of games, crafts, and playtime.

If structured activities for kids and teens are an important consideration in planning your cruise, this is all you need to know.

AREA PRETRIP PLANNING AND RESERVATIONS

WHO'S BETTER: Disney Both cruise lines have good phone-based customer service, but Disney's website is far easier to use than Royal's.

AREA BOARDING PROCESS

WHO'S BETTER: Royal Caribbean Its boarding is faster and more efficient, even on ships such as the *Allure,* which holds 50% more passengers than Disney's largest ships.

AREA GETTING AROUND AND GETTING ORIENTED

WHO'S BETTER: Disney DCL's daily *Personal Navigator* and free companion mobile app let you see quickly what's going on at any time of day. We do like Royal Caribbean's touchscreen maps, near the elevators.

AREA THEMING AND DETAIL OF PUBLIC SPACES

WHO'S BETTER: Tie DCL's stem-to-stern theming, based on the decor of classic ocean liners, makes its ships far prettier than Royal Caribbean's, which, as one of our dinner companions once remarked, feel like "a really nice mall."

That said, Royal Caribbean's largest ships are big enough to host scaled-down versions of New York City's Central Park and Atlantic City's boardwalk. Royal's collection of onboard art, curated from contemporary artists worldwide and found in walkways and stairwells, is more interesting to many adults than Disney's collection, which comes from its animated films.

AREA DINING

WHO'S BETTER: Disney Both cruise lines provide breakfast, lunch, and dinner in standard restaurants as part of your fare. Disney's food is tastier and its restaurants more creatively themed.

On the other hand, Royal Caribbean's larger ships offer more than 20 optional dining locations (where you pay extra to eat), while DCL's

ships have just 1 or 2. If you think you'll tire of eating at the same restaurants again and again, Royal is a better choice.

Service is excellent on both lines.

AREA IN-ROOM DINING

WHO'S BETTER: Disney Royal Caribbean charges guests $7.95 for basic room-service fare (Continental breakfast is free), while most of Disney's offerings are free.

AREA LIVE ENTERTAINMENT

WHO'S BETTER: Royal Caribbean Both lines put on large, splashy stage shows: Royal Caribbean's lineup includes Broadway hits such as *Cats, Grease, Hairspray,* and *Mamma Mia!;* Disney generally rehashes its animated stories. Royal's shows are more varied and appeal more to adults; we also think its performers and musicians are more talented than DCL's.

AREA NIGHTCLUBS, BARS, AND LOUNGES

WHO'S BETTER: Disney Surprised? Where Royal Caribbean's bars tend to be large, open to pedestrian traffic, and barely themed, Disney's are more intimate and have appropriately atmospheric music and decor, and many sit in a dedicated adults-only area, far away from crowded public spaces. (Case in point: Disney's Champagne bars play Édith Piaf and Frank Sinatra in the background, as the good Lord intended; Royal's bars play The Eagles and Gordon Lightfoot.) Plus, service is more personal on DCL.

AREA SHOPPING

WHO'S BETTER: Royal Caribbean Its larger ships carry a wider variety of men's and women's clothing, art, housewares, and more. Both DCL and Royal sell men's and women's jewelry, duty-free booze, and sundries.

AREA SPA

WHO'S BETTER: Disney Another area where DCL wins on theming and detail. While the Senses Spas on the *Dream* and the *Fantasy* are smaller than Royal Caribbean's spas, Disney's overlook the ocean and have more heated-stone loungers, more themed showers, and better steam rooms.

AREA POOLS

WHO'S BETTER: Disney for kids, Royal Caribbean for adults The children's play areas, slides, and water rides on Disney's ships are better than Royal Caribbean's. Royal's newer ships have larger adult pools and more of them, spread across an even wider area than on Disney's largest ships. Both lines take safety seriously, with lifeguards on duty whenever the pools are open.

AREA DEBARKATION

WHO'S BETTER: Royal Caribbean Both DCL and Royal Caribbean can get you off the ship quickly, although Royal does it a bit faster. Disney's baggage-claim area is better organized, however, making it easier to find checked luggage.

AREA GAMBLING

WHO'S BETTER: Depends Many of Royal Caribbean's ships have full casinos with slot machines and tables dedicated to poker, blackjack, roulette, craps, and more. Admission is limited to guests age 18 and older on most sailings. In contrast, the only onboard gambling offered on DCL is a bingo game once or twice a day, at which kids are welcome (see page 214 for details). If you like to gamble—or you don't—the choice is obvious.

AREA HEALTH AND SAFETY

WHO'S BETTER: Disney DCL ships consistently receive the highest marks of any cruise line in **ProPublica**'s assessment of ship health and safety, which includes data on Centers for Disease Control (CDC) inspections, illness outbreaks, crime and accident/incident reports, Coast Guard inspections, and environmental-impact assessments. The *Dream* and *Fantasy* currently have ratings of 100 (on a scale of 0–100); the *Magic* and *Wonder* have ratings of 99. In contrast, Royal Caribbean's ships earned ratings of 92–100, except for *Freedom of the Seas,* which got an 86—but that's just above failing according to ProPublica's criteria. For more information on cruise-line safety, visit projects.propublica.org/cruises.

In the most current CDC inspections, the *Dream* and *Magic* each received a perfect 100, the *Fantasy* scored a 99, and the *Wonder* received a 97, while 15 of Royal Caribbean's 23 ships scored 96 or lower. Four Royal ships did score 100 (*Navigator, Radiance, Rhapsody,* and *Serenade of the Seas*), but two ships (*Allure of the Seas* and *Anthem of the Seas*) got the minimum passing score of 86.

To check the latest inspection scores, see wwwn.cdc.gov/inspectionquerytool (*wwwn.* is correct). Also note that both Disney and Royal Caribbean fare better than some other cruise lines. In late 2017, four Carnival ships—the *Breeze, Liberty, Triumph,* and *Vista*—all failed their inspections, with scores in the 70s.

AREA INTERNET

WHO'S BETTER: Depends Technically, **Royal Caribbean** wins, but that may or may not be what you want depending on what you're looking for in a cruise. Whereas Wi-Fi on the DCL ships is slow, costly, and flaky (see page 110 for details), several of Royal Caribbean's *Oasis*- and *Quantum*-class ships offer land-quality internet at a daily flat rate. It's so fast and stable, in fact, that you can stream your favorite Netflix shows at sea—something you can't currently do on DCL. But if you're booking a cruise with the goal of unplugging, a DCL trip will help you stay on track.

Cost Considerations

Money can't buy happiness, but it can buy you a yacht big enough to pull up right beside it.

—D. L. Roth

Price Differences Between Disney and Royal Caribbean Cruises

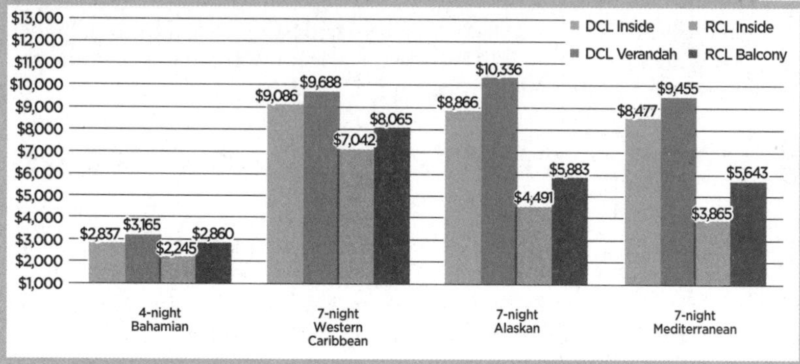

Disney's fares include unlimited fountain soda, plain coffee, tea, and water (bottled soft drinks and water cost extra), while Royal Caribbean charges around $9 per person per day for fountain soft drinks as part of a beverage package (plain coffee, tea, and water are free). That works out to around $252 for a family of four for a seven-night cruise.

We don't recommend Royal's beverage package. For one thing, their free coffee is better than Disney's. Also, while Royal officially prohibits bringing soda aboard, they rarely enforce the rule when it comes to small quantities—say, a six-pack of Mountain Dew. (We're told that security personnel are primarily concerned with contraband booze—enterprising smugglers have been known to replace the contents of bottles of clear soda with vodka or gin.) Finally, it's hard for us to wrap our heads around drinking $250 worth of soda in a week. If you and your family limit soft drinks to the occasional Coke at mealtimes, you probably won't spend anything close to $250 during your trip.

Soda costs aside, the bottom line is that Disney charges a premium for its cruise products. The chart above shows the lowest fares available for summer 2019 cruises to four popular destinations served by Disney and Royal for two adults and two children (ages 6 and 8). Prices are for the cheapest refundable Inside Stateroom and the cheapest stateroom with a verandah (balcony), including all taxes and fees. All cruises except the Mediterranean are round-trip and depart from the same port, except Alaska (Disney uses Vancouver, Royal uses Seattle). The ports visited are either exactly the same or similar.

The cheapest Disney cruise costs 50% more than the cheapest comparable Royal cruises for these destinations. Disney's slightly higher prices are justified for the Bahamian cruises, because Disney's *Dream* is a better ship than Royal's *Mariner of the Seas*. For Western Caribbean

itineraries, we think Royal's *Harmony of the Seas* is every bit as good overall as Disney's *Fantasy,* for $1,600–$2,000 less.

Amenities between the two lines are roughly similar on Mediterranean and Alaskan cruises, however, and the most important features here are the ports you'll visit. For these destinations, Disney's higher prices are more difficult to justify: the price difference is essentially the cost of an entire separate vacation.

HOW *to* CONTACT *the* AUTHORS

MANY WHO USE THE UNOFFICIAL GUIDES write to us with questions, comments, or their own strategies for planning and enjoying travel. We appreciate all such input, both positive and critical. Readers' comments are frequently incorporated into revised editions and have contributed immeasurably to their improvement. Please write or email us at the following addresses:

Erin, Len, and Ritchey
The Unofficial Guide to Disney Cruise Line
2204 First Ave. S., Ste. 102
Birmingham, AL 35233
unofficialguides@menasharidge.com

You can also find us on **Facebook** (@theunofficialguides), **Twitter** (@theugseries), **Instagram** (@theugseries), and **Pinterest** (@theugseries).

When you write, put your address on both your letter and envelope; the two sometimes get separated. It's also a good idea to include your phone number. If you email us, please tell us where you're from. Finally, know that as travel writers, we're often out of the office for long periods of time, so bear with us if we're slow to respond. Unofficial email isn't forwarded to us when we're traveling, but we'll get back to you as soon as possible after we return.

READER SURVEY

OUR WEBSITE HOSTS A QUESTIONNAIRE you can use to express opinions about your Disney cruise, at touringplans.com/disney-cruise-line/survey. The questionnaire lets every member of your party, regardless of age, tell us what he or she thinks about attractions, restaurants, and more.

If you'd rather print out the survey and send it to us, mail it to

Reader Survey
The Unofficial Guides
2204 First Ave. S., Ste. 102
Birmingham, AL 35233

PART ONE

DOLLARS *and* SENSE

WHAT'S INCLUDED *in* YOUR DISNEY CRUISE FARE

A DISNEY CRUISE ISN'T CHEAP. Given the cost, you might be wondering how much more you'll have to pay once you're aboard the ship. Here's a quick rundown of what is and isn't included in your cruise fare. We've included some rough estimates of the optional items to help you with budgeting.

FOOD

INCLUDED: LOTS OF FOOD All meals, including snacks, are free at all of the ship's restaurants except for **Remy** and **Palo.** You can order as much food as you like.

NOT INCLUDED: FANCY RESTAURANTS Meals at **Remy** and **Palo** cost an additional $95 and $30, respectively, for dinner, plus gratuity; Palo also charges $30 for its brunch, while Remy's brunch is $60. Alcoholic beverages are an extra charge beyond those prices, at each meal.

INCLUDED: MOST ROOM-SERVICE FOOD Your fare includes room-service meals, except as noted below. Room service is a great option if you're in the mood for breakfast on your verandah or you don't feel like dressing up for dinner.

INCLUDED: ALL-YOU-WANT SOFT DRINKS AND ICE CREAM Soda, coffee, water, cocoa, and hot and iced tea are free and unlimited at meals, as are beverages served from drink dispensers on deck. Self-serve ice cream from the onboard dispensers is free; note, however, that the specialty ice creams sold at **Vanellope's Sweets and Treats** on the *Dream* and at **Sweet on You** on the *Fantasy* cost extra, as do the smoothies at **Frozone Treats** on the *Dream* and *Fantasy.*

The 10 Best Bangs for Your Buck (*and One Freebie*) on a Disney Caribbean Cruise

1. Rainforest at Senses Spa At $16–$25 per day, the Rainforest Room is a must-do. Only a limited number of passes are sold per cruise, so buy yours as soon as possible. Single-day passes may be available in advance online; multi-day passes must be purchased on the ship. We've never found the Rainforest Room to be crowded and have often had the place to ourselves. This is the ultimate in quiet relaxation for adults—and a total bargain at that.

2. Porters for your bags The $2–$5 per bag you'll tip your porter both boarding and returning home is money well spent. These guys work hard and make our lives so much easier. When you're boarding, not having to handle your own bags is one less hassle in a hectic process. When you debark, it helps you end your cruise on a high note.

3. Oceanview staterooms If the prospect of 3–7 nights in a cabin with no natural light is more than you can bear but a Verandah room is beyond your budget, we happily recommend a room with a porthole. Located on the lower decks, Oceanview staterooms offer a closer view of the sea. Good deals on this category abound, as Oceanview rooms don't sell as quickly as inside rooms (least expensive) and Verandah rooms (often in the highest demand). Oceanview cabins also have the best access to the main dining rooms, Guest Services, and the adult lounge areas.

4. Cabanas on Castaway Cay *Hold up! How can you possibly recommend something that costs at least $400 as a bang for your buck?* Here's the thing: the amenities that come with a cabana ($400 at Serenity Bay for 4 people, $550–$600 at the Family Beach for 6 people, and $900 at the Family Beach for 10 people in a Grand Cabana) equal more than the sum of its parts. If you have enough people to fill a cabana or you can find someone to share with, the free equipment rentals, shelter from the sun, dedicated beach (Family Beach), and personalized service make this something well worth checking out. Our only qualm in including the cabanas here is the fact that they're notoriously difficult to book. See page 264 for more.

5. Palo A quiet, no-rush brunch or dinner for adults with great service and fantastic food for just $30 plus tip? *Yeah, baby!* And besides, your kids are probably ready to spend some time away from you, too. Come for the food, linger for the atmosphere.

NOT INCLUDED: BOTTLED DRINKS, PACKAGED SNACKS, ALCOHOLIC BEVERAGES, AND FANCY COFFEES Bottled water ($3), soda not served as part of meal service or from the self-service dispensers on the pool deck ($3), beer ($6 and up), and wine ($8 and up) cost extra, as do packaged snacks such as popcorn and peanuts. You'll also pay out-of-pocket for specialty coffees, espresso, cappuccinos, and teas from bars and cafés (such as the **Cove Café**). A 15% gratuity is automatically added to bar and beverage tabs. Adults age 21 and older also may bring

6. Adult-beverage tastings For around \$20–\$30, you're treated to several wines, liquors, or cocktails. (*Tip:* Eat before you sip so you don't get smashed.) We've been lucky enough to be the only participants on a few occasions, allowing us to interact with the guides. Our favorite is the Champagne tasting, but we haven't been let down by any of them. One author discovered a new favorite wine during a tasting at Meridian on the *Fantasy*. Another time we were asked, "How would you like to try the most expensive whiskey we sell?" Our reply: "Yes, please!"

7. Castaway Ray's Stingray Adventure This is both less expensive and better organized than stingray encounters in other ports. It's a winner with kids (\$45) and adults (\$56). There's no time wasted getting back and forth to your port adventure because it's on Castaway Cay—just show up at your appointed time and have fun interacting with the rays.

8. It's a Small World Nursery Parents of children younger than age 3 can enjoy some downtime and let the excellent staff watch their little ones for \$9 per hour for the first child and \$8 per hour per additional child in the same family. Feedback from parents is consistently positive.

9. Coffee The swill at the beverage stations can best be described as a tepid, vaguely coffee-flavored substance that may make you question your will to live. Pony up for the real thing at **Cove Café, Vista Café,** or the coffee bar at the buffets. Sure, it's around \$3–\$6 plus tip, but that's less than you'd pay at Starbucks, and it doesn't make you regret your caffeine habit. Ask for a **Café Fanatic** rewards card and get every sixth coffee drink free. (For us, that's sometime early in day two of any cruise.)

10. Castaway Cay 5K This port adventure is free, and you can take pride in knowing you've gotten in your exercise for the day while being among the first to exit the ship at the island. There are race bibs and plastic medals. Try to beat your Castaway Cay personal best every time you come to the island.

11. Gratuities DCL ships are full of enthusiastic cast members, many of whom are far away from home, who work hard to make your trip magical. To ensure great service, generously tip not only your servers and stateroom attendants but also your baristas and bartenders. And don't forget these folks when you're filling out your comment cards at the end of the cruise—it's good karma to boost a deserving person's career.

a limited amount of beer, wine, and liquor aboard in their carry-on luggage; a \$25 corking fee applies if you bring your own wine to a full-service restaurant on board.

NOT INCLUDED: SOME BAR SNACKS Many onboard bars offer free basic snacks in the evening, such as chips and salsa, cut veggies, or mini hot dogs. If you want more-substantial or themed bar food (bangers and mash at **O'Gills,** for example), expect to pay \$8–\$12 per item.

ENTERTAINMENT AND ACTIVITIES

INCLUDED: LOTS OF ENTERTAINMENT There's no extra charge for live performances, movies, and character greetings.

NOT INCLUDED: BINGO, SOME ONBOARD SEMINARS, AND MOVIE SNACKS A few activities, such as bingo, cost money to play. Beverage seminars, which typically offer several kinds of spirits for sampling, cost about $20–$30, depending on the alcohol. Some holiday activities, such as making gingerbread houses, cost $20–$30. Packaged snacks, popcorn, and beverages at the movie theater and main stage cost extra, but you can always grab a free soda, ice cream, or plate of chicken nuggets from the top deck and bring it with you to the show.

INCLUDED: GYM FACILITIES Covered in your fare is use of the fitness center, which has changing rooms with showers and sauna.

NOT INCLUDED: SPA AND SALON SERVICES Spa treatments (including massages, facials, steam rooms, and upscale showers) cost from $115 to upwards of $500 per person, per treatment. Salon services range from $50 to $70 for manicures and pedicures, and from about $35 to $75 for hairstyling, depending on hair length.

INCLUDED: POOLS, GAMES, AND MOST SPORTS These include all of the pools and waterslides and activities, such as miniature golf, basketball, table tennis, and shuffleboard. Board games are available at no charge in some lounges.

INCLUDED: CASTAWAY CAY BEACHES AND RESTAURANTS Food, lounge chairs, and beach umbrellas are free, as is the island's 5K road run.

NOT INCLUDED: CASTAWAY CAY RECREATION AND ALCOHOL DCL charges for bike rentals ($13 for one day, $16 for two days), snorkeling ($18–$34 for one day, $23–$45 for two days), and use of boats ($16–$30 per half-hour) and watercraft ($104 per hour for one rider, $183 per hour for two riders). Pricing for private cabanas varies seasonally and by the size/location of the cabana. Adult beach cabanas start at $399 for up to 4 people; up to 2 additional adults costs $50 per person. Family cabanas for up to 6 people cost $549 late September–early March, $599 mid-March–mid-September; up to 4 additional people costs $50 per person. The grand family cabana is $899 for the first 10 people; up to 6 additional people costs $50 per person. Alcohol pricing on Castaway Cay is comparable to pricing on the ship.

KID STUFF

INCLUDED: KIDS' CLUBS (AGES 3 AND UP) These include the **Oceaneer Club/Oceaneer Lab** for kids ages 3–12, the **Edge** club for tweens ages 11–14, and the **Vibe** club for teens ages 14–17.

NOT INCLUDED: CHILDCARE FOR KIDS UNDER 3 **It's a Small World Nursery** charges $9 per hour for the first child and $8 per hour for a second child in the same family.

NOT INCLUDED: CHILDREN'S MAKEOVER EXPERIENCES All ships have a **Bibbidi Bobbidi Boutique** that provides princess makeovers (plus pirate makeovers on Pirate Nights). Salon services start at about $19 for a boy's hairstyling. For girls, a basic hairstyling, makeup, and nail polish treatment starts at about $60 and can top $600 for a multinight princess package with several costumes. (We have daughters. We love them. But maybe not *that* much.)

NOT INCLUDED: CHILDREN'S SPECIAL DINING EXPERIENCES Some ships offer special dining experiences for children. For example, the **Royal Court Tea** currently costs $280 for one adult and one child (additional children and adults in the same family may be added at an extra charge). The experience includes sweet and savory tea courses, a visit with Disney princesses, and elaborate gifts for the children.

MISCELLANEOUS

INCLUDED: CALLS TO ANYWHERE ON THE SHIP Use of the ships' **Wave Phones** (see next page) is free. Guests may also use the **DCL Navigator app** with their own phones to text other guests for free using onboard Wi-Fi.

NOT INCLUDED: SHIP-TO-SHORE CALLS AND INTERNET Ship-to-shore calls from onboard phones cost a shocking $7–$9.50 per minute. Each stateroom has a landline-style phone (remember those?) with voice mail, plus a **Wave Phone,** a free mobile phone you can use on the ship and Castaway Cay for calls, voice mail, and texting (only from Wave Phone

SCOTT SAYS *by Scott Sanders*

SCOTT'S MONEY-SAVING STRATEGIES

IT'S COMPLETELY POSSIBLE to go on a Disney cruise and not spend a dime aside from gratuities. The ships offer essentially everything you need and more while you're on board, but there are plenty of opportunities to enhance your vacation. That said, I suggest budgeting for some onboard spending—it *is* a vacation, after all.

If you prepay your base gratuities prior to sailing, you can just add any additional tips at the end of your cruise.

My favorite money-saving strategy is to book excursions via third parties. The catch: sticking to the all-aboard time so you don't miss the ship. If that sounds too stressful, just explore on your own (where it's safe to do so).

My top money-saving tip is to book an inside stateroom—the money that you save can go toward onboard splurges. There's no denying that a higher-category room is nice, but if you're only using your room to sleep, shower, and change clothes, why spend more?

to Wave Phone). See page 110 for more about using the internet while on board.

NOT INCLUDED: PHOTOS Similar to its Memory Maker packages at Walt Disney World, Disney offers cruise packages of prints or digital images loaded onto flash drives. Pricing varies depending on the length of your voyage. Typically, a package of 10 prints costs about $150. An unlimited number of JPEG files costs about $200–$400, depending on the number of sail days, with an additional $100 buying you the physical printouts of your images. Photo packages may be prepurchased, sometimes at a discount, at mycruisephotos.com. Onboard staff also will shoot pictures for free with your own camera. Three ships (*Fantasy, Wonder,* and *Magic*) have **Shutters Photo Studio,** where you can book a dedicated photo session for your family for a whopping additional fee: 12 photos cost almost $1,000.

NOT INCLUDED: SHORE EXCURSIONS Known in DCL-speak as "port adventures," these cost anywhere from $13 for a 1-hour bike rental on Castaway Cay to $3,800 per person for a Cork, Ireland, excursion including a helicopter flyover of Dunmore Head, a shooting location for *The Last Jedi.* (The pint of Guinness they throw in makes the cost totally worth it.) Be aware that many shore excursions carry additional optional costs beyond the stated price. For example, many excursion operators offer souvenir photo packages for an additional fee. Also note that meals are not included in the price of many shore excursions.

NOT INCLUDED: LAUNDRY It costs $2 to wash and $2 to dry a load of clothes in the onboard laundry rooms. Soap, fabric softener, and dryer sheets are available for $1 each, per load. Dry-cleaning is also available for an additional fee. Typical pricing is about $6 to dry-clean a man's shirt. Garment pressing is available for about half the price of dry-cleaning.

NOT INCLUDED: GRATUITIES Disney automatically adds gratuities of around $12 per person per day to your onboard account. A 15% gratuity is automatically added to bar and beverage tabs. See page 114 for more information.

NOT INCLUDED: TRANSPORTATION TO THE PORT Round-trip service between Walt Disney World and Port Canaveral runs $70 per person; transportation costs between any city's cruise terminal and airport will vary. See the section starting on page 90 for more details.

CRUISING *with* KIDS

LET US START BY SAYING that your kids will in all likelihood have a great time on a DCL cruise. (See pages 57 and 220 for our advice on cruising with teens and tweens.)

As parents, we know that one of the most difficult parts of planning a vacation with kids is ensuring that they stay entertained throughout

the trip. For us, this usually means making sure that every travel day has at least a couple of things specifically designed to appeal to our kids and their friends—things that we'd prefer didn't involve shopping or sitting passively in front of a screen.

It can be exhausting to plan this way (and we're *professionals*!). In fact, we think this is one of the main reasons why a trip to Disney World is so appealing to parents: Disney's theme parks provide a nearly constant and wide-ranging set of entertainment options for kids and adults. A family that hasn't planned a thing can show up and find something fun to do. Disney cruises work the same way: family activities, including trivia contests, scavenger hunts, and shuffleboard, are scheduled throughout the day, on virtually every day of every sailing.

If you think your kids would benefit from spending some time with their peers, Disney provides organized activities throughout the day for children ages 3–17. Some activities for younger children get started as early as 7 a.m., while activities for older teens can run until 2 a.m. Off the ships, Castaway Cay offers dedicated beach and recreation spots for families, teens, and tweens, plus a splash area for little ones. There are shore excursions created just for families, too. Some sailings also offer teen-only excursions and sightseeing events.

Disney is also keeping up with two recent trends in the cruise industry. The first is setting aside more space per ship for kids' clubs. On the *Dream* and *Fantasy,* these clubs take up substantially more space than on the *Magic* and *Wonder.* Second, Disney frequently runs concurrent, age-appropriate activities within the same club. For example, the Oceaneer Club accepts children ages 3–12; however, Disney may group the younger kids together for a game with marshmallows in one area of the club while the older kids sing karaoke in another.

Our own children have found Disney's kids' activities more fun than hanging around with us on the ship. It may be a cliché, but it's true: we saw the kids only during meals, at bedtime, or when we specifically scheduled things to do as a family. Thanks to the web, our kids are still in contact with the friends they've made on their cruises, even though some are an ocean away.

On the other hand, if your kids aren't interested in the kids' clubs, or if you're determined to make your cruise a time for family togetherness, there are also many activities that you can do together. These include structured things like family game shows and trivia contests, and unstructured things like board games and scavenger hunts. Many styles of family travel can be accommodated on the ships.

CRUISING *Without* KIDS

GIVEN THAT DISNEY IS SYNONYMOUS with family-friendly entertainment, it's natural for those who travel without children to wonder if DCL is a good choice for them. Happily, just as with the Disney parks,

there's something for folks of all ages to enjoy on a Disney cruise. Disney ships have an adults-only pool and coffeehouse, the gym is limited to guests age 18 and up, some entertainment districts are adults-only after 9 p.m., and, with the exception of teens in the Chill areas, the spas are limited to those 18 and up. For those wanting to dine in an adults-only atmosphere, Remy (*Dream* and *Fantasy* only) and Palo (see Part Seven) are likewise restricted to those age 18 and older. Castaway Cay has an adult beach with its own dining, bar, and cabanas (which must be reserved in advance).We recommend traveling when school is in session if you're looking for a more adult-oriented vacation; the good news is that these times tend to be far less expensive.

unofficial **TIP**
DCL rates highly with women cruisers because of its safe atmosphere.

If your idea of a fun cruise is a party barge, then DCL probably isn't for you—there's no casino, and honestly the nightlife is more mild than wild. But we've traveled several times with just adults in our party and had a fantastic time. Spend some time at the spa, get to know the bartenders and baristas at the various bars and lounges, skip the stage shows, dine at Palo or Remy (or both!), and enjoy some downtime.

unofficial **TIP**
According to Disney cast members we've talked to, the long ship-repositioning cruises (such as the Panama Canal itinerary) and transatlantic voyages tend to have the fewest children on board.

WHERE *to* FIND MORE INFORMATION

DISNEY CRUISE LINE'S official website is **DisneyCruise.com** (disney cruise.disney.go.com). Here you can see which itineraries are served by each ship; search for cruises by destination, month, and length; and check staterooms prices. Once you've made a reservation, you can book shore excursions, restaurants, and children's activities through the site.

Free trip-planning videos about DCL, Walt Disney World, Adventures by Disney (including Disney river cruises), and other destinations are available at **DisneyPlanning.com** (you'll need to fill out a short survey first). The DCL video can also be accessed through the My Disney Cruise area of the DCL site (see page 39). Besides being a good planning tool, the video is a good way to prepare kids who've never cruised before.

DCLNews.com posts official news and PR about Disney Cruise Line. Though intended for the media, most of the site is open to the public. The information resources include fact sheets and press releases, as well as photos and videos of the ships.

PassPorter's Disney Cruise Line and Its Ports of Call ($19.95–$44.95 per year depending on the subscription package) provides a good overview of DCL. Go to passporter.com and choose "Disney Cruise Line,"

then "LIVE! Guide" from the menu on the left. Previously a print book (you may still be able to find older editions at your local library or for sale online), the Passporter guide has moved to an exclusively digital subscription format. Kept constantly updated, the book can be viewed on desktop, laptop, and mobile devices or downloaded as a PDF. The higher-priced subscription package entitles you to unlimited access to not only the DCL guide but also PassPorter's Disney World and Disneyland guides. (You may also view the book at no charge minus the bells and whistles—the catch is ads.) The companion website has user-led discussion forums where folks from all over can ask questions and provide answers to almost any cruise-related scenario.

Scott Sanders's **Disney Cruise Line Blog** (disneycruiselineblog.com) posts almost-daily updates, including everything from new-itinerary rumors to new shopping merchandise on board. The site also has a cool feature that lets you see the current location of every ship in the Disney fleet. In addition, look for tips and advice from Scott in the **Scott Says** sections throughout this book. For up-to-the-minute DCL news, the Disney Cruise Line Blog Twitter feed, **@TheDCLBlog,** is a terrific resource.

The **Disney Parks Moms Panel** (disneyworldforum.disney.go.com) features Disney Cruise Line specialists. These moms are veterans of many DCL voyages and have received training from DCL cast members. They're able to answer any individual Disney cruise–planning question, big or small.

Some popular Disney websites with dedicated DCL message forums include **DISboards** (disboards.com), **WDWMagic** (wdwmagic.com; choose "Forums" and then "Disney Cruise Line"), **MiceChat** (micechat.com), and, for Brits, **The DIBB** (thedibb.co.uk; *DIBB* stands for "Disney Information Bulletin Board").

The **US government** offers a wealth of online resources for citizens traveling to other countries. The **Department of State** travel website, travel.state.gov, includes weather and safety advisories, advice on what to do if you've lost your passport, information on visa requirements, and more. The travel website for the **Centers for Disease Control and Prevention (CDC)**, cdc.gov/travel, provides wellness advice specific to foreign destinations, including a section on cruise travel.

The CDC also offers a free email and text service with travelers' health updates (subscribe at cdc.gov/emailupdates), as well as the mobile app **TravWell,** which includes customizable packing lists and emergency phone numbers for every destination. Both apps are free at the Apple App Store and the Google Play Store.

Finally, try searching **Facebook** for a group specific to your DCL sailing. Many cruise-specific groups share tips on excursion booking, pricing changes, and other information, as well as organizing private mixology classes or gift exchanges. If you're a social person, this can be a nice way to meet new friends before you sail. For one Northern

European DCL sailing, we found that voyage's Facebook group to be a good source of information about airfare to Copenhagen.

IS IT WORTH IT?

AS YOU PLAN YOUR CRUISE, you may find yourself asking questions along these lines:

- Is it worth paying a higher price for DCL versus another cruise line?
- Is splurging on a cabana worth the (considerable) expense?
- My daughter wants to go to the princess tea. Is it worth it?
- Is the food at Remy worth the upcharge?
- This photo package seems expensive—should I get it?
- Is that helicopter excursion *really* worth $4,000?
- Should I spring for a second stateroom for my family with teens?

You may also have non-money-related questions:

- Do I keep my preschool-age daughter up late to go to the fireworks show on Pirate Night?
- Should we get off the ship in Nassau?
- Is meeting Cinderella worth the wait in line?
- Is a Disney cruise worth the trouble if I have to take my child out of school to go?

The dirty little secret most travel writers won't tell you is that our answers to these questions is, "We don't know"—and we say that even after having experienced all the things you're asking about and paid for them out of our own pockets.

unofficial **TIP**
In a nutshell, worth is achieved when benefits exceed costs.

Here's what we *do* know: We can tell you what the charge on your Amex card will be. We can tell you our personal perception of the quality of the food, the service, or the attention to detail. We can tell you what other guests we've surveyed have said about the quality of the food, the service, or the attention to detail. We can tell you what the views are like, how long waits are likely to be, and which experiences were worth it *to us*. But we can't tell you whether these experiences will be worth it *to you*. (Heck, even the coauthors of this book disagree about the worth of some DCL activities and expenses.)

We're not unsympathetic to the "Is it worth it?" question. Vacation time and money are scarce commodities. You want to be reassured that benefits you'll gain from your experiences will be greater than your investment in those experiences, both in money and time. You

want to be reassured that your investment will be worth it, but we can't tell you if a Disney Cruise Line experience will be worth it *to you,* because we don't know you.

For example, a Senses Spa Ultimate Indulgence package costs about $600. It includes a fancy facial, a deep-tissue massage, time in the Rainforest Room, and all the herbal tea you can choke down. There's absolutely no way this $600, 3-hour investment would be worth it to coauthor Erin, who doesn't like being touched by strangers and prefers coffee over tea. On the other hand, maybe you have a particular muscle ache that only a deep-tissue massage can fix, or you believe spa treatments are the ultimate form of pampering.

So how can you determine whether any specific Disney Cruise experience will be worth it *to you?* Here are some questions to consider:

1. **What is your income and/or vacation budget?** If you make $50,000 a year, then spending 1% (or a lot more than 1%) of your total annual income on a Concierge-level suite would be a significant expense. Your stay would have to be pretty darn spectacular to be worth it. If you make $500,000 a year, then a Concierge suite would be far less of a bite to your bottom line.
2. **What is the financial opportunity cost of the experience?** Will spending money on a cabana mean that you'll have less money to spend on other things you might like to experience, such as port adventures and adult dining? If push comes to shove, which would you rather have?
3. **What is the time opportunity cost of the experience?** Is going on that 8-hour tour more important to you than getting to experience the ship's amenities to their fullest?
4. **What are the real financial costs of the experience?** Have you done all your research on promotions and discounts? What are the hidden taxes, gratuities, or other fees that would make the experience more costly? Can you think of ways to make the experience *less* costly?
5. **Will you have opportunities to experience this event again, or is it a one-time-only experience?** For example, if Christmas is the only time your extended family, including your aging parents, are available to travel, then the extra expense of a holiday cruise might be well worth it.
6. **Are there aspects of your personality that will affect the experience?** As noted in the Senses Spa example above, Erin is not a massage person, so money not spent on spa experiences would be worth it to her. Other folks might detest wearing a jacket to dinner, so no matter how good the food is, Remy wouldn't be worth it to them. (For us, it's *1,000%* worth it.)
7. **Are there aspects of other family members' personalities that will affect the experience?** What would you do if your child didn't want to go to the kids' clubs? Would your vacation be affected (positively or negatively) if you had less opportunity for adult time versus family togetherness?

8. **Is a reasonable facsimile of this experience available elsewhere?** If, say, you've experienced that cool zip-line course back home, then you can probably skip the zip-line excursion in port.
9. **Why do you want to cruise?** Do you plan to spend as much time relaxing as possible? Then port excursions might not be for you. If you've booked the trip to show your kids Europe for the first time, then taking a long excursion every day might be *completely* worth it, even if it's expensive.
10. **How do you define a good vacation?** Do you value relaxation? Convenience? Novelty? Adventure? Indulgence? Quality or quantity of food? Ease of planning? Family time? Private time? If the cruise doesn't push one or more of these buttons, then it's probably not worth it.
11. **Will you feel frustrated if you have to do without something you're used to?** If, for instance, you dread having to sleep in the same room with your kids, then the extra expense of a second stateroom may well be worth it.
12. **Will these experiences make for great memories down the road?** A princess or pirate makeover for your kids at the Bibbidi Bobbidi Boutique might seem like an unnecessary indulgence. But if you know your Disney princess-obsessed 5-year-old daughter will be overjoyed to get the royal treatment and will talk about it for months afterward, then it could be worth the expense after all.
13. **How disappointed will you be if the cruise doesn't go as planned?** Let's face it—things don't always happen as we expect them to: the weather doesn't cooperate, kids get sick, and so on. If you think the experience will be a total bust if it's not absolutely perfect, then maybe you should reconsider a Disney cruise.
14. **Would you do this even if it were free?** We have friends who are deathly afraid of heights. Even if someone gifted them with a parasailing excursion at Castaway Cay, they wouldn't take it.
15. **Will you feel guilty or foolish if you spend your time or money on the experience?** There can often be waits of well more than an hour for the AquaDuck waterslides on the *Dream*-class ships. If it were Erin's favorite slide in the universe, she had nothing but time on her hands, and she knew that she'd never get to experience it again, she'd still hate herself for waiting that long for a water ride that lasts just a couple of minutes. Likewise, we have family members who think blowing money on fancy food is ridiculous—they would hate themselves if they spent $200 to eat at Remy, even if it was the best food they'd ever tasted.

By asking yourself these and similar questions, you may be able to determine on your own whether a particular DCL experience will be worth it to you. If you still have questions, try these tips:

Get advice from someone in a demographic similar to yours. If you have three daughters, then it's pointless to seek advice from someone

with only sons about whether Bibbidi Bobbidi Boutique is worth the expense. Ditto if you're used to staying in luxury accommodations but you solicit advice about the worth of a Concierge-level suite from someone who stays only at value-priced hotels.

Find someone like you to get information that will be useful. This tactic is particularly important when lurking on message boards, reading reviews at travel sites, and scanning social media posts.

Ask your advisor for a benchmark. If you're asking for DCL advice from someone you don't know personally, then try to get their opinion on something you're both familiar with. If, say, you both like restaurants X and Y, then chances are good that you'll agree with their assessment of restaurant Z.

The importance of sharing perspectives played out in a Facebook DCL group we follow when someone posted, "We're thinking about upgrading. Is it worth the extra money to get a Verandah room?" She got 72 responses within a few hours, with answers ranging from "It's so lovely to walk out into your own open space" to "We spend so little time in our room that we opt for an inside cabin." The opinions ping-ponged back and forth between pro–Verandah room and pro–inside room, with all commenters equally adamant that their view was the right one.

In the end, it was an anti–inside room comment—"Inside rooms are incredibly dark"—that persuaded the original poster, who had provided no previous specifics about her likes and dislikes, to go with the inside room. As it turned out, she loves to sleep in a pitch-black room . . . so much so that she might have even paid extra for maximum darkness.

PART TWO

PLANNING YOUR CRUISE

CHOOSING *an* ITINERARY

DISNEY CRUISE LINE OFFERS ALMOST 50 separate itineraries, ranging from 2-night weekend getaways to 14-night voyages between two oceans using the Panama Canal. The cruise you select is likely to be determined by how much vacation time you have, the ship on which you want to sail, the cost, and the ports that interest you.

unofficial **TIP**
The average DCL cruise lasts five nights, sails somewhere in the Caribbean, and stops at Disney's Castaway Cay island in the Bahamas.

ITINERARY RECOMMENDATIONS FOR FIRST-TIME CRUISERS

WE THINK THE IDEAL ITINERARY for first-time cruisers is four or five nights on the *Dream*. Why? It's a newer ship, with good restaurants, bars, and spa; more space for kids' activities; and more space on deck for pools and lounging. The *Fantasy* is equal to the *Dream* in these respects, but it primarily sails seven-night voyages. If you're not concerned about acclimating to a cruise vacation, then that's another excellent choice.

GENERAL RECOMMENDATIONS

IF YOU'RE TRYING TO DECIDE among Eastern Caribbean, Western Caribbean, and Bahamian cruises, you have just a couple of questions to answer. First, are you interested in exploring the culture of the ports you're visiting? Second, if so, are you more interested in Caribbean towns or Mayan history?

If the answer to the first question is no—if your perfect vacation involves lying on a beach, taking the kids snorkeling, scuba diving, or swimming with dolphins—you can do that in every port from Barbados to Cozumel. Pick any itinerary that includes Castaway Cay and that also fits your schedule and budget, and you're golden.

If you're interested in local color, choose between the **Eastern** and **Western Caribbean** itineraries. The Eastern itineraries feature wonderful ports that seem to be recovering well from the effects of Hurricanes Irma and Maria in late 2017.

On **Western Caribbean** cruises, Costa Maya and Cozumel are notable only for their inland tours of Mayan ruins. If those interest you more than Caribbean towns, pick a Western itinerary.

Now, lest you think we're making an "all those people look the same" argument in advising you how to choose between Bahamian and Caribbean itineraries, rest assured that we're not. Rather, our advice is based on the observation that the cruise industry's overbooking of the same Caribbean ports has led to a certain sameness of experience virtually everywhere. As Julia Cosgrove, editor-in-chief of *Afar* magazine, observes, "There's no sense of 'I should go to this island as opposed to that because I'm going to get this deeper cultural experience by connecting with people in one place versus another.'"

Disney's **Alaskan** itineraries, served by the *Wonder*, are virtually identical. Choose whichever sailing suits your budget and schedule.

Disney's **Mediterranean** cruises are distinguished primarily by their length: 5, 6, 7, and 10 nights in 2019 and 4 and 12 nights in previous years. Most depart from Barcelona, and a few end in other cities. In a change from previous years, Disney has no scheduled stops in Venice or at any port in Greece as of press time.

Northern European itineraries have more variety than those in any other region. These sailings range from 7 to 11 days, with some focusing on Norway and Iceland and others visiting Estonia and Russia or sailing the British Isles. Limited availability of some itineraries makes them particularly popular, with some ports visited on only one or two sailings per year. If you find that your preferred itinerary is fully booked, check back often to see if other guests have canceled, or enlist the assistance of a travel agent who can check for cancellations on your behalf.

unofficial **TIP**
Guests with special needs (see Part Five, page 126) will want to think about the port-adventure options available with the itineraries they're considering. Because some ports have a preponderance of excursions that prohibit wheelchair access, you may not want to book a trip where your choice of off-ship activities could be limited.

SAVING MONEY

IN THE LAST EDITION OF THIS BOOK, we noted that Disney had ended its practice of last-minute fare discounts across almost all of its itineraries. As of late summer 2018, however, that trend has changed for two key destinations.

We analyzed more than 1.5 million fares for this edition. "Book early" is still the best advice for **Bahamian** and **Alaskan** cruises, with

savings of 12%–18% ($1,100–$1,800) if booked more than a year in advance versus booking 60 days before departure. See pages 28–33 for detailed charts.

In this respect, Disney's strategy is similar to that adopted by Royal Caribbean in 2015. Royal Caribbean told customers it would cut back on last-minute deals in favor of cheaper early bookings and dubbed it Pricing Integrity. It took a couple of years for customers to see that they weren't bluffing, but Royal Caribbean has seen both higher fares and higher occupancy as a result. DCL seems to have adopted a similar model for its Bahamian and Alaskan markets.

unofficial **TIP**
When you're combing through the DCL website for discounts, look for stateroom categories with the codes **IGT, OGT,** and **VGT.** These indicate heavily discounted inside, outside, and Verandah staterooms.

The exceptions to this were 2018 cruises to the **Western Caribbean** and the **Mediterranean** (see pages 30 and 32 for their respective charts). Disney's fares for summer Mediterranean cruises were as cheap at 60 days before departure as 400+ days before. Savings weren't quite as good for summer Western Caribbean dates, but fares were still $1,000 cheaper than peak if booked within 30 days of departure.

In general, you have eight primary strategies for saving money on a Disney cruise:

1. **Book as early as possible.** Most cruise fares start low and begin to rise as the ship fills up. You can save 10% by booking a year in advance. See the chart on page 28 for examples.
2. **Book at the last minute.** There seems to be a small but consistent dip in Caribbean and Mediterranean cruise prices starting around 30–45 days prior to departure, especially for staterooms on higher decks. If you can't book a year in advance, check the fares daily starting two months out. Consider booking as soon as you see even a small drop or increase in price. These deals are especially good if you live within a day's drive of the departure port because you can avoid the last-minute price hikes on airline tickets. Offers including last-minute deals can be found on DCL's website (disneycruise.disney.go.com) as well as on our favorite money-saving site, **MouseSavers** (mousesavers.com), under "Disney Cruise Line." This strategy works for all categories of staterooms.
3. **Don't book 7–10 months in advance.** This seems to be about the time when many families start making reservations for their cruises. It also seems to be when prices spike. We wouldn't be surprised if Disney adjusts prices according to spikes in interest in travel, such as that indicated by website traffic, frequency of other bookings, and similar real-time statistics.
4. **Book your next cruise on board.** DCL offers discounts up to 10% off the lowest prevailing rates, occasionally along with onboard ship credits. Stop by the Future Cruise Sales Desk, usually on Deck 4 Midship, for

details. Be aware that discount blackout dates may apply—when we tried to book a cruise coinciding with Easter, we were told that the standard 10% discount was unavailable. We were, however, able to get an onboard credit and a reduced deposit.

5. **Depart from a less popular port at a slow time of year.** Disney offers aggressive discounts on cruises from ports that aren't in great demand. At this writing, off-season seven-night cruises out of Miami on the *Wonder* were selling for around 13% less than similar cruises on the *Fantasy* out of Port Canaveral, for the same stateroom categories. Similar four-night cruises on the *Magic* out of Miami were 20% cheaper than those on the *Dream* out of Canaveral, too. Your travel agent should know which ports aren't selling as quickly as others. (See Part Four, page 90, for more tips on choosing a port.)

6. **Take advantage of onboard credit offers.** While pricing for cruise fares is generally consistent among Disney, independent travel agents, and larger online sites such as Orbitz and Expedia, some outfits can sweeten the pot with generous onboard credits. Shop around for the best deals.

7. **Use your special status.** Members of various groups may have access to discounts that are unavailable to the general public. For example, there are often special rates available for military personnel, Canadian residents, and Florida residents. These will typically be noted on the DCL website's Special Offers page (disneycruise.disney.go.com/special-offers). Additionally, AAA and Costco members may be able to book at a discount through the travel arms of these organizations. If you're traveling with a group of at least eight staterooms or 16 adults (cruising for a wedding or family reunion, for example), you may be eligible for perks like special gifts or private parties. For more information, call ☎ 800-511-6333.

8. **Sail during an off-peak time.** Disney charges a premium for its cruises, and we think they're worth it. But the same cruise on the same ship can often cost twice as much on peak dates than during the off-season. An example follows using the *Fantasy*—an easy ship for comparing fares, because it sails just two itineraries: seven-night Eastern and Western Caribbean cruises out of Port Canaveral. The chart on page 30 shows the cost of the *Fantasy's* standard seven-night cruises for all of 2018, based on two adults and one child in a Category 4A Deluxe Family Oceanview Stateroom with Verandah. (Prices for 2019 show the same seasonal patterns, at generally higher prices.)

There are few surprises here: it's cheapest to sail when the kids are in school, and most expensive over the winter holidays. Specifically, early fall, the beginning of December, and right after New Year's are the least expensive times to take your Disney cruise.

Other than holidays, the middle of summer is the most expensive time to cruise (even ignoring the special 10- and 11-night itineraries). If you have children and want to cruise with them, try to book a cruise that leaves as soon as school gets out for the summer or right before

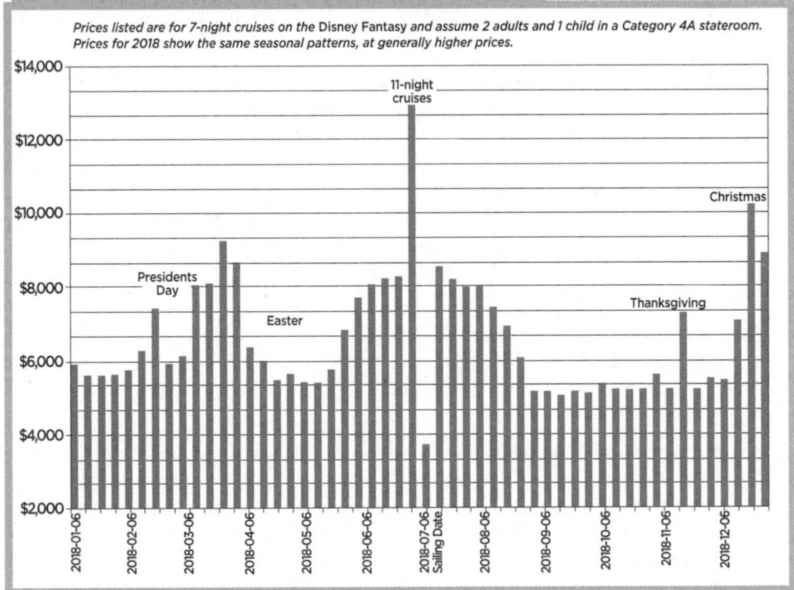

it starts back in the fall. Your fare won't be as low when school is in session, but it's the best you're going to get.

What's truly astounding is the difference in price between December 9 and December 23. That two-week difference will cost you nearly double if you want to toast the New Year aboard the *Fantasy*. Or, put another way, you could sail back-to-back in January—14 nights—for little more than you would for the Christmas cruise. We know which option we'd choose.

PRICE TRENDS BY SHIP AND ITINERARY

YOU NOTICED, OF COURSE, THAT "BOOK EARLY" AND "WAIT" are complementary suggestions—if you can't do one, do the other. In this section, we show how these strategies work for each ship in the Disney fleet on some of DCL's most popular itineraries. The previous and following graphs represent our analysis of more than a million prices gathered from DCL's website, for every combination of family size, stateroom category, ship, and voyage.

To simplify this discussion, we show the pricing trends for two-adult, two-child families in DCL's Deluxe Family Oceanview Stateroom with Verandah (DFOVSV), for sailings in summer 2018, from 15 months to a few days in advance, as follows:

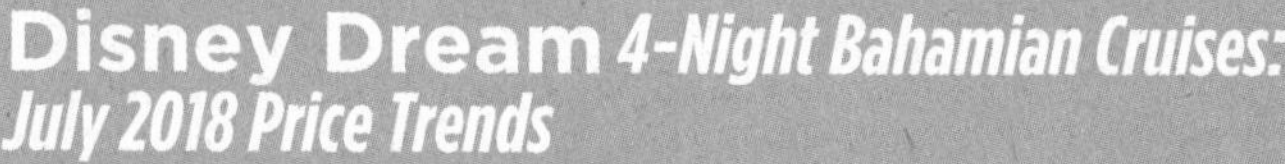

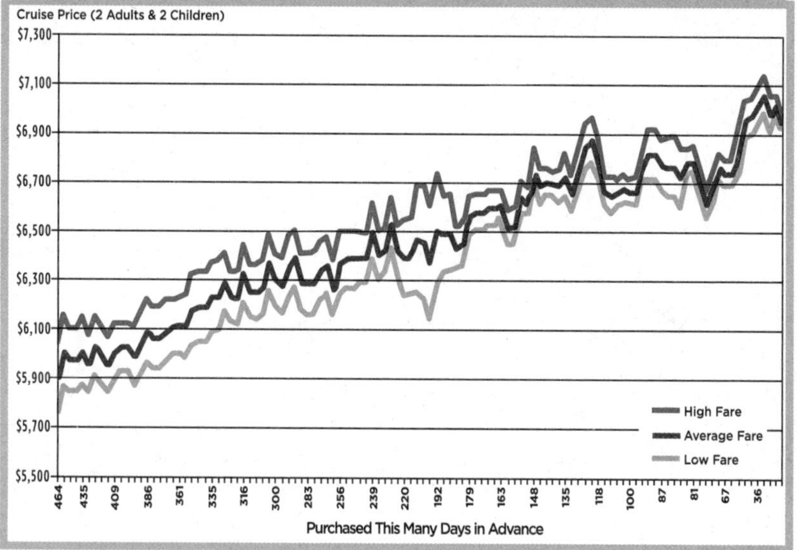

- Four-night Bahamian cruises on the *Dream*
- Seven-night Western Caribbean cruises on the *Fantasy*
- Seven-night Alaskan cruises on the *Wonder*
- Seven-night Mediterranean cruises on the *Magic*

The price of a specific DFOVSV depends primarily on the deck on which it's located; staterooms on a higher deck usually cost more than the same stateroom on a lower deck. In the following charts, we show the price trends for the highest and lowest price of all DFOVSVs on all decks. The charts use a 20-day rolling average for the prices to smooth out tiny variations.

As in years past, "book early" is the best strategy for DCL's **Bahamas** cruises. Our typical family would save around $700, or 11%, on the cost of their cruise by booking a year in advance, compared with booking at around 80 days. The price trend for cabins on higher decks shows a small drop between 120 and 100 days out, and again at day 85. (This trend has appeared in 2017 and 2018 prices.)

The Bahamas price trend for cabins on lower decks generally remains around $200 less than the same category for a higher deck, from the time the cruise goes on sale until about 80 days before departure. For these kinds of staterooms, we think "book now" is the best advice. The average savings you'd get by trying to time any price drop

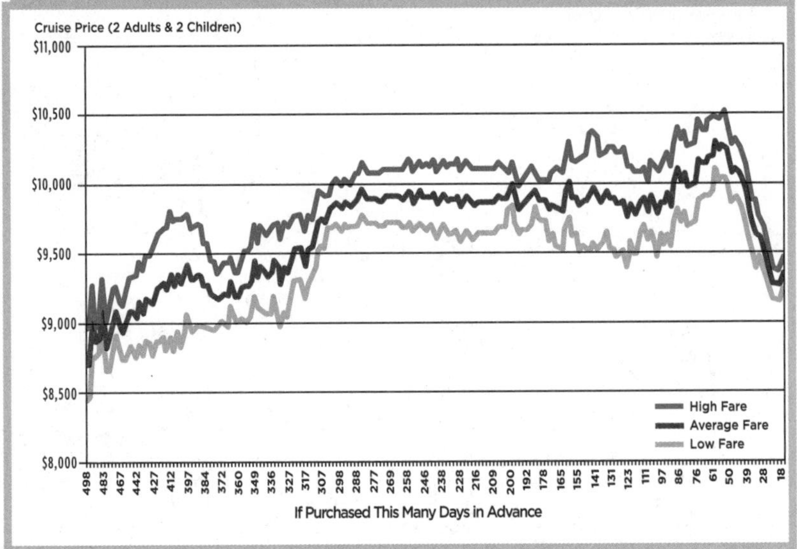

is around $300 or less—no more than 5% of your cruise fare—and it doesn't seem worth the time or stress to do that.

Price trends are similar for Disney's **Caribbean** cruises on the *Fantasy,* with the lowest prices offered a year in advance. As with the *Dream,* the *Fantasy*'s prices tend to fluctuate by around $700 or so from 12 months to 7 months in advance. If you want to be sure of a room on a specific sailing, book as early as you can. If you're less concerned about the exact room you get, it's worth noting that last-minute Western Caribbean cruise prices dropped about $1,000 from their peak.

The same "book now" advice holds true with **Alaskan** cruises on the *Wonder,* as shown on the opposite page. A couple of interesting things to note here: (1) The low fares in 2016 were less than $10,000. They're now more than $14,000. (2) The prices show much less variability. In 2016, stateroom prices could swing by $2,000. In 2017, it's less than $1,600 overall, and around $1,200 for upper-deck cabins. That means Disney's data scientists, who help set these prices, are getting better at matching price and demand further in advance.

Prices for **Mediterranean** cruises on the *Magic* (see chart on page 32) show the most volatility. The best options are to book very early (more than a year in advance) or very late (within 45 days of departure).

Disney Wonder ***7-Night Alaskan Cruises: July 2018 Price Trends***

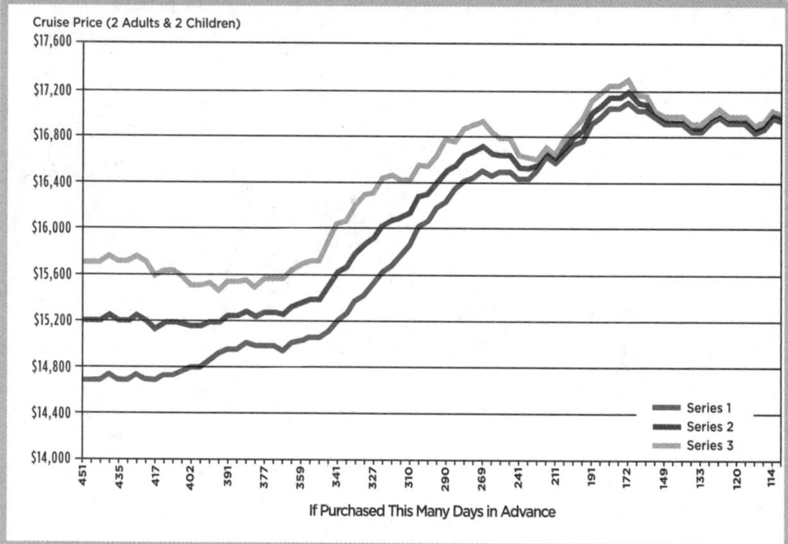

If that's not possible, book whenever you see fares drop to within $500–$700 of their year-in-advance prices.

Finally, if you're trying to decide whether to book a cruise in 2019 or 2020, know that we expect cruise prices to climb substantially higher in 2020 than in 2019. On page 33 is one last chart, showing the price of a standard four-night **Bahamian** cruise on the *Dream,* for every sailing during the year, from 2014 through 2019. Prices are quoted approximately 12 months before departure. Summer cruise fares have increased by around $1,600—almost 33%—since 2017. We expect that trend to continue for the near future.

SURF *and* TURF, DISNEY-STYLE

COMBINING YOUR CRUISE WITH A WALT DISNEY WORLD VACATION

DISNEY SELLS PACKAGES THAT COMBINE A DISNEY CRUISE with a trip to Walt Disney World for cruises departing from Port Canaveral. Called **Land and Sea** packages, these itineraries include the Bahamas, the Eastern and Western Caribbean, and the *Magic*'s Eastbound Transatlantic cruise to Barcelona, Spain.

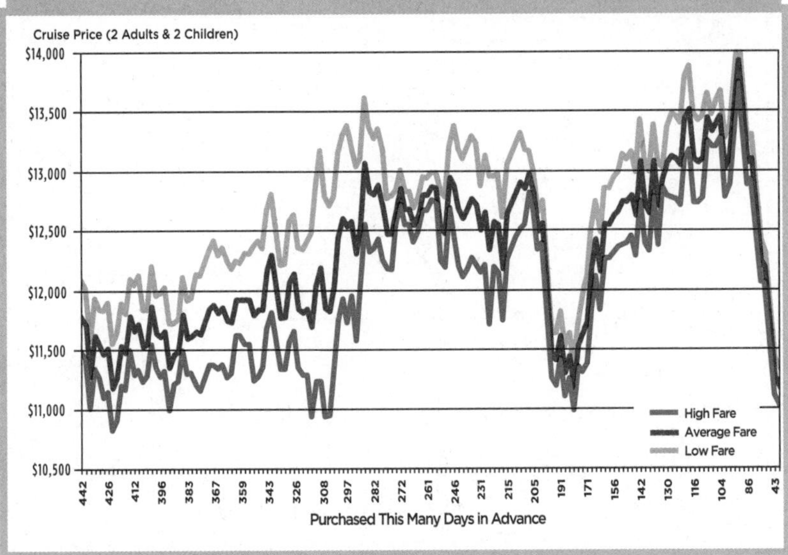

Land and Sea packages include lodging at a Walt Disney World on-property resort; theme park admission, dining plans, and other additional components can be added to the Walt Disney World portion of the trip.

Because of the lack of flexibility with a Land and Sea package booked through DCL, and because you save money when you book components à la carte, we recommend making reservations for each part of a theme park–cruise vacation separately. Regardless of whether you book Land and Sea together or separately, you can arrange bus transportation between Port Canaveral and your Walt Disney World resort for a fee.

unofficial **TIP**
We recommend seeing the World first—chances are that your tired legs (and wallet) will appreciate some downtime at sea.

The most frequent question we're asked about combining a theme park vacation with a cruise is whether to visit Disney World before or after the cruise. The majority of people who've done both say they were more relaxed on the cruise than at Walt Disney World, so they prefer to take the cruise after the park visit. Some families don't have a preference either way. A relatively small number prefer to see Walt Disney World second because they prefer the faster pace of WDW after a cruise.

Disney Dream 4A Cabins

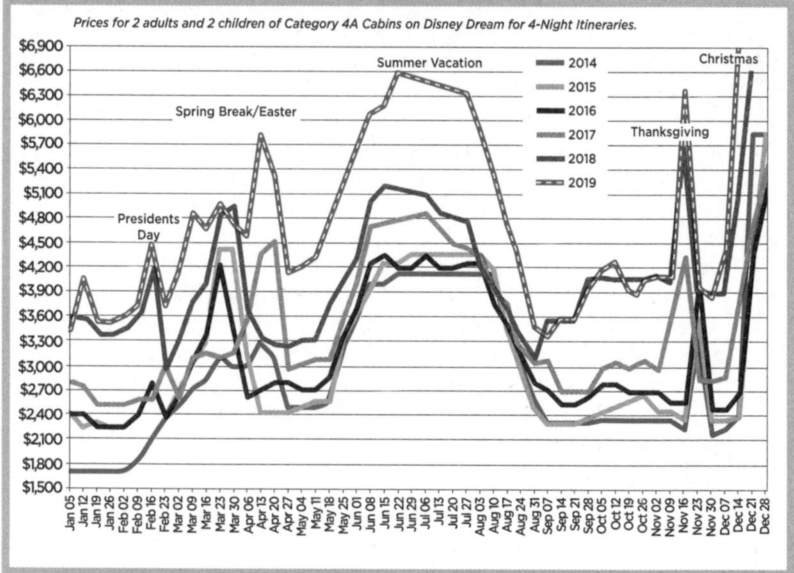

COMBINING YOUR CRUISE WITH AN ADVENTURES BY DISNEY TRIP

SOME EUROPEAN CRUISES out of Barcelona and Copenhagen can be combined with a precruise or onboard **Adventures by Disney** (**AbD**) guided vacation. Precruise AbD trips include lodging, meals, and tours. AbD trips that are concurrent with a cruise include preselected port adventures accompanied by Disney-trained guides, as well as special onboard activities and assistance. For more details, see adventuresby disney.com (click "Cruises," then click "Disney Cruise Line Packages") or read our blog post on what the AbD cruise supplement looks like at tinyurl.com/abdsupplement.

In addition to its DCL supplements, AbD offers **European river cruising** on the Danube, the Rhine, and the Seine. See Part Thirteen for details.

BACK-*to*-BACK CRUISING

HAVE YOU EVER ENDED A CRUISE and thought, "I don't want to go home! Can't I just stay on board?" That's almost exactly what you do when you book back-to-back cruises—cruises on the same ship

SCOTT SAYS *by Scott Sanders*

PLAN OF ATTACK

THERE IS NO RIGHT OR WRONG WAY to pick a cruise. Ultimately, it comes down to where you want to cruise, when you want to cruise, and how much you want to spend. If you're flexible about the where and the when, then you might score a lower cruise fare.

We've discovered that our trips are more enjoyable when we include our daughter in the planning process. One way to do that is to look at *Personal Navigators* from prior sailings with a similar itinerary and ship. (You can find a selection of these on my website at tinyurl.com/dclnavigators.) While activities do change, daily schedules give an idea of what may be offered, and when. Whether you prefer to plan every hour of your vacation or just go with the flow, having a general idea of what might be interesting can make it easier when it comes to packing.

Take some time to review the deck plans for the ship you'll be sailing. The better you know the layout, the easier it will be to move around the ship during your vacation.

where the second cruise begins the day the first cruise ends. And we think it's *glorious*.

Other than not wanting to leave, why might you consider a back-to-back cruise?

1. **The ship you like doesn't offer longer cruises.** Our first back-to-back cruises were three and four nights on the *Dream*. You want a week on the *Dream*? *Voilà!* You got it.
2. **You want to see more ports.** Want to see both the Eastern *and* Western Caribbean? Book two consecutive cruises on the *Fantasy*. The Baltics *and* the Mediterranean? The *Magic* has you covered.
3. **You want to save on transportation costs.** Combining two itineraries can be less expensive (assuming you're planning to do both in the first place). For instance, it was much less expensive for us to fly to Vancouver, British Columbia; do a 7-night Alaskan cruise immediately followed by a 10-night cruise to Hawaii; and then fly home from Oahu than to book round-trip airfare to Canada *and* round-trip airfare to Honolulu.
4. **You're amassing Castaway Club credits.** We're not saying that one of our coauthors booked a back-to-back cruise just because the second cruise was the one that pushed her into Platinum Castaway Club status. But we're not saying she didn't either.
5. **You really love Castaway Cay.** A significant subset of Disney cruisers finds DCL's private Bahamian island to be the best part of their trip. If you're a Castaway Cay devotee and the few itineraries with "double dips" (two stops at Castaway Cay on one sailing) don't line up with your

vacation schedule, then you can cobble together your own double-dip vacation by scheduling a four-night and three-night sailing on the *Dream* back-to-back.

So how does it work?

First a caveat: not every consecutive cruise can be booked back-to-back due to federal maritime law. It's a bit confusing, and it applies only to ships registered outside of the United States, including DCL's ships, which are registered in the Bahamas. If your first cruise leaves from a US port, your last cruise ends in another US port, *and* you haven't visited a "distant foreign port" along the way, you're in violation of the Merchant Marine Act of 1920. (We know, it's complicated.)

unofficial **TIP**
If you're interested in back-to-back cruising, your best bet is to contact Disney before you book—and definitely before you've booked airfare—to be absolutely sure that you'll be allowed on the ship.

Oddly, the Disney website will let you book back-to-back cruises that violate the law, but once DCL catches your mistake, you'll be forced to choose one cruise or the other. Countries that this affects include the United States, Italy, and Norway. Because at this time no Disney cruises depart from Norway (though they do visit there), you'll need to pay close attention if you're booking a back-to-back that travels to either US coast, or if you're booking a back-to-back that includes southern Europe.

Here's a back-to-back example that's OK: an Alaskan cruise starting in Vancouver, followed by Vancouver to San Diego—this works because you're starting in Canada.

Not OK: Honolulu to Vancouver, followed by Vancouver to San Diego—you start in one US city and end in another; plus, Vancouver, despite being in Canada, is too close to the United States to be considered a *distant* foreign port.

unofficial **TIP**
If you're truly a travel-by-the-seat-of-your-swim-trunks cruiser, you can book a back-to-back on board while you're on what would be the first cruise. You'll pay in full at booking, and technically you can't be within 24 hours of the second sail date, but the Future Cruise Sales folks tell us people do this all the time.

Once you've booked successfully, you're going to be in one of two situations: either you were able to book the same cabin for each cruise or you weren't. If you have the same cabin, life is beautiful—you pack a carry-off with any medications or valuables you need with you, leave everything else in your cabin (unpacked, still in the closets and drawers), and walk off with the debarking passengers. Then you check in again (in the Castaway Club platinum lounge), share a smug look with your fellow passengers who are doing the same thing, and walk back on once you're cleared. The ship is so empty when you board again that Len once did carpet angels in the atrium after reboarding.

If you're changing cabins, you'll have to pack as if you're leaving, but DCL will move your bags to your new cabin for you. You still

have to carry off only a day bag, and you won't need to go through customs between cruises. Your room attendant will know ahead of time that you're a back-to-back cruiser, and you'll be given written instructions on the last night for how things will go. Then you just enjoy your next cruise.

Note that if you've bought an onboard internet package (see page 110), none of your unused data will roll over on a back-to-back cruise, so don't make the mistake of buying a new package on the last night of your first cruise thinking you'll be able to keep it.

The BOOKING PROCESS

GETTING STARTED

ONCE YOU'VE SETTLED ON A SHIP, an itinerary, and dates, it's time to book your trip. You have three ways to do this:

1. Use the DCL website. **2.** Call DCL at ☎ 800-951-3532. **3.** Use a travel agent.

There are advantages to each. The main advantage to booking yourself, either online or by phone, is that you can usually do it immediately. If you've booked a cruise before, you have access to each traveler's information, you don't have questions about the ship or itinerary, and you want instant gratification, this may be your best option.

The main advantage of using a travel agent is that he or she can save you time by doing most of the tedious legwork for you; plus, the agent may also offer a discount in the form of onboard credit—money you can use to pay for items like adult beverages, port excursions, photography services, or babysitting. Many agents have booked dozens, if not hundreds, of cruises, and have a single-page form for you to fill out, where you provide your preferences for everything from what time you prefer to board the ship to when you prefer to eat. Some travel agencies will also rebook your cruise automatically if a lower fare becomes available; a travel agent might also be able to save you money because he or she might have access to group space for a particular cruise. (You're not required to participate in any group activities, but you do get the price advantage of the group booking.) Finally, a seasoned travel agent may be able to help you find rooms with special characteristics, such as an oversize verandah, a particular view, or one of the few sets of inside staterooms connected to porthole staterooms.

DEPOSIT TERMS AND CANCELLATION POLICIES

MOST CRUISE RESERVATIONS REQUIRE A DEPOSIT equal to 20% of the cruise's price (not including taxes) for each passenger age 3 and older on that reservation. Some DCL promotions, such as booking a follow-up cruise while you're already on a current cruise, require only

a 10% deposit. Booking a future cruise while you're on the ship almost always includes an onboard credit for the cruise you're booking, too.

Disney Cruise Line's full cancellation policy can be found online at the DCL website; click "Terms and Conditions" at the bottom of the home page. You can cancel a reservation in writing or by phone; also, moving the date of your cruise or changing the name of someone on your reservation is considered a cancellation.

The amount of your refund depends on a variety of criteria (terms were updated in 2018). If you've booked a Concierge-level stateroom or suite, the following policies apply:

CONCIERGE CANCELLATION POLICY: 1–5 NIGHTS
Payment in full required 120 days prior to arrival.
Cancel 90 days or more before sailing, charge is **deposit per guest**
Cancel 89–56 days before sailing, charge is **50% of vacation price per guest**
Cancel 55–30 days before sailing, charge is **75% of vacation price per guest**
Cancel 29 days or fewer before sailing, charge is **100% of vacation price per guest**

CONCIERGE CANCELLATION POLICY: 6 NIGHTS OR LONGER
Payment in full required 150 days prior to arrival.
Cancel 90 days or more before sailing, charge is **deposit per guest**
Cancel 89–56 days before sailing, charge is **50% of vacation price per guest**
Cancel 55–30 days before sailing, charge is **75% of vacation price per guest**
Cancel 29 days or fewer before sailing, charge is **100% of vacation price per guest**

The standard cancellation policies are less restrictive:

STANDARD CANCELLATION POLICY: 1–5 NIGHTS
Payment in full required 90 days prior to arrival.
Cancel 89–45 days before sailing, charge is deposit per guest
Cancel 44–30 days before sailing, charge is 50% of vacation price per guest
Cancel 29–15 days before sailing, charge is 75% of vacation price per guest
Cancel 14 days or fewer before sailing, charge is 100% of vacation price per guest

STANDARD CANCELLATION POLICY: 6 NIGHTS OR LONGER
Payment in full required 120 days prior to arrival.
Cancel 119–56 days before sailing, charge is deposit per guest
Cancel 55–30 days before sailing, charge is 50% of vacation price per guest
Cancel 29–15 days before sailing, charge is 75% of vacation price per guest
Cancel 14 days or fewer before sailing, charge is 100% of vacation price per guest

Cruises booked with a "restricted rate" discount code are always nonrefundable and nontransferable—you eat the cost of the entire cruise if you don't sail.

Airfare and port-hotel bookings made through Disney have unique cancellation policies. Check with DCL or your travel agent for specifics.

AGE REQUIREMENTS FOR BOOKING

DCL ALLOWS ADULTS age 18 and up to travel unaccompanied and book their own staterooms. However, **guests age 17 and younger must be booked into a room with an adult age 21 or older.**

DCL's age requirement is liberal compared with, say, Carnival's, which at this writing allows only adults age 21 and older to book and travel unaccompanied and requires guests under 18 to travel with an adult who's at least 25. Additionally, Carnival imposes restrictions on the number of people of certain ages who may travel together. For example, an adult over 25 may chaperone no more than eight people under 21. The exceptions to Carnival's rules—young married couples and military personnel—must provide careful documentation of their circumstances. Disney's policy affords young married couples, young servicepeople, and most college students the ability to travel unchaperoned and unencumbered by extra paperwork.

Nevertheless, any group that includes minors needs to consider the implications of the age requirement when planning a Disney cruise. For example, a single parent who wants to travel with four minor kids would have to book a suite. That's often more expensive than booking two individual rooms, but it's the only option in this case because DCL doesn't allow minors to stay by themselves in a different stateroom, even if the rooms are connected by an inside door.

In the case of a couple who want to book more than one room but are traveling with just one minor child, Disney requires that one parent be booked into a room with the child. Further, if the parent who is registered in a different room wants to leave the ship with the child, that parent must first sign a waiver at the Guest Services desk.

A few situations would either be a no-go or require altering to meet the age requirement:

- High school and college spring breakers, some of whom are 18 and some of whom aren't
- Young adults ages 18–20 who want to travel with younger siblings but without their parents
- Families traveling with an under-21 childcare provider whom they wish to book in the same room as the child
- Guests wanting to travel with minors who aren't in their immediate family—for example, a child's friend or grandchild whom you're happy to have along but whom you might not want sleeping in the same room as you

In general, DCL requires that guests be age 21 or older to drink alcohol. Guests ages 18–20 may drink on some European cruises with a parent or guardian's written consent, as long as that parent or guardian is present when the alcohol is purchased and consumed.

MY DISNEY CRUISE

INFORMATION ABOUT YOUR CRUISE is stored in a section of the DCL website called My Disney Cruise, similar to the My Disney Experience planning center at the Walt Disney World website. At this writing, My Disney Cruise can be accessed from the top-right corner of the DCL home page (disneycruise.com) or directly at disneycruise.disney.go.com/my-disney-cruise/reservations.

You must pay your deposit and receive your confirmation number before you can use My Disney Cruise. If you've cruised with DCL previously, you may access your reservation without your reservation number through the website's Castaway Club section.

My Disney Cruise includes the following subsections:

- **My Reservations** Provides basic information about your upcoming cruise, including your reservation number and the names of the guests in your party (click "View Details" to see your stateroom number and its location, plus your port arrival/departure times); your assigned dining time (and the ability to change this, pending availability); whether you've purchased the Vacation Protection Plan (Disney travel insurance); whether you've added Disney ground transfers to/from the port; links to activity planning (such as port adventures, spa treatments, or adult dining); a link to a special-request form for lactose-free, low-fat, vegan, or vegetarian dining; and a link to request a free character call to announce your trip. My Reservations also includes links to the following:

    Required documents for your trip

    Packing suggestions

    Download access to the DCL Navigator app (see page 107)

    Driving directions to the DCL ports

    Information about air- and ground-transportation options (see page 90 for additional information)

- **My Cruise Activities** Connects to the "My Reservations" page and becomes active after you've paid in full for your voyage. When you're inside your booking window (based on your Castaway Club level; see page 65), use My Cruise Activities to reserve port adventures (see page 365), adult dining (see page 153), spa treatments (see page 249), infant care (see page 225), adult-beverage tastings (see page 244), and more. Occasionally, port adventures and some onboard activities (notably character meals and some character-greeting experiences) are added as options days or weeks after initial booking begins. Even if you've already booked your supplemental activities, you may want to check back every few days to see if there has been anything new added.

- **My Online Check-In** You may check in online up to three days before your sailing. This is where you'll give DCL specifics about your pre- and postcruise travel, authorize your credit card for onboard purchases, and provide additional information about your party. While Online Check-In isn't mandatory, we strongly recommend it: it can serve as a reminder

about documents you'll need for your trip, and it'll help save you and your party time at the port terminal.

- **My Saved Cruises** Holding spot for cruises that you've marked online that you may be interested in.
- **My Family and Friends** Links to information about family members you're traveling with, including the ability to share your vacation plans with them online.
- **Make a Payment** Here's where you pay for your cruise. After you've paid in full, Make a Payment redirects to My Reservations.
- **My Profile** Links to your online relationship with Disney, including affiliations with Disney theme parks. Includes links for changing your address, updating your password, or tinkering with other biographical information.
- **Cruise Planning Tools** Links to a 1-hour vacation-planning video and e-brochure.
- **DCL Navigator App** This is another way to access the app.
- **Photography Services** Provides information about photo opportunities on the ship, as well as a link to preorder onboard photo packages via My Cruise Photos (mycruisephotos.com/dcl; see page 117).
- **Gifts and Amenities** Lists information about gifts and items you can preorder for your stateroom: floral arrangements, fruit baskets, holiday decor, and beverages (water, beer, and wine). Somewhat incongruously, it's also the place to reserve a one-day pass to the spa's Rainforest Room shower, sauna, and relaxation area (see "Spas," page 249). Another odd twist: to actually order any of these items, you'll need to complete your request by phone, fax, or snail mail. Orders must be placed three days before you sail. Also note that on some sailings you'll find a link here to rent formalwear.
- **Castaway Club** Links to information about your Castaway Club status (see page 65) as well as current details on club benefits. You can also see the dates and stateroom numbers for all your previous sailings. This can be particularly helpful if you want to book a stateroom similar to one you had before but can't remember the exact cabin type.

OTHER PREP WORK

PACKING

HAVING TRAVELED WITH LOTS OF PEOPLE over many years, we realize that asking "What do I need to pack?" is like asking "What is art?" Everyone will have their own answer based on their experience and preferences. Some people assume they're going to do laundry on the ship and pack three days' worth of clothes for a seven-night cruise; others would rather pay for an extra suitcase to carry more clean clothes. Bottom line: it's up to you.

Knowing what to pack is equally important, and the range of opinions regarding packing essentials varies wildly. The DCL website has a helpful page (disneycruise.disney.go.com/faq/preparing-for-cruise/pack-list) with suggestions on appropriate clothing for the ship's restaurants and ports of call, along with a short, reasonable list of incidentals to pack (as well as stuff you can't bring aboard).

When you're looking at the packing tips on the DCL website, be sure to consult the list for your destination—not surprisingly, you'll need to pack a bit differently for Alaska than you would for the Caribbean. In addition to general packing lists, you may want to consider the particular port adventures you've selected. For example, if you're touring in Rome, you may want to dress more stylishly than you would if you're just hanging out at the beach, or if you're planning to visit churches and cathedrals, you'll want to take a moment to research their dress codes.

Beyond that, just type "Disney Cruise Line packing list" into any search engine, and you'll see thousands of lists with hundreds of items. Some of them read like an Amazon jungle-trek prep list (yes, mosquito netting appears on more than one). It's useful to read through a couple of lists to see if they mention anything you can't live without. Our most important packing advice is this: don't drive yourself crazy trying to pack for every scenario. You're going to lug those bags a lot farther than you might think.

unofficial **TIP**
If you're not absolutely sure that you're going to use something on your cruise, *leave it at home.*

You can buy most everyday personal items on board if needed—it's probably not worth a trip to the drugstore to buy motion-sickness pills, antibiotic/anti-itch creams, or over-the-counter pain relievers if you don't already have them on hand at home. The primary exception is remedies for gastric distress, which aren't sold on board. (See page 53 for more on gastric distress and motion sickness.)

Besides appropriate clothing, our short packing list includes the following essentials:

- **Prescription medications** Pack these in carry-on luggage, in their original containers. (See pages 43 and 131.)
- **Tablet computer** Load enough books, music, movies, TV shows, games, and apps for the cruise, plus the trip to and from the port. Remember that onboard internet speed and pricing make video streaming all but impossible. If your child must have access to particular content, then be sure you download it to your device before you set sail.
- **White-noise mobile app** This is useful for drowning out noise from hallways, next-door cabins, and ship machinery. A good one to try is **Sleepmaker Rain** (available in free and paid versions at the Apple App Store and Google Play).
- **Hats, sunglasses, and sunscreen** Sunscreen is reasonably priced on the ships in case you don't want to pack it.
- **Water shoes or flip-flops** You'll need these for the pool and beach.

Some guests may find that they have more luggage than they can reasonably transport to the ship on their own; this often happens to guests with small children sailing on longer voyages with bulky items such as diapers and wipes. In such cases, you can mail a package to yourself at Port Canaveral for delivery to the ship. Only one mailed box is allowed per stateroom. Use the following address for mailing the package:

DISNEY CRUISE LINE WAREHOUSE
[Guest name + stateroom number, or **GTY** if you don't know your room number]
8633 Transport Drive
Orlando, FL 32832
ATTN: Housekeeping

The package must have your name, the ship name, your sail date, and your stateroom number noted on the outside of the box. Your box should also have a packing slip (think a FedEx window envelope) affixed to the exterior, detailing the contents of the package. Boxes should not weigh more than 20 pounds and cannot measure more than 12 inches per side. Packages must arrive at least 24 hours prior to sail-away time. If you have questions about the process, contact DCL at ☎ 407-566-8196.

If you're departing from a port other than Port Canaveral, you may be able to ship a box to yourself at your pre-sail hotel. Check with the hotel directly for address information and other instructions.

Some guests choose to economize on alcohol by bringing their own. Guests age 21 or older may bring a maximum of two bottles of unopened wine or Champagne (no larger than 750 milliliters) or a six-pack of beer (bottles or cans no larger than 12 ounces each) on board at the beginning of the trip *and* at each port of call. These beverages must be packed in carry-on bags—*not* your checked luggage. Alcohol packed in your checked luggage will be removed and stored.

unofficial **TIP**
Food is prohibited in shipped boxes. This includes baby food/formula and alcohol.

If you bring hard liquor, powdered alcohol, or beer or wine in excess of the allowed quantity, it will be stored until the end of the cruise. If you plan on purchasing the local firewater while in port, ask to have it packaged for travel (for example, in bubble wrap) because the ship will hold it for you when you board; the next time you'll see it is when you're getting ready to head home.

While you're packing, it makes sense to take a peek at the fairly extensive list of items that are prohibited aboard the ship. Not surprisingly, you can't bring weapons or fireworks, but did you know that you also can't bring pool noodles, musical instruments, inline skates, fishing gear, or kites? Other prohibited items include candles, clothing irons, DVD players, gaming systems like XBox or PlayStation, balloons, wagons, and Christmas lights. Even if you've cruised previously,

a repeat look at the banned-items list is prudent. Recent additions to the list include toy guns (including Disney-themed guns such as Star Wars blasters), remote-controlled drones (including those intended for photography), and marijuana, even if medically prescribed. Find the complete list of banned items at tinyurl.com/dclprohibiteditems.

Likewise, use common sense and don't bring any items with you that would be difficult or impossible to replace: expensive or sentimental jewelry, or your child's one and only "lovey." We had a daughter's beloved plush bunny go missing on a cruise, much to the distress of the entire family. (Farewell, Pinky, we hardly knew ye.) If items such as these must make the trip, label them with your contact information—sew a soft tag on a stuffed toy—and keep them in the stateroom safe when not in use. This applies to favorite toys as well as jewelry. (Pinky disappeared when a housekeeper inadvertently took her away with the sheets when she stripped the bed.)

TRAVELING WITH PRESCRIPTION MEDICATIONS A hot topic on cruise discussion boards is whether prescription medicines must be transported in their original containers or can be transferred to handy daily-dose containers. Some guests with complex medical conditions argue that they'd need an additional suitcase to pack all of their prescription bottles and claim they've never been questioned about their meds. Honestly, we've never been questioned either over many cruises—but we also realize that it takes just one challenge to derail your otherwise relaxing vacation.

DCL recommends keeping meds in their original bottles, as do the Food and Drug Administration and U.S. Customs and Border Protection. If, like most cruisers, you'll be visiting countries other than your own, be aware that they have their own regulations as well and that foreign airlines may also have restrictions.

In short, err on the side of caution.

unofficial **TIP**
We recommend bringing one converter per person, two if you're traveling alone.

ELECTRICAL OUTLETS

ALL OUTLETS ON DCL SHIPS conform to the North American 110V/60Hz standard. If you live in the United States or Canada, any device you have that operates normally at home should work fine on board. All staterooms have hair dryers, so if you're tight on space or not attached to your own model, you won't need to pack one.

If you're visiting from outside the United States, you may need an adapter or converter for your electric gadgets. What's the difference? An adapter ensures that the plug on your device will fit into the electrical receptacle in the wall, but it doesn't change the electrical voltage. A converter does both (and costs more). Your local version of Amazon likely has an excellent selection.

Be aware that there is a real scarcity of electrical outlets in most staterooms, particularly on the *Wonder.* If two people in your party over age 8 will be sharing a stateroom, you'll almost certainly need to

bring some mechanism to add outlet access—problem is, power strips and extension cords are on DCL's list of prohibited items. A good workaround is a plug-in USB hub. Many inexpensive models allow four or five USB devices (phones, tablets, and the like) to charge on one outlet. If you're bringing a laptop, you can use that as a charging hub, too.

Another possible workaround is an international electrical converter, even if your cruise takes place in the United States. Most staterooms have a 220-volt outlet near the desk, which is intended for the hair dryer provided on board. If you have a converter, you can use this outlet for your 120-volt US devices.

PASSPORTS AND TRAVEL DOCUMENTS

EVERYONE IN YOUR PARTY, including babies and children, must present proof of citizenship before boarding the ship. *A passport is your simplest, safest bet because it covers all your bases.* You **must** have a passport if you're a US citizen flying from home to a foreign cruise port, or vice versa. In other situations, it's good to have but not absolutely necessary.

If you don't have a passport and (1) you're a US citizen traveling from a US port (such as Port Canaveral, Miami, Galveston, San Diego, New Orleans, or New York); (2) you're traveling only within the Western Hemisphere (the US, Canada, Mexico, or the Caribbean); and (3) you're on a so-called closed-loop cruise—that is, you're embarking and debarking from the same US port on the same ship—you may be able to use alternative documentation.

According to U.S. Customs and Border Protection (see cbp.gov/travel/us-citizens/western-hemisphere-travel-initiative), adult cruisers meeting these conditions may present government-issued photo ID *plus* proof of citizenship: an original or copy of a state-issued birth certificate, a Consular Report of Birth Abroad, or a Certificate of Naturalization. US citizens under age 16 (or under age 19 if traveling with a school group, religious group, or other organized youth group) need present only the proof of citizenship. Be aware, however, that you may still need a passport to enter the countries your cruise ship is visiting, so check before you go.

For adult US citizens who don't have a passport, acceptable photo-ID options on a closed-loop cruise include the following:

- **A U.S. Passport Card.** This limited-used document lets you enter the US by land or sea from within the Western Hemisphere. At this writing, a Passport Card costs $55 for adults age 16 and older, versus $135 for a full passport.
- **An Enhanced Driver's License (EDL).** An EDL provides proof of both identity and citizenship in addition to certifying you to drive. Currently available only to US citizens in Michigan, Minnesota, New York State, Vermont, and Washington State, EDLs contain security features such as a radio frequency identification (RFID) chip.
- **A Trusted Traveler Program Card** (NEXUS, SENTRI, or FAST).
- **A Uniformed Services ID Card** for US military traveling on official orders.

We recommend that all members of your party obtain passports if possible, even for a closed-loop cruise. Let's say that you're on a port adventure in Nassau and you learn of an urgent family emergency. If you have a passport, you can hop on a plane and be back home within hours. If you don't, you'll have to go to the U.S. Embassy, shell out the money for an expedited passport, and then wait for it to be processed before you can fly home.

Documentation requirements for Canadian citizens are similar: a Canadian passport, Canadian Enhanced Driver's Licence, or Trusted Traveler Card. Citizens of other countries may be required to present a passport or visa to enter a port even if US and Canadian citizens aren't.

As of 2018, all US citizens flying domestically must provide a **Real ID**–compliant driver's license or ID card at their airport's Transportation Security Administration (TSA) checkpoint. At press time, a number of states and territories weren't fully compliant with Real ID regulations, which are intended to combat terrorism; residents of states that weren't fully compliant as of January 22, 2018, must provide an alternative form of identification, such as a passport or one of the four documents above. Check your state's status at dhs.gov/real-id. If your state isn't in compliance yet, you may not be able to fly using only a standard driver's license as identification—you would need a passport or another form of ID listed on the dhs.gov website.

A particularly confusing area of ID requirements applies to US citizens traveling on Alaskan cruises from Vancouver. With the Western Hemisphere Travel Initiative, you could drive from the United States to Vancouver with only a Real ID driver's license or a US passport *card,* but you may be required to have a passport *book* to board the ship in Vancouver, depending on whether you're on a closed-loop cruise, a repositioning cruise, or a back-to-back sailing. Be sure to confirm your exact documentation needs well before your trip. When in doubt, the passport book is the gold standard.

Check the specifics of your sailing when choosing excursions. Again, if you're an American citizen and your cruise starts from a non-US port, you must have a passport to get there. Also, note that some DCL port adventures on Alaskan cruises require a valid passport because you cross into Canada during the trip. Plus, some foreign ports, notably those in Russia, require not only passports but also special visas for guests who plan to explore the port on their own versus with an approved excursion group or tour guide.

Whichever forms of identification you bring, be sure to secure them when traveling—either in your stateroom/hotel-room safe when you're not in port or on your person when you're out and about. Some guidebooks recommend leaving your passport on board at all times, but we've seen too many instances of people being left behind because of a taxi breakdown or other mishap. If you have your passport and a credit card, you can fly to the next port to meet the ship if needed. That beats searching for an embassy, possibly having to wait

for it to reopen after a weekend or holiday, and then paying for and waiting for an expedited replacement.

Also be sure to take precautions in the unlikely event that your ID is lost or stolen. Make photocopies of your passport or other documents; keep one set of copies in your luggage and another set at home with a trusted friend or relative. We also email digital copies of our ID and travel documents to ourselves or upload them to the cloud.

GETTING A PASSPORT US citizens may obtain passports themselves by following the steps at tinyurl.com/howtoapplyforapassport. Once you submit your application, you should receive your passport within six weeks, but you may be able to get it more quickly by visiting an official passport agency in person. See tinyurl.com/uspassportagencies for locations.

While Disney does not offer additional passport advice beyond working directly with the U.S. Department of State, many other major cruise lines (including Royal Caribbean, Holland America, and Norwegian Cruise Line) refer guests needing passport assistance to **Visa Central** (877-535-0688, visacentral.com). This reputable fee-based service can help with passport processing and offers one-day turnaround on passport renewals. If you find the application process too complicated to tackle on your own, Visa Central may be worth the cost.

TSA PRECHECK If you fly at least a couple of times per year, you may want to consider registering for **TSA PreCheck** (tsa.gov/precheck). This service shortens your waits in line to less than five minutes in most cases; it also lets you skip hassles such as removing your shoes and unpacking liquids and electronics from your carry-on luggage. Membership costs $85 for five years, so it's money well spent.

If you fly more than six times per year, you may want to consider **Clear** (clearme.com/home), a higher-fee service that provides even faster screening, letting you skip to the front of the TSA precheck line. Or, if you make frequent international trips, **Global Entry** (cbp.gov/travel/trusted-traveler-programs/global-entry) could be your best option. We're fans of all of these.

MINOR AUTHORIZATION If you're an adult age 21 or older traveling with someone else's minor child, Disney Cruise Line requires written permission from the child's parent or legal guardian in addition to proof of the child's citizenship. DCL's **Minor Authorization Form** is available as a PDF at tinyurl.com/dclminorauthorization. Present the form at check-in at the cruise terminal.

If you're cruising outside the United States with your minor child but without the child's other parent—whether you're a single parent or your spouse/partner couldn't make the trip—U.S. Customs and Border Protection recommends that you also bring along a signed, notarized letter of permission in addition to proof of the child's citizenship. (See tinyurl.com/childtravel for details.) Adults traveling with someone else's

minor child are advised to do the same in addition to filling out the Minor Authorization Form.

The permission letter isn't legally required, and many cruisers, including Erin, report that they've never been asked for it. That said, customs reserves the right to investigate situations that it deems suspicious, so better safe than sorry.

The letter should include the following information:

- The child's full name and birth date
- Your full name, address, and phone number
- The other parent's full name, address, and phone number
- A description of the entire trip, including dates, countries, and cruise information, plus transportation information if available
- The purpose of the trip
- The other parent's original signature, in ink, and the date of his or her signature

Banks and post offices usually have a notary public on staff, but don't put off this task until the last minute in case you can't locate one easily. The notary will have to witness the other parent signing the form, so it's best to have the other parent present the form to the notary. DCL doesn't require that the Minor Authorization Form be notarized, but if you're already getting a permission letter notarized, it couldn't hurt to get the form notarized as well.

CREDIT CARDS AND PAYMENT METHODS

DISNEY CRUISE LINE SHIPS accept cash, traveler's checks, Visa, MasterCard, American Express, Discover, Diners Club, JCB, and the Disney Visa Card. They also accept Disney gift cards, Disney Rewards Dollars (available to Disney Chase Visa holders), and Disney Dollars (which were discontinued in 2016 but are still redeemable).

Your stateroom key serves as a credit card. Cash is not accepted directly as payment for beverages, spa or salon services, photography, laundry, or retail purchases. If cash is your preferred method of payment, you'll need to stop by the Guest Services desk to set up a Cash Account, which allows you to store cash that will fund the onboard charges made with your stateroom key. Even if you're securing your onboard account with a credit card and plan to make most onshore purchases with a card, you may still like to keep cash on hand to tip luggage attendants and pay for stuff while you're in port. Some guests also like to keep cash on hand to tip for room-service deliveries or to add to gratuity envelopes for their stateroom host or dining-room server. You can cash checks and obtain change from the Guest Services desk; you also can use other credit cards on board.

unofficial **TIP**
To prevent any sudden stops on your accounts, let your bank and credit card companies know that you're traveling abroad before you leave home.

US dollars are widely accepted throughout most of the Caribbean and in the Bahamas, and most prices are quoted in dollars. Credit cards from US-based banks are also accepted at many shops and stores, but don't count on smaller stores, bodegas, markets, and taxis taking them.

If you're traveling to Europe, Mexico, or Canada, you have a few options:

- **Ask your local bank to convert your US dollars before you leave home.** Many banks will do this at a reasonable exchange rate; some charge a small exchange fee. Give your bank about a week to obtain the currency you need, because many branches don't keep euros, pesos, or Canadian dollars on hand. Your bank will likely convert any unspent foreign currency back to dollars when you return, too.
- **Use a local ATM that's part of your bank's network.** If you're traveling in Europe and you're not sure how much cash to bring, you can usually get a fair exchange rate by withdrawing money at a local cash machine. Visa's website has a handy worldwide ATM locator (visa.com/atmlocator), and in our experience there are usually many more ATMs available than the ones listed online. Keep in mind that your local bank will probably add a withdrawal fee and a foreign-transaction fee, so it's better to make a few large withdrawals than lots of small ones.
- **Exchange traveler's checks for local currency when you disembark.** Traveler's checks are safer than carrying cash because they can be replaced if lost or stolen. The downside: converting them to local currency takes more time than using an ATM or obtaining local currency before you leave home.

If you want to convert your traveler's checks to cash, try to find a local bank willing to do the exchange, and verify the exchange calculations by hand. We've heard from readers who were promised one exchange rate outside a local currency-exchange stand (not a bank) and got another, lower rate when the conversion was done inside.

Passengers traveling on DCL ocean cruises and Adventures by Disney (AbD) river cruises in Europe should take particular care to understand the currency used in all of the countries they will be visiting, both during their cruise and during any pre- or postvoyage travel. Of particular note, not all countries in Europe use the euro as legal tender. For example, AbD's Rhine River cruises begin in Switzerland, which uses the Swiss franc, and the AbD Danube River cruises either start or end in Hungary, which uses the Hungarian forint. DCL European ports that do not use the euro include Norway, Iceland, Denmark, Russia, and several others.

The US dollar is unofficially accepted by many markets, bodegas, and taxis throughout Mexico, but you'll rarely get a good deal that way. You'll probably be offered a simple exchange rate of 10 or 15 pesos per dollar, whereas at press time the actual exchange rate was about 19 pesos per dollar, a significant difference from what you're likely to be offered.

If you're a frequent international traveler, it likely makes sense for you to check with your credit card providers to see if they charge a currency-exchange fee for purchases made with your cards in other countries. Some cards don't charge any exchange fees, so it could pay to shop around.

Having a credit card lost or stolen is an annoyance at any time, but it can be particularly upsetting when you're traveling and relying on your card for food and lodging, or for paying off your bingo and bar bill on board. We've had to cancel cards while on vacation more than once due to suspected identity theft. Replacing a compromised card on the road (or in the middle of the ocean) is much more complicated and stressful than simply having a new card delivered to your home or office. For this reason, we strongly suggest that you or members of your party travel with at least two kinds of credit and/or debit cards, with enough access to funds to pay for several days of your trip. Keep one card with you and the other tucked in your stateroom or hotel safe.

Be aware that the ships have no ATMs, but you can exchange small amounts of money (bills only, not coins) at the Guest Services desk, at prevailing exchange rates. DCL takes no commission on these transactions.

HEALTH INSURANCE

US RESIDENTS TRAVELING OUTSIDE OF THE STATES should contact their health insurance providers to check their coverage for emergencies outside the country. While Disney offers trip insurance for its cruises, it currently limits coverage to $10,000 per person for medical and dental emergencies. Ten grand at most hospitals these days is going to get you some ice, a Band-Aid, and a kiss from the doctor to make your boo-boo better . . . if you're lucky. If you're going to pay for additional insurance, make sure it's enough to be helpful in an emergency.

Residents of most European countries who are planning a Disney cruise in Europe should consider the **European Health Insurance Card,** which covers travel through much of Europe (see ec.europa.eu/social/main.jsp?catId=559). If you need additional travel insurance, companies such as American Express offer it for around 3% of the total cost of your trip.

Finally, some websites, such as insuremytrip.com, offer a handy feature for comparing travel insurance policies from different companies. **MouseSavers** (mousesavers.com) also contains some good tips.

PHONE SERVICE

WHEN IT COMES TO STAYING CONNECTED to the outside world during your cruise, you should first decide exactly *how* connected you want to be. Do you want to be accessible only in an emergency? Do you want to check email once or twice a day? Do you want to post to social media? Do you want to enjoy audio or video content? Are you OK with just texting, or do you want to be able to call home? Are you willing to

put in the effort to search for Wi-Fi locations while you're in port, or do you want to be fully connected at all times?

unofficial **TIP**
If you must use your phone to make calls from the ship, keep them brief and infrequent. Texting is cheaper but can still add up.

You also should be aware that connectivity while you're on the ship and while you're in port are two entirely different animals. Depending on your needs, you may actually have to arrange two different phone/data plans—one for use while you're at sea and one for use while you're on land.

ON BOARD **Wave Phones** are cell phones that you can use to call and text other members of your party on the ship and at Castaway Cay. Each stateroom also has a landline-style phone with voice mail.

Regular cellular service is also available through DCL's **Cellular@Sea** network. The rates for pay-as-you-go talk, text, and data roaming on board vary depending on your wireless carrier but are extremely expensive compared with a standard cellular plan—make sure that you have roaming turned off when you don't need it or, better yet, turn off your phone completely when you're not using it. Otherwise, your phone will connect to Cellular@Sea automatically—leaving you open to and possibly liable for hundreds or even thousands of dollars in unexpected charges.

Some carriers offer special cruise-ship plans or bundles that reduce costs. While they're more expensive than a typical wireless plan, rates have come down over the past few years. For example, Erin's AT&T plan now offers a talk–text cruise package that includes 50 minutes of voice calling and unlimited texting for $50—a 10-minute emergency call using your stateroom phone would cost far more, so springing for this package could be well worth its price in peace of mind. Be sure to check the specifics of your plan with your cell carrier so you can make any necessary changes before you board the ship.

If you're trying to unplug on your cruise and you prefer not to use your phone on board at all, you can use your stateroom phone to make and receive ship-to-shore calls in an emergency, but the rates are sky-high—$7–$9.50 per minute—and are charged to your stateroom. On the upside, calls are limited to 10 minutes. The number for incoming calls is ☎ 888-322-8732 in the United States or ☎ 732-335-3281 outside the United States; callers must provide a credit card number along with your ship and stateroom number.

IN PORT Most wireless carriers in the United States offer international talk, text, and data at rates far more reasonable than simply paying onboard roaming charges as you go. Check with your carrier before your cruise, though, to make sure it offers coverage in the countries you plan to visit.

T-Mobile includes free unlimited text and data in more than 200 countries as part of its T-Mobile One, Simple Choice, New Classic,

and Select Choice plans; depending on the plan, free calling within Canada and Mexico may also be included. T-Mobile's international data is too slow for video streaming but fine for emailing, web surfing, social media posting, and such.

Sprint has coverage similar to T-Mobile's and offers free unlimited international text and 2G data as an add-on to a regular plan (calls are 20¢ per minute), plus a separate package with free unlimited talk and text and 1GB of high-speed data covering Canada and most of Latin America (including Mexico). Sprint also has plans that include international LTE data for a flat daily or weekly rate, which varies by region.

AT&T's Unlimited Plus and Unlimited Choice Plans include unlimited talk and text throughout the United States, Canada, and Mexico. They also offer a $10-per-day, per-device International Day Pass, which provides unlimited talk and text in more than 100 countries, with data availablity based on your standard plan.

Verizon's international plans are similar to AT&T's, with daily flat-rate TravelPass options and monthly plans offering talk, text, and data in more than 100 countries.

Our general advice is to thoroughly research your carrier's options, paying particular attention to differences in rates and coverage on the ship versus off of it. Again, international plans used in port are nearly always a better value than onboard wireless bundles, and they're definitely a better value than just letting your phone roam indiscriminately.

If you've chosen either a land package or a sea package but not both, be aware of what type of service your phone is actually using. When the ship's wireless network is on, the display on your device will show **Cellular@Sea, 901-18,** or **NOR-18,** which indicates that you're roaming on Cellular@Sea. When you start roaming on a land carrier, your device will display that carrier's network information.

unofficial **TIP**
Cruise ships are required to turn off their wireless networks when they're 9–12 nautical miles from land and while in port.

The easiest ways to keep your wireless bill from spiraling out of control both on and off the ship are as follows:

1. **Keep your phone turned off when you're not using it.** If you don't have the patience or tech savvy to tinker with settings, this is the simplest way to ensure that your phone doesn't connect to a cellular network without your consent.

2. **Put your phone in airplane mode.** This shuts off your voice, text, and data connections but still lets you take pictures, listen to music, and connect to Wi-Fi (see below).

3. **Disable data unless you absolutely need it.** Look for an icon or button called "Settings" on your phone, and from there look for "Cellular," "Wireless and Networks," or the like. Under that, look for "Data Usage," "Cellular Data," "Data Roaming," "Mobile Data," or something similar—*make sure it's unchecked/turned off.* Otherwise, your phone will connect

to data on board or in port and sync email, cloud storage, and so on in the background. Simply turning off data is easier than tweaking sync settings in individual apps. Airplane mode (see previous page) accomplishes the same thing but also disables talk and text.

4. **Use Wi-Fi for calling and messaging in addition to web and email.** The four major US wireless carriers offer free Wi-Fi calling to the United States from international locations, depending on your plan. You need a phone that supports Wi-Fi calling; check with your carrier for details. You can also use messaging apps such as iMessage and WhatsApp over Wi-Fi. The catches, of course, are finding a hotspot with a strong signal and deciding whether you want to pay for Wi-Fi versus scrounging for free access (try Googling "free Wi-Fi in cruise ports"). If you do find a free hotspot, say, at a restaurant, keep in mind that you may be expected to buy a little something in return. (DCL's onboard Wi-Fi generally isn't reliable enough for making calls.)

unofficial **TIP**
If you use AT&T or T-Mobile, or you own a newer iPhone regardless of the carrier, your phone should work virtually anywhere DCL travels that has wireless coverage.

In addition to watching costs, you also need to make sure that your phone's wireless hardware is compatible with the wireless infrastructure of the countries you plan to visit. Almost all cell phones throughout the world use either **CDMA** or **GSM** to transmit calls.

Within the United States, Verizon, Sprint, and U.S. Cellular use CDMA, while AT&T and T-Mobile use GSM, which is also the standard in most of the rest of the world. Discount carriers such as MetroPCS, Straight Talk, and Tracfone piggyback on the major carriers' networks.

Note that the two technologies don't work together, so a phone that has only CDMA hardware won't work on a GSM network, and vice versa. (If your phone doesn't use a SIM card, it's CDMA, although the latest CDMA smartphones have SIM slots as well.) The currently available versions of the **iPhone,** whether sold unlocked through Apple or through a wireless carrier, have both CDMA and GSM hardware, as do a number of newer Android and BlackBerry devices; check with your carrier or your phone's manufacturer to be sure.

DCL ships have a dedicated desk for questions about internet packages (see page 110). The staff has printouts available detailing specific phone settings that will minimize your data consumption. If you're planning to use any data during your vacation, it's well worth stopping by the internet desk for information.

unofficial **TIP**
Disney's onboard Wi-Fi is free to use with the **DCL Navigator** app (see page 107).

If you have a US-based wireless carrier, using your phone in Alaska and Hawaii won't run up your bill, but you may experience service quality that's different from what you might expect in your hometown. For example, our AT&T service in Skagway, Alaska, was acceptable, but our Verizon service was spotty at best.

MOTION SICKNESS AND GASTRIC DISTRESS

THE DISNEY SHIPS ARE LARGE VESSELS with sophisticated stabilizers and other technology that keep motion to a minimum, and the navigation staff does as much as possible to minimize the impact of weather on ship motion. Most of the time, you'll feel no different on the ship than you would if you were strolling across your own front yard; nonetheless, there may be times when you feel the motion of the ocean. Depending on your level of sensitivity, the ship's route, sea conditions, and other factors, your perception of this situation might range from mild amusement to abject misery.

unofficial **TIP**
News of a guest's GI distress will result in a report to the onboard medical staff and a likely 24-hour quarantine.

If you know that you're prone to motion sickness issues in other situations (such as during long car rides and on roller coasters), you may want to speak with your doctor, and possibly your child's, before you sail. He or she may suggest natural or over-the-counter remedies such as ginger supplements, Queasy Pops, or peppermint essential oil; acupressure tools such as SeaBands; electrical-stimulation tools such as ReliefBands; over-the-counter medicines such as Bonine or Dramamine (available in children's and nondrowsy versions); or, in severe cases, prescription remedies such as the scopolamine patch.

We're not doctors, but in our experience it can be more effective to alleviate motion sickness before it starts than to try to quell a full-blown attack. Erin has had personal success with starting a daily dose of Dramamine two days before sailing and continuing to take it through the voyage. Other guests swear by SeaBands, wearing them throughout their trip. You may have to experiment a bit to find the best solution for you.

unofficial **TIP**
If you find yourself disoriented on the ship, take a look at the design on the carpet. In the stateroom hallways, the point of the star and the north direction of the compass point toward the bow, or front, of the ship.

Regular and kids' versions of Dramamine are available for sale in the ships' gift shops, as well as in single-dose form at Guest Services and at the onboard health center, but you'll likely save a few dollars if you buy it at home.

Another component of motion sickness may be the location of your stateroom. The rule of thumb is that midship staterooms experience the least rocking, followed by aft and then forward staterooms. Lower decks are more stable than high decks. If you're prone to motion sickness, a Deck 2 midship cabin may be more comfortable than a Deck 9 forward cabin. The exception to this might be if you find that fresh air helps you, in which case a midship stateroom with a verandah on Deck 6 might be your best bet.

While motion-sickness medications are available at the onboard shops, you'll have to head to the ship's infirmary to get medicines for gastric distress, such as Imodium or Pepto-Bismol. DCL wants to reassure guests that they're on top of possible outbreaks of norovirus and

the like, so if you have unexpected stomach or intestinal issues, do the safe and sane thing and head to the onboard health center. But if you know that you typically experience minor issues in any travel situation and you don't need a doctor, bring your own over-the-counter GI meds.

Again, preventing "traveler's tummy" is preferable to combating it once it's started. Tips for keeping comfortable at sea include the following:

- **Make good decisions your first day aboard.** If you traveled from home the same day you boarded the ship, chances are you got up several hours before normal, packed yourself onto a plane or into a car, maybe ate something healthy (but probably didn't), and headed to the cruise terminal. What are you going to do first? Head to the buffet, of course! It's a cruise, and you want to start off with a bang. That's great, but perhaps reconsider that second slice of prime rib or plate of crab legs—there's no shortage of food, after all. Snack on some fruit or sip some peppermint tea as a light alternative to dessert.
- **Stay hydrated.** Carry a water bottle and fill it every time you pass a beverage station on the pool deck. Fill it at night and keep it in your cabin's beverage chiller for morning.
- **Take a walk.** Stretch your legs on the outside decks and enjoy the sea air. It may be just what you need.
- **Take an antacid.** Tums and Zantac are typically stocked on board, or you can bring your own.
- **Lay off the soda.** Yes, fountain drinks are included in your cruise fees, but just because you can have all you want doesn't mean you should. Bubbly beverages put air in your stomach, and as anyone who's ever fed a baby knows, that's not a good thing. Water is good. Add some lemon if you like.
- **Eat modestly.** *Remember:* You can always get more food if you're still hungry later. You can also skip dessert, get two appetizers instead of an entrée, or order from the kids' menu. What you eat is up to you, not your tablemates or your servers.
- **Pack some loose-fitting clothing to avoid constriction.** Be sure to pack at least one dinner-appropriate outfit that you know will fit no matter what's going on in your gut. Maybe that's a caftan, a maxi dress, or palazzo pants with a drawstring waist. Guys, you're on your own here—just try to leave a few notches to spare on your belts and you should be OK.
- **Make good choices in port.** Stick with bottled water and cooked food in ports with possible sanitation issues. (Drinking from, say, a water fountain in Mexico is probably playing with fire.) Additionally, if you're prone to motion sickness or GI issues, choose port activities with minimal movement. Avoid stuff like rides on small boats or jeep trips down bumpy dirt roads.
- **Wash your hands.** The disinfecting wipes handed out every time you come within 20 feet of food are only a start. The very best way to avoid major and minor bugs is to wash your hands at every opportunity.

PREPARING YOU AND YOUR HOME FOR TRAVEL

IN ADDITION TO CRUISE-SPECIFIC PREPARATIONS, you also should be aware of general guidelines for international travel. If you want to be comprehensive, **Pinterest** is filled with hundreds of travel-prep hint lists, but a few of our favorite tips are as follows:

- Consult with your doctor about whether you're up to date on all recommended vaccinations.
- Confirm all travel and transportation arrangements; double-check that names match on all documents.
- Consider adding numbers of foreign embassies or consulates to your phone contacts.
- Make sure that your credit/debit cards are compatible with international travel. Most international locations use chip-style readers rather than swipe-style readers.
- Download maps of your destination cities to your phone before your cruise.
- Arrange to stop mail and newspaper delivery.
- Make arrangements for pet sitters or house sitters.
- Unplug appliances such as coffeemakers and toasters.
- Hire someone to maintain your yard or remove snow so that your absence isn't immediately apparent to strangers.
- Clean your refrigerator of perishable items, and arrange grocery delivery for the day of your return.
- Adjust your home's heating/cooling settings to maximize energy savings while you're gone.
- Update your mobile device(s) with games, music, movies, and books for your flight, drive, or poolside lounging.

A WORD ABOUT THE WEATHER

AS MUCH AS WE'RE SURE THEY'D LIKE TO, Disney can't control the weather. You're probably envisioning spending your Caribbean cruise sipping piña coladas on the pool deck, but the reality is that you may encounter inclement weather during your sailing. Don't worry if it rains; there are plenty of indoor activities for children and adults. Disney also does a terrific job of providing extra indoor programming if conditions warrant. Be sure to check the mobile version of the *Personal Navigator,* which is updated more frequently than the print version, for up-to-the-minute additions to the schedule. (See page 107 for more details.)

In extreme situations, DCL will alter plans more substantially than just running a few more games of bingo. Hurricanes and tropical storms do sometimes necessitate significant changes in itinerary. On rare occasions, sailings have left their embarkation port a day or two late, returned to port a day or two early, omitted or substituted a midtrip port stop, ended a voyage at a port other than the one planned, or even canceled a sailing, all in the interest of guest safety.

Noteworthy weather-related itinerary changes include a 2016 sailing of the *Magic,* which was scheduled to head from New York to the Bahamas but was reconfigured to a Canadian Coastline sailing due to Hurricane Matthew. Hurricane Irma forced the cancellation of sailings on the *Dream* and *Fantasy,* as well as midtrip returns of these ships to Port Canaveral. Damage from Hurricanes Irma and Maria also forced some *Fantasy* sailings to change from Eastern Caribbean to Western Caribbean routes.

While Walt Disney World has an official hurricane policy (disneyworld.disney.go.com/faq/hurricane-policy), there is no comparable codification for Disney Cruise Line. DCL does, however, have an admirable record of assisting guests with refunds and remediation for missed sailing days and fees at skipped ports. For example, in the case of the 2016 Hurricane Matthew full-itinerary change on the *Magic,* guests were allowed to cancel their trips for a full refund or rebook a future cruise at a 20% discount. Guests choosing to remain on the new itinerary were automatically given a $100-per-person stateroom credit. For Hurricane Irma in 2017, DCL offered refunds on the missed days for the sailings that returned early and were offered a 25% discount on a future sailing in 2017 or 2018. Those on the canceled sailings were given a full refund and the same 25% discount on future sailings.

If your itinerary changes, it may be easier to get refunds for excursions booked through Disney rather than for those booked on your own (see Part Twelve, page 365). Also, keep in mind that if you're flying to your DCL sailing, weather can also impact your airline, and guests with pre- or postcruise hotel stays may also see those plans affected by weather issues.

If you encounter storms, rest assured that the chance of any real danger at sea due to a hurricane is virtually zero. Weather tracking is such that cruise lines typically know about impending severe weather at least three days before its impact, giving them plenty of time to change course. Captains also have great latitude to reroute ships to avoid areas of concern. Large ships such as the Disney fleet even have the ability to outpace the danger zone of a storm: most hurricanes travel at a speed of about 10 knots, and the ships are able to sail at more than 20 knots.

If you want to delve into the minutiae of maritime weather tracking, **PassageWeather** (passageweather.com) is a terrific source of information about phenomena that affect ships: surface winds, wave height and direction, sea-surface temperatures, and more. The **National Weather Service** also offers detailed current information at its Ocean Prediction Center (opc.ncep.noaa.gov).

Weather issues are possible at any time of year but are more common in the Caribbean and Bahamas from mid-August until early November. But even if you avoid sailing in the Caribbean during that

time, weather might affect your cruise in other ways. In August 2011, Erin sailed on the *Magic* in the Mediterranean. The weather during the voyage was spectacular, with clear skies and calm seas throughout. But when she disembarked in Barcelona, she found that Hurricane Irene, the seventh-costliest hurricane in US history, was busy pummeling the eastern United States, forcing the closure of all the airports near her home. Her European vacation was unexpectedly extended by several days until the airports reopened.

Whenever possible, build in a day or two on both sides of your sailing to account for unexpected weather situations. You may also want to consider whether trip insurance makes sense for your family. Depending on the policy, it may cover flight-change fees and/or unexpected hotel stays. Be sure to read the fine print on any trip-insurance contract to understand exactly what it covers before you purchase (see page 49 for more details).

On the other end of the spectrum, some guests, equating cruising with the tropics, are wary of booking a sailing to colder-weather regions such as Canada, Alaska, and Northern Europe. We've sailed itineraries to these areas and rank them among our favorites. During a Norwegian Fjords cruise on the *Magic*, we often heard the maxim, "There's no bad weather, only bad clothing." As long as you're dressed appropriately, touring in a cooler climate can be a fabulous experience, with more variety in the sights than you're likely to find on a beach-intensive voyage in the Caribbean.

The ships also feel particularly cozy on cold-weather routes. For example, on the glacier-viewing Tracy Arm day of Alaskan sailings, the DCL staff places piles of fleece blankets on deck and rolls around a cart stocked with hot cocoa, Irish coffee, and hot toddies. Cuddling up with your honey, sipping a warm beverage, and watching seals and whales swim by makes for a truly memorable day. We're with Elsa on this one: "The cold never bothered us anyway."

MAKING SURE YOUR CHILD IS READY TO CRUISE

IT'S NO SECRET that many Disney Cruise Line guests are families with young children. Most of these guests have a fabulous time, but the small subset of DCL cruisers who have a neutral or even negative experience while cruising are typically those whose expectations are disconnected from the reality of traveling on a cruise ship.

unofficial **TIP**
Planning, patience, and realistic expectations will go a long way toward helping you have a great trip.

When you're considering a Disney cruise with kids, know first that travel with small children is almost always more challenging than travel with older kids or grown-ups. Adults who are used to traveling solo or with other adults may be surprised at the difficulties they experience when traveling with young children.

Rest assured, however, that whatever issues you encounter aren't specific to Disney or cruising but rather par for the course when it comes to travel in general. Whenever you travel with young kids, you're carrying their stuff, making sure they eat what they're supposed to, hovering over them at the pool, and making sure they get something approximating sleep. This always-on feeling can be hard to reconcile with the "cruise as ultimate relaxation" ethos that many expect.

To figure out if you and your child are ready for a cruise vacation, ask yourself these questions:

- **Is my child a good sleeper?** Are there specific situations in which he or she doesn't sleep, such as the following?

  The ship is moving. Many children find this comforting, but others find motion while they're sleeping to be disconcerting.

  The bedding may be unfamiliar.

  You'll likely be sleeping in the same room as your child. Does this affect his/her ability to sleep, or yours?

- **How does my child react to changes in his or her schedule?** Many younger children have trouble coping with changes in their nap or eating schedule, particularly if that schedule is disrupted for several days in a row. The activities on the ship take place at set times—times that may not suit your child's schedule. Can your child deal with the disruption, or are meltdowns inevitable? Are you willing to forgo eating in the main dining rooms if your child's schedule requires?
- **Do I have any claustrophobia issues? Does my child?** On any cruise ship, space is more compact that you'll find in most land-based locations. Staterooms are smaller than many typical hotel rooms; stateroom bathrooms may be smaller still than what you're used to. (A large guy trying to bathe a toddler in a half-size stateroom bath is a special kind of amusing.)
- **Do I have any issues with crowds? Does my child?** There is a fixed maximum number of people on the ship, so you won't experience the unlimited crowds on board that you might at one of Disney's theme parks. Nonetheless, you will have to deal with crowds and lines from time to time—some of these situations, such as the dance parties, are avoidable, but others, like the mandatory safety muster, are not.
- **Does my child have issues with costumed characters?** By elementary school, most children outgrow any reticence about seeing or interacting with costumed characters. But a moderate percentage of toddlers and preschoolers find the characters to be terrifying, with said terror resulting in a meltdown for the child and subsequently a meltdown from the parent.

  Characters are difficult to avoid entirely on DCL ships. Many of the character-greeting opportunities take place in public areas such as the lobby atria or at the exits to the main theaters, and there are sometimes surprise character appearances in the kids' clubs. Given the narrow hallways and central locations of the characters, you will likely

be quite close to them on several occasions. If your young child has a serious character aversion, you may want to wait a bit before booking.

- **Is my child easily overwhelmed in new situations?** On a ship, there are new foods, new people, new activities, and loud ship horns—the list goes on and on. I've heard several stories about children becoming upset on seeing the yellow lifeboats. It may be difficult to predict what exactly will unsettle a 3-year-old, but chances are that you already know if your child becomes easily upset or overstimulated. Additionally, you may want to consider that on sea days, there may be few options for separating your child from other people other than staying in your stateroom.
- **Will childcare eat into my vacation budget?** DCL's kids' clubs are included in your cruise price for potty-trained children ages 3 and up. The nurseries (for infants–age 3) charge a fee—currently $9 per hour for the first child and $8 per hour for each additional child in the same family. It may be relatively easy to leave your 10-month-old in the nursery while you enjoy the sunshine, but be aware that those fees can sneak up on you over the course of a long sailing.
- **Will I be able to get childcare when I need it?** Children ages 3–17 are allowed unlimited use of the kids' clubs whenever you and they want, with no reservations necessary. The nurseries, however, accept only a limited number of children per hour, and reservations are required. Depending on how crowded your cruise is and what level of Castaway Club status you've attained, you may not be able to arrange babysitting for your young child when you want it.
- **Is my child in a particularly active phase?** Given the constraints of the ship, space is limited for many large-motor activities. Additionally, there are many expectations for restrained behavior while on board (sitting still in a restaurant, for example). The kids' clubs offer some physical activities, but they may not be exactly the type of activity your child is used to.

  Further, opportunities for ball play, climbing, and running are fairly limited for young children, and what there is on board takes place almost entirely in the kids' clubs. If you have a child with separation issues who also needs lots of physical activity, or a child with separation issues with an aversion to water play, then you may want to think hard about whether this is the right time to book a cruise.
- **Does my child require a great deal of gear for personal maintenance or stimulation?** Yet again, it bears mentioning that staterooms are small. Boxes of diapers, strollers, play mats, and similar items may feel particularly large in a confined space. Consider whether it might be more practical to cruise when these items are no longer necessary.
- **Traveling with my child means I wouldn't get to experience everything the ship has to offer. Would I be wasting my money by booking a cruise in the first place?** *Absolutely not*—some of our most memorable cruise experiences haven't involved a specific activity or event. Given factors such as a young child's sleep schedule, however, you may find that most adult and even many family activities are

inaccessible to you. If you're in for the night because your child is asleep at 8 p.m., then you're going to miss the stage shows, family game shows, and many similar experiences that take place later in the evening. There are some partial workarounds—for example, the main stage shows are available on closed-circuit TV in your stateroom.

- **Who else are we traveling with? What are their needs?** Travel with a small child may go better, or worse, depending on your traveling party. Many folks with young children cruise with extended family. This can be a boon for Mom and Dad (or Mom and Mom or Dad and Dad) if Grandma offers to babysit while the parents enjoy Palo or the margarita-mixing class. It can be a struggle for the parents if Grandma expects the entire clan to sit still for a 3-hour dinner every evening, or if Grandma needs physical assistance or medical attention of her own.
- **What ports will the ship be visiting? Are there appropriate excursions or other activities in port?** Some families cruise to spend time enjoying the ship, while others find the port itinerary to be the key enticement. In either case, if you're planning to leave the ship while it's in port, review your port-excursion options carefully. At some stops, there may be limited offerings for children under age 5 or even under age 8. At other ports, excursions may technically be available to younger children but aren't practically appealing. (For example, a 5-hour bike tour probably isn't appropriate for a 4-year-old.) With younger kids, you may want to consider arranging your own excursions or just going for a walk near the dock area. The counterpoint to this is that some families find cruising to be one of the easiest ways for a young child to experience a distant land.

unofficial **TIP**
Also see our thoughts on food issues with young kids on page 155.

By the time a child is 6 or 7 years old, he or she has usually developed strong enough coping skills to deal with separating from family, meeting new people, waiting his or her turn, and sitting still for extended periods of time. Additionally, a school-age child likely has a broader palate, little need for special equipment, and enough language skills to effectively communicate in productive ways. Each of these capabilities will serve to make cruising, or any travel, more relaxing for the entire family.

DISNEY WORLD *vs.* DISNEY CRUISE LINE: HOW TO DECIDE

WHILE MANY DCL GUESTS CHOOSE TO COMBINE a cruise with a visit to Walt Disney World (see page 31), we also get many questions from readers trying to decide if they should choose a Disney cruise *or* Disney World, rather than both. Here are some factors to consider as you make your decision:

- **Travel to the vacation.** Disney World is obviously in just one place, but you can hop on a Disney cruise in many locations. If you live near New York, Galveston, Vancouver, or one of DCL's other departure ports, the savings in time and money compared with traveling to Florida for your vacation could be substantial. You'll also save on time off from work if you board DCL near your home. Erin cruised DCL out of New York and was home, unpacked, and back at work by 9:30 a.m. on debarkation day.
- **Weather.** Some vacationers are wary of sailing during hurricane season, making Disney World potentially more attractive during that time. If you have to travel during the summer (teachers, for example) and are heat averse, one of DCL's many cool-weather itineraries may make sense.
- **Motion sickness.** While most folks find they have minimal motion-sickness issues on a Disney cruise, any cruising may be too much for severe sufferers. Disney World (with a focus on the tamer rides) or an Adventures by Disney river cruise (see Part Thirteen) will make more sense for you.
- **Mobility issues.** The average Disney World visitor walks 7–12 miles per day. Sure, you could rent a wheelchair or an ECV, but that's still a whole lot of mileage to cover each day. The ships are large but contained. If you have difficulty walking long distances or transferring in and out of mobility devices, then DCL could be a convenient solution.
- **Access to health care.** There are basic medical facilities on board the ship (see page 113), but if you have complicated medical needs, you may find that ready access to full hospital facilities makes Disney World a safer option.
- **Variety of accommodations.** There are many stateroom categories, but nearly all of them are variations on a box. If you want to stay with extended family in one unit or have access to residential-style amenities like full kitchens, private communal living spaces, or large outdoor play spaces, then you're out of luck with DCL. With hundreds of thousands of hotel rooms, villas, and rental homes in the Disney World area, there are accommodations to meet every need.
- **Pace of the vacation.** It's a near-cliché to come home from Disney World and say that you need a vacation from your vacation, especially with kids in tow. Disney World trips involve lots and lots (and lots and lots) of running around to take advantage of the countless attractions and entertainment. This is much less true on a Disney cruise, where there are fewer must-do activities and sleeping in and lounging around are much more common.
- **Variety of dining.** The food on DCL is plentiful, all-inclusive, and available anytime you want it, but your choices are limited. If you like exploring a wide variety of cuisines, or if you have an extremely picky eater in your group, Disney World may be a better choice. Guests who follow special/restricted diets may find the lack of personal kitchen facilities challenging on a cruise ship.
- **Access to childcare.** Here's where DCL has the clear advantage. Group childcare was recently discontinued at Disney World, and hiring a

babysitter can get really pricey really fast. Contrast this with DCL, where high-quality group childcare is included in the price of your cruise and is available throughout the day and evening for kids ages 3–17. (Infant and toddler care are available for a small fee.) This may be particularly appealing for a single parent who needs some occasional downtime to recharge during vacation, or for the parent(s) of an only child who might benefit from interacting with other children, rather than just adults, during an extended vacation.

- **Access to exercise facilities for teens.** There are lovely gyms on the Disney ships, but access to these facilities is limited to guests ages 18 and up. If you have a serious high school athlete in training, a fully land-based vacation may better serve his or her needs.
- **Need for planning.** With the advent of computerized FastPass+ reservations and hundreds of restaurants to choose from, planning a trip to Disney World can seem more complicated than planning a military invasion. With DCL, there is much less need to map out your time in advance. You can decide on most shipboard activities at the spur of the moment. And it's perfectly fine to wing it and just wander around in most ports. If you prefer a wholly spontaneous vacation, DCL may be the way to go.
- **Shorter lines.** We're professionals at avoiding lines at Disney World, but even we encounter lengthy waits there from time to time. The only times you might wait in line on a DCL ship are for some character greetings or the occasional turn on the waterslides.
- **Family togetherness.** Because DCL is a smaller-scale proposition than Disney World, family members are less likely to be pulled in different directions due to competing interests. On the other hand, if you want an excuse to separate from your traveling companions, then Disney World is the place to be.
- **Children's age considerations.** Families will find plenty to enjoy together on the DCL ships, but most kids will want to spend at least some time in the onboard kids' clubs. Mostly this is great, but the clubs are strict on age requirements, particularly in the older groups. This could be a challenge if the kids in your party can't go to the same club. If, for example, you have a 10- and 12-year-old, or a 17- and 18-year-old, who want to hang out together on vacation, Disney World will provide more opportunity for this.
- **Pregnancy and babies.** If you're more than 24 weeks pregnant or you have a baby under 6 months old, DCL is off-limits, but you might have a great time at Disney World. Also consider sleeping (or not sleeping) arrangements in a small stateroom with a toddler on an erratic sleep schedule, or feeding arrangements with a baby not eating much solid food. The pros and cons of potty training on a cruise ship are another topic worth considering closely.
- **Connectivity.** Internet access is available on board the ships (see page 110), but it's costly and often unreliable. If you must have reliable 24/7

contact with your work, school, or extended family, then DCL may not be the best choice for you.

- **Cultural literacy (American version).** Even Disney naysayers must concede that having at least a baseline knowledge of Disney World is assumed in much of the United States. If you live within driving distance and have never been, it may be time to make a visit.
- **Cultural literacy (international version).** If you want to show your kids the world, there may be no easier way to do it than via a cruise ship. You can see the highlights of half a dozen countries and only have to unpack once.
- **Disney overload.** If you want your kids to have a Disney experience but you want to limit your own exposure to the Mouse, then DCL is the better choice. If you skip the musical shows and character greetings, your Disney exposure is fairly minimal. Adventures by Disney river cruises (see Part Thirteen) have minimal Disney influence.
- **Price.** Costs will obviously vary depending on your accommodations, the size of your party, and so on. There are bare-bones budget versions and over-the-top luxury versions of both Disney World and DCL vacations. When you're researching costs, try to compare apples to apples (budget DCL versus budget Disney World, not budget DCL versus luxury Disney World or vice versa). Also consider the prices for all ancillary items you'll consider during your trip (things like Park Hopper tickets at Disney World or port-adventure fees on DCL) and whether those are needs or wants.

If you end up choosing a Walt Disney World vacation over a DCL cruise, take a look at our sister publications *The Unofficial Guide to Walt Disney World* and *The Unofficial Guide to Walt Disney World with Kids,* along with their companion website, **TouringPlans.com.** These resources can give you the complete scoop on planning a Disney World visit with minimal hassle and maximum fun.

COMPARING PRICES

WE HAD A HUNCH THAT A DCL VACATION would be more expensive than a WDW vacation, but we weren't sure by how much, so we decided to investigate by spot-checking some DCL prices against WDW prices for the same dates. (All prices were researched in late summer 2018; you'll likely see somewhat different pricing.)

Example 1: We priced the March 16, 2019, seven-night Western Caribbean sailing of the *Fantasy* for two adults and two children, ages 14 and 9. The lowest rate offered for this was $7,457 for an inside cabin. As with all DCL sailings, the price of food and onboard entertainment is included, but not port excursions or other extras. An inside stateroom can be pretty dismal for four people, so we also priced an Oceanview stateroom ($7,821) and a Verandah stateroom ($8,661).

Then we took the same four people and put them in a pool-view room at Walt Disney World's Port Orleans Riverside Resort, which would give them space similar to the Verandah stateroom's, for seven nights beginning March 16, 2019. To that we added seven-day Park Hopper tickets for everyone in the family (to simulate the onboard activities) and a Deluxe Dining Plan (to approximate the included food on DCL). The total price: $6,301, or a savings of about $2,300 over the Verandah stateroom.

Of course, money could be saved or spent on both sides of the equation: you could choose a smaller cabin to save a little money, or add port excursions to spend a lot of money. The theme park–goer could downgrade hotels or skip the Park Hopper add-on to save money, or add special events like tours to spend more money. **Overall winner on price: Walt Disney World**

Example 2: We priced the December 16, 2019, five-night Bahamian cruise on the *Dream* for two adults. This is a holiday-splurge vacation, so we looked at the price for a Concierge suite: $5,643. For a similar level of posh, we priced these folks for five nights in a Club Level Deluxe King room in the main building at Disney's Grand Floridian Resort & Spa. This room, plus a six-day Park Hopper theme-park ticket and the Deluxe Dining Plan, costs $10,078, or nearly twice the price of the DCL version. Yes, the DCL couple will likely add expense for excursions, but probably not $4,000 worth of excursions. **Overall winner on price: DCL**

Example 3: We priced the June 10, 2019, four-night Bahamian sailing on the *Dream* for one adult. It's a budget getaway, so we looked at the inside stateroom price of $3,374. At Walt Disney World, the comparable budget digs are a nonpreferred room at All-Star Music, a Disney Value resort, for those same four nights, plus a Park Hopper ticket and the Deluxe Dining Plan. Total: $1,634, or about half the price of the cruise.

In this scenario, DCL charges nearly the same stateroom rate for one person as for two—our solo traveler is effectively paying for all the food and entertainment her nonexistent companion is not eating or enjoying. With WDW, she only has to pay for the food and entertainment for one person. **Overall winner on price: Walt Disney World**

The differences become more stark when you look at DCL's itineraries outside the Bahamas and the Caribbean. Compared with the price of European cruises, even a luxury-level domestic Walt Disney World vacation looks downright thrifty. But as with all things Disney, it makes sense to sit down with a spreadsheet and a calculator to examine the cost comparisons as they apply to your family's unique circumstances and vacation priorities.

CASTAWAY CLUB

DCL USES THIS PROGRAM TO REWARD REPEAT CRUISERS. It works somewhat along the lines of a frequent-flyer program—the more you cruise with Disney, the better your status and the more perks you get.

Castaway Club status is determined solely by the number of DCL voyages you've completed, not by how much money you've spent. A guest who's sailed on five 3-day cruises in the smallest inside cabin belongs to a higher level than a guest who has spent more money on one 12-day voyage in the largest cabin.

The club levels are as follows:

- If you've never taken a Disney cruise before, you're a **First-Time Guest.**
- Guests who have completed 1–5 Disney cruises have **Silver** status.
- Guests who have completed 6–10 Disney cruises have **Gold** status.
- Guests who have completed more than 10 Disney cruises have **Platinum** status.

Most guests will be able to count all of their cruising toward their status level, with a few rare exceptions, such as a Disney cast member cruising on business. (Tough life, eh?)

A number of perks are available to all Castaway Club members, including "Welcome Back" stateroom gifts and priority check-in at the port terminal. As your membership level increases, so do your benefits. Gold and Platinum guests receive 10% off many onboard merchandise purchases. On sailings of eight nights or longer, Gold and Platinum guests are invited to a special reception with crew members. Platinum cruisers, along with their guests age 18 and older staying in the same stateroom, are treated to a free meal at Palo. While none of these perks are enough incentive to book another trip, they are a nice way to acknowledge loyal customers.

For many guests, one of the chief benefits of Castaway Club membership is that the higher your status level, the earlier you can reserve many aspects of your cruise, including port adventures, onboard dining at the adults-only restaurants Palo and Remy, spa visits, and some childcare situations:

- **First-Time Guests** may make reservations 75 days prior to sailing.
- **Silver** Castaway Club members may make reservations 90 days prior to sailing.
- **Gold** members may make reservations 105 days prior to sailing.
- **Platinum** members may make reservations 120 days prior to sailing.

DCL made one significant change to Castaway Club benefits in 2017. When new itineraries are released, Platinum Castaway Club guests may now book trips three days before they become available

to the general public, Gold guests may book two days ahead, and Silver guests may book one day ahead. This gives loyal customers a greater chance of obtaining their preferred staterooms on new sailings. While cruises seldom become fully booked in the initial days of availability, it is possible that a new cruiser could be locked out of a unique stateroom type on a particularly popular voyage.

Castaway Club status may not make much of a difference in some situations. For example, nearly everyone will be able to rent a bike at Castaway Cay. In other circumstances, however, belonging to a higher level can be a real boon. For example, Castaway Cay has only 21 private cabanas, split between the family and adult beach areas. With several thousand guests aboard your ship, competition for these private oases can be fierce, and Castaway Club members get first crack at them. Other popular perks include dining at Palo and Remy on days at sea and Flounder's Reef babysitting during showtimes.

Sometimes not everyone in a single stateroom has the same Castaway Club status. In that case, the benefits for each guest are determined by the Castaway Club member with the highest status in that room. For example, if I (Erin) have been on a few more cruises than my husband and my status is higher than his, I can make reservations for both of us at my level. (Lucky me!) But if we're also traveling with First-Time Guests staying in another stateroom, they *can't* take advantage of my higher status level, even though they're in our party. Effectively, then, Castaway Club status on any particular cruise is applied by stateroom, not by party. Keep this in mind if you're planning activities for a large group—not everyone will have equal access to reservations if members of your party have different status levels.

If you're traveling with guests in multiple staterooms, there may be situations where their Castaway Club status might influence whom you book into which cabin. For example, let's say Adam and Bob are Gold cruisers but their kids, Carol and Diane, are Silver cruisers. If the parents are booked into one stateroom and the kids into another, the parents can make their port-adventure reservations at the 105-day mark, but the kids won't be able to reserve port adventures until the 90-day mark, leaving open the possibility that the adventure will become fully booked in the intervening 15 days. But if Gold-level Adam is booked into a stateroom with Silver-level Carol and Gold-level Bob with Silver-level Diane, both staterooms will be able to book their port adventures at 105 days, meaning there's a much higher likelihood that they could all enjoy their adventures together. This would also mean that both staterooms receive the Gold-level welcome-aboard gift rather than one Gold and one Silver. (Once you're on the ship, no one will care which family members actually sleep in which staterooms. Your stateroom attendant will be happy to configure the beds however you choose, and Guest Services will issue you keys to both rooms.)

PART THREE

STATEROOMS

DISNEY CRUISE LINE'S SHIPS boast some of the largest cabins in the industry, which helps explain (a bit) why its fares are correspondingly high. An inside cabin, generally the least expensive on any ship, is 169–184 square feet on Disney's ships, compared with 114–165 square feet on Royal Caribbean and 160–185 on Carnival. Disney's Oceanview and Verandah (balcony) cabins are larger than Royal Caribbean's and Carnival's, too.

unofficial **TIP**
On the *Dream* and *Fantasy*, some inside cabins have "virtual portholes"—video screens that combine real-time views from outside the ship with animated snippets of various Disney characters. Many children strongly prefer these to actual Verandah views, and inside cabins are usually much less expensive.

In addition to greater space, DCL's bathroom layout is an improvement over those of other cruise lines. DCL staterooms in Categories 10–4 are configured in a split-bath design, in which the shower and toilet are in separate compartments, each with its own door and sink. The advantage of this design is that two people can get ready at the same time. (Category 11 staterooms have the shower and toilet in the same compartment.)

DCL's clever incorporation of storage space is one of the things we were most impressed with on our first few cruises. Most cabins have two closets, each big enough for one large suitcase or two small ones; under-bed storage for carry-on or soft-sided luggage; and several drawers built in to the cabin's desk area. Other nooks and crannies for storage are scattered throughout the staterooms.

While Disney's staterooms are well designed and large for the cruise industry, most are smaller than the typical hotel room. A room at a Walt Disney World Value hotel, such as Pop Century Resort, is about 260 square feet—about 40% larger than a DCL inside cabin. Even a well-appointed Family Oceanview Stateroom with Verandah is 304 square feet, a little smaller than a room at a Disney Moderate hotel, such as Caribbean Beach Resort.

HOW YOUR STATEROOM CATEGORY AFFECTS *the* PRICE *of* YOUR DISNEY CRUISE

ALONG WITH YOUR DEPARTURE DATE AND HOW FAR in advance you book, the type of stateroom you choose is one of the major factors in determining your cruise's cost.

The chart below shows how much a fare increases, based on the cabin category, for a typical seven-night cruise on the *Disney Fantasy* for two adults and two children.

A Category 4A stateroom—the most expensive non-Concierge category—costs, on average, about $1,000 15% more than the least expensive cabin. With this, you get another 130 square feet of space and a better view.

What's remarkable is the slow, steady slope of the line until you reach Concierge level. This shows that Disney is very consistent in its pricing across stateroom categories. That's interesting, because there

Price-Per-Cabin Categories on a 7-Night Disney Cruise

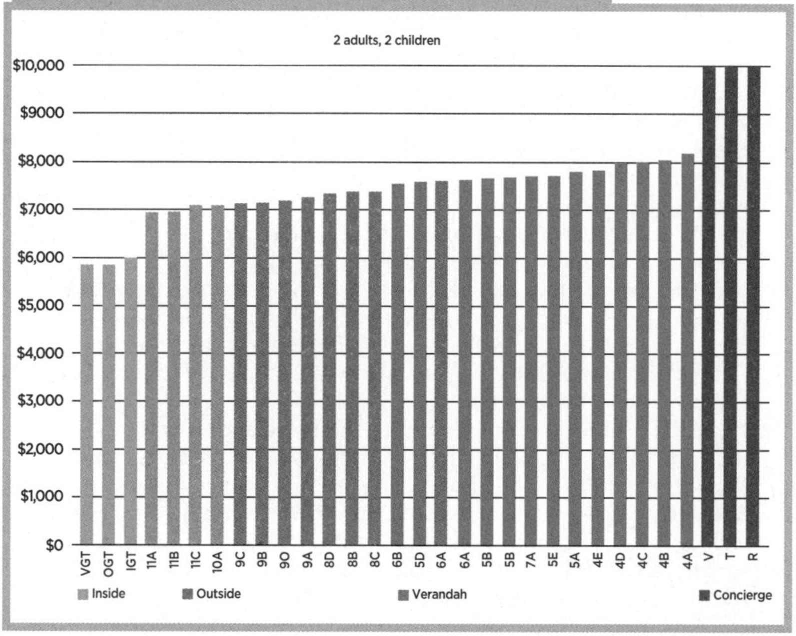

2 adults, 2 children

$10,000
$9000
$8,000
$7,000
$6,000
$5,000
$4,000
$3,000
$2,000
$1,000
$0

VGT OGT IGT 11A 11B 11C 10A 9C 9B 9O 9A 8D 8B 8C 6B 5D 6A 6A 5B 5B 7A 5E 5A 4E 4D 4C 4B 4A V T R

Inside Outside Verandah Concierge

aren't the same number of staterooms in each category—the vast majority are Verandah staterooms, but in this case a larger supply doesn't equal a lower price. Disney seems to have just the right amount of each type of stateroom to meet guest demand.

OUR STATEROOM RECOMMENDATIONS

AT 169–184 SQUARE FEET, an **Inside Stateroom** has enough room for two adults, or two adults and one small child. (Remember: they give you 60 square feet per person in prison.) These are Category 10 and 11 cabins, so a family of this size shouldn't have much contention for bathrooms when getting ready.

If you're a family of three or four and you have two tweens or teens, you'll appreciate the extra space of a **Deluxe Oceanview with Verandah Stateroom** (246 or 268 square feet) or **Deluxe Family Oceanview with Verandah Stateroom** (about 300 square feet). Alternatively, you could book two cabins: two inside connecting rooms or an inside and outside cabin across the hall from each other. The advantage to two rooms, besides the extra space and extra bathroom, is that the kids can sleep late if they want. Additionally, putting the kids in a different room allows the parents to access the television and verandah (both of which are located on what is typically the kids' side of the room) without fear of disturbing anyone. (See page 66 for tips on booking multiple staterooms with differing Castaway Club statuses and page 38 for age requirements for booking children and teens into different staterooms than their parents.)

CABIN APPOINTMENTS

EVERY DCL STATEROOM is outfitted with the following:

- **Bedside lamps**
- **Beverage cooler** Keeps drinks cool, not necessarily cold—no freezer
- **Closet**
- **Coffee table** The top opens for storage (*Dream* and *Fantasy* only)
- **Custom artwork** Usually depicts Disney characters and themes relevant to the cruise line, ships, islands, or travel
- **Desk with chair and dedicated lighting** Big enough for getting actual work done
- **Electronic safe** Just big enough for passports, wallets, and other small valuables
- **Hair dryer**
- **Hooks** (for towels) and **hangers** (for clothes)
- **Ice bucket** and glasses

- **In-room phone** with voice mail
- **In-room thermostat**
- **Life jackets**
- **Privacy curtain** Separates the sleeping area from the sofa
- **Private bath** with sink, toilet, and shower
- **Room-service menus**
- **Satellite television** with remote
- **Sleeper sofa**
- **Toiletries** H2O Plus brand soap, shampoo, conditioner, and body lotion are available in standard guest rooms. Elemis bath products are stocked in the Concierge-level suites. (*Note:* In late 2018, Disney announced that, in an effort to reduce single-use plastic waste, it will be transitioning to refillable in-room amenities in its hotels and on its cruise ships. Expect to see individual bottles replaced with wall dispensers in the coming months.)
- **Wave Phone** A mobile phone you can use aboard the ship (see page 15 for more information)

unofficial **TIP**
An iron and ironing board are available in most of the ships' laundry rooms.

Cabins with exterior windows also include blackout curtains, which do an amazing job of blocking the sun. If you need light to wake up in the morning, don't shut them unless you want to sleep until noon.

WHAT YOU *WON'T* FIND Cabins don't have minibars, coffeemakers, microwaves, teakettles, steam irons, or ironing boards.

Over the past few years, DCL has removed the bedside alarm clocks from most staterooms—most guests nowadays prefer to use their phones as clocks, plus this frees an additional electrical outlet. Alternatively, you can request a wake-up call. If you simply must have an alarm clock, check with Guest Services to see if they have any available.

Note that the primary beds in DCL staterooms are standard queen-size beds, not the split twins that you might find on some other cruise lines. This means that if you have more than two adults in the room, it's likely that two of them will be sharing a sleep surface. This is usually not a problem for a romantic couple or same-gender siblings, but there are other situations in which people who are comfortable traveling together, even sharing a cabin, might not want to sleep in the same bed: say, a father traveling with a teen or adult daughter, stepsiblings, in-laws, opposite-gender adult siblings, and so on. As you make your decisions about what type of stateroom you need, consider the number and type of sleep surfaces as well as stated capacity of the room.

The beds on **Adventures by Disney** river cruises (see Part Thirteen) are split twins, which means that they can be separated with a gap between them. When coauthor Erin traveled with her husband, the bed was made up as a queen; when she traveled with her young-adult child, the bed was configured as two twins.

DOOR DECOR The door to your stateroom is made of metal and is thus magnetic. Repeat cruisers are often fond of decorating their doors with magnets related to family celebrations, the cruise destination, a holiday, or something Disney-related in general. The longer your cruise, the more likely you are to see doors festooned with magnets, sometimes quite elaborately. When cruising in the Caribbean, Erin's daughters like to break out a pirate version of **Magnetic Poetry**'s build-a-sentence kits.

Of course, you're under no obligation to decorate your door, but if you choose to do so, be aware that you can't tape or hook anything to your door, nor may you use sticky-gel wall/window clings. Any damage to your door will result in a charge to your stateroom account.

STATEROOM CATEGORIES

Note: *Due to the shape of the ships, there are minor variations on floor plans even within stateroom categories.*

CATEGORIES 11A–11C: Standard Inside Stateroom

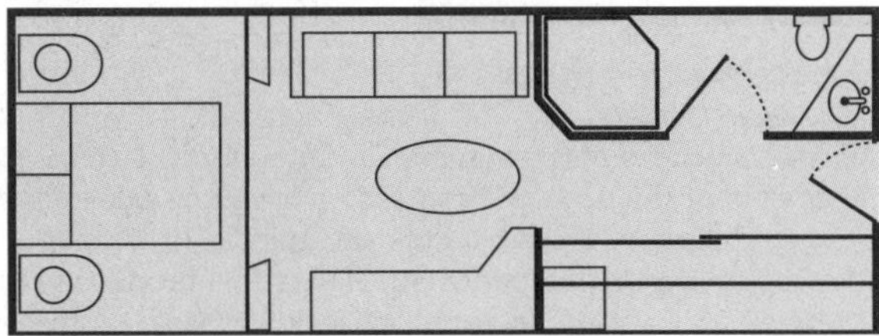

MAXIMUM OCCUPANCY 4 people

SIZE (square feet) *Magic/Wonder,* 184; *Dream/Fantasy,* 169

DESCRIPTION These cabins have one queen-size bed, a sleeper sofa, and combined bath with tub and shower. Some rooms have a pull-down upper berth. These cabins are on Decks 2, 5, 6, and 7 on the *Magic* and *Wonder* and on Decks 2, 5, 6, 7, 8, 9, and 10 on the *Dream* and *Fantasy.*

CATEGORY 10A (all ships), CATEGORIES 10B and 10C (*Magic* and *Wonder*): Deluxe Inside Stateroom

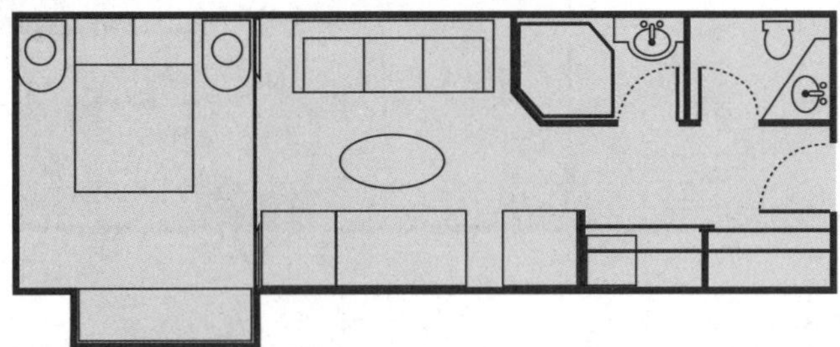

MAXIMUM OCCUPANCY 4 people

SIZE (square feet) *Magic/Wonder,* 214; *Dream/Fantasy,* 204

DESCRIPTION These cabins have one queen-size bed, one sleeper sofa, and split bath. Some rooms have a pull-down upper berth. Category 10C rooms on the *Magic* and *Wonder* are located entirely on Deck 1 Midship and Deck 2 Aft. Category 10B rooms, also found on the *Magic* and *Wonder,* are located entirely on Deck 2 Midship. Category 10A rooms are on Decks 5 and 7 on the *Magic* and *Wonder* and Decks 5, 6, 7, 8, and 9 on the *Dream* and *Fantasy,* anywhere along the ship.

CATEGORIES 9A–9D: Deluxe Oceanview Stateroom

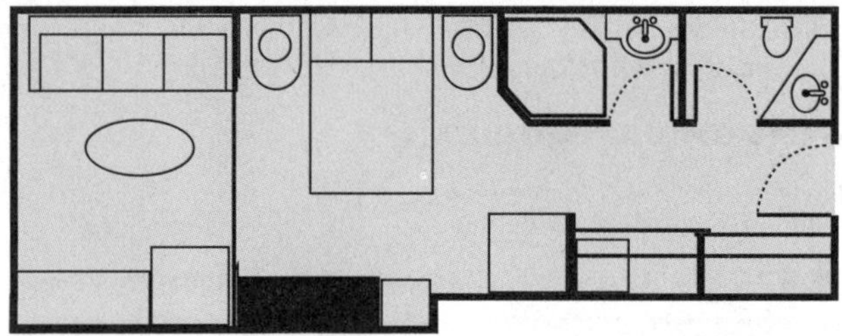

MAXIMUM OCCUPANCY 4 people

SIZE (square feet) *Magic/Wonder,* 214; *Dream/Fantasy,* 204

DESCRIPTION Same size and features as a Category 10 Deluxe Inside, plus a window view of the ocean. These cabins have one queen-size bed. All cabins on all ships have a sleeper sofa and split bath; some rooms have a pull-down upper berth. Categories 9B–9D are found only on Decks 1 and 2 on the *Magic* and *Wonder* and only on Deck 2 Midship on the *Dream* and *Fantasy.* Category 9A cabins are found on the Forward section of Decks 5, 6, and 7 on the *Magic* and *Wonder,* and on Decks 5, 6, 7, and 8 of the *Dream* and *Fantasy.* The 9A cabins on Decks 6, 7, and 8 of the *Dream* and *Fantasy* are interesting because they're at the extreme Forward and Aft ends of the ships, affording them unique views at a relatively low cost.

CATEGORIES 8A–8D (exclusive to the *Dream* and *Fantasy*): Deluxe Family Oceanview Stateroom

MAXIMUM OCCUPANCY 5 people

SIZE (square feet) 241

DESCRIPTION These cabins have one queen-size bed. Most have a one-person pull-down bed in the wall; a few also have one-person pull-down beds in the ceiling. All cabins have a one-person sleeper sofa. Some 8As have a single

bathroom, others a split-bath configuration. Most bathrooms have round tubs and showers.

CATEGORY 7A: Deluxe Oceanview Stateroom with Navigator's Verandah

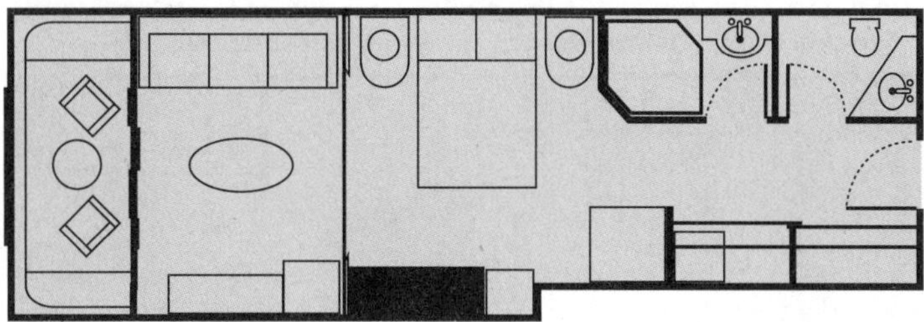

MAXIMUM OCCUPANCY 4 people

SIZE (square feet) *Magic/Wonder,* 268 (including verandah); *Dream/Fantasy,* 246 (including verandah)

DESCRIPTION Found on Decks 5, 6, and 7 on all ships (Fore and Aft on the *Dream* and *Fantasy;* Aft only on the *Magic* and *Wonder*), these cabins have one queen-size bed. All cabins have a one-person sleeper sofa and split bath. The interesting feature about these cabins is the Navigator's Verandah: a small, semienclosed, teak-floored deck attached to the stateroom and featuring either a large exterior window or open railing. The window doesn't open, so in those rooms the extra space and teak deck are the difference between these cabins and the Category 9 staterooms on the *Magic* and *Wonder.* On the *Dream* and *Fantasy,* these cabins have an undersize or obstructed-view verandah.

CATEGORIES 6A (all ships) and 6B (*DREAM* and *FANTASY* only): Deluxe Oceanview Stateroom with Verandah

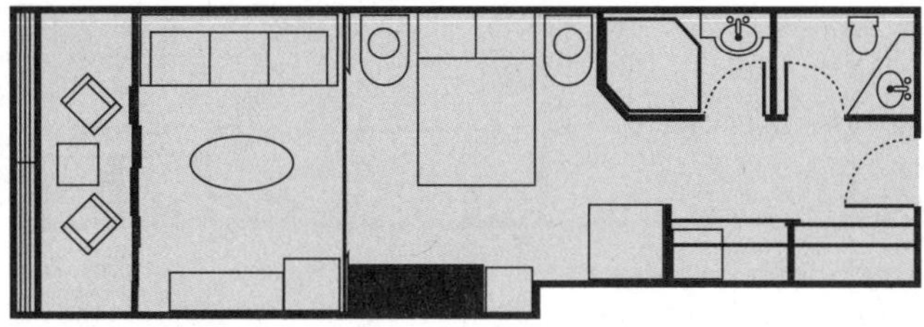

MAXIMUM OCCUPANCY 4 people

SIZE (square feet) *Magic/Wonder,* 268 (including verandah); *Dream/Fantasy,* 246 (including verandah)

DESCRIPTION These cabins have a queen-size bed, a one-person sleeper sofa, and a one-person pull-down bed, typically above the sofa. All have a split bath, most with round tubs and showers. Category 6A cabins are found Aft on Decks 5, 6, and 7 of the *Magic* and *Wonder* and Aft on Decks 8, 9, and 10 on the *Dream* and *Fantasy.* Category 6B staterooms are found only on the *Dream*

and *Fantasy,* Aft on Decks 5, 6, and 7. These staterooms differ from Category 5 staterooms because they have private verandahs with a short white wall instead of a railing with plexiglass. In addition, some of the Category 5 cabins are found Midship, whereas all Category 6 cabins seem to be Aft.

CATEGORIES 5A–5C (all ships), 5D and 5E (*Dream* and *Fantasy* only): Deluxe Oceanview Stateroom with Verandah

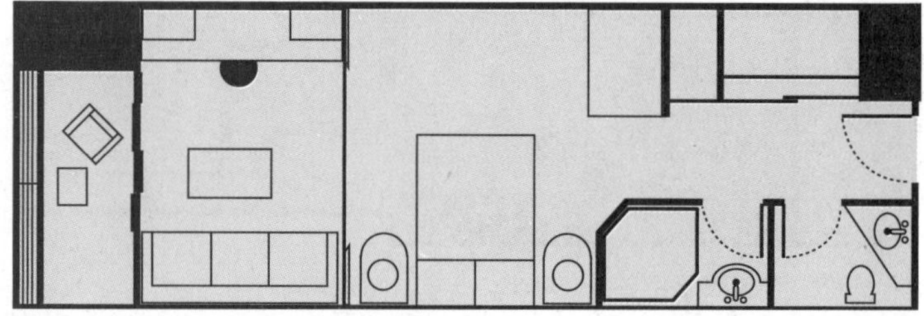

MAXIMUM OCCUPANCY 4 people

SIZE (square feet) *Magic/Wonder,* 268 (including verandah); *Dream/Fantasy,* 246 (including verandah)

DESCRIPTION There seems to be little difference between these and the Category 6 cabins on the *Magic* and *Wonder.* All have the same square footage and amenities, and all are on Decks 5, 6, and 7. Category 5E cabins have oversize verandahs, and some have a white wall instead of a railing with plexiglass. No other Category 5 cabins have a white wall on the verandah.

CATEGORIES 4A, 4B, 4E (All ships), 4C and 4D (*Dream* and *Fantasy* only): Deluxe Family Oceanview Stateroom with Verandah

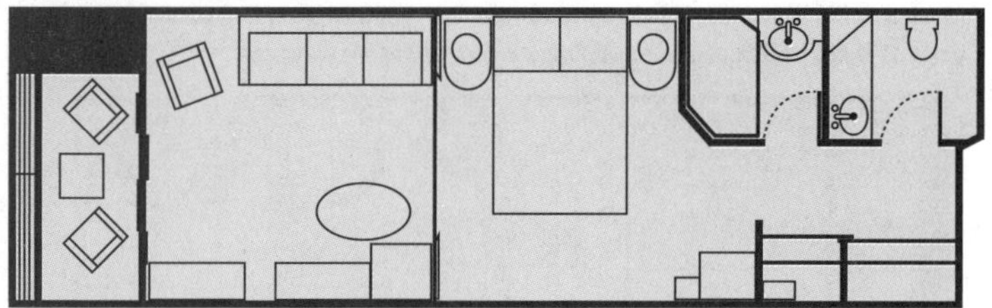

MAXIMUM OCCUPANCY 5 people

SIZE (square feet) *Magic/Wonder,* 304 (including verandah); *Dream/Fantasy,* 299 (including verandah)

DESCRIPTION These cabins have a queen-size bed and sleeper sofa (fits one person); most have a pull-down wall bed (sleeps one). Some also have a pull-down upper-berth bed. All have a split bath, most with round tubs and showers. One issue with the pull-down wall bed in these cabins is that you'll have to move the desk chair in order to use the bed. The Category 4E cabins are found only Aft on Decks 7 and 8 of the *Magic* and *Wonder.* There are only two 4E cabins on Deck 7, and what makes them interesting is that they have an angled view directly off the ship's stern. They're also

adjacent to Deck 7's "secret" sun deck. On the *Dream* and *Fantasy,* the A–D designations for this category represent the deck on which the stateroom is located: 4A staterooms are on Decks 9 and 10 Midship, 4B staterooms are on Deck 8 Midship, 4C staterooms are on Deck 7 Midship, and 4D staterooms are on Deck 6 Midship. The Category 4E staterooms, on Decks 5–10 of the *Dream* and *Fantasy,* seem to represent any section of the ship where the balconies are slightly larger than standard (that is, at the aft of the ship and anywhere the verandahs change shape along the sides).

CATEGORY V: Concierge Family Oceanview Stateroom with Verandah

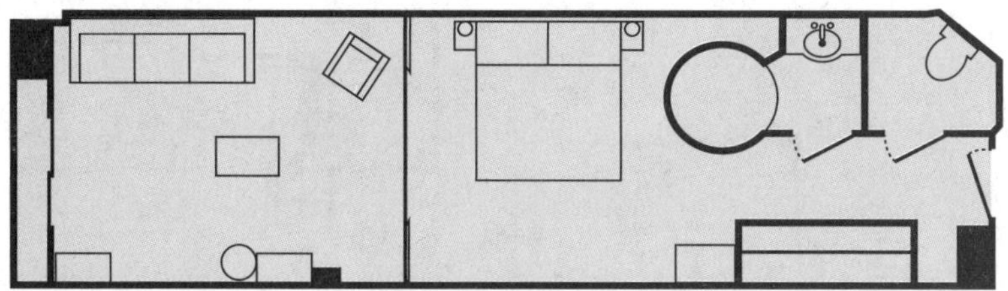

MAXIMUM OCCUPANCY 5 people

SIZE (square feet) 306 (including verandah)

DESCRIPTION These cabins have a queen-size bed, a sleeper sofa for two, and an upper-berth pull-down bed that sleeps one. These rooms have an extra half-bath, giving the shower side of the split bath a sink and vanity. Category V staterooms are on Decks 11 and 12 on the *Dream* and *Fantasy* and on Deck 8 on the *Magic* and *Wonder.*

CATEGORY T: Concierge 1-Bedroom Suite with Verandah

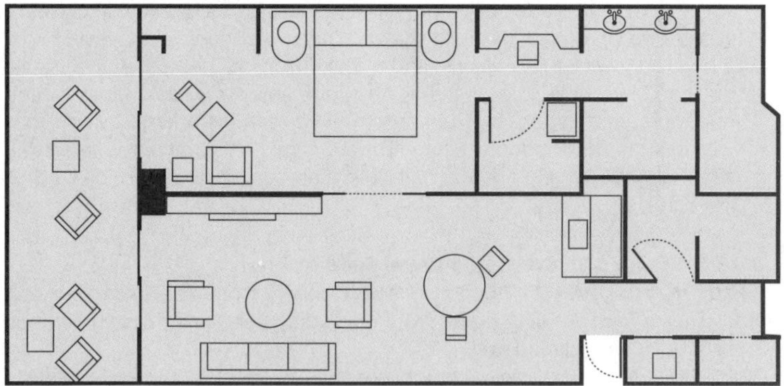

MAXIMUM OCCUPANCY 5 people

SIZE (square feet) *Magic/Wonder,* 614 (including verandah); *Dream/Fantasy,* 622 (including verandah)

DESCRIPTION These cabins feature a separate bedroom with queen-size bed and a bathroom with whirlpool tub and separate shower. The living room has

upholstered chairs and a sofa, plus a separate table and chairs. The living room also sleeps three: two on the convertible sofa and one in the pull-down bed. These staterooms are found all along Deck 8 on the *Magic* and *Wonder* and the Forward sections of Decks 11 and 12 on the *Dream* and *Fantasy.*

CATEGORY S (*Magic* and *Wonder* only): Concierge 2-Bedroom Suite with Verandah

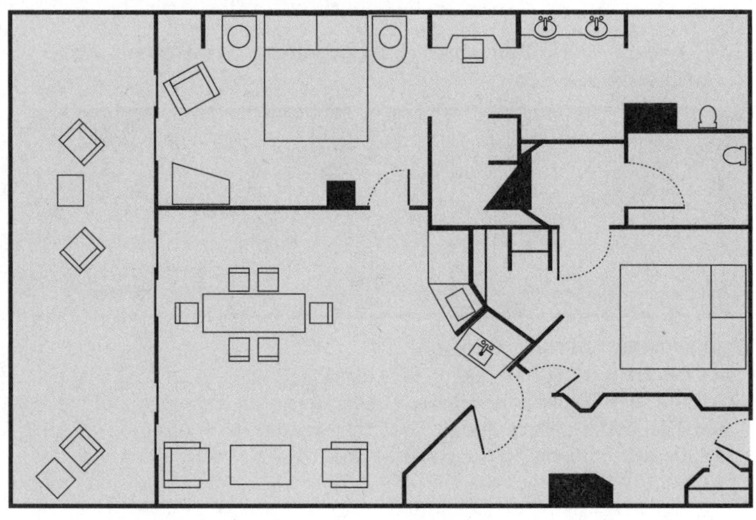

MAXIMUM OCCUPANCY 7 people

SIZE (square feet) 954 (including verandah)

DESCRIPTION The master bedroom has a queen-size bed, a walk-in closet, a vanity, two sinks, and a walk-in shower. The other bedroom has twin beds, a bathroom with tub and sink, and a walk-in closet. Two others can sleep on the convertible sofa in the living room, and a pull-down bed sleeps one more. In addition, the 2-Bedroom Suite features a large living room with seating for 10 people, a huge private verandah suitable for entertaining a few guests, and another half-bath. Category S cabins are on Deck 8 Forward.

CATEGORY R: Concierge Royal Suite *(see next page)*

MAXIMUM OCCUPANCY 7 people (*Magic/Wonder*); 5 people (*Dream/Fantasy*)

SIZE (square feet) *Magic/Wonder,* 1,029 (including verandah); *Dream/Fantasy,* 1,781 (including verandah)

DESCRIPTION On the *Magic* and *Wonder,* the master bedroom has a queen-size bed, a walk-in closet, a vanity, two sinks, and a walk-in shower. The other bedroom has twin beds, a bathroom with tub and sink, and a walk-in closet. Two others can sleep on the convertible sofa in the living room, and a pull-down bed sleeps one more. On the *Magic* and *Wonder,* the Royal Suite includes a separate dining room, living room, and media room, plus

Concierge Royal Suite

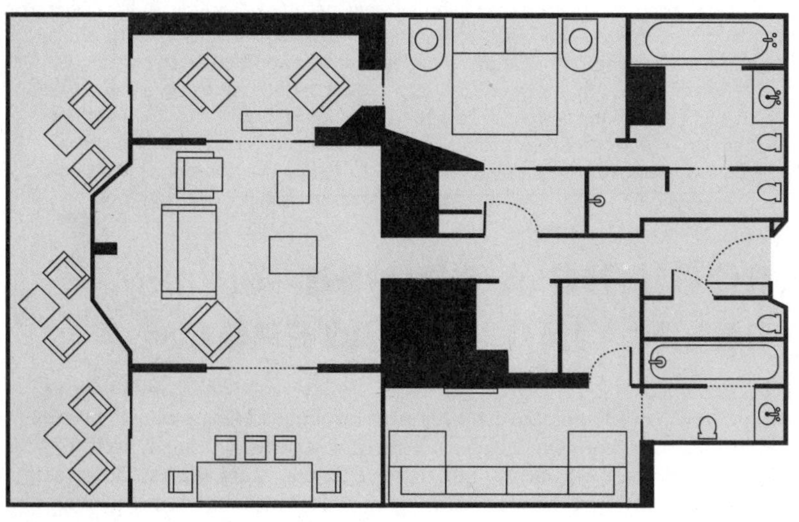

Concierge Royal Suite with Verandah

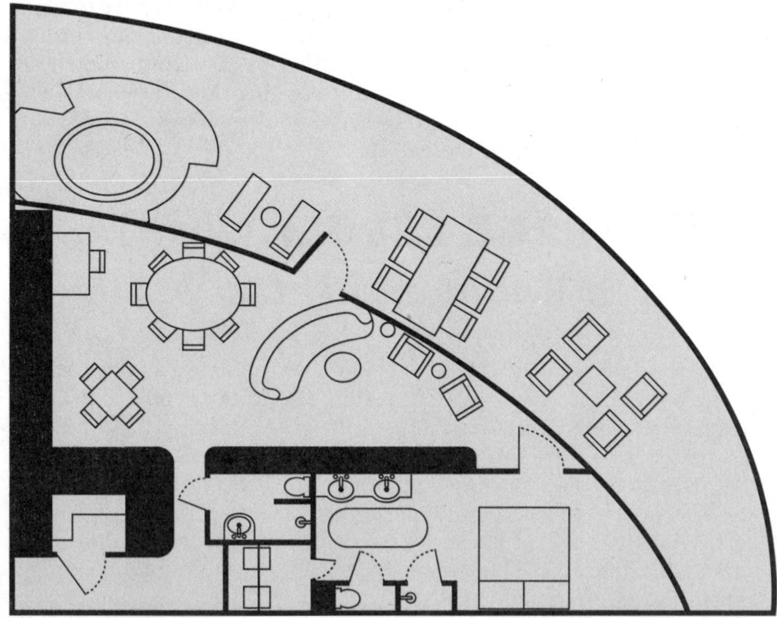

a private verandah that you should rent out to other families for birthdays (it'll fit an elephant!) and another half-bath. Royal Suites on the *Dream* and *Fantasy* have one long room separated into dining and living areas. The master bedroom features a queen-size bed and bath with two sinks, a shower, and a tub. An in-wall pull-down double bed and a single pull-down bed in the living room complete the sleeping arrangements. The most impressive feature of these suites on the *Dream* and *Fantasy* may be the verandah, which curves around the suite to follow the contour of the deck. Besides being large enough to land aircraft on, it includes a whirlpool tub.

BOOKING A CRUISE *Without* SELECTING A STATEROOM

UNLIKE BOOKING A HOTEL, where you typically don't find out your exact room until you arrive, most guests booking a Disney cruise choose a specific stateroom when they make their reservation. When a preferred stateroom category is nearly full, however, DCL offers what's known as a **GTY reservation.** *GTY* stands for "guarantee," meaning you're guaranteed to be in a particular category of room or a higher category, but you won't know exactly which cabin you're in until immediately before you depart. GTY reservations are often offered close to the ship's sail date.

Other acronyms you might see are **VGT** (Verandah Guarantee), **OGT** (Oceanview Guarantee) and **IGT** (Inside Guarantee), which are typically used when DCL is offering a last-minute discount on a cruise that's not selling well. There are a number of restrictions on these fares—the cruise must be paid in full at booking time, for example—but there are often good deals to be had if you're willing to leave your stateroom selection up in the air.

CONCIERGE LEVEL: *What You Need to Know, and If It's Worth It*

A DISNEY CRUISE IS ALREADY A FAIRLY LUXE VACATION, but what do you do when you want to plus it up even more? Booking a stateroom on the Concierge level is one option. The amenities offered to Concierge level guests are substantial, as is the price. Not surprisingly, this is one of the areas of cruising where we are most often asked, "Is it worth it?" See page 20 for our thoughts on this topic, but *spoiler alert*: it depends.

The Concierge levels on the *Dream* and *Fantasy* are nearly identical. The cabins are on Decks 11 and 12, with an exclusive Concierge lounge on Deck 12. The lounge opens to a private outdoor-sunning area (it's right by Satellite Falls).

On the *Magic* and *Wonder,* Concierge staterooms are on Deck 8, while the concierge lounges and staff are on Deck 10.

Concierge categories are as follows:

1. **Category V: Concierge Family Oceanview Stateroom with Verandah** This is the same layout as a Category 4, but with the added bonus of Concierge service. These can connect to 1-Bedroom Suites to make a 2-Bedroom Suite. Category V is available only on the *Dream* and *Fantasy.*
2. **Category T: Concierge 1-Bedroom Suite**
3. **Category S: Concierge 2-Bedroom Suite** (*Magic* and *Wonder* only)
4. **Category R: Concierge Royal Suite**

You can check out the floor plans for a Concierge 2-Bedroom Suite on page 76 and two Concierge Royal Suites on page 77. Prepare to be wowed upon walking in: these are seriously nice cabins, with lots of room to spread out. We already think Disney has great staterooms, but the finishing touches in Concierge are beyond our expectations. In fact, if you're considering booking here, we think you'd do well to choose it for an itinerary and ship you've already taken so you're not torn between exploring the ship and port and just enjoying the Concierge level.

The benefits of booking this level are quantifiable—more space, lounge access, early booking opportunities for specialty dining and port excursions (notably cabanas on Castaway Cay)—but they're also intangible when it comes to the added level of service. Also quantifiable is the cost: expect to pay for all this luxury and space. For an apples-to-apples comparison, plan to pay around 50% more for a Category V versus a Category 4, or around twice as much as a Category 4 for a Concierge 1-Bedroom Suite.

Concierge level has perks that range from "really useful" to "we can take it or leave it." The pampering begins before boarding. The Concierge team will contact you before your booking window for port excursions and dining to ask for your requests. While making Palo or Remy reservations usually isn't a problem no matter where you're booked, getting a cabana on Castaway Cay is nearly impossible if you're not in Concierge.

On boarding day, Concierge guests check in with Platinum-level guests in a separate area (Port Canaveral only) or line (other ports). While Platinum and Concierge guests may both board at will, with no waiting for your boarding group to be announced, Concierge guests are escorted to the lounge by the staff. This helps you get around the usual wait for an elevator on embarkation day.

The lounge itself is fantastic. Snacks and beverages are served all day, and Concierge staff are available from morning to evening to assist with anything you need help with. You'll never need to stand in line at Guest Services for anything. The quiet and calm of the lounge

are pretty much the opposite of the chaos of the nearby pool deck. You may never want to leave.

One of our favorite Concierge benefits is room service from the main dining room. A server will bring your entire meal—you pick from the menu as you would at the table at one of the dining rooms—and serve it course by course in the privacy of your cabin. He or she waits in the hallway between courses.

A good rate for Concierge Family Oceanview Staterooms with Verandah on DCL in 2018 was less than $390 per person per night. For comparison, a good rate for a non-Concierge Deluxe Family Oceanview Stateroom with Verandah was around $240 per person per night. The 2019 Concierge Level prices we checked were running $50–$100 more per person, per night than they were in 2018, while the non-Concierge Deluxe Family staterooms were only about $10 more per person, per night, in 2019 versus 2018. (Comparable concierge staterooms on Royal Caribbean start at $260 per night for seven-night cruises.) Thus, Concierge access costs at least $200 more per person per night on Disney. But you're not cruising with Disney because it's economical—you're doing so because DCL is stylish, with excellent service and kids' clubs.

SO IS CONCIERGE WORTH IT? Being logical types, we like to approach the question methodically. If you accept that (1) a Disney cruise is worth the surcharge you pay over other lines, (2) a verandah room is worth what you pay over an inside room, (3) the expense will neither kill your overall bottom line nor negatively impact other aspects of your vacation, and (4) you enjoy personal attention, then the next linear progression is that, yes, the extra space of a Concierge room (we're talking one bedroom) could be worth the price Disney charges. Basically, staying on Concierge level means not just upgraded accommodations but also avoiding all the little annoyances of a cruise vacation—lines, noise, masses of fellow cruisers—by waving them away with a magic wand made of money.

Personally, we wouldn't sail Concierge every time, but we do find the one-bedroom Concierge level suites worth it, for us, if we're celebrating something special or want to take a particularly relaxing or luxurious vacation. To help with your decision, take a look at our "Is It Worth It?" discussion (page 20). If you decide to pass, don't sweat it—you'll have a great time anyway.

STATEROOM SELECTION *for* LARGER PARTIES

GUESTS TRAVELING WITH NUCLEAR FAMILIES with four or fewer people are often fine staying in one stateroom. DCL offers many options for ship location and stateroom size at a variety of price

points—just choose where you want to be and how much you want to spend, and you're good to go. Guests traveling with parties of five or more, and guests traveling with extended family, blended families, or unrelated friends may have more-complicated decisions to make when choosing their staterooms.

A quick glance at DCL's deck plans and stateroom classifications shows that on, for example, the *Magic,* the lowest stateroom category that will sleep a party of five is a Category 4 Deluxe Family Oceanview Stateroom with Verandah on the upper decks. Let's look at pricing for a hypothetical family of five (two adults, three kids ages 16, 13, and 9) for the 7-Night Bahamian Cruise from New York City on the *Magic* on November 3, 2019. At the time of our search, the lowest price to put this family into one stateroom is a Category 4E stateroom for $9,779. If, however, we try to book that same family of five into two 11B Standard Inside Staterooms, with one adult and two children, ages 13 and 9, in one stateroom and one adult and the 16-year-old child in the other, the total price is $8,451 ($4,789 for the stateroom of three and $3,662 for the stateroom of two). Moving this family from one stateroom to two results in a savings of $1,328.

Of course, you have some tradeoffs to consider. Moving into two of the lowest-priced inside staterooms obviously takes away this family's access to a verandah. On the other hand, they gain about 60 square feet of living space and an additional shower and toilet when they switch to two inside cabins. For many families, the advantages of saving more than $1,300 and gaining a bathroom would well outweigh the loss of a verandah.

Making things even more complicated, the pricing is different if you book those same passengers (two adults and three kids ages 16, 13, and 9) into the same two inside staterooms, but in a slightly different combination. If you put one adult and both teens into one room, with the other adult and the 9-year-old in the other room, the cost is $4,828 for the first room and $3,662 for the second room, for a total of $8,490 for the party of five. But if you book one adult, one teen, and the 9-year-old in the first room, their cost is $4,789, and the cost for the second room (with an adult and the 13-year-old) is $3,662, for a total of $8,541. The difference between the booking strategies saves $51.

The reason behind the difference is that the second person in a stateroom is always charged an adult rate, regardless of age, meaning if that if the 9-year-old is booked into a stateroom with just one other person, he's also priced at an adult rate, but if he's the third person in a stateroom, he's charged a child's rate.

Granted, a $51 savings is a drop in the bucket for a vacation that costs thousands, but if you're traveling with a very large party (a family reunion, for example), small tweaks can add up. Again, however, note that the Castaway Club status of the travelers also has ramifications for room assignments; if members of your party have different

statuses, it may be worth a few dollars to choose a different booking configuration. (See page 66.) Also note that once you're on board, it's easy to tinker with who actually sleeps where, regardless of how the booking was made.

A couple other things to think about when booking staterooms for larger parties:

- **Do we need connecting staterooms?** Guests traveling with small children may prefer them, while guests traveling with well-behaved teens or other adults may find that adjacent rooms or nonadjacent rooms in close proximity are enough.
- **Does it matter if all members of the party have the same type of stateroom?** Is parity needed to keep peace among family members? Are we willing to have an Oceanview Stateroom and an Inside Stateroom, or a Verandah Stateroom and an Oceanview or Inside Stateroom? Is it sufficient if only one room has a verandah that everyone can use?

UNIQUE STATEROOM COMBINATIONS

IF YOU'RE A LARGER FAMILY LOOKING TO BOOK two or more staterooms, you'll quickly see that in most situations involving connecting rooms, both of the rooms are in the same price classification. For example, a Category 9A room is connected to another 9A room.

On the DCL website, you'll find that connecting rooms are indicated on the deck plans in two different ways depending on which version of the deck plan you're looking at: either by a sideways fan–shaped symbol in the downloadable PDF ships' brochures or by a gap between rooms in the interactive deck plans online at disneycruise.disney.go.com/ships/deck-plans.

Only even-numbered rooms are connected. For example, on the *Magic* and the *Wonder,* Room 8004 connects to Room 8006, while on the *Dream* and the *Fantasy,* Room 9666 connects to Room 9668.

In some situations, different categories of staterooms are connected. Booking dissimilar connecting rooms can be a strategy to save money or to experience a variety of amenities or room configurations. Some examples of this are as follows:

On the *Dream/Fantasy*

- **5186/5188, 5688/5686** Category 9A accessible Deluxe Oceanview Staterooms connected to Category 7A Deluxe Oceanview Staterooms with Navigator's Verandahs. Particularly attractive for people with disabilities who are traveling with unrelated caregivers.
- **6186/6188, 6686/6688** Category 9A accessible Deluxe Oceanview Staterooms connected to Category 6B Deluxe Oceanview Staterooms with Verandahs
- **6606/6608, 6504/6506** Category 9D accessible Deluxe Oceanview Staterooms connected to 9A Deluxe Oceanview Staterooms

- **6001/6501** Categories 11B and 10A. Both are inside staterooms, but 10A (Deluxe Inside) is slightly larger than 11B (Standard Inside). Good for families on a budget who don't need full parity between rooms.
- **6178/6180, 6678/6680** Categories 7A and 6B, one with a full verandah and one with a navigator's verandah.
- **7168/7170, 7666/7668** Categories 7A and 5C, one with a full verandah and one with a navigator's verandah.
- **7188/7190, 7686/7688** Categories 6B and 5E, both staterooms with verandahs, but one with a full view off the stern of the ship.
- **8022/8024, 8520/8522** Categories 7A and 5B, one with a full verandah and one with a navigator's verandah.
- **9150/9152, 9650/9652** Categories 7A and 5A, one with a full verandah and one with a navigator's verandah.
- Most Concierge-level rooms can be combined with other rooms to create large suites.

On the *Magic/Wonder*

- Many Concierge-level rooms can be combined with other rooms to create large suites.

GET *to* KNOW YOUR VERANDAH

A *VERANDAH* (NOTE THE FANCY *H* AT THE END) is analogous to a balcony at a hotel. Some cruise lines have verandahs (or *verandas,* depending on the line) that face toward the center of the ship, often toward a pool or open deck stage, but the verandahs on DCL ships face outward toward the ocean.

DCL uses a variety of language to describe the verandahs on its ships. For example:

- **Standard (Family) Verandah** Has a transparent acrylic wall between you and the ocean. You can see the ocean from anywhere, sitting or standing.
- **White-Wall Verandah** An open-air lounge area with a solid white wall from the deck to the railing. You can see the ocean if you're standing up, but you're not likely to if you're sitting down. Most of these staterooms are located in the aft portion of the ship.
- **Navigator's Verandah** An open-air lounge area that has a solid wall from the deck to the railing as well as some enclosure above the railing. Picture a balcony with a large porthole opening to a view of the ocean. You can see the ocean if you're standing up, but you're not likely to if you're sitting down. Most Navigator's Verandahs have one chair and one fixed bench built into the wall rather than two regular chairs.
- **Obstructed-View Verandah** A significant portion of the view is blocked by ship walls or something like the lifeboats.
- **Undersize Verandah** A verandah with smaller square footage than is typical on DCL ships.

THE STATEROOM SCOOP

Tammy Whiting is a travel agent at **Storybook Destinations,** an Authorized Disney Vacation Planner. She offers some great insight into specific staterooms on the DCL ships. (*Magic*-class ships are the *Magic* and *Wonder*; *Dream*-class ships are the *Dream* and *Fantasy*.)

- ***Category T or S, Concierge 1- or 2-Bedroom Suite with Verandah*** On the *Magic* class, I recommend 8032, 8034, 8532, or 8534. These have a layout that puts the twin pull-down bed in the living room instead of in the master bedroom, allowing the master bedroom to have its own closed-off space. On the *Dream* class, there are six suites with oversize verandahs: 12006, 12012, 12506, 12512, 11006, and 11002. For the absolute best view of Castaway Cay, book 12512. I slightly prefer the Concierge staterooms on Deck 12 over Deck 11, because they have easier access to the Concierge Lounge and Sundeck.

- ***Category V, Concierge Family Oceanview Stateroom with Verandah*** Category V staterooms are essentially Category 4 staterooms with Concierge soft goods and Concierge service. On the *Magic* class, I prefer starboard side if visiting Castaway Cay. On the *Dream* class, I have the same starboard answer, while also recommending one of the staterooms on the bumpout. Those are 12008, 12010, 12508, 12510, and 11004. If you're traveling with the party in Stateroom 12512, definitely book 12510 to open the verandah partition between the two staterooms for amazing Castaway Cay views.

- ***Category 4, Deluxe Family Oceanview Stateroom with Verandah*** Category 4 staterooms are the biggest non-Concierge staterooms on the ships. The word "Family" in the title means the stateroom is slightly longer and may sleep up to 5. The A, B, C, and D versions of these staterooms (letter indicates location on the ship) have similar features. Many 4Es are nonconforming, sleeping 4 instead of 5, and, on the *Dream* class, lacking the round tub of the other 4s. The *Dream*-class 4Es do have spacious verandahs, while the *Magic* class 4Es have white-wall verandahs.

- **Extended Verandah** A verandah with greater-than-typical square footage. Instead of room for just two regular chairs, there may be room for lounge chairs or for four chairs.

Also be aware that some staterooms have combinations of these verandah types. For example, many of the far-aft rooms on Decks 7, 8, 9, and 10 of the *Dream* and *Fantasy* have extended verandahs with white walls.

The type of verandah you select can have cost implications. For example, we spot-checked the September 1, 2019, Northern European sailing of the *Magic* for a party of two adults and one child, age 9, in a

- ***Category 5, Deluxe Oceanview Stateroom with Verandah***
Category 5 is my go-to room: a standard-size stateroom with an unobstructed verandah. I'm particularly enthusiastic about the 5Es on the *Dream* class. 5Es are on the far aft (back) of the ship and have huge verandahs, with some of my favorite views on board. There are a few Category 5s on the *Magic* class that have solid-white metal walls, so if that bothers you, avoid 7130–7138 and 7630–7638.

- ***Category 6, Deluxe Oceanview Stateroom with Verandah (Undersize, Obstructed-View, or White-Wall)***
Category 6 staterooms are like Category 5 staterooms, but they all have either an undersize, obstructed-view, or white-wall verandah. Some of these differences are minor, so if you want to save a little from a Category 5, Category 6 may be for you. Category 6 staterooms on Deck 6 have slightly larger verandahs than others on the *Magic*-class ships.

- ***Category 7, Deluxe Oceanview Stateroom with Navigator's Verandah***
There is a significant difference between the *Dream*- and *Magic*-class Category 7s. A navigator's verandah on the *Magic* class is a mostly enclosed verandah, with a large circular or oval window-type opening cut out for viewing purposes. On the *Dream* class, it's just a slightly obstructed view from the verandah. These are slightly more obstructed than the Category 6s, thus the Category 7 designation. On the *Magic* class, there are four such staterooms that are not fully enclosed: 6134, 6634, 7120, and 7620.

- ***Category 8, Deluxe Family Oceanview Stateroom***
Category 8s are found only on the *Dream* class. Once again, the word "Family" means they are bigger staterooms that sleep up to five and have round tubs. They also have very large portholes with seating. The exceptions are 8As, which are almost like suites, with two large portholes and lots of space; many have a divider of some kind between the bed and seating area. Not all have bathtubs.

(continued on next page)

Deluxe Oceanview Stateroom with Verandah. Within seven consecutive staterooms, on Deck 7 Aft, three different verandah configurations are available, all with different pricing:

- **Obstructed-View Verandah:** $6,271
- **White-Wall Verandah:** $6,411
- **Standard Verandah:** $7,111

For a party of two adults and a child, on the October 4, 2019, 5-Night Baja Cruise on the *Wonder,* on Deck 7 Aft, you can get a Deluxe Oceanview Stateroom with Verandah:

THE STATEROOM SCOOP *(continued)*

- ***Category 9, Deluxe Oceanview Stateroom***
Category 9s are Oceanview staterooms minus verandahs. On the *Magic* class, I'd avoid Deck 1 if staying in a Category 9—this is a short deck with no access to the Aft elevators. The Oceanview staterooms on Deck 1 also have two small portholes instead of one larger porthole, which greatly limits your view. The 9C staterooms that are all the way forward, like 2504 or 2510, also have a bit more space due to the curvature of the ship. On the *Dream* class, the 9Bs on Deck 2 outside Enchanted Garden are in a convenient location. The *Dream* class also has some large corner staterooms that are 9Ds: 7006, 7504, 8006, and 8504.

- ***Category 10 Deluxe Inside Stateroom***
Category 10s are basically the same size and have the same setup as Category 9s, but they have no outside views. On the *Dream* class, however, they have virtual portholes, which gives a view (via camera) of what is happening outside (with some occasional Disney magic thrown in). The *Magic* class has its own exciting unnamed category here—secret porthole staterooms. These are inside staterooms that actually have a window, albeit with an obstructed view. If you want some natural light for the price of an Inside Stateroom, these are the staterooms for you. Book 5020, 5022, 5024, 5520, 5522, or 5524 on the *Magic* class. *Warning:* These staterooms are more popular than a Dole Whip on a sweltering day at Disney World, so book early!

- ***Category 11, Standard Inside Stateroom***
There are no split bathrooms, standard in all other categories, in Category 11 staterooms. While I highly recommend the split bath for families, some people prefer having one large bathroom as opposed to two smaller ones. Additionally, on the *Magic*-class ships, some 11Bs have a "sideways" layout—these staterooms are somewhat popular and feel a bit roomier than the typical Inside Stateroom layout.

- **White-Wall Verandah:** $3,745
- **Standard Verandah:** $4,085

The same party size on the August 7, 2019, 3-Night Bahamian Cruise on the *Dream* can choose between four variants of the Deluxe Oceanview Stateroom with Verandah on Deck 6 Aft:

- **Undersize Verandah:** $3,516
- **Obstructed-View Verandah:** $3,540
- **Standard Verandah:** $3,588
- **Extended Verandah:** $3,588

In this last case, note that you can get a stateroom with verandah seating space for two (standard) for the exact same price as a state-

room with verandah seating space for four (extended)—a little tweak that could make a big difference for some families.

If you have dreams of sitting with a glass of wine and staring at the sea, be sure you're getting a verandah configuration that will actually allow you to do this. It may well be worth it to spend a few dollars, or even a few hundred dollars, more for better sight lines. Or if you don't particularly care, you can save yourself a few bucks by choosing a different verandah configuration.

Also note that if your party is staying in two adjacent Verandah Staterooms, you may be able to remove the divider separating the outdoor space between them, effectively creating an extended verandah shared by two rooms. Not all Verandah Staterooms offer this option, so check with your stateroom host to see if the divider is removable.

Although verandahs are your "private" outdoor space, please keep in mind the following rules and courtesies:

- **No smoking.** Cigarette/cigar smoke inevitably drifts to neighboring verandahs. Please smoke only in designated areas of the ship (see page 131). The same rule applies to vaping and electronic cigarettes.
- **No drying clothing or towels.** These items are almost guaranteed to blow away.
- **No nudity, for the love of Pete.** You may be visible from other ships, port locations, or nearby verandahs.
- **No loud music or conversation.** You will be heard in nearby staterooms.

If you're sailing to a cold-weather destination, you may find that a verandah is less of an imperative than if you're traveling to tropical locales. It may be nice to stand out on your balcony to view the trees, wildlife, or glaciers for a few minutes, but it may not be comfortable to read or dine outdoors for an extended period of time.

Some guests with small children may have safety concerns. Verandah doors have a lock that's above adult shoulder-height. It is theoretically possible that an enterprising elementary-schooler could climb on a chair or coffee table to reach the lock, but it would take some real ingenuity and strength to open the door. If you're still concerned that you may have a late-night escape artist on your hands, then you may want to save verandah lodging for when Junior is a bit older.

MAKING CHANGES *to* YOUR STATEROOM RESERVATION

GETTING THE BEST RATE FOR YOUR CRUISE often means booking more than a year in advance (see page 25). But a lot can change in a year, including little things (school and work schedules) and big things (pregnancy, marriage, or divorce). Sometimes these changes mean that

you have to cancel the cruise (see page 36 for more on how to do that), but at other times you'll still want to go on the cruise but you may want or need to travel with different people.

Don't worry: Disney Cruise Line lets you change the actual names on a reservation until close to sail time. When Erin's husband had to bow out of an Atlantic Canada (Canadian Coastline) cruise with her due to an unforeseen business meeting that was scheduled during the sail dates, she was easily able to swap in a friend to sail with her.

You may also make changes to the number of guests in your stateroom until your paid-in-full date. The rule of thumb here is that if you're unsure about exactly which friends or family members you'll be traveling with, you should make the reservation for the larger of the possible party sizes. Here's why:

In some cases, your stateroom can physically accommodate more people but DCL won't let you add them to the room; this typically happens when there is a higher-than-average number of guests in your part of the ship. In such instances, strict rules about lifeboat capacity and other safety issues beyond individual cabin capacity come into play.

Another factor in booking your maximum party size and then paring down is that it locks in your booking rate. Even if DCL will allow you to add someone to your room well after the original booking, they might be charged at a higher cost. As long as you make party deletions before your paid-in-full date, you'll be able to reduce the number of guests in your room.

OTHER STATEROOM CONSIDERATIONS

OVERALL, THE FOLLOWING are things to consider when selecting your stateroom:

- The number of people in your party and whether they are best accommodated in one cabin or more than one cabin—connecting staterooms or not
- The stateroom location on the ship: deck; Forward, Mid, or Aft; Port or Starboard; proximity to pools, theaters, restaurants, and so on
- Inside, Oceanview, or Verandah? If Verandah, which type?
- The need for disability accommodations
- Overall price

A few additional tips and factors to consider:

- Don't book connecting staterooms unless you absolutely need to. The connecting doors are less soundproof than an actual wall.
- Rooms adjacent to or across the hall from laundry rooms may be noisy, both because of the washers and dryers and conversation among guests waiting to use them.

- Rooms directly above the theaters will be noisy during the evenings (Deck 5 Forward on all ships). We've stayed in a room directly above the Walt Disney Theatre on the *Magic* and heard music from the shows loud and clear.
- Some guests find that rooms directly below the pools (Midship Deck 10 on the *Dream/Fantasy,* Midship Deck 8 on the *Magic/Wonder*) are noisy during the day, with guests dragging deck chairs overhead. If you're a daytime napper, avoid this location.
- Elevator mechanical noise is typically minimal, but there will be more foot traffic the closer you are to an elevator.
- Guests with mobility issues may find it helpful to be close to an elevator; those hallways are long and narrow.
- The Starboard side of your ship will face the island if you're docked at Castaway Cay. If you have a room with a view, consider whether you'd prefer to gaze at the island or the water.
- Some guests find the far-aft staterooms on the *Dream/Fantasy* Deck 10 (10158–10658) too noisy—their verandahs are directly below the outdoor seating for the Cabanas buffet.
- Stateroom location may affect your comfort if you have trouble with motion sickness (see page 53).
- Disability-accessible staterooms are available at a number of price points; if, however, you need to use a device like a walker inside your stateroom, this will be challenging in most of the smaller staterooms.
- Some staterooms come preconfigured with enhanced communication for deaf and hearing-impaired guests.
- In addition to the stated room capacity, also consider the number of separate sleep surfaces. Will the members of your party be comfortable sleeping together on the number of beds in the room? (See page 80.)

If the nuances of stateroom features or locations are important to you, you may find it helpful to work with a DCL-specialist travel agent. Many are well versed in the distinct characteristics of particular cabins.

PART FOUR

ARRIVING, GETTING YOUR SEA LEGS, *and* DEPARTING

TRANSPORTATION *to* YOUR CRUISE

CHOOSING A DEPARTURE PORT BASED ON TIME AND MONEY

MOST DISNEY CRUISE LINE ITINERARIES depart from two or three different ports at various times of the year. While the differences in quality are relatively small, your departure port is more likely to affect your trip's transportation cost.

If you live within a few hours' drive of one of Disney's ports, your least expensive option is almost certainly going to be using that port. Otherwise, consider flying in the day before you depart to account for flight cancellations.

If you're taking a European cruise and flying in from North America, consider arriving two days before your cruise. This will protect you against most flight cancellations and also give you a bit more time to adjust to the time-zone difference.

As for quality, Disney's Port Canaveral terminal is the nicest in the United States, with easy, ample parking; good directional signage; and a comfortable waiting area. We wouldn't choose a cruise, however, based on the hour or so spent in the terminal. Instead, factor in the transportation cost to and from the port, plus lodging, in the total cost of the cruises you're considering to see how the overall cost shakes out.

GETTING TO AND FROM THE PORT

MOST NORTH AMERICAN DCL GUESTS have three options when arranging transportation to the cruise terminal: booking transportation through Disney, booking through a third-party service, or driving themselves. This section covers all three options in detail, including driving

directions, GPS settings, and terminal parking rates for those taking their own car.

Using Disney Transportation from the Airport or a Disney-Approved Hotel

If you're flying to Orlando, you can use **DCL's shuttle service** to get to Port Canaveral. The cost is $70, per person, round-trip, free for kids under age 3. You can also use this service in just one direction for $35 per person. DCL recommends that your flight into Orlando arrive by 1:45 p.m. and your flight out depart after 11:30 a.m.

Disney also provides shuttle service from other city airports to and from its cruise terminals, as well as to and from a few select hotels near each port. Depending on the destination, prices range from about $30 to about $150. See tinyurl.com/disneycruisetransfers for details on the exact routes serviced.

While Disney's shuttle service is certainly convenient, particularly if you're in an unfamiliar foreign country, you should nevertheless understand how much of a premium you'll be paying for that convenience. In a particularly egregious case of price gouging, guests staying at the Disney-approved New York Marriott Marquis hotel before the fall 2016 Canadian sailing on the *Magic* were offered transfers to the Manhattan Cruise Terminal for $35 *per person.* For a family of four, this would total $140. The distance from the Marriott Marquis, in Times Square, to the terminal is about a mile—easily walkable if you don't have a lot of luggage. (Disney charges the same $35 price for the 60-mile transfer from Walt Disney World hotels to Port Canaveral.) Taxis and ride-share services, plentiful in midtown Manhattan, typically charge less than $15, including a tip, for four people and luggage to drive from Times Square to the terminal.

If you've purchased ground transfers from Disney, you must give them your flight information; you can do this on the DCL website at disneycruiseline.com/plan. Disney provides few details about where to find your ground-transportation driver. Unless you hear otherwise, assume that a uniformed DCL greeter will be stationed near the airport baggage-claim area holding either a DCL sign or a sign with your party's name on it.

Using Disney Transportation from Walt Disney World to Port Canaveral

Disney provides round-trip transfer service between Walt Disney World hotels at a cost of $70 per person, round-trip. One-way service is also available for $35 per person.

LUGGAGE TRANSFER If you're taking a Disney cruise after staying at an on-site Disney-owned resort at Walt Disney World and you've booked

transportation from the resort to the ship through Disney, cruise representatives can transfer your luggage directly from your hotel room to your ship's stateroom.

Contact DCL at least three days before you leave home to take advantage of this service. They'll ask you for the number of bags and tell you when and where to meet for your drive to the ship. They'll also give you instructions on what to do with your bags; typically, you'll simply leave them in your hotel room, with your DCL luggage tags attached, and Disney will transfer them directly to your stateroom.

Surprisingly, you may not find this service as efficient as might be expected from Disney, as this reader reports:

> *The staff at Pop Century Resort want nothing to do with helping you get ready for your cruise. When I stopped at the Concierge desk to ask about luggage transfer, they simply gave me a card with the DCL phone number on it and told me to call it myself. When I called the number, I got an automated message telling me what time I would be picked up, but there was no indication of the meeting spot or what to do with our bags. We finally did get printed instructions about the port transfer at 9:30 p.m. We were told to leave our luggage in the room, by the door, with the DCL tags attached no later than 8:30 a.m. and that we should meet in the Pop Century lobby at 12:30 p.m. to check in with the cruise-line staff.*
>
> *You really do have to be ready on time—cast members were at our door at 8:31 to collect our luggage. Also, the DCL staff was in the Pop lobby at noon; we left as soon as everyone scheduled to be on the bus was there.*
>
> *One thing to note: If you use Disney transportation to get to Port Canaveral, you don't have any control over what time you get to the port. They tell you where to be and when to be there. So if you want a few more minutes in the parks, you can't leave WDW a bit later, and if you want more time to explore the ship, you can't leave earlier.*

Third-Party Shuttle Services

The easiest, cheapest way to get from the airport to your hotel or to the port is likely **Uber** or **Lyft.** Their prices are typically for up to four people in a single car rather than the per-person rate that Disney charges. If, however, you have more than four people in your cruise group or you have three people with a lot of luggage, you may want to use a third-party shuttle service instead.

GALVESTON Galveston Express (☎ 409-762-4397; galvestonexpress.com) offers both shared and private transfers, with the former being less expensive. From William P. Hobby Airport in Houston to the Port of Galveston, it's about $50 per person, round-trip. **Galveston Limousine** (☎ 800-640-4826; galvestonlimo.com/airport-shuttle.asp) has coach bus service from both Hobby and George Bush Airports several times per day. Round-trip fares are $40–$50 per person, with discounts available for online advance booking.

PORT CANAVERAL Mears Transportation (☎ 407-423-5566; mearstransportation.com) offers private town cars, SUVs, and van shuttles from Orlando to Port Canaveral. Round-trip cost is approximately $320 for up to four people in a town car, $380 for up to five people in an SUV, or $380 for up to eight people in a luxury van. If you have a large party, booking a third-party service like Mears offers cost savings as well as the ability to schedule your departure at your own convenience. Mears now has an app for iOS and Android that lets you track your driver's location and may also offer discount codes or coupons.

SAN DIEGO SuperShuttle (☎ 800-258-3826; supershuttle.com) offers one-way and round-trip transfers from virtually every airport in the region. Cost is about $12 per person between San Diego International Airport and the cruise port. Check the SuperShuttle website for details; type in "San Diego Cruise Ship Terminal" as your destination when you reserve online.

SuperShuttle also serves the airports you may use if you're cruising out of New York City; Miami; New Orleans; Dover, England; or Vancouver, British Columbia. Check the website for pricing information.

Minnie Vans

In 2017 Disney, in cooperation with Lyft, launched this shuttle service as a perk for Walt Disney World hotel guests. Originally limited to trips around Disney World property, Minnie Van service was expanded in mid-2018 to shuttle Disney hotel guests between the World and Orlando International Airport. (Ride service within Disney World proper was also opened to all guests, not just those staying on-property.) Then, in late 2018, service from Disney World or the airport to Port Canaveral was added for guests combining a Disney resort vacation with a DCL cruise.

Minnie Vans are, well, minivans painted red with large white polka dots to resemble Minnie Mouse's signature ensemble. The drivers are Disney cast members who are trained in safety and knowledgeable about the routes, so chances are you'll be getting better service than you would from a random cabbie or ride-share driver.

The vans may be cute, but the price is not: $250 one-way to the port for up to four people. That same group taking the DCL bus transfer to the port would pay $140 one-way. Though the sensible part of our brains understands that paying an extra $110 for a ride to port is foolish, we freely admit that we probably would have done this *once* had Minnie Vans been available when our daughters were 6 years old.

From within Walt Disney World, you arrange a ride by using the Lyft mobile app: confirm your current pickup location, enter your destination, and tap "Request." The app will then display a map tracking the vehicle en route and give you an identifying number to help you spot your car. To arrange service from the airport, call ☎ 407-WDW-PLAY (939-7529); service is available for flights arriving between 7 a.m.

and 10 p.m. and departing from 9 a.m. to midnight. At press time, only one-way rides to Port Canaveral were available, but we expect this to change eventually.

Driving Yourself

The following section provides driving directions to DCL ports in Florida, California, New York, Texas, and Canada, plus information on parking rates at the various cruise terminals. (We'll include information for **New Orleans,** which was announced as a new port late in this book's production schedule, in a future edition.)

unofficial **TIP**
Text the location and a photo of your parking spot to other members of your group before you leave the lot. This will help you remember where you parked when you return from your cruise.

TO PORT CANAVERAL It takes about an hour to drive from Orlando to Port Canaveral under normal conditions. Traffic and road construction on the Beachline Expressway (FL 528), a toll road, can turn that 60-minute trip into a 3-hour ordeal. And because Port Canaveral and Orlando are linked by only three main roads—with only limited connections between them—there are a couple of points along the Beachline where you have no way of taking an alternate route if traffic is delayed. Our advice is to allow at least 2½ hours for this trip. If you get to the port early, Disney's cruise terminal is air-conditioned and comfortable, with enough room for restless kids to run around in while you wait to board.

If you're using a GPS, enter this address as your destination: **Port Canaveral Terminal A, 9155 Charles M. Rowland Drive, Port Canaveral, FL 32920.** If your GPS doesn't recognize Port Canaveral as a city, use **Cape Canaveral** instead in the address above.

If you're not using a GPS, DCL's **My Disney Cruise** planning center (see page 39) has very clear driving directions for getting to Port Canaveral. If you're driving from Walt Disney World, the most direct route uses eastbound FL 536 to the Central Florida GreeneWay (FL 417) and then to the Beachline Expressway. The GreeneWay and Beachline are toll roads, so have $10 in cash on hand for the round-trip.

You'll be on the Beachline almost the entire way to Port Canaveral. Once you arrive, the port's terminals function almost exactly like an airport's. The same kinds of signs for airline terminals are posted for cruise-line terminals at Port Canaveral. DCL ships usually depart from Terminal A, so you'll be looking for road signs to that effect. If you want to see what the drive looks like, **YouTube** has videos showing the exits, terminal, and parking options from a car passenger's perspective.

Once you arrive at Terminal A, you'll park and walk to the security checkpoint. Parking at Port Canaveral terminal costs $17 per day, including the days of arrival and departure. See portcanaveral.com/cruise/directions-parking for details. (Prepayment used to be an option but was discontinued in 2018.)

TO MIAMI Driving here is a challenge because of the traffic, one-way streets, and constant construction. We recommend using a GPS, preferably one with traffic information, to guide you to the port. Use this address: **Port of Miami, 1015 North America Way, Miami, FL 33132.** DCL recommends that you turn off your GPS once you've reached the port's bridge, then staying in the left lane and following the signs to the parking garage closest to your terminal.

Like Port Canaveral, Miami has both parking garages and open-air lots. Parking is $22 per day. If the lots closest to your ship are full, drop off some of your family and luggage near the cruise terminal, then swing around and find a spot in one of the other garages—the nearest open garages can be half a mile from the terminal, and there's no reason to have everyone haul their luggage that far.

Miami's ports are supposed to have shuttles running between the parking garages and terminals, but we've never seen them operating. (We *have* seen giant iguanas running around, though, so keep your eyes open.)

Once you're inside the terminal, you'll be directed to a check-in line. Miami's terminals are older and smaller than Port Canaveral's, but DCL's section is well maintained and efficient. After you check in, you'll go up a set of escalators and then through a long corridor to board the ship.

TO GALVESTON The port is about 71 miles from Houston's George Bush Intercontinental Airport (IAH), roughly a 90-minute drive with traffic. If you're just dropping off passengers, the address to use for your GPS for Terminal 1 is **2502 Harborside Drive, Galveston, TX 77550;** Terminal 2 is at **2702 Harborside Drive.** If you're parking, the GPS address for the parking lots is the **intersection of 33rd Street and Harborside Drive.** Parking costs range from $55 for four days to $170 for two weeks, with a $5 discount if you prepay online at portgalvestonparking.com.

TO NEW YORK CITY The **Manhattan Cruise Terminal** is located at **711 12th Ave., New York, NY 10019,** about a mile from Times Square. The closest cross street is West 52nd Street. Standard yellow-taxi rates (exclusive of tolls and tips) from area airports are as follows: John F. Kennedy International Airport, $52 flat rate; LaGuardia Airport, $25–$35; Newark International Airport, $80–$100 (negotiate the price with the driver in advance). From the Port Authority Bus Terminal, the fare is $8–$10.

If you're driving, note that cars enter the cruise terminal from the north at the intersection of West 55th Street and 12th Avenue (New York Route 9A, also known as the Henry Hudson Parkway and the West Side Highway).

• **FROM NEW JERSEY AND POINTS SOUTH** From the Lincoln Tunnel, follow the signs to West 42nd Street, make a left onto 42nd Street, go three blocks, and make a right onto 12th Avenue. Take 12th Avenue for

a half mile and make a left on West 55th Street, which is the entrance to the terminal. From the Holland Tunnel, take Exit 1 (NY 9A). Go through three lights and make a right onto West Street, which is also 12th Avenue (NY 9A). Take West Street/12th Avenue 1 mile and make a left onto West 55th Street, which is the entrance to the terminal.

• **FROM THE GEORGE WASHINGTON BRIDGE, WESTCHESTER COUNTY, AND POINTS NORTH** Go south on the Henry Hudson Parkway (NY 9A) and then exit to the right at West 55th Street, which is the entrance to the terminal.

• **FROM LONG ISLAND VIA THE QUEENS-MIDTOWN TUNNEL** Go west on 34th Street to 12th Avenue. Turn right onto 12th Avenue and continue north to the terminal on West 55th Street.

• **FROM MIDTOWN MANHATTAN** Take West 55th Street across 12th Avenue to the terminal.

Parking is located above each of the piers. To park at the official port lot, drive up the viaduct ramp at 55th Street to the receiving area adjacent to the cruise vessel's berth. Passengers who are parking a car must enter the terminal and park before bringing in bags to the second level for check-in. The daily rate for up to 10 hours (drop-offs and visitors) is $35; parking for 1–10 nights is $40 per night.

With hundreds of other parking lots located within walking or taxi-drop-off distance to the port, it's quite possible to find nearby parking for substantially less than the port's rates. We're fans of the **Best Parking** app; we have friends who rave about **SpotHero** and **ParkWhiz.** It's worth playing around with the various apps to see if one is better than another for a particular location or a particular day. Using Best Parking, we spot-checked the dates of DCL's 2018 New York sailings and were able to find several lots with rates about 20% cheaper than the cruise terminal's.

The closest New York City–Metropolitan Transit Authority **buses** to the terminal are the **M57–57th Street Cross Town** and the **M31–57th Street/York Avenue.**

The closest **subway trains** to the terminal are the **A, B, C, D,** and **1** at Columbus Circle. From Columbus Circle, walk south on Eighth Avenue and turn right onto 52nd Street. Continue down 52nd Street to 12th Avenue and the terminal.

TO SAN DIEGO You'll need to park in the Economy Lot on Pacific Highway (**3302 Pacific Highway, San Diego, CA 92101**) at San Diego International Airport, then take a shuttle from the lot to the Port of San Diego. Parking is $13 per day.

If you prefer valet parking, use the **Wyndham San Diego Bayside** (**1355 North Harbor Drive, San Diego CA 92101**). Visit sandiegocruiseshipparking.com for more information.

TO VANCOUVER The port is about a 30-minute drive from Vancouver's airport: **Cruise Terminal, 999 Canada Place, Vancouver, BC, Canada V6C 3C1.** Traffic in the several blocks surrounding Canada Place can be quite congested on cruise-departure mornings, so budget an extra 20 minutes for the last three blocks of travel if you're planning to arrive at the port during the late morning of your sail date. The cruise terminal has 775 parking spaces, which cost $26 CDN (about $21 US) or $182 CDN ($145 US) per week. Reservations are recommended and can be made online at canadaplace.westpark.com/reserve-a-space.html.

If you're a group of able-bodied adults with a reasonable amount of luggage, the easiest and cheapest way to get from the airport to the cruise terminal is Vancouver's clean and efficient **subway–light rail service.** The one-way trip costs about $9 CDN (about $7 US) and takes about half an hour, with no transfers needed. Visit translink.ca for more information. (Input **YVR** as your start point and **Canada Place** as your end point.)

Adding Air Travel to Your Package? *Don't!*

While you can purchase airfare through Disney, we don't recommend it—rarely do you save money by doing so, not to mention if you book through Disney, you lose all control of your flight selection.

We've been cautioned by both Disney-specialist travel agents and a travel-specialist Disney cast member that DCL air bookers will get you from point A to point B, but they generally won't pay attention to the presence or length of layovers, fine details about departure times, the size of the aircraft, local airport selection, or other particulars that can turn a good trip into a logistical headache.

You also may find that flight refunds are more difficult to obtain if you arrange your air travel through Disney. Book your flight yourself, or use a travel agent who will consider personal factors and logistics as well as pricing.

The **DAY** *Before* **YOUR CRUISE**

STAYING AT A LOCAL HOTEL THE NIGHT BEFORE

YOUR CRUISE WILL START ON TIME, even if you're not on the ship. One way to minimize the chance of that happening is to arrive at the port the day before your cruise and spend the night at a local hotel. While it adds a night's lodging to your trip's cost and another day to your trip's length, we think the peace of mind you get from knowing you'll make your cruise is worth it.

DCL has relationships with hotels in each of its port cities. You can book your pre- or postcruise hotel stay through Disney as part of your vacation package, no matter which port you're sailing from.

The pros: Disney has vetted the property, so you're unlikely to end up with a real dud, and transportation to/from the port will be seamless if you've also purchased ground transfers. The cons include the limited range of price-point options and a lack of choices at nonmainstream properties—if, say, you've got your heart set on staying at a hip new boutique hotel in Barcelona, you'll likely have to book it on your own rather than through DCL.

If you have Disney book your hotel stay, be prepared to have the process feel somewhat different than if you booked on your own. For example, during a recent DCL Alaskan voyage, we had Disney book our pretrip hotel stay at the convenient Fairmont Vancouver Airport Hotel. Because we booked through Disney, we got no direct information from the Fairmont—not even a confirmation number. This proved slightly problematic when we called about six weeks before our trip to inquire about the type of room we were in: we learned that Disney doesn't even tell the hotel the names of its guests or their room needs until about two weeks in advance. Rest assured that if you've booked a room through Disney, you'll have one. But for hyperplanners used to having every detail mapped out, the process may feel somewhat unsettling.

If you're driving to your cruise, most hotels near cruise ports offer their guests inexpensive parking and taxi and shuttle transportation to the port; some offer these services to the general public, too. The hotel's parking rates are often substantially less than what you'd pay at the cruise terminal. For example, parking at many Port Canaveral hotels costs less than $10 per day, compared with $17 per day at the terminal.

If You're Cruising out of Port Canaveral

You have the option of spending the night at a hotel in Port Canaveral or Orlando. We've done both, and there are advantages to each. The advantage to staying in Port Canaveral is that you're only a few minutes from the cruise terminal. You can have a relaxed breakfast on the morning of your cruise, take a swim in the pool, and pick up any last-minute items at one of Port Canaveral's grocery stores. The one downside to Port Canaveral is that it doesn't offer as many entertainment options as Orlando, and you may find yourself staying at your hotel for the evening, either watching TV or swimming. While many families find this relaxing, some would prefer to maximize their vacation activities.

Our favorite hotel in Port Canaveral is the **Residence Inn Cape Canaveral Cocoa Beach** (8959 Astronaut Blvd.; ☎ 321-323-1100; tinyurl.com/residenceinncanaveral). Its studio, one-bedroom, and two-bedroom suites sleep up to six people, plus there's a free breakfast buffet and internet access at reasonable prices. There's no on-site restaurant, but you have plenty of nearby dining options.

The advantage to staying in Orlando is that you can visit a Disney theme park, Disney Springs, or Universal Orlando before your trip. You'll have a wide variety of entertainment options and dozens of restaurants from which to choose. Some hotels, including the **Hyatt Regency Orlando International Airport** (9300 Jeff Fuqua Blvd.; ☎ 407-825-1234; tinyurl.com/hyattregencymco), offer transportation to Port Canaveral for cruise guests. The downside to staying in Orlando is that you'll still need to allow a couple of hours in the morning for the trip to the cruise terminal. See pages 91 and 94 for more details.

If You're Cruising out of Miami

You'll have many hotel options. We've spent the night before our Miami departures as far away as Orlando. Because there are so many ways to get to the Port of Miami by car, traffic and construction aren't as much of a concern as for Port Canaveral, although driving in a city as large as Miami has its own challenges (see page 95). And unlike hotels in Port Canaveral, most in Miami charge about as much for parking—around $20 per day—as does the Port of Miami ($22 per day), so there's little benefit to parking off-site.

Holiday Inn Port of Miami-Downtown (340 Biscayne Blvd.; ☎ 305-371-4400; tinyurl.com/hiportofmiami) sits within a mile of the port,

SCOTT SAYS *by Scott Sanders*

BABY, YOU'VE ARRIVED!

IF YOU'RE NOT DRIVING YOURSELF TO THE PORT, arrange your pre- and postcruise transportation yourself in advance. Also, while it adds to the cost of your trip, arriving the day before your cruise creates a safety buffer in the event of transportation delays like a delayed flight.

When it's time to go to the port, assign a point person for your party to be in charge of the check-in documents and government-issued IDs. The check-in process is much quicker if you already have all your documents signed through DCL's Online Check-In and have all of them ready to present.

Need to change a dinner seating or you don't like your assigned rotation? Check the *Personal Navigator* and arrive at the designated location before the listed time to increase your chances of having your change request granted. This is also the time to make reservations at Palo and Remy if you didn't do so previously online, or if you want to make additional reservations.

Before the end of your first day on the ship, sign up for the free 50MB internet package even if you don't think you'll use it. At the very least, you'll have it in case you need to get online or check in at home.

with plenty of restaurants, shopping, and activities a short walk or drive away, plus an on-site fitness center and high-speed wireless internet. Its one weakness is the small number of on-site parking spaces: if one isn't available, you'll have to find space at a nearby pay-parking lot and walk back. The **Courtyard by Marriott Miami Downtown** (200 SE Second Ave.; ☎ 305-374-3000; marriott.com/hotels/travel/miadt-courtyard-miami-downtown-brickell-area) is another moderately priced hotel. Near restaurants, shopping, and other activities, the Courtyard has an on-site gym and offers high-speed wireless internet.

If You're Cruising out of New York

There are more than 1,500 hotels in New York City, plus many more in the surrounding area. They range from flophouses to palatial luxury accommodations and everything in between. If you're looking for moderately priced digs in midtown Manhattan, a couple of reliable choices include **The Row NYC** (700 Eighth Ave.; ☎ 888-352-3650; rownyc.com/the-hotel), which is also home to the wonderful **City Kitchen** food court (citykitchen.rownyc.com), and the **Hampton Inn Manhattan–Times Square North** (851 Eighth Ave.; ☎ 212-581-4100; tinyurl.com/hamptoninn-nyc-manhattan). If you have Starwood hotel points, the **Sheraton New York Times Square Hotel** (811 Seventh Ave.; ☎ 212-581-1000; sheratonnewyork.com) is typically the most economical use of your points in midtown, though that may change as their rewards program merges with Marriott's.

If You're Cruising out of Galveston

Wyndham offers two upscale choices. The **Hotel Galvez & Spa** (2024 Seawall Blvd.; ☎ 409-765-7721; hotelgalvez.com) is a century-old beachside hotel with modern rooms, a spa, heated pool, and free shuttle service to the port and Galveston's Strand Historic District, both less than 2 miles away. Rates are as low as $140 per night during the off-season. **The Tremont House,** in the Strand, is only a few blocks from the port (2300 Ship's Mechanic Row; ☎ 409-763-0300; thetremonthouse.com). Like the Galvez, the Tremont House is modern and luxurious; while it doesn't have a pool or spa, its location near downtown is better for people who want to explore the area on foot. Rates are less than $200 per night most of the year. These hotels both offer AAA, AARP, and other discounts; be sure to inquire when booking.

If You're Cruising out of San Diego

You're in luck—it's possible to stay at a **Disneyland** hotel before your trip! Disneyland is typically less than 3 hours (with traffic) from the San Diego cruise terminal. The **Disneyland Hotel** (1150 Magic Way, Anaheim; ☎ 714-778-6600; disneyland.disney.go.com/disneyland-hotel) is our favorite on-property hotel, while **Disney's Paradise Pier Hotel**

(1717 S. Disneyland Drive; ☎ 714-999-0990; disneyland.disney.go.com/paradise-pier-hotel) is usually the least expensive. **Disney's Grand Californian Hotel & Spa** (1600 S. Disneyland Drive; ☎ 714-635-2300; disneyland.disney.go.com/grand-californian-hotel) has the advantage of being adjacent to Disney California Adventure, making it an easy walk if you'd like to enjoy this theme park during the evening.

In addition to Disney's hotels, many good off-site hotels are situated around the park. One of the most popular is the **Howard Johnson Anaheim** (1380 S. Harbor Blvd.; ☎ 714-776-6120; hojoanaheim.com), across the street from Disneyland and a shorter walk to Disneyland's entrance than Disney's own Paradise Pier Hotel.

If You're Cruising out of Vancouver

The **Pan Pacific Vancouver** (999 Canada Place, Ste. 300; ☎ 604-662-8111; panpacificvancouver.com) is located at Vancouver's port. It's posh and pricey, with rates between $400 and $500 US per night. Also pricey (and fabulous!) is the **Shangri-La Vancouver** (1128 W. Georgia St.; ☎ 604-689-1120; shangri-la.com/vancouver), with spectacular views of the ocean and mountains, huge marble baths, and a friendly staff. A more economical option is the **Metropolitan Hotel Vancouver** (645 Howe St.; ☎ 604-687-1122; metropolitan.com/vanc), with rates starting at around $200 US per night.

unofficial **TIP**
If you're planning to fly home from the Vancouver airport, be aware that you can't check in earlier than 3 hours before your flight or later than 1 hour before for international flights—you must check in *exactly* 1–3 hours before your departure.

Vancouver is a worthwhile destination in its own right, combining global sophistication and Canadian charm. The city is easily accessible by foot, taxi, and transit. Cruisers in search of international cuisine should make a point to sample the city's Asian specialties, from sushi to Indian to dim sum. For upscale dining, stick close to the downtown core around **Robson Street** and the cruise terminal. For an authentic experience, head to Vancouver's **Chinatown** (vancouver-chinatown.com), one of the largest in North America. If you're looking for something unique, try a Japanese-style hot dog sold from a food cart. It's Tokyo meets New York meets your belly.

Another must-stop for foodies is the **Granville Island Market** (granvilleisland.com). We've found everything from fresh mangosteens to maple-glazed walnuts here, as well as prepared foods like salmon potpie and gooseberry tarts. Disney geeks will want to keep an eye out for the Dole Whip vendor.

Fashionistas will love hitting the high-end designer shops (**Chanel, Hermès, Louis Vuitton,** and the like), while shoppers looking for a Canadian experience should head to **Roots** (1001 Robson St.; ☎ 604-683-4305; canada.roots.com) or **Hudson's Bay Company** (674 Granville St.; ☎ 604-681-6211; thebay.com), home of the eponymous

blankets. Fans of food souvenirs can pick up maple treats, British sweets and biscuits, and ketchup-flavored crisps all over the city.

If you arrive in the afternoon, walk to **Stanley Park,** along the waterfront, to see the beautiful Canadian Rockies in the distance (vancouver.ca/parks-recreation-culture/stanley-park.aspx). Or check out **Gastown** (gastown.org) and its steam-powered clock. For nightlife, check ahead before your arrival for live theater, musical concerts, or any festivals that are happening during your stay. A few good websites to try are tourismvancouver.com, hellobc.com/vancouver, and timeout.com/vancouver.

If you're a Disney-theme-park nut, you won't want to miss the **Fly-Over Canada** attraction (flyovercanada.com) located at Canada Place, adjacent to the cruise terminal. The experience is nearly identical to Soarin' at Epcot and Disney California Adventure, only with footage of Canada rather than international points of interest. It ain't cheap—about $28 CND for adults (ages 13–64), $23 CND for seniors (age 65 and older) and students (ages 13–21), and $20 CND for kids ages 12 and younger (discounts are often available if you ride before 11 a.m.) for a 10-ish-minute ride—but it may be worth it to see the similarity to Soarin', even in the preshow safety video. Be aware that prices are lower if you purchase tickets online rather than at the gate.

GET *in the* BOAT, MEN *(and Women and Kids)!*

CHOOSING A BOARDING TIME

YOU'LL BE ABLE TO CHECK IN at least 75 days in advance using DCL's **My Disney Cruise** (see page 39). This offers you a chance to verify information, ensure that you have the right credit card on file, and so on. You'll also be able to choose your boarding window—the time when you provide Disney your travel documents and board the ship. (Platinum Castaway Club members and guests in Concierge staterooms may board at any time.) Guests arriving at Port Canaveral via a Disney transfer bus from Walt Disney World will typically arrive at the port at 1 p.m. at the earliest. Choosing an earlier boarding time will not impact when you get there.

The earliest boarding windows are usually around 10:30 a.m. at Port Canaveral (boarding times may vary at other ports). We recommend choosing as early a board time as you can, or after 1:30 p.m. Here are the pros and cons to both approaches:

Early Boarding Time

PROS An uncrowded ship. You'll find smaller crowds at the pools and the buffet, and you'll be among the first in line for coveted character

meet-and-greet tickets, as well as last-minute spa, restaurant, or port-adventure availability.

CONS Most staterooms don't open to guests until at least 1:30 p.m. This means you'll be carrying everything you brought on board with you until you're able to enter your room. Guests with lots of camera equipment or big laptops may find this inconvenient.

Later Boarding Time

PROS The ability to sleep later on your boarding day and the ability to access your stateroom as soon as you board the ship. If you have kids who require an afternoon nap, this may be your best option.

CONS The ship is already full of people, including lines for the pools and food. Moreover, the elevators off the atrium tend to be packed with folks and their luggage trying to get to their rooms. Guests who arrive at the ship late may be locked out of some spa, restaurant, or character-greeting reservations.

CHECKING IN AT THE TERMINAL

HAVE YOUR CRUISE DOCUMENTS and government-issued ID ready as soon as you arrive. Many terminals, including Port Canaveral, have an initial security checkpoint outside the perimeter to ensure that only ticketed passengers enter.

Once you're past that checkpoint, you'll undergo another round of security screening just inside the terminal's entrance. You'll pass through a metal detector, and your luggage will undergo X-ray scanning. If you have bags too large to get through the security screening, use the porters at the terminal.

Disney's cruise terminals, especially those at Port Canaveral and Vancouver, are spacious, clean, and comfortable. (Miami's is a little smaller than the others, New York and Copenhagen have limited seating, and Barcelona's offers Spain's finest folding chairs for you to sit in while you wait.) If you have to wait a few minutes for your group to be called, you'll find enough seating for your family to sit down and relax. Vending machines and bathrooms are available, and Disney provides everything from character greetings to ship models to maps on the floor to keep your kids occupied.

If you haven't already received this by email, once in the terminal look for cast members handing out a mandatory (but mercifully short) health questionnaire. This questionnaire asks if anyone in your travel party is currently suffering from fever or has experienced vomiting or diarrhea in the previous three days. You'll also be asked questions about recent travel to any West African countries or contact with Ebola patients. Answering "yes" to any of the questions means you may be denied boarding, so be sure everyone you're traveling with is in good health.

Head for the check-in desk and have your signed cruise documents, health questionnaire, and IDs ready. (All guests must check in whether they've cruised with DCL before or not.) Concierge has a dedicated check-in desk, and returning DCL guests can use a separate line for its Castaway Club (though given the number of return cruisers DCL sees, it's not always as fast as you'd think).

The check-in desk is where you'll receive your cabin number (if you don't already have one) and get issued your magnetic-stripe Key to the World stateroom cards (see next section). Disney will also take your photo, which will be used for identification purposes when you exit and enter the ship.

Walt Disney World visitors should be aware that the DCL ships still use plastic cards for onboard transactions and identification, much like the pre-2014 key cards used at WDW—there are no MagicBand equivalents on the ship. Children in some of the kids' clubs will be issued a wristband, but they don't have the same functionality as a MagicBand, and they must be returned at the end of the voyage.

The check-in desk also will issue your party a boarding number, usually 1–30. Rather than have everyone try to board the ship at once, Disney organizes passengers into boarding groups of about 25–30 families at a time. Loudspeakers announce every few minutes which group numbers are currently allowed to board.

If you've not yet done so, you'll have an opportunity in the cruise terminal to sign up your children for the kids' clubs before boarding. A good time to do that is while you're waiting for your boarding group to be announced.

Your Key to the World Card Explained

ASIDE FROM SERVING as your stateroom key and a charge card to use on the ship, your Key to the World card contains helpful information about your cruise in abbreviated form.

The first line just beneath the Disney Cruise Line logo lists the dates of your cruise. The second line lists the name of your ship; then either **A** for "adult" or **M** for "minor," indicating whether you're old enough to drink; and then a code indicating whether you've booked Disney transportation: **P** indicates transportation to the port, **R,** transportation to the resort (if you've booked a combination cruise–resort vacation), **A,** transportation to the airport, or a combination of letters.

The next two lines display your name and, if applicable, your Castaway Club status. The next two lines after that show your dining schedule. The first of these lines shows the time of your nightly dinner seating and the number of your assigned table, while the second of these lines lists a series of letters, one for each night of your cruise, representing the first letter of the name of one of the ship's three rotational restaurants. For example, the three-letter code **ERA** indicates a three-night cruise

on the *Dream;* **E** signifies Enchanted Garden, **R** is the *Dream*'s Royal Palace, and **A** is for Animator's Palate.

Finally, a large single letter in the lower-left corner indicates the lifeboat station to which you are to report for the mandatory safety drill, and a code at bottom center shows the number of your check-in line.

BOARDING THE SHIP

YOU CAN BOARD THE SHIP any time after your boarding number is called. Have your room keys out, because they're scanned whenever you come on and off the ship.

Just before you enter the ship, photographers will offer to take a photo of your party. If this is important to you, a quick mirror check in the restroom and dressing in something you'd like recorded for posterity is a good idea. If you don't care to be photographed, breeze on past the people getting photos; they're certainly not mandatory, and lines can back up.

As you step on board, a cast member will ask your family name. Why they do this when so many parties traveling together don't necessarily have the same last name, we don't know. Either give your first names (Thurston and Lovey are our favorites) or make up a portmanteau combining your last names—no one is checking your ID—or just give any old name. What doesn't work is saying you'd rather not, and it's easiest to just board as the Howells if you'd rather not announce your presence. (You know how the paparazzi are.)

YOUR FIRST AFTERNOON ABOARD

IF YOU DIDN'T GET A *Personal Navigator* handout in the terminal, pick one up at Guest Relations while you're still on Deck 3; alternatively, download the DCL Navigator app ahead of time (see page 107). This is also a good time to do any last-minute reservations or change your dining rotation or seating time. If this isn't your first Disney cruise and you're already familiar with the ship, you may choose to split up your group to do these tasks and meet up after you're done. It will save you time running around the ship.

Our first stop is usually Senses Spa to book its Rainforest Room, if we weren't able to book it ahead of time (see page 249). The Rainforest Room has limited availability, so start there if it's a priority for you.

Next, check for any last-minute openings at Palo or Remy if you wish to dine there and haven't booked yet. The location for this check-in desk will be noted in your *Personal Navigator.*

In recent years, Disney has tinkered quite a bit with its procedures for character greetings. You'll now find that you may reserve greetings for a subset of the more popular characters online prior to your trip, just like you'd reserve a meal at Palo. Typically, this elite group of characters includes a group of all the onboard princesses at once, Anna/

Elsa/Olaf, and Marvel or Star Wars characters (on some sailings). If you want to meet these specific characters, and haven't done so online, then you'll want to do this as soon as you get on the ship. Tickets are usually only available on embarkation day. Check the print copy of your *Personal Navigator* for the ticket distribution time and location.

If it's after 1:30 p.m., you can head to your room and drop any bags you carried on. You may also see your room attendant already sprucing up your cabin for the evening. This is a great time to introduce yourself to your stateroom attendant and let him or her know if you have any special requests related to your room. These might include letting them know your child's typical nap hours or your preferred room temperature. We've had some luck "pre-tipping" our stateroom hosts. For example, Erin's daughters have long, thick hair and run through an abnormal amount of conditioner. Tipping our host at the beginning of the trip has worked to ensure that we always had more than enough on hand.

In the afternoon, people will start to swarm the Cabanas buffet as if they've never seen food before. A nearly identical buffet is usually served in Enchanted Garden on the *Dream* and *Fantasy,* and Tiana's Place on the *Wonder* (you'll also find far fewer people at these two restaurants). If all you're looking for is a quick bite to eat and you're all over age 18, try the quick-service Vista Café or Cove Café. We love Cabanas, but there's no shortage of food on the ship, and you've already spent enough of your day in lines.

If you're sailing from a warm-weather location, the pool deck will be full of folks swimming and lounging. And when we say "full," we mean hectic to chaotic. If you want to relax, don't go there. But do pick up a drink at the beverage station to stay hydrated.

The chaos comes to a head with the **Sail-Away Celebration,** the kind memorialized in *Love Boat* reruns, with Champagne toasts, confetti, and Gavin MacLeod in short shorts. It's kind of fun and a nice way to start your cruise, but it's not a must-do for us. (If you're a young whippersnapper who didn't grow up with *The Love Boat,* check out the reruns on MeTV. The theme song may or may not be the reason we're writing about the cruise industry today.)

THE LIFEBOAT DRILL

THIS IS USUALLY HELD around 4 p.m. before the ship leaves port. Every member of your group will need to be present, and you'll need to bring your stateroom keys to the drill; attendance is tracked by computer, which reads your room key to validate your presence.

Many years ago, guests were required to wear their life vests to the drill. This is no longer the case, but it makes sense to do a quick check of your stateroom closet to make sure that it contains the appropriate number and size flotation devices for your party. If you don't have the

proper life vests, address this with your stateroom attendant as soon as possible.

The lifeboat drill is the last mandatory activity for the day. If you're down for an early dinner seating, it will soon be time to dress for dinner. If not, you may choose to attend the first evening show. And with that, your afternoon is done, things calm down, and you can finally relax and start your vacation.

BARE NECESSITIES

THE *PERSONAL NAVIGATOR*

YOU'LL BE GIVEN THIS HANDOUT, shown on the following pages, when you board the ship. The *Personal Navigator* is a daily guide to the ship's activities and events, including times, locations, shop and restaurant hours, and more. You'll receive a new one every night for the following day; extra copies are available at Guest Services and from your stateroom attendant by request.

DCL has been tinkering lately with the format of the paper *Personal Navigator.* In prior years, the *Navigator* was a six-page flyer with daily schedule information, along with announcements, advertisements, and fun facts. Currently, the six-page version is most commonly distributed only on embarkation day, with an abbreviated two-page, schedule-only version distributed on the remaining sail days.

The *Navigator* paper schedule lists the ship's entertainment offerings for every hour of the day, separated into three sections: the top section holds the morning's activities, usually running from 8:30 a.m. until 1:30 p.m.; the middle section contains afternoon activities, from 1:45 p.m. until around 6:45 p.m.; and the bottom section lists the evening's events, from about 7 p.m. to midnight.

Each section is separated into approximately 10 rows of activities, and each row generally corresponds to an age group, location, or event. For example, you'll see rows for special events at the pool, character greetings, movies, family activities, and stuff for adults, plus the schedule for the Vibe, Edge, and Oceaneer Club/Lab kids' activities.

DCL NAVIGATOR APP Yes, there's an app for that! Available free at the Apple App Store and Google Play Store, it works through the ships' onboard Wi-Fi, so you can keep your device in airplane mode while using it.

Note: You won't be charged for Wi-Fi if you're using it only with the Navigator app. To avoid unnecessary data charges, however, be sure to download the app to all your family's mobile devices before you depart.

The app consists of six main categories: Dining Information (including the menus for your ship's dining rooms); Deck Plans (maps showing each floor of the ship); the hours of the various ship services

Disney Cruise Line for Introverts

A quick glance at your print *Personal Navigator* or the DCL Navigator app shows that your cruise includes numerous activities for those with a social bent: singing karaoke, rocking out at a dance party, and so on. That's great if you love being around people, but we've fielded questions from guests who tend toward introversion, nervous that all the activities on DCL might be too overwhelming for them. Here are some tips to make your Disney cruise more comfortable for an introvert or someone prone to sensory-processing overload.

- **Choose the right cabin.** Introverts may prefer a stateroom with a verandah (see page 83), which affords plenty of private space where you can observe the sea without venturing onto the public decks.
- **Request your own dinner table.** DCL sometimes seats small parties at a communal table with others in the main dining rooms. If that's not your cup of tea, call DCL at ☎ 800-951-3532 to request your own table. If the main dining rooms are too much for you in general, try eating dinner at Cabana's, which is typically much calmer, or order room service to your stateroom.
- **Avoid Cabana's during the day.** Dinnertimes are quiet, but the breakfast and lunch buffets are a bustle of activity. Breakfast and lunch in the main dining rooms tends to be less frenetic.
- **Reserve time in the spa's Rainforest Room (see page 249).** This relaxing area is open to a limited number of guests, making it a quiet oasis.
- **Use the adults-only areas as much as possible.** The adult pools on board and Castaway Cay's Serenity Bay are much less raucous than the comparable family areas on both ship and shore.
- **Book your own port excursions, or just explore the ports on your own.** Because Disney's port adventures are all group events, a private or self-guided tour may be more your speed.

(shops, gym, and so on); Activity Schedules; Debarkation Information (what you need to do at the end of your vacation); and Onboard Chat, our favorite feature.

Onboard Chat allows you to text other passengers at no charge using the ship's onboard Wi-Fi. You can choose from DCL-specific emojis featuring Disney, Marvel, and Star Wars characters to spice up your messages.

Before the Navigator app was introduced, guests could access a version of Onboard Chat on the Wave Phones provided in the DCL staterooms, but we find the app's functionality far superior—it makes communicating with family and friends on the ship as easy and intuitive as it is back at home. Here's why:

- It uses a device—your smartphone or tablet—that you and your family are already familiar with.

• **Stay on board while the ship is in port.** If you want to experience the ship's amenities in peace, this is often best accomplished on port days, when most other guests are on land.
• **Keep your celebration to yourself.** Disney tends to make a fuss for milestones. If you don't want to be the center of attention, then don't tell the cruise staff that it's your birthday, anniversary, graduation, etc.
• **Choose a less-popular sailing date on a less-crowded ship.** Sailings during the school year tend to be more empty than those during the summer and holidays. Take a look at stateroom availability—the more cabins available, the less crowded the ship—or ask a travel agent to help you find a sailing that's sparsely populated.
• **Communicate your needs to your stateroom attendant.** If you want quiet time in your cabin during certain hours, let your attendant know so that he or she can give you the space you desire.
• **Make ample use of online check-in and reservations.** This minimizes the need to chat with cast members on board.
• **Bring a quiet project.** Focusing on your knitting, a killer crossword, or that classic novel you've always to read can keep you centered during downtime.

- You'll likely have your phone with you for use as a camera anyway. There's no need to remember to bring a different piece of electronic equipment like the Wave Phone.
- You can chat with every phone owner in your party, even if they're not together.
- You can easily share your chat information and interact with other guests you meet on the ship, if you want to.
- You can create a personalized schedule of your activities for the day and set reminders for when they start.
- Parents can configure children's access to the chat function to meet their own specifications, allowing the level of access that's comfortable for each family.

The app also shows you the complete menus for every restaurant on the ship, usually several days in advance. Of course, you can always wait until they hand you the menu at the restaurant to see what your dining options are, but there may be some instances when knowing the menu in advance, or knowing what's being served in a different restaurant, can be very helpful.

- If the evening menu is particularly appealing (or unappealing), you can adjust your eating for the rest of the day accordingly.
- If you have a particularly picky child in your party, you can plan in advance whether to dine at Cabanas, try room service, or have the child eat at the kids' club.

- If you see a favorite dish on the main-dining-room menu for a night that you have a reservation at Palo, you can try to modify your Palo reservation for a different evening.
- If you see something particularly appealing on the menu of a different dining room, you can ask to have it brought to you at your meal. (Yes, you can order anything served at any of the three main dining rooms—not just the one you're assigned to.)

The onboard-activities section of the app includes information about activities the print version doesn't have room to include. For example, with the Cartoon Physics activity, the printed *Navigator* lists just "Cartoon Physics Class," but the app includes a description of the class and a listing of alternative times for the same activity at other points in the sailing. This is particularly helpful with the kids' club activities, which tend to be labeled with inscrutable names in the print *Navigator*.

Other nice features of the app are the ability to set alarms to remind you when favorite activities are starting, plus real-time updates to the ship's schedule.

INTERNET

FOR MANY OF US, being offline for the duration of a cruise simply isn't an option. The good news is that DCL ships offer **Connect@Sea** internet packages in a variety of sizes that will meet most people's needs. Here are the packages offered and our recommendations:

PLAN	DATA	COST	NOTES
Pay as You Go	1 MB	25¢	Use if you have a one-off need to check or send email
Small	100 MB	$19 (19¢/MB)	For guests who need to check email from time to time but don't need to web-surf during their cruise
Medium	300 MB	$39 (13¢/MB)	For guests who wish to use social media to let their friends know how much fun they're having on board
Large	1,000 MB	$89 (9¢/MB)	For guests who are unable to leave their work at home or who wish to stream music. (Video is another story—most movies take up more than the 1GB allowance, and an HD movie can take up to four times this much. Our advice: don't waste your time.)

So how well does it work? For the most part, we've been happy enough. However, it's not perfect, and at times we've found ourselves with either no connectivity or speeds so slow that there may as well have been no connection. If you think you'll need more than the minimum data, it's likely worth checking with your wireless carrier to see how its data-at-sea rates compare.

Here's what we've learned along the way:

1. Update your apps and download any other content (movies and so on) **before** you're on the ship. To do otherwise is a waste of time and money.
2. The first day of your cruise (and only the first day), you'll be offered 50MB of free Wi-Fi. Every person in your cabin age 18 or older may sign up for this. This is typically enough to do two or three quick email checks,

depending on the number of photos and attachments included. Use this until you need more.

3. Download the latest version of the **DCL Navigator** app (see page 107) before you're on the ship. **DCL Wi-Fi is free for use with this app.**
4. Don't bother trying to stream video content—it just won't work. Wi-Fi calling likely won't work either.
5. The system will throttle your usage if you use too much bandwidth at once. This affects everyone using your package, not just the computer with too many connections.
6. If you have a business-critical need for email, put an auto-responder on your account so people will know there may be a delay in replies. (You may or may not choose to state that the reason is that you're off having a great time on a cruise.)
7. If you have multiple email accounts, turn off syncing for the ones that tend to get a lot of junk mail.
8. If you use Apple's iMessage, you can also use it on the ship for quick texts back to land (to other iMessage users).
9. The more remote the ship's location, the worse your connection is likely to be. Service is usually good in the Caribbean, where you're never too far from pockets of civilization. During a Northern European voyage that included a long day at sea from Iceland to Scotland, service was nonexistent.
10. If you don't want to bring your own laptop or smart device while traveling, there are a few public areas on board where you can use DCL-provided computers to access the internet (with a package). These include **Cove Café,** an adults-only lounge on all four ships; **Vista Café,** a family café on the *Dream* and *Fantasy,* and the **Promenade Internet Café** on the *Wonder.*
11. If you share your Connect@Sea password with members of your party, you can use your account simultaneously. Be cautious, however, about giving internet access to children and teens. Typical teen data usage can be shockingly expensive at sea.
12. To replenish your data after using up a package, stop by the onboard **Connect@Sea** desk. You can upgrade to the next level by paying just the difference in package prices rather than starting from scratch.

The Connect@Sea help desk on each ship should have a printout of helpful tips to bring your extraneous data consumption down to the bare minimum. The instructions are slightly different depending on whether you have an Apple or Android device, but in general the steps you'll want to take include the following:

- Turning off location services
- Turning off background app refreshes
- Turning off music and app updates
- Turning off email sync and cloud backups
- Disabling automatic video playing on social media

ONBOARD SERVICES

A 24-HOUR GUEST SERVICES DESK is just off the lobby on each ship to answer questions, make reservations, and provide other help. You can also contact Guest Services from your stateroom by touching the Guest Services button on your phone.

The best amenity that comes with your stateroom is likely to be your stateroom attendant, who will tidy up your cabin after you depart in the morning, deliver your *Personal Navigator,* and turn down your beds each night. You'll almost certainly see him or her more than any other crew member, and you'll be amazed at how little sleep these hardworking staff seem to need.

Given the nature of a cruise, you'll find that your stateroom attendant is in and out of your room much more often than a typical hotel housekeeper would be. This makes it particularly important to make ample use of your DO NOT DISTURB sign if you plan to sleep late, take an afternoon nap, or otherwise just don't want to be bothered for a while.

AIRLINE CHECK-IN FOR SAILINGS ENDING AT PORT CANAVERAL

EVEN BEFORE YOU BOARD THE SHIP, you can request airline check-in for your flight home by making arrangements at your terminal's check-in desk. To do this, have the airline name, flight number(s), departure time and date, names of passengers as printed on their ticket(s), and the flight confirmation number(s) for each flight segment.

While you're on board, you can ask Guest Services to check you in to your flight if you're flying home the day that your cruise returns to port; just stop by the Guest Services desk before 10 p.m. on your second night to make this request. This service is available to anyone flying out of Orlando International Airport on domestic flights (including the US Virgin Islands and Puerto Rico) on Alaska Airlines, American Airlines, Delta Air Lines, JetBlue Airways, United Airlines, and US Airways.

No matter when you register, your first flight's departure must be after 11:30 a.m. on the day your cruise ends, to ensure the ship has enough time to make it back. There's a limit of two bags per person, and each bag must weigh less than 50 pounds. (According to Disney, a few randomly selected passengers may be required to undergo additional screening at the airport, and thus are ineligible for early check-in.)

The day before your cruise ends, you'll receive printed instructions in your stateroom, along with your boarding passes and temporary luggage tags. Affix the tags to your bags and leave them in the hallway outside your stateroom between 8:30 and 10:30 p.m. The next time you see your bags will be on the baggage carousel at your destination airport. This makes for easy maneuvering at Orlando International (the

airport for most DCL guests) because you simply proceed directly to the security line and on to your gate. Your airline's baggage fee will be added to your DCL bill and will appear on your checkout statement.

LAUNDRY SERVICES

SELF-SERVICE LAUNDRY FACILITIES are available on Decks 2, 6, and 7 on the *Magic* and *Wonder,* and on Decks 2, 5, 6, 7, 8, 9, and 10 on the *Dream* and *Fantasy.* Laundry rooms are furnished with washers, dryers, and detergent for purchase. It costs around $2 to wash a load of clothes and another $2 to dry them; detergent is another $1 per load.

You're likely to find the ships' laundry rooms sparsely used during three- and four-night sailings originating in the United States. Competition for washers and dryers can reach *Hunger Games* intensity on long European voyages, where guests with substantial pre- and post-cruise travel use the machines as a way to keep their packing manageable. You'll find laundry rooms less crowded on non–sea days, after 11 p.m., or before 7 a.m.

In addition to do-it-yourself laundry, each ship offers full-service laundry and dry-cleaning on board, with pickup from and delivery to your stateroom. Simply drop your clothes in the dry-cleaning bag hanging inside your closet and complete the attached paper form with any cleaning instructions. The laundry service usually takes 24 hours, but we've had simple requests—laundering and pressing a couple of shirts—done on the same day.

PORT ADVENTURES

IN ADDITION TO GUEST SERVICES, a separate Port Adventures desk on Deck 3 (*Magic* and *Wonder*) or Deck 5 (*Dream* and *Fantasy*) handles booking for shore excursions. The staff are usually knowledgeable about the most popular excursions at each port. In addition to providing information about cost and time, they can typically answer questions regarding the appropriateness of a particular activity for the members of your family. They also can help you reschedule an activity if needed. (See Part Eleven for details.)

HEALTH SERVICES

EACH SHIP'S HEALTH CENTER employs a third-party doctor and nurse for medical issues. The most common reasons for visiting the Health Center are motion sickness, sunburn, and nausea, although the staff have seen their share of broken bones over the years. The Health Center (Deck 1 Forward; open 9:30–11 a.m. and 4:30–7 p.m.) can provide doses of basic over-the-counter and some prescription medicines; anything serious, such as surgery, will probably require an airlift to the nearest hospital. Also, note that use of the Health Center isn't free, and rates are comparable to those of US hospitals—in other words, expensive—so check your insurance coverage before you leave home

(see page 49 for more on that). However, just like the First Aid Centers in the Disney parks, Health Services will often provide you with a dose or two of over-the-counter medicine, such as aspirin or motion-sickness tablets, for free. The Guest Services desk also has a supply of basic over-the-counter medicines and first aid. If you just need Tylenol or a Band-Aid, that's a good first place to start. Also be aware that during hours when both the Health Center and the ship's stores are closed, Guest Services may be the only place to obtain basic-care items like aspirin, diapers, or feminine-hygiene products; a limited supply of these is typically available at no charge.

SHIP-TO-SHORE CALLS

IF YOU DON'T WANT TO USE YOUR CELL PHONE on the ship, you can use your stateroom phone to make and receive off-ship calls. Friends and family can reach you by calling ☎ 888-322-8732 in the United States or ☎ 732-335-3281 internationally; they'll need to know which ship you're sailing on and your stateroom number. Rates run about $7–$9.50 per minute, with a 10-minute maximum per call, so consider this an emergency-only option.

TRANSFERS TO WALT DISNEY WORLD HOTELS

DISNEY HAS BEEN TINKERING with ship-departure procedures for guests who've purchased transfers from the ship to a Walt Disney World resort hotel. In years past, buses started running to Disney World as soon as the ship cleared customs, usually around 7 or 7:30 a.m. More recently, Disney hasn't begun running its port-transfer buses from Port Canaveral to Disney World until 9 a.m. If you're an early riser, this can feel like a lot of unnecessary waiting around.

We recently used Disney's transfer from Port Canaveral to Disney's Wilderness Lodge resort. Our bus didn't leave the port until about 9:30 a.m. and made several stops at other hotels before ours, so we didn't get to our resort until after 11:30 and didn't get to the Magic Kingdom until well after noon. Had we scheduled our own transportation, we could have been picked up at 7:30 a.m. and been driven directly to our hotel, putting us at the Magic Kingdom much closer to 10 a.m. When time is tight, a couple of extra hours in the theme parks can be a major asset. Next time we'll arrange a town car.

TIPPING

YOU'LL ENCOUNTER CREW MEMBERS throughout your cruise, many of whom you'll see several times per day and who will have a direct impact on the quality of your trip. It's customary to give a small tip to these crew members in recognition of their service. The chart below indicates the suggested tip for these staff for each person in your cabin. Thus, if you have four people in your family and you're taking a seven-night cruise, budget $336 ($84 times four) for the personnel shown, plus any spa, bar, or other dining gratuities you anticipate.

STAFF MEMBER	Suggested Gratuity Per Day	Suggested Gratuity 3 Nights	Suggested Gratuity 4 Nights	Suggested Gratuity 7 Nights
Stateroom Attendant	$4	$12	$16	$28
Dining Room Server	$4	$12	$16	$28
Dining Room Assistant Server	$3	$9	$12	$21
Dining Room Head Server	$1	$3	$4	$7
TOTAL (Per Guest)	**$12**	**$36**	**$48**	**$84**

These suggested gratuity amounts are automatically added to your stateroom account based on the number of people in your cabin and your cruise length. Once on board, you can adjust these amounts or pay in cash by visiting the Guest Services desk (open 24 hours a day) on Deck 3. Lines at Guest Services get long on the last night of your cruise, so plan to make any adjustments sooner rather than later if you wish to avoid a wait. If it makes your budgeting process easier, you're welcome to prepay many of your gratuities weeks or months before boarding the ship. Call DCL or your travel agent to arrange this.

At Palo and Remy, a gratuity is automatically added only for alcohol; an additional gratuity for dining service is left to your discretion. As the service at the adult restaurants is typically impeccable, we tend to tip at Palo and Remy as if we were tipping on what the cost would have been in an on-shore restaurant of that caliber. It's also customary to add a gratuity for room service, again at your discretion. Also note that an automatic 15% gratuity is added to Cove Café and bar tabs, plus any alcohol ordered elsewhere on deck.

CHECKOUT *and* DEPARTURE

YOUR LAST NIGHT ON THE SHIP

unofficial **TIP**
You'll need your Key to the World cards to exit the ship, so keep them handy until you're back on land.

YOU'LL RECEIVE debarkation information—including what to do with your luggage, where you'll be eating breakfast, and when you need to be off the ship—the night before your last night on board (for example, night six of a seven-night cruise). This information is also available at Guest Services the last night of the cruise.

Packing

If you haven't already arranged onboard airline check-in, you'll receive luggage tags in your stateroom on your last night on board, along with instructions for getting breakfast before departing in the morning and gratuity envelopes. Use these luggage tags if you'd like Disney to transport your bags from the ship to the port terminal upon docking. (This enables you to walk off the ship without having to carry bags; you'll pick up your luggage before you go through customs.) The luggage tags

will be in colorful shapes of Disney characters: green Tinker Bell, orange Goofy, blue Donald Duck, and so on. Write your stateroom number, name, home address, and number of bags on each tag, and attach one tag to each piece of luggage you want Disney to transport. Place your tagged bags outside your stateroom during the hours noted on the instruction form placed in your stateroom. For sailings ending at Port Canaveral, this is typically between 8:30 and 10:30 p.m., but other ports may have different instructions.

A few packing tips:

- Don't forget to lay out clothes to wear to breakfast and off the ship the last morning.
- If you're flying home, note that any alcohol you purchased on the ship must be packed in your checked bags.
- Don't pack your passports, birth certificates, Key to the World cards, or any other travel documents in your checked bags. You'll need them before you can pick up your luggage, so keep them in a bag you plan to carry by hand off the ship.
- Remove any old airline or cruise tags from your luggage before you affix any new ones.
- Keep inside your stateroom any luggage you'll carry off the ship by hand. When you've gotten off the ship, you'll find a section of the terminal dedicated to checked baggage. Checked bags will be organized by color and character, with all of the green Tinker Bell-tagged luggage together, all of the orange Goofy luggage together, and so on. Overhead signs will direct you to each section.

  Luggage will be sorted by stateroom number within each section, so look for yours by finding your stateroom number within your section. If you can't find one of your bags, check a few feet up and down the row, too—sometimes the stateroom order isn't exact. Ask a cast member for help if you still can't find your luggage after checking the nearby spaces.

EXPRESS WALK-OFF

FOR GUESTS WHO WISH to be among the very first off the ship—those who need to get straight to the airport or who have other time-dependent plans that day—DCL offers Express Walk-Off. As soon as the ship clears customs, guests may depart the ship.

unofficial **TIP**
Concierge guests may order room-service breakfast the last morning of the cruise.

You must carry all of your own luggage to take advantage of this service; you may not set it out the night before. Be considerate and let your cabin attendant know if you're doing this so he or she isn't waiting for your bags to appear in the hallway the last night of the cruise.

BREAKFAST ON THE MORNING OF YOUR DEPARTURE

YOU'LL HAVE THE CHANCE FOR ONE MORE SIT-DOWN MEAL. The table-service breakfast seatings are assigned based on your seating time for dinner. Guests with the early dinner seating are scheduled for their final breakfast on board at 6:30 a.m. Guests with the later dinner seating get a last-day breakfast assignment at 8 a.m. This effectively means that any guest with a late dinner seating and an early flight will be unable to eat a table-service breakfast on their last morning. For guests in this situation, the Cabanas buffet is open beginning at 6:30 a.m.—expect pastries, fruit, bacon, eggs, cold cereal, and not much else. Cove Café is also open beginning at 6 a.m.

unofficial **TIP**
Guests with flights out of Orlando International Airport before 1 p.m. are required to leave the ship by 8 a.m.

PHOTO PURCHASES

IF YOU'VE PURCHASED A PHOTO PACKAGE (a photo CD/flash drive, photo book, or the like), it will be available for pickup on the morning of your departure. Pickup time usually starts at 7 a.m., and lines begin to form earlier than that. If you have an early flight and are using Express Walk-Off, plan to be in line to grab your photo products by about 6:30 a.m. Have another member of your party grab you a banana and coffee (or one last pastry) from the buffet line for you to eat while you wait.

If you've purchased a photo flash drive and you have a laptop with you, it makes sense to take a moment to verify that the drive is indeed loaded, that you understand the download process, that the photos are yours, and that the package is indeed the one you paid for. We've had a few instances when there were problems. We were able to resolve them once we were home, but it took several weeks of phone calls and emails to get the right photos—something that would have taken just a few minutes had we noticed while we were still on the ship.

Although we don't recommend this, it may be possible to purchase your shipboard photos while you're at home, up to six weeks after your sailing. Check support.mycruisephotos.com for more information.

US CUSTOMS ALLOWANCES

EACH FAMILY WILL NEED to fill out a **Customs Declaration form** (see following pages). Besides the usual name and address, the form asks which countries you've visited, whether you're bringing in prohibited items such as fruits or vegetables, whether you've handled livestock, and whether you're carrying more than $10,000 in cash. (Answering "yes" to all three is probably the start of the next installment in the Hangover series.) See tinyurl.com/customsduty for more information.

continued on page 120

U.S. Customs and Border Protection

Customs Declaration

19 CFR 122.27, 148.12, 148.13, 148.110,148.111, 1498; 31 CFR 5316

FORM APPROVED
OMB NO. 1651-0009

Each arriving traveler or responsible family member must provide the following information (only ONE written declaration per family is required):

1. Family **Name**
   First *(Given)* Middle
2. **Birth date** Day Month Year
3. Number of **Family members** traveling with you
4. (a) U.S. Street **Address** (hotel name/destination)
   (b) City (c) State
5. **Passport issued by** (country)
6. **Passport number**
7. Country of **Residence**
8. **Countries visited** on this trip prior to U.S. arrival
9. **Airline/Flight No.** or **Vessel Name**
10. The primary purpose of this trip is **business**: Yes No
11. I am (We are) bringing
    (a) fruits, vegetables, plants, seeds, food, insects: Yes No
    (b) meats, animals, animal/wildlife products: Yes No
    (c) disease agents, cell cultures, snails: Yes No
    (d) soil or have been on a farm/ranch/pasture: Yes No
12. I have (We have) been in close proximity of (such as touching or handling) **livestock**: Yes No
13. I am (We are) carrying **currency or monetary instruments** over $10,000 U.S. or foreign equivalent: Yes No
    (see definition of monetary instruments on reverse)
14. I have (We have) **commercial merchandise:** Yes No
    (articles for sale, samples used for soliciting orders, or goods that are not considered personal effects)
15. **Residents** — the **total value of all goods,** including commercial merchandise I/we have purchased or acquired abroad, (including gifts for someone else, but not items mailed to the U.S.) and am/are bringing to the U.S. is: $
    Visitors — the **total value of all articles** that will remain in the U.S., including commercial merchandise is: $

Read the instructions on the back of this form. Space is provided to list all the items you must declare.

I HAVE READ THE IMPORTANT INFORMATION ON THE REVERSE SIDE OF THIS FORM AND HAVE MADE A TRUTHFUL DECLARATION.

X (Signature) Date (day/month/year)

For Official Use Only

CBP Form 6059B (10/07)

U.S. Customs and Border Protection Welcomes You to the United States

U.S. Customs and Border Protection is responsible for protecting the United States against the illegal importation of prohibited items. CBP officers have the authority to question you and to examine you and your personal property. If you are one of the travelers selected for an examination, you will be treated in a courteous, professional, and dignified manner. CBP Supervisors and Passenger Service Representatives are available to answer your questions. Comment cards are available to compliment or provide feedback.

Important Information

U.S. Residents — Declare all articles that you have acquired abroad and are bringing into the United States.

Visitors (Non-Residents) — Declare the value of all articles that will remain in the United States.

Declare all articles on this declaration form and show the value in U.S. dollars. For gifts, please indicate the retail value.

Duty — CBP officers will determine duty. U.S. residents are normally entitled to a duty-free exemption of $800 on items accompanying them. Visitors (non-residents) are normally entitled to an exemption of $100. Duty will be assessed at the current rate on the first $1,000 above the exemption.

Agricultural and Wildlife Products — To prevent the entry of dangerous agricultural pests and prohibited wildlife, the following are restricted: Fruits, vegetables, plants, plant products, soil, meat, meat products, birds, snails, and other live animals or animal products. Failure to declare such items to a Customs and Border Protection Officer/Customs and Border Protection Agriculture Specialist/Fish and Wildlife Inspector can result in penalties and the items may be subject to seizure.

Controlled substances, obscene articles, and toxic substances are generally prohibited entry.

Thank You, and Welcome to the United States.

The transportation of currency or **monetary instruments,** regardless of the amount, is legal. However, if you bring in to or take out of the United States more than $10,000 (U.S. or foreign equivalent, or a combination of both), you are required by law to file a report on FinCEN 105 (formerly Customs Form 4790) with U.S. Customs and Border Protection. Monetary instruments include coin, currency, travelers checks and bearer instruments such as personal or cashiers checks and stocks and bonds. If you have someone else carry the currency or monetary instrument for you, you must also file a report on FinCEN 105. Failure to file the required report or failure to report the *total* amount that you are carrying may lead to the seizure of *all* the currency or monetary instruments, and may subject you to civil penalties and/or criminal prosecution. SIGN ON THE OPPOSITE SIDE OF THIS FORM AFTER YOU HAVE READ THE IMPORTANT INFORMATION ABOVE AND MADE A TRUTHFUL DECLARATION.

Description of Articles (List may continue on another CBP Form 6059B)	**Value**	**CBP Use Only**
Total		

PAPERWORK REDUCTION ACT NOTICE: The Paperwork Reduction Act says we must tell you why we are collecting this information, how we will use it, and whether you have to give it to us. The information collected on this form is needed to carry out the Customs, Agriculture, and currency laws of the United States. CBP requires the information on this form to insure that travelers are complying with these laws and to allow us to figure and collect the right amount of duty and tax. Your response is mandatory. An agency may not conduct or sponsor, and a person is not required to respond to a collection of information, unless it displays a valid OMB control number. The estimated average burden associated with this collection of information is 4 minutes per respondent or record keeper depending on individual circumstances. Comments concerning the accuracy of this burden estimate and suggestions for reducing this burden should be directed to U.S. Customs and Border Protection, Reports Clearance Officer, Information Services Branch, Washington, DC 20229, and to the Office of Management and Budget, Paperwork Reduction Project (1651-0009), Washington, DC 20503. **THIS FORM MAY NOT BE REPRODUCED WITHOUT APPROVAL FROM THE CBP FORMS MANAGER.**

CBP Form 6059B (10/07)

continued from page 117

COMMENT CARDS

ON THE LAST NIGHT OF YOUR CRUISE, you'll be given a comprehensive survey asking for your evaluation of the ship's cleanliness, the entertainment offerings, the condition of your stateroom, the children's programming, and a number of other aspects of your cruise. You'll also be asked your perceptions of your dining-service team.

Note that the dining staff's performance reviews and pay are often strongly affected by guest input on these comment cards. Because of this, some servers may give guests a high-pressure sell for "excellent" ratings, basically begging for high marks. If you really do love your servers, then by all means rate them as excellent, but don't feel strong-armed do so if the service is good but not outstanding.

The survey also asks you to name any cast members "who made your cruise experience particularly magical." In addition to the obvious dining, stateroom, and entertainment cast members, we like to keep a lookout for cast in minimally guest-facing roles—maintenance crew, for example—and note when we see them doing a great job.

FLYING OUT LATE ON DEPARTURE DAY

DCL ASKS THAT GUESTS not schedule flights home before 11:30 a.m. If you can fly out in the early afternoon, you're golden: grab some lunch at the airport and you're good to go. But there may be times where you can't or don't want to fly home until later in the day.

So how do you occupy your time if you disembark at 8 a.m. but you're not getting on your plane until 8 p.m. or later? Well, there's no need to wander aimlessly around MCO all day, unless you're just really into reenacting scenes from the woefully underrated Tom Hanks film *The Terminal*. A few suggestions:

- **Rent a room for the day at the Airport Hyatt** (inside the airport) to sleep, swim, shower, and chill.
- **Take a Port Canaveral-area hotel shuttle** from the port to the hotel; then take a cab or ride share to the airport.
- **Rent the cheapest possible room at WDW** and take the DCL bus there. Swim and play at the resort, then take Disney's Magical Express bus to the airport. (Hey, who said you have to sleep?)
- **Visit other Orlando attractions:** NASA at Cape Canaveral, Universal Orlando, SeaWorld, Madame Tussauds Orlando, the outlet shopping centers, or the Icon Orlando wheel; play minigolf or regular golf, go horseback riding at Disney's Fort Wilderness, or experience iFly indoor skydiving in Orlando. Rent a car at the port if you need to store luggage (drop it off at the airport); if you can check all but minimal hand luggage through from DCL to your home airport, then hire a cab, Uber, or Lyft.
- **Purchase a day pass for an executive lounge at the airport,** and get some work done in peace and quiet.

PART FIVE

TIPS *for* VARIED CIRCUMSTANCES

DCL *for* SINGLES

BECAUSE DISNEY CRUISE LINE is targeted to families, roughly 90% of its guests are couples or parents and kids. That's about 10 points higher than the cruise industry's average, and it means that there are around 200 solo travelers per cruise on the *Magic* and *Wonder,* and around 400 on the *Dream* and *Fantasy.*

unofficial **TIP**
US law requires Disney to disclose most claims of crimes alleged to have taken place on board. DCL voluntarily discloses all such incidents.

Like the Disney theme parks, Disney Cruise Line is great for singles. It's safe, clean, and low-pressure. Safety and comfort are excellent, especially for women. If you're looking for places to relax without being hit on, Disney's ships are perfect. The bars, lounges, and nightclubs are clean, friendly, and interesting; the restaurants are welcoming; and the spas are excellent places for grabbing some solo time in public. One aspect that you do have to be vigilant about when traveling alone is shore excursions in foreign countries—more on that a bit later.

If you're interested in meeting other singles, Disney usually runs a **Singles Mingle** session on one of the first few days of each cruise. These informal get-togethers last about an hour and are typically held at the Cove Café in the adults-only part of the ship. We've also seen lunchtime gatherings with the sort-of-depressing name **Cruisin' Solo.** (Don't worry—they're cooler than they sound.)

Single and not-so-single guests ages 18–20 are welcome to attend an **1820 Society** gathering during one night of their cruise. It's a meet-up attended by guests and crew, generally during the evening after the second dinner seating, also usually at the Cove Café.

DINING Single travelers will likely be paired with other groups for dinner at the standard restaurants. When we've cruised solo, our dinner companions are usually one or two couples, which means we're sitting

at a table for four or six. If the cruise is especially popular, Disney may try to squeeze in another single person to your group, too, so that everyone has a table. Our dinners with these new friends couldn't have gone better, and we say that as pretty strong introverts. We've met interesting people from many different places, never run out of things to talk about, and even kept in touch with a few folks when we got back home.

Solo travelers are also welcome at Palo and Remy, and we've had many fine dinners and brunches there. If you're having difficulty making a reservation for one using the DCL website before your trip, try stopping by the restaurant on the afternoon you board. We've found the staff to be exceptionally accommodating for these requests, especially if you're willing to arrive either early or late.

CRUISE FARES While some cruise lines are adding stateroom cabins designed especially for solo travelers, cabins on Disney's ships are all designed to hold at least two people. To make up for the room, bar, and shore-excursion revenue lost when one person books a cabin that could hold two paying passengers, Disney adds a 100% surcharge (or "single supplement," in cruise-industry lingo) to most solo-traveler fares, making the cost equivalent to two people taking the same trip. There's a small chance that you can find last-minute deals on unsold cabins without paying the full 100% supplement. Your best bet is to check the DCL website or have a travel agent research for you.

unofficial **TIP**
If your port adventure involves boating, snorkeling, or any other water-based activity, you'll almost certainly be assigned another traveler or couple as a buddy for safety reasons.

PORT ADVENTURES As with dining, there's a good chance you'll be paired with other couples for shore excursions. But unlike dinner, it's possible for a solo traveler to simply be a quiet observer during many excursions, especially those designed for groups.

We've been single travelers on everything from cooking demonstrations to snorkeling to city tours, and they've all gone well. All of the programs we've tried can accommodate single guests, and the Port Adventures staff makes everyone feel welcome. That said, some excursions run by third-party companies will use private taxi or shuttle services to transport guests from the ship to their activity, and it's possible for a solo traveler to be the odd man out if the vehicle doesn't have enough seats to accommodate the entire group, as Len recounts:

I was once the only solo traveler in a group of nine for an excursion in Mexico that involved a 30-minute bus ride. When we got to the departure point, we saw that not all of us were going to fit on the eight-person bus that the excursion company brought. The couples were placed together, and the Port Adventures staff hurriedly brought around an unmarked, nondescript "taxi" for me.

As I got in this random car on a random street in a random Mexican town, my last words to the others were, "Take a good look—this

is what I was wearing the last time you saw me." Of course, I made it to and from the shore excursion just fine, and we all had a laugh once we were reunited. But I wouldn't recommend that others do this, especially women traveling alone.

In the (unlikely) event that you're asked to travel alone to a shore excursion, decline politely. Ask to be accompanied by a staff member or to be escorted back to the ship. Along the same lines, if you're not comfortable walking back to your stateroom at night, ask a member of the crew to accompany you. And use extra caution walking to and from the parking lot at the cruise terminal.

DCL *"At Large"*

AS WITH ITS THEME-PARK GUESTS, Disney realizes that its cruise guests come in all shapes and sizes and makes many accommodations to ensure that they're treated well.

Your stateroom's personal flotation devices (PFDs, or life jackets) are designed to fit most bodies. With PFDs, chest size, not weight, is the measurement that determines proper fit. Disney's PFDs include a nylon strap that wraps around your body to keep the PFD snug against your chest. Try on your PFD when you first get to your stateroom to ensure that the strap fits around your body. If it doesn't, mention it to your group's leader during the lifeboat drill.

The AquaDuck waterslides on the *Dream* and *Fantasy* seem able to accommodate virtually all body shapes and sizes; we've heard success stories from individuals weighing more than 300 pounds and couples weighing more than 400. The AquaDunk slide on the *Magic* has a weight limit of 300 pounds.

If an activity or port adventure has a weight limit, it will be printed in the details describing the activity; look for phrases such as "Guests must weigh" or "Weight must be" in the activity's listing. Some shore excursions, including kayaking and some scuba and snorkeling trips, have weight limits of 240 or 300 pounds per person. Segway tours generally accommodate persons of up to 250 pounds.

Many Alaskan excursions involving helicopters or seaplanes have a weight limit of 250 pounds inclusive of all gear (clothing, cameras, and such); it may be possible to modify this requirement by paying an excess-weight fee for additional fuel. Other activities have weight limits of up to 350 pounds per person. Again, check the activity's details for more information, or check with the Port Adventures desk on board.

Ask for bench seating or chairs without arms at restaurants and lounges. If you don't see them, the staff should be able to provide them.

Wear comfortable shoes. You'll be surprised at the amount of walking you do on board the ship, not to mention the walking you'll do from the cruise terminal to the ship.

DCL *for* EXPECTANT MOMS

DISNEY PROHIBITS MOTHERS-TO-BE FROM SAILING if they will reach their 24th week of pregnancy at any time during the cruise. For example, a woman who is 23 weeks pregnant would not be allowed by Disney to take a 12-night transatlantic cruise. In addition, note that if you're flying to or from your cruise, airlines may have their own, different policies regarding pregnant travelers.

On board, the AquaDuck and AquaDunk waterslides are off-limits to expectant mothers, as is the waterslide at Castaway Cay. Other shore excursions, such as scuba activities, off-road driving, and parasailing, also prohibit expectant mothers from participating. In addition, some tour operators have restrictions on snorkeling and dolphin encounters.

To understand the risk of disease or injury to you or your baby, talk to your doctor about any shore visits you plan to take. For example, in 2018 (and several years prior), US federal health officials issued warnings for pregnant women (and women hoping to become pregnant) who were visiting areas in Latin American and Caribbean countries where mosquitoes spread the Zika virus, linked to infant brain damage. If you become pregnant after booking a cruise to a Zika-affected area, speak with Disney about remediation. While nothing is guaranteed, we have heard of guests having rebooking penalties waived for postponed trips. (See pages 49 and 53 for additional resources on travel health.)

Also note that some excursions require lengthy drives on pothole-strewn roads—some of them dirt, gravel, or sand—in vehicles that have seen years of use. Even if all you're planning to do is relax on a beach, the drive to get there may be bumpy enough to make you reconsider going. Remember that it's always OK to stay on the ship and take advantage of the entertainment and activities on board.

DCL *for* YOUNGER CHILDREN

DISNEY CRUISE LINE REQUIRES that infants be at least 6 months of age to cruise on most sailings and at least 1 year of age on some longer voyages. Depending on how early you've booked your cruise, a surprise addition to the family may influence whether you're able to sail. If you find yourself in this situation, contact Disney as soon as possible to understand your options.

unofficial **TIP**
For more on cruising with children, see "Cruising with Kids" in Part One (page 16), "Making Sure Your Child Is Ready to Cruise" in Part Two (page 57), and "Special Considerations" in Part Nine (page 220).

Guests with young children should think about the family's sleeping arrangements when planning their cruise. Disney does provide "pack and play" cribs free of charge to guests who need them. Given the small square footage of most staterooms, however, the crib's

footprint will have an outsize impact on the room's usable space for other family members, particularly if the child will be napping during the day. Training your young child to sleep in a bed rather than a crib might enhance your family's enjoyment of their living quarters.

In general, the younger the child, the more you'll want to stick as closely as possible to his usual eating/sleeping schedule, which for most guests with young kids means that you'll want to choose the earlier dinner seating. However, you should also consider the influence of time-zone changes if you're cruising in a locale that's distant from your home.

For sailings outside the United States, the earlier seating is often more popular, becoming fully booked more quickly. On European sailings, where late dining is more common, the late seating may be more popular. If your preferred seating is fully booked at the time you purchase your cruise, keep checking back. It's often possible to make a switch, even in the middle of a trip. To make a change before your sailing, call DCL directly at ☎ 800-951-3532, or speak to Guest Services while you're on board.

Parents of fussy young eaters should understand that while the Disney ships offer a wide variety of food, available virtually around the clock, the limited capacity of a ship's kitchens means that not every possible food will be available in every possible form. For example, the macaroni and cheese served on the ship may not be the same mac and cheese that your child is used to. ("*Orange*? I want white!") If your child is a truly limited eater, you'll need to strategize in advance.

Also note that as part of Disney's ongoing eco-friendly efforts, they've banished plastic straws and cup lids from the ships. This could be a big issue for parents of a small child prone to spilling. If you have a child who is learning to drink from a cup, then you may want to bring your own lidded cups and/straws, as well as a means to clean them. We're envisioning a lot of guests with tiny bottles of dish detergent next to their stateroom sink.

Another potential issue for parents of younger children is separation anxiety. Many young children adore spending time in the nursery or shipboard kids' clubs. However, if your child is in a separation-anxiety phase, you may feel that this isn't the best time to leave him in the care of strangers, even if you're just a deck or two away. If you have a skittish youngster, be realistic about your expectations. Assume that most of your cruise will be family time rather than "Mom and Dad at the spa" time, and be pleasantly surprised if your preschooler ends up spending significant time in the kids' club.

Breastfeeding is allowed in all areas of the Disney ships. Your stateroom is never far away when you're on a ship, but you shouldn't feel like you have to rush back to your room every time your baby gets hungry. You're welcome to nurse in the theaters, in the dining rooms, or in other public areas of the ship; however, the same rules

may not apply when you're off the ship. If you're traveling with a baby, you may want to research the customs and mores of your specific destination(s).

DCL *for* OLDER CHILDREN

SOME FAMILIES WITH 17- AND 18-YEAR-OLD kids may encounter frustration during their trip due to Disney's strict enforcement of age restrictions on teen and adult activities. We recently traveled with a teen just days away from her 18th birthday. Even though she was a high school graduate, she wasn't allowed to dine at Palo (yes, we tried bribery, and no, it didn't work), exercise in the ship's fitness center, or go to some of the adults-only cooking demonstrations. We've seen 17- and 18-year-old cousins unable to do virtually anything together because the older teen wasn't allowed into the Vibe teen club and the younger one wasn't allowed into any of the adult activities. If you have an older teen, consider a slightly different travel date.

DCL *for* SENIORS

MOST SENIORS WILL FIND A DISNEY CRUISE less tiring than a Walt Disney World vacation. First, most seniors find considerably less walking required on the ship versus the parks. Second, the ships' adults-only areas provide a break from children (and their families) when needed. And even the most energetic onboard attraction, the AquaDuck/AquaDunk, isn't as intense as a ride on Space Mountain or Big Thunder Mountain Railroad.

Because of their flexible schedules, retirees can often take advantage of off-peak cruise fares, especially during fall or spring, when the weather is nicest and crowds are lower because school is in session. If you're cruising to the Caribbean, the Bahamas, or Mexico, be sure to bring a jacket and sweater along with your warm-weather clothing. While temperature averages hover around 70°F in most of those locations, a cold front can drop temps into the upper 40s with little notice, and it's not uncommon to have morning temperatures in the lower 50s.

GUESTS *with* DISABILITIES

DCL STRIVES TO MAKE ITS SHIPS accessible to all. Virtually the entire ship, from staterooms to restaurants to nightclubs and pools, is friendly to users of wheelchairs and electric convenience vehicles (ECVs). More accommodations are available for other special needs, too. Your first step to getting the assistance you need is to complete the **Request**

Special Services form, available at disneycruise.disney.go.com/special-services-information-form. This form must be submitted online 60 days before sailing; you may also call DCL's Accessibility Desk at ☎ 407-566-3500 (voice) or 407-566-7455 (TTY) with specific questions.

Overall, guests with mobility issues can expect that their needs will be met with courtesy and good design. One guest writes:

> *I love the accessibility of Disney. I have more freedom and independence at WDW and on board DCL than I do in my own hometown. Being disabled fades into the background, and I can feel just like everyone else.*

Stateroom Furnishings

In addition to the standard stateroom amenities, DCL offers the following for guests with disabilities:

• Close-captioned TV (*most stations*)	• Portable toilet • Raised toilet seat	• Rubber bed pads • Shower stool
• Bed boards and rails	• Refrigerator	• Transfer benches
• Sharps container	• Distilled water for CPAP machines or other medical devices	
• A Stateroom Communication Kit, including an alarm clock, door-knock and phone alerts, phone amplifier, bed-shaker notification, strobe-light smoke detector, and text typewriter (TTY)		

WHEELCHAIR AND ECV USERS DCL suggests that guests using a wheelchair or ECV request a wheelchair-accessible stateroom or suite. Found on every Disney ship, accessible staterooms include the following features:

• Doorways at least 32 inches wide	• Fold-down shower seating and hand-held showerheads	• Open bed frame for easier entry and exit
• Bathroom and shower handrails	• Lowered towel and closet bars	• Ramped bathroom thresholds
• Emergency call buttons and additional phones in the bath and stateroom		

One advantage to having an accessible stateroom is that its wider door lets you store your wheelchair or ECV inside your cabin when it's not in use. This also makes it easier to recharge the equipment when needed. If you find yourself in a standard stateroom whose door isn't wide enough to accommodate your vehicle, you may be asked to park the vehicle in a designated area elsewhere on the ship, even at night. In practice, we've seen many ECVs parked in a corner of each deck's elevator-landing areas. Chances are that your vehicle will be stored within a short walk of your cabin.

Outside of your stateroom, special areas are designated at most ship activities for guests in wheelchairs. At the Walt Disney Theatre, for example, Disney cast members direct guests in wheelchairs to a reserved seating area. Shops, restaurants, bars, and nightclubs

unofficial **TIP**
Service animals are welcome on all DCL ships, and each ship has a designated animal-relief area on an outside deck.

are all accessible, and accessible restrooms are available throughout the ship's public areas. A limited number of sand wheelchairs are available on Castaway Cay, too, on a first-come, first-served basis.

Note that DCL's pools require a transfer from wheelchair to use. For this reason, Disney recommends that guests in wheelchairs travel with someone who can help transfer them to and from the wheelchair.

Another area to be aware of is tendering from ship to shore. Some ports, such as the one at Grand Cayman, aren't deep enough to accommodate large cruise ships such as Disney's. When DCL ships anchor at Grand Cayman, smaller boats, or tenders, pull up next to the ship, and guests board them for travel to and from Grand Cayman.

Some tenders use steps instead of ramps to get guests on board. In those cases, wheelchair passengers must use the steps. Also keep in mind that the Disney ship and tender craft both float freely in the ocean. It's not uncommon for the stairs to move 2 or 3 feet up and down during the course of a transfer. If the seas are too rough, wheelchair guests may be denied transfer.

SIGHT- AND HEARING-IMPAIRED GUESTS In addition to closed-caption TVs, assistive listening devices and printed scripts are available for shows at the ships' main theaters and show stages. Stop by the Guest Services desk to pick those up. In addition, American Sign Language (ASL) interpreters are available for live performances on some cruise dates. One reader remarked:

> *We had two ASL interpreters on board who followed one group around the entire cruise. They signed every show, including the lounge acts. They were spectacular performers, sometimes better than the shows themselves!*

CHILDREN WITH DISABILITIES Disney's youth programs are open to special-needs children ages 3–17. All children must be toilet-trained and able to play well with kids who are about their same age and size.

The number of special-needs children who can participate is limited and is based on the number of available counselors, the number of other children in the programs, the number of special-needs children

SCOTT SAYS *by Scott Sanders*

SCOTT'S SUPER-SPECIAL SPECIAL-PEOPLE TIP

DISNEY IS GREAT ABOUT accommodating the various needs of its passengers. It's usually best to contact DCL before your sailing to discuss your specific needs so they can be appropriately noted on your reservation (or have your travel agent do this for you). In my case, I have a shellfish allergy that I've noted on my reservation, but I always make it a point on the first night at dinner to tell each member of my serving team.

CRUISING WITH AUTISM

ALISON SINGER, president of the Autism Science Foundation (autismscience foundation.org), has cruised several times with a daughter who has autism. She writes:

OUR FIRST FAMILY CRUISE WITH OUR DAUGHTER JODIE, who has very severe autism, was on the Disney *Magic* when she was 12. Trust me when I say I was VERY nervous. As an autism family, we needed a lot more than faith, trust, and pixie dust!

DCL's accommodations for people with autism include expedited check-in, allowing a family member to stand in for the person with autism at the mandatory guest-assembly drill (after a brief appearance by the person with autism), and allowing a family member to save seats in the theater to avoid a wait in line. In my own experience, the cruise staff went well beyond the listed accommodations.

My biggest concern when we first booked the cruise was mealtimes, but the dining staff was incredibly accommodating when I requested the special foods Jodie needed. One of DCL's strengths is that the waitstaff travels with your family to dinner in the various restaurants each night, so I only had to discuss her needs with one person. As soon as we'd arrive at dinner, French fries, iceberg lettuce, and a small bowl of Russian dressing would magically appear on Jodie's plate. I was also able to order her main course the night before, so she never had to wait, and her plate was always refilled with what at times felt like an overabundance of French fries—but hey, it's vacation!

Most importantly, this accommodation enabled our family to sit together for an entire meal and enjoy our delicious dinners all the way through to the Mickey Bars. Also, we found that letting Jodie wear headphones at the table helped her handle the noise of the busy dining rooms.

Unlike some other cruise lines, though, DCL doesn't provide one-on-one aides for youth activities and doesn't permit adult family members to serve as aides. A similarly aged sibling or cousin could provide support at the kids' clubs, but in most situations your child would need to be high-functioning enough to navigate the youth programs independently. In such cases, families report generally great experiences—few demands are placed on the kids in general, and the activities are all fun and engaging.

Overall, my family's experience was extremely positive, and we look forward to our next Disney cruise!

already enrolled, and the specific needs of the child to be enrolled. Check with the Youth Activities team when you get on board for more details. Disney is unable to provide medical attention, one-on-one care, or training for a specific need.

PORT ADVENTURES Many port adventures have mobility requirements. For more information, check at the onboard Port Adventures desk, go

to disneycruise.disney.go.com/port-adventures, or see Part Twelve, Port Adventures (page 365).

Other amenities, such as disabled parking at the cruise terminal, are also available. See DCL's Guests with Disabilities FAQ (disney cruise.disney.go.com/guest-services/guests-with-disabilities) for more information.

EQUIPMENT RENTALS Guests who need medical equipment on board may find it convenient to rent from **Special Needs at Sea** (specialneedsat sea.com). They deliver to the Disney ships at most embarkation ports, including Barcelona, Copenhagen, Miami, New Orleans, New York City, Port Canaveral, and Vancouver. The available equipment includes wheelchairs, ECVs, walkers, oxygen and respiratory aids, and audiovisual aids.

OTHER CONSIDERATIONS Guests who use electronic devices (insulin pumps or pacemakers, for example) to wirelessly transmit information to medical providers should know that connectivity on board can be intermittently spotty and potentially expensive. If you must constantly monitor these devices, you will want to make well-informed decisions when planning your cruise.

Additionally, guests with a specific medical condition or care regimen should carry documentation about the nature of care and the contact information of their medical providers. The location of this information should be known to the guest's travel companions.

As noted earlier, DCL no longer stocks plastic straws and cup lids for drinks. Straws, however, can be crucial to quality of life for guests with mobility, eating, and sensory-processing issues, so bring your own if you or someone in your group needs them.

DIETARY RESTRICTIONS

DCL'S TABLE-SERVICE RESTAURANTS include gluten-free, vegetarian, no-sugar-added, dairy-free, and Lighter Note (lower-calorie) offerings on all menus. With advance notice, DCL can also accommodate low-sodium, kosher, and halal diets, as well as diets that omit food allergens such as eggs, nuts, shellfish, all at no additional cost. Counter-service restaurants and room service may have fewer options for those with dietary restrictions.

Notify DCL of your needs at least 60 days in advance via the Request Special Services form, available when you check in online or at disneycruise.disney.go.com/special-services-information-form. Disney asks that the form be submitted at least 60 days in advance of your cruise.

unofficial **TIP**
As noted in the Request Special Services form, DCL makes every reasonable effort to accommodate its guests' dietary needs, but they don't maintain separate kitchen facilities for the preparation of special meals; therefore, they can't guarantee that the food served is 100% allergen-free. Most cruisers with food allergies give DCL high marks, but you eat at your own risk.

Most sailings host a special informational meeting for guests with food allergies on embarkation day, typically at 1 p.m. Call ☎ 800-951-3532 to inquire about whether this is happening during your cruise.

Your best resource for food issues during your sailing may be your dining-service team. Even if you've completed the Request Special Services form well in advance, always remind all dining personnel you encounter, including your head server. Additionally, some guests have found they are most comfortable if they stick with their serving team, who have been fully briefed on their needs. Staying with the same team during breakfast and lunch as well as dinner, and even on Castaway Cay, can provide an extra measure of security. Feel free to ask your team about their daytime restaurant assignments.

unofficial **TIP**
A wealth of additional information on vacationing at Walt Disney World and Disney Cruise Line is available at **Allergy Free Mouse.** See allergyfreemouse.com/dining/disney-cruise-food-allergy for DCL specifics.

Note that most port adventures are run by independent contractors, not Disney. Your food requests and accommodations will *not* be automatically transferred to excursion contractors, and some providers may not be equipped to work with certain dietary issues. What's more, due to legal and agricultural restrictions, in many ports you won't be able to bring certain types of food off the ship. Check with Guest Services for advice on how best to handle your dietary needs in port.

SMOKING *on* BOARD

SMOKING, INCLUDING CIGARETTES, CIGARS, PIPES, and electronic cigarettes, is prohibited in your stateroom, on your stateroom's outdoor verandah (if it has one), and in any indoor space on the ship. On the *Magic* and *Wonder,* outdoor smoking areas are located on the starboard side of Deck 4 between 6 p.m. and 6 a.m., and on the port side of Deck 9 Forward, excluding the AquaLab area on the *Magic* and the Mickey's Pool area on the *Wonder.*

unofficial **TIP**
Guests found smoking in their staterooms or on their verandahs are charged a $250 cleaning fee.

Smoking areas on the *Dream* and *Fantasy* are on the port side of Deck 4 Aft, also from 6 p.m. to 6 a.m.; the port side of Deck 12 Aft, accessed by walking through the Meridian Lounge; and near Currents Bar on Deck 13 Forward, port side.

TRAVELING *with* MEDICATION

TRANSPORT PRESCRIPTION MEDICINE in its original containers, in your carry-on bag instead of checked luggage. The problem you want to avoid isn't one with Disney but the customs staffs of the countries

you're visiting and US border control when you return: while it's an unlikely scenario, you could be asked to provide either the original containers (with your name on them) or a copy of a valid prescription, to ensure that you're not importing illegal or prohibited drugs. Check tinyurl.com/travelingwithmeds for current federal guidelines; if you'll be taking your meds with you into port, also check the policies of the countries you'll be visiting.

Be aware that your ship's onboard Health Center may not to be able to refill prescriptions (especially for controlled substances) that run out during your cruise, so get them refilled before you leave home.

During our travels, we've had transportation or weather issues delay our arrival home by as many as four days. If you take medication that is critical to your health and well-being, we strongly encourage you to bring several days of extra doses with you whenever you travel, particularly when you travel to countries where medical protocols may be different from what you're used to back home.

FRIENDS *of* BILL W.

BEER, WINE, AND SPIRITS flow freely on cruise ships, even those run by Disney. Daily **Alcoholics Anonymous** meetings are available on each cruise. While the times and locations may vary, they're generally found here:

- 8:30 a.m. at Animator's Palate on the *Magic*
- 8:30 a.m. at the Cadillac Lounge on the *Wonder*
- 8:30 a.m. at the Outlook Lounge on the *Dream* and *Fantasy*

While the Cadillac and Outlook Lounges display and serve alcohol, the ship's bartenders lock up the entire stock every night, so no bottles are out in the open during the meetings.

LGBT+ TRAVELERS

DCL IS VERY WELCOMING TO LGBT+ GUESTS. Many of our gay friends, both with and without children, rave about their Disney cruises. One friend notes:

> *After about the second day, you can start picking out who's "family." We met more gay people traveling on the Disney cruise than on any of our other nongay cruises.*

We've also met several same-sex couples and many LGBT+ staff on our **Adventures by Disney** river cruises (see Part Thirteen).

Unlike other cruise lines, however, DCL doesn't offer onboard activities geared specifically to LGBT+ travelers: you won't find, say,

a Gay Mingle listing in your *Personal Navigator.* As noted previously, many LGBT+ cruisers have good luck finding their tribes while out and about, but if you're traveling solo, it may be worth joining the Facebook group for your cruise or posting to a Disney discussion board to make connections before your trip.

The experiences of LGBT+ travelers in port depend largely on the itinerary. In most places you'll be absolutely fine, but there are a few where it pays to be cautious (socially conservative parts of the Caribbean and Eastern Europe, for example). If you're unfamiliar with the local culture of the ports you'll be visiting, try Googling "LGBT+ travel advice" as a starting point for additional research.

RELUCTANT CRUISERS

IF YOU'RE READING THIS BOOK, chances are you're excitedly planning one of your first cruises. As you plan, one of the challenges you may face is coping with a reluctant cruiser in your family—that person who just can't get on board (ha-ha) with the idea of spending time on a ship.

While we, Erin and Len, love cruising now, we understand where they're coming from, because we were once reluctant cruisers, too: Erin had seasickness concerns, while Len was afraid of being disconnected from work. Rest assured that, despite a few missteps, our fears ultimately ended up being unfounded, and that information and preparation can address almost any cruise concern.

Here's how our issues worked out—we hope our experiences will help reassure your reticent cruiser.

ERIN: I was woefully underprepared for my first Disney cruise—it was hastily tacked on to a Walt Disney World vacation without much forethought. Even though I'm prone to motion sickness and my then-3-year-old daughter was in her separation-anxiety phase, I didn't bother to do any research on how to deal with these issues. Not surprisingly, I did encounter some seasickness, and I didn't know what to do when my daughter didn't want to spend time in the kids' club. After that experience, I didn't think cruising was for me.

Fast-forward about eight years to when my husband decided that the easiest and most efficient way to introduce our daughters to Europe would be on a cruise. With the carrot of a side trip to Disneyland Paris dangling before me, I reluctantly agreed to a Mediterranean sailing on the *Magic*. This time I did my homework: I had an arsenal of motion-sickness-remediation tools suggested by my doctor, my daughters had matured enough to enjoy the kids' clubs (and I had researched things to do with them if they didn't want to go to the clubs), and I found that it truly was easy to see much of southern Europe by cruise ship.

We introduced our children to Barcelona, the French Riviera, Rome, Naples, Florence, and Majorca, and I had to unpack only once. *I was hooked!* I still prefer cruises with calmer waters (typically in Europe and Alaska), but I've gotten my sea legs and am also happy to hop on the *Dream* or *Fantasy* for a jaunt through the Caribbean anytime. Cruising is a terrific way to see the world—as long as you're prepared.

LEN: I'm a workaholic who thinks constant high-speed internet access is an inalienable right. (*True story:* I once tried to charter a helicopter at midnight to extract me from a family camping trip to the Outer Banks of North Carolina because there was no air-conditioning or internet.) So I wasn't looking forward to a weeklong cruise, which I imagined as huddled masses essentially cut off from civilization with Jimmy Buffett playing in the background.

But my first cruise, on the *Fantasy*, couldn't have gone better—there were more than enough activities to keep me busy all day and just enough internet access to stave off any "Get me out of here!" instincts. I even learned to "relax" in the *Fantasy's* Rainforest Spa (if *relax* means "catch up on *The New York Times*'s mobile edition").

If you're like me, you'll appreciate the additional restaurants, lounges, and activities on the *Dream* and *Fantasy*. I don't recommend a seven-night cruise for your first trip on the high seas, but I also think a three-night cruise is too short: you're either packing or unpacking every day. A four-night cruise is the bare minimum for a great experience, as it includes a day at sea so you can explore the ship. A five-night cruise (with two sea days) is probably the best choice.

PART SIX

THE SHIPS *at a* GLANCE

OVERVIEW *and* OUR RECOMMENDATIONS

LAUNCHED IN 1998, the **Disney Magic** holds roughly 2,700 passengers and 950 crew members. The **Disney Wonder** has the same capacity and was launched in 1999. The **Disney Dream** and **Disney Fantasy,** which took their maiden voyages in 2011 and 2012, respectively, hold up to 4,000 passengers and 1,450 crew members. The *Magic* and the *Wonder* are the workhorses of the fleet: The *Magic* covers everything from Mexico to the Mediterranean, while the *Wonder* plies the seas from Alaska to the Caribbean.

unofficial **TIP**
When it comes to choosing a ship, you'll do well with either the *Dream* or the *Fantasy.* We recommend going with whichever has the price or itinerary to meet your needs.

All four DCL ships share sleek lines, twin smokestacks, and nautical styling that calls to mind classic ocean liners, but with instantly recognizable Disney signatures. The colors—dark blue, white, red, and yellow—and the famous face-and-ears silhouette on the stacks are clearly those of Mickey Mouse. Look closely at the *Magic*'s stern ornamentation, for example, and you'll see a 15-foot Goofy hanging by his overalls. (It's Donald on the *Wonder*'s stern, Mickey on the *Dream*'s, and Dumbo on the *Fantasy*'s.) A reader tip:

> *I highly recommend the* **Art of the Ship** *tour [see page 219] for adults interested in the ships' design. We learned all about the interior decorating and decor planning on the ship.*

The ships' interiors combine nautical themes with Art Nouveau and Art Deco inspiration. (Art Nouveau, popular at the turn of the century, incorporates natural shapes, such as from plants and animals, into its geometric designs; Art Deco has the geometry without the

nature—think those sleek interiors from 1930s movies.) Disney images are everywhere, from Mickey's profile in the wrought-iron balustrades to the bronze statue of Helmsman Mickey featured prominently in the *Magic*'s atrium, Ariel on the *Wonder,* Admiral Donald on the *Dream,* and Mademoiselle Minnie decked out in full flapper style on the *Fantasy.* Disney art is on every wall and in every stairwell and corridor. A grand staircase on each ship sweeps from the atrium lobby to shops peddling DCL-themed clothing, collectibles, jewelry, and more.

Ships have two lower decks with cabins, three decks with dining rooms and showrooms, and then three or five upper decks of cabins. Two sports and sun decks offer separate pools and facilities for families and for adults without children. Signs point toward lounges and facilities, and all elevators are clearly marked as Forward, Aft, or Midship.

Our main complaint concerning the ships' design is that outdoor public areas focus inward toward the pools instead of seaward, as if Disney wants you to forget that you're on a cruise liner. On the *Magic* and the *Wonder,* there's no public place where you can curl up in the shade and watch the ocean—at least not without a plexiglass wall between you and it. On Deck 4 of the *Dream* and the *Fantasy,* however, an open promenade, complete with comfy deck chairs, circles the ship. It's shady and fairly well protected from wind, and it offers the opportunity to sit back and enjoy the sea without your having to look through plexiglass barriers.

Speaking of plexiglass, a predictable but nonetheless irritating design characteristic is the extensive childproofing. There's enough plexiglass on all four ships to build a subdivision of see-through homes. On the pool decks especially, it feels as if the ships are hermetically sealed. Plus, verandah doors have a two-part locking mechanism, with one of the two parts 6 feet off the floor—causing even adults occasional consternation in trying to operate them.

DCL CHEAT SHEET

CAN'T REMEMBER, SAY, which ship has the AquaDunk and which has the AquaDuck without looking it up? Neither can we from time to time. These handy charts summarize what's the same and what's different across the ships; see pages 138–139.

FEATURES FOUND ON EVERY DCL SHIP

ALL DISNEY CRUISE LINE SHIPS HAVE AMENITIES in common, including the following:

• Adult pool and deck areas	• Fitness center
• Bars, lounges, and cafés	• Full-service spa and salon, with sauna
• Buffet restaurant	• Guest Services desk
• Family pools and water-play areas	• Health Center

• Infant, child, tween, and teen clubs • Movie theater • Outdoor basketball court, shuffleboard, and other sports areas • Outdoor LED screen for movies, concerts, and videos	• **Palo,** an upscale Italian restaurant • Photo gallery for purchasing onboard photos • Retail shopping, including duty-free alcohol • Theater for live performances

Whereas some amenities are shared by all ships, as listed above, the *Dream* and *Fantasy* have the following features not found on the *Magic* or the *Wonder:*

• **AquaDuck** water coaster • Champagne bar (**Pink** on the *Dream,* **Ooh La La** on the *Fantasy*) • **Chill Spa** for teens. (The *Magic* and *Wonder* have treatment rooms branded as Chill Spa, but they are vastly different from the version on the larger ships.) • **Premium-ice-cream shop** (Vanellope's on the *Dream,* Sweet on You on the *Fantasy*). Other ships have only a soft-serve station on deck.	• **Meridian,** a martini bar • Miniature-golf course • **Remy,** an upscale French restaurant • **Satellite Falls,** an adults-only splash pool and sun deck • Separate decks for Concierge rooms • **Skyline** bar • A **Tiffany & Co.** jewelry boutique. (Yes, shopaholics, *that* Tiffany's.)

FEATURES UNIQUE TO SOME SHIPS

IT SEEMS WITH EVERY DRY DOCK, each DCL ship loses a little more of its unique character. Still, each of the following ships has something that sets it apart:

UNIQUE TO THE *MAGIC* **AquaDunk,** a vertical waterslide. (The **AquaDuck** on the *Dream* and *Fantasy* sounds similar—the name is off by just one letter—but it's a horizontal water coaster.)

UNIQUE TO THE *WONDER* A Concierge-only lounge on Deck 10 with 270-degree views of the sea.

unofficial **TIP**
Disney ships have no casinos or libraries.

RANKING THE SHIPS

IF YOUR CRUISE DESTINATION is the Bahamas or the Caribbean, one decision you'll need to make is whether to sail on either the *Magic* and *Wonder* or on the *Dream* and *Fantasy.* Ignoring the different itineraries each ship serves, here's how we rank the Disney ships:

1. *Fantasy* **2.** *Dream* **3.** *Wonder* **4.** *Magic*

The *Fantasy* and *Dream* have better restaurants, bars, and pools than the older ships, plus more on-deck activities, more space for children's activities, more deck space for tanning, better spas, and more

continued on page 140

WHAT'S THE SAME ACROSS THE SHIPS

DINING

All ships have a **Cabanas** buffet and a **Palo** adult-dining venue.

FAMILY ENTERTAINMENT

All ships have a **D Lounge** family nightclub and a **Bibbidi Bobbidi Boutique** for princess and pirate makeovers.

KIDS' CLUBS

All ships have **It's a Small World Nursery, Oceaneer Club/Lab** for older kids, **Edge** tween club, and **Vibe** teen club. The clubs on the *Dream/Fantasy* are larger than those on the *Magic/Wonder,* but following the most recent dry-dock refurbishments of all the ships, the quality of facilities in the clubs is now comparable.

FITNESS AND SPAS

All ships have a fitness center, an outdoor running track, and a **Rainforest** sauna/shower complex. All ships have a **Senses Spa** for adults and a **Chill Spa** for teens; however, the spa facilities for all ages are substantially larger on the *Dream/Fantasy* than they are on the *Magic/Wonder.*

TECHNOLOGY

All ships have pay Wi-Fi (free to use with the **DCL Navigator** app) and free **Wave Phones** for calling/messaging others on board.

WHAT'S DIFFERENT ACROSS THE SHIPS

SHIP			
Magic	***Wonder***	***Dream***	***Fantasy***
• FEATURE: Dining			
ADULT DINING			
Palo	Palo	Palo, Remy	Palo, Remy
COUNTER SERVICE			
Daisy's De-Lites, Duck-in Diner, Eye Scream Treats, Frozone Treats, Pinocchio's Pizzeria	Daisy's De-Lites, Eye Scream Treats, Pete's Boiler Bites, Pinocchio's Pizzeria	Eye Scream Treats, Flo's Cafe, Frozone Treats, Senses Juice Bar, Vanellope's Sweets & Treats	Eye Scream Treats, Flo's Cafe, Frozone Treats, Sweet on You
ROTATIONAL DINING			
Animator's Palate, Lumiere's, Rapunzel's Royal Table	Animator's Palate, Tiana's Place, Triton's	Animator's Palate, Enchanted Garden, Royal Palace	Animator's Palate, Enchanted Garden, Royal Court
• FEATURE: Family Entertainment			
LIVE STAGE SHOWS (may vary depending on itinerary)			
Disney Dreams, Remember the Magic, Tangled: The Musical, Twice Charmed	*Disney Dreams, Frozen: A Musical Spectacular, The Golden Mickeys*	*Beauty and the Beast, Disney's Believe, The Golden Mickeys*	*Disney's Aladdin, Disney's Believe, Disney Wishes*

WHAT'S DIFFERENT ACROSS THE SHIPS				
SHIP	*Magic*	*Wonder*	*Dream*	*Fantasy*
• **FEATURE: Nightlife and Bars**				
ADULT-NIGHTLIFE AREA	After Hours	After Hours	The District	Europa
CHAMPAGNE BAR	No	No	Pink	Ooh La La
COFFEE BAR	Cove Café	Cove Café, Outlook Café	Cove Café	Cove Café
DANCE CLUB	Fathoms	Azure	Evolution	The Tube
LIVE-MUSIC CLUB	Keys, Promenade Lounge	Cadillac Lounge, Promenade Lounge	District Lounge	La Piazza
MARTINI BAR	No	No	Meridian	Meridian
POOL BARS	Signals *(21+)*	Signals *(21+)*	Currents, Waves *(all ages)*	Currents, Waves *(all ages)*
PUB/SPORTS BAR	O'Gills Pub	Crown & Fin	687	O'Gills Pub
UPSCALE "Craft Cocktail" BAR	No	No	Skyline	Skyline
• **FEATURE: Pools**				
ADULT POOLS	Quiet Cove Pool	Quiet Cove Pool	Quiet Cove Pool, Satellite Falls	Quiet Cove Pool, Satellite Falls
FAMILY POOL	Goofy's Pool	Goofy's Pool	Donald's Pool	Donald's Pool
KIDS' POOLS/ SPLASH AREAS	AquaLab, Mickey's Pool, Nephews' Pool/Splash Zone	AquaLab, Dory's Reef, Mickey's Pool/ Splash Zone	Mickey's Pool, Nemo's Reef	AquaLab, Mickey's Pool, Nemo's Reef
TEEN SPLASH POOL *(ages 14-17)*	No	No	Vibe	Vibe
WATER RIDES	AquaDunk *(vertical waterslide)*, Twist 'n' Spout *(kids' waterslide)*	Mickey's Slide, Twist 'n' Spout	AquaDuck *(water coaster)*, Mickey's Slide	AquaDuck, Mickey's Slide
• **FEATURE: Sports and Recreation**				
GAMES	Basketball, Foosball, shuffleboard, table tennis	Basketball, Foosball, shuffleboard, table tennis	Basketball, Foosball, minigolf, shuffleboard, table tennis	Basketball, Foosball, minigolf, shuffleboard, table tennis
• **FEATURE: Technology**				
"ENCHANTED" *(Interactive)* **ART**	No	No	Yes	Yes
INTERACTIVE GAME *played around the ship*	No	No	Midship Detective Agency	Midship Detective Agency
SHUTTERS PHOTO STUDIO	Yes	Yes	No	Yes
VIRTUAL PORTHOLES	No	No	Yes	Yes

continued from page 137

interactive games. These advantages make up for the slightly smaller cabin sizes on the *Dream* and *Fantasy*, whose non-Concierge staterooms are 2%–9% (5–22 square feet) smaller than corresponding cabins on the *Magic* and *Wonder*. Another minor downside: because the newer ships carry more passengers, Castaway Cay is more crowded when they're in port.

THE *Disney Magic*

THE FIRST DCL SHIP, the *Magic* was launched in 1998 and underwent an extensive renovation—or "reimagining," in Disney-speak—during a two-month dry dock in Cádiz, Spain, during the summer of 2013. The 2013 makeover included cosmetic updates to the *Magic*'s lobby atrium; **Keys** (formerly Sessions), the piano bar; **Palo,** the adults-only, fine-dining Italian restaurant; and **Fathoms** (formerly Rockin' Bar D), the dance club. In addition, Vista Spa became **Senses Spa.** The *Magic* underwent additional dry-dock tweaking in late 2015. Changes at that time included the addition of a **Bibbidi Bobbidi Boutique** children's makeover salon and a location update for the **Edge** tween club.

The *Magic* underwent yet another dry-dock refresh in 2018. The **Vibe** teen club got updated decor; the **Cove Café** coffee bar was spruced up; and, most significantly, the tired Carioca's dining room was rethemed as **Rapunzel's Royal Table,** featuring elements from Disney's *Tangled*.

THE *Disney Wonder*

LAUNCHED IN 1999 as the second of DCL's four current ships, the *Wonder* was beginning to show her age by 2016, with visible wear and tear and dated decor in many guest areas. In late 2016, the *Wonder* underwent a dry dock with significant updating and retheming, emerging in much better condition and with amenities, entertainment, and fittings on par with the rest of the fleet.

The *Wonder* continues to have the most in common with its sister the *Magic*, but with slightly different theming. When you board the ship at Deck 3, you're greeted by Ariel instead of Mickey and an Art Nouveau–style atrium rather than Art Deco. In keeping with the *Little Mermaid* theme, one of the standard rotational-dining restaurants on the *Wonder* is **Triton's,** named for Ariel's dad (its counterpart on the *Magic* is the *Beauty and the Beast*–themed **Lumiere's**).

Before the 2016 dry dock, the *Wonder* was home to our two least favorite dining spots in the Disney fleet: **Beach Blanket Buffet** and **Parrot Cay.** The refurbishment replaced these outmoded venues with the more modern **Cabanas** buffet and a unique restaurant, **Tiana's Place,** inspired

by the film *The Princess and the Frog* and serving New Orleans–style cuisine accompanied by live jazz. Additionally, the *Wonder*'s antiquated version of **Animator's Palate** was retrofitted with an interactive show to match its counterparts on the other ships. Following the dry dock, the *Wonder*'s dining is now on par with that of the rest of the DCL fleet.

Len, whose cold, black heart would make Ozzy Osbourne say "Cheer up, mate," nevertheless thinks the *Wonder*'s ***Frozen: A Musical Spectacular*** is the best stage show in the fleet. Besides good songs, solid stage design, and a snappy pace, there are special effects that had him literally saying "Wow!" out loud.

The kids' clubs were also reimagined. The **Oceaneer Club** now features **Marvel's Super Hero Academy,** in which young guests train to become superheroes (with help from Spider-Man during live character appearances), and **Frozen Adventures,** where a digital Olaf leads kids in games and songs.

From a technological standpoint, the *Wonder* continues to lag a bit behind the newer ships. There is no headliner waterslide like the AquaDunk (*Magic*) or water coaster like the AquaDuck (*Dream* and *Fantasy*) on the pool deck, and inside staterooms on the *Wonder* lack the "virtual portholes" found on the *Dream* and *Fantasy.* Nevertheless, the *Wonder* is Erin's sentimental favorite of the DCL fleet:

> *I prefer the smaller size of the* Magic *and* Wonder. *The smaller capacity of the older ships means there are fewer people jockeying for space on Castaway Cay; I also think the older ships have a more cozy, homey atmosphere. By the end of a long sailing on a small ship, the cast members feel like family—something I haven't experienced as often on the* Dream *and* Fantasy.

The *Wonder* splits its time among Alaska, the California coast, the Caribbean, and sometimes Hawaii. Repositioning cruises also take it through the Panama Canal. She sets sail from Galveston, Miami, San Diego, and Vancouver.

Two-thirds of the **Outlook Cafe**'s area was partitioned off during the dry dock to use as a new Concierge lounge. The remaining Outlook Café space is enough to retain its quiet appeal, and the new Concierge lounge is a fantastic place to get a quiet bite to eat while still enjoying the scenery.

THE *Disney Dream*

FOLLOWING THE SUCCESSES OF THE *MAGIC* AND *WONDER*, DCL ordered two new ships that would more than double the number of guests they could serve, allow them to expand the number of itineraries

continued on page 148

Disney Magic / Disney Wonder DECK PLANS

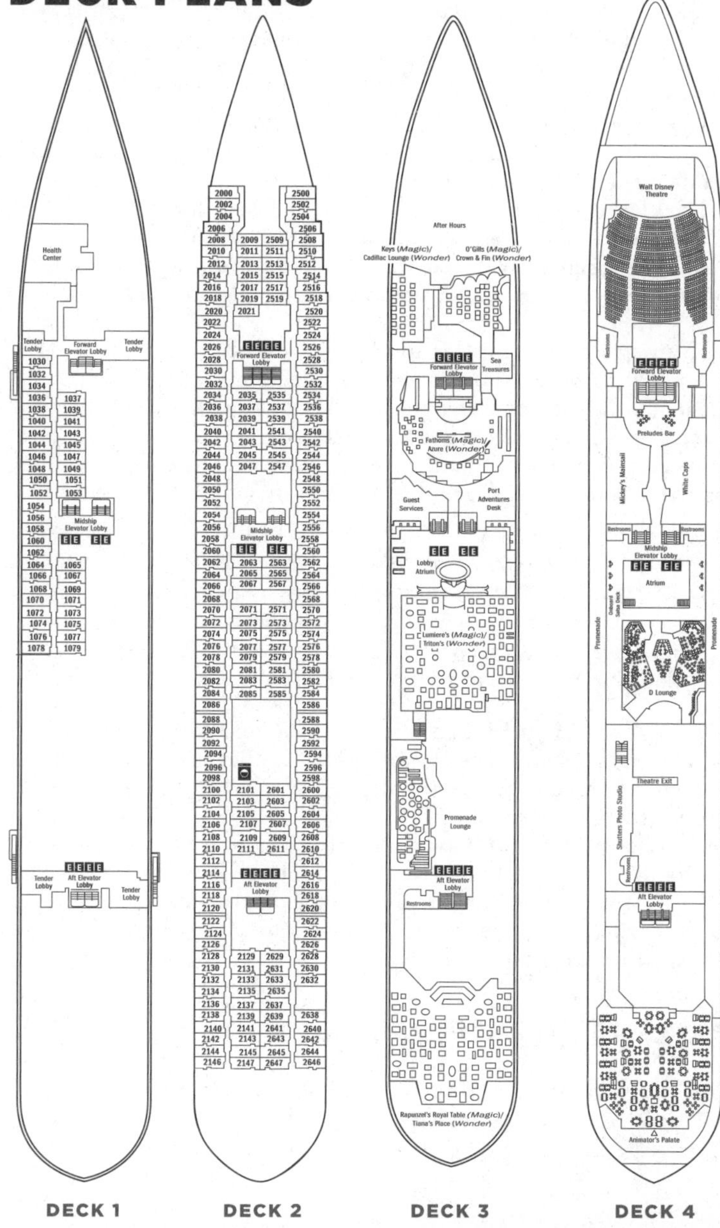

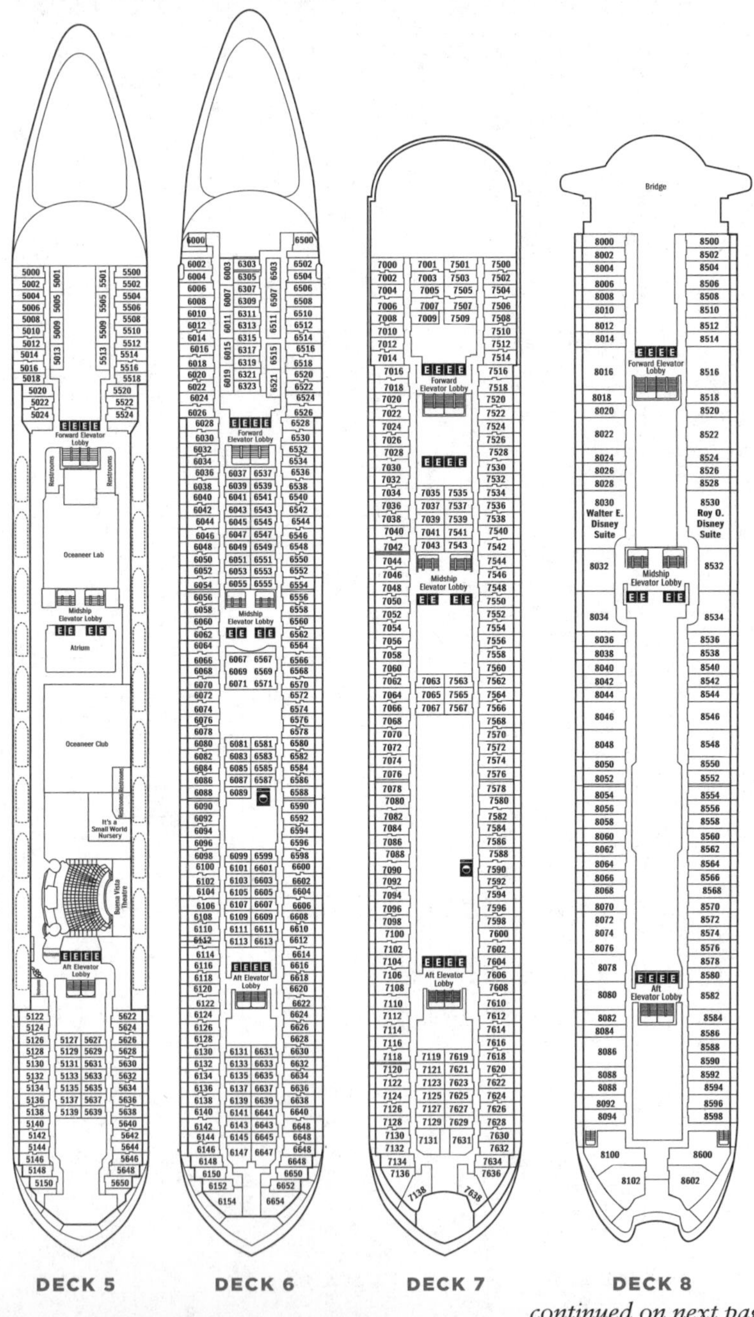

continued on next page

Disney Magic / Disney Wonder
DECK PLANS

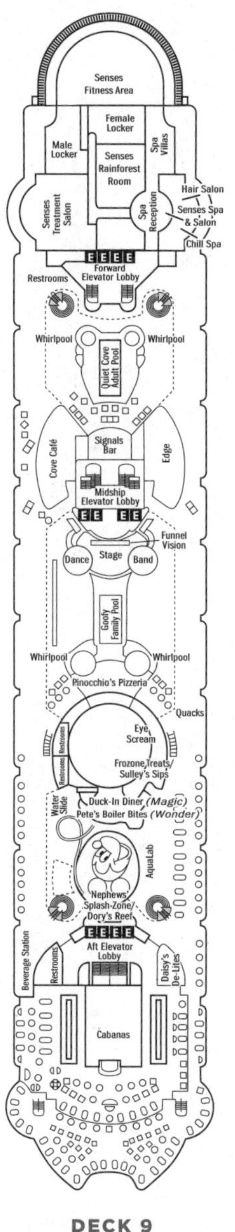

DECK 9

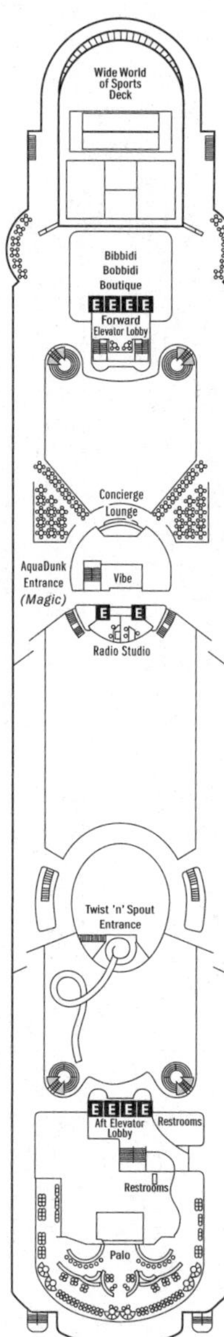

DECK 10

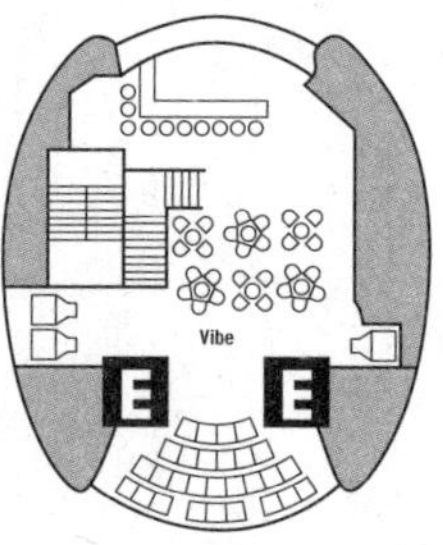

DECK 11

Disney Dream / Disney Fantasy DECK PLANS

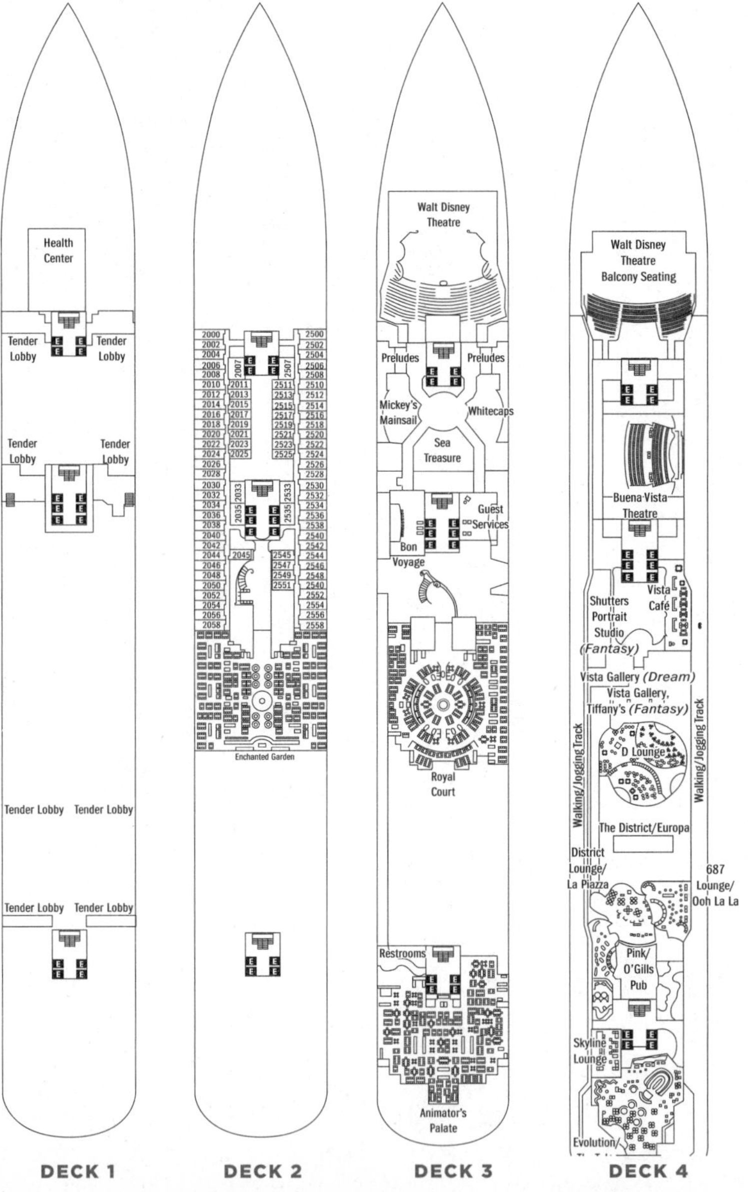

continued on next page

Disney Dream / Disney Fantasy DECK PLANS

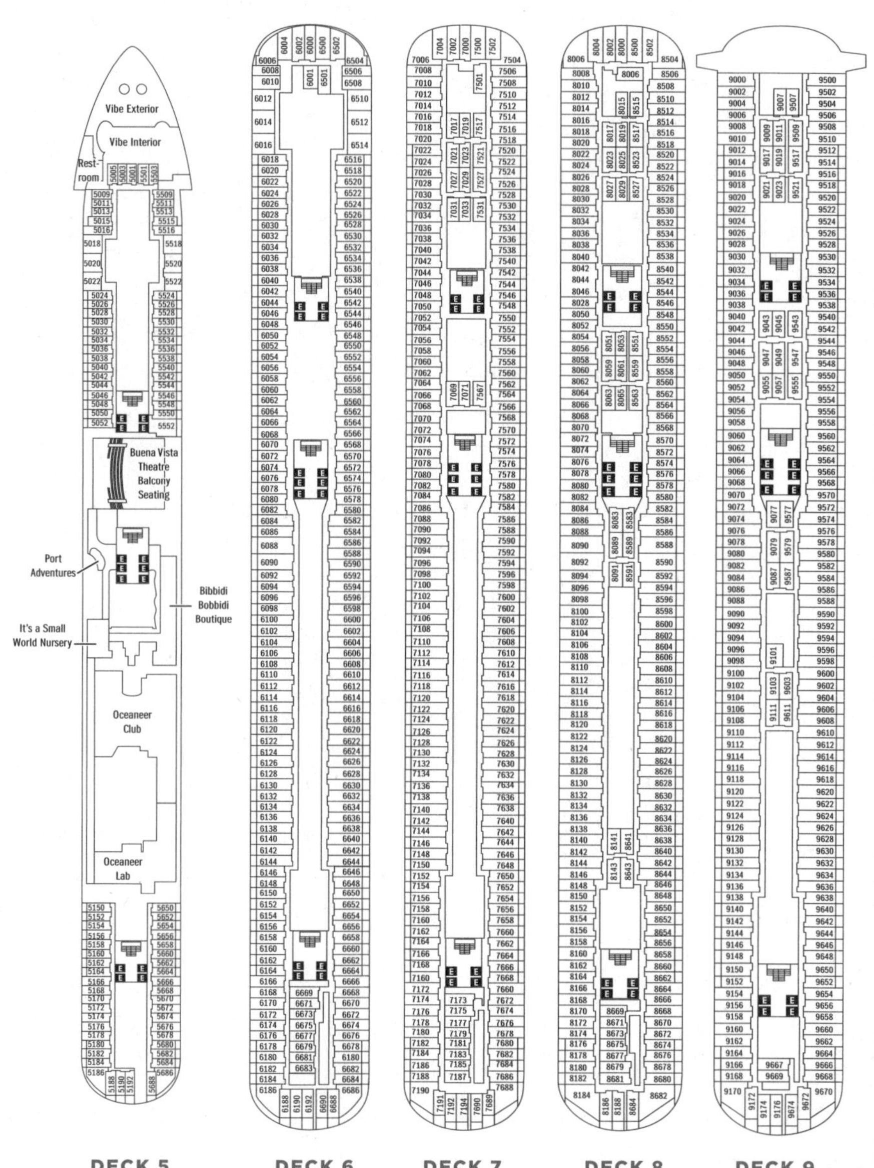

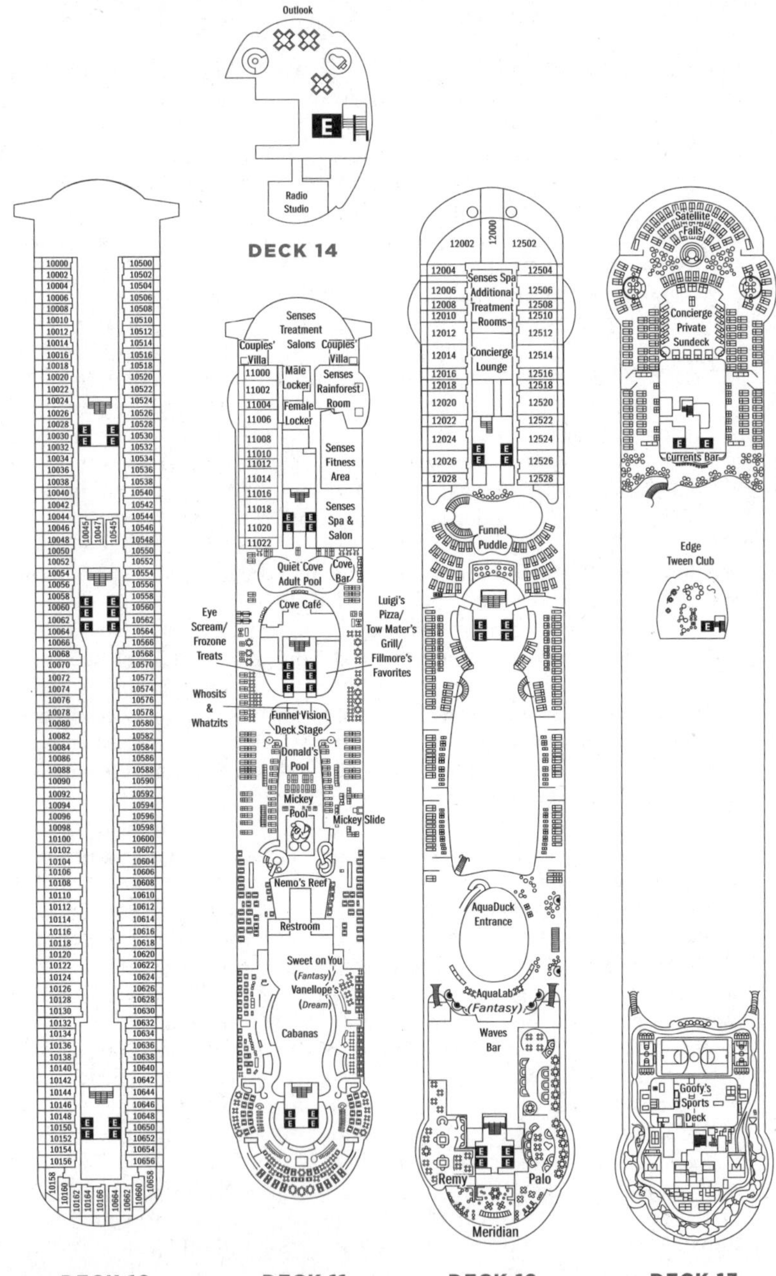
Outlook
Radio Studio
DECK 14
Senses Treatment Salons
Couples' Villa
Couples' Villa
Male Locker
Female Locker
Senses Rainforest Room
Senses Fitness Area
Senses Spa & Salon
Quiet Cove Adult Pool
Cove Bar
Cove Café
Eye Scream/ Frozone Treats
Luigi's Pizza/ Tow Mater's Grill/ Fillmore's Favorites
Whosits & Whatzits
Funnel Vision Deck Stage
Donald's Pool
Mickey Pool
Mickey Slide
Nemo's Reef
Restroom
Sweet on You (Fantasy)/ Vanellope's (Dream)
Cabanas
Senses Spa Additional Treatment Rooms
Concierge Lounge
Funnel Puddle
AquaDuck Entrance
AquaLab (Fantasy)
Waves Bar
Remy
Palo
Meridian
Satellite Falls
Concierge Private Sundeck
Currents Bar
Edge Tween Club
Goofy's Sports Deck
DECK 10
DECK 11
DECK 12
DECK 13

continued from page 141

offered, and bring several first-evers to a cruise ship. The new *Dream*-class vessels were built by Meyer Werft in Germany rather than Italy's Fincantieri, which created the *Magic* and *Wonder.*

The *Disney Dream,* the first of these new ships, set sail in 2011. It's 151 feet longer, 35 feet taller, and 15 feet wider than the *Magic* or *Wonder.* With three additional passenger decks, the ship can hold 50% more passengers and crew than its predecessors, yet it still has the classic lines of the smaller ships.

Disney Imagineering had great fun designing the second-generation ships. Inside cabins were given "virtual portholes," which show the view from the bridge on a round screen. This feature proved so popular with kids that on many cruises, interior cabins had fares higher than those of ocean-view cabins. On the top deck, the **AquaDuck**, a waterslide that circles the ship, was added to the usual pools. Between the pool deck and your cabin, you'll find interactive art that reacts when you pass by it, along with the **Midship Detective Agency**, a scavenger hunt–type game that sends families all over the ship collecting clues.

unofficial **TIP**
We recommend the *Dream* or *Fantasy* over the *Magic* and *Wonder* to travelers who care more about the ships and their amenities than where they cruise.

When it came to dining, **Cabanas** buffet improved on both traffic flow and food quality compared with the dire Beach Blanket Buffet on the *Wonder* (which, thankfully, became Cabanas eventually as well). As for the *Dream*'s three standard dining rooms, **Animator's Palate** was plussed up with new technology as part of the dinner show, **Enchanted Garden** took its place as the prettiest of the three, and **Royal Palace** is a tribute to all things Disney princess, but mostly Cinderella.

Both adults and kids scored big with improvements to the new ship. In addition to the adults-only Palo, **Remy** was added as another upscale-dining option for the 18-and-up crowd. With a subtle *Ratatouille* theme, and not one but two celebrated chefs creating the menus, Remy initially shocked cruisers with its surcharge—now $95 plus alcohol per dinner, the highest in the industry—but diners were pleased nonetheless. The adult lounges, in the area called **The District** on Deck 4, provide more-intimate, better-themed spaces to take the edge off than the old Beat Street on the *Magic* and Route 66 on the *Wonder.* **Skyline,** one of The District's bars, showcases a great use of technology, with a cityscape behind the bar that changes every 15 minutes. It's mesmerizing.

Senses Spa replaced the Vista Spa and outdid it in every way.

Kids got greatly expanded club areas with a Pixar theme. The teen area got a makeover that left it one of the most stylish spaces on board and gave it its own pool (the cast-member pool area from the older ships). Teens also got their own pampering spot, **Chill Spa**.

Though the *Dream* still feels very new, Disney continues to improve the ship. A 2015 dry-dock refresh added the following:

- A **Bibbidi Bobbidi Boutique** makeover salon for children, on Deck 5
- **Vanellope's Sweets & Treats,** a premium-ice-cream shop, on Deck 11. (Think of it as Palo for kids.)
- A **Star Wars**-themed area of the Oceaneer Club. Children "pilot" a faux *Millennium Falcon* and participate in a shipboard version of the *Jedi Training Academy* show at Walt Disney World.

THE *Disney Fantasy*

THE *FANTASY* SAILED ITS MAIDEN VOYAGE in 2012, one year after the *Dream* came into service. The ship is nearly identical to its sister but got some tweaks as a result of guest and cast-member feedback. Both the *Dream* and the *Fantasy* are based out of Port Canaveral and sail the Caribbean. While the *Dream* has mostly three- and four-night itineraries, the *Fantasy* is almost exclusively seven-night sailings.

Walking into the atrium of the *Fantasy*, you see a bronze statue of Minnie Mouse and a striking peacock-inspired carpet—an indication of the Art Nouveau style of the *Fantasy* as opposed to the *Dream*'s Deco look.

The *Dream*'s technology package got some enhancements on the *Fantasy*. The **Midship Detective Agency** has three different storylines (including the Muppets), surpassing the version on the *Dream*, and the show at **Animator's Palate** got a very cool audience-interaction element that we won't spoil here. Other than this addition, the restaurants are identical to the *Dream*'s, with one subtle name change: Royal Palace is **Royal Court** and includes even more princessy goodness. **Cabanas, Enchanted Garden, Palo,** and **Remy** are the same.

On the pool deck, the **AquaDuck** adds the **AquaLab** splash area.

The *Fantasy*'s nightlife area is **Europa. Skyline** is the one constant between the two bar–nightclub areas on the ships, though it displays different cityscapes in this rendition. **The Tube**'s Austin Powers–style decor makes it a very fun place to hang out, but **Ooh La La** is either too high-concept or low-concept for our tastes; we prefer the whimsical look of the *Dream*'s **Pink** for our Champagne needs. **O'Gills Pub** doesn't feel particularly Irish, though it has the same big-screen TVs as **687,** the sports bar on the *Dream*.

PART SEVEN

DINING

NOSHES, NOSHES *Everywhere*

THE FIRST THING MANY CRUISERS DISCOVER when exploring the ships on embarkation day is the buffet. In the way that some people remember the birth of their first child, we remember our first look at the spread at Cabanas. (Sorry, Hannah. Love, Dad.) On one table sat a pile of crab legs that almost reached eye level. Next to this sat a trawler's worth of peel-and-eat shrimp. Surrounding all of this deliciousness were tubs of melted butter and enough cocktail sauce to float the ship itself. On the other side of the aisle, a chef was flash-cooking a steak, the spices, sizzle, and flame making the air smell savory. It was glorious.

unofficial **TIP**
DCL restaurants (except Palo and Remy, naturally) offer kids' menus for breakfast, lunch, and dinner. Kids (except for infants in the nursery) may also dine in their designated clubs free of charge.

You'll never go hungry on a Disney cruise. The variety of dining options is staggering, including everything from coffee shops and pizza stands to Vegas-size buffets to ritzy French and Italian restaurants. That said, we've learned a few ways to increase your chances of enjoying memorable meals on board. This section describes your dining options in detail and includes our advice on how to make the most of them.

ROTATIONAL DINING

ONE OF THE INNOVATIONS that DCL brought to the cruise industry is the concept of rotational dining, in which you visit one of three standard restaurants on each different night of your cruise. As you change from restaurant to restaurant, your server team—your waiter, beverage person, head waiter, and maître d'—all move with you. Your team will quickly learn your dining proclivities, including preferred drinks and favorite desserts, and make menu suggestions. Along with your stateroom attendant, you'll almost certainly rely on your dining team more than any other members of the crew during your trip.

The rotational restaurants have two dinner seatings, typically 5:45 p.m. and 8:15 p.m. Because Disney sets the schedule, there's no need to make reservations each night. You can request either the earlier or later seating when booking your trip or once aboard the ship. You also can request changes to your rotation, specifying which restaurants you visit each night.

Unlike other cruise lines, which may seat several families or groups together, DCL generally keeps families at their own tables. The exception to this would be singles or couples, who are routinely seated with other groups. If you're traveling alone or in a group of two or three and you prefer not to be seated with others during your rotational dining, call DCL in advance to make this request, which is not guaranteed but almost always honored.

On cruises of four nights or longer, you'll repeat at least one of the three standard restaurants. The menus will change each night, but the decor remains the same. Rather than visit the same restaurant twice on a four-night cruise, we recommend using one of those nights to visit **Palo** (on any ship) or **Remy** (on the *Dream* and *Fantasy*). You must pay an additional charge to dine at these restaurants, but the food is stellar, the crowds are small, and the service is impeccable. See page 153 for details.

You may request a particular dining rotation by calling DCL directly at ☎ 800-951-3532. This way, for example, you can pick which restaurant you're assigned to visit twice on a four-night cruise, or three times on a seven-night cruise. You may want to do this if you vastly prefer the decor of one restaurant over the others. Requests aren't guaranteed but are often honored.

Another alternative to rotational dining (besides room service) is dinner at **Cabanas,** the large pool-deck restaurant on each ship. It's less formal and less expensive than splurging on Palo or Remy, and it's your only alternative if you're dining with children. At dinner, Cabanas transforms from a buffet to a full-service restaurant, but you can still show up when you want, and you'll receive generally faster service than you would in the main dining rooms. This would be a good option if, for instance, you had an early dinner seating but you were late getting back to the ship after a port adventure, or if you were assigned to the later seating but your kids are too famished to wait that long.

Finally, note that at least one of the rotational restaurants is open for breakfast and lunch each day—if you're not in the mood to fight the crowds at the buffet, this is a more relaxed option. Check your *Personal Navigator* for more information.

DCL RESTAURANT CATEGORIES

IN GENERAL, FOOD OFFERINGS on Disney Cruise Line are differentiated by freshness, quality, and service:

COUNTER SERVICE Available on each ship's pool deck, fast food includes staples such as burgers, chicken strips, pizza, and sandwiches. In *The Unofficial Guide to Walt Disney World,* we equate the quality

of the counter-service restaurants in the theme parks with that of McDonald's and Taco Bell. With a few exceptions, the food quality at DCL's counter-service restaurants is more like what you'd find in your local supermarket's frozen-food aisle: edible but not as good as something made from scratch. The best items on board are the fresh sandwiches and wraps. Counter-service restaurants for each ship are listed starting with the *Magic*'s, on page 165.

CAFÉS AND LOUNGES Each ship has a dedicated adults-only coffee bar called **Cove Café** that serves espresso, cappuccino, teas, and smoothies, plus wine, mixed drinks, and spirits. A good alternative to a big dinner is Cove Café's small selection of complimentary cold appetizers, available each evening.

Besides Cove Café, a few of the ships' bars and lounges serve appetizers, too. These are described in detail in Part Eight, Entertainment and Nightlife.

BUFFETS Each ship has one large buffet venue, usually open for breakfast and lunch. Buffets tend to serve a bit of everything at each meal and are the easiest way to satisfy disparate appetites. As large and diverse as those at many Las Vegas hotels, the buffets let picky kids (and adults) see exactly what kind of food they're getting. The buffets also offer plenty of seating with ocean views, indoors and out.

FULL-SERVICE RESTAURANTS Each DCL ship has four or five dedicated full-service restaurants. Three of these are part of the standard rotational dinner schedule available to every guest on the ship, with the remaining venues available to adult guests for an additional fee. Additionally, the restaurant on each ship that serves buffet breakfast and lunch also will serve a menu-based dinner that's free and open to all guests.

Along with dinner, one sit-down restaurant is usually open for breakfast and lunch each day, even when the ship is in port. Breakfast and lunch may include both buffet components (an appetizer salad bar, for example) and the option to order from a menu.

Virtually all of the food served at the rotational restaurants will be familiar to American palates. Most dishes, especially at dinner, feature cuts of steak, pork, chicken, and fish similar to those you'd find at a chain eatery. DCL's chefs will add some sort of flavor twist to these, such as soy and sesame if it's an Asian-themed menu, but the basic ingredients will be recognizable to almost everyone. If you want your entrée largely unadorned, look for the **Lighter Note** menu offerings—you'll see here that you can always get plain steak or chicken served with plain rice or a baked potato. Those in the mood for mild need not worry.

Although fresher and of higher quality than the counter-service restaurants, most of the food served at the full-service restaurants is prepared well ahead of time. You get your order faster this way, but it's also well-nigh impossible to customize that order. We've been told, for instance, that we couldn't order a roast-beef-and-mayo sandwich

without the mayo. If you're a moderately finicky eater, you can do the customizing yourself, provided your dish consists of discrete ingredients that you can subtract easily. A BLT without lettuce is probably doable; tomato-and-basil soup minus the basil probably isn't.

The main dining rooms' food quality is on par with upscale American chain restaurants such as P.F. Chang's or Bonefish Grill, with better presentation. If you've cruised on Royal Caribbean or Carnival, you'll probably find DCL's main dining rooms substantially better.

Along with the dining-survey ratings and comments we get, we closely monitor comments about DCL food on social media. A representative sample of recent feedback includes the following:

> *It's a cruise, not a five-star restaurant that serves only 50 people a night. Expect really good "wedding food." It's mass-produced, but it's still pretty darn good.*

> *We live in Chicago and are spoiled with amazing local restaurants. The food we had on the* Magic *wasn't amazing, but considering the constraints of preparing food on a big boat, we were pleasantly surprised.*

> *Compared with other cruise lines, DCL's food is way better.*

> *The food is amazing on all the ships, plus you can ask to get something else or even more than one plate if you can't make up your mind.*

> *We just got off the* Magic *after doing the 12-night British Isles Cruise. They added many interesting regional dishes that I liked.*

> *The food is delightful. They go to the next level to make sure you're satisfied with what you get. We went on our first cruise a year ago, and to this day my daughter still talks about how amazing the food is.*

> *The food is bland—but it has to be to appeal to the masses.*

The consensus seems to be that people's impressions of food are highly subjective but most people like it just fine. Keep your expectations modest, and if you aren't enjoying your meal, speak up—they'll be happy to replace your food with something you might like better.

ADULT DINING The upscale Italian restaurant **Palo,** found on each ship and for which Disney charges an additional fee of $30, serves dinner to cruisers 18 and older. The *Dream* and *Fantasy* have a fifth restaurant, **Remy,** which serves sophisticated French cuisine and levies a $95 surcharge. Both Palo and Remy serve brunch on selected sea days (still adults-only). Both are also difficult to get into, so book a table at disneycruise.com at least 75 days before you sail. See page 162 for more information.

In addition to serving food that's superior to that served in the main dining rooms, the adult-dining restaurants also have a higher level of service. Another reader reports:

> *We went to Palo for dinner on our first night. I asked if the chef could make me chicken parmigiana, which wasn't on the menu. One minute later, the chef himself came out and apologized—he didn't have the ingredients on hand to make it. The next day, I got a call in my stateroom. It was my server from Palo. He said he had something special for me and came down to our stateroom with an entire tray of chicken parm—the chef had made it for brunch that day and wanted me to try his take on it. Truly amazing!*

Disney often tinkers with its adult-dining offerings, testing special events for specific sailings or individual ships. For example, some sailings of the *Fantasy* offer a $279 experience at Palo called **Be Our Chef,** providing guests with the opportunity to learn how to prepare four Palo dishes and take home a special keepsake. Other new or limited-time offerings have included dessert-only tasting experiences at Remy or meals themed to a specific style of food. If you're interested in enhanced adult-dining experiences, check your My Disney Cruise page online (see page 39) or call DCL at ☎ 800-951-3532.

On some sailings, you're limited to just one reservation at Palo or Remy, to give as many guests as possible the opportunity to experience them. If a sailing isn't full or if you elect to dine at one of the adult restaurants on your first night, you may be able to make more than one reservation in advance; check My Disney Cruise online for the specifics of your cruise. Or just stop by the restaurant in person and ask if you can make another reservation—this way, we've been able to eat at the adult restaurants on multiple nights of a single cruise.

ROOM SERVICE

OTHER THAN THE LAST MORNING OF YOUR CRUISE, room service is available on the Disney ships 24 hours a day. With the exception of a few packaged snacks and bottled beverages, there's no charge for room service other than a small tip for the porter who brings your meal ($1 or $2 per person or item ordered is appropriate). Typical lunch and dinner offerings include burgers, pizza, sandwiches, chicken fingers, salads, soups, and fresh fruit. The cheese-and-crackers plate is a particularly popular early-evening snack for guests assigned to the later dinner seating. Continental breakfast items are offered in the morning.

Room service is a great option if you want to eat breakfast quickly before heading out on a port excursion, if you want to dine on your verandah, if you want to eat while enjoying a movie on your stateroom TV, or if you just don't feel like getting dressed for dinner.

If you've brought your own wine on board (see page 42 for guidelines), room service can bring you empty glasses so you can enjoy your beverage in your cabin in style. Room service will also bring you a bucket of ice to chill your wine or Champagne.

The room-service menus always include a selection of warm giant cookies, usually chocolate chip or oatmeal raisin. If you want to be a hero to your kids (or your spouse), have room service bring them surprise cookies and milk as a bedtime snack. Even better, dive into the unadvertised room-service menu and order a round of Mickey ice cream bars for the room. All you have to do is ask.

THEME NIGHTS

unofficial **TIP**
On theme nights, each main dining area serves the same menu, so no one misses out on the fun.

ON CRUISES of longer than three nights, DCL gets festive with themed dinners. These include a **Pirates' Menu** (somewhat Caribbean-influenced on Pirate Night), **Till We Meet Again** (the final night of your cruise), the **Captain's Gala,** and **Prince and Princess Menus.** The menus will depend on your itinerary—for example, DCL Alaskan voyages typically add a seafood-focused night featuring local salmon and king crab.

In 2015 Disney began offering **Frozen-themed days** on some Alaskan and Northern European sailings. The movie-themed menu we were served on the *Magic* in Iceland included items like Sven's Carrot Soup, The Duke of Weselton's Favorite Assorted Meats, Oaken Warm Apple Pudding Cake, and Olaf's White Chocolate Floro Dome. In 2016, Disney started offering **Star Wars–themed days** on some sailings of the *Fantasy.* The themed menu items included Sand People Salad, Bantha Steak Empanadas, Opee Sea Killer Shrimp Cocktail, and Qui-Gon's Crisp Chicken. Dessert offerings included Calrissian Velvet Cake, Cloud City Macaroons, and a Frozen Carbonite Sundae. Finally, **Marvel-themed days** were added to some *Magic* sailings in late 2017. Menu items include Black Widow's Sliced Smoked Salmon, Dr. Banner's Greens and Lobster Salad, Bounty Hunter's Pastry, and Ravager's Devil's Food Cake.

DINING WITH KIDS

ON DISNEY CRUISE LINE, kids are people, too, when it comes to dining. While there are kids' menus featuring standard fare like chicken nuggets and mac and cheese, kids of all ages are welcome to eat from any part of the upper-deck buffet and order any item in the main dining rooms. If *you* want chicken nuggets for dinner and your 6-year-old wants escargot and prime rib, those are both equally fine.

Your serving team should be your partner in planning a strategy on how to best meet your family's dining needs. Do you want your kids' food brought to the table first so they're not ravenous? Do you want the bread basket left off the table so your kids fill up on more protein and veggies than carbs? Do you want only milk and water offered to your kids, not soda? Tell your serving team those things on the first night and they'll make notes about your preferences.

If you've been assigned to the second dinner seating, you can even arrange to have staff from the onboard childcare centers pick your kids up in the dining room so that you can linger over dessert while they're off playing. Speak to the kids' club staff if you'd like to do this. Be aware, however, that there are some special experiences that occur toward the end of the usual dinner hour, some of which your children might not want to miss. For example, at the end of dinner on one night at Animator's Palate on the *Fantasy* and the *Magic*, guests are treated to a short animated film created from diners' drawings. Most kids get a real kick out of seeing their artwork on screen.

In the realm of healthy eating, Disney is taking ongoing positive steps toward offering healthful options at its theme parks and on its ships. **Disney Check** (formerly Mickey Check) meals are available on all the rotational-dining restaurant kids' menus and on the menus posted on the DCL Navigator app. See tinyurl.com/disneycheckmeals for details. The Disney Check symbol indicates that the meal falls within specific dietary guidelines for calorie count; percentages of sugar, sodium, and fat; and recommended amounts of vitamins and other nutrients.

Prepackaged baby food is sold in the ships' gift shops, near the over-the-counter medications. The selection is typically limited, however, to two to four flavors of jarred baby food and one brand of single-serve baby formula. You're also welcome to bring your own packaged baby food aboard the ship. This must be sealed, commercially prepared baby food—homemade foods and open containers of any type are prohibited—and you must bring it with you in your carry-on luggage, not in your checked bags.

unofficial **TIP**
If you want your baby to have warm food, you have two options: ask the kitchen staff to puree food that they've prepared, or heat a jar of baby food in very hot water for a few minutes. (A buffet cereal bowl and hot water from the coffee/tea dispenser will do the trick.)

DCL chefs will also puree any food available on the ship for you. For instance, they can whip up something like pureed peas, carrots, or chicken quite easily. Also keep in mind that many of the soft foods already available on the ship may be fine for older babies and toddlers: mashed potatoes, oatmeal, soups, scrambled eggs, and so on.

If you're planning to bring your own baby food on board, be aware that your child will likely have to eat it cold unless you improvise (see our Unofficial Tip above). (At Walt Disney World, by contrast, guests have free use of microwave ovens in the food courts.) Additionally, you may not bring any cooking appliances on board with you: no electric kettles, rice cookers, hot plates, Sterno cans, or anything else that could be a fire hazard. Further complicating matters, DCL kitchens won't heat any food you've brought onto the ship, nor will they heat baby food that you've purchased in the onboard gift shop.

Children are welcome to eat in the main dining rooms on their own or with young siblings, cousins, or friends in their party. If, for example, the grown-ups are having dinner at the adults-only Palo restaurant, the kids can still have a nice meal of their own in their regular rotational restaurant. Parents will have to assess at what age their kids are ready for this, but we've seen many 8- and 9-year-olds dining together in the main dining rooms while their parents were having a romantic meal elsewhere. Let your server know that you're planning to do this, and they'll be sure to take special care of your child's dining needs. Of course, you could also feed your children room service or have them dine in the kids' club if you'd rather not have them at a full restaurant dinner on their own.

On longer sailings, Disney often offers a character breakfast in one of the main rotational dining rooms. Mickey, Goofy, Pluto, and sometimes other Disney favorites will stop by each guest table to sign autographs and pose for photos. While kids are the main fans of these meals, parties with adults only are also welcome to partake. There is no additional charge for character meals, but they do typically need to be reserved in advance. On some sailings, you can reserve through your My Disney Cruise page online (see page 39); on others, tickets will be distributed on a first-come, first-served basis on embarkation day (see page 237).

DRESS CODE

SHORTS AND T-SHIRTS are acceptable at all meals at the standard restaurants, even for adults. We think most adults will feel more appropriately dressed in pants or dresses at dinner; Bermuda shorts paired with a nice button-down shirt and shoes would probably also work.

A mother of four from Midland, Texas, praises Disney's shorts-tolerant policy:

> *There was no way I was going to pack 8–10 pairs of pants (minimum!) for my kids and my husband for our seven-night cruise. Shorts take up less luggage space and can be worn all day. It's less laundry for me to do when we get home, too.*

Swimwear and tank tops are prohibited at any time, and frankly you'd be freezing for most of your meal.

Many cruises of four nights or longer have a designated **Formal Night.** The food served in the rotational dining rooms is essentially the same as on any other night. But while dress-up clothing isn't required—you won't be refused service for being underdressed—you will find that many people enjoy upping their dinnerwear game for the occasion. The definition of *formal* is fluid: if you own a tux or evening gown that fits, go ahead and bring

> *unofficial* **TIP**
> Remy's dress code requires a tuxedo or jacket for men, along with dress pants. Ties are optional. Acceptable women's attire includes evening gowns, cocktail dresses, blouses and skirts, and pantsuits.

FAQs: What to Wear to Dinner

SOME OF THE MOST FREQUENTLY ASKED QUESTIONS we get from new cruisers have to do with what to wear to dinner. There's just something about seeing zillions of movies and TV shows with cruisers gliding around in tuxes and glamorous gowns that makes the average traveler question his or her sartorial IQ. Here's the lowdown.

What is *cruise casual*? This is DCL's term for acceptable casual attire in the main dining rooms—in short, anything goes except for swimwear and tank tops. We've never seen anyone turned away because of how they were dressed, and the "no tank tops" part seems open to interpretation: Erin has worn slacks or skirts with stylish sleeveless tops without incident.

The main dining rooms have additional dress suggestions depending on the specifics of your sailing—these might include formal, semiformal, pirate, tropical, Frozen, Marvel, or Star Wars attire. *All of these are completely optional.*

What does *formal attire* mean? In the strictest sense, it means tuxedos for men and evening gowns for women. Again, though, it's completely optional. Many guests choose to wear something nicer than cruise casual on formal night, but the range of dress is broad. *Very* broad.

What does *semiformal* mean? We've never seen an official definition of this anywhere, but for men this often means a business suit, with or without a tie; for women this typically means a cocktail dress of approximately knee length. But as with formal night, you'll see a wide range of styles.

Will people judge me if I don't dress up? If they do, that's on them, not you. If you feel self-conscious, you can always eat at Cabanas or order room service. But if you want to wear shorts in the main dining room on formal or semiformal night, go right ahead. It's your cruise. You paid for it. You do you.

What's the scoop with princess gowns? Just as in the Disney theme parks, a sizable subset of girls under age 10 enjoy rocking princess attire while cruising. If

it. We typically opt for a suit and cocktail attire, but you'll also see guys in khakis and pressed golf shirts. Kids should wear whatever nice clothes seem comfortable and appropriate. For girls, a cute sundress is fine; boys may wear a button-down shirt or a tie to look dapper.

Palo's official dress code is more upscale. Dress pants, slacks, and collared shirts are recommended for men, and a dress, skirt, or pants and a blouse are recommended for women. Jeans are permitted if they're in good condition (no holes). Verboten are tank tops, swimsuits/cover-ups, shorts, hats, cutoffs, torn clothing, T-shirts with offensive language and/or graphics, flip-flops, and athletic shoes.

SPECIAL DIETS

TRAVELING WHEN YOU EAT A SPECIAL DIET—gluten-free, vegan/vegetarian, allergen-free, kosher, and so on—can be a challenge. Disney

your daughter is one of them, you can buy dresses on the ship, but in our opinion some of the most charming princess wear is homemade.

What do I need to know about themed events? The most common themed event is Pirate Night, which takes place on almost all DCL sailings in the Caribbean and Bahamas, plus a few other destinations. Every guest gets a pirate-themed bandanna to wear, and the onboard shops have kids' pirate costumes for sale along with related accoutrements such as faux hook hands and eye patches. As with formal and semiformal nights, how much or little you participate is up to you: some guests go all-out, some guests don't dress up at all, and the majority fall somewhere in the middle, wearing, say, an eye patch and a pirate hat with their regular clothes. During Frozen, Star Wars, and Marvel Days (see page 190), about half the ship dresses up to varying degrees, even if it's just a themed T-shirt. If you like dressing up for Halloween, you'll love themed events, but if you don't, it's no big deal.

When are the formal, semiformal, and themed nights on my cruise? To find out what will be happening on your sailing, call ☎ 800-951-3532. In general, however:

- Three-night cruises typically have one standard cruise-casual night, one Pirate Night, and one semiformal night.
- Four-night cruises typically have two standard cruise-casual nights, one Pirate Night, and one semiformal night.
- Seven-night cruises typically have four standard cruise-casual nights, one themed night (Pirate Night or other depending on the destination), one semiformal night, and one formal night.
- Cruises longer than seven nights typically include additional cruise-casual dinners.

Are there times when the dress code isn't just a suggestion? Yes, the adult-dining venues strictly enforce their respective dress codes. We've seen guests get kicked out of Palo for being inappropriately dressed.

as a company has a pretty good reputation for handling special diets, but guests should be prepared (by investigating options ahead of time and noting dietary requests when booking) and be proactive (by making their needs known while on the ship) to ensure the best experience with the dining staff.

In addition to noting any food allergies or dietary requests at booking, you should consult DCL's official guidelines for guests with special diets. You can find this information online at disneycruise.disney.go.com/guest-services/special-dietary-requests. We also recommend that you follow up with a phone call at ☎ 407-566-3602. Other aspects of guest care also may be addressed by consulting Disney's guidelines for guests with disabilities: disneycruise.disney.go.com/guest-services/guests-with-disabilities. Complete the **Request Special Services** form on that page if any member of your party requires unique care or attention. If

HOW TO GET THE MOST FROM DCL DINING

1. Communication is key. Your serving team has been trained to make your happiness their number-one goal. If there's something that would make your meal better, let them know. Want your meal served faster or slower? Tell them. Want a Diet Coke waiting for you when you arrive at the table? Speak up. Don't want your kids to have dessert? Say so.

2. Anyone can order from either the children's or adult menu. If your kid wants filet mignon and you want chicken nuggets, no problem!

3. You can order from any part of the menu. The typical DCL main-dining-room menu is divided into four sections: appetizers, soups and salads, main courses, and desserts. You can order from all of these sections or any subset combination. If all you want is an appetizer and dessert, fine. If you just want two appetizers and a salad, fine. If you want just bread and dessert, fine.

4. All the main dining rooms are "all you care to eat." Seriously. The plated portion sizes are modest by American standards. If you want more of any dish, let them know and they'll bring more. You can order four entrées and three desserts all for yourself and your servers will be happy to make that happen. There is no extra charge for this. Don't be shy—people (read: we) do this every day.

5. Try it—you may like it! A Disney cruise is a fantastic opportunity to try new foods. Not sure you like scallops? Order the scallop dish and your favorite steak. If you try a bite of the scallops and you hate them, you've learned something and no one will take offense. Really, we mean it. And on the plus side, you or your kids may discover a new favorite food.

6. Don't be afraid to say "when." Many servers seem to think that the fuller guests are, the happier they are. so they may try to wheedle you into ordering more food than you really want. If you're full, decline politely but firmly.

7. You can order from a main dining room besides the one where you're currently eating. A full list of menus is available on the DCL Navigator app.

8. You may be able to get off-menu items. It's a well-known "secret" that all the restaurants have Mickey ice cream bars available for dessert, even though they're not listed on the menu. Similarly, you can usually get an unlisted dish of fresh fruit for dessert. If there's a food you like but you don't see it on the menu, ask about it. It may be available.

9. You can get some things for free in the main dining rooms that would cost you extra elsewhere on the ship. For example, kiddie "cocktails" like Shirley Temples and No-hitos cost money if you order them at an onboard bar or lounge, but the waitstaff will bring them to you at no charge during dinner.

10. They'll help you celebrate, but not with candles. DCL loves helping guests celebrate birthdays, anniversaries, graduations, and the like. They'll bring you extra desserts (or extra, extra, *extra* desserts) and an appropriate celebratory button, but open flames are not allowed on the ship, so little Mikey won't be able to blow out a candle.

11. You can order upgraded ice cream desserts for an extra charge. Vanellope's (*Dream*) and Sweet on You (*Fantasy*) will deliver any of their ice cream offerings to the main dining rooms. Early in the day, stop by to place an order, tell them your dining time and table number, and they'll make your child's wildest dreams come true.

you've booked your cruise through a travel agent, he or she may also be able to assist you in your communication with Disney.

Once you're on the ship, your servers also will ask you at the beginning of your cruise about any allergies or special diets. Take advantage of this opportunity to discuss your needs with them.

There are no separate kitchen facilities on board for guests with allergies, nor are there separate dining areas for allergen-free items. Also be aware that you'll need to restate your dining needs to any excursion company or restaurant serving you food while you're not on board. Use particular caution when dining in unfamiliar areas or when communicating in a language other than your own.

unofficial **TIP**
Ask your servers if any off-menu vegetarian items are available. During a recent sailing, we found that Indian food was available but not mentioned in print anywhere. We had a chat with our servers, and they brought us huge bowls of veggie curries and masalas that were tastier than many of the regular entrées.

If you have a specific brand preference—for instance, a type of soy milk or gluten-free waffle—you will most likely be disappointed to find that there isn't much in the way of choice, and there's not a lot that can be done about this when you're at sea. If your child will eat only one brand of something, your best bet is to bring it with you.

Unofficial Guide writer and veteran DCL cruiser **Laurel Stewart** sticks to a vegan diet at home. Here are her tips for non-meat-eaters:

> *I prefer to eat a plant-based diet, but as a travel writer, I often find myself reviewing foods for the sake of research that I wouldn't normally eat, and the last thing I want to do is make a big fuss. For vegetarians who eat eggs and/or dairy, DCL is easy: there are multiple options available to you at each meal, and there's no need to involve the servers. For vegans, however, it's a little trickier. Here are my meal-by-meal tips:*
>
> - **BREAKFAST** *Your easiest and best bet is the buffet, where you can see exactly what you're getting. Ask a server for nondairy milk.*
> - **LUNCH** *There's the buffet again. Also, you can request cheeseless pizza from the pool deck. I've gotten yummy wraps here, along with veggie burgers (vegans, skip the buns) and fries.*
> - **DINNER** *The main dining rooms do a decent job of accommodating special diets, but return cruisers who are vegan or vegetarian will almost certainly get tired of eating the same things again and again. Vegetarian entrées (a separate section of the menu) tend to be vegan, too, but good luck finding an appetizer or dessert that's egg- and dairy-free. Skip the appetizer and choose fresh fruit or sorbet for dessert. You may also be offered a nondairy ice cream like Tofutti or Rice Dream (which is great if you like those—I don't).*
> - **ADULT-ONLY DINING (PALO OR REMY)** *If your whole table is vegan, this is a hard pass: it's expensive, and the vegan options are very limited. Remy in particular seems not to understand the difference between gluten-free and vegan. (Yes, I get it, vegan is not a French thing.) If you're traveling with an omnivore who*

wants to dine at either place, be prepared to miss out. Ovo-lacto vegetarians have more and better choices at both restaurants.

- **CASTAWAY CAY** *You can ask ahead for veggie burgers, many of the sides are vegan, and there's lots and lots of fresh fruit.*
- **MISCELLANEOUS** *Room service doesn't offer the best options right off the menu, but ask when you call if there's anything that can be modified. The antipasti at Cove Café and Vista Café in the evenings are a good choice if you skip the cheeses.*

If you have a specific brand preference, for instance, a type of soy milk or gluten-free waffle, you'll most likely be disappointed to find there isn't much in the way of choice, and there's not a lot that can be done about this when you're at sea. If your child will eat only one brand of something, your best bet is to bring it with you.

For further discussion, see "Dietary Restrictions" in Part Five, Tips for Varied Circumstances (page 130).

MAKING RESERVATIONS

NO RESERVATIONS ARE REQUIRED for any night at any of the three standard rotational-dining restaurants. Reservations are required for Palo and Remy and can be made up to 120 days in advance in some circumstances. Reserve online at My Disney Cruise (see page 39).

Guests in suites or Concierge staterooms can **reserve 120 days in advance.**
Platinum Castaway Club members can **reserve 120 days in advance.**
Gold Castaway Club members can **reserve 105 days in advance.**
Silver Castaway Club members can **reserve 90 days in advance.**
All other guests can **reserve 75 days in advance.**

PRIVATE DINING Private dining rooms are located adjacent to Palo and Remy. These may be reserved by DCL for onboard activities, but if they're not, they may be reserved by guests for private experiences: a small wedding party, for instance, or a big birthday or anniversary party.

To request a private room, download the PDF form at tinyurl.com/paloprivatedining or tinyurl.com/remyprivatedining, and email it to dcl.cruise.activities@disney.com. Requests should be made at least 30 days in advance.

FULL-SERVICE RESTAURANTS: RATED AND RANKED

WE GET MORE THAN 140,000 dining surveys for Walt Disney World every year. Because DCL serves far fewer guests, we get substantially fewer surveys—in most cases, not enough to give a reasonable assurance to the numbers for any individual restaurant. For example, we've received just 21 ratings for **Remy** on the *Dream* and *Fantasy* over the past year, 100% positive. Still, the back-of-napkin confidence interval is somewhere roughly between 83% and 100%, even at an 80% confidence level. Do

we think Remy is fantastic? Absolutely. Do we have the numbers to back that up? Not quite yet.

For a moment, however, let's pretend that we've just sat down together to a nice glass of Glenmorangie and it's just a couple of friends sharing idle, possibly spurious chitchat. Here's what we *think* the surveys say so far:

- The average DCL sit-down restaurant gets a 92.5% thumbs-up from readers.
- **Palo** and **Remy** each get a 96% thumbs-up rating across all four DCL ships.
- The **Cabanas** buffets are rated at 100% on the *Fantasy,* 97% on the *Magic,* and 96% on the *Dream;* the *Wonder*'s Cabanas is rated below average, at 89%.
- Three of DCL's five lowest-rated restaurants are on the *Wonder* (**Triton's** at 81%, **Tiana's Place** at 82%, and the **Cabanas** buffet at 89%).
- The average DCL quick-service restaurant gets an 84.7% thumbs-up from readers.
- The pizza windows across all four ships get below-average marks from readers.
- The average DCL bar/lounge/coffee shop gets an 88.4% thumbs-up from readers.

To help you make your dining choices, we've developed profiles of DCL's sit-down restaurants, grouped by ship and listed alphabetically by restaurant following each ship's counter-service dining coverage. The profiles allow you to quickly check our assessments of a given restaurant's cuisine, star rating, quality rating, and specialties.

SCOTT SAYS *by Scott Sanders*

HOW TO DINE ON DISNEY CRUISE LINE

I SUGGEST THAT EVERYONE NEW TO DCL experience the rotational-dining-room menus first. If brunch at Remy or Palo is offered on your sailing, use that as an opportunity to experience the adult restaurants. Then, on your next cruise, explore the adult-only dinner options. Dinner is also a great opportunity to try something outside of your comfort zone. If you don't enjoy what you've ordered, your servers will bring you a backup dish.

DCL Rotational Restaurants by Cuisine

RESTAURANT	SHIP	OVERALL RATING	QUALITY RATING
AMERICAN/ASIAN			
Animator's Palate	All	★★★	★★★
AMERICAN/GLOBAL			
Rapunzel's Royal Table	*Magic*	★★★	★★★
AMERICAN/SOUTHERN			
Tiana's Place	*Wonder*	★★★	★★★
AMERICAN/CONTINENTAL			
Enchanted Garden	*Dream, Fantasy*	★★★	★★★
AMERICAN/FRENCH			
Lumiere's	*Magic*	★★★	★★★
Royal Court	*Fantasy*	★★★	★★★
Royal Palace	*Dream*	★★★	★★★
Triton's	*Wonder*	★★★	★★★
BUFFET			
Cabanas	All	★★★	★★★

DCL Adult-Only Restaurants by Cuisine

CUISINE / SHIP	OVERALL RATING	QUALITY RATING	VALUE RATING
FRENCH / REMY			
Dream, Fantasy	★★★★½	★★★★½	★★★★½
ITALIAN / PALO			
All ships (**Magic, Wonder, **Dream, Fantasy*)	★★★½* / ★★★★**	★★★½* / ★★★★**	★★★½* / ★★★★**

STAR RATING The star rating represents the entire dining experience: style, service, and ambience, in addition to the taste, presentation, and quality of the food. Five stars is the highest rating and indicates that the restaurant offers the best of everything. Four-star restaurants are above average; three-star restaurants offer good, though not necessarily memorable, meals. Two-star restaurants serve mediocre fare. (No DCL restaurants merit a single star.) Our star ratings don't correspond to ratings awarded by AAA, Mobil, Zagat, or other restaurant reviewers.

QUALITY RATING The food quality is rated on a scale of one to five stars, five being the best rating attainable. The quality rating is based on the taste, freshness of ingredients, preparation, presentation, and creativity of the food served. Price is not a consideration. If you want the best food available and cost is not an issue, you need look no further than the quality ratings.

DISNEY MAGIC DINING

COUNTER-SERVICE RESTAURANTS

Daisy's De-Lites

QUALITY B **PORTION** Small–Medium **LOCATION** Deck 9 Aft

WHEN TO GO Typical hours: breakfast, 6:30–9 a.m.; lunch, 11 a.m.–6:30 p.m. Check your *Personal Navigator* for exact schedule.

SELECTIONS Breakfast includes pastries, croissants, muffins, and yogurt; lunch offerings include sandwiches, wraps, salads, fruit, and cookies.

COMMENTS Daisy's is the highest-rated quick-service restaurant on the *Wonder* and *Magic*. It's a good alternative to the breakfast buffet if all you want is a croissant and some coffee. The wraps are small and tasty, and they make an excellent snack between lunch and dinner.

Duck-in Diner

QUALITY B **PORTION** Small–Medium **LOCATION** Deck 9 Aft

WHEN TO GO Typical hours: 11 a.m.–10 p.m. Check your *Personal Navigator* for exact schedule.

SELECTIONS Middle Eastern meats like chicken or lamb shawarma, served on your choice of pita bread or a tortilla. Burgers and fries are also available.

COMMENTS There are lots of fun toppings and condiments, such as hummus, pickled veggies, baba ghanoush, chile mayonnaise, *kachumber* (an Indian cucumber salad), garlic-mustard aioli, *sambal* (an Indonesian hot sauce similar to sriracha), tzatziki, or a mint-cilantro sauce.

Pinocchio's Pizzeria

QUALITY C **PORTION** Medium **LOCATION** Deck 9 Aft

WHEN TO GO Typical hours: 11 a.m.–6 p.m. Check your *Personal Navigator* for exact schedule.

SELECTIONS Cheese, pepperoni, and specialty pizzas (including veggie). Cheeseless pizza on request. If you're in the mood for fancy pizza, look for offerings labeled "flatbread." This is a more upscale version of pizza, often topped with mushrooms, pancetta, or other items of adult appeal.

COMMENTS About the same quality as frozen pizza . . . but hey, there are plenty of times when that's just what you want.

FULL-SERVICE RESTAURANTS

Animator's Palate ★★★ Deck 4 Aft

AMERICAN/ASIAN **QUALITY** ★★★ **SERVICE** ★★★★ **FRIENDLINESS** ★★★★

Reservations Not accepted. **When to go** Dinner. **Bar** Yes. **Alcohol** Red, white, and sparkling wines, plus mixed drinks and spirits. All alcohol costs extra. **Dress** Casual; no tank tops or swimwear. **Hours** Nightly dinner seatings usually at 5:45 and 8:15 p.m.; check your *Personal Navigator* for the exact schedule.

SETTING AND ATMOSPHERE The idea behind Animator's Palate is that you begin dining inside an old-fashioned black-and-white animated film that is slowly

colorized as dinner goes along. The entrance's walls are decorated with black charcoal sketches of various Disney characters. Inside, the entire color scheme starts out in black, white, and gray from floor to ceiling, including checkerboard-tile floor, black chairs, white tablecloths with black napkins, and black-and-white uniforms for the waitstaff. Even the ship's support columns are dressed up—in this case as white artist's brushes pointed to the ceiling.

Along the outside wall are video monitors that display images and "how to draw" sketches from Disney films. As the evening progresses, you'll notice bits of color being added to the walls and artwork, eventually becoming fully saturated by the end of your meal.

At the beginning of the *Animation Magic* dinner show (typically your second evening at Animator's Palate on a seven-night cruise or your third evening at Animator's Palate on a longer sailing), you're given a sheet of paper and a marker and instructed to draw a self-portrait. (There are guidelines on how to do this.) At the end of the evening, all of the diners' self-portraits are shown in an animated cartoon similar to Disney's 1929 short cartoon *The Skeleton Dance.*

HOUSE SPECIALTIES Pennette Bolognese, grilled tuna steak, ginger teriyaki beef, sesame halloumi parcels (a vegetarian entrée of goat-and-sheep-milk cheese in puff pastry), roasted-garlic dip with bread.

COMMENTS Disney characterizes the cuisine at Animator's Palate as Pacific Rim/American, but it's really just standard chain-restaurant fare. There are probably as many Italian selections—pasta, risotto, focaccia—as Asian. A handful of dishes, such as the vegetable stir-fry, have origins in the East; others are American dishes enrobed in a culinary kimono of sesame, ginger, or teriyaki sauce to make them "Pacific Rim." The food isn't *bad* . . . but it's not Asian either.

Cabanas ★★★ Deck 9 Aft

AMERICAN/BUFFET QUALITY ★★★ SERVICE ★★★★ FRIENDLINESS ★★★★

Reservations Not accepted. **When to go** Breakfast, lunch, and dinner. **Bar** Yes. **Alcohol** Red, white, and sparkling wines, plus mixed drinks and spirits. All alcohol costs extra. **Dress** Casual; no tank tops or swimwear at dinner. **Hours** Daily breakfast buffet, 7–10:45 a.m.; daily lunch buffet, noon–1:30 p.m.; nightly sit-down dinner, 6:30–8:30 p.m. Hours are subject to change, so check your *Personal Navigator* for the exact schedule.

SETTING AND ATMOSPHERE Cabanas is entered from either side of Deck 9 Aft. On either side is a line of buffet tables that run the length of the restaurant. Indoor and outdoor seating are arranged around the buffet. The indoor seating is air-conditioned and features floor-to-ceiling windows, affording excellent ocean views. Outdoor seating is great on mornings when the ship is docking because you're sometimes able to watch the port come into view. Large murals lining the walls display pirate and fish imagery. Coffee, soft drinks, juices, and water are served from dispensers placed at regular intervals throughout the restaurant.

HOUSE SPECIALTIES Made-to-order omelets for breakfast; lunch seafood bar including oysters, clams, crab legs, and peel-and-eat shrimp. Look for special regional breakfast items on Northern European sailings.

COMMENTS The breakfast and lunch buffets easily compare with those at upscale Las Vegas resorts and serve about as wide a variety of items. Breakfast includes everything from fruit, yogurt, and oatmeal to doughnuts, lox, and custom-made omelets. Even cold cereal has options: besides the usual

cornflakes and granola, there's a "build-your-own" muesli bar where you can add ingredients ranging from brown sugar to exotic dried fruits. Don't worry if you skipped dessert last night—you can get several at breakfast here. We haven't asked, but we'd bet hard cash that the staff would make you filet mignon if you requested nicely.

Lunch is a similarly lavish spread, with everything from chicken tenders, sandwiches, and burgers to salmon steaks and pasta. A big draw at lunch is the peel-and-eat shrimp, sometimes complemented by clams, oysters, and crab legs.

Cabanas switches from buffet to sit-down service for dinner. The menu changes frequently, usually along with the menus at the other main restaurants. Appetizers typically include soups and salads, along with meat- and fish-based dishes. Entrées usually include chicken, fish, steak, and vegetarian options. We recommend Cabanas for dinner at sunset on longer cruises as an alternative to dining a second time at one of the main restaurants, especially Lumiere's.

Lumiere's ★★★ Deck 3 Midship

AMERICAN/FRENCH QUALITY ★★★ SERVICE ★★★★ FRIENDLINESS ★★★★

Reservations Not accepted. **When to go** Breakfast. **Bar** Yes. **Alcohol** Limited selection of red, white, and sparkling wines, plus mixed drinks and spirits. All alcohol costs extra. **Dress** Casual; no tank tops or swimwear at dinner. **Hours** À la carte breakfast on select days, 8–9:30 a.m.; à la carte lunch on select days, 11:45 a.m.–1:30 p.m.; nightly dinner seatings usually at 5:45 and 8:15 p.m. Hours are subject to change, so check your *Personal Navigator* for the exact schedule.

SETTING AND ATMOSPHERE Despite the name, there are only a few references to *Beauty and the Beast* inside the restaurant. The most notable are the light fixtures, which contain a single red rose. There's also a mural on the back wall that depicts characters from the movie. Besides these, most of Lumiere's decor is Art Deco, which makes sense given the restaurant's location, just off the ship's atrium.

HOUSE SPECIALTIES Lobster bisque; crispy roasted duck breast.

COMMENTS With 95% thumbs-up among readers surveyed, Lumiere's is the highest-rated main dining room on any Disney cruise ship.

DCL puts escargot and French onion soup on the menus of its French-themed standard dining rooms. Besides these dishes, however, most of the rest of the menu is decidedly un-*français* and would be equally at home at your neighborhood bistro: grilled meats and chicken, a vegetarian tofu selection, and pasta. A couple of entrées, such as the herb-crusted rack of lamb and crispy duck breast, stand out. The Grand Marnier soufflé is the most popular dessert, but we think the brioche bread pudding with toffee sauce is even better.

Palo ★★★½ Deck 10 Aft

ITALIAN QUALITY ★★★½ VALUE ★★★½ SERVICE ★★★★½ FRIENDLINESS ★★★★

Reservations Required. **When to go** Brunch on sea days; dinner nightly. **Bar** Yes. **Alcohol** Large list of Italian wines, listed by region, plus select wines from around the world; mixed drinks and spirits; *limoncello*; grappa; ice wine. All alcohol costs extra. **Dress** Dress pants, slacks, and collared shirts are recommended for men; a dress, skirt, or pants and a blouse are recommended for women. Jeans are OK if in good condition (no holes).

No tank tops, swimsuits, swimsuit cover-ups, shorts, hats, cutoffs, torn clothing, T-shirts with offensive language and/or graphics, flip-flops, or athletic shoes. *The dress code is strictly enforced*—expect to be turned away if you don't comply. **Hours** Brunch on sea days on cruises of 4 nights or longer, 10 a.m.–12:30 p.m.; nightly dinner, 6–8:30 p.m. Hours are subject to change, so check your *Personal Navigator* for the exact schedule. **Special comments** An additional $30/person charge will be added to your cruise bill for each meal at Palo (charge may be waived for Platinum Castaway Club members). If you need to cancel a reservation, you must do so 24 hours in advance or the full per-person charge may be applied to your bill. Guests must be 18 or older to dine.

SETTING AND ATMOSPHERE Palo sits across the entire Aft section of Deck 10, which means that almost every seat has a spectacular view of the ocean sunset during dinner. On the *Magic,* Palo has contemporary decor, with tan-wood panels, round leather benches, and deep-purple fabric on the wood chairs. A small bar is available for guests waiting for their tables to become available; part of the kitchen is open to the view of guests sitting in the middle of the restaurant. Red-and-white-striped poles near the bar, evocative of those used to steer gondolas, call to mind Palo's roots in Venice (*palo* means "pole").

Because Palo is adults-only, it's much quieter than DCL's main dining rooms. The quietest tables of all are on the port side, aft (left and forward), tucked away behind the curve of the restaurant. If you're looking to do some people-watching with dinner, request a table on the starboard (right) side of the ship, near Palo's entrance. Brunch offers open seating, so sit wherever the view is best. Background music is mostly Italian and ranges from Vivaldi to Sinatra, as God intended.

HOUSE SPECIALTIES For a first course at dinner, try the fish-and-seafood soup, laden with mussels, clams, and lobster. The *antipasto freddo,* a selection of familiar cheeses and cured meats, could be a little more adventurous. Our favorite entrées are the pasta in lobster and tarragon sauce; the Dover sole; and the rack of lamb. The chocolate soufflé, by far the most popular dessert, is served with both dark- and white-chocolate sauces. If you're not in the mood for chocolate, there may also be other versions of the soufflé available. We were offered orange or almond soufflé on a recent sailing. It never hurts to ask.

Palo's brunch menu is the best on board. One large table is dedicated to breads, muffins, and pastries, along with sliced fruits and fresh vegetables (the roasted asparagus is tasty). An entire aquarium's worth of fish is available in another section, including shrimp cocktail, cured salmon, smoked-trout mousse, seared tuna, scallops, crab legs, crawfish, and mussels. Eggs cooked in every conceivable way, including Benedict, Florentine, Julia, and customized omelets, are on the menu, too. Not enough? Try the selection of made-to-order pizzas.

COMMENTS Palo, the *Magic*'s one upscale restaurant, is its own little island of adult serenity and food. Service is very good, and don't be surprised if the maître d' and your server are from Italy.

Dinners at Palo are tasty and relaxing, especially with a glass or two of wine. That being said, we think Palo is better for brunch—besides the best selection of midday food anywhere on the ship, the view out of Palo's windows is much better during the day; once the sun sets at dinner, Palo's spectacular windows just reflect the inside of the restaurant. If we could improve one thing at Palo, it would be the coffee served, which is Joffrey's. A restaurant this good can do better.

Finally, note that we rate Palo on the *Dream* and *Fantasy* higher overall, as well as for quality and value. It's undeniably very good on both the *Magic* and the *Wonder,* but the decor on the *Dream*-class ships is more sophisticated, and the kitchens are larger, allowing for better food preparation.

Disney sometimes adds special adult-dining experiences to specific sailings; see page 154 for more information.

Rapunzel's Royal Table ★★★ Deck 3 Aft

AMERICAN/GLOBAL QUALITY ★★★ SERVICE ★★★★ FRIENDLINESS ★★★★

Reservations Not accepted. **When to go** Dinner. **Bar** Yes. **Alcohol** A decent selection of reds, whites, and sparkling wines, plus mixed drinks and spirits. All alcohol costs extra. **Dress** Casual; no tank tops or swimwear at dinner. **Hours** Nightly dinner seatings usually at 5:30 and 8 p.m. Hours are subject to change, so check your *Personal Navigator* for the exact schedule.

SETTING AND ATMOSPHERE During the *Magic*'s 2018 dry dock, Carioca's restaurant was rethemed as Rapunzel's Royal Table—a nod to the popularity of the 2010 Disney film *Tangled.* Performers serenade you with songs from the movie, Rapunzel and Flynn Rider will visit your table, and Vladimir may stop by with his collection of ceramic unicorns. Encourage your kids to stick around to the end of the meal to see the procession of floating lanterns.

HOUSE SPECIALTIES Many dishes have a *Tangled* theme, such as the Snuggly Duckling Platter (sliced meats with pumpernickel and mustard); Maximus Salad (potatoes, carrots, and greens); Flynn Rider Platter (smoked pork loin with braised cabbage); Pascal Punch (Odwalla Mango Tango smoothie with coconut and strawberry yogurt); and the pièce de résistance, Tangled Pasta (angel hair tossed with basil pesto and scallops). Gimmicks aside, the food is quite good.

OTHER RECOMMENDATIONS On longer sailings, Rapunzel's serves German-style dishes in honor of the Brothers Grimm (who popularized Rapunzel and other characters in their bestselling *Children's and Household Tales*): pretzel bread, a grilled-knockwurst appetizer, green-and-white asparagus salad, trio of veal (tenderloin, pulled shank, and pasta with veal sauce), and Sacher torte dessert.

COMMENTS Rapunzel's kids' menu is full of safe bets—macaroni and cheese, mini-burgers, baked salmon, whole-wheat pasta—but much of the adult menu successfully straddles the line between kid-friendly and grown-up. It's a great way to introduce your children to more-sophisticated dishes that aren't totally weird or unfamiliar. (At Lumiere's, on the other hand, we've heard a few kids cry with dismay when they learned what escargot is.)

DISNEY WONDER DINING

COUNTER-SERVICE RESTAURANTS

Daisy's De-Lites

QUALITY B PORTION Small-Medium LOCATION Deck 9 Aft

COMMENTS See profile of Daisy's De-Lites on the *Magic* (page 165) for details.

Pete's Boiler Bites

QUALITY B **PORTION** Medium **LOCATION** Deck 9 Aft

WHEN TO GO Typical hours: 11 a.m.–6 p.m. Check your Personal Navigator for exact schedule.

SELECTIONS Grilled hot dogs and sausages; hamburgers and veggie burgers; chicken strips; chicken sandwiches; tacos; fries.

COMMENTS The tacos are surprisingly good. A nearby fixin's bar provides toppings for your order.

Pinocchio's Pizzeria

QUALITY C **PORTION** Medium **LOCATION** Deck 9 Aft

COMMENTS See profile of Pinocchio's Pizzeria on the *Magic* (page 165) for details.

FULL-SERVICE RESTAURANTS

Animator's Palate ★★★ Deck 4 Aft

AMERICAN/ASIAN **QUALITY** ★★★ **SERVICE** ★★★★ **FRIENDLINESS** ★★★★

COMMENTS See profile of Animator's Palate on the *Magic* (page 165) for details. Technological enhancements to the restaurant in late 2016 brought the *Wonder*'s Animator's Palate up to par with the ones on the other ships, at least when it comes to setting, atmosphere, and entertainment—the food, like that at the Animator's Palates on the other ships, is nothing to write home about.

Cabanas ★★★ Deck 9 Aft

AMERICAN/BUFFET **QUALITY** ★★½ **SERVICE** ★★★★ **FRIENDLINESS** ★★★★

COMMENTS See profile of Cabanas on the *Magic* (page 166) for details.

Palo ★★★½ Deck 10 Aft

ITALIAN **QUALITY** ★★★½ **VALUE** ★★★½ **SERVICE** ★★★★½ **FRIENDLINESS** ★★★★

COMMENTS See profile of Palo on the *Magic* (page 167) for details.

Tiana's Place ★★★ Deck 3 Aft

AMERICAN/NEW ORLEANS **QUALITY** ★★ **SERVICE** ★★★★ **FRIENDLINESS** ★★★★

Reservations Not accepted. **When to go** Breakfast, lunch, and dinner. **Bar** Yes. **Alcohol** Limited selection of red, white, and sparkling wines, plus mixed drinks and spirits. All alcohol costs extra. **Dress** Casual; no tank tops or swimwear at dinner. **Hours** Breakfast buffet on select days, 7:30–10:45 a.m.; lunch buffet on select days, noon–1:30 p.m.; nightly dinner seatings at 5:45 and 8:15 p.m. Hours are subject to change, so check your *Personal Navigator* for exact times.

SETTING AND ATMOSPHERE Tiana's Place is a complete overhaul of this restaurant's previous incarnation, the dismal Parrot Cay. An homage to the dining venue in *The Princess and the Frog,* Tiana's Place evokes a New Orleans supper club, with rustic elements interspersed with purple-and-green fabrics and fixtures of polished gold (think upscale Mardi Gras). Live music—a first for a DCL rotational-dining room—is performed on the main stage and features the jazz, swing, and blues sounds of Louisiana.

HOUSE SPECIALTIES Look for close approximations of New Orleans specialties, including a shrimp-and-grits appetizer, pepper pot soup, and a roasted Creole half-chicken with corn and buttered chard. The buttermilk beignets, served with a chocolate-espresso dipping sauce, are delicious. There's also an appropriately themed Bananas Foster sundae.

COMMENTS Readers rate Tiana's as the second worst sit-down restaurant in the DCL fleet, at 82% thumbs-up. As for us, it's a toss-up: Erin loves the food, while Len wishes for a secret door leading to a quieter restaurant with more authentic flavor.

Triton's ★★★ Deck 3 Midship

AMERICAN/FRENCH **QUALITY** ★★★ **SERVICE** ★★★★ **FRIENDLINESS** ★★★★

Reservations Not accepted. **When to go** Lunch. **Bar** Yes. **Alcohol** Limited selection of red, white, and sparkling wines, plus mixed drinks and spirits. All alcohol costs extra. **Dress** Casual; no tank tops or swimwear at dinner. **Hours** Daily breakfast, 8–9:30 a.m.; daily lunch, noon–1:30 p.m.; nightly dinner seatings at 5:45 and 8:15 p.m. Hours are subject to change, so check your *Personal Navigator* for details.

SETTING AND ATMOSPHERE In case you've forgotten that King Triton is Ariel's father in *The Little Mermaid,* a large tile mosaic of Triton and Ariel sits at the back of this restaurant as a reminder. Besides the art, Triton's blue, beige, and gray color scheme lends a vaguely seaworthy theme to the inside.

HOUSE SPECIALTIES Breakfast features the usual suspects: fruit, cereal, eggs, waffles, bacon, sausage, and pastries. Lunch includes soups, salads, sandwiches, and burgers, plus a couple of alternative offerings such as pasta or fish. Dinner appetizers include escargots and French onion soup; order one of the crispy duck breasts for the table if no one is adventurous enough to try it themselves. The Grand Marnier soufflé is probably the most popular dessert.

COMMENTS With 81% thumbs-up, readers rate Triton's as the worst DCL sit-down restaurant. We're not really sure why, though—there's a decent selection of French-inspired entrées, plus enough standard vegetarian, chicken, beef, and pork dishes to fill up almost anyone. Even more puzzling, Lumiere's on the *Magic* is essentially the same restaurant with substantially higher ratings.

DISNEY DREAM DINING

COUNTER-SERVICE RESTAURANTS

Fillmore's Favorites

QUALITY C **PORTION** Small–Medium **LOCATION** Deck 11 Midship

WHEN TO GO Typical hours: 10:30 a.m.–6 p.m. Check your *Personal Navigator* for the exact schedule.

SELECTIONS Sandwiches, wraps, salads, fruit, cookies.

COMMENTS While the menu can change, it usually includes a roast-beef-and-Cheddar sandwich, a Greek salad veggie wrap, and a chicken Caesar wrap. Fresh fruit, such as whole bananas, grapes, and oranges, is also available.

Luigi's Pizza

QUALITY C **PORTION** Medium **LOCATION** Deck 11 Midship

WHEN TO GO Typical hours: 10:30 a.m.–6:30 p.m. Check your *Personal Navigator* for the exact schedule.

SELECTIONS Cheese, pepperoni, barbecue-chicken, freshly baked pretzels, and veggie pizza slices.

COMMENTS As with the pizza joints on the *Magic* and *Wonder,* you'd never mistake Luigi's for authentic pizza, but it's fine if you need a quick bite. Occasionally open after dinner, when ordering a whole pie is a convenient alternative to room service or restaurant dining.

Tow Mater's Grill

QUALITY C **PORTION** Large **LOCATION** Deck 11 Midship

WHEN TO GO Typical hours: 10:30 a.m.–11 p.m. most days. Check your *Personal Navigator* for the exact schedule.

SELECTIONS Grilled hot dogs, sausages, burgers, and chicken sandwiches; fried-chicken strips; fries.

COMMENTS The fries and burgers serve as sustenance for chlorine-addled kids (that is, if they can be pried out of the pool long enough to eat). The chicken strips and hot dogs are the best things on the menu. A nearby fixin's bar provides toppings for burgers and sandwiches.

Vanellope's Sweets & Treats ★★★

QUALITY B **PORTION** Large **LOCATION** Deck 11 Midship

WHEN TO GO Typical hours: 11:30 a.m.- 10:30 p.m., with a 1-hour closure during the late afternoon. Hours are subject to change; check your *Personal Navigator* for updates.

SELECTIONS Named for *Wreck-It Ralph*'s Vanellope Von Schweetz, Vanellope's Sweets & Treats serves ice cream and house-made gelato with an extensive array of toppings, along with cupcakes, cookies, candy apples, chocolate truffles, and bulk and packaged candies. Ice cream and gelato flavors vary seasonally. Kick your sugar buzz into high gear with espresso-based drinks.

COMMENTS You can get free soft-serve at the **Eye Scream** machine and smoothies at an extra charge at **Frozone Treats,** both around the corner. The more upscale treats at Vanellope's start at $2.50 for a single scoop of ice cream or $2.95 for a scoop of gelato. Toppings are 50¢ each; a waffle cone costs an extra 75¢. Sundae selections are imaginative, and serving sizes are generous—even the smallest sundaes, starting at $4.95, can likely serve two. If you have a large group, indulge in Ralph's (as in Wreck-It) Family Challenge: an eight-scoop, eight-topping sundae served in a souvenir trophy cup. Like Sweet on You on the *Fantasy* (see page 178), Vanellope's delivers to the main dining rooms.

FULL-SERVICE RESTAURANTS

Animator's Palate ★★★ Deck 3 Aft

AMERICAN/ASIAN **QUALITY** ★★★ **SERVICE** ★★★★ **FRIENDLINESS** ★★★★

Reservations Not accepted. **When to go** Dinner. **Bar** Yes. **Alcohol** Red, white, and sparkling wines, plus mixed drinks and spirits. All alcohol costs extra. **Dress** Casual; no tank

tops or swimwear. **Hours** Nightly dinner seatings usually at 5:45 and 8:15 p.m.; check your *Personal Navigator* for the exact schedule.

SETTING AND ATMOSPHERE Each DCL ship has a restaurant called Animator's Palate, and all four pay tribute to Disney's (and Pixar's) animation processes, though each ship has a slightly unique execution of the theme. Animator's Palate on the *Dream* (and the *Fantasy*) features vivid colors throughout. The floor has red carpet with stars of silver, gold, and blue, and the walls are the color of caramel. The backs of the dining-room chairs are patterned after Mickey Mouse's pants, with red backs, yellow buttons, and a black "belt" at the top.

Shelves along the walls hold small toy versions of Disney and Pixar icons in between video screens displaying animation sketches from popular Disney movies. The more interesting ones will show on one screen how one complete animated cell is drawn, starting from sketches of the main characters to how key background elements are drawn, color samples for walls and floors, and the finished art. The art changes throughout the evening, keeping the view fresh for everyone.

At certain points during your dinner, some of the screens will switch from sketches to an interactive video featuring the surfer-dude turtle Crush from *Finding Nemo*. When we say "interactive," we mean it—Crush will ask you questions and react to your responses, allowing you to have an actual conversation with him. Based on the same real-time computer graphics found in Epcot's *Turtle Talk with Crush* attraction (also found at other Disney parks), the technology behind this minishow allows Crush's mouth to move in the appropriate way as his words are spoken. Parents may be more amazed than children.

HOUSE SPECIALTIES Penne Bolognese, grilled tuna steak, ginger teriyaki beef, lemon-thyme chicken, roasted-garlic dip served with bread.

COMMENTS The "wow" factor doesn't extend to the food—as is the case at the other Animator's Palates, the cuisine isn't much different from what you might get at Applebee's or Chili's, despite the Pacific Rim/American designation.

Cabanas ★★★ Deck 11 Aft

AMERICAN/BUFFET QUALITY ★★★ SERVICE ★★★★ FRIENDLINESS ★★★★

COMMENTS See profile of Cabanas on the *Magic* (page 166) for details.

Enchanted Garden ★★★ Deck 2 Midship

AMERICAN/CONTINENTAL QUALITY ★★★ SERVICE ★★★★ FRIENDLINESS ★★★★

Reservations Not accepted. **When to go** Lunch, especially on your embarkation day, when the crowds are headed to Cabanas. **Bar** Yes. **Alcohol** Limited selection of red, white, and sparkling wines, plus mixed drinks and spirits. All alcohol costs extra. **Hours** Breakfast buffet on select days, 8–10 a.m.; lunch on select days, noon–1:30 p.m.; nightly dinner seatings at 5:45 and 8:15 p.m. Hours are subject to change, so check your *Personal Navigator* for the exact schedule.

SETTING AND ATMOSPHERE Designed to evoke a 19th-century French greenhouse, with patinaed cast-iron arches supporting a spectacular ceiling display of plants, sun, and sky, Enchanted Garden is the prettiest of the *Dream*'s three main rotational restaurants.

During lunch, lights in the ceiling simulate the midday sun, and diners see what appears to be ivy climbing up the side of the ironworks; as the sun sets, the "sky" turns to dusk and eventually to dark. Lights, in the shape of flowers and hung from the ceiling, open their "petals" as night falls.

The centerpiece of Enchanted Garden is a burbling concrete fountain, 7 feet tall, topped by Mickey Mouse. The best seats are the round, raised, high-backed booths along the center walk, which allow you to see all the action in one half of the restaurant. Look for framed Hermès scarves outside the restaurant—a posh touch of France. Disney says Enchanted Garden is inspired by the gardens at Versailles, but we think it looks more like the hothouse at Paris's Jardin des Plantes. We could be wrong, though.

HOUSE SPECIALTIES Roast pork tenderloin seasoned with smoked salt; scallops with roasted asparagus; pan-seared sea bass with fava beans and pea risotto; and seaweed with squid.

COMMENTS The menu is more American bistro than Paris brasserie, despite the French setting. Besides substituting brioche for bread, the Frenchiest thing on the menu is the word *julienne* to describe how the vegetables are cut.

There's usually at least one pork dish, such as roast pork tenderloin, one chicken dish (baked or roasted), and a steak or prime rib available, along with several seafood and vegetarian options. Honestly, you could serve these dishes at Animator's Palate or Royal Court without anyone noticing, but maybe the scenery here makes the food taste a little bit better.

Palo ★★★★ Deck 12 Aft and Starboard

ITALIAN QUALITY ★★★★ VALUE ★★★★ SERVICE ★★★★½ FRIENDLINESS ★★★★

Reservations Required. **When to go** Brunch on sea days; dinner nightly. **Bar** Yes. **Alcohol** Large list of Italian wines, listed by region, plus select wines from around the world; mixed drinks and spirits; *limoncello*; grappa; ice wine. All alcohol costs extra. **Dress** Dress pants, slacks, and collared shirts are recommended for men; a dress, skirt, or pants and a blouse are recommended for women. Jeans are OK if in good condition (no holes). No tank tops, swimsuits, swimsuit cover-ups, shorts, hats, cutoffs, torn clothing, T-shirts with offensive language and/or graphics, flip-flops, or tennis shoes. *The dress code is strictly enforced*—expect to be turned away if you don't comply. **Hours** Brunch, 10 a.m.–12:30 p.m. on sea days on cruises of 4 nights or longer; nightly dinner, 6–8:30 p.m. Hours are subject to change, so check your *Personal Navigator* for the exact schedule. **Special comments** An additional $30/person charge will be added to your cruise bill for each meal at Palo (charge may be waived for Platinum Castaway Club members). If you need to cancel a reservation, you must do so 24 hours in advance or the full per-person charge may be applied to your bill. Guests must be 18 or older to dine.

SETTING AND ATMOSPHERE Palo is on the starboard side at the back of Deck 12, opposite the adults-only French restaurant Remy (see next profile) and adjacent to the Meridian bar. Although all four Disney ships have a restaurant named Palo, the restaurants on the *Dream* and *Fantasy* have the nicest furnishings.

The entrance to Palo on the *Dream* has a pretty gold-and-ruby-colored glass chandelier, surely one of the most photographed parts of the restaurant. Guests entering Palo walk past a glass-enclosed wine closet and see the main dining room, decorated with deep mahogany wood-paneled walls and columns

and rich burgundy carpet. One half of the room features deep-green patterned fabric on the booths and chairs, with paintings of the Italian countryside and seashore along the walls. The other half of Palo uses a saturated red fabric for its seating; illustrations of Italian villas hang on the walls. Also within the *Dream*'s Palo, and unique to Disney's larger ships, are small private dining rooms with custom fabrics, wallpaper, and lighting. Stick your head inside if one is empty, and you'll see how the wealthy merchants of Venice might have lived.

Naturally, tables next to Palo's floor-to-ceiling windows afford the best views, but tables near the back wall sit on an elevated platform, allowing diners there to see over the tables nearest the windows. Our favorite table is to the left of the entrance, tucked by itself in a rounded corner along the inside wall and surrounded by a mural depicting Venice from the water. It's a bit high profile, though; quieter seats are available at the far ends of either side of the restaurant. Brunch offers open seating, so sit wherever the view is best.

HOUSE SPECIALTIES Start your dinner with the cioppino, a tomato-based fish stew with squid, clams, and shrimp, or the white-bean soup, with prosciutto and perfectly al dente beans. A complete selection of pasta is available, either as a separate course or as an entrée. One of these, the vegetarian mushroom risotto, is so rich you'd swear it had meat in it. Our favorite entrée is the rack of lamb, which comes in a crispy crust of Parmesan cheese and oregano. For seafood, we like the grilled tuna with potato risotto a bit more than the grilled scallops. The chocolate soufflé, by far the most popular dessert, comes with both dark- and white-chocolate sauces.

As on the other ships, Palo's brunch menu is excellent. One large table is dedicated to breads, muffins, and pastries, along with sliced fruits and fresh vegetables (the roasted asparagus is tasty). An entire aquarium's worth of fish is available in another section, including shrimp cocktail, cured salmon, smoked-trout mousse, seared tuna, scallops, crab legs, crawfish, and mussels. Eggs cooked in every conceivable way, including Benedict, Florentine, Julia, and customized omelets, are on the menu, too. Not enough? Try the selection of made-to-order pizzas. If there's any room left for dessert, small cups of tiramisu will take care of your sweet tooth.

COMMENTS Given what you've already spent on the cruise, dropping another $30 to dine at Palo requires no thought whatsoever.

Remy ★★★★½ Deck 12 Aft

FRENCH QUALITY ★★★★½ VALUE ★★★★½ SERVICE ★★★★½ FRIENDLINESS ★★★★

Reservations Required. **When to go** Dinner. **Bar** Yes. **Alcohol** An extensive selection of French wines and Champagnes. **Dress** Jackets and dress shirts for men; dresses, blouses, and skirts, or pantsuits for women. *The dress code is strictly enforced*—expect to be turned away if you don't comply. **Hours** Brunch on sea days on cruises of 4 nights or longer, 10 a.m.–12:30 p.m.; nightly dinner, 6–9 p.m. Hours are subject to change, so check your *Personal Navigator* for the exact schedule. **Special comments** An additional $60/person charge will be added to your cruise bill for each brunch at Remy, $95/person for each dinner. The wine pairing for dinner is $105/person. A Remy dessert-tasting experience is $55/person, with a Champagne pairing available for an additional $30/person. If you need to cancel a reservation, you must do so by 2 p.m. on the day of your reservation or the full per-person charge will be applied to your bill. Guests must be age 18 and older to dine.

SETTING AND ATMOSPHERE Remarkably elegant and understated for a Disney restaurant—and one named after a cartoon rat at that. The most prominent features at Remy are the floor-to-ceiling windows, which look out over the ocean on the port side of the ship from high on Deck 12; and the Art Nouveau lights, which seem to spring from the floor as thick vines, branching out into yellow lights as they reach the ceiling. Besides those touches, and perhaps the oval mirrors along the wall opposite the windows, the rest is simple and elegant: oval, round, and square tables, all with white-linen tablecloths, and round-backed wood chairs with white upholstery. The olive-green carpet pattern matches the Art Nouveau decor without being distracting. A small teak deck wraps around Remy, allowing you to walk out for a quick breath of fresh air between courses.

HOUSE SPECIALTIES The tasting menu may be one of the best 3-hour dining experiences you'll ever have. Splurge on the wine pairing. If the tasting menu sounds like too much food, Remy's meat entrées usually include Australian Wagyu beef and pork from central France.

Remy also offers an extensive brunch on days when the ship is at sea. Like the brunch at Palo, Remy's has an extensive selection, including fruit, pastries, seafood, beef, pork, pasta, and fish. A Champagne pairing is available for an additional $30 per person. We prefer the dinner experience, but spending the morning at Remy is a lovely way to start a day at sea.

Remy sometimes offers special dining experiences. Recent ones have included the **Pompidou's Patisseries Dessert Experience** (sometimes called the **Remy Dessert Experience**), which includes a sampling of six premium desserts for $55 per person, or $80 per person with a supplementary Champagne tasting, and **Petites Assiettes de Remy** (**Small Plates of Remy**), a six-course savory tasting at a similar price point. During these special offerings, chefs typically describe the history of each item and explain the sourcing of the ingredients. If you're interested in these experiences, check online at My Disney Cruise (see page 39) or call DCL at ☎ 800-951-3532 to see if they'll be offered during your sailing.

COMMENTS What makes a great restaurant such as Remy different from restaurants that are simply very good is that, while the latter usually have a few signature dishes that they do very well, virtually *everything* at Remy is nothing short of exceptional. An appetizer of carrots—yes, the root vegetable—will be the most extraordinary carrots you've ever had, probably in varieties and colors you didn't know existed, and with a flavor that is the pure essence of carrot-ness. Now imagine a meal of three to eight courses, all equally as good, ranging from soups, seafood, and beef, to sides, cheese courses, and desserts. That's your average evening at Remy.

Remy offers both a standard dinner menu and a chef's tasting menu. If you have the time or the inclination, order the latter—it allows you to savor every bit of creativity and technical mastery the kitchen can muster.

A couple of examples from our meals: One course early in the tasting menu was billed as the chef's interpretation of a grilled-cheese sandwich with tomato soup. The entire serving consisted of one small, golden-brown cube, about the size of a postage stamp on each side, designed to be eaten in one bite. The outside of the cube was a cheddar cheese, coated with seasoned breadcrumbs and fried lightly. Inside was a tomato sauce, barely seasoned and reduced to concentrate the flavor. The first bite—it took maybe two to finish the entire thing—tasted

of crispy, butter-fried bread and melted cheese. The second was all tomato: bright, slightly acidic, and sweet at the same time, balancing out the butter and cheese from the outside coating. Remy's chefs had both amplified the flavors to their essence and reduced the size of the dish to its bare minimum.

Another appetizer was the chef's take on cheese pizza. Its base was a small, crispy wafer of baked bread, barely thicker than a sheet of paper. On top of that was a half-inch layer of white foam, about the consistency of whipped cream but made from Parmesan cheese. And on top of that were placed three small basil leaves.

The pizza's tomato "sauce" was presented in a Champagne flute as a clear, intensely flavored liquid. The kitchen had achieved this transparency by repeatedly filtering juice from ripe tomatoes through layers of fine cheesecloth, trapping the red bits and letting the clear juice through. We were instructed to follow a bit of the crust and cheese foam with a sip from the flute, and the flavors combined beautifully.

One last tip on the tasting menu: Remy offers a wine pairing for most courses. The selections are very good, but it's a *lot* of wine that could easily be split between two people. Len's first evening at Remy began with a martini at Meridian and continued with the wine pairing for dinner. The first few courses were memorable, but by the time he realized how much alcohol was involved, it was too late. The last quarter of the meal is a hazy memory that apparently involved Len applauding someone else's cheese cart as it rolled by for dessert. That called for another dinner at Remy, minus the booze.

Royal Palace ★★★ Deck 3 Midship

AMERICAN/FRENCH QUALITY ★★★ SERVICE ★★★★ FRIENDLINESS ★★★★

Reservations Not accepted. **When to go** Lunch. **Bar** Yes. **Alcohol** Limited selection of red, white, and sparkling wines, plus mixed drinks and spirits. **Dress** Casual; no tank tops or swimwear at dinner. **Hours** Daily breakfast, 8–9:30 a.m.; daily lunch, noon–1:30 p.m.; nightly dinner seatings at 5:45 and 8:15 p.m. Hours are subject to change, so check your *Personal Navigator* for the exact schedule.

SETTING AND ATMOSPHERE The most attractive part of Royal Palace may be its entrance, done in gold-and-white-marble tile below a pretty flower-shaped chandelier accented with blue-glass "diamonds" and red "rubies." Inside the doors, gold-and-white faux-marble columns form a circle just inside one ring of tables; royal-blue carpet with gold trim lines the inner part of the restaurant. Drapes cover the windows lining one side of the room, and mosaic-tile pictures of Disney princesses line another.

HOUSE SPECIALTIES Breakfast is standard buffet fare: fruit, cereal, eggs, waffles, bacon, sausage, and pastries. Lunch includes soups, salads, sandwiches, and burgers, plus a couple of alternative offerings such as pasta or fish. Dinner appetizers include escargots and French onion soup; the wild-boar tenderloin entrée is tasty. The Grand Marnier soufflé is probably the most popular dessert.

COMMENTS You know Disney is serious about the French theme when they put snails on the appetizer menu. There are other Gallic influences on the menu—many of the entrées have sauces made with butter, wine, or spirits—plus enough standard vegetarian, chicken, beef, and pork dishes to make anyone happy.

DISNEY FANTASY DINING

COUNTER-SERVICE RESTAURANTS

Fillmore's Favorites

QUALITY C **PORTION** Small-Medium **LOCATION** Deck 11 Midship

COMMENTS See profile of Fillmore's Favorites on the *Dream* (page 171) for details.

Luigi's Pizza

QUALITY C **PORTION** Medium **LOCATION** Deck 11 Midship

COMMENTS See profile of Luigi's Pizza on the *Dream* (page 172) for details.

Sweet on You Ice Cream & Sweets

QUALITY B **PORTION** Large **LOCATION** Deck 11 Midship

WHEN TO GO Typical hours: 11 a.m.–10:30 p.m., with a 1-hour closure during the later afternoon. Hours are subject to change; check your *Personal Navigator* for updates.

SELECTIONS Choose from chocolate truffles (about $2 each), macarons (French meringue cookies, about $2 each), fancy cupcakes (about $4 each), wrapped candy by the pound, and an array of Mickey-themed pastries. The star attraction is the freezer case, stocked with ice cream, house-made gelato, and toppings aplenty. Ice cream and gelato flavors vary seasonally. Kick your sugar buzz into high gear with espresso-based drinks.

COMMENTS You can get free soft-serve at the machine by the pool and free ice cream at dinner in the main dining rooms. If you need a fancier fix, single scoops at Sweet on You start at $2.50 for ice cream and $2.95 for gelato. Toppings cost 50¢ each, and waffle cones cost 75¢. Sundae selections are imaginative and serving sizes are generous; even the smallest sundaes, starting at $4.95, can likely serve two. For a special indulgence, try the create-your-own ice cream sandwich ($4.95): choose any combination of two cookies (white chocolate-macadamia, chocolate-chip fudge, M&M's, chocolate chunk, or peanut butter) and any flavor of ice cream or gelato. Like Vanellope's on the *Dream* (see page 172), Sweet on You delivers to the main dining rooms.

Tow Mater's Grill

QUALITY C **PORTION** Large **LOCATION** Deck 11 Midship

COMMENTS See profile of Tow Mater's Grill on the *Dream* (page 172) for details.

FULL-SERVICE RESTAURANTS

Animator's Palate ★★★ Deck 3 Aft

AMERICAN/ASIAN **QUALITY** ★★★ **SERVICE** ★★★★ **FRIENDLINESS** ★★★★

Reservations Not accepted. **When to go** Dinner. **Bar** Yes. **Alcohol** Red, white, and sparkling wines, plus mixed drinks and spirits. All alcohol costs extra. **Dress** Casual; no tank tops or swimwear. **Hours** Nightly dinner seatings usually at 5:45 and 8:15 p.m.; check your *Personal Navigator* for the exact schedule.

SETTING AND ATMOSPHERE Each DCL ship has a restaurant called Animator's Palate, and all four of them pay tribute to Disney's (and Pixar's) animation processes, though each ship has a slightly unique execution of the theme. Animator's Palate on the *Fantasy* (and the *Dream*) features vivid colors throughout. The floor has red carpet with stars of silver, gold, and blue, and the walls are the color of caramel. The backs of the dining-room chairs are patterned after Mickey Mouse's pants, with red backs, yellow buttons, and a black "belt" at the top.

Shelves along the walls hold small toy versions of Disney and Pixar icons in between video screens displaying animation sketches from popular Disney movies. The more interesting ones will show on one screen how one complete animated cell is drawn, starting from sketches of the main characters to how key background elements are drawn, color samples for walls and floors, and the finished art. The art changes throughout the evening, keeping the view fresh for everyone.

The version of Animator's Palate on the *Fantasy* includes *Animation Magic,* an impressive special effect. At the beginning of the second night you dine there, you're given a sheet of paper and crayon and told to draw a self-portrait. At the end of the evening, all of the diners' self-portraits are shown in an animated cartoon similar to Disney's 1929 short cartoon *The Skeleton Dance.*

At your first scheduled dinner at Animator's Palate, you get a different show. At certain points during your second dinner, some of the screens will switch from sketches to an interactive video featuring the surfer-dude turtle Crush from *Finding Nemo.* When we say *interactive,* we mean it—Crush will ask you questions and react to your responses, allowing you to have an actual conversation with him. Based on the same real-time computer graphics found in Epcot's *Turtle Talk with Crush* attraction (also at other Disney parks), the technology behind this minishow allows Crush's mouth to move in the appropriate way as his words are spoken. Parents may be more amazed than children.

HOUSE SPECIALTIES Ginger-teriyaki beef tenderloin; roasted-garlic or red-pepper dip with bread.

COMMENTS When it comes to the food, it's a tale as old as time—as is the case at the other three Animator's Palates. The dishes are pedestrian chain-restaurant fare, despite the Pacific Rim/American designation. On the *Fantasy,* anyway, the entertainment makes up for whatever the food lacks.

Cabanas ★★★ Deck 11 Aft

AMERICAN/BUFFET QUALITY ★★★★ SERVICE ★★★★ FRIENDLINESS ★★★★

COMMENTS See profile of Cabanas on the *Magic* (page 166) for details.

Enchanted Garden ★★★ Deck 2 Midship

AMERICAN/CONTINENTAL QUALITY ★★★ SERVICE ★★★★ FRIENDLINESS ★★★★

COMMENTS See profile of Enchanted Garden on the *Dream* (page 173) for details.

Palo ★★★★ Deck 12 Aft and Starboard

ITALIAN QUALITY ★★★★ VALUE ★★★★ SERVICE ★★★★½ FRIENDLINESS ★★★★

COMMENTS See profile of Palo on the *Dream* (page 174) for details.

Remy ★★★★½ Deck 12 Aft

FRENCH QUALITY ★★★★½ VALUE ★★★★½ SERVICE ★★★★½ FRIENDLINESS ★★★★

COMMENTS See profile of Remy on the *Dream* (page 175) for details.

Royal Court ★★★ Deck 3 Midship

AMERICAN/FRENCH QUALITY ★★★ SERVICE ★★★★ FRIENDLINESS ★★★★

Reservations Not accepted. **When to go** Lunch. **Bar** Yes. **Alcohol** Limited selection of red, white, and sparkling wines, plus mixed drinks and spirits. **Dress** Casual; no tank tops or swimwear at dinner. **Hours** Breakfast, 8–9:30 a.m.; lunch, noon–1:30 p.m.; nightly dinner seatings at 5:45 and 8:15 p.m. Hours are subject to change, so check your *Personal Navigator* for the exact schedule.

SETTING AND ATMOSPHERE The most distinctive design elements of Royal Court are the gold-colored wood columns on the floor, which rise to attach to the ceiling through flared white glass decorated with plant stems and shaped like flower petals. Along with these, white-marble columns and carpet patterned to look like fancy rugs give Royal Court a formal feel, even when it's half-full of kids. Small, round lamps placed around the room are designed to look like Cinderella's pumpkin coach, and some of the walls feature tile murals depicting scenes from *Cinderella* and other Disney-princess films. Tables near the starboard wall sit under portholes that offer ocean views, although these are partially blocked by a privacy wall running along the inside perimeter of the restaurant.

HOUSE SPECIALTIES Breakfast is standard buffet fare: fruit, cereal, eggs, waffles, bacon, sausage, and pastries. Lunch includes soups, salads, sandwiches, and burgers, plus a couple of alternative offerings such as pasta or fish. Dinner appetizers include escargots and French onion soup; the wild-boar tenderloin entrée is tasty. The Grand Marnier soufflé is probably the most popular dessert.

COMMENTS Only differences in decor distinguish Royal Court from **Royal Palace** on the *Dream* (see page 177).

PART EIGHT

ENTERTAINMENT *and* NIGHTLIFE

LIVE THEATER *on the* SHIPS

LIVE ENTERTAINMENT IS PRESENTED at the **Walt Disney Theatre** most nights, on most itineraries. The shows are generally either Disney-themed theatrical productions (typically musicals) or variety acts such as comedians, magicians, or ventriloquists. The theatrical shows are usually of two types: retellings of familiar Disney stories and so-called jukebox musicals.

Disney's Aladdin: A Musical Spectacular, on the *Fantasy,* is an example of the retelling genre. This is DCL's unique interpretation of the *Aladdin* film—it's not the same *Aladdin* musical that's playing on Broadway, nor is it the same *Aladdin* show that was performed for many years at Disney California Adventure theme park at Disneyland. The cruise version features live actors and multiple Arabian-themed sets reprising key scenes from the animated film, including the most popular songs, in about half the time of the original movie.

The *Wonder*'s ***Frozen: A Musical Spectacular*** is the best of the retelling shows. The character puppets—Sven and Olaf, naturally—are charming, and the lighting and projections are the best we've seen in all the Disney entities, including the parks. We also like the *Magic*'s ***Tangled: The Musical,*** which features new songs from beloved Disney composer Alan Menken. The *Magic*'s ***Twice Charmed: An Original Twist on the Cinderella Story,*** offers a nice twist to the retelling genre, providing more surprises than the standard film reinterpretations. As we were going to press, a new version of ***Beauty and the Beast*** was about to debut on the *Dream,* replacing the long-reviled *Villains Tonight*. We're thrilled that Belle has vanquished that particular monster.

Examples of jukebox musicals include ***Disney Dreams, Disney Wishes, Disney's Believe,*** and ***The Golden Mickeys.*** Each features songs and characters from many different Disney films, with the numbers linked by an original story. We're generally not fans of these shows. The storylines are threadbare, serving to string together unrelated songs

SCOTT SAYS *by Scott Sanders*

GETTING THE MOST FROM A DCL SHOW . . . OR NOT

DCL HAS BEEN TINKERING with its evening entertainment schedule by offering shows on two different evenings instead of unique entertainment each night—the idea is to give guests more opportunities to see a show without the pressure to attend a show each night—but if a show just doesn't float your boat, so to speak, you have a great chance to experience other areas of the ship while they're relatively uncrowded. We've often been the only guests in the lounges during showtimes, and the gift shops are practically empty. Alternatively, you can just watch the show on your stateroom TV.

rather than providing an interesting narrative. Lack of plot, however, isn't our primary objection to these shows—we realize it's a Disney cruise. Rather, they recycle the same handful of characters and songs played in every entertainment venue throughout the ship. If you haven't heard "Be Our Guest" from *Beauty and the Beast* performed a dozen times on board . . . well, have your hearing checked when you get home.

Finally, the *Magic* puts on a farewell show, ***Remember the Magic,*** on sailings of seven nights or longer. Featuring guest photos and a few musical numbers, it's intended as a recap of your cruise, but we think one last trip to the spa would be a better use of what's left of your time on board.

THEATER ETIQUETTE Although it may be tempting to treat the Walt Disney Theatre like your living room at home (your bedroom, after all, could be right down the hall), you should observe standard theater etiquette while you're on the ship. Pretend that you're at *Gypsy* on Broadway and a furious Patti LuPone has just snatched the phone of an audience member who was texting during "Rose's Turn"—or just follow these tips:

- **Arrive on time.** Latecomers distract those around them.
- **Likewise, don't save seats** unless someone in your party has a legitimate medical need to arrive late (see page 127).
- **Don't talk during the show.** You would think this was a given, but you'd be surprised at how many people feel free to chatter away.
- **Turn off your phone or leave it in your room.** Patti LuPone may not chew you out, but don't be surprised if somebody else does.
- **Don't take photos,** especially with a flash. Not only is this rude, it's dangerous for the performers. It's hard enough to execute complex choreography on a ship at sea—it's even harder when you've been temporarily blinded by the flash from a camera.
- **Don't sing along unless invited to as part of the show.** It's *Beauty and*

the Beast, not *Beauty and the Guy in Row 12 with the* RUN LIKE YOU STOLE SOMETHING *T-shirt and a Wicked Sunburn.*

- **Clap at appropriate times.** Show the performers the appreciation they deserve.
- **Consider carefully whether to bring very young children to the show.** As parents, we understand that children aren't robots and their behavior isn't always predictable, but a crying baby or a toddler kicking the seat in front of him detracts from other guests' ability to enjoy the show.

A BIT OF ADVICE You'll probably see at least one musical if you're taking small children on your cruise. (Note that not all productions are performed on every sailing.) Along with reading the show profiles that follow, we recommend watching a few minutes of each show on **YouTube** before your cruise. This will not only help you decide which show is worth your time, but it will also let you know what you're missing in case another entertainment option is available.

DCL describes its theatrical offerings as "Broadway-style," but this doesn't mean you'll see the touring-company equivalent of a Broadway hit (like the versions of *Cats, Mamma Mia!,* and *Grease* staged on some Royal Caribbean sailings). Frankly, as devotees of actual New York City theater, we used to roll our eyes at the "Broadway-style" descriptor, thinking it laughable to compare the simplified shows on board with real Broadway productions such as Disney's own stage version of *The Lion King.*

In discussing our criticisms with Disney cast members, we learned that at least from a technical standpoint, DCL performances actually have much more in common with Times Square than Topeka: the stage mechanics, costuming, special effects, and lighting are as close to state-of-the-art as is practicable at sea. If you find your eyes glazing over when you take your children to the show, try paying attention to the technological aspects of the programming—they'd be top-notch in most locales and are nothing less than remarkable given the constraints of an ocean liner.

If that doesn't enrich your perspective, consider that, as at most Broadway theaters, you can bring a glass of wine with you to your seat.

THE *MAGIC*'S SHOWS

Disney Dreams: An Enchanted Classic ★★★½
Walt Disney Theatre, Deck 4 Forward

PETER PAN SAVES THE DAY

When to go Typical showtimes are 6:15 and 8:30 p.m. Check your *Personal Navigator* for specific dates. **Duration** 55 minutes. **Our rating** Not to be missed.

DESCRIPTION AND COMMENTS Peter Pan must help a young girl named Anne Marie "find her own magic" before sunrise, whisking her through settings from *Aladdin, Beauty and the Beast, Cinderella, The Little Mermaid, The Lion*

King, and *Frozen.* Each story's main characters appear in key scenes from their respective movies and sing their signature songs. The sets are attractive, the special effects are good (expect Elsa to unleash a minor blizzard in the Walt Disney Theatre), and the script is fast-paced and entertaining. The cast seems to enjoy it, too, and it shows.

Remember the Magic: A Final Farewell ★★
Walt Disney Theatre, Deck 4 Forward

RECAP OF YOUR *MAGIC* CRUISE

When to go Typical showtimes are 6:15 and 8:30 p.m. on the night before your cruise concludes. Presented on cruises of 7 nights and longer. **Duration** 25 minutes. **Our rating** Not worth seeing.

DESCRIPTION AND COMMENTS *Remember the Magic* summarizes your cruise with photos and video clips of families taken by Disney photographers and shown on video screens. Expect songs and dances by Disney princesses and jokes about eating too much at the buffet. We recommend skipping this show and spending your last night revisiting your favorite activities on board.

Tangled: The Musical ★★★½
Walt Disney Theatre, Deck 4 Forward

GIRL WITH MOMMY ISSUES USES HER TRESSES TO GET OUT OF SOME HAIRY SITUATIONS

When to go Typical showtimes are 6:15 and 8:30 p.m. Check your *Personal Navigator* for specific dates. **Duration** 50 minutes. **Our rating** A fresh take on a classic fairy tale.

DESCRIPTION AND COMMENTS This faithful retelling of Disney's *Tangled* features songs by Broadway and film composer/demigod Alan Menken (*Little Shop of Horrors, The Little Mermaid, Beauty and the Beast, Aladdin, Hercules, Pocahontas, Newsies,* and many more). Actors, singers, and dancers—and miles and miles of synthetic hair—wend their way through intricate sets. The Snuggly Duckling tavern is particularly charming, the puppetry on the larger-than-life sidekick horse Maximus is good enough to have you believing the operator is actually equine, and the ending lantern scene is among the most charming segments of any DCL production. Having seen this show several times, we think the lighting is more moving and affecting if you sit more to the middle of the theater than right up front.

Twice Charmed: An Original Twist on the Cinderella Story
★★★½ Walt Disney Theatre, Deck 4 Forward

A FRESH TAKE ON A CLASSIC TALE

When to go Typical showtimes are 6:15 and 8:30 p.m. Check your *Personal Navigator* for specific days. **Duration** 55 minutes. **Our rating** A new narrative for a familiar story.

DESCRIPTION AND COMMENTS If you're familiar with Disney's original *Cinderella* movie, you'll recall that the wicked stepmother breaks the first glass slipper just as it's about to be fit on Cinderella's foot. Cinderella, however, produces the second glass slipper, shows that it fits, and goes on to marry the prince.

Twice Charmed begins where that story ends. As the show opens, Cinderella's stepmother and stepsisters are lamenting the fact that they didn't know

Cinderella had the second slipper. A nefarious fairy godfather appears to send Cindy's evil kin back in time and destroy her slipper before the prince's foot-fitting team ever arrives. Cinderella must then figure out a new way to persuade the prince that they're meant to be together.

As is the case with any Disney film, you can guess in the first 5 minutes how it's all going to end, but *Twice Charmed* is interesting anyway because it has a new narrative. The sets are pretty, the songs aren't bad, and it's an enjoyable way to spend an evening.

THE *WONDER'S* SHOWS

Beauty and the Beast ★★★½
Walt Disney Theatre, Deck 3 Forward

TALE AS OLD AS TIME, SONG AS OLD AS RHYME . . .

When to go Typical showtimes are 6:15 and 8:30 p.m. Check your *Personal Navigator* for specific days. **Duration** 50 minutes. **Our rating** We love the score—really, we do—but even we think "Be Our Guest" is overplayed.

DESCRIPTION AND COMMENTS This is an abridged but otherwise faithful version of *Beauty and the Beast*—no, not *that* one, the other one. The set design and costuming are inspired by the 2017 live-action/CGI movie, not the 1991 animated classic.

DCL's *Beauty and the Beast* includes songs from both films. The actors playing the inanimate-object characters—Mrs. Potts, Cogsworth, and the like—wear regular period clothing rather than full-body character costumes, and they carry puppets of the objects they represent. (Example: Mrs. Potts carries a teapot with a painted face and lips that move.) Disney has made this concept work in other shows—*The Lion King* on Broadway, for example—but it doesn't work here: the whole point is that these household items have been magically transformed into sentient beings. Nevertheless, the music soars, Gaston still needs therapy to work out his toxic masculinity, and true love prevails at the end. No, I'm not crying, *you're* crying!

Disney Dreams: An Enchanted Classic ★★★½
Walt Disney Theatre, Deck 4 Forward

PETER PAN SAVES THE DAY

COMMENTS See the profile of this show on the *Magic* (page 183) for details.

Frozen: A Musical Spectacular ★★★★½
Walt Disney Theatre, Deck 3 Forward

SISTERS IN THE SNOW

When to go Typical showtimes are 6:15 and 8:30 p.m. Check your *Personal Navigator* for specific days. **Duration** 50 minutes. **Our rating** The cold is rather enjoyable.

DESCRIPTION AND COMMENTS You know the music—you've heard it over and over and over and over—but if you haven't seen DCL's take on this modern animated classic, you haven't seen the story performed with more heart or better artistry. The puppetry here is critical to the storytelling, adding warmth to what could be an icy rehash. Life-size reindeer Sven and snowman Olaf are your obvious guesses for which characters are portrayed as puppets, but there are several surprises as well.

Frozen's special effects provide a couple of genuine "Wow!" moments; we count them among our favorites in any Disney venue, and no, we're not talking about soap-bubble snow. The costumes are gorgeous too: if you're a costuming geek, try to sit up close to see the detailed fabric; otherwise, a middle-of-the-theater view is the best vantage point from which to take it all in.

The Golden Mickeys ★★
Walt Disney Theatre, Deck 4 Forward

DISNEY SPIN ON AN AWARDS SHOW

When to go Typical showtimes are 6:15 and 8:30 p.m. Check your *Personal Navigator* for specific days. **Duration** 45 minutes. **Our rating** There are better uses of your time.

DESCRIPTION AND COMMENTS The least coherent live show on a Disney ship, *The Golden Mickeys* starts out as an Oscars-style awards presentation, except it's Disney characters giving themselves awards for their own movies in various made-up categories. As each award winner is announced, live performers reenact the movie's key scenes on stage, including songs, as clips from the movies play on the stage's screen backdrop.

This show has many problems. For one, the "awards" stop making sense almost as soon as they're presented: The "Best Heroes" award is simply a montage of main characters from Disney films, and one of the last awards, "A Salute to Friendship," is apparently the only way the show's writers could think of to get Woody, Buzz, and Jessie together on stage. Unless you have a burning need to see yet another rehash of songs from *The Lion King* and *Beauty and the Beast,* skip this one.

THE *DREAM'S* SHOWS

Disney's Believe ★★★
Walt Disney Theatre, Deck 3 Forward

MAGIC TRIUMPHS OVER CYNICISM

When to go Typical showtimes are 6:15 and 8:30 p.m. Check your *Personal Navigator* for specific days. **Duration** 50 minutes. **Our rating** Nice change of pace.

DESCRIPTION AND COMMENTS A botanist father who doesn't believe in magic must learn to believe in order to reconnect with his daughter on her birthday. The father's guide is *Aladdin*'s wisecracking Genie, who takes Dad through time, space, and Disney music on his journey to acceptance.

Believe has one of the most sophisticated sets of any Disney stage show at sea, and there are enough visual elements to entertain almost any kid. Although it's not a holiday show, the plot seems like a loose adaptation of Charles Dickens's *A Christmas Carol,* with a committee of ghosts, including Mary Poppins, Peter Pan, Baloo from *The Jungle Book,* Rafiki from *The Lion King,* and Pocahontas from Scarsdale, judging by her accent. (On the other hand, no princess from Scarsdale would be caught dead in that *shmata.*)

Many other Disney stars appear throughout the show, but, thankfully, *Believe* includes some less-familiar characters and songs. The final stretch has a hit parade of other princesses and ends with performances by Mickey and Minnie.

The Golden Mickeys ★★ Walt Disney Theatre, Deck 3 Forward

DISNEY SPIN ON AN AWARDS SHOW

COMMENTS See profile of this show on the *Wonder* (above) for details.

THE *FANTASY'S* SHOWS

Disney's Aladdin: A Musical Spectacular ★★ Walt Disney Theatre, Deck 3 Forward

SONG-FILLED EXTRAVAGANZA

When to go Typical showtimes are 6:15 and 8:30 p.m. Check your *Personal Navigator* for specific days. **Duration** 45 minutes. **Our rating** Needs more Genie.

DESCRIPTION AND COMMENTS A song-filled retelling of Disney's *Aladdin,* this live show features stage sets of Agrabah, the Cave of Wonders, and the Sultan's palace, along with the film's main characters: Aladdin, Princess Jasmine, Jafar, Iago, and Genie. All of the major numbers are performed, including "Friend Like Me" and "A Whole New World." Because it's an adaptation of an existing film, *Aladdin* has less extreme Disney sweetness than, say, *Believe.*

Having seen the original movie, the Broadway musical, and another live adaptation that ran at Disney California Adventure (DCA) until 2016, we're disappointed in the *Fantasy's* production. The performances are fine, but the script, along with the set design, falls flat.

In the movie, Genie has the most important role: besides providing narrative and background, he tells jokes to keep the action moving. In the DCA show, Genie likewise ad-libbed topical humor into the act, and he delivered so many fast-and-furious zingers that he inevitably got the biggest ovation at the end. Genie's onboard humor, however, has been watered down so much that it doesn't provide the spark the rest of the script needs. (Perhaps the ship's flaky Wi-Fi prevents him from regularly accessing TMZ?) Also, we're surprised that the sets for a stage show on a $900 million cruise ship aren't as nice as those created for a show at a theme park more than 10 years ago.

Disney's Believe ★★★ Walt Disney Theatre, Deck 3 Forward

MAGIC TRIUMPHS OVER CYNICISM

COMMENTS See profile of this show on the *Dream* (opposite) for details.

Disney Wishes ★★★ Walt Disney Theatre, Deck 3 Forward

TEEN-FOCUSED SONG AND DANCE

When to go Typical showtimes are 6:15 and 8:30 p.m. Check your *Personal Navigator* for specific days. **Duration** 50 minutes. **Our rating** Entertaining.

DESCRIPTION AND COMMENTS In *Disney Wishes,* graduating high-schoolers Kayla, Nicole, and Brandon are visiting Disneyland in search of the ride of their lives. This search is complicated by the trio's imminent split for college, as well as Brandon's hush-hush crush on Kayla. Nicole, Brandon's sister, has her own dark secret: she wants to be an artist.

Wishes has young actors, fast-moving dance numbers, and lots of visual razzle-dazzle, so it's entertaining for tweens and teens. It's not bad for parents, either, especially if they can recognize the bits of Magic Kingdom park trivia interspersed in the dialogue. According to maritime law, which requires that Disney stage shows must include at least one song from *Aladdin, Beauty and the Beast, The Lion King,* or *The Little Mermaid,* there's also a rendition of "Under the Sea." But most of the show's songs come from less-familiar Disney films, such as *Hercules, The Jungle Book, Mulan, Pinocchio,* and *Tangled,* making it easier to sit through than most other shows of this type.

OTHER LIVE PERFORMANCES

BESIDES LIVE STAGE SHOWS, the Walt Disney Theatre hosts variety acts, including everything from magicians and comedians to ventriloquists, jugglers, hypnotists, and musicians. Repositioning cruises, with their many sea days, may have guest Broadway artists or other niche celebrities. Many of these acts will do preview shows or short sets at various venues throughout the ship before their major engagement at the theater. We've seen some incredible onboard acts, but also a few for whom *mediocre* would be a kind description. If there are previews, we suggest catching a few minutes (or asking other guests who've seen them) to decide whether the act is worth your time.

In our experience, the best live acts tend to be the magicians and comics, who can adapt their material to the audience as the show is happening and revamp parts of their acts between shows.

MOVIES

RECENT DISNEY MOVIES, including films released during the cruise, are shown at the **Buena Vista Theatre** on each Disney ship. Each theater is equipped with digital film projectors, state-of-the-art sound systems, and the capability to show 3-D films (complete with glasses for guests). Padded, upholstered seats are arranged stairlike behind the screen, allowing good views from almost anywhere in the theater. About half a dozen films (more on longer sailings) are shown on any cruise almost continuously throughout the day beginning at about 9 a.m. and running through midnight. Admission is free. Popcorn and drinks are sold outside the theater before and during each presentation; you can also bring your own snacks and drinks. We've been known to make a quick trip up to the pool deck just before movie time to grab an order of chicken nuggets and a soda to snack on during the film. Why pay for popcorn when you can get movie nugs for free?

In the case of real blockbusters, films may be shown in the larger **Walt Disney Theatre** in addition to, or sometimes in place of, live stage shows. We were on board the *Dream* for opening week of *Star Wars: The Force Awakens;* the entire theater was packed more than once, and the concession stand was doing a brisk business in Darth Vader–helmet drink holders and Han Solo in Carbonite–shaped popcorn buckets.

unofficial **TIP**
DCL shows new Disney, Pixar, and now Marvel film releases on the same day that they're released on land, so there's no need to worry about being late to the party when the next installment of your favorite franchise premieres.

The movie schedule for your entire sailing is available on the DCL Navigator app. The same film may be shown three or four times during your cruise, at different times of day.

Classic Disney films are also shown on a giant 24-by-14-foot LED screen perched high above each ship's family pool (**Goofy's Pool** on Deck 9 of the *Magic* and *Wonder,* **Donald's Pool** on Deck 11 of the *Dream* and *Fantasy*).

Deeper cuts from the Disney film catalog are also shown on the ships' in-room televisions. TVs on the *Dream* and *Fantasy* have dozens of animated and live-action films available on demand, including rarely seen films and documentaries. This can be a nice option if you just want to chill in your room after a long day in the sun.

TELEVISION *and* NEWS

DCL STATEROOM TVs ARE SMALL—think large computer monitor, not home theater—and they don't broadcast anything approaching the programming you're used to at home. (Then again, we hope you didn't book a cruise just so you could spend it holed up in your room watching TV.)

In addition to the aforementioned Disney movies, there's Disney propaganda—for example, advertisements for the Disney Vacation Club and Adventures by Disney—along with shows from the Disney Channel, Disney XD, and Disney Junior.

Aside from Disney programming, your round-the-clock TV lineup includes tips for enjoying the ship, information about port adventures and shopping, a 24-hour live camera that broadcasts from the ship's bridge, and an onscreen account center that lets you keep tabs on your bill without having to trudge to Guest Services.

unofficial **TIP**
If you're a news junkie, plan on checking your favorite websites when you have data/Wi-Fi access in port.

News and sports channels such as BBC News, CNBC, CNN, ESPN, Fox News, and MSNBC are technically included as well, but in practice they may be available only sporadically or not at all depending on your itinerary, due to international broadcasting rights or, more likely, poor satellite reception. To its credit, DCL is up front about this on its website.

Available at Guest Services, the ***USA Times*** is a daily eight-page summary of the top dozen or so Associated Press news stories, plus some sports scores and a bit of celebrity dish.

When it comes to print entertainment, semicurrent editions of a dozen or so non-news magazines are sold in the onboard gift shops—think *People* and *Us Weekly,* not *The Economist* and *Time*—as well as a few fluffy paperbacks and perhaps a crossword compendium. Again, we recommend that you bring your own reading material or stock up in port.

LIVE SPORTS

ON THE *WONDER*, the main sports bar is **Crown & Fin;** it's **687** on the *Dream* and **O'Gills Pub** on the *Magic* and *Fantasy.* These are your primary venues for watching baseball, basketball, and soccer. NFL games are usually shown here, too; some are also shown on the ships' **Funnel Vision** big screen on the pool deck.

Keep in mind that the ships get their TV programming from satellite feeds, which can be affected by weather. If you want to watch a specific game, show up at least 30 minutes beforehand and ask a crew member to find the right station—there are hundreds of channels, and it may take a while to find your game.

If you happen to be sailing during a sporting event of national or worldwide interest, expect that it will be available for viewing in nearly every public space with seating. During one *Wonder* sailing during the World Cup soccer finals, the *Personal Navigator* listed just two viewing venues, but we found screens pulled down from the ceiling in every bar, lounge, and café. And if you're interested in major live events other than sports, rest assured that Disney has you covered. We've been on board during the Oscars and saw the broadcast playing in several of the lounges and the Buena Vista Theatre.

THEMED EVENTS *and* HOLIDAY ENTERTAINMENT

PIRATE NIGHT

THIS IS HELD ON ONE NIGHT on virtually every cruise. The crew, restaurants, and entertainment take on a pirate theme. The ship's transformation begins early in the day, when the usual background music is replaced by songs and audio from the theme parks' Pirates of the Caribbean ride and the spinoff film series. Afternoon craft sessions and family activities are pirate-themed as well. Some time in the afternoon, your stateroom attendant will drop off in your cabin a pirate bandanna for each member of your group to wear, along with booty such as chocolate "coins" covered in gold foil.

On cruises of four-plus nights, each ship's main restaurant will have a special menu for the evening, designed to look like a treasure map. Virtually all of the crew, as well as the ship's officers, will wear special pirate outfits, and families have an opportunity to pose for photos with them before dinner. Many guests pack special outfits just for Pirate Night, including black knee-high boots, capri pants, white puffy shirts, and eyeliner. (The women dress up, too.)

Pirate Night concludes with a stage show and video on the family pool's Funnel Vision screen, accompanied by a short fireworks display. The fireworks are usually shot from the starboard side, so you'll have a better view from there. The best viewing spots are as follows:

- ***Magic*** and ***Wonder:*** Deck 10 Port side. From the port, you can see Mickey on the zip line with the fireworks behind him instead of having to turn back and forth to look at one or the other
- ***Dream*** and ***Fantasy:*** Deck 12 Forward, near Currents bar

FROZEN DAYS

ADDING TO THE AVALANCHE OF *FROZEN* TIE-INS, DCL introduced yet another one to its lineup of themed onboard activities in 2015. Frozen Days are held on sailings headed to Alaska on the *Wonder* and to Northern European countries on the *Magic*. The lobby atrium is bedecked with paper icicles; a special themed menu is served at dinner (including a delightful Olaf-inspired carrot cake); a traditional Scandinavian dance lesson is held in the lobby; a gonna-stuff-some-chocolate-in-my-face-themed scavenger hunt takes place; and a stage show and dance party called *Freezing the Night Away* is held on the upper deck, with appearances by Anna, Elsa, Kristoff, and an animated Olaf and Sven.

We were on hand for a *Freezing the Night Away* deck party in Iceland; the wind speed and chilly outdoor temperature made us question the conviction behind Elsa's "the cold never bothered me anyway" signature statement. Costumes are by no means required, but many children, particularly girls, wore princess gowns. Erin was reminded of her Halloweens growing up in Maine, with parents urging kids to "just put on a jacket already!"

STAR WARS DAYS

IN 2016 DCL INTRODUCED Star Wars Days on several seven-night cruises on the *Fantasy*. These sailings included onboard 3-D showings of *Star Wars Episode VII: The Force Awakens*, guest Star Wars costume celebrations, Star Wars–related crafts and children's activities (Padawan Mind Challenge, anyone?), a guest-participation show called *Star Wars Saga*, and a fireworks-filled stage show called *Summon the Force*.

Additionally, Star Wars characters appeared for scheduled and surprise meet and greets. The ship's horn played the "Imperial March." Even much of the onboard food and drink was Star Wars–themed. The beverages of the day were Galaxy in a Glass and a Planetoid Punch; dinner selections included Sand People Salad (Cobb salad in disguise), Bantha Steak Empanadas (chopped beef in a pastry crust), and a Frozen Carbonite Sundae.

During Star Wars Days in early 2018, the Buena Vista Theatre played older Star Wars films virtually around the clock in addition to showing the latest movie in the series. New activities included a "Porgs on Board" scavenger hunt, lessons on drawing Star Wars characters, and BB-8 races. Star Wars–themed makeovers were available in the Bibbidi Bobbidi Boutique, and even adults and teens could get in on the action with a Rey makeover that included a costume. Finally, guests in inside staterooms got a surprise when the *Millennium Falcon* and several other iconic Star Wars vehicles paraded past their rooms' virtual portholes.

MARVEL DAYS

FOLLOWING THE SUCCESSFUL ADDITIONS of Frozen Days and Star Wars Days, DCL announced the addition of Marvel Days beginning in the fall of 2017. The inaugural Marvel Days, on the *Magic,* included photo ops with superheroes like Iron Man, Spider-Man, Thor, and fan favorite Black Panther; a superhero-filled stunt show on deck; a "Ravagers Night Club" adult dance party; an interactive show where Dr. Strange tutored guests in the Mystic Arts; Disney characters like Mickey and Minnie dressed up in their own superhero costumes; near-constant showings of Marvel films; trivia games; and learn-to-draw character lessons. The menu items offered were standard DCL fare, but with suggestions about which superhero is best associated with each item. Thor would choose Roasted Cod or Pasta with Meatballs, while Scarlet Witch would choose Gingered Soba Noodles or Ricotta Gnocchi. Who knew?

FORMAL NIGHT

MOST CRUISES OF SEVEN NIGHTS OR LONGER have a designated Formal Night. This is a chance for families to put on the ritz. The crew and officers also get into the act by wearing their dress whites. While there are no special meals or activities, you'll see many families getting their photos taken in the ship's atrium before or after dinner.

unofficial **TIP**
Formal Night is very popular for reservations at **Palo** and **Remy**.

If you break out in hives at the very thought of dressing up on a cruise, not to worry: you can still come to dinner in your shorts and running shoes, or you can avoid the whole business altogether by eating at Cabanas or ordering room service. Really, there's no pressure.

As for what *formal* and *dress-up* mean, you're likely to see a wide range of interpretations. Some cruisers opt for the whole nine yards—we've seen entire parties in tuxes and evening gowns—while others go with business or dressy casual wear: for men, suits or jackets with slacks (ties optional); for women, cocktail dresses or stylish tops paired with slacks or skirts. A collared long- or short-sleeved shirt with khakis or dress slacks is appropriate for teen boys; teen girls usually dress as if they're going to a high school dance. Little kids aren't expected to dress up, although many young girls enjoy getting decked out like their favorite Disney princesses.

If you don't have any fancy duds handy, you can rent them before you leave home by visiting **Cruiseline Formalwear** (cruiselineformal.com). Your garments will be delivered directly to your stateroom, and you'll return them to your stateroom attendant at the end of your cruise.

For more information about Formal Nights and themed events, call DCL at ☎ 800-951-3532. For further discussion, see our Frequently Asked Questions in Part Seven, Dining (page 158).

EASTER

EASTER IS CELEBRATED ON THE DISNEY SHIPS, but in a much more low-key fashion than many of the other holidays. There are no Easter decorations on the ship, and the festivities last for only one day rather than throughout the sailing. Religious services will be offered, typically including a sunrise service, a Catholic Mass, and an interdenominational Protestant service. When we sailed on the *Fantasy* during one recent Easter, secular observations of the holiday included appearances by the White Rabbit from *Alice in Wonderland* (as a stand-in for the Easter Bunny), and Mickey and Minnie wearing what was supposed to be their pastel Easter finery but looked to us like what they'd be sporting on the golf course. Other Easter events include themed craft activities, face painting for children, and the distribution of candy and cookies in the lobby atrium.

INDEPENDENCE DAY

DEPENDING ON YOUR SHIP'S ITINERARY, you'll likely see some special onboard activities on July 4. We recently spent Independence Day on the *Magic.* Crew members distributed small American flags to any guest who wanted one. There was a lobby party that started with a truly inspiring rendition of "The Star-Spangled Banner" sung by a Walt Disney Theatre performer and ended with a dance party featuring Mickey in an Uncle Sam hat, Minnie dressed like Betsy Ross, and Chip 'n' Dale in tricorne caps, bopping to patriotically themed songs like "Party in the USA," "Born in the USA," and "American Pie," as well as "Sweet Caroline" . . . because nothing says America quite like Neil Diamond.

Other activities included themed crafts, American-history trivia contests, and face painting. The breakfast and lunch buffets at Cabanas were heavy on red, white, and blue desserts.

Canada Day also occurred during this same cruise. It got a one-sentence acknowledgment in the *Personal Navigator.* Sorry, Canada.

HALLOWEEN

ONE OF THE BEST PLACES TO CELEBRATE HALLOWEEN is on a Disney cruise. The crew and officers dress up, and many families bring special costumes to wear for this one night on board. Even the Disney characters dress up—one of our favorite memories is being "attacked" by Zombie Goofy one Halloween on board the *Magic* while his guide murmured "Brains!" as they shuffled along.

Most of the family activities have a Halloween theme: animation classes feature scary characters, the crafts sessions may be villain-themed, and even the karaoke is spooky. As darkness falls, photographers are stationed in each ship's atrium before and after dinner, so families can get photos of themselves dressed up. Kids can visit various areas of the ship to trick-or-treat.

DCL ships begin celebrating Halloween in September (mercifully a few weeks later than the WDW theme parks, which break out their Halloween decor in August). Expect to see pumpkins, black cats, and other decor starting around the last week of September and running through October 31. Every ship offers Halloween-themed movies, deck parties, craft-making, and more.

Introduce your kids to the audience-participation legacy of *The Rocky Horror Picture Show* at the **Nightmare Before Christmas Sing and Scream.** Sing along with the movie, then meet Jack and Sally after the show. There's also a new Halloween-themed deck party, **Mickey's Calling All the Monsters Mouse-Querade,** along with storytelling sessions for kids. For the grown-ups, the ship's dance club hosts a costume party.

THANKSGIVING

IF YOUR CRUISE DATES INCLUDE THE FOURTH THURSDAY in November, you'll be celebrating Thanksgiving aboard your ship. Expect to see Mickey, Minnie, Goofy, and Donald in their Pilgrim costumes, plus many other Disney characters in seasonal outfits. Don't be surprised, however, to see the rest of the ship already decked out for Christmas. The main dining rooms on each ship will serve a traditional Thanksgiving menu. And it wouldn't be Turkey Day without (American) football, even on DCL. Games are broadcast on each ship's big Funnel Vision LED screen near the family pool, as well as at the sports bars.

CHRISTMAS, HANUKKAH, AND KWANZAA

DCL BEGINS DECORATING ITS SHIPS for the winter holidays in early to mid-November. Dates vary from year to year, but in 2018 **Very MerryTime Cruises** commenced in November. Among the many decor elements on board, expect to see the ship's atrium decked out with a massive Christmas tree, a Hanukkah menorah, and a Kwanzaa kinara. A tree-lighting ceremony typically takes place on the first night of each Very MerryTime cruise.

Family activities include making holiday greeting cards, drawing Disney characters in holiday outfits, building gingerbread houses, and so on. As at Epcot theme park, each ship will have storytellers scheduled throughout the day, along with special holiday-themed merchandise. Expect to see Mickey, Minnie, Goofy, and other characters dressed in winter finery, plus lots of holiday movies on your stateroom TV. Beware that while most holiday activities are included in the price of your cruise, a few, notably decorating gingerbread houses, charge a modest fee to participate.

The most interesting decorations, however, have palm trees decorated with garland, lights, and bulbs, and plastic snowmen sitting on the sand. Disney characters wear holiday-themed island outfits, and even the shuttle bus from the dock is decorated with reindeer antlers.

Religious services are typically offered during each night of Hanukkah. A Catholic Mass is held at midnight on December 24, and a Mass and interdenominational service are held on December 25. Santa Claus distributes small gifts to children in the atrium on Christmas morning, along with milk and cookies. Should you need a little gift-wrapping help, that service is available on board at no extra charge; check your *Personal Navigator* for the location, or ask at Guest Services.

Finally, the ship's onboard music, piped into the hallways and public areas, switches from standard Disney tunes to Christmas-themed tracks. Some people enjoy it; others prefer standard Disney music.

NEW YEAR'S EVE

DURING THE DAY, video screens on each ship's pool deck display a clock counting down the hours, minutes, and seconds until midnight. The pool deck is also the site for a big family-themed party in the evening, with DJs and live entertainment continuing through midnight. Each ship's dance club also hosts a party, complete with DJ, hats, noisemakers, confetti, and bubbly drinks at midnight. Families will want to see the special fireworks display and the atrium's balloon drop at midnight. The ships' kids' clubs host parties early in the evening, allowing the little ones to get to bed at a reasonable hour.

NIGHTCLUBS, BARS, CAFÉS, *and* LOUNGES

EACH DISNEY CRUISE LINE SHIP has a collection of nightclubs and lounges for adults. Nightclubs typically offer dancing and live acts; lounges are oriented to conversation, with smaller spaces and comfortable seating. (Guests must generally be age 21 or older to drink; see page 38 for an exception.) The following section lists the clubs, bars, and lounges found across all four ships; we've included the **Cove Café** coffee bar as well, since it also serves alcoholic drinks. Check your *Personal Navigator* for exact hours.

About Those Drink Prices . . .

If it's been a few years since you cruised with Disney, you may notice that some signature cocktails cost significantly more than they used to. For example, the Shipbuilder's Wife—made with Absolut Pears vodka, limoncello, grappa, agave, and fresh lemon juice—was introduced at O'Gills Pub on the *Fantasy* in 2012 for $5.75. Four years later, in summer 2016, the price had increased by just a dollar, but by early 2017, the same cocktail showed up on the menu of the *Dream*'s 687 bar for a notably higher $8.50.

If you're used to clubbing in a major city, $8.50 might seem like a bargain—we would expect to see a drink like the Shipbuilder's Wife priced more like $12–$14 at a New York City nightspot. But if you're trying to keep tabs on costs, stick with domestic beers, grab a drink-of-the-day on deck, or BYOB. (See page 42 for more info on DCL's alcohol carry-on policy.)

ON THE *MAGIC*

Cove Café LOCATION: Deck 9 Midship

SETTING AND ATMOSPHERE Cove Café on the *Magic* received a complete design overhaul during the ship's 2018 dry dock. The decor now features neutral cushions on dark rattan seating, with green accents on the walls and bar and large potted palms in the corners. Picture it: *The Golden Girls* if it were still in production today (and we consider that a good thing, pussycat). There are open areas for socializing, but you can still find nooks and crannies where you can curl up with a book or magazine and a latte to while away the day.

SELECTIONS Cove Café serves just about every java you can think of: espresso, cappuccino, latte, Americano, and cold drip, in both regular and sugar-free variations. Cove also serves hot teas and has a good selection of wines, Champagnes, spirits, and mixed drinks. Prices for these are the same as throughout the rest of the ship. Service is excellent.

unofficial **TIP**
If you're one of those people who need a coffee or six every day, ask your server for a **Café Fanatic** rewards card; you'll get every sixth specialty coffee free.

Besides beverages, the Cove Café has a self-serve refrigerated case stocked with small bites. Breakfast items usually include plain and chocolate croissants, Danish, and fruit. Afternoon and evening snack service usually consists of cookies, brownies, cakes, crackers, and fruit. Dinner, though, is our favorite because, for a couple of hours, Cove Café brings out a selection of prosciutto, dried sausages, marinated olives, cheeses, and bread. You can make a light supper out of these and a drink; because most families are either at dinner or preparing for it, there's a chance you'll have the café all to yourself.

COMMENTS The Wi-Fi signal here is fairly strong, making it a good spot to catch up on email or the latest news. You'll also find a small selection of current magazines. This is a big part of Cove Café's appeal: the ability to sit in a comfy chair, sip coffee, and page through *The New Yorker* in blessed silence, surrounded by $350 million of luxury cruise ship.

ACROSS THE SHIPS All four DCL ships have a Cove Café. Those on the *Magic* and *Wonder* now have different finishes, but the overall comfort level is still the same, and they're both slightly larger than the Cove Cafés on the *Dream* and *Fantasy*. The Cove on the *Wonder*, however, connects to the **Outlook Café** (see page 202), which is unique to that ship. The Cove Cafés on the *Dream* and *Fantasy* are likewise almost identical twins, but they don't have the televisions found in the cafés on the *Magic* and *Wonder*. Guests at all Cove Cafés must be at least age 18 to enter and at least 21 to drink alcohol.

Promenade Lounge LOCATION: Deck 3 Aft

SETTING AND ATMOSPHERE The Promenade Lounge hosts family activities during the day and live music at night. It's done in the same Art Deco style as

the rest of the *Magic,* with cherry-wood finishes, creamy lighting, and brass accents. Sixteen computers line one wall, providing 24-hour internet access . . . because nothing goes together like booze and email.

SELECTIONS Beer and wine by the glass, spirits, mixed drinks, and coffee. Free snacks are served, starting in the afternoon—mostly chips, salsa, and such.

COMMENTS Though one of the most attractive nightspots on the ship, the Promenade Lounge sits adjacent and open to pedestrian traffic from one of the *Magic*'s main inside walkways, making it louder and less relaxing than it could be. Nighttime entertainment is usually provided by a singing duo, such as a pianist and vocalist, making for an enjoyable way to spend half an hour after a meal. (For the performers, though, it's got to be like singing in a Greyhound station due to the outside noise. Some glass and wood partitions would work wonders here.) We recommend using the Promenade as a meeting place for groups to get a drink before dinner at Carioca's or Lumiere's (see Part Seven, Dining) or to listen to the live music with a nightcap.

ACROSS THE SHIPS There's also a Promenade Lounge on the *Wonder.* Like the Promenade on the *Magic,* it's a nice place to have a before- or after-dinner cocktail, as long as you can deal with all the people promenading past on their way to other parts of the ship. The comparable bar on the *Dream* and *Fantasy* is **Bon Voyage** (see page 202).

Signals LOCATION: Deck 9 Midship

SETTING AND ATMOSPHERE Signals is an adults-only outdoor bar next to the adult pool. It has a few seats for those looking to get some shade, but most patrons take their drinks back to their deck chairs to sip in the sun.

SELECTIONS Much of Signals' menu is devoted to popular beers and frozen drinks, but they can whip up almost anything you can think of. Signals also serves coffee, juices, and bottled water. Soda machines are nearby.

COMMENTS Signals on the *Magic* got a small refresh in 2018, adding some additional areas with shade and a few more televisions. It still doesn't have much in the way of atmosphere, but because it's located near the Quiet Cove Pool, it's a little quieter than other bars.

ACROSS THE SHIPS Only the *Magic* and *Wonder* have Signals bars. The *Dream* and *Fantasy* have a total of four outdoor bars: one on each ship called **Currents** and another on each ship called **Waves** (see pages 203 and 204, respectively). Drinks and service are comparable at all of these, but we think Currents has the best views and the nicest decor. Also, Signals serves guests age 21 and older only, while Currents and Waves welcome kids.

After Hours

This is Disney's name for the collection of bars on the *Magic*'s Deck 3 Forward. It includes **Fathoms,** a venue for live entertainment and dancing; **Keys,** a piano bar; and **O'Gills Pub,** a sports bar. After Hours has a contemporary urban nightclub theme, pulled together by a white-and-silver color scheme and accented by chrome light fixtures.

Some After Hours lounges, such as Fathoms, are home to family-oriented entertainment during the day, but all usually have an adults-only policy (age 18 and up to enter, 21 and up to drink) after 9 p.m.

After Hours's bars generally carry the same wines and beers, although each serves its own unique line of cocktails. O'Gills Pub, the sports bar, also serves a collection of Irish beers not found elsewhere.

The bars in After Hours get much higher reader satisfaction ratings than bars elsewhere on the *Magic*.

Fathoms LOCATION: Deck 3 Forward

SETTING AND ATMOSPHERE Fathoms has an undersea theme: fiber-optic light fixtures shaped like jellyfish, sand-art murals along the bar, and silver-and-black bench seating that undulates like ocean waves. Six sets of couches are built into Fathoms's back wall, providing an excellent semiprivate view of the entertainment stage.

The middle of the club holds a dance floor and a raised stage with a professional sound system and lighting. Armchairs upholstered in silver fabric are arranged in groups of two or three around circular cocktail tables. These help control the echo in Fathoms's large, open floor plan.

SELECTIONS Sea-themed cocktails make up most of Fathom's bar menu, priced at $10–$12, with beer, wine, and spirits also available. Expect to find lots of fruity drinks made with blue curaçao, orange liqueur, and muddled citrus.

COMMENTS Like other DCL nightclubs, Fathoms does double-duty during the day by hosting family-oriented activities, such as scavenger hunts, bingo, and talent shows. At night the stage hosts everything from game shows to live music, dancing, DJs, karaoke, comedians, magicians, and other performers. The game shows' setups follow well-known television models: there's one similar to *The Newlywed Game,* for example, where contestants try to guess how their partner will answer some random set of questions. This being Disney, though, you probably won't hear any questions about "making whoopee."

ACROSS THE SHIPS Fathoms doesn't have an identical sibling on the other DCL ships, but it's most similar to **Azure** on the *Wonder* (see page 200), **Evolution** on the *Dream* (see page 206), and **The Tube** on the *Fantasy* (see page 213).

Keys LOCATION: Deck 3 Forward

SETTING AND ATMOSPHERE Keys features live piano music nightly. Six large porthole windows run along one of the rectangular room's long walls. The bar is in the middle of the opposite wall, and the piano player is between the two, at the far end of the room from the entrance doors.

Keys's theming is supposed to evoke nightspots of Hollywood's Golden Age—think a chic piano bar on Sunset Boulevard circa the late 1940s. The furnishings include midcentury-modern sofas and chairs with curved, radius-style arms and backs. Carpeting is a crisp silver with geometric sunbursts. Over the bar area is a columned pavilion topped with panels of stylized piano keys. The live entertainment's audio levels tend to be loud for such a small space, but it's a pleasant enough experience.

SELECTIONS The bar menu includes specialty drinks with musically themed names, such as the **Moji-Do,** a mojito; the **Bloody Mi-Re,** a Bloody Mary with vodka, yellow-tomato juice, lime, and whiskey-flavored Worcestershire sauce; and the **Rob Roy,** made the typical way (Scotch, vermouth, and bitters), only *Rob* is spelled with the musical symbol for a flat note. Most of these cocktails cost about $11, about $5 more per drink than at O'Gills Pub (see next profile). The

most expensive drink is a $16 Manhattan, made with Jack Daniel's Sinatra Select whiskey, Antica Formula vermouth, and Cointreau. Coffee, cappuccino, and espresso are available, too, but we recommend the Cove Café (see page 196) if you're looking for those.

COMMENTS Live entertainment usually begins with a show around 7:30 p.m.; a typical night's schedule will have more performances around 9:30, 10:30, and 11:30 p.m. The pianists are acceptable, if nondescript, and play medleys of well-known songs by familiar artists. Some nights have themes, such as 1950s and '60s hits, Elvis, or Simon and Garfunkel, and you can always submit requests.

During the day, Keys is often used for group seminars on everything from wine and spirits to acupuncture, Chinese herbs, and back-pain treatments. (We sense a "feel better one way or another" theme here.) Check your *Personal Navigator* for details. The bar typically opens anywhere from 5:30 to 6:30 p.m. Children are admitted to Keys until 9 p.m., when it becomes an adults-only venue until its midnight closing.

ACROSS THE SHIPS The *Magic*'s Keys is most similar to the *Wonder*'s **Cadillac Lounge** (see next page). The entertainment is interchangeable between the two, while Cadillac Lounge's decor is more gimmicky (albeit well done).

O'Gills Pub LOCATION: Deck 3 Forward

SETTING AND ATMOSPHERE This Irish bar's name is a nod to the Disney classic and Sean Connery vehicle *Darby O'Gill and the Little People.* That said, it's an Irish bar in the same way that Lucky Charms cereal is an Irish breakfast. Sure, there's a clover pattern woven into the green carpet and background music that features a lot of fiddle-and-flute and U2, but if you've come here expecting Raglan Road at Walt Disney World, you're in for a disappointment.

Nine wall-mounted televisions provide live satellite coverage of whatever sports are being played around the world. Comfortable burgundy-leather banquettes are built into the wall, and padded leather armchairs surround the tables set within the banquettes. In the middle of the room, about a dozen bar-height tables and stools provide the best views of the most TVs.

SELECTIONS The bar menu includes a beer flight of 5.5-ounce Irish brews. There's also a selection of Irish whiskeys and cocktails using Irish whiskeys, as well as standard beers, wines, and a full bar. Beers are about $6, wines by the glass run about $7–$10, and cocktails are $6–$11 depending on the amount of booze and the level of fancy. We like to have an Irish coffee here after dinner when we're sailing in Northern Europe.

COMMENTS A comfy spot to sit, sip, and watch the game. There are often substantial snacks like chips, crudités, small sandwiches, or pigs in a blanket available in the evening—enough to make a light dinner. More-substantial items are available to buy—bangers and mash, for example—but we found that ordering these could take up to an hour. Stick with the freebie snacks if you're hungry right now.

ACROSS THE SHIPS O'Gills Pub on the *Magic* joins the *Fantasy*'s bar of the same name (see page 210). Along with the *Wonder*'s **Crown & Fin** (page 201) and the *Dream*'s **687** (page 287), these are the DCL fleet's upscale sports bars. The larger televisions at the *Magic*'s O'Gills make it easier to watch events from across the room.

PALO Adults on the *Magic* and *Wonder* also have the option of grabbing a before- or after-dinner drink at Palo (see page 158 for information on the dress code and pages 39 and 162 for booking information). When Palo is open for dinner, guests may sit at the bar, which is full-service and offers a view of the open kitchen. Because many people don't realize they can do this, you could find yourself with the counter to yourself. We love it because it's quiet and you can talk to the bartender and servers while they bring in drink orders for their tables. Because of the brunch setup, bar service is available only during dinner.

ON THE *WONDER*

After Hours

Following the *Wonder*'s late-2016 dry dock, the old Deck 3 Forward bar area, Route 66, was renamed After Hours, matching the nomenclature on the *Magic*. Like its counterpart on that ship, After Hours has a contemporary-urban-nightclub theme, pulled together by a uniform color scheme and similar light fixtures.

After Hours is a much appreciated update from Route 66, which boasted fake-antique road signs affixed to the walls and Rascal Flatts's cover of "Life Is a Highway" on an endless loop in the corridors. Some After Hours lounges are home to family-oriented entertainment during the day, but all usually have an adults-only policy (age 18 to enter, age 21 to drink) after 9 p.m. After Hours's bars generally carry the same wines and beers, although each serves a unique line of cocktails.

The *Wonder*'s bars—**Azure, Cadillac Lounge,** and **Crown & Fin**—are rated below average by readers, and rank among the worst on DCL. We're not suggesting that you should drink alone in your room, but the bar at **Palo** on Deck 10 Aft might be your best bet on the ship.

Azure LOCATION: Deck 3 Forward

SETTING AND ATMOSPHERE Formerly Wavebands, this is the Wonder's dance club. The color palette is creams and blues, with curved wooden beams meant to evoke the undulating sea.

SELECTIONS There doesn't seem to be any particular theming to the bar menu. You'll find standard beers and wines along with some hard ciders and hard sodas. Cocktails include ingredients like sparkling sake, pomegranate puree, elderflower liqueur, and fresh Drinks. Cocktails are on the expensive side here, with most priced at more than $11.

COMMENTS The small stage will likely be the site of your bingo game during the day and some crew-facilitated partying in the evening.

ACROSS THE SHIPS Azure doesn't have an identical sibling on the other ships, but it's most similar to **Fathoms** on the *Magic* (see page 198), **Evolution** on the *Dream* (see page 206), and **The Tube** on the *Fantasy* (see page 213).

Cadillac Lounge LOCATION: Deck 3 Forward

SETTING AND ATMOSPHERE This is the *Wonder*'s piano bar. The decor pays tribute to 1950s-era Cadillac cars by way of leather-upholstered barstools and chairs, couches made to look like automobile rear seats, and a bar built into a

replica of the front of a 1959 Cadillac Coupe de Ville, complete with working headlights.

"Designed by General Motors" isn't something we normally listen for when discussing bar theming, but it works here. The furnishings—with dark woods; carpets in burgundy, gold, and fuchsia; leather-covered walls; chrome accents; and those butter-and-chocolate-colored leather barstools—clearly indicate that this is a bar meant to call to mind a very specific time and place.

The best seats in the house are in the far corner, opposite the main entrance and to the right of the piano player. These include a comfortable leather couch and two leather armchairs, plus a side table to hold drinks. From here you can listen to the music and watch some of the action at the bar, tucked away in your own discreet corner of the lounge.

SELECTIONS The Cadillac Lounge serves beer, wine, spirits, and cocktails, and it's the only bar in After Hours that serves Champagne by the glass (outside After Hours, the **Outlook Café** also serves Champagne; see opposite page). Coffee, cappuccino, and espresso are available as well, but we'd recommend the Cove Café if you're looking for those. Free snacks and appetizers are available all evening.

COMMENTS Live entertainment usually begins with a show around 7:30 p.m.; a typical night's schedule will have more performances around 9:30, 10:30, and 11:30 p.m. The pianists are acceptable, if nondescript, and play medleys of well-known songs by familiar artists. Some nights have themes, such as 1950s and '60s hits, Elvis, or Simon and Garfunkel, and you can always make requests.

During the day, the Cadillac Lounge is often used for group seminars on everything from wine and spirits to acupuncture. Check your *Personal Navigator* for details. The bar typically opens anywhere from 5:30 to 6:30 p.m. Children are admitted to the Cadillac Lounge until 9 p.m., when it becomes an adults-only venue until its midnight closing.

ACROSS THE SHIPS The Cadillac Lounge is most similar to the *Magic*'s **Keys** (see page 198). The entertainment is interchangeable between the two, while Keys's retro-Hollywood decor is more restrained.

Cove Café LOCATION: Deck 9 Forward

COMMENTS See profile of Cove Café on the *Magic* (page 196) for additional details.

Crown & Fin LOCATION: Deck 3 Forward

SETTING AND ATMOSPHERE Formerly Diversions, Crown & Fin is the *Wonder*'s sports bar. In late 2016, it was transformed from a generic bar into an authentic-ish English tavern. The space is adorned with dark woods, plush leather furniture, and brass accents. Subtle nods to classic Disney films set in London can be found in the artwork and props.

SELECTIONS Cocktails and British craft beers on tap. There is also a pub-grub menu available for an extra fee. We're not sure why you'd want to pay $8 for a German pretzel in a British bar . . . but sometimes the sea makes you do things you shouldn't.

COMMENTS Given the size of the ship, the odds are good that you'll be able to find other fans of your favorite teams at Crown & Fin. Besides televised sports, Crown & Fin hosts family-oriented and adult activities throughout the day, ranging from Disney-character-drawing classes for kids to trivia contests and afternoon beer tastings. Check your *Personal Navigator* for the schedule.

ACROSS THE SHIPS The Crown & Fin refurbishment brings this bar in line with the other clubby sports-viewing venues on DCL. We're pretty sure we'd be happy to watch the big game here or just while away a sea day nursing a pint and playing checkers.

Outlook Café LOCATION: Deck 10 Forward

SETTING AND ATMOSPHERE What makes the Outlook Café special is that its seating area is surrounded by large glass windows, making it the perfect venue in which to get some sun in a climate-controlled environment. This means air-conditioning when the *Wonder* is in the Caribbean and heat when it's plying the waters off Alaska.

SELECTIONS Coffees, teas, wine, beer, mixed drinks, and Champagne by the glass. Free snacks are also offered.

COMMENTS An extension of the Cove Café, the Outlook Café, found upstairs via a spiral staircase, is a marvelously atmospheric place to while away some time. There's nothing like it on any other DCL ship.

ACROSS THE SHIPS The Outlook Café is unique to the *Wonder.* As at the Cove Cafés, guests must be age 18 to enter and 21 to drink alcohol.

Promenade Lounge LOCATION: Deck 3 Aft

COMMENTS See profile of Promenade Lounge on the *Magic* (page 196) for additional details.

Signals LOCATION: Deck 9 Midship

COMMENTS See profile of Signals on the *Magic* (page 197) for details.

PALO Adults on the *Magic* and *Wonder* also have the option of grabbing a before- or after-dinner drink at Palo (see page 158 for information on the dress code and pages 39 and 162 for booking information). When Palo is open for dinner, guests may sit at the bar, which is full-service and offers a view of the open kitchen. Because many people don't realize they can do this, you could find yourself with the counter to yourself. We love it because it's quiet and you can talk to the bartender and servers while they bring in drink orders for their tables. Because of the brunch setup, bar service is available only during dinner.

ON THE *DREAM*

Bon Voyage LOCATION: Deck 3 Midship

SETTING AND ATMOSPHERE Sitting just off the atrium, Bon Voyage is one of the prettiest, if not smallest, of the *Dream*'s bars, with just 10 seats at the counter plus 4 covered armchairs a few feet away. The two highlights here are the gorgeous Art Deco mural behind the bar—which shows well-heeled passengers in 1920s formal wear departing their touring cars to board the *Dream*—and the swirled, maize-yellow illuminated bar face, which reflects gold light off the beige-marble floors.

SELECTIONS Bon Voyage's bar menu is similar to that in The District (see page 205) and includes draft and bottled beer; wines by the glass and bottle; spirits; and mixed drinks, including a few special fruit-flavored martinis. Service is excellent.

COMMENTS Open from around noon to 11 p.m. daily, Bon Voyage is a good spot for groups to meet before dinner or to have a nightcap before departing for the elevators. Because it's in a heavily trafficked area, there's no live entertainment, and it isn't our first choice for a quiet drink or conversation, but it is a good place to fortify yourself while standing in those character-greeting lines. (Sometimes you need a little liquid courage to face Chip 'n' Dale.)

ACROSS THE SHIPS The *Fantasy* also has a Bon Voyage just off the Deck 3 atrium; the *Dream*'s Bon Voyage is more appealing, even without live entertainment. The **Promenade Lounge** is the comparable bar on the *Magic* and *Wonder* (see page 196).

Cove Café LOCATION: Deck 11 Forward

COMMENTS See profile of Cove Café on the *Magic* (page 196) for additional details.

Currents LOCATION: Deck 13 Forward

SETTING AND ATMOSPHERE This outdoor area has the best views of any bar on the *Dream.* Built behind and into the structure supporting the forward stairs and elevators, the curved, glossy white face of the bar mirrors the curve along the opposite deck rail and provides some shade during the day. Currents is beautiful at night, when a royal-blue neon sign with CURRENTS rendered in a retro-looking script—think a nameplate on a 1950s car—lights up the bar and bar shelves, accented with matching blue tile.

Ten stationary barstools are spaced far enough apart for easy access to walk-up traffic. Most guests take drinks back to their lounge chairs, but there's also plenty of (unshaded) armchair seating around Currents.

SELECTIONS Currents serves bottled and draft beer, cocktails, and frozen drinks.

COMMENTS The one downside to Currents is that it's next to a smoking section. Depending on the prevailing winds, this is either not an issue at all or a mild annoyance.

ACROSS THE SHIPS Currents is the same on the *Dream* and the *Fantasy.* **Signals** on the *Magic* and *Wonder* is similar (see page 197), but Currents's layout is much more open, with much better views and nicer decor. Also, where Signals is adults-only, Currents welcomes kids and serves nonalcoholic concoctions just for them.

Meridian LOCATION: Deck 12 Aft

SETTING AND ATMOSPHERE Situated between the restaurants Palo and Remy, Meridian is the *Dream's* martini bar. It's also one of our very favorite bars on the ship.

Sitting high up on Deck 12 Aft, Meridian has windows on three sides of its relatively small, square room. Panoramic views of the sunset await early diners who stop in around dusk. Antique ship-navigation maps and instruments adorn the walls and shelves. Meridian's furnishings include rich brown-leather couches and armchairs, as well as cocoa-colored teak floors with brass inlays. Meridian also has outdoor seating on a teak deck that runs along one wall of Remy. It's lovely on warm summer evenings—and in demand around dusk—so don't be surprised if it's standing-room only.

SELECTIONS Meridian's bar menu emphasizes mixed drinks and spirits over beer and wine, although those are also available, as are coffees. The best

thing about Meridian is the bartending staff, who will often offer to make a custom martini for you on the spot. This usually starts with the bartender inquiring whether you like fruit- or herb-based drinks and what kinds of liquors you usually prefer. A couple of minutes of muddling, shaking, and stirring, and you have the first draft of your new drink. And if it's not quite what you expected, they'll be happy to start over.

Meridian on the *Dream* also offers an antipasti tray with wine for guests who want to snack while they drink. Prices: signature wines, $20 per person or $89 per bottle; premium wines, $28 per person or $99 per bottle; you can also omit the wine for $30 per person. We're not sure, though, why guests wouldn't simply choose the free evening antipasti at Cove Café or Vista Café. Meridian also offers a cigar menu, with prices ranging from about $10 to about $50 for individual or small packages of cigars. The smoking area is nearby but outdoors, not in the lounge itself.

COMMENTS We recommend stopping by Meridian for its martini experience alone, even if you don't have reservations for Remy or Palo (see Part Seven). If you're dining at Remy, though, beware of the combined effect of Meridian's martinis and Remy's wine pairings—as Len once found out, it may be more than you bargained for.

Meridian usually opens around 5 p.m. and stays open until midnight. It's one of the few DCL nightspots with a dress code: inside the lounge, men should wear dress shirts and pants, and women should wear dresses, skirts and blouses, or pantsuits. If you're just visiting the outdoor area, jeans and shorts are allowed, but swimwear, T-shirts, or tank tops are verboten.

ACROSS THE SHIPS Both the *Dream* and the *Fantasy* have nearly identical Meridian lounges; the *Magic* and *Wonder* do not. Together with the two Skyline bars (see page 208), the two Meridians rate at the top of reader-satisfaction polls across all of Disney Cruise Line.

Vista Café LOCATION: Deck 4 Midship

SETTING AND ATMOSPHERE This small, Art Deco–themed nook is tucked into a corner of Deck 4.

SELECTIONS Vista Café serves everything from coffee and free pastries in the morning to beer, wine, cocktails, and light snacks at night.

COMMENTS With just four seats at the bar, this isn't the place for large groups. It's most useful as a place for a family to get a drink and a bite to eat on their way to one of the day's activities on Decks 3 or 4.

ACROSS THE SHIPS Vista Cafés can be found on both the *Dream* and the *Fantasy* but not the *Magic* or *Wonder.* Both cafés offer the same food and drink and are about the same size; the only significant difference is the decor—the Vista on the *Fantasy* has that ship's Art Nouveau theme rather than the Art Deco styling of the *Dream.* The marble floor of the *Fantasy*'s version is a bit bigger than the *Dream*'s, making the former Vista Café seem more of an intentionally designed space versus one carved out of an underutilized corner.

Waves LOCATION: Deck 12 Aft

SETTING AND ATMOSPHERE Tucked behind the rear smokestack, Waves is an outdoor bar catering primarily to sunbathers on Deck 12. Waves's eight fixed barstools are arranged around an attractive white tile face, and the back of the bar is decorated with small tiles in varying shades of blue. An overhang

above the bar provides shade for guests seated or standing at the bar, but most of the seating—upholstered blue cushions on glossy, curved-back teak booths, plus various sets of tables and chairs—is directly in the sun.

SELECTIONS The most popular drinks at Waves are bottled beers, frozen cocktails, and mixed drinks. Nonalcoholic smoothies and fruit juices are available for children and teetotalers.

COMMENTS Waves's hours vary, but it's usually open from late morning to late evening. Most visitors are coming from the lounge chairs or sports activities on Deck 13; some are just looking for a quiet spot away from the crowds.

ACROSS THE SHIPS Both the *Dream* and the *Fantasy* have Waves bars, and both are essentially identical. **Signals** is the outdoor bar on the *Magic* and *Wonder* (see page 197); Waves, however, is quieter, has nicer decor, and welcomes kids (Signals is 21-and-up only).

The District

This is the designation for the five bars and lounges on the *Dream*'s Deck 4 Aft: **District Lounge,** in a hallway connecting the different venues; **Evolution,** a dance club; **Pink,** a Champagne bar; **687,** an upscale sports bar; and **Skyline,** a cosmopolitan watering hole.

The theming is meant to evoke images of exclusive urban nightlife. Along the faux-brick walls and behind velvet ropes are black-plastic silhouettes of couples "waiting" to get in. Other walls have similar black-plastic images of paparazzi or simply the logos of the clubs illuminated in a repeating pattern.

Most of The District's bars open between 5 and 5:30 p.m. and stay open until midnight. District Lounge usually opens a little earlier; Evolution operates from around 10 p.m. to 2 a.m. Hot snacks are usually provided throughout the evening in one of The District's circular pedestrian walkways.

Evolution, Pink, and Skyline admit guests age 18 and up only. Families are welcome at District Lounge and 687 until 9 p.m., when the bars become adults-only.

District Lounge LOCATION: Deck 4 Aft

SETTING AND ATMOSPHERE An attractive, contemporary bar and seating area are bisected by a walkway connecting The District's bars. The bar seats six along its curving, white-stone front. Lights hidden beneath the black-marble top point down, creating smoky gray shadows in the stone. Behind the bar is a bronze-colored wall; orange lighting illuminates the bottles and provides this side of District Lounge with its most prominent color.

A lounge with couches and armchairs sits across the walkway opposite the bar; although it's not perfect, it's one of the more stylish places on the *Dream.* While the lounge is completely open to (and exposed to noise from) guests going from club to club, off-white leather couches, Champagne-colored metal poles, and cocoa-colored carpeting provide a visual boundary marking its border. Deeper inside are U-shaped armchairs, covered outside in the same white leather and inside in deep-brown leather, arranged in groups of 4 around small tables. A curving, chocolate-colored, illuminated wall provides a backdrop.

SELECTIONS The bar menu has a bit of everything: draft and bottled beer, cocktails, frozen drinks, whiskeys and tequilas, and wine and Champagne by the glass and bottle. There's also a special martini menu (about $10) not found at other clubs in The District. A few nonalcoholic drinks and coffees are available as well.

COMMENTS The best seats are along the lounge's inside wall, where you can relax in those deep armchairs while watching everyone else shuttle between clubs. This is also the best vantage point from which to watch the District Lounge's entertainment, which includes live singers and pianists later at night. The lounge is also a good meeting place to start out the evening, especially for groups who haven't decided which of The District's bars to visit.

ACROSS THE SHIPS The District Lounge roughly corresponds to the Venetian-themed **La Piazza** on the *Fantasy* (see page 211) but has no relative on the *Magic* or *Wonder.* We like District Lounge more than La Piazza: its recessed seating allows you to enjoy a drink away from the bustle of club-goers walking to their next destination.

Evolution LOCATION: Deck 4 Aft

SETTING AND ATMOSPHERE The *Dream*'s dance club, Evolution is, according to Disney, designed as "an artistic interpretation of the transformation of a butterfly . . . emerging from a chrysalis." What this entails is a lot of yellow, orange, and red lights arranged in the shape of butterfly wings and hung around the club. Pairs of wings hang above the dance floor, and we'll forgive you for comparing slightly tipsy dancing tourists to wriggling pupae. A couple of the walls are wing-patterned, too, bathing guests seated at the leather couches alongside in hues of ginger and crimson.

Fortunately, most of the butterfly theming is concentrated around the dance floor and along a couple of back walls. Between the two, it's not as noticeable; plastic-shell chairs sit in the dimly lit sections, occasionally alongside high-backed couches. Short barstools line the outside edge of the room, surrounding small, round tables. The circular bar has gold-leather seats on one side, allowing guests a view of the dance floor while they drink; the other half of the bar is for walk-up traffic.

SELECTIONS Evolution's drink menu is similar to District Lounge's, offering draft and bottled beer, cocktails, spirits, and wine, and Champagne by the glass and bottle.

COMMENTS Evolution is DCL's lowest-rated lounge, perhaps because of the relatively unusual (and subtle) theming. Because it's one of the largest venues on the *Dream,* Evolution is the site of family activities throughout the day, holding everything from hands-on craft-making seminars to tequila tastings to time-share presentations. Evolution's adults-only entertainment usually starts later than at other bars in The District, around 10 or 10:30 p.m.; check your *Personal Navigator* for details.

Live entertainment includes magicians, comics, singers, and more. In addition to live acts, Evolution's DJs sometimes dedicate an entire night's music to a specific genre. Common themes include classic rock, disco, and something called urban country.

ACROSS THE SHIPS Evolution is most similar to **The Tube** dance club on the *Fantasy* (see page 213), **Fathoms** on the *Magic* (see page 198), and **Azure** on the *Wonder* (see page 200), although it has no direct equivalent. We rate Evolution as the second-best dance club on DCL, behind The Tube. Theming, lighting,

and seating are nicer than at Fathoms and Azure, while The Tube's London Underground ambience is better executed than Evolution's more-conceptual "caterpillar to butterfly" idea.

Pink LOCATION: Deck 4 Aft

SETTING AND ATMOSPHERE Pink, the *Dream*'s Champagne bar, is our favorite nightspot on the ship. Decorated in silvers, whites, and golds, the space is intended to make you think you're sitting inside a glass of Champagne. In the walls are embedded round lights of white and pink, tiny near the floor and larger near the ceiling, imitating the carbon dioxide fizz inside a flute of bubbly. The silver carpet's starburst pattern calls to mind bubbles rising from below, and the rounded, glossy white ceiling is meant to represent the top of the glass. The light fixtures are upside-down Champagne flutes. Behind the bar are a multitude of glass "bubbles," expanding as they rise from the bar shelf to the ceiling.

Around the bar are half a dozen stools, with silver legs and clear, oval plastic backs that continue the bubble theme. Beyond the bar, a couple of burgundy chairs sit among their silver-velvet sisters. After a few drinks, we're pretty sure these are supposed to represent rosé Champagne, of which several are served at the bar. The best seats in the house, though, are on the padded couch inside a dome-shaped cubby in the wall at one end of the lounge. Move a couple of those big chairs in front and you have a private little cocoon, or slide them away for a view of the entire room.

SELECTIONS Pink's Champagne menu includes many recognizable names: Cristal, Moët et Chandon, Taittinger, Veuve Clicquot, and the requisite Dom Pérignon. Champagne-based cocktails are also available; most include fruit juices, such as mango, pomegranate, and peach, while a few include other liquors—the **Elderbubble**, for example, contains raspberry vodka along with Champagne and elderflower syrup. A small selection of white, red, and dessert wines is available by the glass (more by the bottle), along with a dozen or so whiskeys and Cognacs.

COMMENTS If you love Champagne, Pink is a relative bargain. Its markup is generally less than twice the average retail price—usually considerably less than what Disney charges at its theme-park resorts.

ACROSS THE SHIPS Only the *Dream* and the *Fantasy* have Champagne bars, and this is one of the main reasons we prefer these ships over the *Magic* and the *Wonder.* However, we like Pink's relatively understated theming better than the *très feminine* French-boudoir decor of **Ooh La La** on the *Fantasy* (see page 211).

687 LOCATION: Deck 4 Aft

SETTING AND ATMOSPHERE Anytime you see a venue with a dozen flat-panel TVs, chances are it's a sports bar. On the *Dream* it's called 687, and the screens are set in rows above the bar, in a cluster at a far end of the room, and individually in some seating areas.

The bar is set in the middle of 687's rectangular floor. Four porthole windows across from the bar provide light during the day, and moss-colored couches beneath them work to separate the wall into group-size partitions. The scarlet, green, and gold carpet and burgundy-painted, wood-paneled walls give 687 a more masculine feel than the sports bars on the *Fantasy, Magic,* and *Wonder.*

Besides the couches, barstools and tables are arranged around the room to provide good views of either set of televisions. A few leather-covered armchairs are also arranged around the screens and across from the couches. There's plenty of room to stand between these, too, in case you want to just catch up on some scores. Couches arranged in some of the corners provide quieter spots to unwind.

SELECTIONS Bar and table service are excellent. The menu is similar to District Lounge's and includes both draft and bottled beer, cocktails, spirits, and wine, and Champagne by the glass, plus coffees and nonalcoholic drinks. The bar menu was updated in 2017 for a more upscale vibe—think "lunching at the yacht club" rather than "pounding brewskis at the frat house." The signature-cocktail list has been whittled to just two items— the Shipbuilder's Wife (Absolut Pears vodka, limoncello, grappa, agave, and fresh lemon juice) and the Keel (Maker's Mark, Campari, limoncello, orange juice, and fresh ginger, with a mint garnish). Even the beer list is fancified, with a $17 Lindeman's Framboise Lambic and a $9 Trappist Ale at the top of the list. The pub-grub menu includes Wagyu beef sliders and crispy calamari, for $14 and $12, respectively. Or you can get some free chicken fingers from the pool deck snack bar and order a Bud Light if you want to watch football the old-fashioned way (and we often do).

COMMENTS We've spent a few evenings watching games at 687. The seating is comfortable, and it's easy to see and hear the action on the screens. Because of the way the seating is arranged, however, we've found it difficult to start conversations with other patrons. Try sitting at the bar if conviviality is important to you.

Besides sporting events, 687 hosts family activities during the day, including movie, music, and sports trivia. A selection of board games is available in case you want to play rather than watch. Finally, this is usually where runners meet before debarking for the start of the Castaway Cay 5K run when the *Dream* is docked there.

ACROSS THE SHIPS We find 687 more upscale than **Crown & Fin** on the *Wonder* (see page 201) or **O'Gills Pub** on the *Magic* and *Fantasy* (see pages 199 and 210, respectively). While its seating isn't as open, it's a posh place to catch up on the day's highlights in relative quiet.

Skyline LOCATION: Deck 4 Aft

SETTING AND ATMOSPHERE Along with Pink, Skyline is one of our two favorite bars on the *Dream.* The concept is that you're in a lounge high on the edge of some of the world's most famous cities. Behind the bar are seven "windows"—large HDTV screens—affording panoramic views of New York City, Chicago, Rio de Janeiro, Paris, and Hong Kong.

Each city is shown for about 15 minutes across all seven screens; then the scene changes to another locale. The foreground of each view includes close-up views of apartments and offices, while the middle and background show each city's iconic architecture and landscape.

That would be mildly interesting scenery on its own, but Disney has added special effects that make Skyline beautiful. Each view shows the city in motion: cars move along streets, neon signs blink to illuminate sidewalks, and apartment lights go on and off as their residents come and go. (Look closely and you can even see Mickey Mouse waving to you from inside a tiny apartment in Paris.) A second effect is that the scenery changes depending on the time of day you're inside. If you get here in late afternoon, you'll see the sun setting on

these towns. Stay long enough—and we have—and dusk turns to evening, then evening to night.

Last, Skyline has mirrors on the walls perpendicular to the video screens. Because the mirrors are set at right angles to the screens, they reflect the videos and make the bar look longer than it is. It's a well-known decorating trick for making a small room seem larger, but it's still nice to see it included here.

The rest of the decor is natural surfaces: wood panels, ceiling, and floors, in colors ranging from honey to mahogany; dark marble countertops; and leather chairs.

SELECTIONS The specialty is "around the world" cocktails themed to the featured cities. For example, the **1914** (about $9), representing Chicago, pairs Absolut Vanilla and Absolut Kurant vodkas with fresh blackberries and raspberries; the **Zen-Chanted** (about $11), representing Hong Kong, is made with 3Vodka (distilled from soybeans), Zen green-tea liqueur, Cointreau, and guava and lime juices.

COMMENTS Adding movement to the scenery means the view at Skyline doesn't get boring. It also means that the club doesn't need a television to hold its patrons' attention. And the cityscapes are a great way to break the ice with fellow cruisers.

ACROSS THE SHIPS Although there are Skylines on both the *Dream* and the *Fantasy,* their drink menus are mostly different. Drinks at the *Dream*'s Skyline tend toward the fruity, whereas drinks at the *Fantasy*'s Skyline make more use of herbs and spices, such as basil, thyme, coriander, cilantro, and paprika.

ON THE *FANTASY*

Bon Voyage LOCATION: Deck 3 Midship

SETTING AND ATMOSPHERE Just off the atrium and done in the same Art Nouveau style as the rest of the ship, Bon Voyage is one of the prettiest bars on the *Fantasy.* Behind the bar are two gold-and-white peacocks etched in glass, while the bar's face is a translucent gold marble. Cinnamon-colored wood accents complete the look. Bon Voyage has just 10 seats at the counter, plus 2 fabric-covered couches and 6 armchairs a few feet away.

SELECTIONS The bar menu is similar to that at La Piazza (see page 211) and includes draft and bottled beer, wines by the glass and bottle, spirits, and mixed drinks, including a few special fruit-flavored martinis.

COMMENTS Near the atrium and open from around noon to 11 p.m. daily, Bon Voyage is a good spot for groups to meet before dinner or to have a nightcap before departing for the elevators. Because it's in a heavily trafficked area, there's no live entertainment at the bar, and it's not our first choice for a quiet drink or conversation.

ACROSS THE SHIPS The *Dream*'s Bon Voyage is done in Art Deco rather than the *Fantasy*'s Art Nouveau version and is more appealing, even without live entertainment. The **Promenade Lounge** is the comparable bar on the *Magic* and *Wonder* (see page 196).

Cove Café LOCATION: Deck 11 Forward

COMMENTS See profile of Cove Café on the *Magic* (page 196) for details.

Currents LOCATION: Deck 13 Forward

COMMENTS See profile of Currents on the *Dream* (page 203) for details.

Meridian LOCATION: Deck 12 Aft

COMMENTS See profile of Meridian on the *Dream* (page 203) for details.

Vista Café LOCATION: Deck 4 Midship

COMMENTS See profile of Vista Café on the *Dream* (page 204) for details.

Waves LOCATION: Deck 12 Aft

COMMENTS See profile of Waves on the *Dream* (page 204) for details.

Europa

This is the designation for the five nightspots on the *Fantasy*'s Deck 4 Aft: **O'Gills Pub,** a sports bar; **Ooh La La,** a Champagne bar; **La Piazza,** an Italian-inspired lounge; **Skyline,** a cosmopolitan watering hole; and **The Tube,** a London subway–themed dance club.

While the nightlife districts on the other three ships have distinctive theming, Europa has next to none. The ostensible theme is Europe, but the decor consists mostly of just shiny gold walls, with each club's name illuminated and repeated in a pattern. That said, one nice touch found only at Europa lies in the round black-and-white photos on the walls: the images, which feature European icons, including the Eiffel Tower, London's Big Ben, and the Leaning Tower of Pisa, turn into short animated videos. Also, for what it's worth, the restrooms here are decorated fabulously.

Most of Europa's bars open between 5 and 5:30 p.m. and stay open until midnight. La Piazza usually opens a little earlier than that; The Tube operates from around 10 p.m. to 2 a.m. Hot appetizers are usually provided throughout the evening in one of La Piazza's circular pedestrian walkways.

Ooh La La, Skyline, and The Tube admit guests age 18 and up only. Families are welcome at La Piazza and O'Gills Pub until 9 p.m., when they become adults-only.

O'Gills Pub LOCATION: Deck 4 Aft

SETTING AND ATMOSPHERE The *Fantasy*'s sports bar, O'Gills lies just off one side of La Piazza (see next page). It's ostensibly an Irish pub, but it's the least visually interesting bar in Europa. The attempts at theming—Irish music and liberal use of four-leaf clovers—are halfhearted at best; with some paint, antiques-store scavenging, and the right "beer of the month" subscription, O'Gills could pass as a Chicago-, Dallas-, or Green Bay–themed bar.

The centerpiece is a huge high-def video screen in the back corner, which shows sporting events and sports news all day long. Several other smaller screens are distributed throughout the room, and there's plenty of seating and standing room.

SELECTIONS The bar menu includes bottled and draft beer, including a house draft lager and several Irish brews. Wine is available by the glass and bottle, and the friendly bartenders can mix up any cocktail you want. The specialty is Irish whiskey and Scotch; a private-label Irish cream liqueur is on the menu, too.

COMMENTS You wouldn't come here for the Irish ambience, but as a generic sports bar, O'Gills isn't bad.

ACROSS THE SHIPS There's another O'Gills on the *Magic* (see page 199). As a sports bar, however, it's similar to **687** on the *Dream* (see page 207) and **Crown & Fin** on the *Wonder* (see page 201). We prefer 687, O'Gills on the *Magic,* and Crown & Fin because they have better sight lines to the TV screens from the seating areas.

Ooh La La LOCATION: Deck 4 Aft

SETTING AND ATMOSPHERE This is the *Fantasy's* Champagne bar. The French-boudoir theme is enough to make you break out in "Lady Marmalade" from *Moulin Rouge:* rose-colored upholstery on the walls, purple carpet, and chairs lined with gold fabric. Along one wall are a series of padded couches in ivory and green. Gold-edged mirrors and fleurs-de-lis line the walls. A single red chair and a couple of small, red-topped side tables provide a touch of bold color.

The bar, at the far end of the lounge, seats six around its black marble top. In keeping with the boudoir theme, the mirror behind the bar looks like an oversize version of one you'd find on the dressing table of a fashionable Frenchwoman at the *fin de siècle.* And because it's a Champagne bar, hundreds of small glass bubbles fill the mirrors.

SELECTIONS Ooh La La serves reasonably priced Champagnes by the glass and bottle. A couple of these, such as Pommery Rosé Brut and Bollinger La Grande Année, aren't found at Pink, the Champagne bar on the *Dream.* Available along with these are such familiar names as Taittinger and Dom Pérignon. A glass of bubbly starts at around $8 and goes up to $20; bottles cost anywhere from around $50 to $500.

Champagne cocktails, with fruit juices and other liquors, cost around $11, but remember the Second Law of Champagne: if it needs another ingredient, you're drinking the wrong Champagne. (The First Law: Champagne goes with everything!) Sparkling wines, along with reds and whites, are available by the glass and bottle, and the fully stocked bar can furnish virtually any cocktail you like.

COMMENTS The best seats in Ooh La La are on the L-shaped silver couch near the main entrance. It's the perfect private place to do some people-watching. Another nice touch is the use of area rugs to mark off sections of seats—it's possible to mingle within that small area, having individual conversations while still being part of the group. The club has three porthole windows—which we didn't expect—with ocean views and seating below. If you visit during the late afternoon, the light from outside provides a gentle transition from day to dusk.

ACROSS THE SHIPS Only the *Dream* and the *Fantasy* have Champagne bars, and this is one of the main reasons we prefer these ships over the *Magic* and the *Wonder.* However, we like the relatively understated theming of **Pink** on the *Dream* (see page 207) better than the frilly decor of Ooh La La.

La Piazza LOCATION: Deck 4 Aft

SETTING AND ATMOSPHERE This Venetian-themed lounge sits near the front of Europa. Appropriately, La Piazza ("The Plaza") serves as the walkway to O'Gills and Ooh La La, whose entrances sit just off this venue; farther beyond are Skyline and The Tube, so you'll walk by La Piazza on the way.

The bar sits in the middle of a bright circular room. It's themed to look like an Italian carousel, its ceiling decorated with hundreds of carousel lights. Around the bar are rose-colored barstools; lining the wall are golden, high-backed, upholstered couches with small tables for drinks. The couches are separated, elevated, and set into niches in the walls, making them good vantages from which to watch people walk between the clubs.

SELECTIONS La Piazza's bar menu features Peroni and Moretti, two Italian beers, as well as prosecco (Italian sparkling wine) and limoncello (an Italian lemon-flavored liqueur). These ingredients also make their way into La Piazza's five signature cocktails—the **Mercutio**, for example, features Absolut Pears vodka, limoncello, grappa, and fresh lemon juice, with the sweetness of the pear and grappa balancing out the tartness of the citrus.

COMMENTS The couches are good spots for watching La Piazza's live entertainment, which has been an up-tempo jazz trio on each of our cruises. If you're not into music, our favorite pastime at La Piazza takes place starting at 11 p.m., when we start to wager a round of drinks on the number of couples who will stop to take photos on La Piazza's Vespa motorcycle-and-sidecar prop in the next 10 minutes. The over-under on that bet is usually 2.5, and the rules prohibit shouting encouragement to the *ubriachi.*

ACROSS THE SHIPS Somewhat similar to **District Lounge** on the *Dream* (see page 205), La Piazza has a better drink menu, while District Lounge has a better layout. Neither the *Magic* nor the *Wonder* has a comparable bar.

Skyline LOCATION: Deck 4 Aft

SETTING AND ATMOSPHERE Skyline is our favorite bar on the *Fantasy.* The concept is that you're in a lounge high on the edge of some of the world's most famous cities. Behind the bar are seven "windows"—large HDTV screens—affording panoramic views of seven cities: Athens, Barcelona, Budapest, Florence, London, Paris, and St. Petersburg.

Each city is shown for about 15 minutes across all seven screens; then the scene changes to another locale. The foreground of each view includes close-up views of apartments and offices, while the middle and background show each city's iconic architecture and landscape.

That would be mildly interesting scenery on its own, but Disney has added special effects that make Skyline beautiful. Each view shows the city in motion: cars move along streets, neon signs blink to illuminate sidewalks, and apartment lights go on and off as their residents come and go. (Look closely and you can even see Mickey Mouse waving to you from inside a tiny apartment in Paris.) A second effect is that the scenery changes depending on the time of day you're inside. If you get here in late afternoon, you'll see the sun setting on these towns. Stay long enough—and we have—and dusk turns to evening, then evening to night.

Last, Skyline has mirrors on the walls perpendicular to the video screens. Because the mirrors are set at right angles to the screens, they reflect the videos and make the bar look longer than it is. It's a well-known decorating trick for making a small room seem larger, but it's still nice to see it included here.

The rest of the decor is natural surfaces: wood panels, ceiling, and floors; dark marble countertops; and leather chairs.

SELECTIONS The specialty is "around the world" cocktails themed to the featured cities. For example, **El Conquistador**, representing Barcelona, pairs Tanqueray gin and Absolut Peppar vodka with fresh muddled strawberries, basil, and

cracked black pepper; the **Aquincum**, representing Budapest, is made with 901 Tequila, Grand Marnier, paprika, and freshly squeezed lime juice.

COMMENTS Adding movement to the scenery means the view at Skyline doesn't get boring. It also means that the club doesn't need a television to hold its patrons' attention. And the cityscapes are a great way to break the ice with fellow cruisers.

ACROSS THE SHIPS Although there are Skylines on both the *Dream* and the *Fantasy,* the latter one features two more cities in its "windows" than the one on the *Dream.* Also, their drink menus are mostly different. Drinks at the *Dream's* Skyline tend to be flavored with fruits and fruit juices, such as cranberry, pomegranate, lemon, and lime; drinks on the *Fantasy's* Skyline are made with fruits, too, but also with herbs and spices, such as basil, thyme, coriander, cilantro, and paprika.

The Tube LOCATION: Deck 4 Aft

SETTING AND ATMOSPHERE With its London subway-meets-Austin Powers theme, The Tube is the *Fantasy's* dance club. Its decor includes leather couches with prints that look like Underground tickets, 1960s-mod egg-shaped chairs, and a floor painted like a London subway map. We especially like the upholstered leather couch set deep inside the lounge because it's under a set of lights in the shape of a crown and across from two shiny silver armchairs designed to look like thrones. A couple of red phone booths are set on either side of the dance floor. *Oh, behave!*

SELECTIONS The Tube's circular bar, set under Big Ben's clock face, serves a typical menu of bottled beer, mixed drinks, spirits, and wine and Champagne by the glass. The Tube also serves six signature drinks, our favorite of which is **Mind the Gap**, a mix of whiskey, Drambuie, and Coke.

COMMENTS The Tube usually opens around 10 p.m. and sometimes gets things going with a quick game of Match Your Mate (think *The Newlywed Game,* only groovier). Dancing usually gets started around 10:30 or 11 p.m. Most of the music is contemporary dance, but there are themed nights with disco and, of course, British hits. If you want a good view of the stage, particularly if you have a large party, plan to arrive a few minutes early for nondance activities.

ACROSS THE SHIPS The club's closest counterparts are **Fathoms** on the *Magic* (see page 198), **Azure** on the *Wonder* (see page 200), and **Evolution** on the *Dream* (see page 206). The Tube, though, is our favorite dance club on any of the ships.

PART NINE

ACTIVITIES, RECREATION, *and* SHOPPING

BESIDES EAT, DRINK, BE ENTERTAINED, and tour ports, there's lots to do on every Disney Cruise Line itinerary:

- **Family activities** are held throughout the day and include trivia contests, bingo, deck parties, and more.
- **Children's programs,** the strength of Disney Cruise Line, begin as early as 7 a.m.
- It wouldn't be a Disney cruise without **character greetings,** including Mickey, Minnie, and the Disney princesses.
- Each ship's **pools and water-play areas** are the center of activity during the day on most cruises.
- **Onboard seminars** are inexpensive (some are free) and cover everything from cooking demonstrations to wine tastings.
- Runners and sports fans will find a **measured track** on each ship, plus **basketball, volleyball, miniature golf,** and more.
- After a tough day on shore, you can relax at the **spa.**
- **Shopping opportunities** are available on board and in port.

FAMILY ACTIVITIES

BINGO

DCL IS ONE OF THE FEW CRUISE LINES that have no casino gambling on board. What it does have is bingo, played most days on most ships, in one or two hour-long sessions per day. The cost to play is about $30 per paper card per game, with four games played per hour. Prizes range from duffel bags filled with DCL swag to actual cash jackpots of several thousand dollars. On one sailing, we watched a young guy win nearly $9,000 at bingo—enough to pay for his entire vacation and then some.

With that much money at stake, it's no surprise that many people take these games seriously. Games are fast-paced, and players are expected to keep up. Additionally, DCL interjects sound effects, music, dance, and random chatter into the number calling. This makes it fun for the kiddos, but it can be somewhat overwhelming if you were expecting a level of cacophony more suited to old folks at the Elks Lodge. (*Pro tip:* The reason the bingo crew members do a crazy dance every time the B-11 ball is called is that when the machine is in Spanish-language mode, *B-11* is *B once,* pronounced more or less like "Beyoncé.")

Children are allowed to play bingo, keeping track of the numbers and enjoying the merriment, but they must be accompanied at all times by a guest age 18 or older, who will officially be the winner of any cash prizes.

The cost to play varies, even within the same voyage. Pricing is typically higher at the end of each sailing, when the payouts are larger. Buy-in starts at $30 for one set of traditional paper bingo cards per session. However, most guests opt to rent electronic bingo machines, often priced at $40 or $50 for 24 cards per session. The electronic machines receive signals from the bingo console, telling them which numbers have been called. Because the machines keep track of the state of the game, you don't have to be hypervigilant every second.

If you think you're going to be playing frequently, be sure to stick around at the end of each session. The caller will often give out a special one-day-only password that's good for free bingo cards if you mention it at the next session. On longer sailings, the caller will sometimes offer personal touches by asking you to bring in something original, such as a child's drawing of the ship or a phone photo of a specific thing in port, in order to get a free bingo card during the next session.

When we sailed DCL in the Baltic on the *Magic,* our bingo caller asked guests to bring him jokes related to our sailing to get an extra card. Coauthor Erin's daughter Josie brought him, "I'm **TALLIN** you that I'm so sad that my journey **RUSSIAN** around the Baltic is over! It was super **SWEDE,** but now it's **FINNISHED.**" (We visited Tallin, Estonia; St. Petersburg, Russia; and ports in Sweden and Finland.) For her

SCOTT SAYS *by Scott Sanders*

"ARE WE HAVING FUN YET?"

I OFTEN HEAR PEOPLE SAY they're concerned about being bored on a cruise. But if you look over your *Personal Navigator,* you'll see that there's almost always something interesting to do. The trick is to not try to do it all—this is a cruise, after all, not a theme park. Relax a bit and let the day unfold.

effort, Josie not only got a free bingo card for Mom but also a free bingo ball–shaped lip balm emblazoned with her favorite B-11 call number for herself. *Creativity counts, people!*

There may also be frequent-player discounts for reduced fees on cards if you play several times during the same cruise—be sure to ask.

IS THIS WORTH YOUR TIME? Len rarely plays bingo—he doesn't like the noisy atmosphere or gambling in general—but Erin's family plays several rounds of bingo on every sailing. If you don't mind some boisterous silliness and you're OK with gambling relatively small amounts of money, it could be worth a $30 buy-in just once to see if it's your cup of tea. But beware that once you get hooked, costs can add up quickly.

DECK PARTIES

FEATURING DISNEY CHARACTERS, deck parties are usually held several times per cruise, typically near the family pool or in the ship's main lobby. The first party, known as the **Sail-Away Celebration,** happens as you leave port on embarkation day. Additional deck parties will happen any time there is a themed day/evening on the ship (Pirate Night, Star Wars Day, New Year's Eve, and so on). Expect to hear G-rated versions of the pop songs being played at weddings and bar mitzvahs during the year you're sailing. Bonus points if you get a song performed by the former star of a former hit show on the Disney Channel.

All outdoor parties are high-energy affairs, with loud music, dancing, games, and other activities, plus videos displayed on the ship's giant LED screen. The indoor versions omit only the giant video screens. Check your *Personal Navigator* for dates and times.

IS THIS WORTH YOUR TIME? If you were a fan of the old *Love Boat,* it's a near must-do, if only for the kitsch/pop culture factor. Little kids typically love the show if they're able to see the stage. If you're an adult cruising for relaxation, take a pass.

FAMILY NIGHTCLUBS

IN ADDITION TO ITS MYRIAD adult-entertainment offerings (see Part Eight), DCL has what would be an oxymoron in any other context: the family nightclub. Set up like grown-up nightspots, with snazzy decor and their own bars, tables and chairs, and dance floors, these lounges offer daytime and nighttime entertainment, including comedy shows, trivia contests, cooking demos, karaoke, line dancing, and more. (Many of the same activities are also offered during the day at some adult lounges.) Refreshments are served, including cocktails for Mom and Dad and smoothies and sodas for the kids, all at an extra charge.

unofficial **TIP**
DCL prohibits guests from bringing their own musical instruments on board. However, Disney can provide a full-size electronic keyboard for performers, and the ships typically keep an acoustic guitar on hand for use in the teen clubs; ask if you can borrow it for the talent show.

Most of the family-nightclub activities take place in each ship's **D Lounge,** on Deck 4 Midship. Hours vary, so check your *Personal Navigator* for details.

The family activities in the nightclubs (and sometimes in the lobby atrium) vary considerably depending on the length of the sailing, the itinerary, whether it's a special-events sailing (Star Wars, holiday, and so on), and other factors. You'll obviously have a wider array of family activities if you're spending 11 nights on the ship than you will for a quick 3-night trip. Days at sea will have a wider range of programming than days in port, when many guests will be off enjoying the sights on land.

There are, however, a number of activities that show up with some frequency. Among them are the following:

- **Diaper Dash.** All babies of crawling age are invited to participate in a race along a padded mat in the atrium. The cruise staff livens things up with "interviews" with the babies and toddlers. There may be few participants on long European and repositioning sailings, but competition can be fiercely funny on short Caribbean hops. It's great fun to watch, even if you don't have a participating child. Beware, however, of having your child participate if he or she is sensitive to loud noises—the cheering can get intense.
- **Disney Trivia, Cruise Trivia, Sports Trivia, Movie Trivia, and so on.** Trivia is big on longer sailings. It often helps to have team members from different generations, because questions may come from current topics or ancient times (you know, like the '80s). Though the prizes are typically low-value items like plastic medals or keychains, rivalries can get intense. Keep an eye out for Disney know-it-alls who study in advance with the specific aim of wiping the floor with their onboard competition.
- **Disney Tunes Trivia.** Another version of the trivia genre, but look for Tunes Trivia with a live pianist rather than prerecorded music snippets. They can sometimes tweak the music to make it easier or harder to guess. We've also had some fascinating postgame conversations with the performers.
- **Crafts.** These are usually low-mess, cut-and-paste craft-assembly affairs, typically most enjoyed by elementary schoolers. Teens will likely find them boring.
- **Family Karaoke.** Guests choose songs from black loose-leaf binders. Obviously, there are many songs from Disney films among the possibilities, but you'll also find classic and contemporary pop and rock tunes, country hits, American Songbook standards, and a few Spanish-language hits. As you might expect, any song with even a hint of profanity is forbidden in the Family Karaoke selection. (There is often an adult karaoke where the standards are slightly relaxed, with emphasis on *slightly.*) Expect to hear aspiring Idina Menzels belt the showstopper from the latest Disney film at least two or three times per session. (A cast member told us she nearly wept for joy when *Moana*'s "How Far I'll

Go" finally supplanted *Frozen*'s "Let It Go" after a two-year reign as the ubiquitous karaoke selection.) If you want to sing, be absolutely sure to be there at start time; available time slots often fill quickly.

- **Who Wants to Be a Mouseketeer?** An abbreviated (and much less remunerative) version of *Who Wants to Be a Millionaire?* Questions are kid-friendly. More fun to participate in than to watch from the audience.
- **Animation Lessons.** If you're familiar with the animation lessons at the old Magic of Animation attraction at Disney's Hollywood Studios, then you have an idea of what to expect here. Don't expect to become an artist overnight, but you may come out of it with a passable rendition of Mickey. If you have a child who's a perfectionist, this could be a trouble spot—we once had a child melt down when her drawing was less than identical to the instructor's.
- **So You Think You Know Your Family.** Structured a bit like the old *Newlywed Game,* this involves parent-child pairs guessing how the other generation will answer various questions. Typical families chosen to participate have a child in the 7- to 11-year-old age range. May spark some interesting dinner-table discussions about how your family might have answered.
- **Dance Lessons.** Longer sailings may have instruction in some locally flavored dance—Irish step dancing on a Northern European cruise or tango on a Mediterranean cruise, for example. You may pick up a few steps if you have a bit of movement experience or are a natural dancer. We're not, so we just pretend that we're burning off enough calories to have an extra turn at the soft-serve machine by the pool deck.
- **Toddler Time.** Very low-key, usually scheduled in the early morning. Cast members will put out some blocks and small toys for toddlers to explore. You can't leave your child unattended, but you may be able to turn your brain off for a few minutes while you let your first dose of caffeine soak in.
- **MagicQuest (also known as Wonder Quest or Family Dream Quest).** This is a contained scavenger hunt. Cast members will ask for things that might be found in the room—a pen, a sweatshirt, something with a picture of Donald Duck on it, for example. There's a surprising amount of running around. Bring a bag full of random personal items for the best results.
- **Cooking Lessons.** These are more observational than hands-on affairs; you'll be watching someone else describing the steps of cooking rather than handling any food yourself. Printed recipes are usually distributed at the end; we've had good luck re-creating them at home.
- **Chip It Golf.** Usually populated by dads wearing long shorts and their tween sons. Seriously, we've never seen a woman participate in this activity, and we can't figure out why.
- **Mickey Mania.** Disney trivia in a game-show format. Four parent-child teams have to be quick on the buzzer for a chance to answer moderately challenging questions. Most families chosen to compete have kids ages 8 through teens.

- **The Feud.** Think *Family Feud* with Disneyfied questions. Because not everyone is traveling with extended family, you may be playing with people you don't know.
- **Art of the Ship Tour.** Walk around the ship with DCL cast members who will point out construction and design elements of the vessel on which you're cruising. The tour is often interesting, but there's not much in the way of interactivity.
- **Mirror, Mirror.** Game show and story with a vague Snow White theme. We've seen it at least half a dozen times, but we're still not sure we get the point.
- **Family Talent Show.** Some cruises of seven nights or longer host a guest-participation talent show. We've seen some amazingly skilled child gymnasts, dancers, and magicians on board. If you're interested in performing, be sure to sign up at Guest Services early in your trip, and pack whatever shoes, costumes, karaoke tracks, or sheet music you might need to perform. While you're not allowed to bring your own musical instruments onto the ship, you can usually borrow a guitar or keyboard that's kept on hand.

unofficial **TIP**
People tend to enter and leave the family activities with some regularity—don't feel obligated to stick around if you're not having fun.

Your enjoyment of any of these activities may be affected by your mood, the personalities of the other participating guests, and your perception of the staff who are running the event. While the cruise staff who run the family activities are universally enthusiastic and engaging, it's always possible that someone could be having a bad day. Also note that while it's usually good to arrive on time at the beginning of an activity so you can hear the instructions for a game, for example, there's no requirement that you stay for the entire thing. If you know after 5 minutes that an activity doesn't interest you, then you can always look for something else more to your liking.

SPORTS AND FITNESS

THE DISNEY SHIPS have several sports options available for families, covered later in this chapter, beginning on page 247.

CHILDREN'S PROGRAMS *and* ACTIVITIES

WHEN IT COMES TO ENTERTAINING CHILDREN, Disney Cruise Line has no equal. Youth clubs (also known interchangeably as kids' clubs), designed for infants to 17-year-olds, open as early as 7:30 a.m. for babies and close as late as 2 a.m. for teens. Kids can participate in organized activities, ranging from craft-making to trivia contests and

dance parties, or they can play individually with computer games, board games, books, and craft materials. Most of the organized activities last 60–90 minutes, so a new event will likely start soon after your child arrives; this means kids become part of the group quickly. Based on reader feedback, it's far more likely that your child will not want to leave his or her kids' club than not want to go to it in the first place.

Reservations are required for babysitting at the nurseries, but they're not needed for the kids' clubs for children ages 3 and up. Once you've registered your kids at the club, you can drop them off there as little or as often as you like, with no need to let anyone know in advance. It's an incredibly flexible system that allows for a great deal of vacation spontaneity.

Outside of the kids' clubs, there's plenty more for children and families to do. Much like the Disney theme parks, the DCL cruise ships offer a contained environment that gives tweens and teens some autonomy to roam on their own. Wave Phones (see page 15) and the texting function of the DCL Navigator app mean that you'll always be able to reach your children, and the free food on the pool deck and at the buffet means there's no worrying about finding something to eat, or how to pay for it.

Younger children (and older ones who aren't yet pretending they don't know you) and their families have activities scheduled throughout the day, from karaoke to character greetings; check your *Personal Navigator* for times and locations.

Other activities include minigolf (*Dream* and *Fantasy*) and the sports decks, all topside.

SPECIAL CONSIDERATIONS

INFANTS Babies must be 6 months of age or older to sail on most Alaskan, Bahamian, Caribbean, and other cruises of seven nights or fewer. Some longer cruises, often those with multiple consecutive sea days, such as the transatlantic crossings, require that children be at least 1 year old to sail.

TWEENS AND TEENS Don't worry that your preteen or teenager is "too cool" for a Disney cruise. Based on both our own experiences and those of other parents, teens will practically forget you exist once they get a feel for the clubs and activities. In fact, before you even set foot on the ship, you should set some ground rules for how often your teen needs to check in with you. Our rule was that everyone had to eat two meals per day together during sea days and stay together during shore excursions. On Castaway Cay, we reserved morning activities for family time, and the teens were allowed to explore the island on their own after lunch.

ONLY-CHILD SITUATIONS The middle- and high-school kids' clubs are seamless for kids who are traveling with similarly aged siblings, cousins, or friends. They have a built-in companion for activities and can sample

DCL YOUTH CLUBS IN BRIEF
IT'S A SMALL WORLD NURSERY
• LOCATION Deck 5 Aft • AGES 6/12 months (depends on itinerary)–3 years • OPENS Varies • CLOSES 11 p.m. • FEE $9/hour for first child, $8/hour for each additional child • MEALS Bring your own food, milk, and formula
OCEANEER CLUB/OCEANEER LAB
• LOCATION Deck 5 Midship • AGES 3–12 years • OPENS Varies • CLOSES Midnight • FEE None • MEALS Lunch and dinner
EDGE
• LOCATION Deck 9 Midship (*Magic, Wonder*), Deck 13 Forward (*Dream, Fantasy*) • AGES 11–14 years • OPENS Varies • CLOSES 1 a.m. • FEE None • MEALS None
VIBE
• LOCATION Deck 11 Midship (*Magic, Wonder*), Deck 5 Forward (*Dream, Fantasy*) • AGES 14–17 years • OPENS Varies • CLOSES 2 a.m. • FEE None • REFRESHMENTS Sodas (free), smoothies (extra charge) • EXTRAS Sun deck with splash pools (*Dream, Fantasy*)

the club offerings at will, with no fear of being the odd kid out. Our (multiple) children were able to pop in and out of the teen clubs whenever an activity seemed interesting, never feeling alone or out of place.

For a middle-schooler or teen traveling as the only one of his/her age group in the family, the youth clubs can be more challenging, as was the case with one of our teens on a recent trip. She was completely fine joining in the introductory games during the Sail-Away Celebration, where the fun was orchestrated by a counselor. Several other times, however, she dropped in at Vibe and found just a few kids who were obviously paired off into subgroups. Because of this, our normally social and extroverted daughter had trouble slotting herself in.

Our teen's observation was that the "single" kids who did best at Vibe were the ones who participated in absolutely every activity there, including the teen activities on Castaway Cay, thus giving them the opportunity to pair off with someone. Because she was doing so much stuff with us, she found it harder to participate at Vibe on an ad hoc basis. For solo teens and tweens, then, the youth clubs might best be thought of as an all-or-nothing proposition: those who just want to sample the clubs, as opposed to immersing themselves in the activities, should expect the social scene to be harder to break into.

ACTIVE KIDS As a parent, you're the best judge of how much physical activity your child needs. We've rarely seen truly bad behavior on the Disney ships, but when we have, it's usually been an active child running in circles around other guests after sitting in passive activities all day.

To ensure that your kids burn off their excess energy in a positive way, keep an eye out for ways to add physical activity to their day, particularly if you're spending several consecutive days at sea. The

A YOUNG CRUISER'S TAKE ON KIDS' CLUBS

THIRTEEN-YEAR-OLD CRUISE BLOGGER **Kieran Sweeney** shares his thoughts on DCL's youth clubs:

SPENDING TIME IN THE YOUTH CLUBS is one of my favorite things to do on a Disney cruise. They really show how much effort Disney has put in to ensure that every kid on the ship has a good time. For example, all the Edge counselors on my most recent cruise knew all the kids' names. Not only that, but they greeted us by name whenever we came in. This made it feel welcoming and friendly.

The kids' clubs really are for anyone (except adults).* If a kid really likes to draw and create art, there are special activities for them; in fact, the Oceaneer Lab even has a whole room for art! If a child likes to play video games, there are tons of games to choose from! If a kid is super-energetic, there are activities for that (Gaga Ball is a personal favorite).

When I'm on a cruise, I spend most of my free time in the kids' clubs. No matter what ship I'm on, the *Personal Navigator* always includes tons of fun things. I check it daily to plan what I want to do in the clubs that day. I especially like the activities held outside the clubs. For example, Edge and Vibe have scavenger hunts that make teams go around the ship, solve puzzles, and look for the next clue. It's a great way to explore the ship and make new friends.

**Authors' note: The kids' clubs all have open-house hours when kids can play there with their parents or when adults can just pop in to see the facilities. We're not ashamed to admit that we've lingered at the* Millennium Falcon *bridge replica at the* Dream*'s kids' club. (We are maybe a* little *ashamed that we've loudly spoken the words "Traveling through hyperspace ain't like dusting crops, boy" while doing so.)*

pool and sports deck are obvious solutions, but these may sometimes be unavailable due to weather or temporary maintenance issues. The many onboard dance parties can be a good way for an active child to let off steam; also carefully check your *Personal Navigator* for movement opportunities.

USING THE KIDS' CLUBS WHEN YOU'RE OFF THE SHIP Guests are welcome to use the kids' clubs whenever they're open, including when the ship is in port. There's no requirement that you remain on the ship while your child is in the care of the kids' club, nor is there any limit to the number of consecutive hours a child can remain in a club.

This can play out in a number of ways. Some parents might choose to leave their sand-phobic 6-year-old on the ship for an hour while they're a Wave Phone call and a 10-minute walk away on Castaway Cay. On the other end of the spectrum, coauthor Erin met a guest on an 11-hour-long excursion to Rome while the ship was in Civitavecchia, a 90-minute drive away. The guest had left her 7-year-old daughter at the

kids' club on the ship because she thought her child would be bored with the long ride and sightseeing.

While this isn't something we would do ourselves, it's perfectly acceptable within the rules of DCL. And only you know what's right for your family: that guest on the Rome excursion was the single mother of an independent and articulate child who enjoyed spending time in the kids' club. She had saved for years to make the cruise happen, and visiting Rome was a lifelong dream for her. It was a win–win for them both.

If you do decide to leave your child for an extended period of time, communicate your plans to the counselors at the club and possibly also to the cast members at Guest Relations. Let them know where you'll be, when you'll return, your cell number, and any pertinent medical information, as well as contact information for the child's home medical providers and other general emergency contacts.

Also note that this might be a situation where you'd be better served by taking one of Disney's port adventures rather than a self-booked excursion. In the event that you encounter delays in getting back to the ship, chances are that the crew will wait a few extra minutes for a large group on a DCL port adventure versus a lone guest on a third-party excursion.

Occasionally a ship will leave stragglers behind at the port. This is panic-inducing for most people; having it happen while your child is back on the ship is orders of magnitude more distressing. Keep your passport with you at all times—should this worst-case scenario happen, having your passport handy should expedite your reunion with your child.

YOUTH CLUBS

THE BULK OF DCL'S CHILDREN'S ACTIVITIES take place at the youth clubs on the ships. They're organized by age group, as follows:

• **Oceaneer Club** and **Oceaneer Lab** for children ages 3–12	
• **Edge** for ages 11–14	• **Vibe** for ages 14–17

We provide profiles of the clubs starting on page 225, organized by ship and ordered from the youngest to oldest age groups.

Children in the following age groups may choose which club they wish to participate in: 3-year-olds can choose the nursery or (as long as they're potty-trained) Oceaneer Club/Lab; 11- and 12-year-olds can choose between Oceaneer Club/Lab and Edge; and 14-year-olds can choose Edge or Vibe. This flexibility is helpful when siblings who are close in age want to be in the same club. Once a choice is made, however, it may not be changed. Disney is also strict about making sure that kids stick to the club for their age group—that is, no sneaking into Vibe if they're not old enough, or if they're even slightly too old.

Children in the nurseries, Oceaneer Club, and Oceaneer Lab will be asked to wear a wristband while they're on the premises, and parents will be given an electronic pager. The wristbands look somewhat

similar to the MagicBands in use at Walt Disney World, but they work differently. Parents will see a $12.95 charge per band on their bill if the bands are not returned at the end of the sailing.

Sensors at each club's doors will trigger an alarm if your child tries to leave without a parent to deactivate the wristband. In the event that Disney or your child needs to contact you, club staff will call you on your Wave Phone. Kids ages 8–12 may check themselves out with their parent's permission.

Children registered at the Edge and Vibe clubs (kids ages 11–17) are free to come and go as they please—no check-in or checkout is necessary. If your kids get bored, they may leave to visit a character greeting, go to the pool, grab a snack, go back to the room, or just roam around. (Rest assured that they won't be allowed to leave the ship without adult accompaniment, unless you've specifically completed a special form allowing them to do so.) Parents enjoying some alone time while their kids are at Vibe or the Edge may run into them before they expect it.

For some kids, this is an unprecedented amount of freedom, which may cause discomfort for the parent or child. Be sure to set ground rules for your kids about notifying you where they are; these might include periodic checking in via Wave Phone, sending texts using the DCL Navigator app, or leaving notes on a whiteboard posted on your stateroom door.

All kids must be registered to use the youth clubs. Parents can sign up their children either before boarding through online check-in (see page 39) or on embarkation day in the clubs' open houses. Signing up online has the advantage of giving busy cruisers one less thing to worry about after boarding the ship. Open houses are a great way for parents to check out the various clubs in person. (*Warning:* The spaces are so well themed that adults will be sad when they have to leave.) Once a child is registered for a club, he or she may use its facilities for the entire cruise.

Some activities, such as board games, computer games, and crafts, are generally available on an ad hoc basis; kids can access them whenever they're in the club. Throughout each day there are also planned themed activities, which will be noted in your *Personal Navigator.* Some of the listed activities are self-explanatory: You can easily figure out what "Magic Show" or "Dance Party" means.

Other activities, however, are more cryptic. Case in point: we'd been wondering for years what the mysteriously named "4th Pig's Pasta Palace" was until we were finally clued in by reader Lori Ketcherside:

> *4th Pigs Pasta Palace in the Oceaneer Lab is when the fourth pig (in addition to the original Three Little Pigs) uses science to test different options to build his home. This involves using macaroni to create houses that will withstand damage when bumped, hit, or dropped.*

This sounds awesome, but there's no way we would have figured out what it was from the title alone. Lori adds:

> *My daughter loves it, but when my son was on a gluten-free diet, they wouldn't let him participate for fear that he would put one of the pasta pieces in his mouth. He never felt left out, though, because they always had other special projects for kids with food allergies.*

Lori's comments here are a good reminder for families with special diets to double check what's happening with food during all activities on the ship.

Nurseries

These operate under a reservation system and charge an hourly rate for services; parents will need to book specific times. The charge is $9 an hour for the first child and $8 an hour for each additional child in the same family. You should bring your own milk, formula, and baby food, along with diapers and wipes, a change of clothes, and a blanket and pacifier if your child needs those to nap.

Space is limited at each nursery; reservations are required and are first-come, first-served:

- **Concierge guests and Platinum Castaway Club members** (see page 65) can make reservations **120 days** in advance.
- **Gold Castaway Club members** can make reservations **105 days** in advance.
- **Silver Castaway Club members** can make reservations **90 days** in advance.
- **All other guests** can make reservations **75 days** out.

If you haven't made your nursery reservations by the time you board the ship, either stop by before dinner or call from your stateroom or Wave Phone: dial ☎ **7-5864** on the *Magic, Dream,* and *Fantasy* or ☎ **7-18500** on the *Wonder.*

Hours vary, especially when the ship is in port, but on most sea days the nurseries are open 9 a.m.–11 p.m., with open-house tours 8–9 a.m.; check your *Personal Navigator* for details. The nurseries are sometimes open noon–3 p.m., and usually 5:30–11 p.m. on the first afternoon of your cruise.

The *Magic*'s Youth Clubs

It's a Small World Nursery LOCATION: Deck 5 Aft

OVERVIEW This is the *Magic*'s onboard nursery for infants and toddlers ages 6 months–3 years (some longer sailings may require children to be 12 months of age or older). Trained staff play with the children throughout the day. Unlike the activities at the clubs for older kids and teens, activities at the nursery are unstructured but may include movies, story time, crafts, and occasional visits from Disney characters.

DESCRIPTION AND COMMENTS Too cute. Decorated with brilliantly colored murals inspired by the art of Mary Blair, the Disney animator who designed It's a Small World at Disneyland and Walt Disney World, the nursery is cleverly divided into three sections. Up front is the "acclimation zone," a welcome area where kids can get used to their surroundings; this leads to a long, narrow, rectangular, brightly lit play area, off of which is a darkened, quiet room for naps. The play area is stocked with pint-size activities, including a 2-foot-tall playground slide on a padded floor, a small basketball hoop, plenty of leg-powered riding vehicles, play mats with large toys, and adorable miniature craft tables that you'd swear came from the Lilliput IKEA. A one-way mirror lets parents check up on their tots discreetly.

Around the corner, at the far end of the nursery, is the resting room, with six cribs and three glider chairs (sort of like rocking chairs, except they move linearly). Murals in soothing blues and golds adorn the walls. This room is kept dark most of the day, and the staff ensures that activities in the main room happen far enough away that noise isn't a problem. Just outside are a sink and changing area.

ACROSS THE SHIPS All DCL ships have It's a Small World Nurseries. The version on the *Magic* has a larger nap room than the nurseries on the other ships.

Oceaneer Club and Oceaneer Lab LOCATION: Deck 5 Midship

OVERVIEW The Oceaneer Club and Oceaneer Lab are connected spaces that host the 3- to 12-year-old set. Activities for older kids usually take place in the Lab and are often educational or participatory in nature (such as cooking demonstrations or science experiments). Younger children's programs are generally held in the Club and include story time, character greetings, and movement activities. Disney designates 7 as the border age for the Club and Lab and provides details in your *Personal Navigator* about each area's different activity tracks. During open houses, one side remains open for activities while the other side is open to the public. Lunch and dinner are provided.

Parents must check kids up to age 7 years in and out of the club. With parental permission, 8- to 12-year-olds may check themselves in and out—just designate your preference when you register your kids.

DESCRIPTION AND COMMENTS The Oceaneer Club and Lab are separate areas connected by a short private hallway, allowing children to go from Lab to Club and back. Besides providing kids twice as much space, this arrangement separates younger and older children while giving siblings of different ages the chance to stay in contact.

The Oceaneer Club consists of four distinct sections branching off from a central "library" decorated with oversize children's books and outfitted with a huge plasma TV for movie screenings. **Andy's Room** is *Toy Story*–themed and is for smaller children. Its main feature is a tall, circular, gentle playground slide in the shape of Slinky Dog. There's also a large pink Hamm (the piggy bank) sitting in the middle of the play floor, and a giant Mr. Potato Head with equally large plug-in pieces, all scattered about.

Club Disney Junior, the second themed room, serves as the Oceaneer Club's primary activity center. The grass-green carpet is surrounded by sky-blue walls painted with clouds. The room has a large video screen on one wall and sturdy kid-sized furniture in bold colors.

Club Disney Junior connects to both Andy's Room and **Marvel Avengers Academy,** where you'll find Thor's hammer, Captain America's shield, and a life-size Iron Man suit, as well as another video screen and computer collection. Avengers Academy activities follow a multiday story in which kids embark on a recruitment experience that has them team up with various Avengers, hang out with Captain America, and suit up like Iron Man to battle the evil Red Skull.

Opposite Marvel Avengers Academy is **Pixie Hollow,** a Tinker Bell–themed dress-up and play area with costumes, an activity table, and a few computer terminals with themed games.

The Oceaneer Lab is done in a 19th-century nautical theme, with lots of exposed woods, red-leather chairs, navigation maps, and sailors' tools. More than a third of the space consists of one long room, filled with kid-size tables and stools, which serves as the primary area for arts and crafts. At the far end of this space is a set of computer terminals.

Next to the craft space, in the middle of the Lab, is a large screen for watching movies. Facing the screen is a collection of comfortable beanbags. Finally, the left side of the Lab is a set of small rooms. A couple have computer terminals or video-game consoles; one is a smaller crafts room, and another is an animation studio where kids can learn to draw Disney characters and create their own computer animations.

ACROSS THE SHIPS All DCL ships have an Oceaneer Club/Lab. On the *Dream* and the *Fantasy,* the Club is also subdivided into themed areas, but they differ somewhat from those on the *Magic.* The Lab has a similar nautical theme and layout but is distinguished by a central "interactive floor," composed of individual video screens surrounded by foot-operated touch pads and used to play different interactive games.

Following the *Wonder*'s 2016 refurbishment, its Oceaneer Club and Lab are now on par with those on the *Magic.* Recent additions to the *Wonder*'s play areas are the **Marvel Super Hero Academy** (which is slightly different from the *Magic*'s Avengers Academy), Andy's Room, **Club Disney Junior** (an area for storytelling and games), and **Frozen Adventures** (for play related to everyone's favorite fake Scandinavian country, Arendelle).

Edge LOCATION: Deck 9 Midship

OVERVIEW Tweens and early teens rule at Edge. Unlike at the Oceaneer Club/Lab, kids can come and go as they please. Activities range from drawing and cooking classes to scavenger hunts and computer games. Parents may be surprised to see that things are scheduled past midnight on some nights.

DESCRIPTION AND COMMENTS The Edge is the rec room your kids dream of. There are sections for electronic gaming, active play, and lounging. You'll see both a high-tech zone and comfy couches. Kids can move freely between both.

Edge is likely to be the first of the youth clubs in which the staff will treat your kids as peers to interact with rather than as children to be supervised. The staff generally does a great job of getting to know each child and will even compete in games alongside the kids. If you ever want to feel old and slow, watch the cup-stacking competition, where the object is to stack and unstack a pyramid of 15 plastic cups as quickly as possible. Some kids can do both in less than 10 seconds total.

ACROSS THE SHIPS All DCL ships have an Edge. The amenities and layout of Edge on the *Magic* are more or less the same as those on the *Wonder,* and following the *Magic*'s dry dock, the decor is similar as well. On the *Dream* and the *Fantasy,* Edge is inside the ships' forward (nonfunctioning) smokestack. The decor and atmosphere are ultramodern and high-tech, versus the homier feel of Edge on the *Magic* and *Wonder.*

Vibe LOCATION: Deck 11 Midship

OVERVIEW Vibe is one of the coolest spots on the *Magic.* Even if you don't have a kid traveling with you, it's worth checking out during an open house. Counselors lead the activities (dance parties, karaoke, group games, and the like), but teens are given plenty of autonomy in their structure. Parents should note that the only curfew for teens on board is whatever one they impose themselves. One rule of note that's strictly enforced: no public displays of affection.

DESCRIPTION AND COMMENTS Vibe sits up a flight of stairs in the ship's forward smokestack, but your teens probably won't mind the climb. Inside is a two-story-tall lounge with exposed brick walls, leather furniture, and a smoothie bar. A 2018 redesign removed a lot of the clutter, giving the area a more modern, streamlined look. There are still lots of board games, magazines, and video games, but they're more likely to be put away when not in use. We think there should be a Vibe for adults.

ACROSS THE SHIPS All DCL ships have a Vibe. The layout and amenities are more or less identical on the *Wonder.* On the *Dream* and the *Fantasy,* Vibe is dramatically different but just as cool. The theming and decor are urban ultralounge rather than funky rumpus room, and teens get an indoor/outdoor space, complete with a grown-up sun deck and splash pool.

The *Wonder*'s Youth Clubs

It's a Small World Nursery LOCATION: Deck 5 Aft

OVERVIEW This is the *Wonder*'s onboard nursery for infants and toddlers ages 6 months–3 years (some longer sailings may require children to be 12 months or older). Trained staff play with the children throughout the day. Unlike the activities at the clubs for older kids and teens, activities at the nursery are unstructured but may include movies, story time, crafts, and occasional visits from Disney characters.

DESCRIPTION AND COMMENTS The *Wonder*'s Small World—the cruise industry's first nursery at sea—is divided into two sections. One is a brightly lit play area, the other a darkened quiet area for naps. The play area is stocked with play mats, toys, books, large motor-play equipment, baby swings, and a TV/DVD player. The color scheme and decor reflect the design of the It's a Small World attraction at the Disney theme parks. A one-way mirror outside lets parents check up on their tots discreetly.

At the back of the nursery is the resting area, furnished with cribs. This room is kept dark most of the day, and the staff ensures that activities in the main room happen far enough away that noise isn't a problem. A sink and changing station are adjacent.

ACROSS THE SHIPS All DCL ships have It's a Small World Nurseries. The version on the *Magic* has a larger nap room than the nurseries on the other ships.

Oceaneer Club and Oceaneer Lab LOCATION: Deck 5 Midship

OVERVIEW The Oceaneer Club and Oceaneer Lab are connected spaces that host the 3- to 12-year-old set. Activities for older kids usually take place in the Lab and are often educational or participatory in nature (such as cooking demonstrations or science experiments). Younger children's programs are generally held in the Club and include story time, character greetings, and movement activities. Disney designates 7 as the border age for the Club and Lab and provides details in your *Personal Navigator* about each area's different activity tracks. During open houses, one side remains open for activities while the other side is open to the public. Lunch and dinner are provided.

Parents must check kids up to age 7 years in and out of the club. With parental permission, 8- to 12-year-olds may check themselves in and out—just designate your preference when you register your kids.

DESCRIPTION AND COMMENTS The *Wonder's* Oceaneer Club and Lab, once significantly outdated and low-tech, got a major refurbishment in late 2016, bringing it up to speed with the Clubs and Labs on the other Disney ships. The refurb added **Marvel Super Hero Academy,** an interactive play area where children can train to be superheroes and interact with current stars of the Marvel family; Spider-Man makes regular appearances. Artifacts on display in this area include Captain America's World War II shield, Iron Man's helmet, Spider-Man's web shooters, and Black Widow's gauntlets.

Other Oceaneer spaces include the **Frozen Adventures** area for creative and interactive play. A key feature of the Frozen zone is a digital screen when an animated Olaf leads games and songs; character experiences include the requisite visits by Anna and Elsa. **Club Disney Junior** offers storytelling and games featuring *Disney Junior* characters, including Doc McStuffins. **Andy's Room** is a *Toy Story*–themed play zone with larger-than-life toys to play on.

ACROSS THE SHIPS All DCL ships have an Oceaneer Club/Lab. On the *Dream* and the *Fantasy,* the Club is also subdivided into themed areas, but they differ somewhat from those on the *Magic* and *Wonder.* In addition, the Lab on the two newer ships has a central "interactive floor," composed of individual video screens surrounded by foot-operated touch pads and used to play different interactive games.

Edge LOCATION: Deck 9 Midship

COMMENTS See profile of Edge on the *Magic* (see page 227) for details.

Vibe LOCATION: Deck 11 Midship

COMMENTS See profile of Vibe on the *Magic* (see previous page) for details.

The *Dream's* and *Fantasy's* Youth Clubs

It's a Small World Nursery LOCATION: Deck 5 Aft

COMMENTS See profiles of It's a Small World Nursery on the *Magic* (see page 225) and *Wonder* (see previous page) for details.

Oceaneer Club and Oceaneer Lab LOCATION: Deck 5 Midship

OVERVIEW On the *Dream* and *Fantasy,* the Oceaneer Club and Oceaneer Lab are connected spaces that host the 3- to 12-year-old set. Activities for older

kids usually take place in the Lab and are often educational or participatory in nature (such as cooking demonstrations or science experiments). Younger children's programs are generally held in the Club and include story time, character greetings, and movement activities. Disney designates 7 as the border age for the Club and Lab and provides details in your *Personal Navigator* about each area's different activity tracks. During open houses, one side remains open for activities while the other side is open to the public. Lunch and dinner are provided.

Parents must check kids up to age 7 years in and out of the club. With parental permission, 8- to 12-year-olds may check themselves in and out—just designate your preference when you register your kids.

DESCRIPTION AND COMMENTS The Oceaneer Lab and Club are separate areas connected by a short private hallway, allowing children to go from Lab to Club and back. Besides providing kids twice as much space, this arrangement separates younger and older children while giving siblings of different ages the chance to stay in contact.

The Oceaneer Club consists of four distinct sections branching off from a central rotunda painted royal blue; on the ceiling are "constellations" of Disney characters made up of small, twinkling electric lights. **Andy's Room** is *Toy Story*–themed and is for smaller children. There's a crawl-through tube—think a Habitrail for humans—in the shape of Slinky Dog, along with a giant pink Hamm (the piggy bank) sitting in the middle of the play floor, and a large Mr. Potato Head with equally large plug-in pieces, all invariably scattered about.

The next area is **Pixie Hollow,** a Tinker Bell–themed dress-up and play area with costumes, an activity table, and a few computer terminals with themed games. The *Dream* and *Fantasy* Oceaneer Clubs both have **Star Wars–themed immersive play areas**—on the *Dream,* it's a life-size *Millennium Falcon,* and on the *Fantasy* it's a "Command Post" holo-table where children can train with X-Wing pilots. The *Falcon* on the *Dream* lets kids pilot a remarkably well-done simulator—yep, it goes into hyperspeed—and participate in a shipboard version of the *Jedi Training* activity at Walt Disney World's Hollywood Studios. Adult guests can take a turn in the captain's seat of the *Falcon* during regular club open-house times (check your *Personal Navigator*). Wearing a black vest and knee-high boots is completely optional.

The Oceaneer Lab is done in a 19th-century nautical theme, with lots of exposed woods, red-leather chairs, navigation maps, sailors' tools, and inlaid images of sea horses and compasses on the floor. The main hall features a celestial map on the ceiling and a huge "Magic Play Floor," composed of 16 high-definition video screens surrounded by foot-powered touch pads and used to play interactive games. (If you remember the giant piano from the movie *Big,* you get the idea.)

Surrounding the main hall are the **Media Lounge,** for relaxing and watching movies; the **Animator's Studio,** where kids can learn to draw Disney characters and create digital animations; **The Wheelhouse,** with computer stations and interactive games; the **Sound Studio,** where kids can record their own music; and the **Craft Studio.**

ACROSS THE SHIPS All DCL ships have an Oceaneer Club/Lab. On the *Magic* and *Wonder,* the Club is subdivided into themed areas, but they differ somewhat from those on the *Dream* and *Fantasy;* also, the Lab on the two older ships is missing the nifty interactive floor.

Edge LOCATION: Deck 13 Forward

OVERVIEW Tweens rule at Edge. Unlike at the Oceaneer Club/Lab, kids at Edge can come and go as they please. Activities range from drawing and cooking classes to improv-comedy sessions and ghost-hunting and role-playing games. Parents may be surprised to see that things are scheduled past midnight on some nights.

DESCRIPTION AND COMMENTS Built into the *Dream*'s and *Fantasy*'s forward (nonfunctioning) smokestack, Edge has an open layout and a clean 21st-century feel. The walls are papered in a geometric Mickey-head design. The centerpiece of the space is a huge video wall, more than 18 feet wide and nearly 5 feet tall. Across from it are tables with built-in screens for playing interactive games, surrounded by bright-red seating that looks like something out of *The Jetsons;* behind those are cubbyholes outfitted with flat-panel TVs and Wii consoles. Recessed shelves between the game nooks are stocked with books and board games. Next to the game tables are an illuminated dance floor (think *Saturday Night Fever*) and a lounge area with beanbags arranged next to floor-to-ceiling windows. On the other side of the video wall are laptop stations loaded with video games and an onboard social-media app.

Edge is likely to be the first of the youth clubs in which the staff will treat your kids as peers to interact with rather than as children to be supervised. The staff generally does a great job of getting to know each child and getting in on the fun.

ACROSS THE SHIPS All DCL ships have an Edge. On the *Magic* and *Wonder,* it has a totally different layout and atmosphere—more like a cozy family rec room than a high-tech hangout.

Vibe LOCATION: Deck 5 Forward

OVERVIEW Up a flight of stairs from Deck 4 to Deck 5 Forward, Vibe is one of the coolest spots on the *Dream* and *Fantasy.* Even if you don't have a kid traveling with you, it's worth checking out during an open house. Counselors lead the activities (dance parties, karaoke, role-playing games, and the like), but teens are given plenty of autonomy in their structure. Parents should note that the only curfew for teens on board is whatever one they impose themselves. One rule of note that's strictly enforced: no public displays of affection.

DESCRIPTION AND COMMENTS Accessed through a neon-lit hallway, Vibe has a decidedly adult look and feel—if you didn't know better, you'd think you were in a trendy urban nightspot. The central indoor gathering spot is the theater-cum-TV lounge, accented with soft pink neon lighting and featuring a 103-inch flat-panel television. Two rows of couches are arranged in a semicircle in front of the screen; giant throw pillows scattered on the floor make for additional places to lounge. Behind the couches and built into the rear wall are a row of podlike, porthole-shaped nooks for playing video games, watching videos, or hooking up an electronic device. Just off the row of pods is a smoothie bar with a multicolored floor in Day-Glo hues; ultramodern stools with low, curved backs; and white banquette seating.

Off the TV lounge is another sleek space for socializing. The walls are covered in alternating black-and-silver horizontal bars. Black leather-look benches line the walls; next to those are retro-mod tables and chairs arranged nightclub-style. Video-game booths stand nearby. Across from

the seating area are a dance floor and DJ booth, a karaoke stage, and another large video screen.

The main attraction, though, lies outside: the **Vibe Splash Zone,** a private deck with two splash pools, chaise longues, sets of tables and chairs, and recessed seating. Furnishings and decor share the same ultramod style as the indoor spaces.

ACROSS THE SHIPS All DCL ships have a Vibe. On the *Magic* and the *Wonder,* Vibe is dramatically different but just as cool. Built into the ships' forward smokestack, the two-story-tall lounge features brick walls and leather furniture. It looks more like the lounge at a college student center than something you'd find on a cruise ship.

WHAT GOES ON IN A KIDS' CLUB?

IN ADDITION TO FREE PLAY AND OPEN HOURS, all levels of kids' clubs offer a range of physical, quiet, creative, collaborative, and competitive age-appropriate activities. If your kids prefer directed activity to self-initiated play, be sure to keep a careful eye on the DCL Navigator app and the print *Personal Navigator,* both of which list the times of planned activities at the Oceaneer Club/Lab, Edge, and Vibe. Additionally, the app provides a sentence or two of description about the activity, plus alternate times during the cruise when that activity will be offered again. Activities vary, but some sample activities from recent cruises, along with their Navigator app descriptions, include the following:

OCEANEER CLUB AND LAB
• **Anyone Can Cook:** Anyone can cook as we work together to create some of our favorite treats.
• **Big Top Fun Fest:** Come rediscover the circus Disney-style, with clowns, jugglers, and classic Disney cartoons.
• **Craft Corner:** Imagination is the key. It's time to get creative and put your crafty skills to use!
• **Cruisin' with Crush:** Be sure to check out Disney's Oceaneer Club to see Crush when he stops by!
• **Gaga Ball:** Come take part in this great game as you try to outlast your opponents. [*Note:* According to coauthor Ritchey's research, this is the Israeli version of dodgeball, not a sport with a Lady Gaga theme.]
• **Once Upon a Time:** Join Bartleby the Bookmaker for a magical, musical story time featuring a Disney princess.
• **Parachute Games:** Have a blast playing fun games with our colorful parachutes.
• **Piston Cup Challenge:** Design your own race car and see if you've got what it takes to end up in the winner's circle.
• **Super Sloppy Science:** Join Professor Make-O-Mess in some the most extreme experiments you'll ever see.
• **Wacky Relays:** Show off your wacky skills in some of the wackiest races at sea.
• **Wii Challenge:** Take on the challenge in this fun interactive computer game.

EDGE
• **Animation Cels:** Learn what it takes to be a Disney animator, then put your skills to the test as you create your very own animation cel.
• **Cards Tournament:** Join your friends for a game of cards.
• **Crowning of the Couch Potato:** Do you think you know your movies, TV, and commercials? Well, it's time to test your knowledge.
• **Foosball Tournament:** Come show us your Foosball skills and see who's the best of the best.
• **Gaga Ball:** Try to outlast your opponents in this dodgeball-style game.
• **Gender Wars:** Join us as we find out who really are the kings or queens of the castle.
• **Goofy's World Records:** Goofy and his pals have created a variety of games and contests for a wild time.
• **Pathfinders:** A path has been chosen for you. Can you find it?
• **Pelican Plunge:** Enjoy some sliding with your Edge team.
• **Profiles:** Show off who you really are and make some new friends while you do it.
• **Scattergories:** See who can think of the most creative answers.
• **That's Hilarious:** Ever wanted to show off your comedy skills? Then be a part of the cast for this crazy improv show.
• **Volleyball**

VIBE
• **Dream Now! Sea How! Animal, Science, and Environment:** Ever wonder how man and animal can connect and live in harmony? In an interactive session, you will dive into the background, education, mentors, and dreams that sent animal-care workers into their profession.
• **Gotcha!:** Compete in a sophisticated game of hide-and-seek.
• **Homecoming:** Come join your fellow teens in our own version of Homecoming, and dance the night away!
• **Ice Cream Social:** Make your own frosty treat with your counselors.
• **Ninja:** How fast and stealthy can you be?
• **Ping-Pong Tournament**
• **Smoothie Hour:** Create your own custom smoothie.
• **Sports Deck Fun:** The topside sports deck is reserved for teen use.
• **Teen Choice Movie Viewing**
• **Trivia Time:** Test your gray matter with fun trivia.
• **Zombified:** Create an actual zombie movie that will premiere on board.

Additionally, Edge and Vibe may take kids in groups to some of the all-ages performances, game shows, or other events on board.

OTHER KIDS' ACTIVITIES ON BOARD

On the *Magic* and *Wonder*

Many activities take place in the **Promenade Lounge** on Deck 3 Aft, including the following:

• *Playhouse Disney* Dance Party	• Pirate Scavenger Maps	
• Pirate Trivia Quest	• Pop Decades Dance	• Wildcat Bingo

On the *Dream* and the *Fantasy*

Midship Detective Agency is a self-guided interactive game in which kids help Disney characters solve a mystery. Similar to Sorcerers of the Magic Kingdom at Walt Disney World, this is one of the most fun onboard activities in the fleet. You begin by signing up on a computer inside a small desk on Deck 5 Midship. There you'll obtain a small, numbered cardboard game piece. One side of the game piece holds a 2-D bar code and your agent number; the other side displays a detective's badge icon.

Along with your badge card, you'll receive a pamphlet describing each of the agency's suspects behind the mystery. The pamphlet also includes a map of the ship that shows where to find clues to solve the mystery. Once you've signed up and obtained your game material, you'll watch a short video that explains the mystery you're solving. You'll also be told where to go to find your first clue.

Each clue is presented on an "Enchanted Art" video screen somewhere on the ship. The video screens look like ordinary wall art to anyone not playing the game—it's only when you hold up your badge that the screen comes alive with video and sound. (The technology embedded behind the screens' frames includes a bar-code reader for your badge, speakers, and a network of computers to keep track of your accomplishments.) To obtain the clue, you'll first have to solve a simple puzzle or win a simple game. You do this by using your badge as a sort of game controller while you're playing, tilting and moving the badge to guide the action on the screen. It takes a little practice to get used to, so tell your kids before they start that their first try at each screen is just a dry run. You can repeat the action as often as needed.

Once you've obtained the clue, you can eliminate one of the suspects from the mystery; then it's off to another section of the ship to get another clue. Make no mistake: playing this game involves climbing a lot of stairs. However, you get to see a lot of the ship, and it's good exercise for the kids. You'll see them playing at all times of the day and night, and lines often form in front of each video screen, especially on sea days.

There are three different games: **The Case of the Plundered Paintings** and **The Case of the Missing Puppies,** both featuring Mickey and friends, and **The Case of the Stolen Show,** starring the Muppets.

We think the last one is the most fun—the game's designers expertly incorporate the Muppets' humor into the scenes.

Bibbidi Bobbidi Boutique

All DCL ships have varying incarnations of this wildly popular Disney-theme-park makeover spot for kids ages 3–12. Bibbidi Bobbidi Boutique sessions take about 45 minutes; makeover variations for girls have included Disney Diva, Pop Princess, and Fairy Tale Princess. Pricing currently starts at about $65 for the **Crown Package,** which includes hairstyling (but not washing or cutting), nail polish, shimmering makeup, and a face gem. The **Castle Package,** currently about $200, includes all of the above plus a princess sash, a tiara, a wand, and choice of princess costume. There's also a special *Frozen* version of the makeover for about $165, which includes your choice of Anna or Elsa hairstyling and costume, plus shimmering makeup, a face gem, nail polish, a princess sash, a princess tote, and a plush Olaf doll.

Young princes may sign up for the **Royal Knight** package (about $19), which includes hairstyling plus a sword and shield.

On Pirate Night (see page 190), the boutique becomes **The Pirates League** and gives buccaneer-themed makeovers to any guest age 3 and up (guests 17 and younger must be accompanied by an adult). Variations on the pirate makeover are priced between $45 and $100 and include items such as swords, earrings, and costume elements, depending on the package chosen.

For the princess who has everything, there's the **Royal Sea Package,** which gets her three nights of makeovers plus a gift delivered to her bedchamber, um, stateroom. It can be hers for $595 and must be booked by email; go to tinyurl.com/royalseareservations and click "Download the Royal Sea Package reservation form" (a Microsoft Word file), or ask your travel agent for details.

Parents of 2-year-olds should note that the BBB age requirement on ship is a hard rule. While a kind Fairy Godmother at Walt Disney World might look the other way and agree to do a makeover on a child who's not quite in the stated age range, the cast members on the DCL ships won't break the rules because they know exactly how old your child is.

CHILDREN'S PERFORMANCE OPPORTUNITIES

DURING MOST SAILINGS OF SEVEN DAYS OR MORE, the Oceaneer Club and Lab invite kids ages 3–12 to participate in a show performed on stage in the Walt Disney Theatre. The show, often called ***Friendship Rocks!,*** mostly involves having the little ones sit on stage and sing along with a few Disney classics. Mickey will make an appearance. Many younger kids (and their parents) think that being on stage with Mickey makes them rock stars, while others will be completely overwhelmed by the experience—use your best judgment.

Kids with a real yen to perform can check out **karaoke** opportunities on most sailings or **talent-show** opportunities on many longer sailings (see "Family Nightclubs" on page 216).

CHILDREN'S ACTIVITIES IN PORT

WHEN BOOKING PORT EXCURSIONS, look for activities that are specified for families. Some tours will be specially designated for those traveling with kids. All excursion descriptions (see Part Twelve) include a recommendation for ages (or a requirement, depending on the type of activity) and an indication of the amount of stamina needed to participate. Another option for days when you're in port is to stay aboard and enjoy the smaller crowds at the pools and waterslides.

CHILDREN'S ACTIVITIES AT CASTAWAY CAY

DCL'S PRIVATE ISLAND (see Part Ten) has designated areas just for children and families. The teen area, **The Hide Out,** is tucked away, though not on the beach, and offers sports, such as volleyball and table tennis, and scheduled activities. **Scuttle's Cove,** a play area for young children, has youth-club counselors on hand to direct activities. Both The Hide Out and Scuttle's Cove are monitored by Disney cast members to ensure that only children and their parents enter.

CHILL SPA FOR TEENS

EACH DCL SHIP HAS A **Chill Spa,** a dedicated area inside Senses Spa & Salon that's just for guests ages 13–17. Chill Spa on the *Dream* and *Fantasy* is spacious and plush, less so on the *Magic* and *Wonder* (where it's a single treatment room).

Spa services for teens must be booked on board; you can't reserve them in advance online at My Disney Cruise (see page 39) as you would for adult spa services. If you have a stressed-out teen who needs a massage, you're going to incur a bit of stress yourself high-tailing it up to the spa on embarkation day to score a reservation before they fill up.

Officially, a parent or guardian must be present during all Chill Spa treatments; in practice, however, this varies depending on the ship. When coauthor Erin's teen daughter was getting a massage on the *Dream,* Erin was asked to stay in the actual treatment room with her. When the same daughter got a massage on the *Magic* a few months later, Erin was required to wait in the spa lounge because the *Magic*'s treatment room is too small. (Bring a book if you're the designated waiting parent.) If you have a strong preference about whether you stay in the same room with your child at all times, be sure to inquire about the ship's practices when you book the appointment.

If you don't want your teen to be offered any additional spa services or ancillary lotions and potions, note that when you make your reservation. Read more about the DCL spas on page 249.

WHERE TO MEET CHARACTERS

DISNEY CHARACTERS ARE AVAILABLE for photos and autographs several times per day at various locations on the ships; they also make occasional visits to the nurseries and kids' clubs. A complete schedule is usually posted on the **Character Information Board** in your ship's atrium; it's also printed in the Character Appearances section of each day's *Personal Navigator,* listed in the DCL Navigator app, and available by calling ☎ **7-PALS** (7257) from your stateroom phone.

unofficial **TIP**
If you're trying to meet the Disney princesses without a timed ticket, arrive at least a half-hour ahead of the scheduled greeting. We've arrived 45 minutes ahead to get a spot for our kids to meet Belle—and we weren't even the first people in line.

Disney has begun offering free timed tickets for meeting the hugely popular *Frozen* characters Anna, Elsa, and Olaf, a selection of Marvel superheroes, and what we call the "princess bomb," where four or five of the Disney princesses appear in the atrium at once. Previously, lines for these coveted characters would begin forming more than an hour in advance, resulting in crowded walkways and cranky families. Thankfully, the timed tickets have cut down on much of the chaos.

There are two possible modes of ticket distribution: in advance online or in person on embarkation day. We haven't yet figured out a rhyme or reason for why particular sailings use one method or the other, but many cruises now offer both online and in-person character-greeting tickets. If your sailing offers advance character greetings (and onboard character dining experiences), this option will appear in your My Disney Cruise for your sailing on the Disney Cruise Line website. This option may become available days or weeks after your standard port-adventure and adult-dining selections appear. If you're interested in reserving character experiences, keep checking back. If your specific cruise doesn't offer prebooking, then be sure to check your *Personal Navigator* for a note about whether character-greeting ticket distribution is in effect for your specific sailing.

Tickets for the most popular greetings are generally available for just a few hours on embarkation day and not at any point after that, but be aware that **you absolutely will need them** if they're being used on your voyage. Some princesses may greet guests individually during your cruise, but Anna, Elsa, Olaf, and the Marvel characters are unlikely to make any general public appearances.

There may also be nonticketed character greetings, for which guests will begin queuing up far in advance of the posted start time. (Captain Jack Sparrow is always a big draw on Pirate Night, for example.) Unique characters will have long lines; we had quite a wait to see the White Rabbit from *Alice in Wonderland,* who was serving as the de facto Easter Bunny on Easter Day on the *Fantasy.* You can also expect longer waits for common characters appearing in unusual

costumes. For example, Mickey Mouse wearing red, white, and blue on the Fourth of July or Goofy wearing a parka during an Alaskan voyage will be more popular than those characters wearing their standard theme park gear.

Most onboard character greetings are limited to 15 minutes or half an hour. The line will be closed once it's been determined that no more guests can be accommodated in the character's remaining time. If your child is intent on meeting a specific character, your best bet is to get in line 15–30 minutes before that character is scheduled to appear.

On longer cruises, Disney characters such as Mickey, Minnie, Donald, Goofy, and Pluto may make onboard appearances many times throughout the voyage (albeit usually in different attire). The lines for these Disney classics are typically shorter later in the trip, when most folks have already had their fill of photos with the Big Cheese and company.

On **Castaway Cay,** photo ops featuring the Disney gang in beach attire take place near the ship's dock, weather permitting.

Private Character Greetings

If you have a special event taking place on your cruise, you may want to consider booking a private character greeting. For about $500–$600 for a "fur" character (like Mickey or Minnie) or about $1,000 for a "face" character (like a princess), you can book a private room with 30 minutes of character time. While pricey, this may be an attractive option if you're hosting a small wedding, a large family reunion, or a big birthday party for a fervid Disney fan. A private character greeting lets you get every family combination in a photo without your feeling that you're inconveniencing other guests. Call DCL for the latest pricing and details.

A Note About Autographs

A significant subset of Disney-theme-park and Disney Cruise Line guests collect character autographs as souvenirs. Some of the autographs are quite fanciful and can provide a decorative element to objects. The medium for collection is not required to be an autograph book; guests often have characters sign items such as photo mats, pillowcases, T-shirts, and the like. (One of Erin's favorite signature-collection devices was a pair of canvas shoes: see tinyurl.com/autographshoes.) In the theme parks, guests wait in line to meet the characters, present them with an item to be signed, pose for a photo, and then head on their way.

A few years back, DCL had an unofficial autograph program known as "Mickey Mail," in which guests could drop off an item with Guest Services and have the item signed backstage. Initially a nice little-known extra, Mickey Mail became a hot topic on Pinterest and DCL chat groups, which resulted in sometimes thousands of elaborate items being left for signatures at Guest Services on a single cruise. (We've

heard of more than one guest asking for signatures on a full-size replica ship's anchor!) Unable to keep up with demand, DCL discontinued Mickey Mail in August 2015. Now if you'd like an item signed on your cruise, you have to stand in line at the character-greeting points, just as you would in the parks.

What's more, DCL imposes limits on the specific types of items that may be signed. Characters will sign the following:

• Any autograph book
• Disney-branded items that are appropriate to the character doing the signing. For example, Cinderella would be unable to sign a Buzz Lightyear item.
• A Disney-approved photo. Only characters in the photo can sign the photo.
• Disney note cards
• Disney Dollars. Once signed, a Disney Dollar becomes a souvenir and can no longer be used as currency. (Note that distribution of new Disney Dollars was discontinued in 2016; existing Disney Dollars are still redeemable, however.)
• Clothing (must not be worn while being signed)

Characters will *not* sign the following items:

• Flags of any nation	• Receipts or banking slips
• Money other than Disney Dollars	• Skin
• Non-Disney merchandise	• Non-family-friendly or sexually explicit items

POOLS *and* WATER-PLAY AREAS

EACH SHIP HAS SEPARATE FRESHWATER POOLS designed for small children, families, and adults. All are heated to a minimum temperature of 75°F.

REAL TALK ABOUT CRUISE-SHIP POOLS

IF YOU'VE NEVER BEEN ON A CRUISE SHIP BEFORE, you may think you know what the pools are like because you've seen glossy brochures or enticing aerial photography on TV. In the ads, it looks like you could swim luxurious laps on board, working off your morning pastry binge or last night's mai tais. In reality, there is no way possible to exercise in the ships' pools; you can barely even splash in them.

DCL doesn't publish the dimensions of its pools. Erin has taken to carrying a small tape measure when she sails, attempting to take measurements herself, but she has been shooed away by cast members every time ("Don't measure! Don't measure!").

There is no pool on a Disney ship that has a capacity of more than 80 people (and most pool capacities are much smaller than this), even on the *Dream* and *Fantasy,* which carry 4,000 guests each, many, many of whom will be children looking to take a dip in the water. There is an

adult pool respite for grownups to escape to when they can, and there are AquaLab play areas to distract kids who want to be wet, but no matter how you slice it, there's just not a whole lot of room for actual swimming.

In a highly unscientific study, we've shown photos of the pools, with varying numbers of guests in the water, to several noncruising acquaintances. The consensus seems to be that the pools start to look crowded when occupied by about half the stated capacity. We can attest that that's the way they feel, too. One Ohio mom writes:

> *We call it "pool soup."*

A North Carolina mom comments:

> *The pool situation depends on the itinerary and weather. For our cruise on the* Dream, *the pool was my only semi-complaint. The pools were PACKED with kids, I couldn't have gotten in if I wanted to, and it was just myself and my then-6-year-old. I'm thinking (hoping!) that Alaska won't be quite as bad. We love Disney, but the crowds at the pools will definitely be a turnoff for my husband, and I'm not sure I'll be able to persuade him to book another with all of us if they're that crowded.*

And a Virginia cruiser says:

> *We just left the* Magic *in Dover [UK] for the Norway and Iceland cruise. There were folks in the pools on the days warm enough to swim, but nothing at all like the crowding in the pools in the Caribbean!*

The adult pools, on the other hand, are rarely raucous, and the pool situation is more relaxed during cooler-weather itineraries. You can also find more room to enjoy the pools if you visit on port days or during evening show times. All that said, many people find it pleasant to lounge on the pool deck during their Caribbean vacation—sipping cocktails, reading a novel, and enjoying the sun and the Funnel Vision big screen. Lots of kids have fun running between the soft-serve machines and the pools, maybe stopping off for some chicken nuggets on the way. It can be a lovely way to spend an afternoon—it's just not swimming.

RULES ABOUT POOLS

DCL HAS A FEW STRICT POOL REGULATIONS designed to protect the health and safety of its guests. Anyone under age 16 must be supervised at the pools at all times, height and weight restrictions for the waterslides are strictly observed, and snorkels and full-face masks are prohibited (though they are welcome at Castaway Cay). Water wings and other Coast Guard–approved flotation devices are allowed, but rafts, floats, and foam noodles are not.

DCL's swim-diaper policy states: "The U.S. Public Health Service requires that only children who are toilet-trained are permitted to enter swimming pools and spas aboard cruise ships. Swim diapers are not

permitted in hot tubs, spas, or any Disney Cruise Line pools or waterslides, including the AquaDuck, AquaDunk, and AquaLab." Little ones wearing swim diapers *are* permitted at Nemo's Reef on the *Dream* and *Fantasy,* at the Nephews' Splash Zone on the *Magic,* and at Dory's Reef on the *Wonder.*

If poop happens in the pool, all guests must evacuate and the pool must then be drained, cleaned, refilled, and tested for bacteria and chemical balance. The entire procedure takes about 4–5 hours depending on the size of the pool—so don't be that parent who let your almost-but-not-quite-potty-trained child into the water and then ended up spoiling an afternoon for hundreds of other families. Remember, too, that on a cruise even potty-trained kids may be distracted, overwhelmed, and experiencing new foods that may make new digestive demands.

THE *MAGIC'S* AND *WONDER'S* POOLS

THE *MAGIC'S* **AquaDunk,** a variation on the AquaDuck water coaster found on the *Dream* and *Fantasy* (see page 244), is short and mildly fast, with a vertical start. It starts with your entering a vertical tube. You lean against one side of the tube while a clear plexiglass door closes opposite you to seal the tube. Suddenly, the floor drops away and you plunge nearly vertically down the tube, through a quick 270-degree turn and into a braking pool of water. The entire experience takes perhaps 7 or 8 seconds, but the initial sensation of falling is fun enough to make it worth repeating. The AquaDunk usually opens at 9 a.m. and closes around 11 p.m.

> *unofficial* **TIP**
> Unlike the other ships, the *Wonder* doesn't have a headliner water attraction.

Because the AquaDunk has an hourly capacity of only around 120 riders, long lines develop quickly; we've seen 80-minute waits posted. If you're not there first thing in the morning, try during lunchtime or the first dinner seating around 6:15 p.m.

Parents of children with sensitive eyes should be aware that while swim goggles may be worn in the ships' pools and on the smaller slides, goggles and face masks are prohibited on the AquaDunk—the force of the drop all but guarantees that you would lose the goggles/mask.

AquaLab, the *Magic*'s and *Wonder*'s water-play area for small children (age 3 and up), is on Deck 9 Aft. It consists of four areas: AquaLab proper, the Twist 'n' Spout waterslide (age 4 and up and over 38 inches tall), the Nephews' Pool, and the Nephews' Splash Zone.

Every inch of AquaLab is covered in water, which comes out from both vertical and horizontal surfaces. Overhead buckets, slowly filling with water, will dump their contents periodically on anyone standing below, while sprays from faux ship-plumbing will drench anyone walking within 10 feet. Your kids will probably spend hours here, so it's a good thing that both covered seating and refreshments are available nearby.

Next to the main AquaLab area is the **Nephews' Splash Zone,** a water-play area for kids up to 3 years old. This plexiglass-enclosed area has water spouting from pint-size Huey, Dewey, and Louie figures. Padding on the ground allows kids to jump and run around safely, and you'll find parents sitting and relaxing nearby while the little ones get soaked.

A three-story spiral waterslide, **Twist 'n' Spout** is a lot longer and slower than AquaDunk, making it perfect for kids not quite tall enough for the big slide. Twist 'n' Spout starts above Deck 11 and ends on Deck 9 next to AquaLab. The top part of the slide isn't usually staffed, but a camera system there allows the attendant at the bottom of the slide to monitor both the start and the end simultaneously. Kids must be 4–14 years old and 38–64 inches tall to ride. There's plenty of nearby seating for parents to get some sun while watching the little ones splash around.

The **Nephews' Pool** is a shallow, circular pool in the middle of the deck, touching both AquaLab and the Nephews' Splash Zone. Small children can splash around to their hearts' content while parents sit on ledge seating. Just past the forward end of AquaLab is **Pete's Boiler Bites** (*Wonder*) or **Duck-in Diner,** and on the aft end is **Daisy's De-Lites.**

Goofy's Pool, the *Magic*'s and *Wonder*'s family pool, is on Deck 9 Midship. It's the focal point of outdoor activity on the ship. The pool is 4 feet deep at every point, and deck chairs and lounges are arranged on both sides along its length. At the forward end of the pool is the **Funnel Vision** LED screen, which plays movies, TV shows, and videos almost constantly. At the aft end are **Pinocchio's Pizzeria** and two covered whirlpools. Both Goofy's and the Nephews' Pools are typically open 8 a.m.–10 p.m. every day; check your *Personal Navigator* for specific hours.

The adults-only **Quiet Cove Pool** is on Deck 9 Forward. Like Goofy's Pool, it's 4 feet deep throughout, and two adults-only whirlpools are nearby. Teak lounge chairs are provided for relaxing. Just past the aft end of the pool are **Signals** bar and **Cove Café.**

unofficial **TIP**
The ships' swimming pools are relatively small. On the *Magic,* for example, Goofy's Pool is about the size of a typical suburban home's pool.

The *Wonder*'s pool deck got a refurbishment as part of the ship's 2016 dry dock. While the *Wonder* still lacks a thrill-style feature slide, the ship now has a spiral Twist 'n' Spout waterslide. As on the *Magic,* the slide starts above Deck 11; it ends next to a new **AquaLab** children's play area on Deck 9.

On both the *Wonder* and the *Magic* you'll find **Mickey's Pool,** for children age 3 and up, toward Deck 9 Aft. Divided into three smaller pools corresponding to Mickey's face and ears, the pool has a maximum depth of 2 feet, and the bright-yellow spiral **Mickey's Slide** rises about one deck high (about the same level as Deck 10). Kids must be 4–14 years old and 38–64 inches tall to use the waterslide. There's plenty of nearby seating for parents to get some sun while watching the little

ones splash around. Just past the forward end of Mickey's Pool is **Pete's Boiler Bites** snack bar, and on the aft end is **Daisy's De-Lites.**

Children who don't meet the requirements for Mickey's Pool on the *Wonder* can play in nearby **Dory's Reef,** on the port side of the pool. Surrounded by short walls and themed to *Finding Nemo,* this water-play area for kids age 3 and under features gurgling sprays, jets, and sprinkles of water bubbling up from fountains in the floor. Best of all, there's plenty of covered seating nearby. Kids playing in Dory's Reef must be supervised.

THE *DREAM*'S AND *FANTASY*'S POOLS

LIKE THE *WONDER,* the *Dream* and the *Fantasy* have **Mickey's Pool** for children age 3 and up, roughly midship on Deck 11. Divided into three smaller pools corresponding to Mickey's face and ears, the pool has a maximum depth of 2 feet, and the bright-yellow spiral **Mickey's Slide** rises about one deck high (about the same level as Deck 12). Kids must be 4–14 years old and 38–64 inches tall to use the waterslide. There's plenty of nearby seating for parents to get some sun while watching the little ones splash around.

Children who don't meet the requirements for Mickey's Pool can play in the nearby **Nemo's Reef,** toward the aft end of the pool. Larger and wetter than the Nephews' Splash Zone on the *Magic* and Mickey's Splash Zone on the *Wonder,* this *Finding Nemo*–themed water-play area for kids age 3 and under features gurgling sprays, jets, and sprinkles of water bubbling up from fountains in the floor and from kid-size replicas of some of the movie's characters. A set of restrooms is just behind Nemo's Reef.

Found on Deck 11 Midship is the *Dream*'s family pool, **Donald's Pool.** Like Goofy's Pool on the *Magic* and *Wonder,* it's the center of outdoor activity on the ship. The rectangular pool is about a foot deep close to its edges; in the middle is a roughly circular section that drops to a maximum depth of around 5 feet. The different depths allow younger swimmers to relax in the shallows without having to get out of the pool.

Deck chairs and chaise longues line both sides of Donald's Pool. At the forward end of the pool is the **Funnel Vision** LED screen, which plays movies, TV shows, and videos almost constantly. At the aft end is the Mickey Pool. Just beyond the Funnel Vision stage are the counter-service restaurants: **Fillmore's Favorites, Luigi's Pizza,** and **Tow Mater's Grill** on the starboard side, and the **Eye Scream** ice-cream station and **Frozone Treats** smoothie station on the port side. Both Donald's and Mickey's Pools are typically open 8 a.m.–10 p.m. every day; check your *Personal Navigator* for specific hours.

Like the *Magic* and *Wonder,* the *Fantasy* (but not the *Dream*) has an **AquaLab** water-play area. On Deck 12 Aft, it's similar to Nemo's Reef in that its entertainment is provided by water splashing out at you,

but where the water comes up from the floor at Nemo's Reef, it comes down from above at AquaLab. High above your head are water pipes filling buckets and buckets of water, which are counterbalanced so that they spill down on unsuspecting (and suspecting) kids below. In fact, water comes at you from every angle in AquaLab, and that's exactly the appeal. AquaLab is for kids too old or too large to play in Nemo's Reef.

The adults-only **Quiet Cove Pool** is on Deck 11 Forward on both the *Dream* and the *Fantasy*. This pool is 4 feet deep throughout. Rather than wasting space on whirlpools, the *Dream*'s designers wisely placed an outdoor bar, **Cove Bar,** at one end of the Quiet Cove Pool. The area around the bar is a splash-friendly nonslip surface, with white bench seating and a round ottoman-like seat in the middle; there are also a few seats directly at the bar. Behind the pool is the lovely **Cove Café;** on either side is covered seating with chaise longues and chairs.

unofficial **TIP**
The best time to visit the AquaDuck is between 5 and 7 p.m., when most families are either at dinner or getting ready to go. You'll also find smaller crowds on days when the ship is in port.

Both the *Dream* and the *Fantasy* have an **AquaDuck** waterslide, a 765-foot-long clear-plastic tube that's almost as popular as the Disney princesses. Riders board an inflatable plastic raft at the aft end of Deck 12. The raft is shot forward through the plastic tube by high-pressure water faucets below and to the sides, making the AquaDuck a water-powered miniature roller coaster. There's enough water pressure here to propel your raft up two full decks' worth of height, followed by a descent of four decks into a landing pool. Guests must be at least 42 inches tall to ride, and children under age 7 must ride with someone age 14 or older who also meets the height requirement.

The AquaDuck's track sits at the outside edge of Deck 12 and goes as high as one of the ship's smokestacks. If you can keep your eyes open (and your wits about you), it offers some awesome views of the surrounding ocean and any nearby islands.

The *Dream* and the *Fantasy* also have **Satellite Falls,** an adults-only splash pool and sun deck on Deck 13 Forward. Covered with long, vertical tiles in different shades of blue and green, the pool looks great at night. In the center, a structure that looks like a giant Doppler radar receiver (and mimics a pair of actual satellite receivers on either side of the pool) pours a gentle stream of water into the pool below.

ONBOARD SEMINARS

LED BY CREW MEMBERS and attended by a limited number of passengers, onboard seminars are 30- to 60-minute interactive talks. Topics vary, but most involve food, wine, shopping, fitness activities, or how the ship is run. The shopping seminars and tours of the ship are usually free of charge; some of the cooking demonstrations are also free. A small

fee—about $15–$25—is charged for seminars involving alcohol, and for some of the fitness activities.

Cooking demonstrations where wine is served, along with fitness activities, are restricted to guests age 18 and up. Wine and spirits tastings are only for guests age 21 and up, except during cruises that sail solely in Europe, where participants may be 18 if a parent or guardian (1) is traveling with them, (2) has provided written permission for them to drink, and (3) is present when they do so.

The crew members who lead these seminars generally also have duties related to the subject. Wine presentations, for example, are usually run by either a restaurant sommelier or an experienced bartender; cooking demonstrations are run by one of the ship's chefs. Not surprisingly, the crew members' presentation and speaking skills are the most important factor in determining the quality of the seminar. On one cruise, a well-versed chef butterflied three dozen shrimp in slow motion so we could all take notes on proper knife technique. On another cruise, a bartender apparently not used to public speaking ran us through seven tequila shots and margaritas in 35 minutes, rendering us wasted for the rest of the afternoon (not that we minded).

Several **wine-tasting sessions** are usually held on most cruises, especially those of more than four nights. The first session is typically an introduction to wine and covers the basics: grape varietals, flavor characteristics, vocabulary, and such. Subsequent sessions may concentrate on a particular style of wine, or those from a particular region. Most tastings serve 2- or 3-ounce pours from four or five varieties. The Champagne bars on the *Dream* and *Fantasy* hold tastings, too. In addition to wine, Champagne, and tequila, cruises may offer Cognac, whiskey, martini, mojito, and beer tastings as well as general classes on mixology.

The **cooking demonstrations** are some of the best presentations on board. Like the wine sessions, cooking demos often follow a theme: the first day, for example, may show how to prepare an appetizer; the second involves an entrée; and the third will be dessert. Each of these is led by a member of the kitchen staff, usually a chef. These presentations are typically held in one of the ship's nightclubs so more people can attend. To make it easy for everyone to see what the chef is doing, several video cameras are often mounted above the chef's work table, providing a view of the preparations.

We've attended many cooking demonstrations on the Disney ships, and they've all been presented better and had more interesting foods than comparable classes elsewhere. We're always amazed at the number of ingredients used in some of these dishes, too. One shrimp-and-lobster appetizer we prepared consisted of 31 separate ingredients! Trust us, you wouldn't be making these for a church potluck.

If you're looking for exercise instead of food or shopping, the **walking tours** of the ships are a great way to keep moving and see the inner workings of the ship. Most tours begin somewhere on the pool deck

and wind their way down and back up the ship. Areas covered may include the bridge, engine room, kitchens and restaurants, and entertainment areas. One great thing about these tours is that you get to ask questions of the cast members staffing each section. If you want to know what it takes to prepare 800 appetizers at the same time, you'll find the person to ask on this tour.

Shopping seminars are usually held on sea days when the ship will be docked at a port the following day. (The seminars are also videotaped and available on your stateroom's television 24 hours a day.) Most seminars last 60–90 minutes, with multiple sessions held per day. Each session usually covers one kind of item, such as watches, or a particular kind of gemstone available at the next port. The seminar on diamonds, for example, explains how cut, color, carat, and clarity combine to form the basis of each stone's price.

Along with statements of fact, bear in mind that you may hear alternative facts as well. During one shopping seminar on the *Wonder,* we heard the presenter say, "You don't really need to pay attention to things like clarity or gem imperfections if you love a stone, because no one will know about it except you." Of course, she didn't mention that it really *does* matter if you're buying the piece as an investment or if you ever want to sell it or insure it. You also won't hear any negative statements about the products being shilled—while your presenter may extol the virtues of the bright-blue tanzanite, what she won't say is that this gemstone is too soft and scratch-prone to be worn regularly.

Bear in mind that the shopping seminar leader is likely an independent contractor, hired by port retail associations, rather than a DCL cast member. You can tell this by noting that their name tag does not have the Disney logo on it. The seminar leader is representing vendors' interests, not necessarily yours.

We don't understand why anyone would attend a shopping seminar. If you're considering a major purchase such as diamonds, jewelry, or an expensive watch, you're almost certainly better off postponing it until you're back at home and can do your own research. Further, with the vast array of goods available on the internet (usually with better consumer protections), it's unlikely that you'll find many things with prices low enough to justify the risk. (See our Shopping section on page 254 for more information.)

The spa and fitness center host **wellness seminars** most mornings. Topics include everything from stretching exercises and acupuncture to group cycling and Pilates. Many of the sessions, such as stretching and cycling, are free, although space is limited and you're strongly encouraged to sign up well in advance to guarantee a spot. Personal-training sessions, available in 30- or 60-minute increments, cost roughly $45–$80, respectively, before tip.

Finally, the **Disney Vacation Club** (**DVC**) hosts presentations on its Walt Disney World time-shares during the cruise; check your *Personal*

Navigator for the schedule. A DVC representative is often stationed at a desk somewhere just off the lobby. On sea days, you'll probably find the rep roaming the halls of the ship to get the word out on an upcoming seminar. And while you may or may not want to sit through a time-share presentation on vacation, the DVC reps are very generous in giving out free stuff, as this reader found:

> *We didn't want to sit through the DVC sales pitch, but we're suckers for swag. We stopped by the DVC desk and they practically threw goodies at us. Despite me saying that there were just two of us on board, the rep insisted on giving me four DVC baseball caps and four sturdy drawstring backpacks.*

SPORTS *and* FITNESS

EACH SHIP OFFERS AN ARRAY of outdoor and indoor sports and fitness options. While it's no substitute for your local megagym, there's enough equipment and variety on board for almost everyone to maintain muscle tone and cardio conditioning during the cruise.

unofficial **TIP**
The Fitness Center is on Deck 9 Forward on the *Magic* and *Wonder*, and on Deck 11 Forward on the *Dream* and *Fantasy*.

Use of the fitness center is generally limited to guests age 18 and up. While the Vibe teen club may bring a group of 14- to 17-year-olds to the gym for a group activity, a high school varsity athlete shouldn't expect to be able to use the equipment at a training level, even with parental permission or supervision.

Each DCL ship has a comprehensive **Fitness Center** with modern, well-maintained weight machines, free weights, treadmills, stair-climbers, elliptical machines, stationary bikes, and more.

These gyms provide yoga mats, large plastic step-aerobics benches, exercise balls, and elastic bands for stretching. Also provided are a water fountain, a basket of fresh fruit, cloth towels, paper towels, and spray bottles of sanitizer to clean the equipment when you're done. Men's and women's locker rooms have showers, a sauna, sinks, robes, towels, personal-grooming items, and lockers with electric locks. There is no charge to use these facilities.

unofficial **TIP**
The locker rooms at the Fitness Center can be helpful even if you're not working out. During one cruise where we had four adults in one stateroom, we ended up sending some folks up to the Fitness Center to shower, speeding our daily prep time considerably.

We've spent a lot of time in the gyms on every ship, and we've been happy with the variety of equipment available. Nautilus-style weight machines are available for working every major and minor muscle group. Virtually all of the electric cardio machines have video monitors

so you can watch the ship's television while working out, along with plugs for your headphones.

The Fitness Center is usually open from around 6 a.m. until 11 p.m.; check your *Personal Navigator* for the exact schedule. It tends to be most crowded in the morning between 8 and 11 a.m., and least crowded between 5 and 11 p.m. Group- and personal-training sessions are available, including weight training, Pilates, and other courses, for an additional fee. Group sessions start at around $12 per workout, typically about 45 minutes each. Individual training sessions cost around $82 for a 1-hour session. To arrange personal training, stop by the gym on embarkation day.

The only thing we've found disconcerting in the gyms is that the treadmills on the *Dream* and *Fantasy* face the port (left) side of the ship, not the bow. If the ship is moving while you're running on one of these treadmills, the scenery in front of you will be passing from left to right, but your brain expects to see the scenery moving toward you. Some people—including Len—instinctively twist their bodies left in an attempt to line up the scenery with the way their minds think they should be going. This makes for awkward running (walking doesn't seem to be much of an issue). If you find yourself unable to run correctly on the treadmill, try the outdoor course described next.

unofficial **TIP**
If your itinerary includes a trip to Castaway Cay, Disney usually hosts a 5K run around the island starting at 9 a.m. There's no cost to run. Water is provided at several points throughout the course, and Disney usually hands out Mickey-shaped plastic medals to finishers. Check your *Personal Navigator* the night before your stop for where to meet on board.

Runners and walkers will appreciate the **0.3-mile track** circling Deck 4 of the *Magic* and *Wonder* and the **0.4-mile track** on Deck 4 of the *Dream* and *Fantasy.* One of the great things about running laps on the ship is the amazing scenery, which (almost) makes you forget that you're exercising while you're seeing it. We've run a few laps on both ships, and the track is certainly good enough to get in a few miles to start your day. Some sections take you through some relatively narrow corridors, and there's a good chance that you'll be running past groups of other tourists who are out enjoying the deck, too. Finally, keep an eye open for water on the deck, which can make the track slick.

If running isn't your thing, every DCL ship has **outdoor basketball courts** surrounded by woven rope fencing to keep errant balls from leaving the ship. These are popular with kids and parents looking to shoot around a bit—we've never seen a competitive game played at one. The basketball courts can be converted to a miniature soccer field or volleyball court, too, if you can find enough people to play.

Each ship also has **shuffleboard courts** near midship on Deck 4. Since the only time we ever play shuffleboard is on a cruise, we tend to forget the rules in between sailings and then make them up as we go

along while we're on the ship. There are no official rules posted near the courts, so if you're looking to play a regulation game and need a refresher, take a peek here before you sail: www.shuffleboardcourt.com/rules-shuffleboard-game-us-ca.

If you're up for a challenge, **ping-pong tables** are available, too (Deck 9 Forward on the *Magic* and *Wonder;* Deck 13 Aft on the *Dream* and *Fantasy*). Readers report that the windy conditions on deck make it difficult to play, but perhaps your game will benefit from a bit of unpredictability.

The *Dream* and *Fantasy* both have Disney-themed **miniature-golf courses** outdoors on Deck 13 Aft; these are a lot of fun for the entire family. The *Dream* and *Fantasy* also have **Foosball tables** outdoors. As with the table tennis, we find it helpful to have the following list available when our game fails us:

HANDY EXCUSES FOR RECREATIONAL INEPTITUDE
• Gust of wind changed ball trajectory
• Rough seas caused ship to list suddenly
• Sunglasses aren't made for the UV rays at this latitude (*note:* you must be wearing sunglasses when saying this)
• Concentration broken by sound of pirate-ship cannon in distance
• Giant-squid tentacle was seen reaching up behind opponent

If you're looking to get in some individual practice time on the *Dream* and *Fantasy,* **virtual sports simulators** are available on Deck 13 Aft for golf, basketball, soccer, football, hockey, and baseball. These indoor facilities have a large movie screen set up in a dedicated room; a computer projects a simulated soccer field, basketball court, or other appropriate venue on the screen. You're given actual sports equipment to kick, throw, or swing. Your movements, and the movements of the ball, are tracked by computers and displayed on screen—there's a slight lag in the display, but it's not enough to be distracting. Half-hour sessions cost $28 for golf and $13 for other sports; hour-long sessions are $49 for golf and $22 for other sports.

SPAS

SOME OF THE MOST RELAXING TIMES we've spent on DCL's ships have been in their spas. Whether you're looking for a massage, a manicure, a new hairstyle, or just some time to unwind in a hot sauna, you'll find it at the spa.

unofficial **TIP**
The best time to visit the spa is during dinner or when the ship is in port.

This section summarizes the major spa and salon services offered on each ship, but note that many more are available. We recommend visiting the spa on your first afternoon aboard

to sign up for any last-minute treatments and check for specials. *Note:* Prices listed are approximate and do not include a tip, typically 15%–20% of the cost of your treatment. There's a 50% cancellation charge if you cancel within 24 hours of your appointment.

Salon services must be booked after 1 p.m. on your first day aboard—you can't book them online. If you're trying to book spa services before your cruise, Disney's website may not let you book some services, such as facials, for two people at the same time of day. (We think the website assumes that only one person per ship is qualified to do these tasks, and that this person is unavailable once the first service is booked.) If you run into this problem, try booking the services online one after the other, and then visit the spa in person when you board to explain what you want done.

Along the same lines, one thing that's different about spa treatments on the Disney ships versus on land is that the same person is likely to be your masseuse, facialist, and manicurist—there's simply not enough room on the ship for a whole squadron of beauty experts, so roles have to be combined. Some readers like the continuity of having one person to talk with throughout their treatments; others think that one person can't provide the same level of service as multiple dedicated professionals.

ON THE *MAGIC* AND *WONDER*

ON DECK 9 FORWARD is **Senses Spa & Salon.** The reception area and check-in desk are just behind the forward elevator lobby, past the adult Quiet Cove Pool. Senses has a hair salon, treatment rooms for individuals and couples, and a complex of steam baths and showers. Men's and women's locker rooms, shared with the Fitness Center, provide storage lockers with electric locks, showers, robes, slippers, and towels.

Senses Spas on all four ships have a **Chill Spa** for guests ages 13–17. However, the versions on the *Magic* and *Wonder* are nothing like the versions on the *Dream* and *Fantasy*—they're single treatment rooms off the beauty salon. To call them spas is a stretch.

Senses's hair salon has services for men and women. Options for men include haircuts (around $35); the **Elemis Express Shave** with hot-towel wrap (around $45); and the wordy **Elemis Pro-Collagen Grooming Treatment with Shave** (around $95), billed as "the shave of all shaves"—an almost hour-long treatment including the towel wrap, a shave, a minifacial, and massages for your face, scalp, and hands. Men who use electric shavers for their daily toilette should be aware that a hand-held razor shaves much closer than an electric blade and can cause razor burn, even on men who aren't normally susceptible. Your face will be as smooth as a baby's bottom, though.

Women can get a literal head-to-toe makeover, starting with hairstyling. A simple shampoo and blow-dry runs about $32–$48 depending on hair length; adding a cut and style is about $56–$75. Separate conditioning treatments are available: the **Frangipani Hair and Scalp Ritual,** which sounds like it's part of a tribal initiation, starts at around $30; most other standard conditioning treatments cost around $50 each. Senses also offers a treatment for color-treated hair for around $30; hair coloring starts at about $55.

If you're headed to Palo for dinner, you can get your makeup done for your big night out, starting at $75. Manicures (around $50) and pedicures (around $70) come with a heated stone massage of your various digits. There seems to be no discount for a combined mani–pedi. Additional services include adding polish ($25), removing polish ($20), paraffin baths ($15), and acrylic nails ($82).

Facials and massages are administered in private, individual treatment rooms or in one of the dedicated Spa Villas for singles and couples. Five different facials are offered, including ones with microdermabrasion, fruits and herbs, enzymes, and something that involves "amazing micro-currents applied at a high frequency" to your skin . . . *voluntarily.* Treatments cost $115–$170 for a 50-minute session.

unofficial **TIP**
Some treatment rooms at Senses on the *Magic* and *Wonder* sit directly under the basketball courts. If someone is playing, you'll hear through the ceiling every time someone bounces a ball or lands after jumping. If noise is a no-go for you, inquire ahead of time about the location of your treatment room.

Massages include the traditional deep-tissue kind; a variation accompanied by heated, scented stones placed on various parts of your body; and another where warmed bamboo sticks are rolled over you in addition to the massage. Prices range from $129 for a basic 50-minute rubdown to $244 for 100 minutes. Besides these are massages combining hands-on therapy with slatherings of spices, minerals, and herbs designed to make you feel like a Thanksgiving turkey with a healthy glow. Among the offerings are the **Aroma Ocean Wrap with Half-Body Massage** ($188), the **Thai Herbal Poultice Massage ($195),** and the **Exotic Lime and Ginger Salt Glow with Half-Body Massage** (part of two $400-plus treatment packages for couples).

Services in the Chill Spa room for teens range from the **Magical Manicure** at the low end ($29) to the **Hot Chocolate Wrap** at the high end ($141).

Besides these spa services, 30-minute teeth-whitening treatments are available for individuals (around $150) and couples (around $260). They're not especially popular, though, probably because you're told to abstain from drinking coffee and wine after the whitening.

Our favorite spa experience is the **Rainforest,** which costs around $16 per person, per day. This gets you access to three separate steam

unofficial **TIP**
We don't recommend the length-of-cruise Rainforest pass on the *Magic* and *Wonder.* Get the cheaper one-day pass instead.

rooms, arranged around a quiet tiled room with heated stone lounge chairs. Each steam room has its own scent, temperature, and steam setting. Outside the steam rooms are Rainforest showers, with push-button settings that allow you to vary the intensity, pattern, and temperature of the water flow.

Unfortunately, the Rainforests at Senses on the *Magic* and *Wonder* aren't as nice as the versions on the *Dream* and *Fantasy:* they're considerably smaller and less spacious, with fewer showers and lounge chairs, and unlike their larger siblings, they don't have outdoor hot tubs or an ocean view. That said, it's still the most relaxing thing you can do on the ships, and because DCL sells a limited number of passes per cruise—we've heard estimates of as few as 20 on the entire ship—you're unlikely to share the Rainforest with more than a handful of other people on any day. Also, a day pass at the Rainforest on the *Magic* and *Wonder* is less expensive than on the *Dream* and *Fantasy:* $16 versus $27 on the larger ships.

ON THE *DREAM* AND *FANTASY*

DISNEY'S TWO NEWEST SHIPS each have a **Senses Spa & Salon** on Deck 11 Forward. Both are gorgeous, incorporating dark woods and intricate tile and stonework, with comfortable leather chairs and soft bed linens.

Senses on the *Dream* and *Fantasy* is considerably larger than its counterparts on the *Magic* and *Wonder.* Some of the treatment rooms and spa areas afford sweeping views out over the sides of each ship; also, Senses on the *Dream* and *Fantasy* has two covered outdoor whirlpools available to those with a Rainforest pass. On the *Magic* and *Wonder,* ocean views and outdoor features are available only to those who book a pricey treatment in one of the private Spa Villas.

The salon services, facials, and massages offered are about the same as those at the Senses spas on the *Magic* and *Wonder.* Here are the major differences:

More luxurious than its counterparts on the two smaller ships, the **Rainforest** (about $27 per person, per day) gives you access to three saunas with varying levels of heat and humidity: the Laconium, a dry sauna with mild heat and low humidity; the Caldarium, with medium heat and humidity; and the Hamam, a full-on steam bath, with the hottest temperatures and lots and lots of steam. In addition to different levels of steam, each sauna has its own scent and music.

While most guests find the Rainforest peaceful, indulgent, and relaxing, one reader had a different experience:

> *Some guests enter the Rainforest thinking it's Blizzard Beach [at Walt Disney World], screeching and laughing like they're in a theme park.*

I wish Disney would spend 45 seconds educating them on what to expect and explaining that this is a relaxation/quiet area for adults.

We haven't experienced this ourselves, but speak to a cast member if you encounter rowdy behavior in the spa.

We enjoy hopping between these saunas and the nearby Rainforest showers—tiled circular cutouts hidden behind the walls along the path leading to the saunas. Each shower has different options for water temperature, pressure, and spray pattern, each of which you select by pushing a button. For example, one option might be a light, cool mist, perfect for when you've just jumped out of the sauna. Another is like a warm, steady downpour in a tropical jungle.

unofficial **TIP**
Bring a towel to sit on in the saunas, and wear sandals—the seats and floors are very hot.

Had enough of the steam rooms and showers? Then repair to one of the two covered outdoor whirlpool tubs or one of the stone lounge chairs in an adjacent room. The ocean views here are perhaps the biggest selling point over the Rainforests on the *Magic* and *Wonder.*

The best thing about the Rainforest package is that Disney sells only a limited number of them per cruise. We hear that number can be as low as 40 people on the *Dream* and *Fantasy.* Not 40 at a time, not 40 per day—40 people *on the entire ship.* While we haven't actually fact-checked that number ourselves, we can tell you that we've never seen more than two other people in this part of the spa on any cruise. It's the single most relaxing thing you can do on board.

Senses on the *Dream* and *Fantasy* also has a juice bar offering freshly blended juices and smoothies for about $5. We're amused that Disney has gone with the Anglophile spellings of *soya* and *yoghurt* on the menus (because they're classy that way). Exercisers and spa fans can refuel with choices like a spinach, carrot, avocado, ginger–basil, and manuka honey beverage or concoctions including everything from kale to chia seeds, spirulina, matcha, and turmeric powder. We don't know if they really "restore harmony and balance" . . . but they are pretty tasty.

Finally, exclusive to the *Dream* and *Fantasy* is the teens-only **Chill Spa,** a spa-within-a-spa entirely inside Senses. (The *Magic* and *Wonder* also have areas that they call Chill Spa—but they're single treatment rooms.) Designed for guests ages 13–17, Chill has its own array of facial, massage, exfoliating, and mani–pedi packages. Prices start at around $90 for a massage, $95 for a facial, and $45 and $65 for manicures and pedicures, respectively. Hairstyling and fitness sessions in the gym are also available.

Parent–child massages are offered as well ($99 for half-body, $195 for full-body). Let us know if you've tried these with your teens, please: when we told ours about them, one replied, "Gross!" and the other gave us a look like she'd prefer being rubbed with angry ferrets.

SHOPPING

WHETHER YOU'RE AT SEA OR IN PORT, your daily *Personal Navigator* handout highlights your shopping opportunities for the day.

ONBOARD SHOPPING

ONBOARD SHOPS GENERALLY AREN'T OPEN when the ship is in port. If there's any possibility that you're going to run out of something critical during the day, be sure to stock up on it while the shops are open.

As Disney-theme-park fans, we were surprised at the relatively modest amount of retail space on the DCL ships. Each ship has dedicated shopping spaces for children, women, and men. Look for them on Deck 4 Forward on the *Magic* and *Wonder* and Deck 3 Forward on the *Dream* and *Fantasy,* on either side of the walkway to the Walt Disney Theatre.

The shops sell a little bit of everything, from T-shirts and stuffed animals to snacks, bathing suits, and towels. You'll also find sunscreen, aspirin, toothpaste, diapers (in limited sizes), and other travel supplies. The onboard shops may also stock location-specific items; for example, during our Alaskan cruise, the shops stocked mittens, knit caps, binoculars, and books about local wildlife. In addition, an onboard store sells duty-free alcohol by the bottle, including wines and spirits served on board, though you won't be able to take possession of your purchase until the last night of your cruise.

In case you neglected to pack your eye patch for Pirate Night (see page 190), the shops can outfit the entire family head to toe, buccaneer-style. You'll find a variety of the same merchandise found in Disney theme parks, as well as DCL-specific souvenirs. Some of our favorites are china and brush-shaped butter knives from Animator's Palate—the cynics among us wonder if this wasn't in response to these items walking off the ships on their own—and T-shirts with mash-up images of Star Wars characters in cruise situations (surfing Stormtroopers, anyone?).

Bear in mind that a shopping-seminar leader is likely an independent contractor, hired by port retail associations, rather than a DCL cast member. (As noted earlier, you can tell this by the speaker's name tag, which doesn't have the Disney logo on it.) The seminar leader is representing vendors' interests, not necessarily yours. Besides the retail spaces, each ship has an art gallery with limited-edition Disney-character and theme park art, along with **Shutters** photo gallery, where you can purchase snaps from your cruise.

The biggest advantage to buying on board or in port is that you don't pay US or local sales taxes, which can be significant on large purchases. US residents are still required to declare these purchases when they return to the States, and they may be subject to import duties. See page 117 for more details.

IS IT REAL?

YOU PROBABLY REALIZE that "Louis Vuitton" bag on sale for $25 at the Straw Market in Nassau is a fake, but know as well that perfume and sunglasses are among the most counterfeited items out there. Many luxury brands, such as Gucci and the aforementioned LV, do have actual stores in the Caribbean and European ports, so you can buy with confidence there. Another thing to look out for is out-of-season merchandise being sold at full price: on one trip to Nassau, we found an authentic Kate Spade bag being sold at MSRP, but it could be found 30%–50% off stateside because it was from the previous season. With all purchases, do your due diligence ahead of time to know what a fair price is for anything you're considering buying.

We find that the amount of time spent bargaining in port isn't worth any potential savings, and so we don't spend a lot of time shopping on our cruises. That said, our Ports chapter (Part Eleven) highlights any especially good deals we've been able to find along the way.

TYPICAL PRICING FOR DCL SOUVENIRS DCL- and Disney-branded souvenirs sold on the ships—T-shirts, mugs, plush toys, princess costumes, autograph books, and the like—are priced the same as souvenirs sold in US Disney theme parks. For example, a Mickey Mouse T-shirt sold on the *Dream* costs the same as if you bought it at Epcot. To get a feel for what you might spend, 2018 pricing for typical DCL souvenirs was approximately as follows:

• Baseball cap: $25	• Spirit jersey: $65
• Adult T-shirt: $30	• Plush Mickey or Minnie: $30
• Disney coffee mug: $20	• Disney trading pin: $10–$18
• Autograph book: $15	• Beach towel: $25

CASTAWAY CAY

THE SHOPS HERE SELL SOME ITEMS that are exclusive to the island, such as T-shirts and beach towels. We've purchased last-minute cords for our sunglasses, water-resistant pouches for our phones, and other beach supplies on Castaway Cay. Note that no sales tax is charged on the island or on board, which makes purchases cheaper than if you bought them at a Disney park.

IN PORT

MANY TRAVELERS FIND SHOPPING IN PORT as essential to the cruising experience as gambling is to the Las Vegas experience. If you approach buying things with this attitude, you won't be disappointed.

You'll be surrounded by retail opportunities at each port from the moment you step off the ship; bargaining is expected, so assume that the price you're quoted the first time you ask isn't the final one. If you need T-shirts, handmade woodcrafts, or other tchotchkes to bring back as inexpensive souvenirs, you'll have no trouble finding them within a few hundreds yards of the ship.

The Northern European ports are the exception to the schlock-shopping onslaught. For instance, while Diamonds International shops are virtually everywhere in Alaska and the Caribbean, we were thrilled not to see a single solitary one during our recent Scandinavian and Baltic cruises. But here, as in every port, the real trick is to ask pointed questions about what you're about to purchase. If you're buying mittens in Norway, ask if they're made from local wool. Are they hand- or machine-knit? Were they knit in Norway or in a factory in China? It's up to you to understand what you're paying for.

JEWELRY Buying jewelry in port is popular with many cruisers. The problem we have with doing this is that fair prices vary greatly with the quality of the gems purchased, and you really need to be an informed shopper to know what's a good price for an item. Our recommendation is to pre-shop online (**Amazon** and **Blue Nile** [bluenile.com] are great places to start) to know the going prices for gems of the weight and quality you're interested in. One brand in particular, **Effy,** is already sold on Amazon and through its own website (effyjewelry.com), so check it out before you leave.

ALCOHOL Duty-free alcohol is available on board the ship as well as at many ports. If you're thinking about purchasing spirits during your cruise, be sure to do a little pricing research before you travel. Depending on your place of residence and its tax situation, the duty-free pricing may not be much different than what you'd pay at home. Look at the per-ounce price and make sure you're comparing apples to apples, or rather tequila to tequila.

For example, a silver tequila and a *reposado* will be priced differently; be sure you know which you're buying. On the other hand, price may not be as much of an issue if you're making a sentimental purchase (the bottle of wine you learned about during a port-adventure vineyard tour) or if you're buying a noncommodity item like a liqueur made from a local flower and sold only in a particular region.

If you decide to buy alcohol during your trip, remember to review DCL's rules for bringing it on board (see page 42). In many cases, you won't have access to your purchase until the last night of the cruise.

SHOPPING DCL FROM HOME You can do some shopping for your Disney cruise before you leave home. The DCL website has a section (disney cruise.disney.go.com/gifts-and-amenities) where you can order items in advance to be delivered to your stateroom. Items can be pricey, but this

may be helpful if you want to mark a celebration without carrying a lot of stuff on board with you.

If you discover that you forgot to get something once you're back home, a limited selection of DCL-logo items is available online at disneystore.com and through the official Disney shopping app, **Shop Disney Parks** (for Apple and Android). We've found DCL-branded clothing, pins, pillows, towels, jewelry, and toys in both locations. Be aware that the website and the mobile app often carry different items, so check both if you're looking for something specific.

RELIGIOUS SERVICES

CRUISES OF SEVEN NIGHTS or longer hold a nondenominational Christian service on Sunday mornings and a Shabbat service on Friday evenings. Worship times depend on when the ship is in port or, in the case of Jewish services, when sunset occurs. There are no dedicated chapels on the ships—services are typically held in a lounge or theater, depending on the number of guests on board and the ship's other offerings. Guest Services can recommend houses of worship in port.

In addition to regular weekly services, there will be additional services added during religious holiday seasons. For example, during Easter week, you'll typically find a Catholic Mass offered on Good Friday morning, as well as sunrise, Catholic, and interdenominational services offered on Easter morning. Similar events will happen during the Christmas season. Check your *Personal Navigator* for details.

Many DCL ports have houses of worship as key points of interest. If you'd like to attend services while in port, check the institution's website in advance to view hours of operation or specific dress code rules (common in many European churches). Guest Services on board may also be able to offer some advice.

WHAT TO DO *During* A DAY AT SEA

SOME OF THE MOST FREQUENTLY ASKED QUESTIONS we hear from new cruisers are variations on, "What happens during a day at sea?" and "Won't I be bored staying on a ship all day?" To that we say, "There are zillions of things to do for all ages and interests" and "You'll only be bored if you want to be." On the next page are just some of the things we've done on sea days. (Note that not all DCL-organized activities are available on all sailings—the longer your sailing and the more sea days you have, the more options there will be.)

On a Day at Sea, You Can . . .

- Meet characters.
- Get a mani–pedi.
- Sleep.
- Watch old Disney films.
- Watch new Disney films.
- Read a novel.
- Write a short story.
- Go for a run.
- Get in a game of pickup basketball.
- Play bingo.
- Take a spin-cycling class.
- Shop for souvenirs.
- Play a round of minigolf.
- Play shuffleboard.
- Learn to mix drinks.
- Drink the drinks we mixed.
- Enjoy fine dining.
- Play board games.
- Learn to draw Disney characters.
- Watch a Broadway-style show.
- Meet a Broadway star.
- Hunt for Hidden Mickeys.
- Get your face painted.
- Learn the fine art of towel folding.
- Play cards.
- Take a cooking class.
- Lift weights.
- Go for a swim.
- Take a tour of the ship.
- Attend a religious service.
- Participate in a scavenger hunt.
- Be on a game show.
- Have your teeth whitened.
- Cheer at a deck party.
- Play Foosball.
- Play video games.
- Hang out at a piano bar.
- Get an acupuncture treatment.
- Buy art.
- Stare at the sea.
- Attend a history class.
- Go to a dance party.
- Take a ballroom dance class.
- Sit in a sauna.
- Sit in a hot tub.
- Knit a scarf.
- Have your golf swing analyzed.
- Finish an adult coloring book.
- Get a professional shave.
- Make a jigsaw puzzle.
- Catch up on the news.
- Get a family portrait taken.
- Go on a waterslide.
- Order room service.
- Watch a comedy show.
- Get hypnotized.
- Learn the art of knot tying.
- Buy fine jewelry.
- Trade pins.
- Look for wildlife.
- Sing karaoke.
- Watch the big game.
- Learn origami.
- Experiment with your camera.
- Get a massage.
- Try a new food.
- Do the entire *New York Times* Sunday crossword puzzle in one sitting.
- Have your hair braided.
- Play in a trivia competition.
- Chat with other guests.
- Chat with your family.

PART TEN

CASTAWAY CAY

CASTAWAY CAY IS LIKELY TO BE YOUR FAVORITE ISLAND on your Bahamian or Caribbean cruise. The weather is almost always gorgeous; the shore excursions are reasonably priced (mostly); and, as is the case with Walt Disney World, there's little of the real world to get in the way of a relaxing day. And that's before the free food and (nonalcoholic) drinks. We provide additional coverage of Castaway Cay in Part Eleven, Ports, and Part Twelve, Port Adventures.

WHAT *to* BRING

THE SUN AND HEAT ARE INTENSE, so bring plenty of high-SPF sunscreen and water. Insulated sports bottles are a great idea. Other solar protection you may need includes light-colored, long-sleeved, lightweight shirts; sweatpants; swimsuit cover-ups; hats; lip balm; and sunglasses. See page 262 for a list of additional items that you may want to bring along.

Disney will provide you with medium-size towels for use while on Castaway Cay—as many as you can carry. If you'd rather use a full-size beach towel, bring one of your own or buy one while you're on the island. Disney also provides life jackets (free) for use while on the island. Strollers, wagons, and sand-capable wheelchairs are available for rent on a first-come, first-served basis.

WHAT *to* DO

THERE ARE MORE THINGS TO DO than you'll have time for in a single day or even two. A list of our favorite Castaway Cay shore activities follows; see Part Twelve for details.

continued on page 262

Castaway Cay

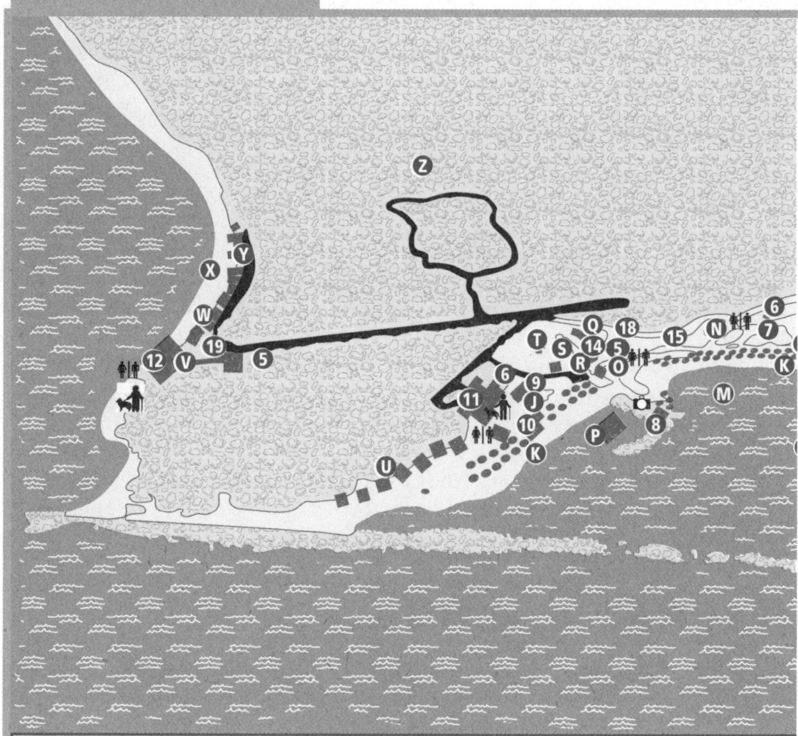

ATTRACTIONS

A. Arrival Plaza
B. Post Office
C. Marge's Barges and Sea Charters Dock
D. Boating Harbor
E. Scuttle's Cove
F. Boat Beach
G. Monstro Point
H. Castaway Ray's Stingray Adventure
I. Gil's Fins and Boats
J. Gazebos
K. Castaway Family Beaches
L. Snorkeling Lagoon
M. Swimming Lagoon
N. In-Da-Shade Games
O. Flippers and Floats
P. Pelican Plunge

ATTRACTIONS

Q. The Hide Out (teens only)
R. Bike Rentals
S. Beach Sports
T. Spring-a-Leak
U. Family Cabanas 1–21
V. The Windsock Hut
W. Massage Cabanas
X. Serenity Bay Adult Beach
Y. Adult Cabanas 22–25
Z. Observation Tower

FOOD AND DRINK

1. Pop's Props and Boat Repair (Covered Seating)
2. Dig In (Covered Seating)
3. Cookie's BBQ
4. Conched Out Bar

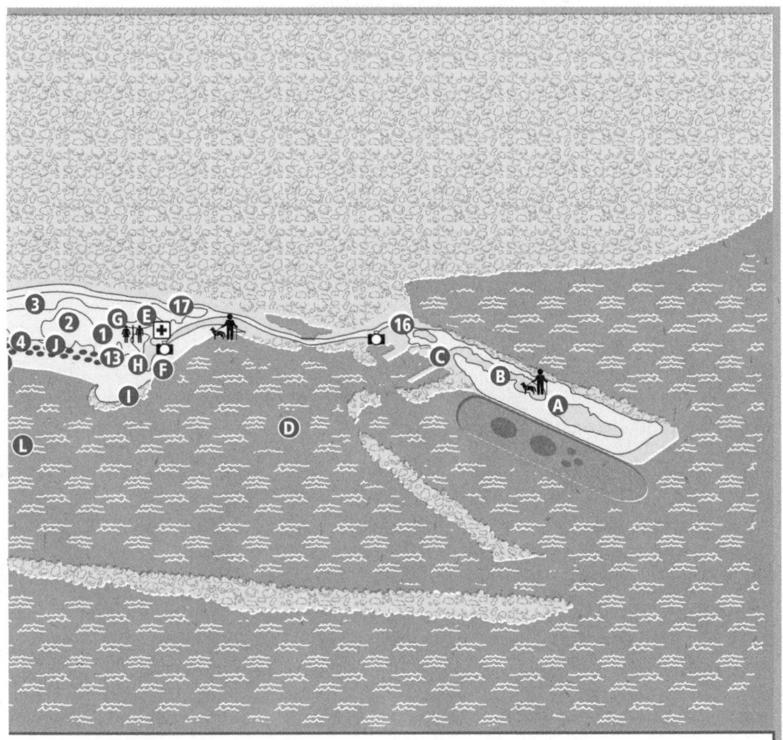

FOOD AND DRINK

5. Summertime Freeze
6. Outdoor Seating
7. Gumbo Limbo (Covered Seating)
8. Heads Up Bar
9. Grouper (Covered Seating)
10. Sand Bar
11. Cookie's Too BBQ
12. Castaway Air Bar

SHOPPING

13. She Sells Sea Shells . . . and Everything Else
14. Buy the Seashore
15. Bahamian Retail

MISCELLANEOUS

16. Kargo Handling Tram Stop
17. Scuttle's Cove Tram Stop
18. Pelican Point Tram Stop
19. Serenity Bay Tram Stop

Animal-Relief Area
Bike/Nature Trail
First Aid
Photo Opportunities
Restrooms and Outdoor Showers

continued from page 259

OTHER ITEMS YOU MAY FIND USEFUL TO BRING TO CASTAWAY CAY
• **A watch or cell phone** for checking how long everyone has been in the sun and when it's time to reapply sunscreen. Also useful for knowing whether the island's restaurants are open (usually 11 a.m.–2 p.m.).
• **An underwater or waterproof camera** for taking photos while swimming, snorkeling, or participating in other activities.
• **A small cooler** to keep medicine, baby formula, and other perishables cool. Fill it with ice before you leave the ship, and refill it from the restaurants' ice machines on the island. The cooler must be soft-sided and no larger than 12 x 12 x 12 inches.
• **Water shoes** will protect your feet from sharp rocks and coral and provide some insulation from hot sand and pavement.
• **Small beach toys,** such as a shovel and pail, though pails might present some packing issues. Toys are also available for purchase on the island.
• **Your own snorkeling gear** if you already have it, or if the idea of sharing a snorkel tube just grosses you out. DCL provides flotation vests for free.
• **Swim diapers,** if you have little ones who like the water.
• **A hairbrush or comb.** It's windy on the island, and you'll want to look good in your vacation photos.
• **Insect repellent.** Disney does a good job of keeping the bug population under control, but in case your family is especially sensitive to bites, however, it's a good idea to bring something like Off or Repel. With heightened concerns about Zika virus, it's a good precaution in any case. Disney now provides insect repellent at many ports, but if you're brand-sensitive or you prefer a particular application method, bring your own.
• **Something to read—a book or e-reader.** Be careful, however, about leaving expensive electronics alone on the island.
• **A portable music player.** Especially useful if you're going for a jog around the island's 5K course.
• **Athletic shoes and socks.** If you want to play basketball on the island, you'll also want proper footwear.
• **A change of clothes.** While Castaway Cay's sun will dry your swimsuit in a hurry, you may want dry clothes to wear while you're walking around the island, sitting down for meals, or riding bikes. You can also return to the ship to change, but going through security takes time.
• **A small amount of cash.** Castaway Cay has its own official Bahamian post office from which you can mail home postcards and letters. The post office takes cash only (no room charges), so bring a few dollars for postage. (This is the only place on the island for which you'll need cash.)

Castaway Cay's lagoons are shallow, with small, gentle waves. Anchored within a short swim from shore is **Pelican Plunge,** a floating platform with two waterslides and a water-play area. The waterslides begin on the platform's second story (accessed by stairs) and end with a splash back into the lagoon. Each slide offers a different experience: one is a long, open slide with moderate turns, while the other is a shorter, enclosed slide with plenty of tight turns and twists.

Along with the slides, Pelican Plunge's water-play area includes pipes, nozzles, and plumes of water spraying out from every direction. The main feature is a giant overhead bucket, which is constantly being filled with water from the lagoon. The bucket is counterbalanced so that when the water reaches a certain level, the bucket tilts over suddenly, pouring gallons of water on anything nearby.

If you have small children who enjoy water but you're concerned about ocean currents, consider letting the little ones run around at the inland **Spring-a-Leak** water-play area, just beyond the Pelican Point tram stop, near the middle of the family beaches. Like Pelican Plunge, Spring-a-Leak has plenty of burbling, spraying, misting water to keep kids wet and happy all day long.

Scuttle's Cove, an additional area for the little ones, offers supervised activities, yet another water-play area, and a giant-whale-bone excavation site. Teens have their own dedicated area inland: **The Hide Out,** with volleyball, tetherball, and other activities. Some teens, however, may not like the fact that The Hide Out is away from the beach and has no water features or water-play areas. Note that kids and teens must be registered at their respective youth clubs on board (see page 223) to play at Scuttle's Cove and hang out at The Hide Out.

OUR FAVORITE FUN STUFF ON CASTAWAY CAY
• **Castaway Ray's Stingray Adventure** affords you the opportunity to pet and feed small and medium-size stingrays in a dedicated lagoon.
• The **snorkeling lagoon** features underwater sights, such as a replica of the *Nautilus* submarine from *20,000 Leagues Under the Sea,* other shipwrecks and shipping artifacts, plus statues of Minnie and Mickey. Common marine life seen in the snorkeling lagoon includes stingrays, blue tang, and yellowtail snapper (plus the occasional barracuda).
• Rent **sailboats or paddleboats, personal watercraft,** or **inflatable floats and tubes.**
• Runners may want to start their day with the **Castaway Cay 5K,** a free (as in no-cost) jog through the developed parts of the island.
• Single-speed **bicycle rentals** allow you to fully explore the island, including its observation tower and trails, which can be accessed only on foot or bike.

HEIGHT AND AGE REQUIREMENTS AT CASTAWAY CAY
• **Pelican Plunge waterslide:** No official height or age requirement listed; life jackets encouraged. Tweens (ages 11–13) have scheduled time to hang out (supervised by youth counselors) at both Pelican Plunge and the **In-Da-Shade Games pavilion.**
• **The Hide Out:** Ages 14–17; must be registered for Vibe on board
• **Scuttle's Cove:** Ages 3–12; must be registered for the Oceaneer Club/ Oceaneer Lab on board

WHERE *to* RELAX

CASTAWAY CAY IS ALSO A GREAT PLACE TO SIT BACK, listen to the ocean, feel the sea breeze on your face, and smell the salt air. Two family beaches are available, while adults ages 18 and up have **Serenity Bay,** a private beach with its own outdoor barbecue, bar, rental cabanas, and more.

FAMILY BEACHES Most of Castaway Cay's developed beachfront is reserved for families. If you're taking the tram from the dock, get off at the first stop, **Pelican Point,** and you'll find yourself in the middle of both family beaches.

A small, hook-shaped peninsula juts into the lagoon and effectively separates the family beaches. If you're going to rent floats or boats or do some snorkeling, you'll want to head to the left of the peninsula once you're off the tram. If you're going to play in the water, especially at the Pelican Plunge waterslide, bear right.

Both family beaches offer free lounge chairs and towels, with restrooms, food, and drink dispensers a short walk away.

CABANAS The Pelican Plunge side of the beach has 21 private cabanas for rent. The typical price is $549 per day for up to six guests. In 2016, Disney added a seasonal supplement to the base price, making the cost $599 from late April until late September. The Serenity Bay side of the beach has five cabanas available at a cost of $399 per day for up to four guests. There is also one Grand Cabana that can accommodate up to 16 guests ($966 for the first 10 guests, $54 for each additional guest).

The cabanas are covered and furnished with cushioned chairs, chaise longues, a hammock, and a bar area. Cabanas are also supplied with fresh towels, water and soft drinks, some snacks, a selection of sunscreens, a refrigerator, a private safe, an outdoor shower, and a shaded deck.

While the financial bite of a cabana is substantial, consider that a cabana rental also includes free use of snorkeling equipment, floats, and bikes. Those three things total $49 a person. If you have six people in your cabana, that's a $294 value. If you'd normally spring for that equipment and several soft drinks, the price of some private shade and

comfort seems a lot more reasonable. (*Note:* Snorkeling equipment is currently not included with the Serenity Bay cabanas.)

The cabanas are so popular that they're often fully booked in advance by Concierge and Platinum Castaway Club members before the general public gets a crack at them. However, cancellations do happen. If you're interested, ask at the Port Adventures desk as soon as you board the ship, and periodically check back a few times before the ship docks at Castaway Cay.

SCOTT SAYS *by Scott Sanders*

CASTAWAY CAY DONE RIGHT

DISNEY'S PRIVATE ISLAND is an extension of the cruise-ship experience, because the ship's crew works in various roles on Castaway Cay. You may, for instance, see your serving team barbecuing at one of the lunch locations.

On the island, there are plenty of loungers and beach chairs for everyone, even if you sleep in and get a late start on the island. Hammocks are more scarce, so arrive early (or look for one around 3 p.m.) if that's part of your island dream.

My favorite time to explore the snorkeling lagoon is in the morning before it gets crowded. As for seeing the rest of the island, the bike rental is a relatively inexpensive way to cover the trails and quickly get to the observation tower.

Not interested in going ashore? No problem. There are plenty of activities on board, and the lines for the waterslides are much shorter—sometimes nonexistent!

As far as renting a cabana goes, I'm not gonna lie—the experience is amazing, but it comes at a price if one is even available to book. Unless you plan to spend most of your day on the island in and around the cabana, I wouldn't recommend renting one.

PART ELEVEN

PORTS

THE FOLLOWING SECTION outlines the ports visited by Disney Cruise Line. Grouped geographically, each profile summarizes the port's history, weather, port information, tourist highlights, food, and shopping opportunities.

Just for the record, some ports as classified by DCL aren't technically part of the geographic area in which they're listed; rather, they're part of an itinerary with a significant part or a majority of its route within that area. For example, Dover, England, United Kingdom, is listed in the "Mediterranean" section because it's on an itinerary that begins there; heads south along the Atlantic coast, visiting Lisbon, Portugal; and then travels north and east along the Mediterranean coast to Barcelona, Spain. Also, note that a few ports are listed in multiple areas—Dover, for instance, appears in the "Northern Europe, British Isles, and Norway" section in addition to the "Mediterranean" section.

Our Itineraries Index (page 420) lists the specific itineraries that visit the ports described here and also includes maps of each area.

ALASKA

CRUISES SAIL FROM Vancouver

SHIP *Wonder*

CRUISE LENGTHS Mostly 7 nights, occasionally 5 or 9

DATES Summer

SPECIAL TOUCHES A naturalist on board who talks about the glaciers and wildlife you'll see, mulled wine on the bar menu, blankets to keep warm on the upper decks, hot soup at the counter-service food venues. A "Taste of Alaska" menu with Alaskan seafood is a big hit.

WHAT TO PACK Warm clothing, including gloves, hats, and scarves; waterproof shoes (that you can hike in); binoculars; sunscreen

PROS	CONS
■ **Vancouver,** one of the most beautiful cities in North America, is a worthy destination in its own right, one that we recommend visiting for a few days before or after your cruise.	■ Waters may still be iced over early in the season, so you may not be able to enter Tracy Arm.
■ Breathtaking scenery.	■ The weather can range from chilly to downright cold—and it *will* rain at some point during your cruise.
■ Ports are fairly low-key, though you can still buy that tanzanite ring you've been eyeing.	■ If shopping is a big part of your cruise experience, you'll be disappointed.
■ If you've ever wanted to see a glacier from a hot tub, here's your chance!	■ The length of the cruise plus travel time to and from Vancouver may be more than you can schedule (at least 9 days).
■ Very relaxing vibe on board.	■ Just one DCL ship, the *Wonder,* cruises Alaska, and then only during the summer.
■ West Coasters, this is an easy trip for you.	

SIGNATURE PORT ADVENTURE Dogsledding. It's pricey, but you'll *love* it.

COMMENTS We realize that Caribbean-cruise fatigue is the ultimate in first-world problems, so if you're rolling your eyes at us when we say that an Alaskan cruise is the cure for too many trips to Nassau, we're there with you. That said, for the opposite of the Caribbean experience without leaving the United States, we heartily recommend seeing the 49th state by ship. *Heads-up:* Marijuana is legal only for medical use in British Columbia, but recreational pot smoking is rarely prosecuted. You may find your kids asking "What's that smell?" as you walk the streets.

Hubbard Glacier, Alaska

HISTORY Hubbard Glacier—the largest tidewater glacier in North America and one of eight Alaskan glaciers—is located on Disenchantment Bay, at the head of Yakutat Bay. Defying the global trend of glacial shrinkage, it is actually *increasing* in total mass and is advancing at a rate of about 85 feet per year. In 2002, the glacier advanced across the entrance to the 35-mile-long Russell Fjord, temporarily turning it into a lake. The nearest land settlement is a sport and commercial fishery located in the town of Yakutat, Alaska.

WEATHER DCL visits Hubbard Glacier in July. Average daytime highs at this time are in the mid-50s, with nighttime lows averaging in the high 40s. (*Note:* All temperatures listed in this chapter are in degrees Fahrenheit.) Typical rainfall is about 8 inches per month.

THE PORT Ships don't dock at Hubbard Glacier—there is no port. Rather, the experience is the view from aboard your ship.

TOURIST HIGHLIGHTS Hubbard Glacier is a behemoth: nearly 76 miles long, 6 miles wide, and 300 feet tall. The glacier frequently calves icebergs that are often 3–4 stories tall, sometimes as many as 10 stories. Ships must keep a safe distance—the calved icebergs sometimes splash into and shoot out of the water dramatically.

Icy Strait Point, Alaska

LANGUAGES English and Tlingit

HISTORY Icy Strait Point is located on Chichagof Island, near the town of Hoonah, Alaska. Native tribes have inhabited the area for thousands of years, primarily as fishers and hunters. In 1912, the Hoonah Packing Company built a salmon cannery nearby, becoming the major employer. The area foundered when the cannery closed in the 1950s; later, as part of the Alaska Native Claims Settlement Act of 1971, the Huna Totem Corporation was founded to stimulate job creation in the area. Huna Totem, owned by some 1,400 Alaskans with ties to native peoples (primarily the Tlingit), operates Icy Strait Point, the only privately owned tourist-cruise destination in Alaska. Cruise-ship visitors provide about half the income to the local economy.

WEATHER In 2019, DCL visits Icy Strait Point in July, August, and September. Average daytime highs during summer and early fall are in the low 60s, with average nighttime lows in the high 40s. Average precipitation for the month is about 3 inches in July, about 7 inches in August, and about 9 inches in September.

THE PORT Icy Strait Point accommodates just one cruise ship at a time, so there is little chance of overcrowding on excursions or at area sights. Passengers are tendered into port at the Icy Strait Point dock, where you'll find basic services. The town of **Hoonah,** a mile away, is accessible on foot.

TOURIST HIGHLIGHTS Wilderness adventures are the focus in Icy Strait. It's located near **Point Adolphus,** one of the world's best locations for whale-watching—whales favor this area as their summer habitat so frequently, in fact, that sightings here are guaranteed by excursion operators. Icy Strait also boasts the highest density of brown grizzly bears anywhere in Alaska. Thrill seekers will enjoy the **ZipRider,** the longest zip line experience in the United States. July is prime season for fishing, with silver, pink, and keta salmon abounding. Kayaking and other water sports are also available, as well as a small museum and a beach area.

WHAT TO EAT The waterfront restaurants buy their seafood from local fishermen. A specialty is Dungeness crab, often butchered and cooked while you watch.

WHAT TO BUY The historic cannery building houses 12 locally owned shops that sell such items as wood carvings, jewelry, and leatherwork. Expect to find true local crafts and few imported items. Halibut fishers may pay to have their catch processed and shipped home to them, making this a particularly personal souvenir. Other foodie take-homes include jams and candies made from local berries.

Juneau, Alaska

LANGUAGES English and Tlingit

HISTORY Juneau began as a mining camp. Gold mining was the major industry from the 1880s until the 1940s, when the last official gold mine was closed. Juneau has been the capital of Alaska since 1906, first as a district and then remaining as the government seat when Alaska became a state in 1959. Growth accelerated in the 1970s with the construction of the Trans-Alaska Pipeline. Central Juneau is close to sea level and is surrounded by natural elements, including mountains, glaciers, and the

Gastineau Channel. No roads lead into or out of town—travel to other areas is accomplished almost exclusively by boat or plane.

WEATHER Disney cruises dock in Juneau May–early September. Average daytime highs during this period range from the mid-50s to the low 60s; nighttime lows during these months are in the low to mid-40s. Precipitation is fairly steady throughout the year. Typical rainfall ranges 4–5 inches per month during the summer.

THE PORT Ships dock within walking distance of downtown Juneau. Within a mile, you'll find the **Federal Building,** the **Governor's House,** the **State Capitol,** the **Alaska State Museum,** the **Visitor Center,** and other attractions. Shuttles and taxis service key attractions beyond downtown.

TOURIST HIGHLIGHTS **Mendenhall Glacier** is a primary attraction. Check at the visitor center for a guide to **walking trails** maintained by the U.S. Forest Service. In addition to natural features, you may see **bears** fishing for salmon in glacial streams. The **Mount Roberts Tramway** ferries guests 1,800 feet up the peak for scenic views and hiking. Points of historic interest include **St. Nicholas Russian Orthodox Church,** the oldest operating church in Alaska. Also stop by the **Red Dog Saloon,** a remnant of the mining era with an Old West atmosphere. For a walking tour that covers many of these points of interest, see page 383.

WHAT TO EAT Fresh fish is a key part of menus throughout the area. Salmon and halibut are most common, but shellfish is also easy to find. Our favorite restaurant in Alaska is **Tracy's King Crab Shack,** just steps from the dock. A moderately covered outdoor venue with a view of the harbor, Tracy's serves Alaskan king crab significantly bigger than your head. We like the sampler platter of crab chowder, crab cakes, and a monster crab leg, washed down with an Alaskan Brewing Company ale. A little pricey, but delish. If you ask the cook nicely, he may let you hold a crab for a fun photo op.

WHAT TO BUY Carved Alaskan jade is abundant in souvenir shops. Also look for native arts and crafts that use natural elements such as stone, wood, and fur.

Ketchikan, Alaska

LANGUAGE English

HISTORY Ketchikan was first settled by native tribes lured by the seaside location. The area has one of the world's largest collections of standing totem poles, found both in town and scattered throughout the region, most created by the town's native founders. In the late 1800s and early 1900s, fishing and fish processing, along with lumber and lumber processing, began to attract settlers from other parts of the world. The town embodied a freewheeling, frontier spirit, with saloons and brothels aplenty. Today, Ketchikan is known in Alaska as the Salmon Capital of the World and caters to a booming tourist trade.

WEATHER Disney cruises dock in Ketchikan May–early September, when the average daytime highs range from the mid-50s to the mid-60s and nighttime lows from the low 40s to the low 50s. While precipitation is lowest during the summer months, Ketchikan lies within a maritime-rainforest area, with abundant rainfall and cloud cover. Expect it to be wet: typical rainfall is 6–9 inches per month during May, June, July, and August.

THE PORT Ships dock adjacent to the center of town. The town itself is just three blocks wide, and most points of interest are easily accessible from the port.

TOURIST HIGHLIGHTS An in-town highlight is a seasonal live show where professional lumberjacks demonstrate ax throws, log rolling, and pole climbing. Those wishing to stay near port can enjoy several small museums, including the **Totem Heritage Center,** the **Tongass Historical Museum,** and the **Southeast Alaska Discovery Center.** (For a walking tour that covers these and other points of interest, see page 385.) Take a ride on the **Cape Fox Lodge** funicular, which affords spectacular views of the port and surrounding areas. Outdoor activities include kayaking, hiking, and wildlife observation.

WHAT TO EAT The local fresh fish is a must-try. Fishermen bring in frequent hauls of salmon, shrimp, crab, octopus, and more.

WHAT TO BUY Alaskan crafts such as miniature carved totems, silver and bronze sculptures, wool clothing, and regional foods are typical Ketchikan souvenirs. Our favorite souvenir purchased on any vacation is the beaver pelt we got at **Tall Tale Taxidermy,** run by the Szurley family, longtime Ketchikan residents. A stop at Tall Tale convinced Erin, a squeamish New Yorker, that taxidermy is a true art form.

Skagway, Alaska

LANGUAGE English

HISTORY Skagway was originally settled by the native Chilkoot and Chilkat peoples. Beginning in the late 1800s, Skagway became a center for gold exploration. In 1896 gold was found in the region, leading to an influx of prospectors, miners, and associated service providers. Competition among prospectors was fierce, leading to a lawless Wild West atmosphere. The gold rush was over by 1900, but the spectacular wilderness inspired many to stay and maintain the new town.

WEATHER Disney cruises dock in Skagway May–early September. Average daytime highs during these months range from the mid-50s to the mid-60s, with nighttime lows averaging from the low 40s to the low 50s. Typical rainfall is 1–2 inches during the summer.

THE PORT There is no dedicated passenger terminal—cruise ships dock alongside industrial sea vessels. On the upside, the dock is an easy walk from town; there are also inexpensive buses. The entire town is accessible from one main street, **Broadway.** For a walking tour that covers the area, see page 387.

TOURIST HIGHLIGHTS At the **Klondike Gold Rush National Historical Park,** the visitor center has educational materials about the area's mining heyday. For more-hands-on learning, try panning for gold yourself at the **Liarsville Gold Rush Trail Camp** (see page 382 for details). **White Pass and Yukon Route Railroad,** a narrow-gauge train line, offers scenic views of mountains, waterfalls, and gorges; in **Haines,** a ferry ride away, you can enjoy watching the whales and American bald eagles. Other outdoor adventures include horseback riding, hiking, rock climbing, and dogsledding.

WHAT TO EAT Fresh fish appears on menus throughout the area. Also try the local Alaskan king crab and elk meat. *Note:* Due to the cost of shipping nonlocal food to this remote location, you may find prices here higher than you'd expect in other parts of the US.

WHAT TO BUY Skagway is a small town, catering mostly to the tourist trade, with abundant small souvenirs on offer. Typical finds include mining and railroad artifacts, hand-knit woolen garments, ceramics, carved wood, and jewelry made by local artisans. Most shops in Skagway don't open until 9 a.m. at the earliest, and there are few notable breakfast spots in town. Unless you have an early excursion, feel free to sleep a little late without worrying that you're missing something.

Tracy Arm, Alaska

HISTORY Tracy Arm is a fjord—a long, narrow inlet with steep cliffs on both sides, created by glacial movement. Part of Tongass National Forest, Tracy Arm is more than 30 miles long, and ice covers about one-fifth of it. In the summer, the fjord may have significant icebergs floating in its waters.

WEATHER The weather is similar to Juneau's: average daytime highs May–September range from the mid-50s to the low 60s, nighttime lows during these months are in the low to mid-40s, and typical rainfall is 4–5 inches per month.

THE PORT Ships don't dock at Tracy Arm—there is no port or town. The experience is the view from aboard your ship.

TOURIST HIGHLIGHTS Tracy Arm is all about the scenery of the **Sawyer Glaciers.** Take in the granite cliffs, icebergs, and forested mountains. You may spot wildlife such as bears, whales, bald eagles, mountain goats, and more. About once per hour, the glaciers calve, sending massive ice sheets into the waters below. The impact of the glaciers is vastly different on different decks. Soaring vistas are best viewed from Decks 9 and 10; to spot animals, try the outdoor areas of Deck 4. If your stateroom is on a lower deck, look out your porthole from time to time. Periodically vary your location on the ship for a fuller experience.

Vancouver, British Columbia, Canada

LANGUAGE English

HISTORY Europeans first visited Vancouver in the late 1700s. The gold rush in the late 1800s brought the city's first long-term settlers. Early industry focused on logging, mining, and transportation, due to the natural port. Immigrants came from England, Scotland, Ireland, and Germany, followed by an influx from China and other areas of Asia. Vancouver is now a major industrial center and cosmopolitan city, bustling with high-rises, shopping, restaurants, and entertainment.

WEATHER Cruises depart from Vancouver during the summer and early fall. The average daytime highs May–September range from the low 60s to the low 70s. Average nighttime lows during those months range from the mid-40s to the mid-50s. This moderate climate makes Vancouver one of the warmest cities in Canada. Vancouver's rainfall is lowest in the summer, averaging fewer than 3 inches per month May–September.

THE PORT Disney cruises embark at the **Canada Place Cruise Terminal,** adjacent to downtown Vancouver. Within walking distance you'll find the **Pan Pacific Hotel,** along with many restaurants and bars.

TOURIST HIGHLIGHTS The **Vancouver Lookout,** near Harbour Centre, affords a panoramic overview of the city. For additional visual stimulation, check

out the **Vancouver Art Gallery,** which displays more than 10,000 pieces of art. Other local attractions include **Science World,** with interactive exhibits and an Omnimax theater, and the **Vancouver Aquarium,** home to 70,000 sea creatures and where whale, dolphin, and sea otter shows happen daily. The **Dr. Sun Yat-Sen Classical Chinese Garden** is the first authentic Chinese garden built outside of China. A 15-minute SkyTrain ride from Vancouver will take you to **Metropolis at Metrotown,** British Columbia's largest shopping center.

WHAT TO EAT You can find nearly every world cuisine represented in the restaurants of Vancouver. Local seafood is a must. For authentic Asian dishes, visit the **Chinatown** district. **Granville Island** is a public market with fresh local seafood and produce; walk among the dozens of stalls to taste the best from local vendors.

WHAT TO BUY No trip to Canada would be complete without the purchase of something maple—syrup, candy, even mustard. Find silk robes in Chinatown, local crafts at Granville Island, and gear representing the Vancouver Canucks hockey team everywhere.

Victoria, British Columbia, Canada

LANGUAGE English

HISTORY British settlement in Victoria began in the mid-1840s as a Hudson Bay trading post. Not long after this, the Fraser Canyon Gold Rush brought an influx of prospectors. The port then became a naval base and the commercial center of British Columbia. Victoria was designated the capital of British Columbia after the territory became a Canadian province in 1871. Today, the city is home to thriving fishing and shipbuilding industries and is a nascent technological hub. The scenic harbor is also a major tourist destination.

WEATHER DCL visits Victoria in early October in 2019. Daytime highs for October average in the mid-50s, with nighttime lows in the high 40s. Expect monthly rainfall of about 3 inches in October.

THE PORT The terminal is about 1 mile from downtown but has no facilities. Take a scenic walk through **Beacon Hill Park,** or take a shuttle or taxi.

TOURIST HIGHLIGHTS For lovers of flora, the sunken garden at **Butchart Gardens** is just one of the popular beauty spots in Victoria, known as the City of Gardens. Many remnants of Victoria's British heritage—including double-decker buses and horse-drawn carriages—remain, and the **Fairmont Empress Hotel** serves a proper English tea. **Craigdarroch Castle,** a 19th-century edifice, affords panoramic city vistas and displays an impressive collection of antique furnishings. For a dose of history, visit the **Royal British Columbia Museum,** which owns more than 7 million artifacts, including an intact woolly mammoth. Outdoors enthusiasts will enjoy walking trails along the Pacific Ocean, as well as scuba diving, kayaking, and marine-life observation. Victoria is also home to a vibrant **Chinatown.**

WHAT TO EAT Victoria is a modern city, with restaurants serving most major cuisines. Pacific cod, salmon, and halibut are on menus throughout Victoria. For Asian favorites such as noodles and broth, venture into Chinatown.

WHAT TO BUY Look for native crafts such as jewelry and carvings. You can find tea and tea-service items in the Anglophile shops. **Fort Street** is known as Antique Row. Visit Chinatown for silks, fans, and Asian ornaments.

ATLANTIC CANADA

CRUISES SAIL FROM New York City

SHIP *Magic*

CRUISE LENGTHS 4–7 nights

DATES Early fall

WHAT TO PACK Rain jacket, umbrella

SIGNATURE PORT ADVENTURE Boat trip plus a lobster dinner

COMMENTS Cruises along Canada's Atlantic coast are a great option for anyone who can easily get to New York City—which is most of us. (DCL confusingly designates this region as "Canadian Coastline"—as if Canada had just one coast.) Because these stops aren't primarily tourist destinations, you get a special experience that isn't focused first and foremost on selling you stuff. Your ship will often be the only one in port, which makes for a relaxing day ashore. This cruise is a perfect fall-break vacation if you just want to get away for less than a week and be pampered while someone else does the cooking and makes your bed.

PROS

- Nice change from beach-based cruises.
- Canada residents: no need for currency exchange. US residents: remember to pick up some "loonies" (Canadian dollar coins) before you embark.
- Lots of competition for transportation to New York City, whether by air, train, or car. Good deals can be found.

CONS

- Not much shopping in the smaller ports.
- Just a couple of ports.
- Your kids may not be keen on a cruise where a highlight is looking at lighthouses.
- Itinerary is offered only on the *Magic*, and then not every year.

Bar Harbor, Maine

LANGUAGE English

HISTORY Bar Harbor is located on Mount Desert Island, named in 1604 by French explorer Samuel du Champlain when he looked at the mountains that rise up from the sea. He called this place Île des Monts Deserts, or "Island of Barren Mountains"—a misleading appellation considering that the island is actually covered in forest. A few years later, French Jesuits set up a mission on the island, which was contested by the British. The French and British regularly swapped control of the area until France's defeat in the Seven Years' War, which ended in 1763. In the 1840s, American landscape artists Thomas Cole and Frederic Church visited the region. Their paintings kindled the imaginations of the American public and spurred interest in the natural beauty of the island. The mid-1800s saw an influx of tourists, including Gilded Age millionaires, and the construction of numerous hotels and mansions to accommodate them. To prevent the area from becoming an overbuilt playground, locals petitioned the federal government for protection, and in 1916 much of the island was declared a national park. Bar Harbor, however, reinvented itself during the last half of the 20th century as a mecca for travelers in search of pristine wilderness.

WEATHER Disney Cruise Line visits Bar Harbor in early October. During this time, daytime highs average in the mid-60s, with nighttime lows averaging in the high 40s. Average rainfall is 5 inches per month.

THE PORT Bar Harbor is a tender port. Ships anchor in the harbor and passengers are transported to land on smaller boats, or tenders, which dock at **Town Pier,** adjacent to downtown Bar Harbor. The shopping district, which has cafés, banks, and other services, is within a 10-minute walk from the dock. A small number of taxis may be available at the pier, but there are no rental-car agencies in town—the closest place to rent a car is at the Bar Harbor airport, about 30 minutes away from town via taxi or shuttle. A free shuttle bus called **Island Explorer** links Bar Harbor with Acadia National Park and other communities on the island; see exploreacadia.com for schedules.

TOURIST HIGHLIGHTS The area's primary draw is the great outdoors. Explore the coastline by kayak, or embark on a whale-watching tour. **Acadia National Park** is Bar Harbor's island neighbor. Use the hiking and biking trails to see the park's attractions, including **Cadillac Mountain,** the highest peak on the East Coast; **Sand Beach,** covered with pulverized shells; and **Thunder Hole,** where the surf races into a naturally carved inlet and explodes high into the air. On an autumn port stop, your visit may occur during prime leaf-peeping season—don't forget your camera. If you'd rather stay close to town, nearby **Agamont Park** has a shore path that follows the sea wall for more than a mile and from which you can see mansions of a bygone era, as well as the rocky coast. Bar Harbor is also home to a few small museums. The **Abbe Museum** is dedicated to the history of the native Wabanaki people. The **George B. Dorr Museum of Natural History** includes exhibits on Maine's natural ecosystems. The **Mount Desert Oceanarium** is a working museum that offers tours of a lobster farm.

WHAT TO EAT When in Maine, get "lobstah" steamed with butter, broiled with breadcrumbs, baked into a pie, spun into a creamy bisque, or mixed with mayo and piled on a toasted hot dog bun. Order a side of corn on the cob and finish off your with a hefty slab of blueberry pie, and you've consumed the quintessential Maine seashore meal. Not in the mood for seafood? Several spots offer wood-fired pizzas. Wash it all down with beer from the local **Atlantic Brewing Company.**

WHAT TO BUY The classic Maine souvenir shop is **Cool as a Moose,** which sells everything from boxer shorts to sweatshirts emblazoned with cartoon bears and moose. Kids will find plush bears, moose, and even lobsters to cuddle. More-substantial items include kitchenware, such as coasters and cutting boards made from the wood of nearby forests. If you venture into the Bangor area, look for wearables from the **University of Maine** emblazoned with its black bear mascot. If you're in the mood for edible souvenirs, try one of the many jams, sauces, syrups, or baked goods produced by Maine's **Stonewall Kitchen.**

New York, New York

LANGUAGE English

HISTORY With a population of 8.4 million in the city proper and 23 million in the greater metro area, New York is the largest city in the United States

and the eighth-largest urban agglomeration in the world. Many would also argue that it's the world's most important and exciting city.

The first European exploration of the New York area began in the mid-1500s. Henry Hudson rediscovered the area in 1609, later claiming it for the Dutch East India Company. Permanent European presence in the area took root in the mid-1600s. New York was a center of conflict during the Revolutionary War, falling to British invaders in the late 1700s. By the early 1800s, the city had become one of the largest ports in North America, and its famed grid system of streets and avenues was developed. Immigrants from all over Europe arrived throughout the 1800s, creating unique ethnic enclaves. Along with immigration came the additional influx of commercial enterprise and cultural dominance in areas such as art, publishing, and fashion. New York's pivotal moment in recent history, of course, was the destruction of the World Trade Center in lower Manhattan on September 11, 2001.

WEATHER DCL cruises stop in New York in the fall. The weather at this time of year can be lovely, with daytime highs in September averaging in the low to mid-70s and fading to the mid-50s during November; expect nighttime lows to be about 10–15 degrees cooler. Precipitation is consistent most of the year, with an average of 4–5 inches of rain per month in the fall. The city's first snow generally falls in December, although it occasionally arrives as early as October or November.

THE PORT Cruise ships dock in midtown Manhattan, on the West Side. Within a 10-minute walk you'll find restaurants, shops, banks—you name it. The port itself is served by taxis and buses, and the subway is just a few blocks away, giving you access to the entire metropolitan area.

TOURIST HIGHLIGHTS We only have space to scratch the surface. Bustling **Times Square** and the **Theatre District** are just a few blocks from the port. Museum lovers have their pick of the **Museum of Natural History,** the **Museum of Modern Art,** the **Metropolitan Museum of Art,** the **Guggenheim,** and scores more. **Central Park** and its zoo are a doable walk or short cab ride away. And of course, the **Statue of Liberty,** the **Empire State Building,** and the **World Trade Center Memorial** are must-dos for many visitors. For a bird's-eye view of Manhattan, visit **Top of the Rock** at 30 Rockefeller Plaza.

If you're in town for a few days before or after your sailing, then you'll want to explore coauthor Erin's other passion, Broadway theater. **Playbill.com** lists and describes all shows currently running. Don't be intimidated by the pricing: for all but a handful of shows (notably *Hamilton, Dear Evan Hansen,* and *The Lion King*), you'll almost always find discount tickets available. Some good resources are the **TodayTix** app, **TKTS** booths, **Theatermania.com, Broadway Roulette.com,** and ticket lotteries at the individual shows. Immediately following the show, you can head to the stage door for a chance to meet some of the performers and have them sign your program.

unofficial **TIP**
In Times Square, beware of pushy hucksters dressed as animated characters ranging from Mickey and Minnie to Dora the Explorer and the Power Rangers. Unless you're prepared to offer them a substantial tip for taking a selfie with you, give them a hard pass.

If you have time to explore farther afield, take along a good city guidebook. We recommend Ellen Levitt's ***Walking Manhattan*** and Adrienne Onofri's ***Walking Brooklyn*** and ***Walking Queens,*** both published by Wilderness Press, the Unofficial Guides' sibling imprint.

WHAT TO EAT If you can eat it, someone in New York can cook it. You truly can find nearly every cuisine in the world represented in the kitchens of New York restaurants: dim sum in Chinatown, Greek specialties in Queens, soul food in Harlem, sushi on nearly every corner, and outposts of Paris's famed **Ladurée** macaron shop on the Upper East Side and in SoHo. For an "only in New York" experience, eat a "dirty-water dog" and a hot pretzel from a cart in Central Park, grab some real coal-oven thin-crust pizza from **Patsy's,** or choose a deli delight at **Zabar's** on the Upper West Side—for noshes such as bagels, lox, knishes, blintzes, pastrami on rye, and sour pickles, this is *the* place. And *shhhh,* don't tell anyone else, but our favorite cookies in the universe come from **Levain Bakery,** on 74th Street near Columbus Avenue. They're big enough to share . . . but why would you want to?

If you want to sample a bit of everything, make a stop at **Urbanspace** (urbanspacenyc.com), a food court with stations from dozens of the city's finest purveyors of deliciousness. Enjoy Beijing-style street crêpes from **Mr. Bing,** a bowl of steaming fresh ramen from **Kuro-Obi,** Japanese-inspired Mexican fare from **Takumi Taco,** or a *dulce de leche* doughnut from **Dough,** and wash it all down with a seasonal ale from **Brooklyn Brewery.** Located at East 45th Street and Vanderbilt Avenue, Urbanspace is steps away from **Grand Central Station,** a classic New York destination in its own right, made even more iconic by the summer 2018 addition of **Art Bird & Whiskey Bar,** which serves the same perfect fried chicken and biscuits as Art Smith's Homecomin' in Walt Disney World.

WHAT TO BUY As if we even needed to mention it, New York is a shopper's paradise, with giant stores, like the 11-floor **Macy's** in Herald Square, and tiny ones, like **CW Pencil Enterprise** (15 Orchard St.), a shop on the Lower East Side that sells only pencils—from vintage graphite to simple children's tools for school. (And trust us when we say the staff is amazing. One of the self-described "pencil ladies" earnestly spent a full 20 minutes helping Erin's daughter choose the best possible No. 2 pencil for taking the LSAT.) Designer goods are everywhere, as are lower-priced sample sales of designer goods, low-priced knockoffs of designer goods, and low-priced goods that are better than their designer cousins. Shoppers who really like to haggle should visit the **Diamond District,** near Times Square. Quintessentially New York gifts include Broadway memorabilia, **Yankees** or **Mets** gear, and wearables emblazoned the names of local colleges such as Columbia, NYU, and Fordham. Many area museums have interesting gift shops—our favorite is the **Museum of Modern Art (MoMA),** which sells books and gifts in the museum itself but also has an entire design store across the street.

Saint John, New Brunswick, Canada

Note: *Saint John should not be confused with **St. John's, Newfoundland and Labrador,** which has been a stop on DCL Canadian cruises in previous years.*

LANGUAGE English

HISTORY The original inhabitants of New Brunswick were the Passamaquoddy and Malecite peoples. Among the first Europeans to visit in the area was Frenchman Samuel de Champlain, in 1604. French fortifications

were in place by the 1630s. Various French, British, and New England factions scuffled about during the 17th and 18th centuries. In 1785, by royal charter, the City of Saint John became the first incorporated city in Canada.

In the mid-1800s, Saint John served as a quarantine station for European immigrants, particularly Irish, to receive medical screening before being admitted to North America. Shipbuilding became a major industry in the later 1800s and remained so into the early 21st century.

WEATHER DCL visits Saint John in early October. Daytime highs during these months average in the high 50s to low 60s, with nighttime lows in the low to high 40s and average rainfall of about 4 inches per month.

THE PORT The ship docks near the city center. The port area has basic services. Many tourist attractions lie within a 15-minute walk of the terminal; taxis are readily available. For a romantic twist, let a horse-drawn trolley take you around town.

TOURIST HIGHLIGHTS **Saint John City Market** is a large structure housing independent vendors who sell everything from baked goods, cheese, and chocolate to jewelry, sculptures, and scenic photography—bring cash, because many vendors don't take plastic. **The New Brunswick Museum** has exhibits devoted to logging, shipbuilding, and whaling; special kids' experiences may be available depending on when you visit. If you can time it right, the **Reversing Falls** are a unique natural phenomenon in which high tides in the Bay of Fundy cause the Saint John River to reverse its flow. You can watch the river run backward from one of several lookouts. Another outdoor possibility is **Irving Nature Park,** which has walking trails and lovely views. **Moosehead Brewery,** Canada's oldest independent beer producer, offers tours and samples. (*Note:* You must be of legal drinking age back home to tour.) **Stonehammer Geopark,** in southern New Brunswick, is the only North American member of the UNESCO-supported Global Geoparks Network. To experience it, take a guided tour at **Rockwood Park.**

WHAT TO EAT The seafood is wonderful here: baked oysters, fish chowder, bacon-wrapped scallops, lobster rolls. A local variation on Quebeçois poutine (fries, cheese curds, and gravy) is *poutines râpées*—dumplings made with raw grated potato, cooked potato, and salt pork, formed into balls, simmered, and served with brown sugar or molasses. Other traditional dishes of the region include *fricot à la poule,* chicken cooked with summer savory, potato, and dumplings; *fricot aux coques,* or clam stew; and *tourtière,* a savory pie of ground pork seasoned with cinnamon and cloves. (Nobody makes *tourtière* as good as Erin's grandma's Christmas-morning version, but you can find good facsimiles in Saint John.) Many desserts are flavored with locally harvested apples or maple. If you want a truly Canadian edible experience, stop by the local **Tim Hortons** for coffee and doughnuts.

WHAT TO BUY **Moosehead** beer rules—bring home a T-shirt, cap, or stein emblazoned with the brewery's logo. Other popular items include books about the area, depictions of the Canadian flag, and maple products such as candies and syrups.

CARIBBEAN, BAHAMAS, *and* BERMUDA

Note: *Please see our Mexico travel advisory on page 323 and our Nassau travel advisory on page 376.*

CRUISES SAIL FROM Port Canaveral, Miami, Galveston, New York, New Orleans, San Juan

SHIPS *Dream* and *Fantasy* (year-round), *Magic* and *Wonder* (fall, winter, and spring)

CRUISE LENGTHS 3-7 nights, occasionally 8, 10, and 11

DATES Year-round

WHAT TO PACK Sunscreen, shorts, swimsuits, shoes that you don't mind getting sandy

SIGNATURE PORT ADVENTURE Castaway Cay

CLASSIC DISNEY ADD-ON Walt Disney World, Disney's Vero Beach Resort

COMMENTS Chances are if you're cruising Disney, you're on a Caribbean or Bahamian cruise. Given that two of DCL's ships sail the Caribbean and Bahamas exclusively and the other two spend half the year there, the numbers are in your favor if you're looking for sun and fun. You may ask yourself, why is Bahamas singled out from the rest of the Caribbean? Because the *Dream* cruises only to Nassau and Castaway Cay, which are both Bahamian ports.

HEALTH CONSIDERATIONS In 2016, the U.S. Centers for Disease Control and Prevention issued health warnings regarding **Zika,** a mosquito-borne virus, in Mexico, South America, Central America, and the Caribbean. Because the virus causes severe birth defects in developing fetuses, pregnant women were urged to avoid nonessential travel to these locales. As of press time, the CDC still lists several DCL ports where Zika is of "enhanced concern," which means that while the risk of infection isn't high enough to warrant avoiding travel to these places altogether, cruisers should nonetheless take precautions against getting bitten by mosquitoes. (Because the virus can also be sexually transmitted, these precautions apply to men and women alike.) Check wwwnc.cdc.gov/travel/page/zika-information for the latest information (*wwnc.* is correct).

Another mosquito-borne virus, **chikungunya,** was confirmed in the Bahamas in 2018. The symptoms—high fever, severe joint or muscle pain, headache, fatigue, and nausea—usually subside after a week, but young children and seniors are at risk of more-serious illness. As with Zika, prevention is key. See cdc.gov/chikungunya for more information.

Basseterre, St. Kitts and Nevis

LANGUAGE English

PROS	CONS
■ Nearly all major cruise lines operate in the Caribbean, which means Disney has to keep its pricing somewhat in line with other companies'.	■ The port experience (except at Castaway Cay) is *very* commercial.
■ Ports are easy to get to.	■ Your ship will most likely be one of many others in port.
■ The US dollar is accepted in all ports, and English is spoken nearly everywhere.	■ If you're not at least a little creative, DCL's Caribbean port stops can blend into one big duty-free-jewelry/hair-braiding/frozen-cocktail blur.
■ Castaway Cay is on nearly every Caribbean itinerary.	■ The summer heat can be oppressive.
■ Cruises can be combined with WDW vacations.	
■ You have your choice of ships and cruise lengths.	

HISTORY The earliest inhabitants of St. Kitts were the Saladoid people, followed by the Igneris, Arawaks, and Caribs. The first European claim, in 1493, was by a Spanish expedition led by Christopher Columbus. About 50 years later, a French settlement ruled the area. This was replaced in 1623 by an English colony, which was almost immediately usurped by the French again. During the 17th and 18th centuries, island rule repeatedly flipped between the English and French. In 1783, the British finally wrested control. In 1883, St. Kitts joined with Nevis and Anguilla under one independent government (Anguilla left this arrangement in 1971).

WEATHER In 2019, DCL visits Basseterre throughout the year. Temperatures are consistent year-round, with daytime highs averaging in the 80s and nighttime lows averaging in the 70s. Rainfall varies from an average low of 2–3 inches per month during the winter to a high of about 5 inches during the fall.

THE PORT Built in 2005, the St. Kitts cruise terminal houses several restaurants and shops. The town of Basseterre is a 15-minute walk from the pier. Taxis are readily available.

TOURIST HIGHLIGHTS **Brimstone Hill Fortress** is a 17th-century military fortification from which you can see six neighboring islands in clear weather. **Romney Manor** is a colonial estate from the same era; adjacent **Wingfield Estate,** a onetime sugarcane plantation and rum distillery that's now home to a popular zip line attraction, is one of four locations on St. Kitts where Carib petroglyphs have been discovered and preserved. The town center of Basseterre, the **Circus,** is home to art galleries, bookstores, and craft shops. Sun worshipers will find several local beaches on which to loll.

WHAT TO EAT Fresh fish, often served with rice and beans, is a staple in this island nation. Jerk and Creole seasonings are prevalent on most menus. The national dish is stewed saltfish with plantains and coconut dumplings. Other typical foods include roast pig or goat, goat stew, *rikkita* (beef marinated with curry and hot pepper), and mango-glazed chicken. Popular side dishes are sweet potatoes, breadfruit, and cassava. Sweets include jam cake, pineapple cake, and tropical fruit. Rum is the adult beverage of choice.

WHAT TO BUY St. Kitts is home to the **Caribelle Batik Factory,** offering colorfully dyed fabric and clothing. Also look for woven hats and bags, pottery, paintings, and carved statuary. Foodies will want to take home packaged sugar cakes and bottles of local rum.

Bridgetown, Barbados

LANGUAGE English

HISTORY The first Europeans in Barbados were Spanish explorers in the late 1400s, but neither they nor a Portuguese expedition in the early 1500s established permanent outposts. An English ship, the *Olive Blossom,* arrived in 1624, claiming the island for James I, and Barbados remained a British dependency until 1966. Even post-independence, British influence is still pronounced here: cars drive on the left side of the road, and most churches are Anglican.

WEATHER In 2019, DCL visits Barbados in January and August. Temperatures remain constant throughout the year, with daytime highs in the mid-80s and nighttime lows in the mid- to high 70s. Expect January rainfall of less than an inch per month, and July rainfall of about 2–4 inches per month.

THE PORT Basic services, including a duty-free shop and a tourist-information desk, are located at the terminal. The village of Bridgetown is about 1 mile away from the pier. Grab a taxi if you don't feel like walking.

TOURIST HIGHLIGHTS Nature enthusiasts should visit **Harrison's Cave,** with natural stalactite formations and waterfalls. **Orchid World** inspires gardeners. History lovers will enjoy the **Barbados Museum,** home to artifacts related to Barbadian heritage. For a taste of agricultural history, visit the **Morgan Lewis windmill,** one of only two remaining functional sugar windmills in the world. The **Mount Gay Distilleries,** renowned for its rum, conducts factory tours and offers tastings and mixology classes (book online at mountgayrum.com/booknow). There are also many nearby beaches for sunning and snorkeling.

WHAT TO EAT The food of Barbados shows influences from England, Portugal, Spain, and West Africa. Fish, of course, is abundant here; look for it in flying fish (with a mustard-and-onion sauce) and fish cakes. Other popular dishes include pepper pot (a spicy stew made with beef, chicken, or seafood, enriched with coconut and hot pepper), peas and rice, candied sweet potatoes, and pudding and souse (pig intestines stuffed with sweet potatoes). Side dishes may include macaroni and cheese or locally grown asparagus and okra. Local sweets include tamarind balls, guava cheese, chocolate fudge, coconut bread, and peanut brittle. The adult beverage of choice is Mount Gay rum.

WHAT TO BUY Popular Barbadian take-home items include replica monkey jars, which were traditionally used to keep water cool. Other desired souvenirs include carved wood, leather goods, jewelry in the shape of fish or dolphins, and handmade soaps and lotions. Epicureans will want to bring home local rum, bottled local hot-pepper sauce, or packaged rum cake.

Castaway Cay, Bahamas

(Also see our coverage in Parts Ten and Twelve.)

LANGUAGE English

HISTORY In 1999 Disney Cruise Line entered into a 99-year lease agreement with the government of the Bahamas, giving the cruise line the rights to develop what was then called Gorda Cay. Renamed Castaway Cay by Disney, the island measures about 1.5 square miles and sits in the Atlantic Ocean, roughly 80 miles north-northeast of Nassau, at about the same latitude as Fort Lauderdale, Florida (100 miles west).

WEATHER Castaway Cay is a year-round destination, but no matter when you visit, it's gonna be either warm or hot. Average high temperatures gradually increase from around 76 in late December–January to a peak of 89 in August before they drop again. Low temperatures are also moderate, from 62 in late January to 76 throughout the summer. Rain patterns follow the Atlantic hurricane season, with peak rainfall occurring late August–early November. Precipitation is lightest December–May.

TOURIST HIGHLIGHTS Less than 10% of Castaway Cay has been developed for cruise guests, but Disney packs plenty of activities into that relatively small space, including two family beaches; one adults-only beach; separate lagoons for boating and snorkeling; a teens-only hangout; basketball, soccer, and volleyball areas; and bike trails. Two open-air trams connect the dock with these areas.

WHAT TO EAT Castaway Cay has three all-you-care-to-eat outdoor restaurants: **Cookie's BBQ, Cookie's Too,** and **Serenity Bay BBQ.** Each restaurant serves the same menu of grilled hot dogs, hamburgers, veggie burgers, chicken, fish, and ribs. Sides include corn on the cob, coleslaw, various salads, and similar picnic food, plus cookies and soft-serve ice cream for dessert. They're generally open 11 a.m.–2 p.m. Serenity Bay BBQ is at the adults-only Serenity Bay beach—no guests under age 18.

All of Castaway Cay's bars serve similar drinks. **Conched Out Bar,** near the gazebo, is the largest bar but has only outdoor seating.

Sand Bar, near the Castaway Cay family beach, is a small shack with a couple of serving windows, specializing in beer and frozen drinks. A limited amount of shaded bench seating is available. **Castaway Air Bar,** near the Serenity Bay adult beach, is the quietest of Castaway Cay's bars, and the view is pretty good, too. **Heads Up Bar,** near Castaway Ray's Stingray Adventures, sits at the far end of the pier. The one downside to Heads Up is the lack of shade—it can get very hot here very quickly, so lingering with a drink isn't always enjoyable. The views are great, though.

WHAT TO BUY Castaway Cay offers little in the way of shopping. Two Disney-operated souvenir stands offer merchandise similar to what you'll find in the onboard shops, such as T-shirts, flip-flops, and baseball caps, as well as fun-in-the-sun basics including plastic buckets, sunscreen, and goggles. If you're looking for something that specifically says CASTAWAY CAY on it, buy it on the island. In addition to the Disney shops, one building houses a few stalls run by Bahamian merchants. You'll find items here much like you'd find at the Straw Market at Nassau: bags, sun hats, and figurines. The one item that many guests find to be a true must is a postage stamp. The island's teeny post office will imprint your letters with a special Castaway Cay postmark. The post office accepts cash only (US currency is fine), not your Key to the World Card, so be sure to carry a few bills onto the island.

Castries, St. Lucia

LANGUAGES English and Creole French

HISTORY The first known settlers in St. Lucia were the Arawak Indians, circa A.D. 200. The first Europeans in the area were the French, who visited in about 1650 and who remained in place until a massive hurricane 130 years later. British settlers acquired the land in the late 1700s and used

the island for sugarcane plantations, worked by enslaved natives and imported Africans. Slavery was finally abolished in the mid-1800s. In 1958, St. Lucia joined the West Indies Federation as a self-governing nation; it is also part of the worldwide British Commonwealth of Nations.

WEATHER DCL visits St. Lucia in January in 2019. Average daytime highs during that period are in the low-80s and average nighttime lows in the mid-70s. Average precipitation is about 2 inches for the month.

THE PORT DCL ships usually dock at **Pointe Séraphine,** within walking distance of the center of town; occasionally, cruise ships must dock farther out, at **Port Carénage,** if the main port is too crowded. The big draw as you debark is the **Pointe Séraphine Shopping Centre,** a slice of duty-free heaven right on the pier, with an emphasis on high-end watches and jewelry. Plenty of taxis stand at the ready.

TOURIST HIGHLIGHTS The 18th-century city of **Soufrière** features both charming gingerbread architecture and naturally colorful sulfur pools. Near Soufrière is **Diamond Botanical Gardens and Waterfall,** which allows swimming in mineral baths in a lush setting. **Pigeon Island,** a former pirate lair, has a museum, beaches, a restaurant, and panoramic views. Snorkelers will love **Jalousie Beach** and **Anse Chastanet Beach.**

WHAT TO EAT West Indian, Creole, African, British, and French cultures influence the cuisine of St. Lucia. Popular dishes include pepper pot, callaloo (a souplike stew of leafy greens), and fried cod. Fresh seafood is on most menus. Vegetable accompaniments may include cassava, taro, or sweet potatoes. Local fruits include banana, coconut, guava, mango, passion fruit, and pineapple. Common beverages are fruit juices as well as local beer (**Piton**) and rum.

WHAT TO BUY The **Castries Market** features stalls with many local vendors. Look for screen-printed clothing, leather goods, carved wood, rag dolls, and handmade jewelry. Gourmands may want to purchase local spices, a jar of the regional banana ketchup, or, of course, rum.

Costa Maya, Mexico *(Please see our travel advisory on page 323.)*

LANGUAGE Spanish

HISTORY Mayans resided in this area beginning in about 200 B.C. The Mayans first had contact with Spanish explorers in the early 1500s, battling them for control of the area. This was followed by a period of invasion by English pirates. The British claimed the region until the end of the 19th century, when the Mexican Navy came to rule. The Mexicans developed a port system, improving trade and communications. Today the primary industry is tourism.

WEATHER The temperature in Costa Maya is fairly constant throughout the year. Average daytime highs year-round fall in the mid-70s to mid-80s, and average nighttime lows year-round are in the mid-60s to low 70s. In 2019, DCL visits Costa Maya during July, when rainfall averages about 8 inches for the month, and October, when rainfall averages about 7 inches.

THE PORT Costa Maya first became a tourist-cruise destination in 2001. The port was built from scratch and then significantly rebuilt in 2007 following Hurricane Dean. Though the facility is thoroughly modern, it was designed to look like an ancient Mayan city. Steps away from the terminal, you'll find restaurants, bars, shops, and saltwater pools catering to tourists.

TOURIST HIGHLIGHTS History buffs will want to visit the fourth-century Mayan ruins at **Chacchoben.** Sun lovers should venture to **Uvero Beach** to lounge on the white sands. More-adventurous types may want to try diving in the nearby coral reefs.

WHAT TO EAT Seafood prevails on most menus. Try it raw in seviche, prepared in dishes such as fish tacos or fish quesadillas, or simply grilled. Many dishes are served with rice or with corn tortillas and guacamole. *Remember:* peel all fresh fruits, and drink only beverages in sealed bottles. Sweets include ices and ice creams based on local fruits.

WHAT TO BUY Much of what is sold in Costa Maya near the port is tourist-grade. You'll find silver jewelry and metalwork (much of it silverplate), along with fabrics, rugs, fragrances, and liquor. Vendors may be open to bargaining.

Cozumel, Mexico

Note: *In 2018 DCL canceled several port adventures in Cozumel due to crime warnings issued by the U.S. Embassy in Mexico. Also see our general Mexico travel advisory on page 323.*

LANGUAGE Spanish

HISTORY Cozumel was a Mayan outpost from the first century A.D. Mayan legend describes Cozumel as the home of Ixchel, a love and fertility goddess. When temples were dedicated to her, she released her favorite birds, swallows, to show her gratitude. (*Cozumel* is derived from *Cuzamil,* Mayan for "Land of the Swallows.") The Spanish arrived in the early 1500s, unfortunately bringing with them diseases that decimated the Mayan population. For years after this, the region was besieged by pirates. In the late 1800s, Abraham Lincoln briefly explored the possibility of making Cozumel a relocation point for freed American slaves. The city's popularity as a tourist region exploded in the 1960s after explorer Jacques Cousteau mentioned it in a documentary as one of the most beautiful places in the world for scuba diving.

WEATHER Temperatures remain consistent throughout the year. Average daytime highs are in the 80s in every season; average nighttime lows range from the high 60s to the mid-70s. Precipitation, on the other hand, varies widely: the driest season is October–March, with an average of fewer than 5 inches of rainfall during each of those months. Rainfall increases to an average of 8 inches per month in the spring and up to 10 inches per month in the summer.

THE PORT Disney ships generally dock at the **Punta Langosta Pier,** at the southern end of the downtown area. A sky bridge leads to **Punta Langosta Mall,** across the street from the dock; here you'll find shops, restaurants, and a Starbucks. Taxis travel to all outlying points.

TOURIST HIGHLIGHTS It's all about the water in Cozumel. Snorkeling and diving in the coral reefs are a popular draw, particularly at **Cozumel Reefs National Marine Park.** For history buffs, the pre-Columbian ruins at **Xelha, Chichén Itzá,** and **Tulum** offer a window into ancient Mayan culture. **Chankanaab National Park** offers opportunities to interact with marine animals, as well as walking trails that wind among a large iguana population. Cozumel

is also the perfect place to enjoy the sun as you lounge at one of its many white-sand beaches.

WHAT TO EAT Fish is plentiful here, as is familiar Mexican fare such as tacos and fajitas. Many restaurants offer barbecued pork. Margaritas are served in most watering holes, some of which boast their own house-made tequilas. Also try the local *michelada,* beer mixed with lime juice.

WHAT TO BUY Jewelry, Mexican handicrafts, and tourist T-shirts are all sold close to the cruise terminal. You may also find good-quality leather sandals, bags, and hammocks. For a food-related gift, look for Mexican vanilla. Tequila and Xtabentun, a honey-based liqueur, are popular purchases. (If you decide to buy spirits, have them wrapped for shipping. You can bring alcoholic beverages onto the ship, but they'll be held for you until debarkation.)

Falmouth, Jamaica

Note: *In 2018 the Jamaican government declared a nationwide state of emergency in response to escalating gang violence. Most of the criminal activity has been confined to Kingston, Montego Bay, and Spanish Town, all well away from Falmouth, but exercise caution: avoid straying too far from port or exploring on your own, and stay apprised of the latest developments.*

LANGUAGES English and Patois

HISTORY Falmouth was founded in 1769. During the late 18th century, it served as a major distribution point for rum, sugar, coffee, and molasses. In trade for crops, Falmouth received many Africans. The port's business declined with the end of slavery in the 1800s, but tourism brought a resurgence of visitors in the late 1900s.

WEATHER Temperatures in Falmouth are consistent year-round. During all months, the average daytime high is in the 80s, and the average nighttime low is in the 70s. Falmouth averages fewer than 3 inches of rain per month January–April, but rainfall picks up later in the year, with an average of about 6 inches per month May–November. Rainfall decreases again in December, to about 4 inches.

THE PORT Falmouth's cruise port opened in 2011 to much fanfare. When ships are docked, local vendors set up stalls nearby to sell their wares. The terminal also has several permanent shops and duty-free vendors. Walking about 5 minutes past the port brings you to Falmouth proper and access to restaurants and more shops.

TOURIST HIGHLIGHTS The **Good Hope Great House,** a former sugar plantation, offers estate tours, horse-and-buggy rides, dune-buggy excursions, river tubing, and zip lining. Many of these activities are also available at **Mystic Mountain** adventure park. **Dunn's River Falls** is a spectacular natural phenomenon. As you walk through town, stop to see the **Water Square Fountain,** the **Anglican Parish Church,** and the **Falmouth Court House.** A few beaches lie within a 10-minute taxi ride; **Montego Bay**'s famed party beaches are about a 30-minute taxi ride away (see our earlier note, though).

WHAT TO EAT Jerk-style preparations are a staple of Jamaican cuisine. Meat, chicken, or fish is rubbed with spices and sugars and then grilled over a wood fire. Rice and peas is a typical side dish. To cool off, try fresh local mango, guava, and the national fruit, ackee. Also look for Jamaican

patties, turnover-like pastries stuffed with meat. With many yam farms nearby, you'll also find yams on many restaurant menus. Rum and rum punch are a potent way to jump-start your relaxation. The national beer, Red Stripe, is served throughout the area.

WHAT TO BUY Many visitors bring home jarred spices, jerk seasoning, or coffee. Local artwork, jewelry, wood carvings, and woven goods are also popular. Many guests consider Jamaican rum to be a must-purchase item. If you decide to buy spirits, have them wrapped for shipping.

Fort-de-France, Martinique

LANGUAGE French and Antillean Creole

HISTORY The earliest known settlers in Martinique were the Arawak people. Early control of the area alternated between the Arawaks and the Caribs. The Caribs called the island *Madiana,* or "Island of Flowers." Christopher Columbus charted the island in 1493 and visited it in 1502; however, the island was deemed uninteresting by the Spanish, who decided not to colonize there. During the mid-17th century, French settlers arrived, creating fortifications and sugar mills, enslaving many natives, and establishing trade with Europe. In the 18th and 19th centuries, control of the island changed hands between Britain and France as the power of these nations fluctuated. The island became an official *département d'outre-mer* (overseas territory) of France in 1946; as such, Martinique is part of the European Union (read: bring your euros).

unofficial **TIP**
English is spoken much less widely in Martinique than in the rest of the Caribbean, so it helps to know or learn some French.

WEATHER In 2019, Disney visits Fort-de-France in August, when daytime highs average in the high 80s and nighttime lows average in the high 70s. Expect average rainfall of about 6 inches per month in August.

THE PORT **Pointe Simon Terminal** lies within a 10-minute walk to town; follow the signs to Centre de Ville. The terminal has basic facilities including restrooms, ATMs, and Wi-Fi, as well as duty-free shopping. Expect to find numerous tourist stalls nearby, as well as cafés and restaurants. Taxis at the port often accept US currency as well as euros.

TOURIST HIGHLIGHTS History buffs will want to visit the **Musée de la Pagerie,** the birthplace of Marie Josèphe Rose Tascher de la Pagerie de Beauharnais, who would later become Napoleon's Empress Joséphine. The architectural attractions include **Fort Royal, the Palais de Justice,** and the **Cathédrale Saint-Louis,** with its distinctive spire. The **Musée Départemental d'Archéologie** in Fort-de-France displays the island's pre-Columbian history, while the **Musée Regional d'Histoire et d'Ethnographie** features Creole furnishings, clothing, jewelry, and musical instruments.

Nature lovers will enjoy hiking on **Mount Pelée,** an active volcano, or relaxing on one of the area's many beaches. (Be aware that topless sunbathing is common.) Shoppers should head to the **Place Monseigneur Romero** to find outposts of French boutiques or visit **Rue Blénac at Rue Antoine Siger** for the covered market featuring island-produced goods.

WHAT TO EAT The food of Martinique blends French and Creole influences. Breakfast may be typically French, with baguettes and croissants. Crêperies and brasseries are common throughout the island. Open-air markets

sell locally grown fruits (bananas, coconuts, guava, pineapples, mangoes) and vegetables (breadfruit, Chinese cabbage, yams). Much Martinican cuisine is prepared from seafood and shellfish, including salted cod, *lambi* (conch), octopus, *blaff* (boiled fish with chives), and the national dish, *court-bouillon* (fish in a spicy tomato sauce). Martinique has seven active distilleries, which primarily make rum. *Ti'* punch (rum, sugarcane juice, and lime) and planter's punch (rum, fruit juice, and lime) are two popular beverages made with the local spirits. French wines are also readily available.

WHAT TO BUY **Rue Victor Hugo** is home to purveyors of French luxury goods such as clothing, perfumes, and housewares. For island mementos, look for madras fabric, local artwork, and ceramics. The most popular souvenirs here may be food items including rums, fruit candies, and jams made from locally grown bananas.

Galveston, Texas

LANGUAGE English

HISTORY Galveston Island was first inhabited by the Karankawa and Akokisa Indians. The Spanish first explored the area in the early 1500s, and the French held force there for much of the 1600s. In 1816, the first permanent European settlement was founded by pirates, who used Galveston as a base of support for the Mexicans against the Spanish in the region. By 1860, Galveston was part of the Republic of Texas and a major port in the slave trade. Later, it became the first city in Texas to provide a secondary school for African Americans. Galveston has been subjected to several major hurricanes, including a catastrophic 1900 storm that remains the deadliest natural disaster in US history. More recently, Galveston saw damage and flooding from Hurricane Harvey in 2017, but its beaches, historical sites, and attractions emerged mostly unscathed.

WEATHER Disney cruises depart from Galveston October–January. Average daytime highs in October hover around 80, with average nighttime lows in the high 60s. Daytime highs in November–January average in the 60s, with nighttime lows in the high 40s to low 50s. Precipitation is fairly constant in the winter: expect average rainfall of 2–4 inches per month.

THE PORT The cruise terminal has basic services. About two blocks from the terminal, you'll find several hotels with shops and restaurants.

TOURIST HIGHLIGHTS **Pleasure Pier,** on the Galveston Seawall, is a low-key carnival area. For bigger thrills, head to **Schlitterbahn** water park. **Moody Gardens** is a botanical preserve and theme park with 3-D and 4-D theaters. Small museums in the area include the **Railroad Museum,** the **Texas Seaport Museum,** and the **Offshore Drilling Rig Museum.** If you're spending time in **Houston** before cruising, check out the **Houston Zoo,** the **Houston Museum of Natural Science,** the **Downtown Aquarium,** and of course the **Johnson Space Center.**

WHAT TO EAT Look for seafood, particularly crab and shrimp; Texas barbecue (brisket and chicken); and New Orleans–style jambalaya and po'boys.

WHAT TO BUY Along the beach, you'll find shops selling the requisite T-shirts and sunglasses, along with jewelry made from shells or coral, beachwear, wind chimes, and beach toys. If you're visiting Houston

before your cruise, look for NASA-related items and clothing emblazoned with the logos of the city's sports teams.

Grand Cayman, Cayman Islands

LANGUAGE English

HISTORY Christopher Columbus accidentally discovered these islands during a voyage in 1503. The Caymans came under British control following the 1670 Treaty of Madrid; during this time, they also saw an influx of settlers from Jamaica, and slaves were brought to the island beginning in the 1730s until slavery was abolished in 1834. The region was besieged by periodic attacks from pirates into the late 18th century. Jamaica (a British colony at the time) governed the islands until 1962, when Jamaica became independent and the Caymans elected to stay under British rule.

WEATHER Temperatures stay consistent throughout the year. Daytime highs average in the 80s and nighttime lows average in the 70s. Precipitation, however, varies considerably: during December–April, you can expect an average of fewer than 3 inches of rainfall per month, while May–August experiences an average of about 6 inches of rainfall per month. September–November may see up to 9 inches of rainfall per month.

THE PORT Grand Cayman is a tender port—you have to take a smaller vessel to get from the ship to land. The tender brings you to the edge of downtown **George Town.** Shops and restaurants are within walking distance of the dock.

TOURIST HIGHLIGHTS **Stingray City** offers opportunities to swim with rays. The **Cayman Turtle Farm** is a research facility that studies green sea turtles; here, you'll be able to observe the 16,000 inhabitants and watch turtle hatchlings feed. Water lovers will find abundant scuba and snorkeling opportunities, including excursions to swim near the wreck of a sunken 1940s schooner. History buffs will enjoy the **Pedro St. James Historic Site** and the **Cayman Islands National Museum.** Numerous beaches afford opportunities for sunning and relaxation.

A field of jagged black-limestone formations in Grand Cayman's West Bay—locally known as **Hell** due to its sinister appearance—has inspired nearby points of interest that have silly fun with the name, such as a gift shop where you can snap a selfie in front of a WELCOME TO HELL sign while wearing devil horns and holding a pitchfork.

WHAT TO EAT Seafood—including the traditional national dish, turtle—is plentiful here. Look for rock shrimp and conch in many dishes. Jerked meats are popular on the island, as are many grilled meats. Many of the desserts, such as sticky pudding and rum cakes, have a British influence. Other sweets may include fruit, honey, and coconut.

WHAT TO BUY Decorative conch shells make a nice reminder of the area. If you've interacted with the stingrays or turtles, a carved replica of these creatures makes a good souvenir. Also look for local artwork and woven hats and bags. Gourmets will want to bring home some Tortuga rum cake.

Key West, Florida

LANGUAGE English

HISTORY The original inhabitants of the area were the Tequesta and Calusa peoples. Juan Ponce de León was the first recorded European visitor, arriving in 1521. Cubans and British used the island as a fishing spot before it was claimed by Spain; however, Spain exerted little control over the area. In 1822, Matthew C. Perry claimed the Keys for the United States. The islands became more prosperous when they were connected to mainland Florida by an overseas railway bridge in 1912. Key West sustained significant damage from Hurricane Irma in 2017, but most major tourist attractions and services have since reopened.

WEATHER Daytime temperatures average in the 80s April–November, with nighttime lows during that time in the 70s. December–March, daytime temperatures average in the 70s, with nighttime lows in the 60s. Precipitation is lowest in the winter and spring, with average rainfall of fewer than 3 inches per month November–May. The summer gets wetter, with average rainfall of 3–5 inches per month in June and July. August, September, and October average 5–7 inches of rain per month.

THE PORT The entire island measures just 2 miles by 4 miles, so many services lie within a brisk walk from the port. **Mallory Square,** on the waterfront near the docks, offers bars, restaurants, and basic shopping. To get around without walking, rent golf carts, bicycles, or a pedicab near the port. The **Conch Tour Train** (tickets may be available at a discount if you buy online in advance at conchtourtrain.com) allows visitors to hop on and off for personalized island touring, but some may find the drop points inconvenient. For less kitsch and more charm, explore a bit beyond the immediate port area.

TOURIST HIGHLIGHTS The must-do for literary types is a stop at the **Ernest Hemingway Home and Museum** (at press time they were only accepting cash for admission). See Hemingway's studio and visit with the beloved polydactyl cats descended from the author's many feline companions. For excellent views of the Keys, visit the nearby **Lighthouse and Keepers Quarters Museum.** Nature experiences are available at the **Key West Aquarium** and the **Key West Butterfly Conservancy.** And no trip to Key West would be complete without some relaxation time on the beach.

WHAT TO EAT Fresh seafood is abundant here, with oysters, clams, lobster, grouper, and shrimp appearing on many menus. Conch fritters are a specialty. There is a large Cuban influence in the food culture here: look for sandwiches of Cuban bread stuffed with meats and cheeses. Beef stews, plantains, and yellow rice are all served with a Cuban flair. The signature dessert, of course, is Key lime pie, made with the juice of local citrus. In addition to pie, you're likely to find dozens of other lime-accented foods during your visit, including cookies, candy, salsa, and barbecue sauce. Rumrunners, mojitos, and margaritas can help you ease into the island lifestyle.

WHAT TO BUY Most of the shopping is casual and beachy: T-shirts, sunglasses, swimsuits, and surf- and sun-related trinkets. Epicures can take home a bottle of Key lime juice to use in their own cooking. If you want a permanent souvenir, you could get a tattoo at one of the many shops on the island.

Kings Wharf, Bermuda

LANGUAGE English

HISTORY The first known European exploration of Bermuda—an island in the Atlantic Ocean about 700 miles due east of Savannah, Georgia—took place in 1511, by Spanish explorer Juan de Bermúdez. Real colonization of the island began in 1609, when a group of British colonists became shipwrecked on a nearby reef. The first slaves, primarily Africans and Native Americans, were brought into Bermuda in the 1620s, which began the island's agricultural economy. When the American Revolution ended, the British used Bermuda's harbors as a staging ground for attacks against the United States. Because of its proximity to the southern United States, Bermuda was also used during the Civil War by the Confederate army as a place to evade Union ships. Following World War II, Bermuda began to function as a tourist destination. The island created its own constitution in 1968. (Though, like the Bahamas, Bermuda isn't technically a Caribbean country, it has an unmistakably Caribbean feel.)

WEATHER DCL visits Bermuda in the early fall. Daytime highs during that period average in the low 80s, with nighttime lows averaging in the low 70s. Rain averages about 4 inches per month in the fall.

THE PORT The dock area has modern conveniences, a tourist-information center, and ready access to shuttles and taxis. Shopping and restaurants are a 10-minute walk away. **Snorkel Park Beach** is located near the terminal, just a few minutes' walk from the pier. An admission fee is charged, but it's a nice beach option if you don't want to stray far from the ship. A ferry dock near the piers affords easy access to Hamilton, Bermuda's capital. Motor scooter rentals are also popular, but be aware that Bermudans follow the British custom of driving on the left side of the road.

TOURIST HIGHLIGHTS Outdoor recreation is a big draw in Bermuda. Hike or swim on the many beaches, or book a round at one of the many fantastic golf courses. **The National Museum of Bermuda** contains exhibits related to Bermuda's culture and maritime history. **St. George's Island,** a UNESCO World Heritage Site, is the earliest continuously inhabited English settlement in the Western Hemisphere. Enjoy the town's architecture, including **St. Peter's Church,** built in 1612. Or pop into one of the small local museums. **Crystal and Fantasy Caves** offer tours 100 feet below ground, with views of a subterranean lake and massive crystal formations. **Bermuda Aquarium,** with its sea turtle exhibit, is a draw for kids.

WHAT TO EAT Fish in all its forms. Bermuda fish chowder is a classic dish, but it's nothing like the heavy, dairy-and-potato-based chowder we're used to in the States: rather, it's a spicy seafood-and-vegetable soup that's traditionally made with fish such as snapper, rockfish, or sea bass; tomatoes; celery; various herbs and spices (black pepper, bay leaf, cloves, curry); a dash of rum; and the island's trademark sherry pepper sauce. (Sherry peppers are a Bermudan variant of bird peppers—they pack a bite but won't have you writhing in agony.) Also look for fried-fish sandwiches served on raisin bread—sounds weird, tastes delicious. For dessert, look for rum cake, and then buy one to take home.

WHAT TO BUY When in Bermuda, buy (what else?) Bermuda shorts. Look for long styles for men and women in Easter-egg hues, as well as matching or contrasting tailored jackets. (*Fun fact:* Bermuda shorts with jackets, ties, and over-the-calf socks are standard men's office wear on the island.) Other popular textile items include Irish linen tablecloths and tea towels.

Sea-glass jewelry and art make lovely souvenirs. For these and other local handiworks, try the **Bermuda Craft Market, Bermuda Clayworks,** and **Dockyard Glassworks,** all near the port. If you want to enjoy a taste of the islands back home, buy a bottle of Gosling's Black Seal, Bermuda's signature rum.

Kralendijk, Bonaire

LANGUAGES Dutch, English, Papiamento, and Spanish

HISTORY Bonaire's native inhabitants were the Caquetio Indians, a branch of the Arawak who came by canoe from Venezuela in about A.D. 1000. The first European settlement occurred in 1499, when Amerigo Vespucci arrived in Bonaire and claimed it for Spain. In 1526, Juan de Ampies imported Spanish domesticated animals such as cows, donkeys, goats, horses, pigs, and sheep; goats and donkeys remain an island mainstay. Starting in 1623, ships of the Dutch West India Company stopped at Bonaire to obtain meat, water, and wood. During the period of 1799–1816, referred to as the "Time of Confusion," the island was occupied off and on by a succession of countries, including the United Kingdom and several others. In 1816, Bonaire was returned to the Dutch. Bonaire was part of the Netherlands Antilles until that country's dissolution in 2010, when the island became a special municipality within the nation of the Netherlands.

WEATHER DCL visits Bonaire in January, when daytime highs average in the mid-80s and nighttime lows average in the mid-70s. Rainfall is typically minimal in the winter, with less than an inch of precipitation for the month.

THE PORT The Bonaire cruise terminal is just south of downtown Kralendijk, which is within easy walking distance. ATMs, a pharmacy, and a small grocery store, as well as several restaurants, are located in the shopping area. Taxis are available near the port. If you want to lounge on the beach, expect to pay $10–$20 per chair.

TOURIST HIGHLIGHTS Bonaire is renowned as a diver's paradise, with crystal-clear waters, minimal current, and abundant sea life; **Bonaire National Marine Park** is a great place to get your fix. Another popular outdoor experience is a kayak trip through a rare mangrove forest. If you're more in the mood to imbibe, the **Cadushy Distillery** tour affords a look into the production of liqueur from the cadushy cactus. For a historical perspective, visit the 1850s-era huts that housed slaves who toiled in Bonaire's aboveground salt pyramids. Kids who love animals will enjoy the **Donkey Sanctuary Bonaire,** where they can feed adorable rescue donkeys.

WHAT TO EAT Other than seafood and goat, Bonaire relies primarily on imports for food, so prices can be higher than you might expect. Goat soups and stews are a favorite local staple. A few small-scale orchards grow such fruits as soursop (tastes like a mashup of strawberry, pineapple, coconut, and banana), limes, mangoes, a local variety of cherry (shimaruku), and a brown fruit called mispel. The sap from the mispel tree is a source of chicle, the original base ingredient used to make chewing gum. For Americans, perhaps the most exotic common food on Bonaire is iguana, which is eaten in soups or stews, or sometimes roasted or sautéed. What does it taste like? Well, some call it "chicken of the trees."

WHAT TO BUY Bonaire's salt pyramids provide a steady supply of sea salt, which is not only used to season food but also mixed with essential oils

to create exfoliating bath products. Bath and beauty products are also derived from the island's aloe vera crop. Cadushy cactus liqueur, available throughout the island, makes an interesting take-home treat.

Miami, Florida

LANGUAGES English, Spanish

HISTORY The Tequesta Indians inhabited the area until Spain claimed it in 1566. Spain ceded Florida to the United States in 1819. Named after the Miami River, the city became a force to be reckoned with following the 1896 southward expansion of Henry Flagler's Florida East Coast Railroad. The population boomed until the Great Depression, and, after a pause, the area saw another surge in population from Cuban exiles during the 1960s and '70s. The Miami metro area sustained widespread flooding and power outages in the wake of Hurricane Irma in 2017 but has since recovered.

WEATHER Average daytime highs in Miami are in the 80s May–October, with nighttime lows in the 70s. Average daytime highs are in the 70s December–April, with nighttime lows in the 60s. Precipitation is greatest during the summer. November–April, expect an average monthly rainfall of about 3 inches or less. May, July, and October average 4–5 inches of rainfall per month, while June, August, and September see average rainfall of 6–9 inches per month.

THE PORT The **Port of Miami** is 9 miles from Miami International Airport and about 5 minutes from downtown. **Bayside Market,** a shopping and dining center, is a 15-minute walk from the port. A park with a small sand beach is also nearby. Major hotels and restaurants are within walking distance.

TOURIST HIGHLIGHTS **South Beach** is where the beautiful people go. Take a stroll there to check out the Art Deco architecture, or stop in a bar or club for a drink. Another interesting neighborhood is **Little Havana,** imbued with old-world charm. Learn about Miami's immigrant history at the **American Museum of the Cuban Diaspora.** Gardeners will like the **Fruit and Spice Park,** which grows more than 500 species of edibles, while kids will love exploring the **Miami Children's Museum** and the **Seaquarium.** And, of course, you can soak in the sun at many other area beaches.

WHAT TO EAT Many local establishments serve food with a Cuban flair. Look for stewed chicken or lamb and grilled fish or pork accompanied by tomatoes, vegetables, and rice. Seafood gumbo with rice is also popular, as are stuffed Cuban sandwiches. For an eye-opening pick-me-up, try industrial-strength Cuban coffee. For a slow-me-down, try sangria, mojitos, and other fruity cocktails.

WHAT TO BUY Miami is a cosmopolitan city with luxury chain stores and chic boutiques in abundance—in particular, **Aventura Mall,** just north of Miami Beach, is a retail Holy Grail, with Bloomingdale's, Cartier, Chanel, Gucci, Prada, and Tiffany's among its tenants. You'll also find the requisite beachside T-shirt and trinket shops. For off-the-beaten-path ideas, try the **Tropicana Flea Market,** open on weekends. Sports fans can pick up jerseys and other gear celebrating the **Miami Dolphins,** the **Miami Heat,** or the **University of Miami Hurricanes.** Hand-rolled cigars are sold around the city. A classic, and classy, choice for gentlemen would be a ***guayabera,*** the loose-fitting Cuban-style shirt. Ladies can start their cruise with some new swimwear.

Nassau, Bahamas *(Please see our travel advisory on page 376.)*

LANGUAGE English

HISTORY Originally called Charles Town, Nassau was destroyed by fire in 1684 during an attack by the Spanish. It was rebuilt and renamed 10 years later by the Dutch and English. Over the next few decades, the Bahamas became a pirate stronghold. In 1718 the Brits ousted the pirates and reclaimed the area. During the American Revolutionary War, there was a brief occupation by Americans and then another Spanish occupation in 1782. Spain surrendered the land back to England a year later. In 1807 the slave trade was outlawed, and thousands of freed slaves eventually made the island their home. Today, Nassau is a major tourist destination, visited by every major cruise line.

WEATHER Daytime highs average in the 80s March–November. Temperatures drop slightly in winter, with daytime highs averaging in the 70s December–February. Nighttime lows average in the 70s June–October and in the 60s November–May. Precipitation is lowest in the winter, with average monthly rainfall of fewer than 3 inches November–April. A moderate rise occurs in May, with average monthly rainfall of fewer than 5 inches. Precipitation increases substantially in the summer and fall, with up to 9 inches of rainfall per month June–October.

THE PORT Ships dock at **Prince George Wharf,** on which is located the **Festival Welcome Center,** with basic tourist services. Downtown Nassau is a 10-minute walk away.

TOURIST HIGHLIGHTS Our walking tour (see page 388) takes in such points of interest as the **Queen's Staircase,** the **Government House,** and **John Watling's Distillery.** Museum and history lovers will enjoy the **National Art Gallery of the Bahamas,** the **Pirate Museum,** and **Fort Charlotte.** Numerous beach, water-sports, and animal-encounter excursions are available. Casinos offer the full complement of opportunities to lose your shirt.

WHAT TO EAT For a taste of typical Bahamian food, try conch, fish stew, or crawfish. These are often served with a side of grits, rice, macaroni and cheese, or potato salad. Desserts may include pastries flavored with pineapple, guava, or coconut.

WHAT TO BUY There is no shortage of trinket vendors aimed at the tourist trade. You'll find inexpensive T-shirts on every corner. If you visit the **Straw Market,** keep a sharp eye out for authentic handmade straw pieces rather than ones imported from China. Other popular items include decorated conch shells and carved wood pieces. Foodies may desire rum cakes or guava jams and jellies. Shoppers should also note that in 2018 Bahamas increased its value-added tax (VAT) rate from 7.5% to 12%.

New Orleans, Louisiana

LANGUAGE English

HISTORY The first known inhabitants of what is now the state of Louisiana were the Eastern Woodlands American Indians. The name *Louisiana,* however, once referred to a much, much larger region. In the late 17th century, explorer Jean-Robert Cavalier, Sieur de la Salle, claimed for France a swath of land stretching from the Great Lakes to the Gulf of Mexico and from the Mississippi River to the Rockies. He named it Louisiana (*La*

Louisiane) in honor of King Louis XIV. Further French settlement took place through the first half of the 1700s. In 1718, the city of New Orleans (*La Nouvelle-Orléans*) was founded by Jean-Baptiste de la Moyne de Bienville; just four years later, it was designated the capital of the Louisiana Territory, which was ceded to Spain in the early 1760s, returned to France in 1800, and finally sold to the United States in 1803. To this day, French influence looms large in New Orleans, from its architecture to its food to the names of its streets. (The French language, once widely spoken, has virtually disappeared from the city proper, however.)

New Orleans boomed in the early 1800s, becoming one of the wealthiest cities in the US. A Confederate outpost, it was captured by the Union in 1862, just a year after the Civil War began; as a result, it was spared the widespread destruction that befell other Southern cities.

Given that the city lies below sea level and is surrounded by water, New Orleans's early civic leaders recognized the need to build a network of canals, levees, and pumping stations to help protect it from flooding. Built piecemeal from the mid-1800s into the mid-1900s, the drainage system was partially successful in warding off flooding during Hurricane Betsy in 1965, but by 2005, the aging infrastructure was no match for Hurricane Katrina, which flooded 80% of the city and claimed hundreds of its residents. Recovery has proceeded slowly but steadily since.

WEATHER DCL visits New Orleans—a brand-new port for the cruise line—during February and March in 2019, when daytime highs range from the mid-60s to the low 70s and nighttime lows average in the low to mid-50s. Rainfall is moderate, averaging about 5 inches per month.

THE PORT The **Riverwalk,** a shopping and dining complex, is about 10 minutes from the port. Shuttles and taxis are readily available.

TOURIST HIGHLIGHTS Head straight for the **French Quarter** (aka the **Vieux Carré**) to admire its architecture and soak in the atmosphere (and liquid refreshments) of its many restaurants, bars, and nightclubs, some playing the iconic regional jazz. **St. Louis Cathedral,** the oldest Catholic cathedral in the US, with its soaring center spire, is one of the most filmed and photographed spots in the city. For a behind-the-scenes look at Mardi Gras, take a tour of **Mardi Gras World,** the world's largest parade-float-construction facility. History buffs will enjoy touring the antebellum estates along the **Great River Road** west of the city, including **Destrehan, Laura,** and **Oak Alley Plantations.** The **Garden District,** long home to New Orleans's elite, is also the former nabe of novelist and NOLA native Anne Rice. Family attractions include the **Audubon Zoo;** the **Louisiana Children's Museum;** and **Carousel Gardens Amusement Park,** inside expansive **City Park.**

If you have some time to spare for exploring in greater depth, we recommend Barri Bronston's ***Walking New Orleans,*** a guidebook from the publishers of the Unofficial Guides.

WHAT TO EAT Um, what *not* to eat? "Noo Awlins" is home to a veritable treasure trove of world-renowned restaurants, but you're just as likely to find delicious fare from a food truck or street stall. Classic savory dishes include jambalaya, crawfish étouffée, and gumbo, as well as red beans and rice and muffuletta and po'boy sandwiches. (For the uninitiated: a muffuletta is round, made with Italian-style cold cuts and cheeses, and topped with a tangy olive salad; a po'boy is the more familiar-looking elongated

sub sandwich, typically larded with crisp fried shrimp, plump fried oysters, or tender roast beef.) For dessert, beignets—square powdered doughnuts minus the hole—will hit the spot, as will flaming bananas Foster. If your DCL cruise visits the city during Mardi Gras season, buy a festive king cake to celebrate (but don't eat the plastic baby inside). Sweets pair beautifully with **Café du Monde** coffee—that is, if you're not already slurping down a Hurricane from **Pat O'Brien's.** *Laissez les bons temps rouler!*

WHAT TO BUY Anything foodie: **Tabasco** sauce and related paraphernalia, Café du Monde beignet mix and coffee, and Cajun- or Creole-inspired spice blends. Also look for sports jerseys for the local college and professional sports teams; recordings of New Orleans jazz and soul; Mardi Gras swag, from the tasteful to the tacky; and souvenirs related to the city's centuries-old voodoo tradition.

New York, New York *(See page 274 for full profile.)*

Oranjestad, Aruba

LANGUAGES Dutch and Papiamento

HISTORY The Arawak Indians were the first inhabitants of Aruba. The Spanish explorer Alonso de Ojeda, the first known European visitor, reached the island in 1499. With the arrival of the Spanish, many indigenous peoples were enslaved and relocated to Hispaniola (present-day Haiti and the Dominican Republic). In the mid-1600s, an 80-year war between Spain and Holland ended with the Dutch assuming possession of Aruba. Dutch military personnel were sent to maintain the island, but contrary to their living conditions under their previous masters, the Indians were allowed to remain free. In the early 1800s, the British and Dutch wrestled for control of the island, with the Dutch ultimately retaining control. Gold mining was a key industry throughout the 1800s. Gold, along with aloe (at one time, Aruba produced 70% of the world's crop), created a stable economy. Following the discovery of offshore oil deposits in 1928, the Royal Dutch Shell and Lago Oil companies built major refineries. These were a resource for the Allies in World War II, but they temporarily ceased operations in the 1980s due to a worldwide petroleum surplus.

Aruba became part of the island nation of the Netherlands Antilles in 1954 (it was disbanded in 2010) and then became a constituent country of the Kingdom of the Netherlands in 1986. (The four current constituent countries—Aruba, Curaçao, the Netherlands, and Sint Maarten—are roughly analogous to the United Kingdom. The three island constituencies are self-governing, but they defer to the Netherlands on matters of foreign policy and national defense.) Today, tourism is Aruba's major industry.

WEATHER Temperatures are constant throughout the year. Daytime highs average in the high 80s and nighttime lows in the low 80s. DCL visits Aruba in January; expect moderate rainfall averages of 1–2 inches during both months.

THE PORT The port of Oranjestad has three air-conditioned terminals with ATMs and several small shops. Taxis and shuttles are available, and **Royal Car Rental** and **Smart Rent A Car** have desks at the port, but the town of Oranjestad—less than 10 minutes away—is easily reachable by foot.

TOURIST HIGHLIGHTS The beaches are a key draw in Aruba for relaxing, marine-animal encounters, and water sports, particularly diving and snorkeling in one of many shipwreck ruins. For those who want a richer form of gambling than DCL bingo, you'll find full casinos in several of the island's hotels. Children will love the **Donkey Sanctuary,** where they can spend an hour feeding carrots and apples to these charming creatures. **Alto Vista Chapel,** dating to 1750, offers a chance for visitors to follow a winding road marking stations of the cross. **Fort Zoutman** comprises the earliest remains of the Dutch settlement and Aruba's oldest building, now a historical museum that showcases artifacts from throughout Aruba's history. The island's many cacti, along with its free-roaming iguanas, make for excellent photo opportunities.

WHAT TO EAT As is the case at most tourist destinations in the Caribbean, you'll be able to find hamburgers and pizza at many locations, but to get a true taste of the island, you'll want to try some traditional Aruban cuisine. Typical dishes include goat meat, often prepared with curry; *stoba,* a stew of vegetables and fish; and *keshi yena,* a sort of Aruban take on a stuffed pepper: the rind from an Edam cheese is filled with meat, onions, celery, raisins, peppers, tomatoes, and spices. A favorite snack is *pastechi,* an empanada-like fried pie filled with beef or cheese. Also try *ayaca,* a dish of dough-covered banana or plantain leaves filled with chicken and pork and seasoned with curry and soy. Simpler foods include fresh grilled or broiled sea bass or other fish. Finish your meal with locally grown fruit.

WHAT TO BUY **Aruba Aloe** skin-care products are of excellent quality; look for lotions, lip balms, and other beautifiers. There are several Aruba Aloe retail stores on the island, as well as the factory itself. Items of Dutch origin are plentiful here, including Delft Blue pottery, *stroopwafel* cookies, and Edam cheese. Also look for carvings, housewares, and jewelry made by local artisans. Out-of-circulation Aruban license plates are another popular take-home item—they're inscribed with the cheery motto ONE HAPPY ISLAND. Cuban cigars are available in many shops; as noted earlier, as of press time it's legal to bring limited quantities into the United States for personal use. See tinyurl.com/cubancigarimportpolicy for details, and periodically check the U.S. Customs and Border Protection website for updates.

Philipsburg, Sint Maarten

Note: *Sint Maarten/Saint-Martin was among the islands hit hardest during the 2017 Caribbean hurricane season. The port is now back to nearly full functionality, however, and many tourist sites are well on their way back to normal operations. DCL made several port calls here in 2018 (using it as a replacement for most of the stops originally scheduled for Tortola), and guests were offered a wide array of port adventures. Check the status of attractions as recovery continues.*

LANGUAGES Dutch, French, and English

HISTORY The island was originally occupied by the Carib Indians. Christopher Columbus later found and named it for the medieval bishop St. Martin of Tours, which is now aptly fitting. In the early 1600s, Dutch colonists used the island as a source of salt for export. The Dutch were then ousted by the Spanish, who were subsequently removed by the French. In 1648 a treaty divided the area in half, with shared control and occupancy. Parts

of the territory changed hands between the Spanish and the Dutch 16 times in about 200 years. At several points in the early 1800s, British pirates attacked and brought the area under English rule. The slave trade was a large part of the island's economy in the 17th and 18th centuries; when slavery was abolished, plantation owners imported low-wage earners from China and the East Indies.

The island is currently divided and called by two names: **Saint-Martin,** controlled by the French, and **Sint Maarten,** controlled by the Dutch. It is one of the smallest landmasses overseen by more than one country. English is widely spoken on both sides of the island.

WEATHER The climate in Saint-Martin/Sint Maarten is mild, with average year-round temperatures between 82 and 89 degrees. DCL is currently scheduled to visit Sint Maarten in January, when rainfall averages less than an inch per month. The highest levels of rainfall occur in October, with a still relatively modest monthly average of less than 3 inches per month.

THE PORT DCL ships dock near Philipsburg, on the Dutch side of the island (Sint Maarten). One mile away, accessible on foot and by taxi, is downtown Philipsburg, which is a major duty-free-shopping destination.

TOURIST HIGHLIGHTS Gamblers will enjoy the island's many casinos; be sure to brush up on the rules of roulette, baccarat, craps, blackjack, and poker before you arrive. Guests looking to get their gamble on will find casinos on the Dutch side near the airport and Simpson Bay, and around downtown Philipsburg. The Boardwalk area on **Great Bay,** on the Dutch side, offers beachside lounging and a long string of bars and restaurants. From **Maho Beach,** also on the Dutch side, watch planes fly incredibly low to land at nearby Princess Juliana International Airport, which reopened in October 2017 despite having been largely destroyed by Hurricane Irma. (For your safety, please heed the signs warning beachgoers not to get too close to approaching and departing aircraft.) Water sports available here include snorkeling, scuba diving, and fishing.

For a quieter and more European experience, catch a cab right off the dock (as opposed to the nonlicensed "tour operators" in downtown Philipsburg) to **Marigot,** on the French side. At **Orient Beach,** women can go topless and some sections allow both sexes to bare it all, but the posteriors *en promenade* tend more toward Joe the Plumber than Jennifer Lopez.

WHAT TO EAT Seafood, particularly conch fritters, is plentiful here. Other dishes may have West Indian, French, and Dutch influences. The island also has numerous Chinese restaurants. Try such regional favorites as callaloo (a beef- or crab-based stew), crab cakes, and johnny-cake biscuits. Dessert often includes coconut pies and guava tarts.

WHAT TO BUY Saint-Martin/Sint Maarten is known for its shopping, particularly electronics, cameras, liquor, fragrances, and cigarettes. These will likely be big-name European brands. If you're looking for local flavor, typical tourist souvenirs include artwork, carvings, and woven goods.

Port Canaveral, Florida

LANGUAGE English

HISTORY In 1929, Congress approved construction of a deepwater port at Port Canaveral, completed and dedicated in 1953. Initially this was

a cargo center, with a primary mission of taking orange juice to points north. Concurrent with the rise of shipping in the area was the building of the nearby space center. The first passenger ships arrived in the 1970s to see the area's newly developed theme parks on their ports of call. The first home-ported cruise ship sailed from Port Canaveral in 1982.

WEATHER It's hot here during the summer. (*Surprise!*) May–October, average daytime highs range from the mid-80s to the low 90s; nighttime lows range from the upper 60s to the low 70s. November–April, expect average daytime highs in the low 70s to low 80s, with nighttime lows in the low 50s to low 60s. Precipitation varies considerably throughout the year. The dry season is November–May, with average monthly rainfall of about 3 inches or less. June–October, monthly rainfall averages 5–8 inches. Summer storms are common.

THE PORT Disney cruises dock at **Berth 8,** at a comfortable dedicated terminal with basic facilities. **Jetty Park,** just east of the port, has a lifeguard-patrolled beach, a snack bar, and a playground. The **Cove** area at Port Canaveral is home to several restaurants and shops. Port Canaveral is currently undertaking a $150-million expansion and upgrade, expected to be complete in 2020. New facilities will include an additional ship berth, a terminal structure, and an 1,800-car parking garage. The new terminal, which will be partially used by Disney, will have integrated mobile passenger check-in and a U.S. Customs and Border Protection screening area.

TOURIST HIGHLIGHTS The main attraction here is **Kennedy Space Center.** Visitors can tour the facilities, ride in a space simulator, and participate in special programs with astronauts. Beach lovers will want to head over to **Cocoa Beach** and relax in the sun. Twenty minutes away, in Titusville, you'll find the **Brevard Museum of Natural History and Science,** the **Great Florida Birding Trail,** and the **US Space Walk of Fame.** Of course, the Orlando theme parks are about an hour west of Port Canaveral. Many cruisers make a pre- or postvoyage visit to **Walt Disney World, Universal Orlando,** or **SeaWorld.**

WHAT TO EAT Seafood is served at most restaurants. Look for oysters, conch, and grouper. Many other cuisines, including Italian, Cuban, Asian, and German, are represented in the waterfront area. Fast food such as burgers and pizza is readily available, too.

WHAT TO BUY Look for souvenirs related to the US space program: model rockets, patches depicting moon missions, and pieces of meteorites. For a unique food experience, buy a package of dehydrated astronaut ice cream. Near the beach, stock up on swimsuits, sunglasses, sunscreen, flip-flops, and other last-minute cruising essentials. You'll find that prices on land are significantly lower than in the shops on board. And if you're visiting the theme parks before or after your trip, you'll find a nearly limitless supply of souvenirs.

San Juan, Puerto Rico

Note: *Puerto Rico sustained catastrophic damage from Hurricane Maria in 2017. Recovery has been slow but steady, and DCL has resumed port stops in and departures from San Juan; during several stops in 2018, guests were offered a wide array of port adventures. Check the status of attractions as recovery continues.*

LANGUAGES Spanish and English

HISTORY Juan Ponce de León was the first European explorer to mention visiting the island of Puerto Rico. The city of San Juan was founded in 1521 by Spanish colonists who used it as a stopover on their way to the Americas. Throughout the 17th and 18th centuries, the island withstood various attacks by the English, including Sir Francis Drake, and the Dutch. In 1815, the island was opened to immigration as part of the Royal Decree of Graces. In 1898, United States warships attacked San Juan, eventually resulting in Spanish cession of Puerto Rico to the United States in the Treaty of Paris. In 1917, Puerto Ricans were granted American citizenship. Not quite a state (although 61% of its residents favored statehood in a 2012 referendum), the island sends a nonvoting representative to Congress and maintains a local legislature.

WEATHER As is the case elsewhere in the Caribbean, weather here stays consistent year-round. Average daytime highs are in the 80s throughout the year, with average nighttime lows in the 70s. Precipitation is lowest in the winter, with an average of fewer than 4 inches of rainfall per month January–March. During the rest of the year, rainfall averages 4–6 inches per month.

THE PORT DCL ships dock in **Old San Juan,** across the street from a Sheraton hotel and just steps away from the main city.

TOURIST HIGHLIGHTS History buffs will want to explore **El Morro,** a fortress built to protect the island from attack by sea, and **El Castillo de San Cristóbal,** designed to protect San Juan from overland attacks (see our San Juan walking tour on page 399). The **Museum of Contemporary Art** showcases modern artists from Latin America and the Caribbean. For fun in the sun, explore the beaches in the nearby towns of **Condado** and **Isla Verde.** Many visitors will want to stop by the **Casa Bacardí** distillery (also known as the Cathedral of Rum) for a tour and a taste (or two).

WHAT TO EAT Puerto Rican cuisine is a melting pot of Spanish, Cuban, Mexican, African, and American flavors. To start your meal, try conch fritters or *empanadillas* (pastries filled with meat or seafood). Entrées include meat or seafood stews, steak or veal, barbecued pig, broiled chicken, grilled seafood, and *mofongo* (a mound of mashed green plantains flavored with garlic and pork cracklings). Beans, rice, and plantains are typical sides. Desserts include coconut or caramel flan (custard); sweets may also be flavored with guava, papaya, or mango. Coffee and local rum are the beverages of choice.

WHAT TO BUY Dominoes is a popular game here; a domino set makes a nice souvenir. Also look for hand-tooled leather goods, scented soaps, and woven hats and bags. Take home some rum or coffee.

St. John's, Antigua and Barbuda

Note: *Antigua escaped major damage during the 2017 hurricane season, but its sister island of Barbuda (not a DCL port) was rendered mostly uninhabitable, and its full recovery may take years. We encourage readers to aid Barbuda in its recovery efforts.*

LANGUAGES English and Spanish

HISTORY This Caribbean nation comprises the inhabited islands of Antigua and Barbuda, along with several uninhabited ones. The first residents were the Ciboney Indians; later settlers included the Arawaks and

Caribs. Christopher Columbus "discovered" Antigua during his second voyage in 1493. The first real European settlement took place in 1632 by an English party vacating St. Christopher Island (St. Kitts). In subsequent decades, the island became home to massive sugar plantations, farmed by enslaved native peoples. By the mid-1700s, slaves outnumbered their European masters. The American War of Independence in the late 1700s disrupted the sugar trade. Britain abolished the slave trade in 1807, and all Antiguan slaves were emancipated by 1834. In 1981 Antigua and Barbuda cut ties with Britain and are now an independent entity.

WEATHER In 2019, Disney cruises visit Antigua in January and October. Daytime highs throughout the year are in the 80s, with nighttime lows in the 70s. Precipitation is low in the winter, with January rain averaging less than an inch per month. October rain is heavier, with average precipitation of 4–5 inches per month.

THE PORT Ships dock at **Heritage Quay.** The town of St. John's, which has all basic services, shopping, and dining, lies within a 5-minute walk.

TOURIST HIGHLIGHTS If you're in the mood to gamble, St. John's is home to several casinos, notably the **King's Casino** near Heritage Quay. History buffs will like **Nelson's Dockyard,** which once housed 17 Royal Navy warships. **Betty's Hope** is a refurbished sugar plantation, showing life as it was during the 17th century. Several beaches offer surfing, swimming, and snorkeling.

WHAT TO EAT Antiguan food is typically Caribbean. The national dish is pepper pot (a stew of meats, vegetables, greens, and hot peppers) with *fungi* (a cornmeal mush similar to polenta). Other frequent menu items are *ducana* (sweet-potato dumplings), seasoned rice, and fresh seafood. Grilled meats, often served with side dishes of macaroni pie or plantains, are popular. Dessert may include fudge, tamarind stew, or peanut brittle. Locals drink tamarind juice, mango juice, and coconut water. For adult beverages, try local beers and rum.

WHAT TO BUY Many goods for sale in St. John's are imported from elsewhere. Look for duty-free perfumes, linen, watches, and electronics. For local flavor, consider hand-carved wood objects, natural soaps, artwork, and pottery. Those with an interest in food may purchase locally produced jams and jellies, as well as local rums.

St. Thomas and St. John, US Virgin Islands

Note: *The US and British Virgin Islands sustained extensive damage from Hurricanes Irma and Maria in 2017. Recovery efforts are well under way, and DCL has resumed port stops at St. Thomas. During several stops in 2018, guests were offered a wide array of port adventures. Check the status of attractions as recovery continues.*

LANGUAGE English

HISTORY The original occupants of the Virgin Islands were the Ciboney people. Christopher Columbus first sighted the islands in the late 1400s, and the Dutch West India Company founded a settlement here in 1657. This was shortly followed by occupation by the Danish West India and Guinea Company. Sugarcane, harvested by slaves on St. Thomas and the nearby islands of St. John and St. Croix, became the primary export. In 1848 slavery was abolished and the sugar trade declined. In 1917 the United States

purchased St. Thomas, St. John, and St. Croix from Denmark as a means of controlling the Panama Canal during World War I, and the islands remain a US territory today (the other Virgin Islands are now under British control).

WEATHER Temperatures are constant year-round. Daytime highs average in the high 80s throughout the year, with nighttime lows in the 70s. Precipitation is lowest in the winter, with an average monthly rainfall of fewer than 3 inches December–April. A moderate rise occurs May–August, with an average monthly rainfall of fewer than 4 inches. Precipitation increases to about 6 inches per month September–November.

THE PORT From the cruise docks, it's a 10-minute taxi ride to **Charlotte Amalie,** the main city on St. Thomas. If you'd rather walk than take a cab, just follow the waterfront path for around 20 minutes to downtown. Pedestrians should note that although this is a US territory, drivers observe British road rules and use the left side of the road—so watch carefully when crossing streets.

Directly at the dock, you'll find outposts of many local shops, as well as some American chain stores. Some cafés, a bank, and a pharmacy are also in the immediate dock area.

TOURIST HIGHLIGHTS The **Paradise Point Skyride** offers views of the harbor. At the top, enjoy lunch and walk along trails inhabited by local wildlife. For another beautiful scene, beachgoers will want to visit beautiful **Magens Bay. Coral World** is a nearby attraction with an underwater observatory, animal interaction with sharks and stingrays, and water sports such as parasailing. For history lovers, **Fort Christian** is worth a visit; reopened in 2017 after having been closed for more than a decade, this museum houses local artifacts in a 17th-century redbrick Danish fortress. (The structure easily withstood Hurricanes Irma and Maria and reopened for tours in early 2018.) Another historic site, **Blackbeard's Castle,** was used as a lookout by Danes to protect the harbor from early pirates; today it's part of a resort complex. (Our St. Thomas walking tour, page 393, visits both Fort Christian and Blackbeard's Castle.)

WHAT TO EAT Local dishes include fresh seafood such as conch and lobster. Stewed beef, goat, and chicken are also popular. For a portable bite, try a meat *pate* (a pastry filled with ground pork and beef). Side dishes may feature plantains, yams, rice, beans, and lentils. Fruit and fruit juices are available in abundance. If you're drinking alcohol here, it's likely rum made from sugar and molasses grown in the Caribbean.

WHAT TO BUY St. Thomas is the largest shopping port in the Caribbean. Most goods, including electronics, fragrances, jewelry, tobacco, crystal, and china are widely available in the States. If you're planning to shop for these, you should be familiar with discount pricing from vendors at home. Shop in the open-air markets for local artwork, carved wood, and hand-pieced leather. Foodies will want to take home Caribbean rum-ball candy.

Tortola, British Virgin Islands

Note: *The US and British Virgin Islands sustained extensive damage from Hurricanes Irma and Maria in 2017. Due to concerns about guest safety, DCL altered itineraries to avoid Tortola for much of 2018 (the* Fantasy *alone missed 25 Tortola stops due to hurricane damage) but finally resumed visits later in the year. Check the status of attractions as recovery continues.*

LANGUAGE English

HISTORY Christopher Columbus was the first European to chart the area. Local lore holds that Columbus himself gave the island its name, which means "land of the turtle dove." Pirates Edward "Blackbeard" Teach and Captain William Kidd were among the first Europeans to actually settle in the region. The Dutch ruled the island for a time; then, in the 16th century, the English took power and established a permanent plantation colony on Tortola and the surrounding islands. The sugarcane industry, dependent on the slave labor of Africans transported from the continent, dominated Tortola's history over the next 180 years but diminished in the mid-19th century with the abolition of slavery. Today tourism is the dominant industry.

WEATHER Temperatures in Tortola remain consistent throughout the year, with daytime highs averaging in the mid-80s and nighttime lows averaging in the low to mid-70s in all seasons. Precipitation varies seasonally: expect monthly average rainfall of 2–4 inches during the winter and early spring. Rainfall averages 4–5 inches during late spring into early summer, increasing to an average of 6–8 inches per month during late summer and fall.

THE PORT Ships dock at **Road Town Harbor,** a 5-minute walk into town. Basic shopping and ATMs are within this walking distance; taxis and rental cars are available at the port. Be aware that residents of Tortola and the British Virgin Islands drive on the left side of the road, as per UK custom.

TOURIST HIGHLIGHTS In town, look for the **Sugar Works Museum,** once part of a cotton plantation. For active recreation, visit **Sage Mountain National Park;** wear sturdy shoes if you want to do some hiking. Beaches abound, with some of the best including **Cane Garden Bay, Smuggler's Cove,** and **Apple Bay.** Many excursions feature water sports such as sailing, surfing, and scuba diving. Ferry rides to smaller nearby islands are a popular choice for day trips. The **Tortola Botanic Gardens** are in the process of replanting. While their gardens may not be as lush as they were prior to the hurricanes, they do need your support, and the recovery efforts may be particularly interesting to home gardeners

Note: Locals (particularly the older generation) can be conservative when it comes to social mores and etiquette, and some consider it unseemly for tourists to wear beach attire away from the beach. A few establishments might even turn you away if you show up in swimwear, so bring a change of clothes if you want to eat or explore in town. Think dressy casual rather than formal—say, a polo shirt and pressed Bermuda shorts for men and a nice sundress for women.

WHAT TO EAT Seafood is on most menus. Look for conch fritters or mahimahi, along with crab, shrimp, and lobster. Jerk spices season many meat preparations. Several area restaurants serve *roti,* an Indian-style curry wrap. Vegetable sides include yam, sweet potato, and okra. Fresh fruit abounds. Pusser's is the local rum—drink it straight or in a fruity punch.

WHAT TO BUY The beachwear, batiks, and baskets found on Tortola are typical of those sold throughout the Caribbean. Local crafts, and recordings of local musicians, along with bottles of Pusser's rum, make for truly authentic souvenirs.

Willemstad, Curaçao

LANGUAGES Dutch and Papiamento

HISTORY Curaçao's first inhabitants were the Arawak and Taino peoples. The Spanish colonized in 1499 and retained their claim until 1634, when the Netherlands declared independence from Spain and the Dutch East India Company usurped control. Curaçao attracted both Dutch and Jewish merchants, each of whom brought their architectural influences to the island. During the early 18th century, the island's deep port and strategic position attracted the British and French. In the early 1800s, the British and Dutch exchanged control of the area several times. The 1815 Treaty of Paris gave Curaçao back to the Dutch West India Company. Soon after the Dutch retook the island, it languished for a century. Slavery disappeared, and social and economic conditions were harsh. In 1920, oil was discovered off the nearby Venezuelan coast. This signaled a new era for Curaçao and its sister island, Aruba. They became centers for distilling crude oil imported from Venezuela, and Curaçao's Royal Dutch Shell Refinery became the island's biggest business and employer. During WWII, the Allies established an American military base at Waterfort Arches, near Willemstad.

In 1954, Curaçao, along with Bonaire, Saba, Sint Eustatius, and Sint Maarten, became the nation of the Netherlands Antilles, with Willemstad as its capital. In 1986, Aruba became a constituent country of the Kingdom of the Netherlands; in 2010, Curaçao and Sint Maarten followed suit, and the islands of Bonaire, Saba, and Sint Eustatius became special municipalities within the smaller nation of the Netherlands. (The four constituent countries of the Kingdom of the Netherlands—Aruba, Curaçao, the Netherlands, and Sint Maarten—are roughly analogous to the United Kingdom. The three island constituencies are self-governing, but they defer to the Netherlands on matters of foreign policy and national defense.)

WEATHER DCL visits Curaçao in January during 2019. Temperatures in Willemstad are consistent all year long: daytime highs average in the low to mid-80s, and nighttime lows average in the mid- to high 70s. Expect moderate rainfall, averaging 1–2 inches per month.

THE PORT Ships dock at a pier directly adjacent to town. Taxis and shuttles are readily available. Basic services such as ATMs, shops, cafés, and several attractions lie within a 10-minute walk of the port.

TOURIST HIGHLIGHTS Downtown Willemstad, designated a UNESCO World Heritage Site in 1997, features charming Dutch architecture that reminds us a lot of the Nyhavn waterfront in Copenhagen, Denmark. The city is split into two districts on either side of a narrow channel, connected by a landmark floating pedestrian bridge. Historical sites include **Landhuis Brievengat,** a museum and replica of an island plantation. **Mikve Israel–Emanuel Synagogue** is a Jewish cultural museum that's also an active house of worship. **The Curaçao Museum** displays exhibits that touch on the geological history of the island, pre-Columbian artifacts, details about the time after the abolition of slavery, antiques, paintings, and a replica of a traditional plantation kitchen. If you're interested in the alcohol-distilling process (or you want to sample the product thereof), you might enjoy a visit to the **Curaçao Liqueur Factory** at **Landhuis Chobolobo.** If you're a gaming buff, several of the area hotels have full casinos. Children will enjoy the **Curaçao Ostrich Farm** and the **Curaçao Sea Aquarium.** And of course, the island offers an array of lovely beaches for sunning and water sports.

WHAT TO EAT The food of Curaçao is a blend of Dutch, Indonesian, and Caribbean, with hints of other world cuisines in the mix. Traditional fare includes *funchi,* or half-and-half, which is a polenta-like side dish of half cornmeal pudding and half rice; *pika hasa,* or red snapper; and a Dutch dish called *keshi yena,* which is a Gouda or Edam cheese rind stuffed with meat or fish. A local favorite is iguana stew, which is said to taste like chicken if you're brave enough to try it. Also look for *ayaka* (meat tamales wrapped in banana leaves) and *kabritu* (stewed goat). But never fear—if you're not an adventurous eater, there are plenty of places to get pizza and burgers. The most popular alcoholic beverage is Curaçao liqueur, made from the peel of the bitter Lahara orange mixed with a variety of spices. For something without a kick, try the local fruit juices.

WHAT TO BUY Dutch Delft Blue ceramics and figurines of Curaçao's historic buildings are some of the more substantial collectibles for sale in local shops. Look also for locally made artwork and musical instruments crafted from driftwood, calabash, and coconut. Other popular souvenirs include books of local lore and photographs of the island. The most traditional consumable purchase is Curaçao liqueur. You can also find Cuban cigars for sale here.

unofficial **TIP**
The US government allows cruise tourists to bring home Cuban cigars, but you may not resell them.

WHAT ABOUT CUBA?

IN 201, THE UNITED STATES AND CUBA normalized relations for the first time in 50 years. In 2017, however, the Trump administration announced that it was tightening travel restrictions that the previous administration had loosened; the renewed hard line on US tourism has had a detrimental effect on burgeoning tourism-related businesses such as restaurants, bed-and-breakfasts and vacation rentals, and transportation providers. Carnival, Holland America, Norwegian, and other cruise lines are making port stops here, but given today's muddy political waters, it's difficult to say whether DCL will move forward with plans to add Cuba to its own itineraries.

HAWAII

CRUISES SAIL FROM Vancouver or Honolulu

SHIP *Wonder*

DATES April and May

CRUISE LENGTH 9 or 10 nights

SPECIAL TOUCHES Cultural ambassadors on board give seminars on lei-making, hula, ukulele, and Hawaiian entertainment with music and dance. Hawaiian menu.

SIGNATURE PORT ADVENTURE Renting a car and seeing the islands for yourself, on your own time

PROS

- Cruises stop at 4 islands.
- You can see everything from blue oceans to mountains, rainforests, and volcanoes.
- Weather is mild (but often rainy).
- Sailing from **Vancouver** eases you into the 5-hour time difference.
- You can add a stay at **Disney's Aulani Resort** if you want to keep the magic going. This is a very popular option, so don't expect reduced rates.
- **Honolulu** has world-class shopping.
- US residents: you may be able to use your own bank's ATM in port. Another bonus for US residents: no cellular roaming in port.
- Ten nights helps you really get to know your cruise staff.

CONS

- If you're sailing from Hawaii, be prepared for jet lag that ranges from heavy-duty (if you're traveling from the West Coast) to crushing (if you're traveling from the East Coast).
- Airfare to or from Honolulu can cost an arm and a leg.
- To really experience Hawaii, you're better off flying to one island and staying there.
- Disney cruises tend to hit Hawaii during the rainy season.
- Because everything has to be shipped into the islands, food and other necessities are very expensive. ("Fun" fact: Hawaii has the highest cost of living of any state.)
- A 10-night cruise is a major time commitment when you factor in transportation before and after the cruise.
- Your only choice is the *Wonder,* and only during limited dates throughout the year.
- What's more, 10 nights means at least $240 in gratuities, plus more Internet to purchase if you need it while you're away, multiple opportunities for dinners or brunches at Palo, before- and/or after-dinner drinks, trips to the gift shop and spa . . . you get the idea.

DEFINITELY VISIT Volcanoes National Park, on the Big Island of Hawaii

CLASSIC DISNEY ADD-ON Disney's Aulani Resort & Spa on Oahu

WHAT TO PACK A variety of clothing for warm to chilly weather; suitable shoes for hiking if you plan to venture beyond the beaches

COMMENTS The 50th state is more than just sand and surf. If you have time, stay a few days before or after your cruise to experience the islands beyond the port adventures.

Hilo, Hawaii

LANGUAGES English, Hawaiian, and Pidgin

HISTORY Hilo is the largest city on the island of Hawaii, aka the "Big Island." Archeological evidence indicates settlement by Polynesian peoples from the Marquesas Islands as early as A.D. 300. Centuries-old local chiefdoms were consolidated under the Hawaiian Islands' first monarch, King Kamehameha the Great, in 1782. The late 18th century also saw the arrival of British Captain James Cook as well as explorers and traders from China. In the 1820s, US missionaries arrived in Hilo, further complicating the cultural influences. During the mid-1800s, sugar plantations thrived, and sugar became a key export. In 1893, a coalition of American and European business and political leaders forced Hawaii's last monarch, Queen Lili'uokalani, to step down, and in 1898 the islands were annexed by the United States. The early 1900s saw a major influx of Japanese immigrants, followed by the arrival of many Korean immigrants. The mid-20th century saw several natural upheavals, including earthquakes, volcanic eruptions,

and tsunamis. Hawaii became the 50th state in 1959. The closure of area sugar plantations during the 1990s led to a downturn in the local economy, but tourism has been fueling the rebound.

WEATHER DCL visits Hilo in April and May during 2020. Average daytime highs during this period are in the high 70s and low 80s, with average nighttime lows in the mid-60s. Precipitation on the Big Island is heavy throughout the year, with April and May averaging 6–8 inches per month.

THE PORT Cruise ships dock at piers on **Kuhio Street,** about 2 miles east of downtown Hilo. There is very little in the way of services near the dock, but taxis can take you into town; there's also a public bus system. Shuttles take guests to the local farmers market or to **Hilo Hattie,** a retailer of Hawaiian-themed clothing.

TOURIST HIGHLIGHTS The **Pacific Tsunami Museum** chronicles the 1946 and 1960 tsunamis that destroyed much of the town; a wave machine lets you experience the feel of rushing water. The **Lyman Museum** features exhibits about Hawaiian geography and history. Nature enthusiasts will want to visit **Hawai'i Volcanoes National Park,** home of Kilauea—the most active volcano on the planet—and Mauna Loa. If you're looking for natural beauty with little exertion, **Rainbow Falls** is small but close to downtown, and it requires no hiking. The **Mauna Loa Macadamia Nut Factory** offers tours and tastings.

WHAT TO EAT If you visit the large farmers market, look for unfamiliar fruits such as mangosteen, durian (*warning:* an acquired taste!), and rambutan; many vendors will allow you a small bite before buying. Some stalls sell prepared foods such as taro pastries and *musubi,* a sushilike snack made with Spam (a Hawaiian delicacy), chicken, or hot dogs. Most menus will have local fish served grilled, broiled, or in tacos. Tropical fruits abound: pineapple, bananas, guava, papaya, mango, and coconut. A great beachside refresher is a shave ice, a tropical take on a snow cone that's topped with a variety of sweet, fruity sauces and sometimes ice cream or sweetened condensed milk. Kona coffee is especially rich and delicious. Macadamia nuts are sold all over the island—try some dipped in chocolate.

WHAT TO BUY Typical Hawaiian souvenirs include floral shirts (match the whole family!), art prints of the local scenery, carved wooden objects, ukuleles, and hula accessories such as skirts and leis. Food finds are everywhere: macadamias in every form, jams and jellies, and packaged Kona coffee beans.

Honolulu, Hawaii

LANGUAGES English, Hawaiian, and Pidgin

HISTORY The capital of Hawaii and both the southernmost *and* westernmost major city in the United States, Honolulu is located on the island of Oahu. Archaeological evidence indicates settlement of the Hawaiian Islands by Polynesian peoples from the Marquesas Islands as early as A.D. 300. The first known foreigner to enter Honolulu Harbor was William Brown, captain of the English ship *Butterworth,* in 1794. King Kamehameha I (The Great), who conquered the islands in 1782, moved his court from the "Big Island" of Hawaii to Waikiki in 1804; he relocated to what is now downtown Honolulu five years later. In 1820, a group of New England missionaries arrived, bringing with them their religion, education,

and economics. Later, immigrants from Asia, Portugal, and Puerto Rico helped make Hawaii a true cultural melting pot. King Kamehameha III proclaimed Honolulu the capital city of his kingdom in 1850. In 1893, the US overthrew the monarchy and in 1898 annexed the islands, creating the Territory of Hawaii. In 1941, the Empire of Japan bombed the Pearl Harbor military base just west of Honolulu, hastening America into World War II. Hawaii became the 50th state in 1959.

WEATHER DCL visits Honolulu in April and May during 2020. Average daytime highs during this period are in the low to mid-80s, with average nighttime lows in the low 70s. Precipitation on Oahu in April and May averages 2–3 inches per month.

THE PORT Cruise ships dock adjacent to **Aloha Tower Marketplace,** which has shops, restaurants, and all basic services. The top floor of this 10-story building houses an observation deck (free admission) offering panoramic views of the harbor. Taxis and rental cars are readily available, and a reliable public bus system covers much of Oahu. The **Waikiki Trolley** is similar to San Francisco's cable-car system.

TOURIST HIGHLIGHTS The main draw in Oahu for many guests is the **World War II Valor in the Pacific National Monument** at Pearl Harbor, encompassing the **USS *Arizona* Memorial** and a museum complex. Tours are a must, and tickets may be purchased in advance (call ☎ 877-444-6777 or visit recreation.gov; *note:* the USS *Arizona* Memorial was closed for structural repairs at press time but was scheduled to reopen in late 2019). A vibrant **Chinatown** is chockablock with unique shops and restaurants. In the Capitol District, visit historic **Iolani Palace,** the only royal residence in the United States. Culture mavens will enjoy the **Hawaii State Art Museum,** which features Hawaiian art across all media. Nature lovers will enjoy the **Lyon Arboretum,** with walking paths that border more than 600 plant species, more than 80 of which are rare or endangered. If you'd like to learn about pineapple production, the **Dole Plantation** is a worthwhile excursion nearby (buy tickets at doleplantation.com). **Waikiki Beach** is abuzz with hotels, shops, and restaurants, flanked by the distinctive **Diamond Head** crater. Disney fans may want to check out the company's **Aulani Resort & Spa,** part of the larger Ko Olina resort complex about 45 minutes west of Honolulu.

WHAT TO EAT Hawaiian cuisine reflects the state's natural bounty as well as its wildly diverse cultural heritage. Most menus will have local fish served grilled, broiled, or in tacos. Tropical fruits abound: pineapple, bananas, guava, papaya, mango, and coconut. Sticky rice serves as the base for everything from a *loco moco* (a burger and fried egg over rice) to the ubiquitous Spam *musubi* (think sushi, only with Spam). If you visit a luau, you're sure to encounter *kalua* pig served with a side dish of *poi* (mashed taro root). Signature sweets include *malassadas* (Portuguese-style doughnuts) and desserts and candies based on the locally grown macadamia nut. A great beachside refresher is shave ice, a tropical take on a snow cone that's topped with a variety of sweet, fruity sauces and sometimes ice cream or sweetened condensed milk. Kona coffee is rich and delicious. Kids will love POG (passion fruit, orange, and guava) juice. Bars and restaurants serve the requisite fruity cocktails, often accompanied by a paper umbrella. Hey, when in Honolulu . . .

WHAT TO BUY There's no more iconic souvenir than the classic Hawaiian shirt. If you're looking for something other than the typical floral print, the gift shop at the USS *Arizona* Memorial often sells Hawaiian-style shirts with military-themed prints. Foodies will want to bring home macadamia-nut candies, Hawaiian sea salt, tropical fruit jams, or a package of local coffee beans. Other popular items include carvings or housewares made from koa wood, leis made from shells, and recordings by Hawaiian musicians.

Kahului, Hawaii

LANGUAGES English, Hawaiian, and Pidgin

HISTORY Kahului is located on the island of Maui. Polynesian and Tahitian settlers were among the first known inhabitants. Until the late 1400s, the island was ruled by tribal chiefdoms, which were united in the mid-1550s under the rule of a single royal family. Europeans began to visit in the mid-1500s, but they did not become a significant presence until the early 1800s. In the 1820s, Christian missionaries began teaching and preaching, altering the island's traditional religious and educational systems. The 1800s saw massive deaths among the indigenous peoples due to the introduction of Western illnesses. Crops such as sugar and pineapple became mainstays of the local economy in the mid-to-late 19th century. Maui served as a recreation and training base during WWII, and the first tourist hotel was built here in 1946. Hawaii became the 50th state in 1959.

WEATHER DCL visits Kahului in April and May during 2020. Average daytime highs during this period are in the mid–80s, with average nighttime lows in the high 60s to low 70s. Precipitation on Maui in April and May averages less than 2 inches per month.

THE PORT Kahului is an industrial port. Within a 15-minute walk you'll find the **Maui Mall**, which houses a grocery store, a movie theater, and shops. A public beach is also within walking distance. Taxis service the harbor, but there is little public transportation—renting a car may be more efficient and less expensive than taking a cab. Shuttles can take you to the Kahului Airport, which has desks for most major auto-rental agencies.

TOURIST HIGHLIGHTS The **Road to Hana** is an internationally famous leisure drive. The narrow, twisting road requires skilled driving, and perhaps some Dramamine. Along the way you'll see tropical vegetation, waterfalls, sea caves, and swimming holes. Many guests will want to explore **Lahaina,** a historic town with numerous art galleries, shops, restaurants, and bars. For shopping and snorkeling, venture to **Ka'anapali,** which features an upscale outdoor mall called **Whalers Village** and the **Pu'u Keka'a (Black Rock)** ocean-diving area. The 112-acre **Maui Tropical Plantation** offers tram tours. For panoramic views, take a **helicopter tour** of the region's volcanoes and waterfalls.

WHAT TO EAT Fresh fish abounds on most menus. Look for coconut shrimp, fish tacos, ahi tartare, ahi *poke* (a raw-tuna salad), and sushi of every sort. The Road to Hana is populated by fresh-fruit stands and vendor shacks that sell delicious banana bread. Pork is often prepared shredded with a sweet sauce on the side. Typical side dishes include pounded taro, rice, or macaroni salad. The locally made potato chips have a cult following (the **Kitch'n Cook'd** brand is particularly addictive). For a refreshing treat, try

shave ice topped with fruit-flavored sauces. Favorite beverages include coffee-based drinks and cocktails made with rum and fruit.

WHAT TO BUY Typical Hawaiian souvenirs include wearables such as Aloha shirts, sarongs, and swimwear, along with recordings by local musicians and prints by local artists. Look for crafts made from koa wood such as carvings, bowls, or hair ornaments. Gourmands will want to buy unusual flavors of Spam (a beloved regional delicacy), coffee beans, macadamia-nut candies, and jams made from local fruits.

Nawiliwili, Hawaii

LANGUAGES English, Hawaiian, and Pidgin

HISTORY Nawiliwili is located on the island of Kauai. Indigenous peoples have inhabited the island since at least 1000 A.D. Continuous European visitation began following Captain James Cook's landing in 1778. The mid-1800s saw an expansion of agricultural trade. Nawiliwili Harbor officially opened in 1930. Hawaii officially joined the United States in 1959. Kauai's beautiful scenery has served as a backdrop for numerous Hollywood films, including *South Pacific* (1958), *Raiders of the Lost Ark* (1981), *Jurassic Park* (1993), and *The Descendants* (2011).

WEATHER DCL visits Nawiliwili in April and May during 2020. Average daytime highs during this period are in the mid-80s, with average nighttime lows in the high 60s to low 70s. Precipitation on Kauai in April and May averages 2–3 inches per month.

THE PORT The port itself has little in the way of services, but the shops and restaurants of the **Harbor Mall** and **Anchor Cove Shopping Center** are within walking distance. Free shuttles are also provided. **Kalapaki Beach,** adjacent to the malls, provides an area for sunning and water play. Taxis service the port, but a rental car may be the most efficient way to see the area.

TOURIST HIGHLIGHTS **Nawiliwili Beach Park** provides beaches for sunning and swimming. The natural wonders of Kauai are also evident at **Waimea Canyon** and **Koke'e State Park. Kilohana Plantation** provides a look into the lavish lifestyles of Hawaii's sugar magnates; a train trip around the plantation functions as a guided tour. Lovely **Wailua Falls** was featured in the opening shots of the 1970s TV staple *Fantasy Island*. The **Kilauea Point Lighthouse** offers sweeping ocean views, and the **Kilauea Point National Wildlife Refuge** offers prime bird-watching.

WHAT TO EAT In a word, fish. Look for *poke,* a raw-seafood salad made with *tako* (octopus) or ahi tuna; *lomi-lomi* salmon, a raw-salmon-and-tomato salad; fish tacos; and *poi,* or mashed taro root. Locals favor *musubi* (Spam or other meat served over sushi rice) and *saimin* (a noodle soup similar to ramen or lo mein). Many meat dishes show an Asian influence. Typical sides include rice, potato salad, and macaroni salad. Fresh fruit, particularly local guava, pineapple, and coconut, is found in abundance. Regional sweets include *lilikoi* (passion fruit) pie, shave ice (like a snow cone), and *haupia* (a luscious coconut pudding that's often used as a pie filling). Coffee and fruit-based drinks are excellent here.

WHAT TO BUY A prized—and pricey—local purchase is a **Ni'ihau shell lei,** handcrafted from shells found on a lightly inhabited nearby island. Musicians may be interested in buying a handcrafted ukulele or CD of local songs. Aloha shirts and hula skirts are great for guests who want to wear

a bit of the islands at home. Look also for candies, cookies, and jams made from locally grown fruits and nuts.

Vancouver, British Columbia, Canada

(See page 271 for full profile.)

MEDITERRANEAN

Note: *The U.S. Department of State is now classifying many European countries at Travel Advisory Level 2, with a note to "exercise increased caution due to terrorism." While no specific threats are mentioned, numerous terrorist incidents, both large and small, have occurred throughout Europe over the past several years. Countries mentioned in the advisories include Spain, France, and Italy, among others, but it's worth noting that the United Kingdom and several other countries have similar safety and terrorism advisories for their citizens traveling to the United States. Consult the country-specific information at travel .state.gov as you make decisions related to your family's travels.*

CRUISES SAIL FROM Barcelona

SHIP *Magic*

CRUISE LENGTHS 5, 7, or 10 nights

DATES Summer

WHAT TO PACK Good walking shoes, lots of euros

SIGNATURE PORT ADVENTURE City tour

CLASSIC DISNEY ADD-ON An Adventures by Disney tour or a side trip to Disneyland Paris

COMMENTS Mediterranean cruises are very popular with families who want to see a lot of southern Europe with minimal hassle. Dining has an international flair.

PROS
- A Mediterranean cruise is a good way to sample lots of ports without having to move your luggage.
- Shopping opportunities abound.
- You have lots of family-friendly port adventures from which to choose.

CONS
- If you're coming from North America, round-trip airfare may put a serious dent in your budget.
- You're only scratching the surface of all there is to see in this part of Europe.
- Your budget will likely be affected by currency-exchange rates.

Ajaccio, Corsica, France

LANGUAGES French, Corsican, Italian, and Ligurian

HISTORY The island of Corsica—an offshore region of France just north of the Italian island of Sardinia in the Mediterranean Sea—has been occupied continuously since the Mesolithic Era. The first historical record of settlement in what is now Ajaccio, Corsica's capital city, dates from the second

century A.D. It became a holy site of the early Catholic church in the early 600s, following which time it was alternately occupied by the Greeks and the Romans. In the late 15th century, the Genoese transformed Ajaccio into a full-fledged city. Ajaccio was subsequently occupied by France during the mid-1500s, but the Genoese soon regained power. Genoa kept the area until 1755, when the French once again prevailed. Napoléon I (Napoléon Bonaparte), emperor of France from 1804 to 1814, was born in Ajaccio in 1769 and in 1811 made it the capital of the newly created French *département* (administrative district) of Corsica. (Today, the island comprises two *départements:* Haute-Corse, or Upper Corsica, and Corse-du-Sud, or Lower Corsica.)

In the 19th century, Ajaccio became a popular tourist destination for European aristocracy. During World War II, it was among the first French towns to be liberated from the Germans.

WEATHER DCL visits Ajaccio, a town of about 68,000 people, in July during 2019, when daytime temperatures average in the low 80s and nighttime lows average in the mid-60s. Summer is the dry season, with less than an inch of rain for the month.

THE PORT Cruise ships dock immediately adjacent to the town. Basic services, including cafés, shops, and banking services, are located in Ajaccio, a 5-minute walk from the ship. Taxis and shuttles are located near the port.

TOURIST HIGHLIGHTS **Musée Fesch** exhibits one of the largest collections of Italian Baroque and Renaissance paintings in France; the museum is also home to more than 700 works depicting the Bonaparte family. **Maison Bonaparte,** Napoléon's birthplace, is also nearby, as is the **Cathedral of Our Lady of the Assumption of Ajaccio,** where the French emperor was baptized. If you want to enjoy some natural beauty, travel 5 miles beyond the city to **Plage de Capo di Feno,** a scenic beach area. Families with children will likely enjoy **A Cupulatta,** a turtle-and-tortoise sanctuary that cares for nearly 3,000 animals from 170 related species.

WHAT TO EAT Ajaccio takes great pride in its local meats, often in the form of sausages, and cheeses, such as the goat cheese Brocciu. Typical seafood dishes include sea bass stuffed with vegetables; fried trout; grilled salmon; and salads composed of squid, mussels, lobsters, and sea urchins. Ajaccio is also well known as a source of fine honeys and jams.

WHAT TO BUY Leather, pottery, and jewelry from local artisans is available throughout the port area. Olive oil and jarred jams are a nice food reminder of the area. Scented soaps are another popular take-home item.

Barcelona, Spain

LANGUAGES Catalan and Spanish

HISTORY Barcelona was founded as a Roman city. Subsequently, Visigoths and then Moors controlled the area until the early 800s. Franks held the region through the 10th and 11th centuries. From the 12th century, Barcelona and Catalonia became allied with the Kingdom of Aragón, and the Port of Barcelona became a trading thoroughfare. A period of decline ensued with the arrival of the Black Death in the 14th century, followed by the expansion of the Hapsburg monarchy as well as the rise of Turks in the region. The early 1700s brought a rejuvenation of the Barcelona dock system and then the arrival of the industrial age in the 1800s. By the mid-1800s, Barcelona was again a flourishing European port. Periods of

unrest and rebuilding took place throughout the early 1900s. Barcelona hosted the 1992 Summer Olympics, a boon for the entire region.

Barcelona is the capital of Catalonia, an autonomous community of Spain with its own language (Catalan) and culture; independence from Spain has been a goal off and on for decades. The modern Catalonian independence movement began in 1922, with Spain granting the region autonomous status as a concession. In 1938, Francisco Franco, Spain's longtime dictator, revoked Catalonia's autonomy, which was restored in 1975 after his death.

A renewed push for independence took hold in the mid-2000s and intensified further in 2017, with Catalonian President Carles Puigdemont announcing a referendum and 90% of Catalonians voting in favor of independence. The Spanish government declared the referendum illegal and seditious, resulting in sometimes-violent demonstrations. During the summer of 2018, Spain's Constitutional Court again blocked a motion approved by Catalonia's parliament to resume measures toward independence. The region's political climate remains volatile at press time, so avoid areas where demonstrations are taking place, and exercise common sense regarding your personal safety.

WEATHER Disney cruises visit Barcelona in the summer and early fall. Daytime highs average in the mid-70s to low 80s, with nighttime lows in the low to mid-60s. Even when temperatures peak, coastal breezes typically keep things comfortable. Precipitation is usually minimal during this period, with an average of fewer than 6 inches per month.

THE PORT There is little here to entice tourists, but a 5-minute taxi ride or brisk 20-minute walk from the port brings you to **La Rambla,** a pedestrian mall bustling with restaurants and smart shops. Taxis are plentiful.

TOURIST HIGHLIGHTS The premier attractions are La Rambla and **La Boqueria,** an open-air market with dozens of food stalls. The influence of artist Antoni Gaudí is in evidence throughout the area, principally in the can't-miss **Sagrada Família** cathedral and the **Park Güell** garden complex. (Our walking tour of Barcelona, page 399, includes a stop at the church.) Gothic architecture abounds in the old section of town. Art aficionados will enjoy the **Salvador Dalí Theatre and Museum,** the world's largest Surrealist object (*trippy* doesn't begin to describe it). Foodies will relish the **Museu de la Xocolata** (Museum of Chocolate). The **Poble Espanyol,** a walled city within the city, showcases architecture, artisans, and food from each of Spain's 15 regions. Sun worshippers will appreciate the city's public beaches.

WHAT TO EAT In a word: *¡tapas!* Most restaurants offer some version of these small plates. Look for seafood, olives, artichokes, egg dishes, breads, and local hams and sausages. La Boqueria's many sweets vendors peddle intricately shaped chocolates and marzipans.

WHAT TO BUY You can find virtually anything for sale in Barcelona, from high-end leather goods and shoes to handblown glassware. Great take-home choices include packaged foodstuffs, such as candy, olives, olive oil, and wine; sportswear featuring the local *futbol* (soccer) teams; and Gaudí-inspired artwork.

Cádiz, Spain

LANGUAGE Spanish

HISTORY Founded by the Phoenicians, Cádiz is the oldest continuously inhabited city in Spain. In its early years, it was variously controlled by the

Romans, the Visigoths, and the Moors. Christopher Columbus used Cádiz as a starting point for two of his voyages. The 16th century saw minor raids by Barbary corsairs and the Englishman Sir Francis Drake. More-serious attacks came at the end of the 16th century, when Cádiz was captured by the English. The city changed hands between the Spanish and the English several times over the next two centuries. Spain maintained dominance in the 18th century, whereupon Cádiz gained prominence as a trading port.

In the early 19th century, the city became the seat of Spain's military high command. In recent years, Cádiz has undergone much reconstruction—many monuments, cathedrals, and landmarks have been cleaned and restored, adding to the charm of this ancient city.

WEATHER During 2019, DCL visits Cádiz in May and July. Daytime highs in May are in the low to mid 70s, with nighttime lows in the high 50s; daytime highs in July are in the high 70s to low 80s, with nighttime lows in the high 60s. Expect rainfall of less than an inch per month throughout the spring and summer.

THE PORT Ships dock near the center of town. Across the street from the dock, you'll find **Plaza San Juan de Dios,** with shops, restaurants, ATMs, and other services. Many shopping and tourist sites are accessible on foot, and taxis are available. Many guests use Cádiz as a jumping-off point for a visit to **Seville,** which is about 2 hours away by train (the rail station is across the street from the port).

TOURIST HIGHLIGHTS The **Catedral de Cádiz** has a glittering gold dome and striking Baroque facade. The **Museo de Cádiz** includes an archaeological section with Phoenician artifacts. You can also explore the four quarters of the city: the **City Center,** which features colorful plazas and gardens; **La Viña,** dotted with bars and nightclubs; **El Populo,** replete with monuments; and **Santa María,** epicenter of the art of flamenco dancing.

If you're heading to Seville, the main draw is the **Alcazar,** an elaborate Moorish palace. The **Catedral de Sevilla** is the largest cathedral in Spain as well as the largest Gothic building in the entire world. The **Museo de Bellas Artes** exhibits paintings by Diego Velázquez and El Greco. And Seville's **Jewish Quarter** is home to many antiques shops, outdoor cafés, and traditional whitewashed homes.

WHAT TO EAT Cold tomato gazpacho is a typical meal-starter. Seafood is plentiful: shrimp, anchovies, squid, and whitefish fried in olive oil. Restaurants in Cádiz also serve dishes made of beef, pork, goat, lamb, or game birds. Cured ham is a specialty. Meat and fish dishes may be accompanied by bread, potatoes, rice, olives, and roasted vegetables. Any savory dish may be served as tapas, small plates meant for tasting or sharing. Desserts may include *pestiños* (deep-fried pastries with honey), *amarguillos* (almond cookies), wine doughnuts, or *pan de Cádiz,* a marzipan treat stuffed with fruit. Sherry and sweet wines are typical of the area.

WHAT TO BUY Intricately embroidered silk shawls are prized in the area. Other popular local crafts include pottery, worked silver, and leather goods. Painted fans are displayed in many shops. Examine the work and the origin of the fan before paying top dollar; some are lovely hand-painted items, while others are imported from China. Young girls will likely want a colorful flamenco dress or flamenco-inspired apron.

Cannes, France

Note: *DCL typically docks along the French Riviera at* ***Villefranche, France,*** *but during a few sailings the* Magic *docks directly at Cannes, about 20 miles away.* *See Villefranche, page 322, for an in-depth profile.*

THE PORT Renowned for its annual film festival, which attracts A- to Z-listers from around the world, Cannes has few services directly at port. Its tender dock lies within a 10-minute walk of town, and most points of interest are located within a several-block radius. A tourist-information office is about five blocks from the dock, on the ground floor of **Palais des Festivals** (1 boulevard de la Croisette; ☎ +33 4 92 99 84 22; cannes-destination.com).

You can explore Cannes by foot or by tram; **Le Petit Train du Cinéma** departs regularly from **Boulevard de la Croisette,** Cannes's main thoroughfare, across from the Majestic hotel. Le Petit Train offers three tram tours: one along La Croisette (35 minutes); another in **Le Suquet** (Cannes's old quarter; 35 minutes); and a combination hour-long ride. Tours are available in English; visit cannes-petit-train.com for more information.

Taxis are easy to find but can be pricey. **Thrifty** and **Hertz** both have desks at 147 rue d'Antibes, about a 15-minute walk from the dock, but be aware that they close for several hours for lunch.

Civitavecchia (Rome), Italy

LANGUAGE Italian

HISTORY Rome is a major metropolis with a lengthy past. According to myth, the city was founded by the twins Romulus and Remus, who were abandoned as infants and suckled by a wolf until a shepherd found them and raised them as his own. From 290 B.C. to A.D. 235, Rome was the dominant force in the Western world, controlling most of Europe and the Mediterranean. Later, the Bishop of Rome (the Pope) established the city as the worldwide seat of the Roman Catholic Church. During the Renaissance, Rome became a hub for art and science.

WEATHER DCL stops at Civitavecchia, about 37 miles northwest of Rome, in June. Summers are hot, with average daytime highs in the low to upper 80s; temperatures in the high 90s aren't unusual. Nighttime summer lows average in the low 60s. Summer is the dry season, with rainfall averaging fewer than 2 inches per month.

THE PORT The pier offers nothing of note. It's a 10-minute walk from here to the train station, from which it's a 90-minute journey to Rome by bus or train.

TOURIST HIGHLIGHTS Rome is a major world city, and it's impossible to take in all it has to offer in a day—choose one or two highlights and plan to come back. Among the main attractions are **Vatican City,** home of the **Sistine Chapel** and **St. Peter's Basilica** (be aware of dress codes); the **Colosseum;** the **Spanish Steps;** the **Pantheon;** the **Trevi Fountain;** the **Catacombs;** the **Arch of Constantine;** and the myriad museums.

If you choose not to visit Rome or the countryside, you'll find smaller but still interesting sights in Civitavecchia itself. The most popular local attraction is **Fort Michelangelo,** built in 1503 to protect the village from invaders. Another

spot in town is the ancient baths, or **Terme Taurine,** built around natural hot sulfur springs. A seafront market that sells souvenirs, food, and, of course, gelato is open during the summer. A public beach is located near the Civitavecchia promenade.

WHAT TO EAT Pizza is available almost everywhere, as is pasta in almost every conceivable shape and size. Roasted or fried artichokes are a popular side dish. Salt cod, zucchini blossoms, and fresh and aged cheeses may be served as an appetizer. For dessert, gelato is a specialty—look for unique flavors such as licorice, melon, apple, or hazelnut.

WHAT TO BUY With every major fashion designer represented in Rome, haute couture and leather goods abound. In and around the Vatican, you'll find religious artifacts, books, and artwork for sale. Sports enthusiasts will want to purchase jerseys of the local soccer teams.

Dover, England, United Kingdom

LANGUAGE English

HISTORY Renowned for its stark white seaside cliffs, Dover enjoys an enviable location in the south of England: it's about a 2-hour drive from London and a Chunnel trip of less than an hour to Calais, France. The city's proximity to France has made it a strategic stronghold for centuries, with evidence of occupation by various tribes and sects dating back to medieval times. During the Tudor years, Dover was fortified to withstand Continental invasion, and the Napoleonic Wars saw the development of further defenses against the French.

In the mid-1800s, Dover endeavored to become a tourist center with seaside amenities. During the 20th century, the city saw extensive fighting during both World Wars as it defended the English Channel, with the aforementioned white cliffs inspiring a worldwide pop hit by British singer Vera Lynn during World War II.

WEATHER Disney cruises visit Dover during the summer and early fall. In July and August, temperatures average in the low 70s during the day and in the low 50s at night. September temperatures are slightly more brisk, with highs in the mid-60s and lows still in the 50s. Precipitation is low throughout the year, with typically less than 2 inches of rain per month from January through September.

THE PORT The town center is about a mile from the docks, which offer basic services. Taxis and a shuttle bus are readily available. Stop at the **Visitor Information Centre,** inside the **Dover Museum** on Old Town Gaol Street, for directions. Buses and trains, available within a mile of the town center, provide access to London, 2 hours away.

TOURIST HIGHLIGHTS If you're staying in town, a visit to **Dover Castle,** atop those famed white cliffs, is a must. Explore secret wartime tunnels, or interact with costumed docents who reenact aspects of King Henry II's court. **Canterbury Cathedral**—the mother church of the worldwide Anglican Communion and the site of religious pilgrimages since the days of Chaucer—is about a half hour away by car.

Many guests make their stay in Dover brief and focus instead on the sights of **London.** Must-sees there include the bustling **West End** theater district, **Buckingham Palace** and the Changing of the Guard, **Westminster Abbey,** the

British Museum, the **Tower of London,** the gigantic **London Eye** Ferris wheel, and much, much more.

WHAT TO EAT British food isn't limited to fish-and-chips and meat pies—to the contrary, it's exceedingly cosmopolitan. Restaurants serve most global cuisines: French, Indian, Italian, Spanish, and more.

WHAT TO BUY In Dover, look for mugs, T-shirts, and books related to the castle and the cliffs. London, of course, has shops offering nearly everything imaginable. Woolens such as sweaters and caps are popular items, as are depictions of the royal family and the city's famed red double-decker buses. And no trip to London would be complete without a stop at **Harrods,** where you can buy everything from gourmet meats and cheeses in the downstairs food halls to haute couture and pet puppies upstairs.

Genoa, Italy

LANGUAGE Italian

HISTORY Recorded history in Genoa begins in the third century B.C. The city was destroyed in the Punic Wars and later reconstructed as a defense point against the Carthaginians. During the Roman Empire and the Middle Ages, Genoa suffered various attacks from the Byzantines, the Lombards, and the Franks. In the 11th century, Genoa became an oligarchic republic, governed by members of several aristocratic families, who divvied up the city in a scenario worthy of an HBO series.

For the next five centuries, Genoa expanded its territory, both physically and via trade. In the early 1500s, an alliance between Genoa and the Spanish empire led to even more growth and ushered in the era of construction on the grand and grandiose palazzos and villas. A century later, conflicts with various European rulers resulted in a period of decline. In 1815, the Congress of Vienna ruled that Genoa be annexed to the Kingdom of Savoy, which several decades later became part of a united Italy. Between the 19th and 20th centuries, Genoa experienced urban growth and became an industrial port center. In 2004, Genoa was selected as one of two European Capitals of Culture by the European Union.

WEATHER DCL visits Genoa in June, when daily highs range from the mid-70s to the low 80s and nighttime lows average in the mid-60s to low 70s. Rainfall is low at this time, averaging just 1–2 inches per month.

THE PORT Basic services are available at the terminal, including taxis and shuttles; the train station is adjacent to the port. The pier is a 5- to 10-minute walk from town, where you'll find restaurants, shops, and other services. Guests with mobility issues should be aware that there are a number of steps on the way from the port into town.

TOURIST HIGHLIGHTS **Piazza de Ferrari** is the city's main square. The approach is via narrow cobblestone alleys, ending in a plaza with a large decorative fountain and a historic church. **Palazzo Ducale,** the seat of power for the *doges* (dukes) who ruled the city in the Middle Ages, is today an arts complex of galleries, restaurants, and a bookstore. Christopher Columbus spent his childhood in Genoa, in a stone house near the **Cloister of Sant'Andrea.** For students of architecture, points of interest include the **Cathedral of San Lorenzo,** which dates to the 6th century B.C.; **Palazzo San Giorgio,** the 15th-century home of the Bank of Saint George; and the **Palazzo Reale,** built in the 17th century. Kids may enjoy the **Acquario di Genova,** a large aquarium with a touch pool, as well as **Galata Museo del**

Mare, a maritime museum with many interactive exhibits including replica boats that you can walk inside. **La Lanterna** is the oldest operational lighthouse in the world.

WHAT TO EAT Genoa is known for its flavorful pestos, served on pasta, meat, or focaccia; also find focaccia topped with cheese, olives, and herbs. Other pasta options include *pansotti* (ravioli stuffed with ricotta and Parmesan cheeses and *prebuggion,* a mixture of leafy greens such as spinach and Swiss chard) and infinity symbol–shaped *corzetti. Torta pasqualina* (Easter tart) is a savory quichelike pie of vegetables, eggs, and cheese. Try the local vegetable minestrone soup for a classic taste of the region. Other popular soups make use of the region's plentiful fresh seafood: *ciuppin* (a fish stew similar to Italian-American cioppino) and *buridda,* a Ligurian favorite. Fish is fried, roasted, and served on large mixed platters, or in a *cappon magro,* an elaborate composed salad. Veal may be served rolled or stuffed with vegetables or herbs. Desserts often include apples or nuts. Italian wine, of course, makes a fine accompaniment to all parts of a meal.

WHAT TO BUY Olive oils, specialty vinegars, and wines are popular food purchases in every Italian port (have your alcohol purchases wrapped for travel). Cookware, ceramic pasta bowls, and serving tools are also in demand. Books and videos related to the life of Christopher Columbus are must-buys for many guests. Locally made gold and silver jewelry are typically lovely.

La Spezia, Italy

Note: *DCL uses both La Spezia and* **Livorno** *(see next profile) as ports for the Florence/Pisa region.*

LANGUAGE Italian

WEATHER DCL visits La Spezia in June during 2019, when daytime highs are in the mid-70s and nighttime lows are in the mid-60s. Average precipitation is about 2 inches per month in June.

THE PORT Cruise ships dock at the **Molo Garibaldi.** The train station and La Spezia proper are a 15-minute walk away.

TOURIST HIGHLIGHTS La Spezia is a charming town with several cafés and public beaches. The most popular attraction in the port is **Cinque Terre,** five small villages built into the rocks between the water and the hills. The villages are connected by a walking trail at **Riomaggiore,** a brief train ride away. La Spezia is also easily accessible by boat to the elegant resort of **Portfino.** For highlights of Florence and Pisa, see below.

Livorno, Italy

LANGUAGE Italian

HISTORY Florence and Tuscany are considered the birthplace of the Italian Renaissance. From about 1300 to 1500, it was the most important city in Europe. Its factious history includes several changes of government, including a period of rule by the storied Medici family. For part of the 1700s, Tuscany was an Austrian territory and then later a prefecture of the French department of Arno; in the 1800s, Italian rule returned. In modern times, Tuscany has become a center of tourism, trade, and financial services.

WEATHER DCL visits Livorno in May, June, and July. Daytime highs for this period average in the high 70s to low 80s, with nighttime lows ranging from the high 50s to mid-60s. Precipitation is moderate with an average rainfall of about 2 inches per month in the spring and summer.

THE PORT Large ships like the *Magic* dock in Livorno's container terminal. There are few nearby services, and pedestrian access is limited. Shuttle buses are provided for the 5-minute trip to **Piazza Grande** or the 10-minute trip to the bus or train station. Trains to **Pisa** depart about every half-hour, with the trip taking about an hour each way. Travel to **Florence** takes about 1½–2 hours each way.

TOURIST HIGHLIGHTS Museums abound in Florence, the most famous being the **Uffizi Gallery.** Other museums include the **Bargello,** the **Pitti Palace,** the **Museo dell'Opera del Duomo,** and (for all you fashionistas) the **Gucci Museum.** The city's iconic building is its cathedral, the **Duomo di Firenze,** where for a fee you can climb to the top for a bird's-eye view of the city. A stroll along the **Ponte Vecchio** is achingly romantic. The **Boboli Gardens** feature lush plantings and an interesting sculpture garden. In Pisa, you *must* see the **Leaning Tower.** The cathedral there, constructed of colorful hand-carved marble, is gorgeous as well.

WHAT TO EAT Try antipasto, which often consists of thinly sliced salami, pickled vegetables, and crostini. Most menus include pasta or risotto, salads, grilled meats, and olives. Florentine desserts may include gelatos, *schiacciata con l'uva* (a sweet grape bread), and *castagnaccio* (chestnut cake).

WHAT TO BUY Florence is a city of high style, with most major luxury retailers in evidence. Leather goods are ubiquitous; look for jackets, gloves, wallets, briefcases, and handbags in traditional and boldly colored dyes. Gold jewelry can be a lovely buy, but make sure it's a good deal. Crafty types may enjoy hand-marbled papers or wax letter seals. Murano glassware and jewelry are popular purchases. Marionettes are wonderful takeaway items for kids.

Lisbon, Portugal

LANGUAGE Portuguese

HISTORY Lisbon has long been a major trading port between Europe and North Africa. Its first inhabitants were pre-Celtic peoples, during the Neolithic Era; successive centuries brought occupations by the Iberians, Phoenicians, Greeks, Carthaginians, Romans, and Visigoths. During the eighth century A.D., Muslim Moors gained control of the region and ruled until Christian Crusaders arrived about 400 years later. Maritime exploration was a primary focus until the early 1700s.

In 1755, a major earthquake, attended by fires and tsunamis, destroyed most of the city's buildings; thus, much of Lisbon's architecture is newer than that of other large European cities. The area was rebuilt under the leadership of then-Secretary of State Sebastião José de Carvalho e Melo. Napoleon occupied Lisbon from 1807 until 1814, after which a new constitution was developed and the territory of Brazil was granted independence.

The early 20th century was a time of unrest, beginning with the assassination of King Carlos in 1908. In 1910, a coup d'état overthrew the monarchy and established the Portuguese Republic. The next 20 years saw more than 40 separate changes of government. The authoritarian Estado Novo (New State, aka

Second Republic) regime ruled from 1926 to 1974, when it was deposed in a military coup known as the Carnation Revolution. In 1986, Portugal joined the European Community, a decision that spurred major redevelopment.

WEATHER DCL visits Lisbon in summer, when daytime highs average in the low 80s and nighttime lows average in the low to mid-60s. Summers are dry, with average rainfall of less than an inch per month. Expect sunny skies.

THE PORT The terminal, which has basic shops, ATMs, and a few cafés and restaurants, lies on the Tagus River, a 20-minute walk from tourist sites. Shuttles and taxis are readily available, as are light-rail and bus service.

TOURIST HIGHLIGHTS The **Alfama** neighborhood is a hilly enclave composed of tiny shops, restaurants, and clubs where traditional *fado* music (think Portuguese blues) is played and sung. While you're in the area, visit the **Castelo de São Jorge,** a Moorish church on Lisbon's highest hill—the views are spectacular. Reach it using **Tram 28,** Lisbon's version of a San Francisco cable car.

The **Belem** district is home to several notable attractions, including the **Monastery of Jerónimos,** the **Monument to the Discoveries,** and the **Museu Nacional dos Coches,** home to the world's largest collection of royal coaches. The **National Tile Museum** displays paintings as well as intricate mosaics. The **Oceanarium,** Europe's largest indoor aquarium, features birds as well as fish and is popular with kids. **Casa das Histórias,** in the seaside suburb of Cascais, showcases the work of Surrealist artist Paula Rego.

WHAT TO EAT Contrary to what you might expect, Portuguese food isn't particularly spicy, but it's definitely delicious. Fish and shellfish dominate many menus. The national dish is *bacalhau,* or salt cod. You can find it prepared with vegetables or fried with rice, eggs, onions, and olives. *Porco alentejana* is pork loin cooked with clams and potatoes. Warm up with *caldo verde* ("green soup"), made with cabbage, onions, potatoes, and *chouriço* sausage. Snack on *presunto,* a dry, cured ham that's somewhat like Italian prosciutto, along with local cheese made from cow, sheep, or goat milk. For a sweet treat, try *pasteis de nata*—egg-custard tarts that are typically topped with cinnamon and powdered sugar; try to get some fresh from the oven. Adult beverages include *ginjinha,* a strong sour-cherry liqueur that's sometimes served from a chocolate shot glass. And no trip to Lisbon would be complete without sampling some port or the many other varieties of fortified wine.

WHAT TO BUY Ceramic tiles are a typical Portuguese souvenir; look for hand-painted tiles in shops throughout Lisbon. Variations may include framed ceramic artwork or coasters. Portugal is a major exporter of cork; take-home treasures made with it include housewares and handbags. Fragrant **Claus Porto** soaps are a thoughtful gift to bring back for a friend or a housesitter—not only do they smell wonderful, but the ornate wrapping paper is beautiful in itself. Foodies will want to take home local olive oils or bottles of port.

Marseille, France

LANGUAGE French

HISTORY Marseille was founded by Greek traders in the seventh century B.C. and thereafter quickly became a trading center for the region; the

port has continued to be important to the city throughout its existence. In 480 B.C., the city became a Roman holding, after which it was conquered in turn by the Visigoths, the Ostrogoths, and the Franks. From the seventh to ninth centuries A.D., Marseille was ruled by the Merovingian and Carolingian Dynasties. In 1214, a part of town known as the Ville Basse became an independent republic. In the early 18th century, Marseille lost about half its population to the Black Death (bubonic plague). In the 19th century, the conquest of Algiers in northern Africa and the opening of the Suez Canal in Egypt led to increased port activity at home. Today, Marseille serves an industrial and commercial center for southern France.

WEATHER DCL visits Marseille in June and July, when daytime highs average in the high 70s to mid-80s and nighttime lows average in the low to mid-60s. Rainfall during this time is particularly low, averaging less than 1 inch per month.

THE PORT Ships dock in an industrial area with few nearby services. The city proper, about 5 miles away from the pier, is accessible by shuttle, bus, or taxi. The central tourist district is quite hilly, with narrow streets and steep staircases, so visitors with mobility issues should take note.

TOURIST HIGHLIGHTS **Vieux Port,** Marseille's old town, is the perfect place for a harbor stroll, with many cafés, restaurants, and shops; the waterfront is home to both yachts and fishing vessels, which make for lovely photographs. The **Basilica of Notre Dame de la Garde** sits atop one of Marseille's highest points, affording stunning views, It's the most important city landmark that's visible from afar. A large, gilded Madonna tops the belfry. The **Abbey of St. Victor,** one of the oldest buildings in the area, dates to early-Christian and Carolingian times and shelters a 13th-century Black Madonna (a wooden sculpture depicting a dark-skinned Virgin Mary). Another impressive religious structure is the **Cathédrale de la Major,** notable for its massive domed towers. The **MuCEM** (Musée des Civilisations de l'Europe et de la Méditerranée) focuses on the history of Mediterranean civilization, and the **Musée d'Histoire de Marseille** covers Marseille in particular.

WHAT TO EAT The signature dish of Marseille is bouillabaisse, the well-seasoned fish stew. The traditional Marseillais version is a two-course meal—fish soup followed by the fish that was used to make the soup—so expect it to be expensive. A rather more acquired taste is *pieds et paquets,* slow-cooked lambs' feet accompanied by tripe. Side dishes often include couscous, a flavorful result of Marseille's commercial connection with North Africa. In addition to French bread, try *navettes,* boat-shaped cookies flavored with orange. French wine is an excellent—nay, near mandatory—choice. For something stronger, sip *pastis,* an anise-flavored liqueur.

WHAT TO BUY *Santons* ("little saints") are traditional Christmas nativity figurines typical of the area. For the active family, look for a *pétanque* set—wooden or metallic balls and other accoutrements used for playing an outdoor game similar to lawn bowling or Italian bocce. When it comes to apparel, striped sailing sweaters and other nautical clothing will remind you of the French seashore. If you want a consumable gift, a bottle of pastis or tinned sardines will put you in a Mediterranean mood.

Naples, Italy

LANGUAGE Italian

HISTORY Naples has been continuously inhabited since at least the second millennium B.C. During the first century B.C., Naples played a role in the merging of Greek and Roman cultures. Following the fall of the Western Roman Empire, Naples became the capital of the Kingdom of Naples and remained so from the late 1200s to the early 1800s. (Today's Italy consisted of assorted independent states until the process of unification began in 1815.) During World War II, Naples was the most bombed Italian city. Many buildings in outer sections of the city were constructed as part of Naples's restoration.

WEATHER Daytime highs during late spring and early summer, when DCL visits, range from the mid-70s to the mid-80s. Nighttime lows during that period fall into the low 60s. Rainfall averages less than 2 inches for the month.

THE PORT Few services are available directly at the port, but from here it's a 15- to 20-minute walk into the city.

TOURIST HIGHLIGHTS In Naples proper, see the **Museo Archeologico Nazionale.** Other historic sites include the **Castel Nuovo,** the **Museo di Capodimonte,** and the **Duomo di Napoli.** Fifteen miles southeast of Naples are the ruins of **Pompeii,** where you can wander the streets of an ancient town preserved in time by the volcanic eruption of Mt. Vesuvius. If you're in the mood for a beach day, take a hydrofoil boat to the island of **Capri.**

WHAT TO EAT Naples is the birthplace of pizza, and **Antica Pizzeria Port'Alba** (founded in 1738) was the first establishment to serve it, though it's certainly not the only one you should consider. The classic version is the *pizza margherita,* a simple pie of tomato, basil, and fresh mozzarella. Neapolitan cuisine is also rich in seafood, often sauced with tomatoes, garlic, and olive oil. House-made mozzarella is sold in many shops. *Limoncello* (lemon liqueur) is the adult beverage of the region; sip it alone or mixed into refreshing cocktails. Regional desserts include *baba* (a small cake soaked in rum or other spirits), *zeppole* (like a doughnut, often filled with custard), and *sfogliatelle* (a shell-shaped pastry). **Odin-Gay** chocolatier is a local favorite.

WHAT TO BUY Bring back some limoncello if you want to taste Naples at home. If you're looking for jewelry, artisans here work in 18-karat gold and carved coral. Many visitors bring home replicas of the historical artifacts they see in Pompeii. Various shops sell locally carved wooden Christmas ornaments. In Capri, handmade sandals are a stylish find.

Salerno, Italy

LANGUAGE Italian

HISTORY Salerno was established as a Roman colony in the second century B.C.; before that, it was inhabited by the Etruscans and the Samnites. The region was later variously occupied by the Goths, Byzantines, Longobards, and Normans. The oldest medical school in Europe was founded here in the 11th century. The 16th century saw a period of conflict with Spain which resulted in a regional economic decline. In the late 1600s, the city suffered several catastrophes, including earthquakes and plague, causing significant population decline. The Spanish slowly revived the city, and by the 18th century the region was largely rebuilt. In 1799, Salerno became part of the Parthenopean Republic and saw a period of Napoleonic rule. Following

the unification of Italy (1815–1871), building and development continued until World War II, during which the town sustained much damage.

WEATHER DCL visits Salerno in June. Daytime highs for the month average in the low 80s, with nighttime lows in the mid-60s. Rainfall is minimal; expect less than an inch per month during the summer.

THE PORT Most cruises dock about 2 miles from town. Services at the port are minimal. Shuttles are available, as are taxis and a ferry service to the Amalfi coast (the typical fee is €8 per person).

TOURIST HIGHLIGHTS Many guests take the ferry to the gorgeous seaside town of **Amalfi.** In Salerno, the **Duomo di Salerno** is a landmark church that features a crypt with the tomb of St. Matthew, adorned with lovely frescoes. The **Museo Diocesano San Matteo di Salerno** houses more relics of St. Matthew, as well as an extensive art collection. **Minerva's Garden** is a terraced orchard at the base of a medieval castle; plants in the gardens were used for therapeutic purposes when Salerno was one of the first centers for medical education. **Museo Roberto Papi** is a quaint museum comprising the collection of a physician who was interested in medical equipment. Trace the history of surgery and medical cleanliness practices in its halls. If you have teens with a macabre sense of humor, **Panic Room Horror Bakery** may be the escape room that's the highlight of their vacation.

WHAT TO EAT Salerno is an Italian-food lover's paradise. Freshly made pizzas and pastas are typically topped with marinara, garlic, oil, and basil. You'll see familiar pasta shapes, but one indigenous to the region is long, hollow *perciatelli.* Most meats are served grilled with vegetables. Popular fish dishes include fried anchovies, steamed mussels with garlic and parsley, and octopus cooked in tomatoes. Fresh cheeses are available everywhere. Local chestnuts, hazelnuts, and walnuts are found in many desserts.

WHAT TO BUY Salerno is known for its lace, which is often sold as table coverings or women's clothing. Pair a lace dress with leather sandals purchased on the street. Find pottery shaped like local citrus fruits, or take home a bottle of locally crafted limoncello.

Toulon, France

Note: *See the earlier entry for* ***Cannes*** *(page 313) and the entry for* ***Villefranche*** *(see next page) for information on additional attractions in the region.*

LANGUAGE French

HISTORY Greek settlers occupied what is now Toulon as far back as the seventh century B.C. By the second century B.C., the Romans had taken over; subsequent centuries saw control of the region bounce back and forth between the Arabs and the Romans. Christianity took root in the first century A.D., and an era of cathedral building began. The area became part of France in the 1400s, and Toulon later became a key naval port and military stronghold. Shipbuilding became a primary industry in the 18th century. During World War II, the French destroyed much of the city's harbor and shipyards to prevent them from being seized by occupying Germans; in 1944, Toulon was the first French city liberated by Allied forces. Today, the area is again known for naval construction as well as winemaking, fishing, and tourism.

WEATHER DCL visits Toulon in June. Daytime highs for the month average in the high 70s, with nighttime lows averaging in the mid-50s. Rainfall is typically minimal, averaging less than an inch per month in June.

THE PORT The cruise terminal was built in 2016, but services are minimal. Toulon proper is about a 10-minute drive from the port. Taxis and shuttles are readily available.

TOURIST HIGHLIGHTS Take a cable car to the top of **Mont Faron** for lovely views. The **Fondation Carmignac** gallery exhibits works from artists such as Andy Warhol and Jeff Koons. Kids will enjoy area beaches such as **Plagues du Morillon.**

Toulon is home to several museums, including the **Musée d'Art,** featuring paintings from the 1400s to the present; the **Musée Mémorial du Débarquement et de la Libération en Provence,** a WWII museum atop Mont Faron that commemorates the Allied liberation of the city; and the **Musée de la Marine,** with a focus on shipping. The city of **Marseille** (see profile on page 318) is about an hour away by train or car.

WHAT TO EAT The region's food is typically Mediterranean. Traditional seafood dishes include octopus stew and mussels with garlic. Fresh vegetables seasoned with thyme, rosemary, lemon, and olive oil appear on many local menus. A tapenade of puréed olives on crusty French bread and accompanied by a glass of wine, or a hearty bouillabaisse seasoned with Provençale herbs, is as Toulon as a meal can get. For a bite of something sweet, try *chichi frégi,* fried dough flavored with olive oil and orange blossoms (think a French take on a Mexican churro).

WHAT TO BUY Locally produced goods include flavored sea salts and perfumed soaps. The luxury-clothing brand **Souleiado** has an outpost in Toulon. If you're shopping for food gifts, lavender honey is a lovely representation of the area.

Villefranche, France

LANGUAGES French, Italian

HISTORY The Greeks were the first organized human presence on what is now known as the French Riviera. They were followed by the Romans in the eighth century B.C. Before the Dark Ages, the region saw invasions from the Visigoths, Burgundians, and Ostrogoths, later followed by threats from the Saracens and Normans.

Stability came in the 13th century with the House of Grimaldi, which took power in what is now Nice, Antibes, and Monaco. Tourism took hold in the late 1700s, when wealthy Brits began arriving to take advantage of the climate and fine air quality.

WEATHER DCL visits the French Riviera in June and July, when it's warm and dry. Daytime highs average in the low 70s to low 80s; nighttime lows average in the mid-60s. Precipitation is low, with less than 2 inches of rainfall for the month.

THE PORT Disney ships anchor in the harbor and tender to the terminal in central Villefranche. Several small shops and cafés, along with train and bus stations, are within walking distance. A soap factory in town, **La Savonnerie de Villefranche,** lets visitors watch its work. If you're staying in port and looking for relaxation, the public beach is about a 10-minute walk away from the old town.

TOURIST HIGHLIGHTS Most major and minor points on the French Riviera are less than an hour from port. In **Nice,** stroll along the **Promenade des Anglais,** or visit the **Cours Saleya** market for sweet and savory treats. In **Cannes,** look for art galleries on the **Rue d'Antibes. Monte Carlo** is famous for luxury shopping, soap opera–worthy royalty, and the **Grand Casino,** where you can try your hand if you're in a gambling mood. **Èze** is a medieval-era hilltop village from which you can see into neighboring Monaco and Italy. **Grasse,** the perfume capital of the world, offers tours of various fragrance factories where you can concoct your own signature scent.

WHAT TO EAT Food along the French Riviera tends to be lighter than other regional French cuisines. Representative dishes include bouillabaisse (fish stew), salade niçoise (tuna, tomato, eggs, and olives), pizzalike pissaladière, crêpes, and, of course, lots of pastries.

WHAT TO BUY In Monte Carlo, look for souvenirs associated with the late Princess Grace and other Grimaldis, as well as trinkets representing the Grand Prix auto race. In Cannes, you'll find many items emblazoned with the logo of the city's world-renowned film festival. Throughout the area, look for fine wines, linens, and fragrances.

MEXICO

Note: *In 2018 the U.S. Department of State issued an update to its previous warnings about travel to Mexico. In a nutshell: US citizens traveling in certain parts of Mexico have been the victims of violent crimes, including homicide, kidnapping, carjacking, and robbery. Most of the homicides appear to have been targeted hits related to organized crime, but turf battles between rival criminal groups have resulted in shootings during daylight hours, injuring innocent bystanders. This general warning applies in addition to the separate State Department advisory for* ***Mazatlán*** *on page 326.*

CRUISES SAIL FROM San Diego

SHIP *Wonder*

CRUISE LENGTH 3, 5, and 7 nights

DATES March, April, September, and October

WHAT TO PACK These DCL cruises have a "Halloween on the High Seas" theme, so bring along your costumes of choice in addition to sunscreen and such if you want to join the fun on board.

PROS

- Can be very affordable, particularly if you live on the West Coast.
- Short cruises are easy on your schedule.

CONS

- These cruises are marketed to families, but the fact that they take place while school is in session could make scheduling a problem.
- There's really nothing that sets these itineraries apart from comparable ones on any other cruise line.
- The Mexican holiday that corresponds to Halloween in the United States—**Día de Los Muertos,** or Day of the Dead (November 1)—doesn't have our holiday's months-long commercialized buildup. Chances are you won't find any preliminary festivities going on while you're in port, even on sailings taking place in mid-October.

SIGNATURE PORT ADVENTURES The usual: sightseeing, dolphin excursions, beach pursuits, shopping, partying

CLASSIC DISNEY ADD-ON Disneyland

COMMENTS These ports are standard stops for most cruise lines—the selling point for the autumn sail dates is Disney's onboard Halloween decor. For the spring sail dates, there's little to differentiate these cruises from those offered by other lines.

Cabo San Lucas, Mexico

LANGUAGE Spanish

HISTORY Native inhabitants of the Cabo San Lucas region include the Pericu peoples. European influence was minimal until the early 1800s. Industry and trade took hold in the early 1900s, when commercial fishing companies began to capitalize on the local tuna. The 1970s saw a surge in tourism, due in part to the completion of Federal Highway 1, linking Cabo to other parts of Mexico.

WEATHER Disney cruises visit Cabo San Lucas in spring and fall. Average daytime highs in March and April are in the low to mid-80s, with night-time lows in the mid-60s. Rainfall is minimal in the spring, averaging less than an inch per month. Average daytime highs in the fall are in the high 80s, with nighttime lows in the low 70s. Rainfall averages about 3–4 inches per month in September, and 2–3 inches in October.

THE PORT Cruise ships anchor in the harbor and tender guests into the marina. Once at the marina, the downtown area is a 10- to 15-minute walk away. Taxis are also readily available. A large mall near the marina offers basic services, as well as an array of luxury-brand outposts such as **Tiffany** and **Cartier.** For those looking to stock up on necessities, there's a **Walmart** at Plaza San Lucas.

TOURIST HIGHLIGHTS The cruise ship anchors in the harbor and tenders guests into the marina. White-sand beaches are the major attraction—relax on the sand or take part in active water pursuits such as snorkeling, sailing, parasailing, or sport fishing. For those wishing to be active and dry, Cabo is a golf paradise, boasting numerous world-class courses. Zip lining is a wonderful excursion for guests with a daredevil streak. Whale-watching and interactive dolphin experiences are popular activities. Those looking to enjoy art and culture will want to visit the **Vitrofusion Glass Blowing Factory** to watch artisans create recycled glassworks, or stay in town to explore the **Iglesia de San Lucas,** a Spanish mission with many of its original features still intact.

WHAT TO EAT Cabo is home to fine-dining establishments serving a variety of cuisines, including Italian and American, but for an authentic taste of Mexico, try some street tacos, quesadillas, or tortas. Rocker Sammy Hagar's **Cabo Wabo Cantina** offers a more touristy take, featuring shrimp, steak, and chicken dishes as well as catch-of-the-day specials, served with a heaping earful of rock and roll on the side.

WHAT TO BUY Along with the typical seaside tourist trinkets, shirts, caps, and shot glasses emblazoned with the Cabo Wabo logo are an obligatory purchase for many visitors. Foodies will want to take home the local hot sauce;

look also for soaps and lotions made with imitation turtle oil or scented with local spices. Mexican tequila and Damiana, a liqueur made with an herb that supposedly has aphrodisiac qualities, are must-buy items for some.

Ensenada, Mexico

LANGUAGE Spanish

HISTORY The Yuma Indians were the first known inhabitants of the region. Portugal's João Rodrigues Cabrilho (Juan Rodríguez Cabrillo in Spanish) conducted the first European exploration of the area in the mid-1500s. Ensenada was founded September 17, 1542, as San Mateo. In 1602 it was renamed Ensenada de Todos Santos ("Bay of All Saints") by Sebastián Vizcaíno, a Spanish explorer and diplomat. The Jesuits were the city's first permanent settlers, in the 17th century. Following a Jesuit ouster in 1768, Dominican brothers took control of the region. Ensenada became the capital of Baja California in 1882; its growth was interrupted by the Mexican Revolution. In the 1920s, prohibition of alcohol in the United States played a role in the eventual rebound of the area, as thirsty Americans began to look south of the border for sources of booze. Today, tourism and fishing are prominent industries.

unofficial **TIP**
Many cruisers use a stop in Ensenada to stock up on medications for which a prescription is needed in the United States but not in Mexico. To help ensure that your purchase doesn't get confiscated by U.S. Customs, carefully review the information at these websites: tinyurl.com/fdadrugimporting, tinyurl.com/deadrugschedules, and tinyurl.com/cbpprohibitedrestricteditems.

WEATHER DCL visits Ensenada in the spring and fall. Average daytime highs in the summer bookend months are in the mid-70s, with average nighttime lows in the mid- to high 50s. Rainfall averages fewer than 2 inches per month throughout the year.

THE PORT Cruise ships dock in the same area as commercial and fishing vessels. Near the dock, numerous pop-up vendors sell typical tourist items; there is also a drugstore along with a few cafés. From here it's a 15-minute walk to the **Avenida López Mateos** tourist area. Taxis and shuttles are also available.

TOURIST HIGHLIGHTS **La Bufadora** is a natural marine blowhole about 20 miles south of town. The best beaches are 5 miles south of Ensenada, in the small town of **Chapultepec.** Activities there include horseback riding, surf fishing, and Jet Skiing. **Riviera del Pacífico,** formerly an exclusive and glamorous hotel (and, according to local lore, the birthplace of the margarita), is now a civic center. If you're in the mood for some culture, try the **Museo de Historia** or the **Estero Beach Museum** for a look at local art and artifacts.

WHAT TO EAT Two words: fresh fish. Look for halibut, clams, oysters, abalone, tuna, and more. The signature dish is the fish taco, typically prepared with batter-fried white fish, shredded cabbage, avocado, and a spicy mayonnaise. (If you order from a stand or a street cart, exercise caution—if there's a crowd, indicating rapid turnover, then the food is generally safe to eat.) When it comes to tipples, you'll find a large selection of beers in most restaurants, as well as the ubiquitous margarita in all manner of incarnations. Or pick up a bottle of vino at one of the area wineries.

WHAT TO BUY Tacky-T-shirt stands abound near the dock—make a game of trying to find the most cringe-worthy examples. You'll also find the usual piñatas, painted maracas, and straw hats. Blankets, leather goods, and logoed shot glasses are everywhere. Note that many items advertised as silver are really silver-plated tin or other soft metal. Numerous stores sell Cuban cigars.

Mazatlán, Mexico

Note: *The U.S. State Department urges caution when visiting this port and its environs; see details below.*

LANGUAGE Spanish

HISTORY The original occupants of Mazatlán were the native Totorames. The first European settlers were the Spaniards, who arrived in 1531. During the early 1600s, English and French pirates used the area's sheltered coastline to ambush passing merchant ships. In 1821, Mexico gained its independence from Spain, and Mazatlán began to prosper as a port city as well as the capital of the state of Sinaloa. In the second half of the 1800s, Mazatlán changed hands multiple times, moving from US occupation during the Mexican-American War in 1847 to French domination a few years later, culminating with Mexican independence in the 1860s. Port growth continued in the later 1800s with the construction of a series of lighthouses and a link with railway systems. The Mexican Revolution, which lasted from 1910 to 1917, put a hold on growth in the early 1900s. While a slight rebound occurred after the revolution, the Great Depression and WWII dampened Mexico's economy. The economy stabilized with an influx of tourism beginning in the 1960s, followed by the growth of the area fishing industry.

WEATHER DCL visits Mazatlán in April, May, and October. Daytime temperatures in the spring and fall average in the mid- to high 80s, with nighttime lows dipping only into the low 70s. Spring rainfall is minimal, with precipitation averaging less than an inch per month. Rain is heavier in October, when average rainfall is 4–5 inches per month.

THE PORT Ships typically dock at a commercial port, with guests transported to the cruise terminal by tram. The terminal has shops, liquor stores, and (depending on when you go) some rather aggressive pitchmen trying to entice you to buy into time-share condos. **Old Town Mazatlán** is a 1-mile walk from the cruise terminal; taxis are plentiful and can provide a 5-minute ride to the center of the city. The **Zona Dorada** ("Golden Zone"), where the beaches and touristy stuff are centered, is a 20-minute cab ride away. There are rental-car desks at the pier.

Note: In July 2018, the U.S. State Department issued an updated travel warning for parts of Mexico. The state of Sinaloa, in which Mazatlán is located, is rated Warning Level 4—Do Not Travel. The warning states:

> *Violent crime is widespread. Criminal organizations are based and operating in Sinaloa state. U.S. government employees are prohibited from travel in most areas of the state. In areas where travel is permitted, the following restrictions are in place: For Mazatlán, U.S. government travel is permitted only in Zona Dorada, the historic town center, and direct routes to and from these locations and the airport or cruise ship terminal.*

If you decide to disembark in Mazatlán, exercise caution late at night and in the early morning, and don't stray beyond the main tourist areas.

TOURIST HIGHLIGHTS The beaches in Mazatlán are top-notch. **Las Gaviotas Beach** and **Sabolo Beach** are popular and, as a result, crowded—**Olas Altas Beach** is a more relaxing choice. **Stone Island** offers horseback riding and snorkeling expeditions. Architecture enthusiasts will want to visit **Immaculate Conception Basilica,** with its ornate domed ceilings. The **Teatro Ángela Peralta,** a 19th-century theater named for a beloved Mexican opera singer, has elaborate wrought-iron balconies and an ornate period interior; today, it shows movies and presents concerts and dance performances. The **Archeological Museum of Mazatlán** offers a look into the pre-European history and culture of the area. Kids will like the **Acuario Mazatlán,** an aquarium housing more than 250 species of sea life. **El Faro Lighthouse,** at 500 feet above sea level, is the second highest natural lighthouse in the world and makes for a nice hike.

WHAT TO EAT Mazatlán is a fishing town; you'll find all manner of seafood in its restaurants and cafés. Shrimp is a specialty: shrimp cocktail marinated in green chiles and lime, shrimp quesadillas, fried shrimp, shrimp ceviche, bacon-wrapped shrimp stuffed with cheese . . . shades of Bubba Gump! Also try *posole,* a soup made with hominy and sometimes pork; *birria,* a stew of goat or lamb; or *chorreadas,* thick corn tortillas covered with meat, onions, and cheese (think a rustic quesadilla). Your side dish may include prickly pear cactus.

You'll find many varieties of beer here; if you want something sans booze, look for *agua de jamaica,* a berry-colored, tealike drink made from boiled hibiscus flowers mixed with sugar and lime, or creamy, rice-based *horchata,* flavored with sugar, vanilla, and cinnamon.

WHAT TO BUY The **Mazatlán Arts and Crafts Center,** in the Zona Dorada, sells a wide array of artisanal products from all over Mexico. Popular items include textiles, such as beach wraps, embroidered shirts, and serapes. Leather sandals and handbags are popular purchases as well, along with handmade housewares and decorative items in wood or pottery. Silver jewelry is everywhere, but weigh the quality against the price. *Heads-up:* Diamonds are tax-free in Mexico! In addition to crafts, the **Mercado del Centro** has food vendors who sell spices and local spirits; bargaining is customary, so put on your haggling hat.

Puerto Vallarta, Mexico

LANGUAGE Spanish

HISTORY The native settlers were the ancient Aztlán peoples. European influence began in the early 1500s, when Spaniards, including Hernán Cortés, took control of the region. During the 17th and 18th centuries, the area was a known shelter for pirates and smugglers. Organized trade began to blossom in 1859, when the Union en Cuale mining company started operating in the region. In the early 1900s, the mining trade gave way to fruit farming, which then ceded influence to the growing tourism industry. Since the 1950s, Puerto Vallarta has been a resort and cruise destination.

WEATHER Disney cruises visit Puerto Vallarta in spring and fall. Average daytime highs during those seasons are in the mid-80s to low 90s, with average nighttime lows in the low to mid-70s. Precipitation is relatively

low in May, averaging fewer than 2 inches of rainfall. October is slightly wetter, averaging about 3 inches for the month.

THE PORT From the **Marina Vallarta Terminal,** it's an easy walk to several restaurants, small shops, and hotels with bars. A full-size **Walmart** is about a 10- to 15-minute walk from the port, allowing you to pick up any basic necessity at a relatively reasonable price. Downtown Puerto Vallarta is about 3 miles from the port, accessible via taxi or bus.

TOURIST HIGHLIGHTS The beaches are the big draw here. Snooze by the waves or enjoy more-active pursuits such as snorkeling or biking. Animal lovers can enjoy dolphin excursions or watch whales and turtles. **El Centro,** Puerto Vallarta's downtown, features churches with charming colonial detail. Tequila manufacturing and tasting is a big draw to this area. Be sure to sample several varieties; you'll be amazed at the differences.

WHAT TO EAT Not surprisingly, you'll find tacos, taquitos, tostadas, and enchiladas on local menus, along with fresh seafood (try red snapper or marlin served with spices and lime). Those in the mood to party will find no shortage of margaritas, daiquiris, and beer.

WHAT TO BUY Puerto Vallarta shopping caters to the tourist trade. You'll find silver, ceramics, leather, and woven goods in many forms, as well as the ubiquitous T-shirts and trinkets portside. Haggling is common with vendors by the beaches, so if you don't like the price you see, feel free to propose something lower. Several modern malls in the area sell brand-name cruise wear at typically reasonable prices. Foodies will want to bring home local chocolates or Mexican spices.

San Diego, California

LANGUAGE English

HISTORY San Diego is the site of the first European settlement in what is now California, a result of exploration conducted in 1542 by João Rodrigues Cabrilho of Portugal. Subsequent European visitors were primarily from Spain. The first permanent mission in the area was established in 1769, with a population of Spanish settlers arriving in 1774. In 1821 Mexico claimed the area in the Mexican War for Independence. In 1850, California became a state. A significant naval presence began in 1901, solidifying San Diego as a major West Coast port. Today, San Diego is a center of high-tech industry.

WEATHER Disney cruises visit San Diego in April, May, September, and October. The average daytime high temperatures in April and May are in the mid- to high 60s, with average nighttime lows in the mid- to high 50s. Average daytime highs in September and October are in the mid-70s, while average nighttime lows are in the mid- to low 60s. Precipitation during all four months is minimal, with an average of less than an inch of rainfall per month.

THE PORT Cruise ships dock at the **B Street Cruise Terminal,** directly adjacent to downtown. An upscale mall, **Horton Plaza,** is a 10-minute walk away. Public transportation and taxis are readily available for more-distant jaunts.

TOURIST HIGHLIGHTS **Balboa Park** is home to gorgeous gardens and 15 different museums, including the **San Diego Museum of Art** and the **San Diego Natural History Museum.** The **San Diego Zoo** is one of the few places in the United States where you can see giant pandas. Theme-park fans will want to visit **SeaWorld** and **Legoland.** The **Gaslamp Quarter** and the

San Diego missions provide insight into the history of the area. **Tijuana, Mexico,** is 17 miles south of San Diego; check on legal restrictions if you plan to drive there.

WHAT TO EAT San Diego is a major metropolitan area whose restaurants serve all major cuisines. The offerings at many local restaurants are influenced by nearby Mexico: quesadillas, tacos, burritos, enchiladas, and such. Because of the city's seaside location, fresh fish is another local menu staple. A regional favorite is cioppino, a stew with fish, clams, shrimp, squid, and mussels, often served with toast.

WHAT TO BUY Sports fans will want to purchase jerseys of the local **Padres** baseball team or the **San Diego State University Aztecs** sports teams. Pick up clothing or shell-based jewelry, or choose some art reflecting the surf culture. Local tequila is another popular gift.

NORTHERN EUROPE, BRITISH ISLES, *and* NORWAY

CRUISES SAIL FROM Dover, Copenhagen

SHIP *Magic*

CRUISE LENGTHS 7–12 nights

DATES Summer

WHAT TO PACK Binoculars, warm clothing

SIGNATURE PORT ADVENTURE It's all about the fjords.

CLASSIC DISNEY ADD-ON If you have any money left after your cruise, **Adventures by Disney** will gladly snap it up.

COMMENTS There was this movie called *Frozen* that was mildly popular a few years ago. We're not saying that Disney decided the best way for DCL to take advantage of this was to sail to Arendelle—sorry, *Norway*—but there are definitely a lot of tie-ins on the cruise. But there's also scenery that can be appreciated only from a cruise ship.

PROS	CONS
■ The scenery is spectacular.	■ We really hope you enjoyed *Frozen*.
■ It's a family-friendly way to see Northern Europe.	■ Food in port can be quite expensive.
■ Most of your meals are included in what are some very expensive places to visit.	■ These are among the most expensive cruises DCL offers—and that's not including airfare.

Akureyri, Iceland

LANGUAGE Icelandic

HISTORY The first known Viking settlement in Iceland occurred in the ninth century A.D. Transient fishing camps formed and dissipated for many hundreds of years, with the first permanent settlement established in 1778; even so, the population numbered fewer than 100 for many more years.

Growth in earnest began in the mid-1800s, when Icelanders began to appreciate the sound natural port and fine agricultural conditions. During World War II, the island served as an air base for British and Norwegian troops, and the U.S. Air Force maintained a presence here until 2006. (Iceland, however, has no armed forces of its own and is considered the most peaceful country in the world.) Today, fishing and fish processing are Iceland's main industries, with a growing tourism sector. Perhaps the country's best-known export is Björk, the aggressively quirky singer-songwriter.

With a population of just under 20,000, the town of Akureyri is small by US standards, but it's the second-largest urban area in Iceland.

WEATHER Disney cruises visit in July, when daytime highs average in the mid-50s and nighttime lows average in the mid-40s. Typical July rainfall is 2–3 inches per month.

THE PORT Services at the port are few, but much of Akureyri is accessible by foot or bike. Taxis and free buses will take you on the short ride into town, where bike rentals and bike tours are available.

TOURIST HIGHLIGHTS Akureyri is home to several small but notable museums, including the **Safnasafið New Folk and Outsider Art Museum,** the **Aviation Museum,** and the **Industry Museum.** For an outdoor experience, try whale-watching, fishing, horseback riding, or taking a dip in a geothermal pool.

WHAT TO EAT Not surprisingly, seafood is a specialty of many restaurants in this fishing nation. Salmon, char, and mussels are particularly popular. Fish is prepared sushi-style or in traditional smoked, salted, and cured forms. (*Hákarl,* or fermented shark, is best left to Andrew Zimmern wannabes.) Beef and dairy are also popular. *Skýr* is a tangy dairy product native to Iceland; similar in flavor and consistency to Greek yogurt, it's technically a cheese. Burgers are easy to find; locals like them topped with béarnaise sauce and French fries. You can also try exotic game such as puffin, reindeer, and whale. Several local bakeries sell a variety of breads, pastries, and doughnuts. The only microbrewery in Iceland, **Kaldi,** is a 20-minute drive from Akureyri.

WHAT TO BUY A popular stop is the **Christmas Garden** shop, which offers a wide array of candles, ornaments, decorations, and ginger-scented snacks. Viking and troll memorabilia can be found almost everywhere. Knit textiles such as sweaters and mittens make for cozy mementos of your trip. You can even buy a reindeer hide to serve as a rug or blanket back home.

Ålesund, Norway

LANGUAGE Norwegian

HISTORY Ålesund has existed as a fishing village since Viking times. According to local lore, the Viking chief Rollo hailed from the area. In 1904, a major fire destroyed much of the town, leaving nearly 10,000 residents homeless. Germany's Kaiser Wilhelm assisted in the rebuilding effort by sending ships full of construction materials. Many of the structures that stand today were built circa 1904–07 in the Art Nouveau style. But despite Germany's influence, Ålesund sided with the Allies during World War II. Today, fishing is its primary industry.

WEATHER DCL visits Ålesund in July and August. Average daytime highs during this period are in the low to mid-60s, with average nighttime

lows in the low 50s. Average rainfall is about 5 inches per month during mid summer.

THE PORT Ålesund's port is small, but within an easy 10-minute stroll you'll find shops, cafés, and local points of interest.

TOURIST HIGHLIGHTS Trek up the stairs from the town park to **Fjellstua,** a mountaintop lodge and café, for panoramic views of the harbor. **Vasset Outdoor and Sports Park** offers fishing and horseback riding. The **Sunnmøre Museum** displays numerous styles of fishing boats as well as 40 historic structures. The municipal **Aalesunds Museum** provides information and exhibits about the city and about the Arctic in general.

WHAT TO EAT This is Scandinavia, so seafood is a given. Try the local delicacy *klipfish,* split, salted, and dried cod. Salted smoked herring is also popular. Adventurous types can buy prawns directly from the fishing boats and eat them raw on the docks. Cheeses and game meats are readily available as well. If you're not in the mood for unfamiliar food, several local places serve pizza.

WHAT TO BUY Hand-knit woolen hats, mittens, and sweaters are easy to find in Ålesund. Blown glass and pottery stock the shelves in shops and galleries. Depictions of trolls and moose adorn all manner of objects. Foodies will want to take home some local jam or honey.

Amsterdam, The Netherlands

LANGUAGE Dutch; English widely spoken

HISTORY Amsterdam was founded as a fishing village in the 13th century. Rapid growth occurred during the 14th and 15th centuries, with extensive building of timber-frame dwellings (most later destroyed by fire) and the development of the trading port. The 16th century brought a rebellion by the Dutch against the Habsburg King Philip II of Spain and the religious intolerance of the Spanish.

The rebellion led to the Eighty Years' War and Dutch independence; subsequently, people were substantially free to believe what they wanted. In years when religious wars raged throughout Europe, many people sought refuge in the Dutch Republic and Amsterdam, making the area a haven for immigrants of many persuasions. By the mid-1600s, trade and commerce converged in Amsterdam, making it a major hub for art and agriculture. The negative byproduct of this cultural melting pot was an outbreak of the bubonic plague in the 1660s, with more than 10% of the city's residents falling to the disease.

Prosperity declined in the 1700s and 1800s, with Amsterdam's fortunes reaching a low during the Napoleonic wars. Reinvigoration came in the form of the Industrial Revolution. The 19th century also saw the construction of many public buildings and a series of 42 protective forts. The Netherlands was a neutral territory during World War II, when German troops invaded. More than 100,000 Jews were deported, devastating the area's Jewish community and decimating the region's diamond trade.

Today, Amsterdam is renowned for its relaxed social attitudes, most famously demonstrated by its red-light districts and "coffee" culture. *Pro tip:* ***Coffeeshops*** (English word) sell cannabis, ***koffiehuizen*** (Dutch word) sell the hot caffeinated beverage. Don't take Aunt Fern to a coffeeshop if all she wants is a cappuccino with light foam.

WEATHER DCL visits Amsterdam in August. Average daytime highs during this period are in the low 70s. Nighttime lows average in the high 50s. Rainfall during this time averages 2–3 inches per month.

THE PORT Cruise ships dock at **Passenger Terminal Amsterdam.** Shuttles and taxis are plentiful at the port. A tram stop is located just outside the terminal, and it's a 15-minute walk to **Central Station,** the city's main transportation hub. Biking is a major form of transport in Amsterdam; bike rentals are plentiful throughout the city. Cafés and shops are within an easy walk of the port. The public library opposite the railroad tracks from the Passenger Terminal offers free Wi-Fi.

TOURIST HIGHLIGHTS The **Rijksmuseum** is one of the world's premier art museums, featuring works by masters such as Rembrandt and Vermeer. The nearby **Van Gogh Museum** is another must-see for art lovers. Literature and history buffs will want to see the **Anne Frank House,** the Frank family's hiding place during WWII. (While the museum is undergoing restoration in 2018–19, tickets may be purchased two months in advance at annefrank.org/en/museum/tickets.) The **Resistance Museum** covers WWII history from other perspectives. The **Homomonument,** a memorial in the center of the city comprising three pink-granite triangles set in the ground, honors LGBT+ people from around the world who have suffered persecution, including those who perished in the Nazi concentration camps. Canal tours are a must for many, as are strolls or bike excursions through the well-manicured parks and tulip gardens. A windmill tour is another iconic experience. **The Heineken Experience** is a brewery tour and tasting for those in the mood to relax. A bit outside of town is **Zaanse Schans,** a replica 18th-century village with cheesemaking demonstrations, windmills, a clog-factory warehouse, cafés, and a petting zoo—making it a big hit with kids. Visit dezaanseschans.nl/en for more information.

WHAT TO EAT *Krokets* (croquettes) are meat-filled dumplings, covered with breadcrumbs and then deep-fried; find them in chicken, shrimp, and ragout (meat stew) variations. A somewhat similar fried bite is the *bitterbal,* typically filled with beef and butter. Other savory dishes include sausages and fried fish. *Patat* is the Dutch version of French fries, served in a paper cone and offered with toppings such as chopped onions, spicy mayonnaise (*fritesaus*), or peanut sauce (*pindasaus*). *Stroopwafels,* thin wafflelike wafers stuck together with caramel syrup, are the Dutch signature sweet; buy them from street vendors or at any café or bakery. Another area favorite is licorice, available in many varieties from soft and sweet to chewy and intensely salty. Pastry offerings include *pannenkoeken,* somewhat like crêpes, and *poffertjes,* puffy miniature pancakes served with powdered sugar or fruit.

WHAT TO BUY **Albert Cuyp Market** is the busiest outdoor market in Europe. Delft pottery in classic in blue and white can be found in simple tiles, decorative objects, home decor, and kitchenware; knockoff pieces will set you back just a few euros, but large, authentic pieces may cost thousands. Depictions of tulips or tulip bulbs are reminders of the familiar Dutch flower. Books about the life of Anne Frank or reproductions of Van Gogh's artwork are fitting remembrances of some of the area's most famous residents. Wooden clogs may be a bit cliché, but some folks consider them a must-buy in the Netherlands—look for high-quality handcrafted pieces if you actually plan to wear them. Hard cheeses, flavored with herbs and

spices, are ubiquitous; buy them vacuum-packed for convenient transport and storage.

Belfast, Northern Ireland

LANGUAGES English and Irish (Gaeilge)

HISTORY What is now Belfast has been inhabited since at least the Iron Age. English occupation began in the 1300s but picked up in earnest in the 1600s, when long-held Irish lands were confiscated by the English and Scottish as part of the Plantation of Ulster. Belfast thrived in the 18th century as a mercantile town, exporting linen to Great Britain, but by the 19th century, the city had developed into a center for industry, namely shipbuilding. (Harland and Wolff, founded in 1861, would later attain fame as the birthplace of *Titanic* and other legendary ocean liners.)

In the second half of the 1800s, tensions began to simmer between Belfast's Protestant majority and an influx of Irish Catholics who had migrated north in search of economic opportunities. A long period of intermittent violent unrest began in the early 1900s. Between 1912 and 1922, the area saw numerous conflicts related to Irish independence. Compounding problems a bit later on, Belfast was particularly hard-hit by the Great Depression. Additional devastation came during World War II, when more that 50% of the city's housing was destroyed.

A period of postwar calm was followed by the reignition of strife between Protestants and Catholics in 1969. Violence escalated further in the early 1970s, with rival paramilitary groups carrying out assassinations and deadly bombings. "The Troubles" continued into the 1980s, with intermittent outbreaks of violence. A ceasefire initiated in 1994 still holds today, but the challenges of recent history remain on the minds of residents and visitors alike.

WEATHER DCL visits Belfast in September, when average daytime highs are in the high 50s and nighttime lows average in the high 40s to low 50s. Rainfall during September averages less than 2 inches for the month.

THE PORT The immediate area is under development, with the Marriott-owned **AC Hotel Belfast** having opened in 2018. Taxis and shuttles are readily available to take you to the city center, about 2 miles away.

TOURIST HIGHLIGHTS **Titanic Belfast** is a museum dedicated to the construction of the *Titanic* in Belfast and the subsequent history of the ship; the star-shaped museum building symbolizes White Star Line, of whose fleet the doomed liner was the crown jewel. The **Ulster Museum** comprises typical museum fare such as art and ancient artifacts, as well as detailed exhibits chronicling the history of The Troubles.

If you want more information on The Troubles, try one of the many **black-taxi tours,** which take passengers to key points of historical interest, or visit **Crumlin Road Gaol,** which housed women and children prisoners during the conflict. **St. Anne's Cathedral,** designed in 1898, is the mother church of the (Anglican) Church of Ireland. For lighter touring, try the **Belfast Zoo** or the **Botanic Gardens.**

WHAT TO EAT The Ulster fry is a Northern Irish variation on the full English breakfast: bacon, eggs, sausages, tomatoes, and mushrooms, accompanied by wedges of crisp griddled bread (typically soda or potato bread) called *farls.* Later in the day, look for fish and chips or pasties, deep-fried patties made from sausage, onions, and mashed potato. Other potato-based

dishes include boxty, a traditional potato pancake, and champ, mashed potatoes loaded with green onions, butter, milk, and cheese.

WHAT TO BUY Many visitors consider Irish linen the must-buy souvenir from Belfast. Look for handmade items, but expect them to be pricey. If it doesn't spook you to take *Titanic* memorabilia back on your ship, look for books and models of the famous voyage. **Bushmills** is the whiskey of choice in Northern Ireland (Bushmills Distillery Reserve, a legendary 12-year-old single-malt, is sold only at the distillery itself). The trip from Belfast to the distillery takes about an hour by car or train. **St George's Market,** built between 1890 and 1896, is one of Belfast's oldest attractions, with an array of fresh food, crafts, and antiques for sale depending on the day.

Bergen, Norway

LANGUAGE Norwegian

HISTORY Bergen, the second-largest city in Norway, with about a quarter-million people, was founded circa A.D. 1030 as a Viking settlement and served as the national capital during the 13th century; it was superseded in population by the eventual capital city of Oslo only in the mid-1800s. Over the centuries, Bergen has withstood a multitude of challenges: in the 1300s it was decimated by the Black Plague, English and Dutch forces battled in its harbor in the 17th century, a series of fires spanning hundreds of years devastated it, and Germany occupied it for several years during World War II. Bergen has long been a Scandinavian center of trade, in particular the seafood industry.

WEATHER DCL visits Bergen in September, when average daytime highs are in the mid-50s and average nighttime lows are in the mid-40s. Rainfall can be substantial, averaging about 7 inches per month in the early autumn.

THE PORT The port lies within a 10-minute walk of town. Restaurants, cafés, and shops are all nearby, as are many of Bergen's tourist attractions. Taxis are plentiful, but many people choose to walk. The wharf area is particularly picturesque.

TOURIST HIGHLIGHTS Many visitors enjoy browsing in the local fish market. Others take the funicular to **Mt. Floyen** for breathtaking views of the surrounding islands. **Bergenhus Festning,** at the entrance to Bergen's harbor, is one of the oldest, best-preserved castles in Norway, with dungeons on the ground floor. **Bryggens Museum** displays archaeological finds from the 12th century. **Bergen Aquarium** houses one of Europe's largest collections of fish and invertebrates from the North Sea. The **Fantoft Stavkirke,** about 3 miles from town, is a painstakingly reconstructed 12th-century stave church: built around 1150 in the town of Fortun, it was moved to Bergen and reassembled in 1883, burned by arsonists in 1992, and finally reopened in 1997 after an extensive restoration. Classical-music enthusiasts will want to visit **Troldhaugen,** the home of composer Edvard Grieg, which is preserved in its 1907 state, complete with Grieg's own Steinway piano.

WHAT TO EAT As a seaport, Bergen specializes in many forms of seafood, including prawns, octopus, salmon, and even smoked whale. Cod plays a starring role in fish cakes, fish balls, and fish pudding (tastes better than it sounds). Root vegetables such as carrots, potatoes, turnips, and onions are a common accompaniment. Pork and game meats are served in the form of chops or meatballs or in stews. Fresh berries are popular

for breakfast or dessert. Several British-style pubs serve beer and ale in a cozy atmosphere—they'll also have a bottle or three of aquavit behind the bar. For the homesick, there's even a TGI Friday's in town.

WHAT TO BUY Knit woolens abound in every form: sweaters, caps, mittens, and socks. Trolls are depicted on every possible item, including clothing, kitchenware, and knickknacks. Also look for unique cheese knives and pewter serving pieces.

Brest, France

LANGUAGES French and Breton

HISTORY With about 300,000 people, the port city of Brest is the largest municipality in Brittany (Bretagne), an administrative region of France on the country's northwest coast. Brittany was settled in the fifth and sixth centuries A.D. by Celts who had been pushed out of Great Britain by invading Anglo-Saxons. Culturally distinct from the rest of France, Brittany maintains a uniquely Celtic identity; its regional language, Breton (Brezhoneg), is related to Welsh and Cornish. (The name *Brest* is thought to derive from a Celtic word for "hill.")

The earliest historical record of the region dates to the 13th century, when it was ruled by John I, Duke of Brittany. One hundred years later, a descendant of the duke surrendered Brest to the English. A royal marriage later passed Brest to the French crown. In the 1600s, Brest became a seaport and then a naval stronghold. In World War I, Brest was the port at which many US soldiers entered Europe; in World War II, the Germans gained control of the port and stationed U-boats there. Following the Allied invasion of Normandy and the Battle for Brest, the city was almost entirely destroyed. Much of the current architecture reflects a rapid utilitarian rebuild after the war—few historical buildings remain.

WEATHER DCL visits Brest in July during 2019. Daytime highs for the month average in the high 60s, with nighttime lows in the high 50s. Average rainfall in July is 1–2 inches per month.

THE PORT Brest is a commercial port, with minimal services near the dock. Shuttles and taxis are available into town, about a mile away.

TOURIST HIGHLIGHTS The **Tanguy Tower Museum** displays a collection of dioramas representing the city on the eve of World War II. Kids will enjoy **Océanopolis,** an aquarium featuring displays of live animals, including European sea otters, a wall of coral, sea turtles, penguins, and seals, along with educational and scientific information. **The Museum of Fine Arts** exhibits European paintings from the late 16th century to modern times; art enthusiasts also might enjoy the **Centre Atlantique de la Photographie,** which showcases works by local photographers. **La Pointe Saint-Mathieu,** a clifftop coastal overlook about 16 miles west of the city, was named a Biosphere Reserve by UNESCO and is home to a 19th-century lighthouse and medieval monastic ruins.

WHAT TO EAT Lobsters, crabs, oysters, clams, shrimps, and periwinkles (sea snails) are available everywhere, served steamed or fried or in soups and stews. Unsurprising for France, a regional specialty is crêpes. The preferred version here is savory, with ham, egg, and cheese—a much classier take on the McMuffin. Breton hard cider is a wonderful accompaniment. For an authentic Breton dessert, try *kouign-amann,* a buttery pastry topped with apples and sugar.

WHAT TO BUY Brest has an outpost of **Printemps,** the famed Paris department store. **Librairie Dialogues** carries a nice selection of books in English if you need to pick up something new to read during your vacation. For fans of comics and anime, visit **Excalibulle,** a shop specializing in European comic collectibles, particularly books and figures of Tintin.

Copenhagen, Denmark

LANGUAGES Danish; English widely spoken

HISTORY Copenhagen (*København* in Danish) was founded as a Viking fishing village in the 11th century. The first fortresses in the area were built circa 1160. In the mid-1400s, the city was designated as the capital of Denmark, the country's first king (Christian I) was crowned, and the University of Copenhagen was founded. The mid-1600s and early 1700s were a time of turmoil and destruction, with a siege by Sweden and a series of devastating fires.

In the early 1800s, Copenhagen withstood an attack by Britain. Most of the 1800s and early 1900s were a period of growth, with art and public beautification as a focus; the Tivoli Gardens amusement park and the writings of the beloved children's author Hans Christian Andersen also came about during this time. The Nazis occupied the city during World War II, following which came another period of artistic growth and development of infrastructure.

Copenhagen is simply lovely. The beautiful scenery, the gorgeous, friendly people, the terrific, reasonably priced food, and the fact that nearly everyone speaks fluent English have prompted Erin's teenage daughter to muse about moving here.

WEATHER DCL visits Copenhagen in August and early September. Average daytime highs during this period are in the high 60s to low 70s; average nighttime lows are in the mid-50s. Monthly rainfall averages about 2 inches.

THE PORT The **Frihavnen (Freeport) Terminal,** about 2 miles from town, has little in the way of services. Taxi stands are nearby, or you can take a 15-minute walk to the nearest train station to get to local sights. Copenhagen Airport is less than 10 miles from the port, making for an easy transfer.

TOURIST HIGHLIGHTS Children will love **Tivoli Gardens,** an intricately landscaped amusement park that provided inspiration to Walt Disney during a 1950s visit. The park offers charming, gentle rides as well as thrills for braver souls. Speaking of Disney inspirations, a visit to Copenhagen wouldn't be complete without a stop at Edvard Eriksen's iconic ***Little Mermaid*** statue, near the harbor. **Rosenborg Castle** houses artifacts of Danish royalty, including many of their crown jewels. The **Latin Quarter** makes for a nice walk; you'll pass the oldest church and synagogue in the city, as well as the university. The **Staten Museum for Kunst** is the country's premier fine-art repository, and the **Nationalmuseet** is Denmark's largest museum of cultural history. Fans of **Hans Christian Andersen**'s fairy tales will want to visit one of the many places he called home in Copenhagen or pay their respects at his grave.

WHAT TO EAT Not surprisingly, Danish pastries are the thing to get for breakfast. Look for local breads and jams as well as *snegl* (snail), a type of buttery cinnamon roll. Seafood, including scallops, cod, salmon, whiting, and oysters, is served fresh, smoked, salted, and pickled. Sausages, cheeses, and deli-style meats are popular, too, particularly as part of a

smørrebrød, or open-faced sandwich. Pork or veal meatballs, accompanied by boiled or roasted potatoes, are classic Danish comfort food. Side dishes are often cabbage- or onion-based. The local beer is **Carlsberg;** the brewery holds daily tours and tastings during the summer.

WHAT TO BUY **Legos** were invented in Denmark; look for unique sets that aren't available back home. Danish fashion is gaining a reputation as world-class thanks to hot designers like **Baum und Pfergarten, Bruuns Bazaar, Henrik Vibskov,** and **Stine Goya.** Clean lines and eco-friendly materials have long been hallmarks of Danish furniture and housewares. **Royal Copenhagen** porcelain is a perennial favorite of collectors. Viking-themed toys, statuary, and books are popular touristy souvenirs.

Cork, Ireland

LANGUAGES English and Irish (Gaeilge)

HISTORY Cork was founded in the seventh century by St. Finnbar, who built an abbey. In A.D. 820, the Vikings raided the abbey and the nearby settlement. Following the 1171 Norman invasion of Ireland, Cork was surrendered to Henry II of England. During the Middle Ages, Cork was a bustling port town, but in 1349, the Black Death came, killing about half of the population. In 1491, Perkin Warbeck arrived in Cork, claiming to be the rightful king of England, and a year later, he tried to overthrow Henry VII. The mayor of Cork and several important citizens went with Warbeck to England, but when the rebellion collapsed, they were all captured and executed. After the attempted rebellion, the city earned the moniker "Rebel Cork." Oliver Cromwell captured Cork for England in the mid-17th century, and in the late 17th century, Cork was subjected to a five-day siege by the army of Holland's William of Orange.

The 18th century saw the arrival of French Protestants (Huguenots) who had fled religious persecution back home. During the early 19th century, the city's population exploded; by the middle of the 19th century, Cork had about 80,000 people, a number that then declined somewhat due to deaths from famine and attendant emigration from Ireland. During the 20th century, however, growth picked up again. In the early 1920s, the city was rocked by unrest stemming from the Irish War of Independence; a British counterrevolutionary outfit called the Black and Tans burned large parts of Cork's city center, including its city hall. (In 1922, Ireland gained independence from the UK.) Later in the 20th century, Cork experienced an industrial decline that was reversed by an influx of food-processing businesses, as well as an uptick in tourism.

WEATHER DCL visits Cork in September. Daytime highs for the month average in the low 60s, with nighttime lows in the low 50s. Monthly rainfall for the month averages 4 inches.

THE PORT Ships dock close to town, near the **Cobh Heritage Center.** Basic services and the small town of Cobh (formerly known as Queenstown) are a pleasant walk from the pier. The train station, at the port, offers service to Cork proper, about 10 miles away.

TOURIST HIGHLIGHTS The **English Market** is a roofed food emporium that's been in operation since the late 1700s. Today run by Cork's city council, it's one of the world's oldest municipal markets. Artisanal breads, along with fresh fruits and seafood, are just some of the delicacies on offer. **St. Fin Barre's Cathedral** is an Anglican Early Gothic–style church designed by

William Burges and consecrated in 1870. The interior is richly decorated with fine mosaics in the choir loft and sumptuous artwork in the chancel. The **Church of St. Anne, Shandon,** is known for its eight bells, which visitors can ring on their way up the tower. For an unusual museum experience, stop at the **Cork Butter Museum,** which chronicles the ups and downs of the butter trade in Ireland. (Trust us, it's more interesting than it sounds.)

For a quintessentially Irish moment, venture about 6 miles out of town to **Blarney Castle,** home of the world-famous Blarney Stone, said to instantly bestow *blarney*—the Irish "gift of the gab"—upon those who kiss it. It helps, however, to be *really* comfortable with heights. While a guide holds you in place, you lie on your back while bending your head back and over the edge of a narrow stone walkway, as you grip vertical iron bars on either side of you. The wall in which the stone is embedded lies just across a narrow, exposed gap from the edge of the walkway—it's a 100-foot drop to the ground outside, but there are iron crossbars below you to break a potential fall. (Visitors used to depend on the guides to hold them by their ankles. *Yikes.*)

WHAT TO EAT All kinds of seafood: smoked salmon, fried cod, seafood chowder, fresh oysters, and more. Lamb roasts and stews are hearty and filling. Potatoes are served roasted, fried, or mashed. The adventurous should try *drisheen,* a type of sausage made from a mixture of blood (cow's, pig's, or sheep's), milk, salt, fat, and breadcrumbs, all stuffed into a pig's or sheep's intestine. (Think Scottish haggis minus the organs.) To wash it down, we recommend Murphy's & Beamish Stout, produced locally and renowned internationally.

WHAT TO BUY Ireland is famous worldwide for the quality of its textiles, including linen, lace, and woven and knitted wool. Woolen blankets, sweaters, and caps are popular gifts. Ceramic and crystal housewares are produced in the area. CDs of Irish music are nice reminders of your trip. A tin whistle makes a fun souvenir for a creative child.

Dover, England, United Kingdom *(See page 314 for full profile.)*

Dublin, Ireland

LANGUAGES English and Irish (Gaeilge)

HISTORY Documented history in Dublin begins with Viking raids in the eighth and ninth centuries A.D., leading to the establishment of a settlement on the south side of the River Liffey. (The city's name in the Irish language, *Baile Àtha Cliath,* means "town of the hurdled ford.") Despite fortifications, the town was sacked many times over the next two centuries. By the 11th century, trading relationships with the English towns of Chester and Bristol brought prosperity to Dublin. Seven hundred years of Norman rule began in the late 12th century. Then, from the 14th to 18th centuries, Dublin was incorporated into the English crown and became the "second city" of the British empire for a time. In 1650, a plague outbreak killed nearly half of Dublin's citizens, causing a major setback in civic development. The early 1700s saw a rebound as the wool and linen trades with England grew. A period of rapid expansion in the 1700s was followed by overpopulation, checked by disease and poverty in the 1800s. The break from England came with the 1916 Easter Rising, the War for Independence, and the subsequent Civil War, eventually leading to the establishment of the

Irish Free State (later renamed the Republic of Ireland) in 1922. Since the mid-1990s, an economic boom christened the "Celtic Tiger" has brought massive expansion and development to Dublin; it also brought many new ethnic groups into the city and created a more international feel, particularly in the north inner city.

WEATHER DCL visits Dublin in September. Daytime highs for the month average in the low 60s, with nighttime lows averaging in the low 50s. Rainfall during September is typically 3 inches per month.

TOURIST HIGHLIGHTS The **Guinness Storehouse** offers lessons on the history of the brew and provides a free pint at the end of the tour. Children will enjoy the **Dublin Zoo** and its elephants, tigers, and gorillas, along with the **National Aquatic Center,** home to one of the best water parks in Europe. Art lovers will want to make a stop at the **National Gallery of Ireland,** with holdings that include works by Monet, Picasso, Van Gogh, and Vermeer. The **National Botanic Gardens** is a nice spot for a relaxing stroll. History buffs will want to see the **Book of Kells** at Trinity College Dublin, as well as **St. Patrick's Cathedral** and the **National Museum of Ireland.**

WHAT TO EAT Dublin is a metropolitan city with a sophisticated culinary scene and most major cuisines represented in its restaurants. If you're looking for traditional Irish fare, however, ask for fried fish or seafood pie, served with some form of potato. Irish cheeses from goat, sheep, or cow milk are in abundant supply. Meat eaters will want to try a classic stew of mutton, lamb, or beef or tuck into some hearty corned beef and cabbage. If you're looking for sweets, have some lemon-vanilla curd cake, a sort of Irish take on cheesecake. And no trip to Ireland would be complete without a pint of Guinness Stout for hoisting, a glass of Irish whiskey for sipping, or a mug of Irish coffee for warming you up.

WHAT TO BUY Textiles are the main retail draw in Dublin. Irish linens are a nice choice, as are hand-knitted sweaters, caps, mittens, and scarves. The traditional Irish fisherman's sweater is bulky, warm, and expensive—make sure you're buying the genuine article and not some machine-knit knockoff. If you want branded items, look for jerseys and tees sporting the logo of a local pub or football (soccer) team, or buy a mug with the Guinness name on it. If you want to take some libations on board, a bottle of **Jameson** whiskey will set you right.

Fredericia, Denmark

LANGUAGE Danish

HISTORY Fredericia was founded in the mid-1600s when a fortress was constructed to protect lands overseen by King Frederik III of Denmark. The fortress successfully defended the Danish islands from Swedish invaders several times during its early history. In the 19th century, Fredericia became one of the most important industrial towns in Denmark. The iron and metal industries flourished in the 20th century, along with textile manufacturing and tobacco processing.

WEATHER DCL visits Fredericia in August, when daytime highs average in the high 60s and nighttime lows average in the mid-50s. Rainfall averages about 2 inches per month during the summer.

THE PORT The terminal has are minimal services. The town proper, with restaurants, shops, and banking, is a 10-minute walk away. Taxis and shuttles are readily available. Some guests choose to rent bicycles at the port.

TOURIST HIGHLIGHTS The primary draw in Fredericia is its **ramparts,** or city walls. It takes about an hour to stroll through the centuries-old fortress, which is surrounded by old cannons as well as historical statues commemorating battles past. The **White Water Tower** offers sweeping cityscapes. **Royal Jelling,** a UNESCO World Heritage Site, is Denmark's largest Viking complex, featuring rune stones, burial grounds, and a museum. Fredericia's most famous landmark is **Landsoldaten,** a tribute to the Danes who protected the city during historical conflicts. **Legoland** is a 1-hour drive away. If you're looking for a family attraction that isn't a theme park, the **Hans Christian Andersen Museum** in Odense is also an hour's drive from the ship. If you'd rather just stay in town, **Madsby Legepark** has playgrounds, a go-kart track, and a petting zoo.

WHAT TO EAT Typical Danish foods include open-faced sandwiches, usually served on a base of sturdy rye bread with toppings of egg, meats, or vegetables. Sausages of all sorts are served at breakfast, lunch, and dinner. Meatballs and potatoes are other savory items appearing on many menus. For dessert, look for layered pastries of sponge cake, cream, and fresh fruit.

WHAT TO BUY Look for **Lego** sets that are unavailable in the United States, along with Danish fabrics and fashions, as well as ceramics.

Geiranger, Norway

LANGUAGE Norwegian

HISTORY Geiranger was quite isolated, inhabited by only a handful of people, until the mid-1800s, when the first steamships and tourist boats stopped to take in views of the fjords, which are now listed as a UNESCO World Heritage Site. During the late 1800s, construction began on several hotels so that visitors could stay to enjoy the natural wonders for longer periods. Since then, Geiranger has functioned as a tourist destination from May to October each year, but it reverts to a typical Norwegian small town in the winter, with fewer than 500 permanent residents.

WEATHER Disney Cruise Line visits Geiranger in August during 2019. Average daytime highs in this period are in the mid-60s, and nighttime lows are in the low to mid-50s. Precipitation in August averages 2–3 inches for the month.

THE PORT Ships anchor in the harbor, and cruisers tender into port. Geiranger is tiny; you can walk from one end of town to the other in less than 20 minutes, or you can take a taxi. Several shops and cafés are steps away from the docking area.

TOURIST HIGHLIGHTS The natural beauty of the fjords is the main attraction of the area; explore it by biking or hiking. **Brudesløret (The Bridal Veil)** is one of the most scenic waterfalls in Norway. Take in the views from the **Dalsnibba** mountain plateau or from **Flydalsjuvet,** a jutting rock formation. History buffs may enjoy **Herdalssetra,** a 300-year-old goat farm that provides a modern view into an ancient agrarian lifestyle; the goats are adorable, too. **Geiranger Church** is a lovely example of traditional architecture. Geiranger is also home to the **Norwegian Fjord Center** as well as a small local art gallery.

WHAT TO EAT Local markets sell cloudberries, strawberries, fruit juices, *sylte* (head cheese), cheeses, goat meat, and *morr,* a preserved sausage similar

to salami. Restaurants and cafés serve traditional Norwegian dishes, including fish prepared in many styles, smoked whale, venison, and elk. Pastry lovers will enjoy the local sweet waffle served with berries and cream.

WHAT TO BUY Geiranger shops sell the ubiquitous Norwegian knit goods and troll souvenirs. Also look for carved rock jewelry, painted wood, and tin kitchenware.

Gothenburg, Sweden

LANGUAGE Swedish

HISTORY Gothenburg (*Göteborg* in Swedish) was built during the 1600s by the Dutch. The original city was built inside a large zigzag-shaped city wall, making 17th-century Gothenburg one of Northern Europe's most fortified cities. During the 1700s, the port's importance grew due to trade from the Swedish East India Company. A series of fires in the later 1700s destroyed many of the town's important buildings, resulting in building codes allowing only stone houses near the city center, many of which remain. Today, fishing is a key industry, and Gothenburg is the home of Scandinavia's largest fish auction.

WEATHER DCL visits Gothenburg in July. Daytime highs during the month average in the high 60s, with nighttime lows in the mid-50s. Rainfall averages about 3 inches per month in July.

THE PORT Gothenburg's new port terminal, opened in 2018, is replete with modern amenities and located about a mile from the city center. Taxis and shuttles are available.

TOURIST HIGHLIGHTS **Lisberg Park** is a charming amusement park built in 1923. Its wooden roller coaster was voted the best in the world in 2003 and 2005. The **Volvo Museum** traces the history of the automaker and includes an on-site café. Two attractions with free admission are the **Gothenburg Botanical Garden,** a peaceful place to enjoy the regional flora, and **Slottsskogen,** a rambling city park featuring pretty ponds and a children's zoo. **Queen Christina's Hunting Lodge,** the oldest stone structure in Gothenburg, is known for its period stone-and-wood interior.

WHAT TO EAT **Saluhallen,** a large indoor food market, has dozens of stalls selling cheeses, coffees, spices, fruit, and prepared foods. Smoked fish can be found on most local menus in the form of herring or salmon. Fresh fish and oysters are also abundant. For a sweet treat, cinnamon buns are the way to go. If you're in the mood for an adult beverage, look no further than the local akvavit (a potent clear liqueur flavored with caraway seed).

WHAT TO BUY The most traditional Swedish souvenir is the **Dala Horse,** a carved, painted wooden toy that is also a symbol of the country. Akvavit and vodka are popular adult purchases. Other typical food take-home items include cloudberry jam, *knäckebröd* (crispbread, keeps for ages), ginger biscuits, and the potent local licorice.

Greenock (Glasgow), Scotland, United Kingdom

LANGUAGES English, Scots, and Scottish Gaelic (Gàidhlig)

HISTORY The area was renowned as a fishing port as early as the 12th century. Organized ownership began in 1296, when Hugh de Grenock was created a Scottish baron. Greenock became a fishing village in the early

1600s; harbor access was also important to the growing tobacco trade. In the early 1700s, shipbuilding became a prominent industry. In 1812, Europe's first steamboat service included Greenock as a stopping point, making it an attractive area for expansion of the paper, cotton, and sugar-refining trades. The mid-1800s saw the expansion of rail lines to Glasgow and other points within Scotland. Greenock was the site of torpedo manufacturing during the World Wars. Several of the area industries saw closures in the mid-1900s, and unemployment was rampant in the latter part of the last century. Over the last several years, tourism has provided a boost to the community.

WEATHER DCL visits Greenock/Glasgow in September. Average daytime highs average in the high 60s. Average nighttime lows are in the high 40s to low 50s. Rainfall during July is typically 3 inches per month.

THE PORT The **Greenock Terminal** offers basic services such as snacks, currency exchange, ATMs, and car-rental desks. If you decide to rent a car, remember that driving here takes place on the left-hand side of the road. Taxis and shuttles are readily available. Fast-food restaurants and a few banks are located within a 10-minute walk of the port. The train station is a 10- to 15-minute walk away, with regular service to **Glasgow,** just under an hour away. **Edinburgh** is 2–3 hours away by train, depending on the number of stops.

TOURIST HIGHLIGHTS Most visitors to Greenock decide to tour in Glasgow. Dating from 1197, **Glasgow Cathedral** is one of the most complete medieval churches in Scotland, but it hasn't actually been a cathedral since the late 17th century. (Originally built as a Catholic bishop's seat, it now serves the Church of Scotland, a Calvinist–Reformed denomination.) If you're looking to add a touch of the Magic Kingdom's Haunted Mansion to your visit, stop at the **Necropolis,** an atmospheric Victorian cemetery. The **Burrell Collection** is an eclectic museum housing everything from ancient tapestries to Impressionist paintings. The **Kelvingrove Art Gallery and Museum** is home to works by many major artists, but it's perhaps best known for its room dedicated to the work of Scottish architect and designer Charles Rennie Mackintosh, the leading exponent of the Art Nouveau movement in Great Britain. To learn about the local spirits, try a tour of the **Glengoyne Distillery** or the **Tennents Wellpark Brewery.**

WHAT TO EAT Traditional Glaswegian dishes include cullen skink, a stew made from smoked haddock, potatoes, and onions. Haddock also can be found deep-fried or broiled and served with tatties and neeps (mashed potatoes and turnips). Many main dishes are based on venison, lamb, or beef and may be accompanied by colcannon, a mashed-potato-and-cabbage mixture, or Yorkshire pudding, a bready side dish made with a batter of eggs, flour, and milk. To truly experience Scottish cuisine, you'll want to go into *Fear Factor* mode and partake of some black pudding (blood sausage) or haggis, a boiled, minced mix of onions, oatmeal, and organ meats. (This is probably a good place to emphasize that *pudding* in the UK can refer to something savory as well as sweet.) Scones and oat cakes are popular snacks. Be sure to follow any meal with a good Scotch whisky or a local beer.

WHAT TO BUY Scotland is famed for its high-quality knitwear and textiles. Get yourself a tartan for a traditional look. A jersey from a local football

(soccer) team is another popular fabric souvenir. Celtic-themed jewelry is sold throughout the region. And, of course, you can't go wrong with a good bottle of Scotch.

Helsinki, Finland

LANGUAGES Finnish and Swedish

HISTORY Helsinki was founded in 1550 by King Gustav I of Sweden as a trading port. During its early years, the city experienced war, poverty, fires, and the plague. More-prosperous times began with the construction of a naval fortress during the 18th century. In 1809, Russia annexed Finland after defeating Sweden in the Finnish War. Czar Alexander I of Russia named Helsinki the capital to reduce Swedish influence and bring the seat of Finnish government closer to St. Petersburg. Finland declared its independence in 1917, which was followed by a brief period of unrest and a longer period of growth and renewal. A highlight of the modern era was Helsinki's hosting of the 1952 Summer Olympics.

WEATHER Disney cruises visit Helsinki in August. Temperatures during this period average in the mid-60s during the day and in the low 50s at night. Precipitation averages about 2 inches per month.

THE PORT Services at the port are basic: a few souvenir shops, an ATM, and a currency exchange. Taxis and shuttles are available to take you to **Kauppatori (Market Square),** about 2 miles away. Once you're in town, you'll find many attractions within walking distance.

TOURIST HIGHLIGHTS Market Square contains many open-air stalls featuring food and flowers. Also note the architecture, which shows both Swedish and Russian influences. To get a feel for the native culture, visit a public sauna, where you can wear your birthday suit and sweat with the locals. Museum lovers have plenty of options here. The **Designmuseo** spotlights Finnish design; the **Kiasma Museum of Contemporary Art** showcases art, design, and technology; and the **National Museum of Finland** focuses on the nation's history. Area churches of note include the **Lutheran Cathedral of Finland,** a palatial white Neoclassical structure topped with green copper domes, and the **Uspenski Cathedral,** an Eastern Orthodox house of worship with a traditional golden onion dome. **Suomenlinna (Finland's Fortress),** a UNESCO World Heritage Site, is a 15-minute ferry trip from town; dating from 1748 and built on six islands, it comprises not only a fortress, museums, and gardens but also a residential community where about 800 people live year-round. Children will like **Linnanmäki,** an amusement park, or the **Helsinki Zoo.**

WHAT TO EAT Smoked and salted fish of every sort is available on menus throughout Helsinki. Look for herring, salmon, perch, and whitefish. Cheese is a staple. *Leipäjuusto* ("bread cheese"), a Finnish specialty, is a rich cow's-milk cheese that's baked or grilled as part of the manufacturing process; the browning makes it resemble a pizza or flatbread. Typical meats include lamb, elk, reindeer, duck, and goose. Potatoes, carrots, turnips, and mushrooms are common side dishes. Summer fruits include strawberries, blueberries, lingonberries, and cloudberries.

WHAT TO BUY Among the most recognizable souvenirs are bags, clothing, and housewares from the internationally famous Finnish design house **Marimekko.** The bold colors and patterns are unmistakable. All manner of

reindeer-related products can be found in Helsinki—blankets and rugs, as well as practical and decorative objects made from bone and horn. Canned reindeer meat is a unique takeaway. Sweet-and-salty Finnish black licorice is another popular purchase.

Kirkwall, Orkney Islands, United Kingdom

LANGUAGE English and Scots

HISTORY Kirkwall, which has about 9,200 people, is the capital of the Orkney Islands, a chain of more than 70 islands just to the north of Scotland. Archaeological evidence dates human habitation of the Orkneys to about 3500 B.C. Residents during the Iron and Medieval Periods included the Picts, the Norse, and the Scots. The area was under Norwegian rule from the 9th to 13th centuries A.D. In 1468, Orkney was promised by Christian I, king of Denmark, Norway, and Sweden, as collateral against a dowry to be paid to James III of Scotland, who was betrothed to Christian's daughter, Margaret. Scotland has largely retained rule (the dowry was never paid). In the late 1600s, Oliver Cromwell's troops were stationed in Orkney and taught the locals various industrial arts and methods of agriculture. Centuries later, the Orkneys held naval bases in both World Wars.

Though the Orkneys are part of Scotland, Norway is only about 300 miles away, and the culture and landscape feel distinctly Nordic rather than Celtic: many place-names have Scandinavian origins, Gaelic has never been spoken here, clans and tartans aren't a thing, and *udal law*—a centuries-old Norse legal code pertaining to property ownership—is still in effect.

WEATHER Disney Cruise Line visits Kirkwall in July, when daytime highs average in the high 50s to low 60s and nighttime lows in the mid-40s. Summer is the dry season, with an average of about 2.5 inches of rain during July..

THE PORT Basic services and cafés can be found within walking distance of the dock. Free shuttle service is available from the terminal into town, about 2 miles away. There's also an auto-rental service near the dock, but availability is limited, so book early. Most of the town can be easily explored on foot.

TOURIST HIGHLIGHTS **St. Magnus Cathedral** is a stone masterpiece dating from 1137. The **Orkney Museum** features historical artifacts from the region. **Highland Park Distillery,** the northernmost distillery in the UK, offers samples at the end of its tour. **Skara Brae,** a UNESCO World Heritage Site, is a well-preserved Stone Age village. The **Orkney Wireless Museum** focuses on the history of radio and recorded sound. The **Ring of Brodgar** is a Stonehenge-like assemblage of 36 gigantic stones. Ferry service is available to other nearby islands.

WHAT TO EAT Fresh seafood is on many Kirkwall menus. Look for oysters, clams, lobster, and scallops, as well as less-familiar local favorites such as torsk, sea witch, and megrim. Meats include local beef, pork, and lamb; in particular, the meat from North Ronaldsay sheep, which feed mainly on seaweed, is a popular treat for visitors. Typical sides include root vegetables and potatoes. Many meals are accompanied by cheese and oat cakes (like crackers or flatbread). Orkney fudge is a prized treat, as are scones with rhubarb jam. Beer, ale, and spirits are easy to find; try the output from the two local breweries or the nearby **Highland Park**

Distillery. The **Orkney Wine Company** produces wine fermented from fruit such as raspberries and elderberries.

WHAT TO BUY Typical Kirkwall souvenirs include hand-knitted woolen goods such as sweaters and mittens. Carved wooden objects and hand-crafted jewelry are also popular. Take home a taste of the islands with some Orkney fudge or oat cakes.

Kristiansand, Norway

LANGUAGE Norwegian

HISTORY Archaeological evidence suggests that the Kristiansand area has been inhabited since at least 6500 B.C. Most of the settlement was small farms until the development of an active trading port in the 1400s. In the mid-1600s, the town was named in honor of King Christian IV (*-sand* refers to the sandy headland on which the city is built). The late 1700s were boom times, with Kristiansand serving as a center of shipbuilding.

Like a number of Norwegian cities, Kristiansand suffered a series of devastating fires in the 18th and 19th centuries that destroyed parts of the town, necessitating rebuilding. In the early 1900s, mining and mineral processing became key industries. Recent years have seen surges in technology and off-shore drilling.

WEATHER DCL visits Kristiansand in early September. Average daytime highs during this period are in the low 60s, with average nighttime lows in the high 40s to low 50s. September precipitation averages just shy of 3 inches.

THE PORT The cruise terminal lies within walking distance to the city center and the **Strandpromenaden (Boardwalk).** You'll find shops, cafés, and basic services within a 10-minute stroll of the ship. Taxis and buses service the port as well.

TOURIST HIGHLIGHTS Children will enjoy **Dyrepark,** a combination zoo-amusement park that is the most frequently visited attraction in Norway. **Posebyen** is the oldest part of town, with many lovely buildings that have withstood past fires. The **Setesdalsbanen,** a railway between Kristiansand and the town of Byglandsfjord, offers rides on a vintage steam train. The Neo-Gothic **Kristiansand Domkirke (Cathedral)** is a center of community activity as well as a house of worship. If the sun is out, walk over to the sandy beach area for some relaxing people-watching. The Strandpromenaden features shops and a fish market.

WHAT TO EAT The quayside area is home to many cafés and restaurants, as well as an open-air market and indoor stalls. Look for seafood offerings such as smoked salmon, mackerel, and cod cakes. Snack like a local—buy some prawns (shrimp) from the market and eat them while you enjoy the harbor view. You'll find moose, elk, venison, and other game meat on many menus. Expect to find a variety of cheeses for sale as well. Several varieties of berries are offered for breakfast and dessert.

WHAT TO BUY Kristiansand retailers sell many of the traditional Scandinavian souvenirs such as knit goods, carvings, and metalwork. Trolls, moose, and elves adorn all manner of trinkets. Jam made from local cloudberries makes a tasty gift.

Liverpool, England, United Kingdom

LANGUAGE English

HISTORY The first known settlement on the banks of the River Mersey dates to the first century A.D. (Theories abound regarding the origins of the name *Liverpool,* one of the most common being that it comes from the Old English *liuer pul,* or "pool of dark water.") In about 1200, King John of England advertised the establishment of a new borough at Liverpool, inviting settlers to take holdings there. For centuries, Liverpool was relatively unimportant, regarded as only a minor port and seeing only modest skirmishes. As trade from the West Indies increased in the 1700s, Liverpool's seaside location became advantageous, and by the beginning of the 19th century, 40% of the world's trade was passing through the docks at Liverpool.

During World War II, the Liverpool area was hit with dozens of air raids, with almost half the homes in the metropolitan area sustaining some damage and thousands more destroyed outright. (Beatle John Lennon was born in Liverpool during an air raid on October 9, 1940.) After the war, a decline in industry in the area precipitated an economic decline, which is now reversing with an influx of tourism.

WEATHER DCL visits Liverpool in September, when daytime highs average in the mid-60s and nighttime lows average in the low 50s. Liverpool typically sees an average of 2–3 inches of rainfall during the month.

THE PORT Ships dock at the **Port of Liverpool,** directly adjacent to the city proper. Major services are available within a 10-minute walk, including shops, cafés, and local attractions. Taxis are readily available. Buses, including the hop-on-and-off sightseeing services, are a 5-minute walk from the port. Additionally, ferry and rail stations are accessible on foot.

TOURIST HIGHLIGHTS Follow the footsteps of Liverpool's favorite sons in **The Beatles Story,** where you can watch scenes from their lives and see personal artifacts, including the trademark glasses John Lennon wore when he composed "Imagine." Art lovers will enjoy the Liverpool outpost of the **Tate Gallery** or the **Walker Art Gallery,** whose holdings include works by Rembrandt and Rubens. **Liverpool Cathedral** is the largest church in northern Britain; climb the 331-foot tower for impressive views of the Mersey and surrounding areas. If it won't upset your sensibilities while sailing, pay a visit to the **Titanic Memorial** in the Pier Head area. Exhibits on the *Titanic* and the *Lusitania* are also on display at the **Merseyside Maritime Museum.**

WHAT TO EAT Liverpool is a meat-eating town. Main dishes are traditionally made with chicken, pork, lamb, fish, and beef. A classic meal is bubble and squeak, a sort of hash brown made with potatoes, cabbage, carrots, green beans, Brussels sprouts, or other vegetables left over from a roast dinner; "bubble and squeak" describes the sound of the veggies frying in the pan. Another popular dish is scouse, a hearty lamb stew. Also look for cottage pie, made with ground veal and mashed potatoes, and toad in the hole, sausages coated with Yorkshire pudding.

If you're in the mood for a uniquely British sweet, try the black-and-white-striped hard candies called **Everton mints,** created by an enterprising 19th-century soccer devotee so that fellow fans of the Everton Football Club would have a snack to enjoy whilst watching the matches. If you need fortification, stop in a pub and ask for a pint of whatever's on tap.

WHAT TO BUY Beatles memorabilia is the key must-purchase item in Liverpool. If you're looking to add some fun to your shopping, make a game

of finding the oddest item embellished with a Beatles-related image. T-shirts and hats are easy; you get bonus points for edible items or Beatles gear for your dog.

Nynäshamn (Stockholm), Sweden

LANGUAGE Swedish

HISTORY During the Iron Age, what is now Nynäshamn was a population center, as evidenced by 27 still-standing rune stones distributed throughout the town and its environs. The area saw little development, however, until the 20th century, when rail lines first connected the port to industrial regions.

WEATHER DCL visits Nynäshamn in August. Daytime highs average in the high 60s, with nighttime lows averaging in the mid-50s. Rainfall averages about 3 inches for the month.

THE PORT The cruise terminal has minimal facilities. The town of Nynäshamn is a little less than a mile away; the route is walkable, and taxis and shuttles are readily available. The train station is adjacent to the port; two trains per hour run to Stockholm, about an hour away.

Those interested in cruise technology will be interested in the pier itself. In 2016, Nynäshamn introduced the **SeaWalk,** a fully retractable dock. About 250 yards long and 450 tons, it's supported by 10 pontoons, each 30 feet wide. When no ships are in port, the SeaWalk is fully retracted; when they arrive, it takes just 10 minutes to fully extend the pier alongside a ship and allow passengers to disembark.

TOURIST HIGHLIGHTS Most cruisers make their way to **Stockholm,** a city with scores of museums. Some notable ones include **Fotografiska,** showcasing contemporary photography; the **Nationalmuseum,** with prominent Rembrandt and Nordic-art collections; and **Moderna Museet**, which houses works by Dalí, Picasso, Kandinsky, and others. **Kungliga Slottet,** the royal palace, is home to the crown jewels and exhibits on weaponry, as well as a charming changing of the guard. Our favorite spot is the **Vasa Museum,** home to a fully preserved 17th-century warship. (Erin's daughter Louisa says that seeing the ship was the closest thing to actually being in a Pirates of the Caribbean film.) For a taste of the outdoors, visit **Rosendal's Garden,** where you can pick your own flowers from lush beds, paying by weight, as well as enjoy a light meal at the café. Children will enjoy **Junibacken,** an indoor park celebrating the life and work of Astrid Lindgren, the author of the Pippi Longstocking books, or **Tivoli Gröna Lund,** a small amusement park.

If you're staying in Nynäshamn and you're in search of relaxation, visit **Nynäs Havsbad,** a hotel, spa, and restaurant with indoor and outdoor pools, hot tubs, and saunas. Those who appreciate kitsch will get a kick out of **Mopedum,** a pop-culture museum focusing on the period 1952–1979, when mopeds dominated Swedish youth culture. Popular outdoor activities include kayak tours and hiking along the shore.

WHAT TO EAT Many eateries serve locally smoked salmon, trout, and prawns. Non-meat-eaters will want to make their way to **Ärlan Mat & Trädgård,** a vegetarian restaurant with a Scandinavian touch. The local brewery is **Nynäshamns Ångbryggeri;** stop by for a tour and a taste.

WHAT TO BUY Clothing, housewares, and textiles are popular souvenirs.

Olden, Norway

LANGUAGE Norwegian

HISTORY Olden is a sleepy little village of about 500 year-round residents. In ancient times, it was home to fishing camps. Permanent settlement began in the mid-1600s. In the late 1990s, Olden became a popular tourist destination.

WEATHER Disney Cruise Line visits Olden in August, when daytime highs average in the mid-60s and nighttime lows average in the low 50s. Rainfall averages 2–3 inches per month during the summer.

THE PORT Olden is a tender port. The tenders dock at the edge of the main village, which measures slightly more than half a mile square. You can get anywhere you want to go in town quickly and easily.

TOURIST HIGHLIGHTS Natural beauty is the draw here—you won't find much in the way of cultural sites, architecture, dining, or shopping. Olden is the gateway to the **Briksdal Glacier**—the largest glacier on the European mainland—in **Jostedal Glacier National Park.** Bring your camera to capture the stunning scenery. "Troll cars," small motorized vehicles reminiscent of golf carts, take tourists around town and up to the glacier.

WHAT TO EAT A few restaurants in town serve seafood and sandwiches. For a more substantial meal, visit the restaurant at the **Olden Fjordhotel,** which offers a typical Scandinavian *smörgåsbord.*

WHAT TO BUY Some shops sell local handicrafts, and there's a boutique or two; otherwise, it's outdoor stalls selling the typical tourist gewgaws.

Oslo, Norway

LANGUAGE Norwegian; English widely spoken

HISTORY A city of about 600,000 people (1.5 million including its suburbs), Oslo is the capital of Norway and also its economic, commercial, and social center. It was founded around A.D. 1000, and while it's changed names—and nations—a few times, it has served as a seat of government since 1300. Like many other European cities, Oslo lost much of its population (about 75%) to the Black Death during the Middle Ages. As a consequence, church membership and revenue dropped significantly, allowing merchants and traders to take over Oslo's economy—a role they never relinquished.

From about 1500 to 1905, Norway was a possession first of Denmark and later of Sweden. It achieved independence from Sweden in 1905. Germany occupied Norway during World War II, establishing its own government from 1940 until the German surrender in 1945.

Like many other European countries, Norway is politically much more liberal than the United States. (The Høyre, Norway's *conservative* party, for example, supports a generous welfare state, universal health care, marriage equality, and membership in the European Union.) Unlike many ports visited by DCL, Oslo is not heavily dependent on tourism; shipping, oil and gas production, fishing, manufacturing, and services are the main drivers of Norway's economy. As a result, there's much more to see and do in Oslo than, say, a typical DCL Caribbean port.

WEATHER DCL visits Oslo in September, when daytime highs average in the low 60s and nighttime lows average in the high 40s. Rainfall averages 3–4 inches per month in the early autumn.

THE PORT The *Magic* docks at the southern end of downtown Oslo, within half a mile of Oslo's **Central Station,** which provides bus, subway, taxi, and train service throughout the city. Public transport is clean and efficient.

TOURIST HIGHLIGHTS Oslo is one of Len's favorite cities. The typically European architecture has a sleek Scandinavian aesthetic. The tree-lined streets have wide, spotless sidewalks. You could spend an entire day just walking around doing nothing in particular and have a perfectly lovely time.

If you're a fan of Walt Disney World and of Epcot in particular, try our walking tour of Oslo (page 397), which visits the original inspirations for three World Showcase icons. The **Gol Stave Church,** in Oslo's Norwegian Museum of Cultural History, is the model for the stave church in front of the Norway Pavilion; **Castle Akershus,** near the port of Oslo, is the model for Restaurant Akershus; and the **Viking Ship Museum,** part of the University of Oslo Museum of Cultural History (a different museum from the one that houses the stave church), was seen in the *Spirit of Norway* film that used to be shown after the old Maelstrom boat ride.

Art and architecture fans should take a short walk west along the waterfront, to the **Tjuvholmen** neighborhood, which features cafés, restaurants, art galleries and museums, outdoor sculpture, and some really interestingly shaped buildings.

Finally, within a short walk of the cruise port, at the west end of Karl Johans Gate (Oslo's main thoroughfare), is the 173-room **Royal Palace,** the official residence of Norway's royal family. For information on guided tours, visit royalcourt.no (click "The Royal Residences," then "Palace Tours").

A short walk from the Royal Palace is the **Nobel Peace Center,** which awards the annual Nobel Peace Prize. The center includes a museum with displays honoring past winners, along with multimedia presentations on current projects. See nobelpeacecenter.org/en for hours and admission prices.

WHAT TO EAT You'll find familiar cuisines represented in the cafés and restaurants along Karl Johans Gate—everything from Northern European to North American, and a fair bit outside. (A friend of ours swears that the best chimichanga he's ever eaten anywhere was in Oslo, at **Taco República.**)

Len recommends dining at one of the **Grand Hotel'**s two restaurants. The **Grand Café** serves a modern interpretation of the Norwegian breakfast, including smoked herring, wild salmon, and local lamb. Expect to pay around $40 per person for breakfast and $80 for dinner, excluding alcohol. If you're feeling fancy, try the Grand's **Palmen** restaurant for afternoon tea, which includes three plates of pastries, cookies, and sweets, along with dainty sandwiches and lots of tea. Cost is around $42 or up to $80 with Champagne.

WHAT TO BUY Norway's currency is the krone (abbreviated NOK), with current exchange rates running about 8–9 NOK to $1 US. Because Oslo is a big town for banking and finance, you'll find ATMs conveniently located around town. Type "Oslo ATMs" into your favorite search engine, and look for your bank's map in the search results.

Be forewarned that prices for everything from food to clothing are as high as the cheekbones of the city's intimidatingly attractive citizens. (Len, ever the cultural anthropologist, muses, "I believe that the trolls in Norwegian folklore are actually based on the looks of foreign tourists.") When it comes to food, it's not uncommon to pay $50 per person for a basic burger, fries, and beer at a sit-down restaurant, or $30 per person for a small pizza, side salad, and drink. If you're on a budget, we recommend just grabbing a snack and some bottled water at a corner store or from a street vendor.

Oslo's main shopping district stretches along **Karl Johans Gate,** about a quarter mile from the port. For a multitude of retail and dining options, try **Oslo City Shopping Centre** (Stenersgata 1; visit oslocity.no for stores and hours), which looks like a Norwegian space port. For high-end threads, try **Eger Karl Johan** department store (23-B Karl Johans Gate; egerkarljohan.no).

Portland, England, United Kingdom

LANGUAGE English

HISTORY Portland is in the central part of England's so-called Jurassic Coast, known for its significant limestone deposits. The area was inhabited by humankind as early as the Middle Stone Age and, later, by the ancient Romans. Motivated by Viking raids, King Henry VIII erected Portland Castle in the 16th century to protect the land from foreign threats. Portland's man-made harbor—the second-largest such harbor in the world, built between 1848 and 1905—was originally a Royal Navy base and is now a popular recreation area.

Stonehenge—perhaps the world's most famous prehistoric monument—is Portland's biggest tourist draw and has been for at least 200 years. It was built in several stages: the first monument was an early henge monument, built about 5,000 years ago, and the unique stone circle was erected in the late Neolithic period, in about 2500 B.C.

WEATHER DCL visits Portland in summer and early fall. Daytime highs during that period are in the low to mid-60s, with nighttime lows in the mid-50s. Typical rainfall is about 2 inches per month when DCL is in port.

THE PORT Ships dock directly quayside at **Portland Harbor;** expect to be greeted by a town crier in historical garb. Taxis and shuttle buses are available to take you to **Portland Castle** or the nearby town of Weymouth, which has many quaint shops and cafés. The port itself has minimal cruise-ship services, as it serves primarily to meet the needs of the many freighters that dock nearby.

TOURIST HIGHLIGHTS Located about an hour away, the key point of interest near Portland is **Stonehenge,** a UNESCO World Heritage Site. Archaeologists believe this ancient circle of standing stones was constructed from 3000 to 2000 B.C. Closer in is the charming seaside town of **Weymouth.** Its attractions include **Nothe Fort, Abbotsbury Swannery and Gardens, Sandworld Sculptural Park,** and **Sea Life Adventure Park.** Attractions in Portland proper include **Portland Castle** (small as castles go), a quaint lighthouse, and several lovely stone churches.

WHAT TO EAT Pub fare and seafood are the culinary highlights. Haddock, mackerel, sea bream, and shellfish are fried or cooked up in stews and casseroles. Locally raised sheep and lamb are prized for their tender meat. Dorset sausage, similar to American meatloaf, is served as an appetizer or entrée. Local blueberries and gooseberries make their way into pastries and ice creams. Dorset Blue Vinney is the local blue cheese. And if at all possible, you should partake of a proper English tea, complete with scones topped with jam and clotted cream.

WHAT TO BUY You'll find all manner of Stonehenge-related souvenirs in the area, from the erudite (coffee-table books and historical tomes) to the kitschy (keychains, snow globes, and trilithon flash drives). Also look for

clothing and housewares decorated with emblems of the British monarchy, fine woolens, and scented soaps and bath products.

Reykjavík, Iceland

LANGUAGE Icelandic

HISTORY The year A.D. 871 brought the first recorded settler to Iceland: Ingólfur Arnarson, a fugitive from Norway. Almost no development beyond basic farming happened for the next 900 years. Industry and infrastructure picked up steam in the mid-1700s with the development of a textile industry based on tanning, wool harvesting, dyeing, and weaving; other early industries included fishing and shipbuilding. The first Icelandic constitution was adopted in 1874, and the island achieved independent statehood in 1904 under the crown of Denmark.

Iceland asserts neutrality in global conflicts but did house Allied forces during World War II. Full independence was reached in 1944, when the first president of Iceland was elected. In more recent times, finance and technology have become key industries. A city of about 120,000 people, Reykjavík is the world's northernmost capital of a sovereign state.

WEATHER They don't call it Iceland for nothing, but in 2019 DCL visits in July, when the weather is surprisingly mild: daytime highs average in the mid-50s and nighttime lows are in the bearable mid-40s. (The highest recorded temperature: a steamy 78°.) Precipitation averages 3–4 inches during July.

THE PORT The **Skarfabakki** cruise dock is about 2 miles from the center of town. There is little of interest near the dock itself, but taxis and a free shuttle will take you to the commercial district. The **Cruise Welcome Center** can direct you as well as provide information about local attractions. Once you're in Reykjavík proper, most attractions are accessible on foot.

TOURIST HIGHLIGHTS Reykjavík is a wonderful blend of urban sophistication and outdoor adventure. Because the island is nearly treeless, many Icelandic buildings are constructed from materials such as driftwood, corrugated iron, volcanic rock, and sod, making for an eclectic and fascinating architectural mix. In town, visit the **Menningarmiðstoð Kópavogs,** a cultural complex with a natural-history museum; the **Hafnarborg,** a modern-art museum; and the **Hallgrimskirkja,** a Lutheran cathedral built in the Expressionist style (meaning it looks like something out of *Star Trek*). About 30 miles from the city, the **Blue Lagoon** mineral spa has interesting geothermal features. An active volcano, **Hengill,** is within a 20-minute drive and features natural hot springs. Wildlife excursions afford opportunities to see whales, birds of prey, and thousands of the island's adorable puffins.

WHAT TO EAT Seafood stews, chowders, and kabobs are local specialties. Lobster, crayfish, salmon, trout, and scallops are abundant. Sushi-style restaurants are popular. Whale meat is a treat for the adventurous. Meats may include duck, horse, and eel, as well as pork and veal served in thin slices or as cold cuts. For those in need of something less exotic, pizza and burgers are easy to find.

Icelanders are also proud of their hot dogs, which have a slightly different (but nonetheless delicious) flavor than their American equivalents—they're made mostly from Icelandic lamb, supplemented by pork and beef. Favorite toppings include raw or crispy fried onions, ketchup, brown mustard, and a caper-herb rémoulade. Pastries, bread, and eggs are morning staples. Cheese

and yogurt made from both cow and sheep milk are popular; *skýr,* a tangy dairy product, is similar in flavor and consistency to Greek yogurt, but it's technically a cheese. Vegetarianism is relatively rare in Iceland, with the most prevalent plant-based foods being potatoes, cabbage, turnips, rutabagas, and other root vegetables. Hot chocolate and coffee are ubiquitous.

The local firewater is *brennivín,* a powerful unsweetened schnapps distilled from potatoes and flavored with caraway, cumin, and other botanicals. It packs a wallop, and thank goodness for that—*brennivín* is the traditional beverage to accompany the Icelandic specialty *hákarl,* or fermented shark.

"Fermented" doesn't really tell the whole story, though. A Greenland shark is cleaned, buried in sand and weighted with stones, then left to cure (read: decompose) for 6–12 weeks. Then the flesh is cut into strips and hung up to dry for several months. The reason for all this advance, um, preparation? The meat is poisonous when it's fresh.

If you still think you might like to sample *hákarl* after reading this far, we'd be remiss if we didn't apprise you of the following: (1) Wikipedia advises, "Those new to it will usually gag involuntarily on the first attempt to eat it because of the high ammonia content." (2) A food blogger who was brave enough to try it likened the taste to "a tramp's sock soaked in urine." (3) It made Gordon Ramsay retch.

WHAT TO BUY Puffins, trolls, and elves are depicted on everything from clothing to housewares. Fine-quality Icelandic wool sweaters are a prized souvenir. Look for hand-knitted items as well as jewelry and carvings made from area driftwood, lava, and found items. Note that shopping in Iceland can be expensive due to high sales taxes, so be sure to ask the *full* price of something before buying.

St. Petersburg, Russian Federation

LANGUAGE Russian

HISTORY The area that is now St. Petersburg has been occupied since at least the ninth century A.D. by a succession of Slavs, Finns, Swedes, and other ethnic groups. Real turbulence in the area began during the 16th century with a series of border disputes between Russia and Sweden. Russia gained control of the region, and the city proper was founded in 1703 by Tsar Peter the Great. After Peter died in 1725, several rulers jostled for position. Eventually Peter's daughter, Elizabeth, took the crown and a period of growth and prosperity occurred in what was now the Russian capital. Catherine the Great assumed power following a 1762 coup d'état; her reign saw the growth of trade and a flowering of the arts. Subsequent rulers Paul I and Alexander I made the government more bureaucratic. Bureaucracy further increased under Nicholas I in the early to mid-1800s. The next ruler, Alexander II, was assassinated in 1881, and the country entered a period of capitalism.

Uprisings in the early 1890s were followed by revolution and destruction during the first World War. Communism prevailed post-World War I, and the city's

unofficial **TIP**
If you'd like to explore St. Petersburg on your own, you **must** obtain a valid Russian tourist visa before your trip; for details, go to washington.mid.ru/en (under "Consular Services," choose "For U.S. Citizens" and then "Visa to Russia"). Guests taking part in organized tours or excursions, such as DCL's own port adventures, don't need a visa.

name was changed to Leningrad in 1924. After a German siege in 1941, food was scarce and famine common. The Soviets resumed control in 1944, but the effects of World War II lasted until well into the 1960s. With the fall of communism in Russia in 1991, the city's original name was restored.

WEATHER DCL visits St. Petersburg in August in 2019. Average daytime highs during this period are in the low 70s, with nighttime lows averaging in the low 50s. Precipitation averages 2–3 inches of rainfall per month during August. During the "white nights" of summer, the sun barely sets.

THE PORT A port terminal finished in 2011 houses passport control, a café, several shops, an ATM, and other basic services. Taxis are at the ready to take you on the 15-minute drive into town or to the transportation arranged by your port-adventure escort.

TOURIST HIGHLIGHTS Many visitors consider the **State Hermitage Museum** their highest priority. The scope and quality of the collections are easily comparable to those of the Louvre or the Metropolitan Museum of Art. The **Peter and Paul Fortress** houses a museum of Russian history. **St. Isaac's** is the largest domed cathedral in the world. The **Church of the Savior on Spilled Blood,** despite its ghoulish name, houses a gorgeous display of mosaics.

WHAT TO EAT You'll find many cuisines represented in St. Petersburg. For Russian fare, try one of the many soups, either cold ones such as beet-based borscht or warm ones made with meat and cabbage. You'll often find meat boiled, served cold, or minced in a pastry or pie. Carp, salmon, pike, and trout are typical seafood offerings. Blinis and pancakes are used as a base for fillings ranging from eggs, chopped meat, and onions, to cottage cheese and jam.

Most Russians drink tea on a daily basis. A popular beverage is *kvass,* which is made from fermented bread; it has an extremely low alcohol content and is sometimes flavored with fruit or spices. Vodka is plentiful, natch.

WHAT TO BUY Russian nesting dolls, or *matryoshka,* are a virtually mandatory purchase. In addition to traditional-style dolls, expect to find many painted with European and American pop stars, athletes, cartoon characters, and, yes, world leaders. Bargaining is common in outdoor stalls. Lacquered papier-mâché boxes, painted with scenes from Russian folk tales, are a popular purchase. Look for jewelry made with amber or detailed silver filigree.

Those knowledgeable about rugs or antiques may encounter some unique finds, but always ask about shipping before you buy. Pick up a book or two on local art and architecture. Of course, you'll want to take home a bottle of vodka (have it wrapped for shipping).

Stavanger, Norway

LANGUAGE Norwegian

HISTORY Stavanger has been a fishing port since the time of the Vikings. The town's official founding date is A.D. 1125, which coincides with the building of the local cathedral. Fishing and small-village life continued for centuries until the development of the petroleum industry, which is a key employer today. The mainland base for several offshore-drilling operations, Stavanger has one of the lowest unemployment rates in all of Europe.

WEATHER DCL visits Stavanger in July and August, when daytime highs are in the mid-60s and nighttime lows are in the mid-50s. Rainfall averages about 4 inches during the month of August.

THE PORT Ships dock at the edge of town. Many services and points of interest are within a 10-minute walk. Taxis, buses, and bike rentals are all located nearby.

TOURIST HIGHLIGHTS Stavanger's **Old Town** is home to charming white-washed cottages, perfect for photo opportunities. For those interested in the local fishing industry, a visit to the **Norwegian Canning Museum** is in order. Other area educational sites include the **Maritime Museum, Printing Museum,** and **Petroleum Museum.** Visitors interested in religious history may want to visit **Utstein Abbey,** Norway's only extant medieval monastery.

WHAT TO EAT Fish, shellfish, lamb, beef, and cheese figure prominently in local menus, as do moose, reindeer, and duck. Locally grown vegetables include tomatoes, cucumber, potatoes, and parsley. Look for lamb ragout and fish stew at the scenic **Flor & Fjœre** restaurant, on the nearby island of Sør-Hidle. Popular cafés in town include **Ostehuset** (Cheese House), where the raclette is locally sourced, and **Sjokoladepiken** (Chocolate Girl), which serves chocolate in nearly every form imaginable. A number of pubs in town serve beers from around the world.

WHAT TO BUY Textiles, knitwear, and handwoven items are popular purchases. Pewter goods are readily available; the work of area glassblowers and potters is also popular.

Tallinn, Estonia

LANGUAGE Estonian

HISTORY The first known large-scale building in Tallinn was a fortress constructed in 1050. Danes ruled this trade port, then known as Reval, during the 1200s. During the Protestant Reformation in the 1500s, Swedes controlled Estonia; then, in the early 1700s, Russians took control. Following World War I, Estonia declared its independence in 1918, but this ended during World War II, when the Soviet Union annexed the country. Estonia regained its independence in 1991, with the collapse of the USSR, and in 2004 the Baltic nation joined the European Union.

WEATHER DCL visits Tallinn in August during 2019. Average daytime highs for the month average in the high 60s, with nighttime lows in the low 50s. Rainfall averages about 2 inches for the month.

THE PORT Completed in 2012, the cruise terminal houses ATMs, a currency exchange, several small shops, and a tourist-information desk; free Wi-Fi is provided. The center of town is about 15 minutes away on foot. Once you get there, most attractions are easily walkable within a 0.6-square-mile area.

TOURIST HIGHLIGHTS **Raekoja Plats** is Tallinn's town square. The weathervane atop the Town Hall has been in place since 1530. **Kiek-in-de-Kök** ("Peep in the Kitchen") is a grand six-story structure housing historical displays and an art museum; built as an artillery tower in 1475, it gained its name because soldiers on duty could snoop on the residents of neighboring houses from its upper floors. **Toompea Castle** is a lovely example of medieval architecture. The top floor of the **Sokos Hotel Viru** was once a secret lair where the KGB eavesdropped on guests; today it houses a

small spy museum. If you'd like to get away from the city, coastal **Pirita** offers boat excursions.

WHAT TO EAT Estonian cuisine is heavy on meat (particularly pork) and potatoes, and on seafood in coastal areas. Soups, both broth- and cream-based, are popular as starters and main courses alike. Cabbage and dark rye bread are typical accompaniments. Local delicacies include marinated eel, *sült* (jellied pork), sliced tongue, and blood sausage served with berry jam. *Kali* is a lightly carbonated nonalcoholic beverage similar to unfermented beer. *Kama,* a dairy drink made with kefir (like liquid yogurt) and ground grain, has a milkshake-like texture. The local adult beverage is **Vana Tallinn,** a rum-based, cinnamon- and vanilla-flavored liqueur with an alcohol content of up to 50%.

WHAT TO BUY Handcrafted woolens are a popular take-home item. Look for sweaters, caps, mittens, and scarves adorned with geometrics or reindeer-related designs. Simple linen shirts and tunics are typical of the area. Area craftspeople expertly carve wooden items, particularly from juniper. Also look for local pottery and blown glass. **Kalev** is the biggest candy manufacturer in Estonia; pick up a box of chocolate to bring home. You also may find Soviet-era artwork and antiques, plus you may see Cuban cigars for sale.

PACIFIC COAST

CRUISES SAIL FROM San Diego or Vancouver

SHIP *Wonder*

CRUISE LENGTHS 7 days or fewer

DATES Before and after the Alaskan runs

WHAT TO PACK Walking shoes, sunscreen

SIGNATURE PORT ADVENTURE City tour—but you're better off exploring on your own.

CLASSIC ADD-ON Disneyland

PROS

- These cruises are among DCL's shortest and can therefore be very affordable, particularly if you already live on the West Coast.
- Short cruises are easy on your schedule.

CONS

- In our opinion, these cruises aren't the best way to see California.

San Diego, California *(See page 328 for full profile.)*

San Francisco, California

LANGUAGE English

HISTORY The first European settlers in the area were Spaniards, who arrived in 1769 and established the Presidio of San Francisco in 1776. By the early 1800s, the Bay Area had become part of Mexico. In 1846 the United States claimed California in the Mexican-American War, and two years

later, the gold rush brought an influx of miners and prospectors to the West, resulting in massive and rapid growth of the area.

In 1906 a major earthquake and fire destroyed much of the city. Many edifices were rebuilt in a grand Beaux Arts style. The Golden Gate and Oakland Bay Bridges were built in 1936–37, allowing farther expansion to outlying areas. In the 1950s and '60s, San Francisco's North Beach and Haight-Ashbury neighborhoods became the Meccas of America's counterculture.

WEATHER DCL visits San Francisco in April. The weather is mild to moderate year-round. When you visit, you can expect average daytime highs in the mid-60s and average nighttime lows in the mid-50s. Rainfall in April averages 1–2 inches for the month. The (in)famous San Francisco fog doesn't hit until summer.

THE PORT Disney cruises dock at **Pier 35,** which has minimal services. Steps away, however, you'll find the **Fisherman's Wharf** shopping and dining area. Also nearby, taxis, buses, and the **Bay Area Rapid Transit** system can take you into the heart of the city, just 10 minutes away.

TOURIST HIGHLIGHTS Watch the ships, eat the snacks, and gaze at the Golden Gate from Fisherman's Wharf. For a somber look into American penal history, take the nearby ferry over to the infamous **Alcatraz** penitentiary. Wander into **Chinatown** to dine and shop. Take in a museum, such as the **San Francisco Museum of Modern Art,** the **Fine Arts Museum of San Francisco,** or the **Walt Disney Family Museum.**

For an outdoor experience, take a hike among the giant redwoods of **Muir Woods National Monument.** Or drive out of town for a visit to the Napa and Sonoma wine country. To immerse yourself in the city's famed gay culture, visit the **Castro District.** Of course, no trip to San Francisco would be complete without a ride on a cable car past **Lombard Street,** said to be the crookedest street in the world.

For more jumping-off points, we suggest Kathleen Dodge Doherty's ***Walking San Francisco,*** published by our sister imprint Wilderness Press.

WHAT TO EAT Virtually all major cuisines are represented in San Francisco. Along Fisherman's Wharf, look for seafood in all forms, particularly chowder. Sourdough bread is an area specialty, often serving as a chowder bowl as well as a side dish. The vineyards north of the city make San Francisco a wine lover's paradise. Authentic Chinese dishes abound in Chinatown. The **Ghirardelli** chocolate factory no longer offers tours, but the ice-cream shop is still out of this world.

WHAT TO BUY For children, a toy cable car is a fun gift. Pick up some silks or carved stone in Chinatown. Sports fans will want jerseys representing the local teams, and foodies will want to pick up some Ghirardelli chocolate, a sourdough starter, or a fabulous bottle of wine.

Vancouver, British Columbia, Canada

(See page 271 for full profile.)

Victoria, British Columbia, Canada

(See page 272 for full profile.)

PANAMA CANAL

Note: *Please see our Mexico travel advisory on page 323.*

CRUISES SAIL FROM Miami, San Diego

SHIP *Wonder*

CRUISE LENGTH 14 nights

DATES Spring and fall as the ship heads to Alaska from Florida; westward in the spring and eastbound in the fall

WHAT TO PACK Your formalwear—14-night cruises give you lots of chances to dress up.

SIGNATURE PORT ADVENTURE It's all about going through the canal.

CLASSIC DISNEY ADD-ON Disneyland

COMMENTS Going through the Panama Canal is a classic itinerary for cruising, and you can let your friends and family know when they can see the ship in one of the great engineering achievements of the world by sending them to pancanal.com/eng/photo/camera-java.html. Be sure to wave to the camera!

PROS

- On a per-night basis, longer cruises are less expensive than shorter ones.
- Two weeks gives you lots of time to get to know the crew.
- This is a great way to see the Panama Canal.

CONS

- With just one trip each way per year, this itinerary can be hard to schedule.
- Other than the canal itself and **Cartagena, Colombia,** the ports are kind of a snooze—they're the same ones visited by every other line.

Cabo San Lucas, Mexico *(See page 324 for full profile.)*

Cartagena, Colombia

LANGUAGE Spanish

HISTORY Cartagena has been inhabited since 4000 B.C. Spanish explorers founded the city proper during the early 1500s. Periodic plundering followed, courtesy of pirates and privateers from France and England; Sir Francis Drake later led a major invasion. During the 17th century, the Spanish constructed a series of fortresses to protect the city. Throughout the 17th and 18th centuries, Cartagena was a major trading outpost. In 1811, what is now Colombia declared its independence from Spain, resulting in nearly a century of crisis. The new nation, known at the time as the United Provinces of New Granada, was reconquered by Spain in 1816; Colombian independence was finally achieved for good in 1883. Today, Cartagena is a prosperous tourist destination.

WEATHER In 2019, DCL visits Cartagena in February and November, but it's hot here year-round: expect daytime highs in the upper 80s, and average nighttime lows in the 70s. Rainfall is minimal in the winter; less than an

inch falls in February, with much heavier precipitation in the fall, averaging about 5 inches per month in November.

THE PORT The cruise terminal has basic services but not much else. A landscaped park near the dock gates has a café and small shops. Buses and taxis are available to take you to the main part of town.

TOURIST HIGHLIGHTS **Old Town** is a popular exploration spot. Look for the **Plaza de Bolívar** and the giant bronze statue of Simón Bolívar, who helped Bolivia (named after him), Colombia, and other South American countries secure independence from Spain. Nearby are the **Museo del Oro y Arqueología** and a 16th-century cathedral. The fortress **Castillo San Felipe de Barajas** presents a look into the area's past. The **Palacio de la Inquisición** exhibits artifacts from the Spanish Inquisition, including some very creative torture devices. Many beaches are located within a 10- to 20-minute taxi ride away from town; divers will find scuba and snorkel equipment available for rent.

WHAT TO EAT Restaurants serve food representative of most major world cuisines. Traditional local foods include grilled fish, meat, and rabbit; rice, cassava, and plantains are common side dishes. Street vendors sell *butifarras* (meatballs), *buñuelos* (cheese balls), and *arepas de huevo* (fried dough with an egg inside). *Mote de queso* is a soup made from yams, eggplant, and cheese. Fruit juices are available in abundance, both in restaurants and in street shacks. The local beer is **Club Colombia.**

WHAT TO BUY You'll find plenty of jewelry, particularly emeralds, for sale here. Many vendors are open to bargaining. Ornate (and sometimes obscene) wood carvings are common finds. For local flavor, search out loose-fitting traditional dresses, baskets, or handmade musical instruments. Java junkies will naturally want to take home some Colombian coffee.

Cozumel, Mexico *(See page 283 for full profile.)*

Galveston, Texas *(See page 286 for full profile.)*

Grand Cayman, Cayman Islands *(See page 287 for full profile.)*

Miami, Florida *(See page 291 for full profile.)*

New Orleans, Louisiana *(See page 292 for full profile.)*

Panama Canal, Panama

HISTORY The government of Spain first authorized the construction of a canal across the Isthmus of Panama—a narrow strip of land separating the Caribbean Sea from the Pacific Ocean—in 1819. Progress was scattershot for several decades thereafter, with planning beginning in earnest in 1876 and construction starting in 1881, this time spearheaded by the French government. Engineering struggles plagued early efforts to dig the canal, eventually resulting in the plan for a system of raised locks. Disease and construction difficulties led to the bankruptcy of the original funders and a long stall in the work process. The project was revived following

strategic interest from US President Theodore Roosevelt, with the United States taking formal control over the canal in 1904. Several years were spent creating an infrastructure capable of supporting the materials and assembling the labor force required to complete the task. Lock building commenced in 1909 and was finished in 1913. In 1914, a French boat, the *Alexandre La Valley,* became the first to completely traverse the canal. The Panama Canal subsequently revolutionized world trade patterns, cutting nearly 8,000 miles off a sea journey from New York to San Francisco.

In 1977, the United States began to reduce its role in the region. (The Panama Canal Zone, a strip of land paralleling the canal immediately to its north and south, was an unincorporated territory of the US from 1903 until 1979, when it reverted to Panama.) Today, the Panama Canal Authority, an agency of the Panamanian government, oversees the canal. In 2016, a nine-year, $5 billion expansion project was completed, widening and deepening the canal's locks and adding a new lane of traffic.

WEATHER Warm, wet, and oppressively humid. In 2019, however, DCL's early Panama Canal crossing is in February, which is significantly drier than the spring, with less than an inch of rain. If you or your hair has an aversion to humidity, then the February sailing is the one for you.

THE PORT The ship moves through the canal without letting off passengers.

TOURIST HIGHLIGHTS The highlight of the voyage is watching how the canal's locks fill and release water to move the ship up and down through the terrain. It takes 8–10 hours to get through all of the locks, so you have plenty of time to catch the action.

Port Canaveral, Florida *(See page 296 for full profile.)*

Puerto Vallarta, Mexico *(See page 327 for full profile.)*

San Diego, California *(See page 328 for full profile.)*

TRANSATLANTIC

CRUISES SAIL FROM Barcelona, Dover, New York City

SHIP *Magic*

CRUISE LENGTHS 10 or 13 nights

DATES Spring and fall as the ship heads to Europe from Florida; eastward in the spring and westbound in the fall

PROS	CONS
■ This can be a cost-effective way to travel to Europe if you have the time to spare.	■ You may not have 2 weeks to dedicate to a transatlantic cruise.
■ A transatlantic crossing is on many cruisers' bucket lists.	■ This is one-way transportation. Even if you can find a good deal on the cruise itself, remember that you'll have to leave room in your budget for your airfare home.
■ You can sometimes find great last-minute deals on these cruises.	

WHAT TO PACK Your formalwear—you'll have plenty of opportunities to dress up—and a steamer trunk, if you have one.

SIGNATURE PORT ADVENTURE When it comes to transatlantic cruises, it's all about the journey rather than the destination.

CLASSIC DISNEY ADD-ON Disneyland Paris

COMMENTS Wanna travel to or from Europe without jet lag *and* pretend that you've gone back in time? Crossing the Atlantic by ship is the old-school way to do it, harking back to the era of the grand ocean liner.

Barcelona, Spain *(See page 310 for full profile.)*

Cádiz, Spain *(See page 311 for full profile.)*

Cartagena, Spain

LANGUAGE Spanish

HISTORY What is now Cartagena has been inhabited since approximately 200 B.C. The city had its ancient heyday during the late Roman Empire, when it was variously known as Carthago Nova and Carthago Spartaria, capital of the province of Hispania Carthaginensis. Following this period, Cartagena was variously occupied by the Visigoths, the Umayyada Caliphate, the Caliphate of Cordóba, the Taifa of Murcia, and several other would-be conquerers. In 1296, Cartagena was annexed to the Kingdom of Aragón.

As far back as the 16th century, the city has been one of the most important defensive ports in the Mediterranean. More recently, during the Spanish Civil War of the 1930s, Cartagena was the main base of the Spanish Republican Navy and one of the last cities of the Republican (loyalist) faction to surrender to nationalist rebels led by Generalissimo Francisco Franco. The city saw increased industrial activity during the 1950s and today is a major cruise-ship destination.

WEATHER DCL visits Cartagena in May. Temperatures are consistent throughout the year, with daytime highs averaging in the high 80s and nighttime lows in the mid-70s. Rainfall averages about 2 inches a month in late spring.

THE PORT Most cruise vessels moor at **Pier Alfonso XII Cruise Terminal,** about a 10-minute walk into Cartagena proper, which hosts restaurants, shops, and other services. The terminal itself has a taxi stand, ATMs, and information booths. Shuttles into town are also available.

TOURIST HIGHLIGHTS The **Roman Theatre** is a well-preserved architectural relic from the first century B.C. The **Portal Museo Arqueológico Municipal de Cartagena** is built on the site of a necropolis, or burial ground, dating from the 400s A.D.; the exhibits include pottery, sculpture, fossils, and other ancient artifacts. The **Castillo de la Concepción** is the highest point in the city, offering panoramic views of the region. Built on the site of a Roman temple, the castle was later turned into a Moorish fortification. **Cala Cortina Beach** is a nice place to relax in the sun.

WHAT TO EAT The region's long growing season ensures fresh vegetables in abundance throughout the year. A favorite dish is artichoke hearts sautéed in beef stock and served with pine nuts. Other veggie highlights include broad beans, fried with onion or cooked in ham-and-chorizo stew; tomato-and-chard omelettes; thistle in almond sauce; and

roasted-pepper salad. Seafood specialties include fresh cod and tuna with tomatoes. Rice is a typical side dish.

WHAT TO BUY Leather goods, jewelry, rugs, and ceramics are popular souvenirs. Look for locally crafted items rather than machine-made imports.

Cork, Ireland *(See page 337 for full profile.)*

Dover, England *(See page 314 for full profile.)*

Halifax, Nova Scotia, Canada

LANGUAGE English

HISTORY The first known settlers of the Halifax area were the Acadians and the Mi'kmaq people. European settlement began in earnest when the British staked claim in the mid-1700s, leading to "Father LeLoutre's War," a dispute between the native peoples and the British. The French and Indian War spurred the establishment of the Halifax Naval Yard in 1759. The late 1700s saw a modest immigration boom comprising Germans, Dutch, New Englanders, and residents of Martinique and many other areas. During the American Revolution, Halifax became a staging area for British invasions of the colonies. The British naval stronghold remained throughout the Napoleonic wars and the War of 1812.

Throughout the 1800s, Halifax was a key point for trade between Canada and Europe. In 1912, recovery efforts for the *Titanic* disaster were based in Halifax, and during both World Wars, Halifax was a launch point for British efforts against their enemies. Current industries include tourism, shipping, and fishing.

WEATHER DCL visits Halifax in late September, when daytime highs average in the high 50s and nighttime lows average in the high 40s. Typical rainfall in autumn averages fewer than 1.5 inches per month.

THE PORT The dock has minimal services., and the waterfront area is easily accessible on foot. Shops, restaurants, and banking services are all within a 10-minute walk. Taxis are available near the pier, as are bicycle rentals. Car-rental desks can be found near the **Westin Nova Scotian** hotel, a 5-minute walk from the ship.

TOURIST HIGHLIGHTS **Halifax Citadel National Historic Site** is a star-shaped naval station in the center of the city. Costumed guides lead tours of musket galleries, earthen ramparts, garrison cells, and guard rooms. The **Canadian Museum of Immigration at Pier 21** is a National Historic Site focused on the experiences of immigrants as they arrived in Canada. The **Maritime Museum of the Atlantic** includes an extensive exhibit on the *Titanic.* Beer lovers will want to sample the wares at **Alexander Keith's Brewery,** a local brewhouse since 1820; the **Garrison Brewery Tour** offers another view of beer-making. Also look for a pop-up farmers market near the pier that sells fresh and prepared food for purchase. For a look at classic maritime scenery, take a drive to nearby **Peggy's Cove,** a fishing village known for its picturesque lighthouse. Animal lovers will want to book a whale-watching excursion during their time in Halifax.

WHAT TO EAT Seafood reigns. Look for lobster prepared in many styles, including in lobster rolls as well as boiled and broiled. Other favorites include scallops, haddock, crab, mussels, smoked eel, and jarred pickled

fish. Lunenburg pork sausage is often used as the base of hearty stews or fresh fried. Many main dishes are served with cabbage or root vegetables including potatoes, carrots, and onions. Rappie pie isn't a pie at all; rather, it's a casserole of potatoes and chicken broth, often served with butter or molasses. Tasty local blueberries are baked into muffins, pancakes, and other goodies. A locally legendary sweet treat is the "Fat Archie," a giant cookie made with molasses, cinnamon, and (usually) raisins. Look for local ales to accompany your meal, particularly selections brewed by Alexander Keith.

WHAT TO BUY Halifax is known for its fine crystal; look for hand-blown pieces. Pewter items are also popular, as are kitchen items embellished with images of lobsters or nautical symbols. A jar of blueberry jam makes a nice take-home gift.

Lisbon, Portugal

(See page 317 for full profile.)

Málaga, Spain

LANGUAGE Spanish

HISTORY Málaga was founded by the Phoenicians in about 770 B.C. Later invasions resulted in periods of rule by the Carthaginians, Romans, Arabs, and Spanish. The city experienced a period of rapid development in the 19th century, becoming one of the most industrialized cities in Spain, but this progress faltered when later leaders focused more energy on cities to the north. Today, Málaga is part of the Spanish autonomous community of Andalusia.

WEATHER DCL visits Málaga in May, when average daytime highs are in the mid-70s and average nighttime lows are in the mid-50s. Precipitation is minimal during the month, with average rainfall of less than 1 inch.

THE PORT Málaga has a cruise terminal with basic services. Visitors can reach the city's main commercial district on foot in about 5 minutes.

TOURIST HIGHLIGHTS **La Alcazaba** is a spectacularly preserved Arab fortress, boasting more than 100 towers and wonderful views of the city. **Gilbralfaro Castle** is a Moorish ruin with vistas of distant Gibraltar. The **Roman Theater of Málaga,** uncovered in 1953, is a fine example of Roman architecture from the first century B.C. Other popular sights are the **Cathedral of Málaga; La Malagueta,** the city's bullring; and the **Mercado Central,** a covered market that sells local meat, produce, and tapas. Fans of Pablo Picasso will enjoy the **Museo Picasso Málaga** as well as the **Museo Casa Natal,** the artist's birthplace. If you're in a theme park mood, **Tivoli World** has fun rides and gardens.

WHAT TO EAT Food in Málaga is typical of Andalusia. Soups include gazpacho, *porra antequerana* (a sort of thick gazpacho with ham), *ajoblanco* (a cold soup with bread, garlic, and ground almonds), and *sopa de ajos* (a hot soup with garlic, bread, and poached eggs), as well as various fish stews and chowders. Seafood—including anchovies, mackerel, hake, shrimp, sardines—is served grilled or fried. For dessert, try almond biscuits or honey pastries. Be sure to sample some of the local sangria.

WHAT TO BUY Málaga has outposts of most major Spanish retailers. Local items to look for include leather goods, ceramics, woven shawls, and jewelry. Olive oil–based soaps are popular gifts, as are religious accoutrements

such as incense, candles, and statuary. Edible souvenirs include sweet Málaga wine (similar to port), olive oil, and candy made with almonds and honey.

Miami, Florida *(See page 291 for full profile.)*

New York, New York *(See page 274 for full profile.)*

Ponta Delgada, Azores Islands, Portugal

LANGUAGE Portuguese

HISTORY The first known human habitation of the Azores—a chain of nine islands in the North Atlantic Ocean about 850 miles west of Portugal—occurred during the mid-15th century, with most settlers arriving from the mainland. Other early residents were Flemish sailors. English incursions onto the islands failed, but the Spanish were more successful and held control for a period in the early 1600s. The Portuguese later resumed rule of the area.

During the 18th and 19th centuries, the Azores served as a trade and travel way station, and during WWII, they were home to a British naval station that performed aerial U-boat surveillance. In 1976, the islands became the Autonomous Region of the Azores, which, together with mainland Portugal and the Autonomous Region of Madeira, makes up the Portuguese Republic.

WEATHER DCL visits Ponta Delgada in May, when daytime highs average in the mid-60s and nighttime lows average in the mid-50s. Rainfall averages about 3 inches for the month.

THE PORT There are few basic services at the cruise terminal itself, but there are many shops and restaurants within a 5-minute walk of port. Taxis and car-rental desks are available at the port area. Public buses service much of **São Miguel Island,** on which Ponta Delgada is located.

TOURIST HIGHLIGHTS Ponta Delgada is a picturesque place for a stroll, its lovely whitewashed topped with red roofs. The **Convent of Esperança** and the **Church of Santo Cristo** are located near the city center. The convent has an ornate public chapel as well as a more modest one for the nuns' use. Many Azores visitors are interested in the islands' geological activity—**Fire Lake** has interesting craters and lush greenery, while **Sete Cidades Crater Lake** is another nice option for hiking or photography. Two tea plantations, both in the northern part of the island; offer tours and tastings. The **Arruda Açores Pineapple Plantation** is another place to learn about the island's agriculture. Whale- and dolphin-watching excursions are also offered. The **Formigas Islets Nature Reserve,** a cluster of rock outcrops at the eastern edge of the island chain, is a nationally designated marine-life habitat and a popular diving destination.

WHAT TO EAT Azorean cuisine, like Portuguese cuisine in general, is homey and hearty. A typical family meal includes *caldo verde,* a kale soup studded with chunks of potato and *linguiça* sausage. Seafood figures heavily in traditional dishes, *bacalhau* (salt cod) being a staple. The Azores are also known for their rich dairy products—yogurt is a typical breakfast staple, coffee is served with steamed milk, and the local cheeses are top-notch. Pineapples grown in the Azores are often exported to the Portuguese mainland, but

you will find them in many desserts on the islands. *Massa sovada,* or Portuguese sweet bread, originated in the Azores but is familiar to Americans as Hawaiian bread (Portuguese laborers brought their culinary traditions with them to Hawaii in the 1870s–early 1900s).

WHAT TO BUY Azorean embroidery and lace work are world-renowned, adorning tablecloths, bedspreads, and clothing. Other local crafts include wicker baskets and furniture, along with gorgeous hand-painted ceramic ware: dishes, vases, teapots, mugs, and more.

Portland, England, United Kingdom *(See page 350 for full profile.)*

Sydney, Nova Scotia, Canada

LANGUAGE English

HISTORY The indigenous residents of the area were ancestors of the Mi'kmaq people. In the 1700s, the colonial town of Old Sydney was founded by British loyalists fleeing the American Revolution. It served as the English capital of Cape Breton from its founding until 1820, when the island colony and its rich coal fields became part of Nova Scotia. Coal mining brought industry to the region, and in the early 1900s Sydney become a major steel-manufacturing center. But the prosperity brought by coal and steel diminished as plants closed in the second half of the 20th century. Today, Sydney's primary industries are tourism and call centers.

WEATHER DCL visits Sydney in September, when daytime highs average in the mid-60s and nighttime lows average in the mid-40s. September typically sees about 3 inches of rain over the course of the month.

THE PORT The dock is adjacent to town. Expect a 5-minute walk to **Charlotte Street** and the city center. Services are all within walking distance, but taxis may be available. One quirk of the port is the world's largest fiddle: **Fidheal Mhor A' Ceilidh**—the Big Fiddle of the Ceilidh. (You can't miss it.) The cruise pavilion itself is home to a market that houses craft vendors, along with a small museum dedicated to Cape Breton Island history.

TOURIST HIGHLIGHTS A highlight of the Sydney area is the **Alexander Graham Bell National Historic Site,** which focuses on Bell's life and work. The **Fortress of Louisbourg National Historic Site** is the largest historical reconstruction in North America; see soldiers' living quarters, cannons, and additional exhibits related to the fishing industry. At the **Cape Breton Miners Museum,** you can follow a retired coal miner below ground to observe what his average workday was like. For outdoor fun, sail the **Bras D'Or Lake** for bird-watching, or drive the **Cabot Trail** for stunning vistas.

WHAT TO EAT Fresh seafood is plentiful. Boiled lobster is common, as are many variations of fish chowder. Blueberries are plentiful in the summer; eat them as is or find them prepared in muffins, cobblers, and pies. Maple syrup and maple candies make nice take-home treats.

WHAT TO BUY Nova Scotia is known for its fine woolen goods: hats, scarves, and mittens as well as woolen home goods such as tablecloths. Pewter mugs and plates are common. Also find the work of local artists sold in shops near the port.

PART TWELVE

PORT ADVENTURES

DISNEY CRUISE LINE OFFERS more than 600 shore excursions—or "port adventures," in Disney-speak—for guests to experience while their ship is docked. While it's impossible for us to have tried them all, we have embarked on quite a few. We've also interviewed scores of families and DCL employees to learn which are the most popular and which ones they'd recommend to friends.

Because most Disney cruises stop at **Castaway Cay** (see Part Ten), this section includes detailed reviews of its port adventures. These generally last 1–3½ hours; others, such as snorkeling or biking, are self-guided. Disney staff leads most (but not all) of these excursions.

Beyond Castaway Cay, most port adventures last about 3–6 hours, including transportation time, and all are designed to fit comfortably into the ship's schedule. Third-party companies based near the port run virtually all of the port adventures, except the ones on Castaway Cay. On the day of your activity, you'll be instructed to gather somewhere on the ship, such as a restaurant or lounge, at a predetermined time. Once you're there, a Disney cast member will ensure that you have the correct port-adventure tickets and identification to reboard the ship. You also may be asked to sign a liability waiver to participate in a particular activity.

When those tasks are complete, everyone signed up for the activity will be escorted by cast members off the ship to a meeting point on the port's docks. There, representatives of the third-party company running the port adventure will meet you. You'll be in their care until you're returned to the port after your activity.

FINDING PORT ADVENTURES

IF YOU'VE BOOKED A CRUISE, you can see your port-adventure options on the DCL website in the **My Disney Cruise** section for your

20 QUESTIONS TO ASK WHEN CHOOSING A PORT ADVENTURE
1. Have I looked at all the physical requirements of the excursion?
2. Does this excursion's price make sense to me?
3. Are there hidden fees that increase the cost of the excursion—for example, add-on photo packages or meals?
4. How does the price of this individual excursion fit into my overall excursion budget?
5. What percentage of the excursion will be spent in transportation?
6. What percentage of the excursion will be spent with a guide versus on my own?
7. Is there an adult-only or teen-only version of this excursion? Do those variations make more sense for me?
8. Does the excursion's mode of transportation make sense for me? (Guests who get motion sickness or who are afraid of heights, for example, may want to avoid helicopter excursions.)
9. Is a meal or snack provided as part of the excursion? Do I want there to be?
10. Will adverse weather conditions drastically affect my enjoyment of the excursion?
11. Does the excursion take place in a port where guests tender to shore? (Tender excursions are more likely to be canceled.)
12. Are there similar excursions at other ports during my itinerary? (For example, numerous ports have dolphin encounters—is this particular port the best for such an excursion?)
13. Are there similar excursions at the same port? (For example, several dogsledding variations are available in Juneau—consider which one appeals to you the most.)
14. How long is the excursion? What percentage of my day will it encompass? Are there other things I'd rather do in port?
15. Is a similar experience available close to home or at another frequently visited vacation spot? (For example, zip-line and go-kart experiences are available in several ports—ask yourself whether you want to spend cruise time for these when you could easily do them elsewhere.)
16. What is the level of activity involved in this excursion?
17. Is this excursion too similar to something I'm doing in another port?
18. Will the timing of the excursion interfere with my child's dining or nap schedule?
19. Can I bring a stroller on the excursion?
20. Are there elements of the excursion specifically designed with children in mind?

voyage (see page 39). But before you book, you can also see full lists of options that may help you choose a specific itinerary.

Your typical starting point for researching port adventures is the DCL website; see disneycruise.disney.go.com/port-adventures/overview. Click on the region where you'll be cruising, and then select a port under the "Ports of Call" tab. From here you can further sort excursions using the "Experience Type" tab (nature, sightseeing, culinary, and so on), the "Activity Level" tab (athletic, moderate, or mild), the "Accessibility" tab (wheelchair-accessible, and so on), and the "Price Range" tab. Clicking on any individual port adventure lets you drill down to specifics like price, age requirements, clothing requirements, length of the adventure, and so on. Some ports offer dozens of choices at a full range of activity levels and price points.

Of course, you're not limited to Disney's offerings: you can explore on your own (see Part Eleven for general suggestions in the profile for each port), or you can book an alternative excursion through another vendor. If you don't see something that strikes your fancy on the DCL website, check the shore-excursion information for other cruise lines. There will likely be overlap, but Norwegian or Carnival, for example, may have identified a third-party vendor that better suits your style.

If you're not up for a full port adventure but you also don't want to hang out on the ship all day, you can also book a day pass to a hotel or resort in port. A safe and convenient alternative to finding a beach on your own, a resort pass gives you access to amenities such as pools, beaches, spas, and the like; some packages include transfers and meal vouchers as well. The best source we've found for passes is **Resort for a Day** (resortforaday.com).

Still another option is to try our **custom walking tours.** See page 383 for details.

Finally, remember that you're under no obligation to participate in *any* organized adventures. Feel free to hang out on the ship or just amble aimlessly around the port city. Your vacation, your call.

EVALUATING A PORT ADVENTURE

THE PORT ADVENTURES OFFERED through Disney Cruise Line have all been vetted by DCL staff for quality and reliability. When you book your excursion through DCL, it's unlikely that you'll end up with

SCOTT SAYS *by Scott Sanders*

PLANNING YOUR PORT ADVENTURE

I'M A BIG PROPONENT of putting together my own port adventures, either with just my family or a small group. It's easy to plan a walking tour with public transportation, and not much more difficult to book a private tour—also significantly cheaper than those offered by Disney. Just remember that it's your responsibility to get back to the ship on time.

No matter how you explore a port, it's a good idea to take water and snacks ashore. In a pinch, you can grab some boxed cereal from the breakfast buffet. If you're traveling with kids and the tour involves traveling on a bus or van for a considerable amount of time, consider bringing an activity for them to do during the trip. We've been on excursions where the total travel time was pushing 4 hours—and not all of it was scenic.

Finally, take some cash to tip your tour guides if appropriate for the excursion; US dollars are almost always welcome worldwide.

an experience that's *completely* without merit. That said, just because an excursion is right for one person doesn't mean it's right for you. If you ask yourself the questions in the chart on page 366, you should increase your odds of choosing the best option for your needs.

Our research shows that two of the most important factors that affect a guest's enjoyment of an excursion are the weather in port and the quality of the guide. Even with the best planning, you may find that a sudden storm or an inexperienced guide dims the quality of the adventure. Of course, if the excursion turns out to be a total wash or the guide is a jerk, you should speak to the tour provider and to Disney, but try not to let normal ups and downs derail your enjoyment.

BOOKING EXCURSIONS ON YOUR OWN VS. THROUGH DISNEY

AS WE'VE MENTIONED, YOU CAN BOOK port adventures on your own or through Disney. Some advantages to booking through Disney include the following:

- **CONVENIENCE OF SELECTION.** To book through Disney, just head over to the DCL website (see page 39). For each port, you'll see a menu of options; it's a one-stop spot for information, including activity descriptions, age/height/weight restrictions, costs, and related data. If you find an excursion appealing, you can book it with just a few clicks.
- **CONVENIENCE OF BILLING.** When you book through Disney, the fee appears on your stateroom bill, which you can pay using any of the acceptable DCL methods, or in US dollars, British pounds, or euros. As an added bonus, you don't pay a deposit and you don't pay until you sail. If you're booking an excursion in another country on your own, you may have to pay a large deposit, you may have to pay in another currency, or you may be limited to a particular credit card or other form of payment. And remember that if you're using Disney Gift Cards as a payment method on the ship, you may get an effective 5% discount if you've purchased your gift cards through Target; plus, you may be eligible for other discounts when you buy through Sam's Club, Costco, or another retailer.
- **SAFETY.** Of course, you'll want to exercise an abundance of caution on *any* port adventure, but if you book a Disney-vetted excursion, you know that they've done some of the work for you. Disney verifies that the excursions they offer are through legitimate businesses. They make sure that the transportation used is safe and that the guides are accountable for your whereabouts. If you book an excursion on your own, the onus is on you to do that research.
- **COMMUNICATION WITH THE SHIP.** When you book an excursion through Disney, they know where you are. If something unforeseen happens, they have representatives who can contact your group and vice versa. If you book your excursion on your own, cast members on the ship will likely have no idea where you are. And they're not going to wait up for you if you're not back by sail-away time.

- **LANGUAGE ISSUES.** Booking your excursion through Disney means that the transaction will take place in English. If you're booking an excursion on your own for a port in another country, the website or phone representative may use another language or speak limited English.
- **CANCELLATION POLICIES.** DCL's port-adventure cancellation policy is clearly stated on its website (also see the section below). If you book on your own, you may be subject to an entirely different set of policies, which may or may not be clearly outlined—or fair.

unofficial **TIP**
Port adventures booked on your own or through non-Disney vendors may have different cancellation policies, so always ask when booking.

On the other hand, some advantages to booking your port adventures through an outside vendor are as follows:

- **PRICE.** Many guests have found that they can save money by booking excursions similar to Disney's on their own.
- **MORE OPTIONS.** While Disney offers a wide range of excursions at each port, the list of options is certainly finite. If you book on your own, there's no limit to the number of choices you might have.
- **CUSTOMIZATION.** When you book on your own, you can often work with a vendor to put together an excursion custom-tailored to your interests or hobbies. You might be able to combine visits to two disparate sites in one excursion. You might be able to skip part of a standard tour that doesn't interest you. You might be able to linger longer at a favorite venue. Or you might be able to arrange for transportation that accommodates a physical need, such as wheelchair use.
- **BOOKING WINDOW.** On the DCL website, your ability to access excursion booking is based on your Castaway Club status (see page 65). First-time cruisers booking through Disney might be locked out of some popular activities because they've become fully booked before they had access. When booking excursions on your own, you're not subject to any waiting period.

CANCELING A PORT ADVENTURE

DEPENDING ON YOUR CASTAWAY CLUB LEVEL, you may make port-adventure reservations up to 120 days in advance. Once you make a reservation, you may cancel it with no penalty up to three days before you sail—no refunds after that. Of course, you're not charged if Disney or the tour provider cancels the excursion due to weather or other unforeseen circumstances.

The only other exception to the cancellation penalty occurs if you decide to upgrade your excursion. You may change a previously booked port adventure to one that's more expensive; you'll simply pay the difference in excursion fees without any penalty. To upgrade on board, visit Guest Services or the Port Adventures desk.

PORT ADVENTURES *on* CASTAWAY CAY

WE CONSIDER CASTAWAY CAY'S SHORE EXCURSIONS among the best values of any that DCL has to offer. Here's a quick rundown of what's available.

BICYCLE RENTALS

THESE SINGLE-SPEED ROAD BIKES with plump tires are good for getting some exercise while exploring the island. Men's and women's models are available, and the seats are designed for comfort. The seats can be adjusted up and down to suit your leg length, although years spent on the island have rusted many of the metal cams used to loosen the seats. Ask a cast member to help (they have wrenches!) if yours won't budge.

Pick up your bicycles just past the Pelican Point tram stop, near the middle of the family beaches. You can also rent bikes next to the Serenity Bay adult beach, just behind the Castaway Air Bar. Cost is $13 for a one-day rental or $16 for two days.

BOAT RENTALS

VARIOUS WATERCRAFT, including one- and two-seat kayaks, sailboats, and paddleboats, are available for rent in half-hour increments. Costs range from $15 for a single-seat kayak to $29 for a Hobie Cat catamaran. The paddleboats require an extraordinary amount of leg power to get anywhere, and 30 minutes is going to be plenty for most people. Previous sailing experience is required to rent a sailboat.

CASTAWAY CAY 5K RUN

ONE OF THE BEST PORT ADVENTURES to start your day on Castaway Cay is fun, well organized, and totally free. Runners and walkers who wish to participate in the 5K meet around 8:15 on the morning the ship arrives at the island. The meeting location is almost always one of the bars in the adult area of the ship, because that's the way the best races begin. Check your *Personal Navigator* the night before for details on when and where to meet.

Sign up for the 5K at the Port Adventures desk anytime; you also can just show up at the designated meeting place on the morning of the race. Two cast members will meet you there—make sure you have your Key to the World Card and ID. They'll give you a runner's bib (a nice touch for this unchipped race) and safety pins; then you'll walk off the ship with the rest of the runners toward the start of the race, by the Pelican Point tram stop. Parents who need to drop their kids off at Scuttle's Cove will be given time to do so on the way.

CASTAWAY CAY 5K RUN FAQS

- **What should I pack?** Don't forget your running shoes and clothes.
- **Can my kid join me?** Sort of. Disney officially restricts participants to guests age 12 and older, so your child won't get a bib or medal. Because of the informal setup of the race, though, there's no way to stop kids under 12 from running along with you. Parents are given time during the walk to the race start to drop off kids at Scuttle's Cove.
- **Is it a race?** This 5K brings out people of all abilities and dedication to their running. Take it at your own pace and just enjoy it.
- **Is there a time limit?** Not officially, but the cast members would probably appreciate it if you wrapped up within 40–45 minutes. (There's also a Castaway Cay Power Walk if that's more your speed.)
- **Can I buy a souvenir?** Yes. When RunDisney began sponsoring this event, we got "medals" (plastic) and the opportunity to buy T-shirts at the end (in addition to the race bibs you receive). The T-shirts, while attractive, are cotton instead of tech material, so they're not ideal apparel for serious running.
- **Can I shower after the race?** There are no private showers on the island, just the ones by the restrooms for knocking off the sand. If you didn't bring a swimsuit with you and don't plan to get right into the water, you'll need to go back to your stateroom to shower.
- **How's the weather?** Hot. Drink lots of water. Wear sunscreen. Eating at Remy or Palo the night before probably isn't the best idea. Did we mention that it's hot?
- **What about itineraries with two stops at Castaway Cay?** You get two opportunities to run. *Yay!* You can do both or either.
- **Is water available?** Yes. Not only does a cast member offer water on the course, but the 5K also begins and ends by a regular water stop. Drink up!

Once you arrive at the start, everyone is given a chance to hit the restroom and drop anything they don't want to run with in the storage area by the bike rentals. This is unsecured, so don't leave your gold doubloons, but other stuff is fine.

Once everyone is ready, you're off and running. The route includes a trip up and down the airstrip and two loops out to the viewpoint. You'll be sharing the road with the trams as well as folks on bicycles, so be aware of your surroundings. One cast member will be at the entrance to the loop with water—take advantage of it, because this run is *hot.*

The other cast member will be stationed by the digital timer at the end of the race to congratulate you on your spectacular finish and give you a medal. Wear it proudly for the other folks who were still at the breakfast buffet while you were out running 3 miles in the heat.

The 5K and snorkeling are the two port adventures that we always do on the island. They're two fun and affordable ways to enjoy your day.

BOTTOM FISHING

A 3-HOUR CATCH-AND-RELEASE fishing excursion ($184 per person) takes place in the waters around Castaway Cay, with Disney-provided fishing rods and bait. Your boat's captain will take you into the waters around the island; the most commonly caught species are yellow jack, grouper, various porgies, and snapper. It's not unheard of to hook a

barracuda or small shark, too. Most charters leave around 9 a.m. and are back in time for lunch. Cruisers who are prone to seasickness shouldn't take this excursion; kids must be age 8 or older to participate.

CASTAWAY RAY'S STINGRAY ADVENTURE

THIS IS YOUR CHANCE TO PET AND FEED small- and medium-size stingrays in a supervised, structured setting on the shore of the Stingray Lagoon. Disney keeps dozens of these stingrays in a sectioned-off part of Castaway Cay's lagoon, and the stingrays are trained to use a special feeding platform at mealtimes. The cost is $56 for guests age 10 and up, $45 for kids age 5–9.

Holding a specially formulated pellet of food between two fingers, you'll place your hand, palm down, on the platform. A stingray will swim up to the platform, glide over your hand, and grab the food in its mouth. You'll also have the chance to pet each ray as it swims by. There's plenty of food and plenty of stingrays for everyone. Besides the feeding, you'll get a brief introduction to stingrays, skates, and sharks before you begin, when a cast member reviews rules and procedures.

Many children are worried about being bitten by the stingrays, and let's face it: the word *sting* in their name doesn't exactly make rays seem cuddly. But rays don't have teeth, and the only thing that seems to get them excited is the prospect of feeding time. Calling them rays may help your kids find these animals more approachable (their fears might also be assuaged by a mention of the friendly Mr. Ray in *Finding Nemo*). Be aware that the stingray adventure is prone to cancellation in windy conditions.

FLOAT AND TUBE RENTALS

INNER TUBES AND RECTANGULAR FLOATS are available for $13 for one day or $16 for two days. You can swap out one type for the other during the day.

GLASS-BOTTOM-BOAT EXCURSION

GUESTS BOARD A SMALL MOTORIZED WATERCRAFT that holds about 25 people and ventures about 15 minutes out into the ocean. You can observe sea life below through several "windows" in the floor of the boat. During the trip, you're accompanied by a local guide who discusses the fish and other natural elements you'll encounter.

The highlight of the tour takes place at approximately the midpoint of the journey: guests are given a cup filled with about 1 ounce of oatmeal, which they toss overboard to attract fish. During the feeding portion of the tour, several hundred tropical fish of various species surround the boat, and the guide points out the characteristics of as many fish as possible. The feeding lasts about 5 minutes, after which the fish disappear quickly. Sightings of fish at other points of the tour are sporadic.

The trip takes about 45 minutes to an hour (about 15 minutes out, 15 minutes back, and around 15 minutes parked at viewing spots along the reef adjacent to Castaway Cay). Cost is $49 for adults and $34 for kids ages 9 and under, including infants and toddlers. Guests must be able to climb five steps to board and debark and must also stand aboard the boat for the duration of the excursion.

PARASAILING

GUESTS LOOKING FOR A BIRD'S-EYE VIEW of paradise should check out this excursion. Floating hundreds of feet in the air, you're master of all you survey, or at least it seems that way for several minutes.

You board a speedboat and travel several hundred yards away from land. Then, in singles or pairs, you stand at the back of the boat and are harnessed to a line-bound parachute that is slowly let out until you and the parachute are 600–1,000 feet above the water. Enjoy panoramic views of your ship, Castaway Cay, and beyond.

Each excursion takes about 10 people onto the boat. There are no ride-alongs—every guest on the boat must pay. Your actual parasail event will last about 5–7 minutes. Depending on the number of other guests, the entire experience lasts 45 minutes–1 hour.

Open to guests age 8 and up, parasailing excursions cost $110 for both adults and kids. Guests must weigh between 90 and 375 pounds; those who weigh less than 90 pounds may be able to ride if they fly in tandem with another guest, but their combined weight may not exceed 375 pounds. Determination of single or tandem rides is at the discretion of the staff.

Kids under age 13 must be accompanied by a paying adult age 18 or older. Guests ages 13–17 may go on the excursion unaccompanied but must be escorted to the Marge's Barges meeting area by an adult age 18 or older. All guests must sign a safety waiver.

You must leave your shoes on the dock and are strongly discouraged from wearing a hat or glasses during your sail; a storage area is provided on the boat for your personal belongings. Wheelchairs and other wheeled mobility devices cannot be accommodated.

No photography service is provided during the excursion—you're welcome to bring a camera along, but you assume all liability if you lose it. (Understandably, anything that falls into the ocean can't be retrieved.)

SNORKELING

THIS IS ONE OF THE LEAST EXPENSIVE, most rewarding shore excursions offered on a Disney cruise. We recommend it for every family. Cost is $18 for kids ages 5–9 for one day, $23 for two days; guests age 10 and up pay $34 for one day, $45 for two days.

First, find some chairs on the family beach, where you can store your stuff while you're in the water. If possible, choose something near

a vertical landmark such as a tree; it will be easier to find when you come back to shore.

Next, pick up your snorkeling gear at Gil's Fins and Boats, a short walk from Scuttle's Cove, the island's first tram stop. You'll be given a mask, snorkel, fins, and an inflatable buoyancy vest to make swimming easier. Also pick up a blue-mesh gear bag, which makes it easier to haul your stuff back to your beach chairs.

Put on your vest before you get in the water, but don't inflate it just yet. Wait until you're in hip-high water to put on your flippers, because it's impossible to walk in them on shore (and they'll get sandy). Don't put your mask on until you get into the water.

If you're snorkeling with younger children, plan on spending 10–15 minutes adjusting the fit of masks and vests. Inflate a kid's vest by blowing into the vertical tube on the left side of the vest, adding just enough air to keep the top of the child's head above water. (If you overinflate the vests, kids will have trouble getting their masks below the surface.) Also, practice using the flippers, which work best with slow, deliberate leg movements.

Once everyone's gear is working, take one last look at the lagoon to get your bearings. Disney has placed orange-and-white buoys above the underwater sites, so head for those.

There usually aren't a lot of fish in the first 30–40 yards nearest the shore, though it's possible to see almost anything once you're in the water. Fish species in the lagoon include yellowtail snapper, sergeant major, banded butterfly fish, blue tang, and barracuda.

If you've snorkeled before and you enjoy it, Castaway Cay offers another excursion in the waters off the island. You board a 28-foot Zodiac rigid-hull inflatable boat and head 30 minutes offshore for a 90-minute open-water snorkeling session. Cost is $122 for adults, $109 for kids ages 6–9.

WALKING AND KAYAK NATURE ADVENTURE

THIS PORT ADVENTURE BEGINS at Marge's Barges, where everyone boards a tram to the Serenity Bay adult beach. Next you walk behind the adult beach cabanas to a nature trail, which leads to the beach beyond. During the walk, your guide will point out interesting plants and animals and talk about the history of the Bahamas.

Upon reaching the beach, participants don their life jackets and head out in their kayaks. This is the part where you're at Mother Nature's whim. We took this tour after a friend raved about it. She headed out in the morning and was able to kayak to the interior of the island. Our own tour was later in the afternoon as the tide was going out. The interior of the island was inaccessible by kayak, and the tides made piloting our single kayak very difficult. We wouldn't book this adventure in the afternoon again, even if it were the only time available.

Even if you're able to book this in the morning, however, the tour is 3–3½ hours long—time you could spend snorkeling, biking, or lazing on the beach. Ideally, you would book this on the morning of the second stop of a five-night Castaway Cay cruise.

Be sure to bring walking shoes, sunglasses, a hat, sunscreen, and a waterproof or water-resistant camera; consider gloves for paddling to avoid blisters. Wear a swimsuit under your clothes for swimming. You must stow your belongings on the beach for the kayaking, so leave the doubloons in the cabin. Water is provided. Cost is $73 for guests age 10 and up.

WATERCRAFT SKI ADVENTURE

BOOKING THIS PORT ADVENTURE is the only way that guests can use WaveRunner watercraft on Castaway Cay, and that fact alone makes it worth your while if you're willing to spend the money.

Riders begin this port adventure at the Boat Beach (the beach closest to where the ship docks), where they're given life jackets and a safety briefing. While you must be at least 18 years old to drive the WaveRunner, kids as young as age 8 may ride along. Our advice for two adults is for each to ride as a single unless one is truly afraid of piloting a craft alone—a single rider will go much faster than two adults due to the weight difference.

If you've never piloted a WaveRunner before, don't worry; it's fairly easy. It's actually easier to maneuver once you get up to speed than when you're idling or going slowly at the beginning of the excursion. If you know how to drive a motorcycle or motor scooter, then you've got this down. Most participants get the hang of things quickly.

As you head out, riders will start in single file with a guide leading and one more assistant bringing up the rear. Try to avoid hitting the wake of the craft in front of you because the bumpiness can be a little scary when you're up to speed, which tops out at a little more than 30 miles per hour at full throttle.

Unless you choose to swim or tip your craft, you won't get especially wet, though you will want to wear waterproof shoes or sandals or go barefoot. Flip-flops aren't allowed, because they're likely to come off in the water (along with hats). You may store anything that you don't want to take with you in an unlocked chest at the beginning of the tour. We recommend taking a waterproof camera for photos on the beach; just secure it around your neck for the trip out.

Disney says the hour-long tour may have two stops, but ours had just one—the same beach you visit on the Walking and Kayak Nature Adventure. The fact that you can visit this beach on the WaveRunner without having to kayak there is a plus, but perhaps we're still bitter about the blister we got kayaking. The other stop is an island opposite the beach.

When you arrive, your tour guide will give you a very brief history of the islands and point out any interesting flora and fauna, much like an abbreviated version of the Walking and Kayak tour. Then you can swim in the ocean for a bit before heading back to the Boat Beach to end your port adventure. The piloting of the WaveRunners, not the nature talk or the beach visit, is the real highlight.

Would we book this again? *Maybe*. This is one of the more expensive port adventures for its length. The WaveRunners are fun, but the Boat Beach is far enough away that just getting there and back will cut into your time on the island.

If you have the chance, you may want to book this for earlier in the day as you're just getting off the ship, or later as you're heading back. Price is $183 for either one or two riders on a single watercraft.

NASSAU

A NOTE ABOUT NASSAU SAFETY

unofficial **TIP**
If you want to explore Nassau on your own, **exercise the utmost vigilance about your surroundings,** and let family remaining on board (or DCL Guest Services staff) know of your on-shore plans.

WE'VE NEVER HAD A BAD EXPERIENCE in Nassau. We acknowledge, however, that we've been lucky: crime is a real problem here—more so than in other cruise ports.

In its 2018 Crime & Safety Report for the Bahamas, the **U.S. Overseas Security Advisory Council (OSAC)**, a division of the U.S. Department of State, doesn't mince words: "THE U.S. DEPARTMENT OF STATE HAS ASSESSED NASSAU AS BEING A CRITICAL THREAT LOCATION FOR CRIME" (emphasis theirs). Here are the specifics:

> *Many criminals carry firearms or edged weapons. . . . In many snatch-and-grab crimes involving purses, jewelry, cell phones, and/or cash, the assailant was armed. If confronted by someone demanding valuables, comply and make the encounter as brief as possible. Remain calm, clearly display your hands, and do not make any sudden moves that could be interpreted as resistance. Armed robberies, property crimes, purse snatchings, theft, fraud, and sexual assaults remain the most common crimes perpetrated against tourists. Use an ATM/credit card for payments when possible (instead of carrying large amounts of cash). Avoid using ATMs in isolated areas. Skimmers—devices fitted over ATMs and used to record card data—have been reported throughout Nassau.*

A recent security notice about the Bahamas from the **UK government** states:

> *There have been incidents of violent crime including robbery, which is often armed and sometimes fatal, in residential and tourist areas. Be*

vigilant at all times, and don't walk alone away from the main hotels, tourist areas, beaches, and downtown Nassau.

The **Canadian government** offers similar warnings:

Sexual assault occurs frequently, particularly near hotels, in hotel rooms, in casinos, on cruise ships and on the beach. Avoid excessive consumption of alcohol, do not consume any drugs, and don't accept rides from strangers or from unlicensed taxi drivers. Due to incidents of sexual assault, it is recommended to be wary when embarking on Jet Ski rides with licensed or unlicensed operators.

Opportunistic crime, including petty theft and purse snatching, occurs frequently in tourist areas.

Never leave food or drinks unattended or in the care of strangers. Be wary of accepting snacks, beverages, gum, or cigarettes from new acquaintances, as the items may contain drugs that could put you at risk of sexual assault or robbery.

Her Own Way: A Woman's Safe-Travel Guide, a government publication, is available at Canada's official travel and tourism website: travel.gc.ca/travelling/publications/her-own-way.

Finally, **DCL** includes safety advisories in the *Personal Navigator* for cruises that stop in Nassau. A recent advisory stated:

While you will find many great experiences in Nassau, there have been reports of increased crime, including assaults and robberies involving tourists in the area. As in any large city, you'll want to take some basic precautions to make the most of your time ashore. . . . Avoid shortcuts, narrow alleys, or poorly lit streets. We recommend that guests visit only the downtown shopping areas and other tourist locations. Leave valuables in your room. . . . Cameras and handbags should be carried out of sight. . . . Use only licensed taxi operators.

If you're participating in a port adventure at **Atlantis** (see next section), which has its own security staff, or another Disney-vetted excursion, your odds of trouble are quite low. If, however, you haven't signed up for any port adventures and relaxation is your number-one vacation priority, **we recommend that you stay on the ship if your cruise stops at Nassau.**

unofficial **TIP**
Don't book watercraft excursions in Nassau.

Remaining on board lets you experience more of the ship's amenities than you'd have time to otherwise during a brief sailing: you can get pampered at the spa, stuff yourself at the buffet, or have your kids participate in activities at the youth clubs. Also, remember that many onboard activities are included in the cost of your sailing, so staying put can be an easy way to save some money you might otherwise spend on tacky souvenirs.

NASSAU PORT ADVENTURES

AFTER CASTAWAY CAY, the port most visited by DCL is Nassau. Virtually all *Disney Dream* sailings stop here, as do many sailings of the *Magic, Wonder,* and *Fantasy.*

The DCL website currently lists about 45 port adventures for Nassau, with 15 of them taking place at **Atlantis,** a Las Vegas–style resort about a 25-minute drive from the port (☎ 888-877-7525; atlantis bahamas.com). In addition to Disney cruisers, you'll encounter guests of other cruise lines, Atlantis guests, and guests of other area hotels—it's a high-volume operation. The resort generally does things well, but due to the sheer number of people who cycle through every day, it can feel a bit like a factory for fun. We're Disney-theme-park fans, so we don't necessarily think that's a *bad* thing, but if you're in the market for privacy or quiet, you'll want to look elsewhere.

Crowd levels vary substantially at Atlantis depending on how many cruise ships are in port on a specific day. If your ship is the only one in port, you'll find plenty of open lounge chairs and short lines for the slides; if there are eight large ships in port, you'll be fighting for a place just to lay your towel on the sand.

Most Atlantis-based excursions are variations on a theme: spend time with a dolphin, visit the beach, visit the waterpark-like **Aquaventure,** go shopping, or some combination thereof. The animal encounters receive generally moderate-to-high marks from guests. They're a commodity item, with almost all of the variations in opinion based on whether they thought their specific guide was funny, what the weather was like, if they were aware in advance that just a small part of the excursion would be spent interacting with the animal, and if they were aware in advance that there would be a substantial upcharge for photos and video of their animal encounter. The weather and your rapport with your guide are the luck of the draw, so adjust your expectations accordingly and you're likely to have a positive experience.

unofficial **TIP**
Many websites track the number of ships that will be docked in a given port on a specific day. We like **ports .cruisett.com**—select the region and port, in this case Bahamas and Nassau, and then select the date of your scheduled port stop at that location. The more ships in port on a given day, the more crowded Atlantis will be.

Here's a rundown of the different port adventures at Atlantis:

- **Discover Atlantis Tour** Free for kids under age 4; $56 ages 4–9; $68 age 10 and up. Includes transportation, an aquarium tour, and access to the casino and shopping. Does not include access to the beach, pools, or Aquaventure.
- **Atlantis Beach Day and Discover Atlantis** Free for kids under age 4; $83 ages 4–9; $98 age 10 and up. Includes everything on the Discover Atlantis tour, plus beach access. Does not include access to the pools or Aquaventure.

- **Atlantis Aquaventure** Free for kids under age 4; $146 ages 4-9; $204 age 10 and up. Some sailings may offer a half-day version of Atlantis Aquaventure priced at $161 for ages 10 and up, $111 ages 4-9, and free for kids under age 4. Includes everything on the previous two tours, plus access to Aquaventure—a mini-waterpark with 11 pools, several waterslides, and a lazy river—as well as a voucher for a fast food-style lunch.
- **Atlantis Aquaventure and Kayak with Dolphins** Kids age 10 and up only; $298. Includes an education segment about dolphin life and 30 minutes in a glass-bottom kayak in the dolphin habitat, plus access to Aquaventure.
- **Atlantis Aquaventure and Paddleboard with Dolphins** Kids age 10 and up only; $298. Includes an education segment about dolphin life and a paddleboard lesson in the dolphin habitat, plus Aquaventure.
- **Atlantis Snorkel the Ruins and Aquaventure** Cost is $244 for kids ages 8 and 9; $282 age 10 and up. Spend 30 minutes on a guided snorkel experience in the marine habitat (like a giant fish tank) with rays, sharks, and tropical fish. Includes transportation, access to the casino and shopping, a voucher for a fast food-style lunch, and access to Aquaventure.
- **Atlantis Dolphin Cay Shallow Water Interaction and Discover Atlantis** Kids under age 4 admitted free but not permitted in the dolphin experience; $200 ages 4-9; $213 age 10 and up. Includes transportation, a self-guided tour of the aquarium, and access to the casino and shopping; no access to pools (other than the dolphin pool) or Aquaventure. Includes an educational segment about dolphin life and a 30-minute wading-depth "meet and greet" with dolphins (you don't actually get to swim with them).
- **Atlantis Dolphin Cay Shallow Water Interaction and Aquaventure** Kids under age 4 admitted free but not permitted in the dolphin experience; $275 ages 4-9; $306 age 10 and up. Includes everything in the Atlantis Dolphin Cay Shallow Water Interaction and Discover Atlantis, plus access to Aquaventure.
- **Atlantis Dolphin Cay Deep Water Interaction and Aquaventure** Kids age 5 and under not permitted; $317 ages 6-9; $348 age 10 and up. Includes transportation, a self-guided tour of the aquarium, and access to the casino and shopping, plus Aquaventure. Also includes an education segment about dolphin life and a 30-minute swim in a dolphin habitat, including one dolphin "push" across the lagoon.
- **Observer at Dolphin Cay and Discover Atlantis** Kids under age 4 admitted free but not permitted in the dolphin experience; $56 ages 4-9; $68 age 10 and up. Includes transportation, an aquarium tour, and access to the casino and shopping; does *not* include access to the beach, pools, or Aquaventure. This can be booked only if other members of your party are doing the Dolphin Cay Shallow Water or Deep Water Interaction. The observer is allowed to stand at the edge

of the dolphin facility and take photos but may not interact with the animals. This is a good choice for parents who don't want to swim with the dolphins but whose kids do.

- **Observer at Dolphin Cay and Aquaventure** Kids under age 4 admitted free but not permitted in the dolphin experience; $149 ages 4–9; $215 age 10 and up. Includes transportation, an aquarium tour, and access to the casino and shopping, plus access to Aquaventure and a voucher for a fast food–style lunch. Again, the observer is allowed to stand at the edge of the dolphin facility and take photos but may not interact with the animals.
- **Private Cabana at Atlantis** For $344, up to six guests have one-day use of a private poolside cabana with a guest host, personal safe, fan, refrigerator, electrical outlets, and private changing area. Note that food is not included in the price; also, each cabana guest must be booked on one of the following tours: Atlantis Aquaventure, Atlantis Dolphin Cay Shallow Water Interaction and Aquaventure, Atlantis Dolphin Cay Deep Water Swim and Aquaventure, or Observer at Atlantis Dolphin Cay and Aquaventure.
- **Ultimate Trainer for a Day** Cost is $564 for guests age 10 and up. Take a behind-the-scenes tour of the veterinary hospital and lab for the dolphins and sea lions. Swim in deep water with the dolphins, and do a double dorsal tow and "foot push." Feed predatory nurse sharks and cow-nosed stingrays; then snorkel with them and hundreds of other tropical fish. Includes lunch and photos.

If you want to use the beach, pools, or Aquaventure without adding a dolphin experience, you may end up saving money, depending on the size of your party, if you actually book a hotel room for the day at Atlantis (the **Beach Tower** is the least expensive part of the resort) or at the nearby **Comfort Suites** (comfortsuitespi.com/atlantis-paradise-island.php), a 5-minute walk away. Atlantis now has a two-night minimum booking, with rates starting at about $140 per night; rates start at about $275 per night at the Comfort Suites, depending on the time of year.

On the face of it, you may think it's wasteful to pay for a hotel room that you won't be staying in overnight. But consider the convenience: for a few hours, you get a quiet place to relax or nap, free Wi-Fi, a place to store your valuables, and a private shower, among other perks. And you'll note that $300 is still cheaper than a less-well-equipped private cabana at Castaway Cay. On the downside, you'll spend valuable time walking from the pools to your room—Atlantis is *huge,* so this is a real consideration.

unofficial **TIP**
The Atlantis website misleadingly states in a few places that Aquaventure Day Passes must be purchased in person at the resort—actually, advance booking is available at atlantisbahamas.com/daybooking.

If you don't want to book a hotel room, consider an **Aquaventure Day Pass,** available through Atlantis and **Resort for a Day** (see

page 367). In 2018, passes were priced at $156–$166, depending on the season, for guests age 13 and up; passes for kids ages 4–12 cost $104. Guests for whom kids' passes could be particularly appealing are those with 10- to 12-year-olds: Disney considers them adults for monetary purposes, but Atlantis still gives them a discount.

If all you want to do is eat and browse the shops without using the pools, beach, or water park, you can do so at no charge. Taxis from the port to Atlantis typically run in the ballpark of $10 per person.

The Atlantis website lists a few variations on activities that don't appear on the DCL site. For example, Atlantis offers a junior version of its Ultimate Trainer package for 6- to 10-year-olds, along with a sea lion encounter, but the DCL site doesn't mention either.

Also note that Atlantis's pricing for most of its dolphin encounters is significantly less than booking through Disney. DCL includes transportation and a few other items in its packages, but for many guests, booking directly through Atlantis and using a cab makes more sense. See atlantisbahamas.com/daybooking for more information.

After Atlantis, the next largest block of Nassau excursions takes place at **Blue Lagoon,** a beach area about 40 minutes away from the port, via catamaran. You can spend your day at the beach, have a dolphin or sea lion experience, or enjoy some combination thereof. Prices are quite a bit less than the Atlantis equivalents. If you don't mind a longer transit time or the lack of a water park, then you'll probably be happier at Blue Lagoon than Atlantis. Again, the animal encounters are typically well rated, with most of the variation coming from rapport with a specific guide, the weather, and the guest's awareness that photos cost extra.

Other Nassau excursions that receive high marks from cruisers include the following:

- **Catamaran Sail and Reef Snorkeling** A well-priced ocean-snorkeling experience.
- **Graycliff Escape** A relaxing pool area and a lovely place for a meal.
- **Nassau Forts and Junkanoo Discovery** A relatively painless history lesson for kids.

Nassau excursions that garner less-than-stellar reviews include the following:

- **Ardastra Gardens and City Tour** A small, underwhelming "zoo." Avoid this tour if birds weird you out.
- **Seaworld Explorer Semi-Submarine** The windows of the sub are often so dirty that you can't see the animals.
- **Sunshine Glass Bottom Boat Tour** Guests must stand for the entire tour. There's not much viewing space, and you get to see the fish for just a few minutes while they're being fed.

For a place to relax close to the ship without all the bells and whistles of Atlantis, try the **British Colonial Hilton Nassau** (tinyurl.com/britishcolonialhilton), which often sells day passes at $79 per person, including a $40 food credit. You can use the Hilton's pools, private beach, lounge chairs, umbrellas, towels, snorkel gear, and kayaks in a safe environment.

OUR SUGGESTIONS *Beyond* CASTAWAY CAY

DOLPHIN ENCOUNTERS

THESE ARE THE MOST POPULAR shore excursions for families. Every port in Mexico, along with Nassau; Falmouth, Jamaica; and Grand Cayman, Cayman Islands, offers one. If your Caribbean or Bahamian cruise includes a port besides Castaway Cay, you'll almost certainly have a chance to book one.

Because of the dolphins' popularity, these port adventures aren't cheap, generally starting at around $180 for adults and $160 for children, or roughly $700 for a family of four.

Most dolphin-related port adventures last 4–7 hours, roughly 30 minutes of which are actually spent in the water with a dolphin and 10–20 other tourists. During our visits, we took turns with the rest of the group in petting, feeding, and taking photos with the dolphin.

In hindsight, the remarkable thing is that we spent perhaps 1 minute each in direct contact with the animal. The rest of your time is taken up by transportation to and from the port, a background class and instruction on how to interact with the dolphin, a short show during which the dolphins demonstrate their jumping skills and tricks, and some beach or pool time once your encounter is done.

MAYAN PYRAMIDS

DCL TOURS OF TULUM MAYA RUINS take place in **Cozumel, Mexico.** Be aware that the trip involves considerable transportation time: 4 of its 7½ hours are spent on ferries or buses. Prices are $149 ages 10 and up, $108 ages 8–9.

SKAGWAY, ALASKA

LONG-WINDED NAME ASIDE, the **Liarsville Gold Rush Trail Camp and Salmon Bake Featuring Exclusive Disney Character Experience** is a fun port adventure for families (2½–3 hours; $119 ages 10 and up; $70 ages 3-9). Guests board a bright-yellow school bus and take a 15-minute drive through downtown Skagway to Liarsville, a re-created mining camp at the foot of White Pass. When you arrive, you're greeted by "locals" dressed in period attire and escorted to the Hippodrome, a covered

pavilion where you'll see a puppet show that highlights the history of the Gold Rush in Alaska, including how Liarsville came to receive its name.

After the show, you'll receive instructions on how to pan for gold—*scoop, swirl, spill*—before you're released to your very own "handler" and set out to seek your fortune. The pans are prepared and handed out as you approach the mining troughs. Getting the hang of the technique isn't as easy at it looks, but your handler is there to help. While you're panning, Chip 'n' Dale stop by to steal some gold, and Donald, dressed in flannel and a hunting cap, pays a visit. Gold in every pan is guaranteed, but even the most successful panning won't make you rich, or even earn you enough to help pay off your stateroom balance.

The salmon bake is set up across the way, buffet-style. Guests trickle over to the food after they strike it not-so-rich, so crowds aren't a problem. Choose from rotisserie chicken, baked beans, rice pilaf, coleslaw, and salads, plus bread and blueberry cake. Wild-caught salmon is served from an open-air grill; the fish is tasty, but be aware that it contains small bones—we guess that's what makes it wild.

This reader liked (but didn't love) the experience:

> *The Liarsville gold panning was fun, and it was a huge hit with my stepson (age 8). I felt the price could have been a bit more affordable, the puppet show a bit shorter, and the gold panning a bit longer and more involved. For us it was a one-time experience, but an enjoyable one.*

WALKING TOURS

FOR THOSE WHO WANT TO STEP OFF THE BEATEN PATH of organized excursions, we've created our own walking tours of DCL ports around the globe. Each tour includes not only things to see and do but also recommendations for places to eat. These tours are less expensive than almost any port adventure, offer a more flexible schedule, allow you to see a great deal of the port, and offer a wider choice of dining options.

Alaska

Juneau Walking Tour

Duration About 3 hours depending on your pace, how much you stop to shop, and how long it takes you to eat. Add another 1–2 hours if you decide to take the tram to Mount Roberts. **Walking distance** About 2.5 miles. **Cost** Lunch varies. Mount Roberts Tramway: $34 adults, $17 kids. Museum: $12. **Accessibility** This is a walk up paved roads with several large hills. Nothing is specifically inaccessible, but guests using wheelchairs might find the route somewhat strenuous. **Kid-friendliness** Best for adults—kids will probably get bored hiking past municipal buildings and museums; plus, there's an optional detour into a bar. **Map** See tinyurl.com/downtownjuneaumap2017.

STEP 1 Depending on which dock the ship is using, you're about 0.75 mile down a nondescript service road from the port to town. You can walk the road or take the free shuttle bus that continuously ferries cruisers

from the ship. Start touring at the **Downtown Public Library** (292 Marine Way). Nearby, look for the bronze sculpture of the city's founders, **Joe Juneau, Richard Harris,** and **Chief Kowee.**

STEP 2 Proceed toward town up South Franklin Street. Depending on the time of day, you may need some fortification to start your tour. If that's the case, the **Red Dog Saloon** (278 S. Franklin St.) has so-so food, but the elegantly named Duck Fart—a layered shot of Kahlúa, Bailey's Irish Cream, and Crown Royal—is one of those things that you just have to try in Juneau.

STEP 3 Continue up South Franklin, stopping in whatever shops strike your fancy along the way. We like the **Alaska Brew Company Depot** (219 S. Franklin St.) for T-shirts and to see the brewery information upstairs; the **Alaskan Fudge Company** (195 S. Franklin St.) to check out and sample the creatively named candies (puffin paws, sea otter paws, husky paws, and huckleberry jelly sticks); and the **Mt. Juneau Trading Post** (151 S. Franklin St.) for pelts and native artwork. If you have room in your luggage, you can buy a woolly-mammoth tusk. Pop your head into the **Alaskan Hotel** bar (167 S. Franklin St.) to check out the Victorian-era decor.

STEP 4 South Franklin becomes North Franklin after Front Street. Proceed up North Franklin to Fifth Street and make a right to see **St. Nicholas Russian Orthodox Church** (326 Fifth St.), built in 1894. Walk back down Franklin and take a left onto Fourth Street. The **Alaska State Capitol** will be a few steps up on your left, at 120 E. Fourth St. Cross Main Street and see the **Juneau-Douglas City Museum** (114 W. Fourth St). Note the large totem pole out front, and spend a bit checking out the exhibits. *(Hours: Tuesday–Saturday, 10 a.m.–4 p.m.; free admission; juneau.org/library/museum.)*

STEP 5 Bear right at the end of Fourth Street as it turns into Calhoun Avenue. At Calhoun and Seventh Street, see the **Alaska Governor's Mansion** (716 Calhoun Ave.). No, you can't see Russia from this house.

STEP 6 Continue on Calhoun, making a left onto Capitol Avenue. Follow Capitol until it dead-ends at Willoughby Avenue. Take a left onto Willoughby and a quick right onto Whittier Street. The **Alaska State Museum** (395 Whittier St.) reopened in June 2016 after a major renovation. The newly redesigned museum joins the Alaska State Library and Alaska State Archives in one comprehensive research facility, with many exhibits open to the public. *(Summer hours: daily, 9 a.m.–5 p.m.; admission: $12 adults, $11 seniors age 65+, free for kids age 18 and younger and military personnel with ID; museums.alaska.gov.)*

STEP 7 Continue down Whittier Street to Egan Drive. The **Centennial Hall Convention Center** (101 Egan Drive) is a good place to pick up maps and get general information.

STEP 8 Egan Drive turns into Marine Way. Note **Juneau City Hall** at the corner of Marine and Seward. Continue on Marine Way to end up back at the Downtown Public Library. Continue down Marine and bear right as Marine turns into the lower part of South Franklin Street—you've walked a large circle.

STEP 9 If you want to eat light, grab something at one of the food carts near the port, but we highly recommend **Tracy's King Crab Shack** (432 S. Franklin St.), our favorite Alaskan cruise-stop restaurant. The Crab Shack Combo (about $39) will feed one hungry or two not-so-hungry people with a cup of crab chowder, a giant king crab leg, and four mini crab cakes. Add a side of slaw, and you can definitely feed two. Seating is at covered outdoor picnic tables. While you're waiting for your order, pop behind the order-prep station to watch the cooks tend to the 9- to 10-pound crabs.

STEP 10 If you're tuckered out, grab the shuttle back to the ship. If not, head to the **Mount Roberts Tramway** station (490 S. Franklin St.). Buy tickets for the tramway and take the 5-minute ride to the top of Mount Roberts. While you're at the top, check out the film in the visitor center, snap photos of the view, scout for bald eagles, or take a brief nature hike. Back at the tramway station, you'll see the ship; take the shuttle from there or walk back. *(Hours, May–September: daily, 8 a.m.–9 p.m.; tickets: $34 adults, $17 kids ages 3–12, free for kids age 2 and younger; mountrobertstramway.com.)*

Ketchikan Walking Tour

Duration About 2–3 hours. **Walking distance** About 3 miles. **Cost** About $35 per person, including admission to the Tongass Historical Museum, admission to Dolly's, and a bowl of chowder or sandwich along the way. For the *Great Alaskan Lumberjack Show,* add $38 for each adult and $18.50 for kids ages 3–12. **Accessibility** While not technically wheelchair-inaccessible, this is a walk of several miles, up several steep hills. Use your best judgment. **Kid-friendliness** Young children may get antsy during Steps 6–8. Skip Dolly's (Step 9) if you have kids along. **Map** Go to experienceketchikan.com and click "Ketchikan Maps" on the left side of the page.

STEP 1 Exit the ship and head to the end of the pedestrian-only dock area. Start at the corner of Mill and Front Streets, near the **Fish Pirate's Saloon.** Walk one block down Mill Street and turn right down Main Street to the **Southeast Alaska Discovery Center** (50 Main St.), operated by the U.S. Forest Service. Check out the exhibits on the Alaskan rainforest, native peoples, and natural resources; there also may be classes or lectures for kids. *(Summer hours: daily, 8 a.m.–4 p.m.; admission: $5 adults, free for kids age 15 and younger; alaskacenters.gov/visitors-centers/ketchikan.)* While you're at the Discovery Center, note that you're adjacent to the ***Great Alaskan Lumberjack Show*** (420 Spruce Mill Way); if you're so inclined, stop in and buy tickets for a show later in the afternoon (see Step 10).

STEP 2 Go back to the corner of Mill and Front streets. If you need maps or information, stop at the **Ketchikan Visitors Bureau** (131 Front St.). Proceed up Front Street, away from the ships, to Mission Street. Turn left onto Mission and take a photo under the glamorous and exciting KETCHIKAN: THE SALMON CAPITAL OF THE WORLD sign.

STEP 3 Step back on Front Street and stop at **Alaska Fine Art** (224 Front St.) to see an incredible mammoth-tusk carving by sculptor Eddie Lee. Also look for eagles, bears, mountain goats, and other carved animals.

STEP 4 If you're hungry, grab a bite at **Annabelle's Famous Keg & Chowder House** (326 Front St.). The three-chowder sampler is a popular choice. When you're done, take a look farther down Front Street to see the **Ketchikan Tunnel.** Locals like to brag about the tunnel because it was once noted in the *Guinness Book of World Records* as the only tunnel in the world that you could go completely through, over, and around. To us, though, it looks like a minor traffic pass-through.

Just on the other side of the tunnel is **Burger Queen** (518 Water St.). The name is catchy, and every local we've talked to raves about it, but we think the burgers are just so-so, and it has ambience perhaps only in an ironic sense: it's a shack with the Tasmanian Devil cartoon character painted on the front.

STEP 5 Go back down Front Street to Mission Street, and then head down Mission away from the water. If you find yourself hungering for canned salmon, buy some at the **Salmon Market,** on the corner of Mission and Main. At 503 Mission St., note **St. John's Episcopal Church,** which has stood in its current location since 1904. Turn around and enter the **Cape Fox Marketplace** at 500 Mission St. Inside this (very) mini mall, you'll find **Tall Tale Taxidermy,** a family-run furrier and taxidermist. We bought a beaver pelt.

STEP 6 Proceed back up Mission Street and bear left as it turns into Dock Street. Just ahead, at 629 Dock St., visit the **Tongass Historical Museum.** View artifacts and photos of Ketchikan's history as a fishing port and mining center. Check out the native totem pole out front. *(Summer hours: daily, 8 a.m.–5 p.m.; admission: $5 seniors, $6 adults, free for kids age 17 and younger; ktn-ak.us/tongass-historical-museum.)*

STEP 7 Proceed up Dock Street and follow it as it turns into Bawden Street. Bawden soon forks—take the right fork onto Park Avenue. Continue on Park to see the **salmon-spawning river.** In season, see salmon struggle to get back to their native streambed; a concrete "fish ladder" aids their passage.

STEP 8 Continue on Park, past Venetia Avenue, Harris Street, and Freeman Street, then turn right at Woodland Avenue (Herring Way will be on the left). Continue on Woodland until it dead-ends at Deermount Street. Turn right onto Deermount. Along the way, you'll pass one of Ketchikan's Alaska Native–American Indian neighborhoods. Deermount dead-ends into Stedman Street—turn right and proceed along Stedman. Pass the **Sun Raven Totem Pole,** just beyond Inman Street, and the **University of Alaska Southeast** campus.

STEP 9 Continue on Stedman Street until you get to Thomas Street. Turn left down Thomas to view the harbor from the wood-planked dock. Continue on Stedman until you get to the red trestle bridge, just past the New York Hotel. Instead of crossing the bridge, take the small path on the right that turns into board-walked **Creek Street,** the old red-light district, which once had more than 30 houses filled with "working girls." Stop in at **Dolly's House** (24 Creek St.), where, as the sign on the side of the building advises, "men and salmon came upstream to spawn." Legendary madam Dolly Arthur and her staff plied their

trade here; period, um, artifacts and photos are on display. *(Hours: daily, 8 a.m.–4 p.m. when ships are in port; closed in winter; admission: $10.)*

STEP 10 Exit Creek Street onto Dock Street, back near the Tongass Historical Museum. Proceed down Dock toward the water. Make a left onto Bawden Street, then a right onto Mill Street. If you've had enough, head back to the ship. Or if you want some more Alaska fun, make a left onto Main Street and head back to the ***Great Alaskan Lumberjack Show.*** The lumberjacks impress with their feats of skill, and anyone who appreciates male eye candy will be delighted—one online reviewer sums them up as "hot guys with chainsaws." *(Buy tickets in person or at alaskanlumberjackshow.com.)* If you're hungry, make a pit stop next door at the **Alaska Fish House** (5 Salmon Way) for a cod burger or some halibut tacos.

Skagway Walking Tour

Duration About 3 hours, depending on the timing of any shows/presentations you partake of. **Walking distance** About 2 miles. **Cost** About $50 per person; includes $25 admission to the *Days of '98* show, $10 admission to a Red Onion Saloon brothel tour, a burger lunch, and a beer at the end. **Accessibility** Most of Skagway is on level surfaces. Wheelchair users shouldn't find it a problem. **Kid-friendliness** The Red Onion allows kids on its brothel tours—use your discretion. **Map** See tinyurl.com/skagwaymap. The entirety of Skagway is about 7 blocks long by 2 blocks wide—you can see your ship from anywhere in town, so it's virtually impossible to get lost. **Special comments** Be aware that while the ship will likely dock at about 7:30 a.m., most of the shops in town, including the restaurants, won't open until after 9 a.m., so unless you have an excursion, there's no reason to rush in the morning. If you want to go farther afield, stop by the **Chilkoot Trail Center,** on Broadway between First and Second Avenues. *(Hours, June 1–Labor Day weekend: daily, 8 a.m.–5 p.m.)* Run jointly by the National Park Service and Parks Canada, it offers maps and advice on day hikes in the surrounding area.

STEP 1 Assume that you're exiting the ship from the Ore Dock (the most likely option). Directly ahead, you'll see the **White Pass & Yukon Route** train tracks.

STEP 2 Follow the tracks up Broadway until just before First Avenue. Take a photo at the WELCOME TO SKAGWAY, ALASKA sign. Walk forward about 30 feet to view the old **Yukon Engine #52** (1881) and **Rotary #1 Snowplow** (1899), which was capable of clearing up to 12 feet of snow off the tracks.

STEP 3 Proceed up Broadway and turn right onto Second Avenue. Stop into the **White Pass & Yukon Route** headquarters (231 Second Ave. at Spring Street) to see exhibits about Alaskan train travel. The souvenirs sold here are slightly less tacky than those sold elsewhere. If you didn't book a train excursion on the ship but would like to do one, buy your tickets here; note that some trips visit Canada and require a passport. *(Hours: weekdays, 8:30 a.m.–5:30 p.m.; wpyr.com.)*

STEP 4 Also on Second Avenue at Broadway is the **Klondike Gold Rush National Historical Park Visitor Center.** Check out the exhibits discussing the Gold Rush experience in the Klondike Region. Stay for the free 30-minute movie, *Gold Fever: Race to the Klondike,* or a 45-minute

ranger presentation. Rangers are also available to answer general questions about Alaska and mining. *(Hours, May–September: 8:30 a.m.–5:30 p.m.; nps.gov/klgo.)*

STEP 5 Head back out to Broadway and walk toward Sixth Avenue, browsing in the shops along the way. Poke your head into the **Mascot Saloon** (corner of Broadway and Third Avenue), a National Park Service reproduction of a Gold Rush–era watering hole. If you've forgotten any basics for your trip, stop in **Skagway Hardware,** on the corner of Fourth Avenue and Broadway. They have everything from mouthwash to suitcases and power strips.

STEP 6 On the corner of Broadway and Sixth Avenue, take in the hour-long ***Days of '98*** stage show. This campy musical tells the tale of Soapy Smith, a notorious con man who duped many prospectors during the late 1800s. *(Reservations: thedaysof98show.com.)* If you have time to kill before the next show, grab a muffin at the best bakery in town, **Bites on Broadway,** directly across Sixth Avenue. Or cross to the other side of Broadway to snap a photo in front of the **Skagway Post Office,** which has one of the highest zip codes in the country: 99840.

STEP 7 After the show, turn right down Sixth Avenue (away from town) and take a look at the **William and Ben Moore Cabin & Homestead,** a National Park Service–restored Gold Rush–era home.

STEP 8 Back on Broadway, find the **Skagway Bazaar,** on the post-office side of the street between Fifth and Sixth Avenues. Scoot down the narrow passageway to find the **BBQ Shack,** which serves caribou, elk, buffalo, and venison burgers, as well as halibut or smoked-salmon chowder.

STEP 9 Return to Broadway, heading back toward the ship. Stop in the **Red Onion Saloon** (205 Broadway), once Skagway's premier house of joy, at the corner on Second Avenue. Relax with an Alaska Brewing Company beer on tap, or try the Fire Dance, an Alaskan-moonshine shot sprinkled with real gold flakes. The curious—including, kind of surprisingly, kids of any age accompanied by an adult 21 or older—can take one of the various **bordello tours,** which offer a look at the upstairs "cribs." Free garters with every tour! *(Reservations: redonion1898.com.)*

STEP 10 Revisit any interesting sights and shops, and then return to the ship via Broadway.

Bahamas and the Caribbean

Nassau Walking Tour

If you decide to do this walking tour, use common sense: walk with a partner or group, avoid deserted areas, don't carry large sums of cash, don't use ATMs by yourself or in out-of-the-way places, leave expensive jewelry and electronics on the ship, secure your passport and other documents, and don't engage with anyone who seems sketchy. See "A Note About Nassau Safety," page 376, for more advice.

Duration About 3 hours. **Walking distance** 4.5 miles. **Cost** Around $20/person (including lunch and a cocktail at the distillery). **Accessibility** Good except for the Queen's Staircase, which is inaccessible. **Kid-friendliness** Best for adults—while children are allowed on

Nassau Walking Tour

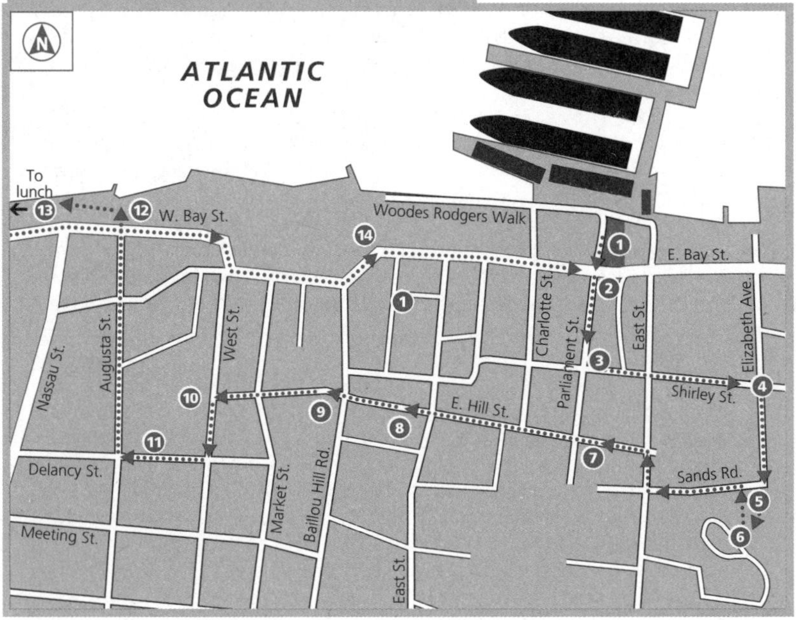

the distillery tour, they'll probably be bored to tears there and at the various cultural sites. **Map** See above for a map coded to the steps below, or pick up a city map in Festival Place as you leave the port. **Special comments** Wear good walking shoes, bring swimwear if you intend to enjoy the beach, and **heed our previous advice.**

STEP 1 Exit the cruise ship through Festival Place. You can pick up a map of Nassau here.

STEP 2 Outside Festival Place, take Parliament Street across Bay Street to Parliament Square.

STEP 3 Continue on Parliament Street to Shirley Street, and take a left.

STEP 4 Continue on Shirley Street across East Street to Elizabeth Avenue.

STEP 5 Take a right onto Elizabeth Avenue to continue to the base of the **Queen's Staircase.** Named for Queen Victoria, this is perhaps the most tranquil spot on our tour. Enjoy the cool shade, the junglelike greenery, and the artificial waterfall cascading to the left of the stairway before you ascend the 65 steps to the entrance of Fort Fincastle. The stairs, while steep, aren't overly challenging, but alternatively you can take East Street to Prison Lane to the top of the staircase. Be careful, though, because there's no sidewalk along this route.

unofficial **TIP**
Note: Self-appointed "tour guides" at Fort Fincastle may try to hustle you for tips. Give only if you feel like it.

STEP 6 Climb the Queen's Staircase to reach the **Water Tower** and **Fort Fincastle.** Intended to protect Nassau from invasion and constructed to resemble the bow of a paddlewheeler, the fort—built in 1793 by Lord Dunsmore, aka Viscount Fincastle, then-royal governor of the Bahamas—never actually saw any skirmishes. *(Hours: Tuesday-Sunday, 8 a.m.-4 p.m.; admission: $1.)*

The Water Tower, built in 1928, no longer holds any water and is closed to the public pending a renovation announced in 2016. (Visitors used to be able to climb 216 steps to an observation deck affording panoramic views.) Nevertheless, it's a great landmark to let you know early on that you were headed in the right direction to reach the staircase and the fort.

STEP 7 Descend the staircase and take a left on Sands Road. Follow Sands Road to East Street, and make a right. Visit the **General Post Office,** at the corner of East Street and East Hill Street. Postage stamps make a nice, inexpensive souvenir whether you're a collector or not; US currency is accepted.

STEP 8 Continue on East Hill Street and take a right on Market Street. Take a left on Duke Street to **Government House**, the seat of the Bahamian government—you can't miss this pink-stucco, white-columned building with the big statue of Christopher Columbus out front. The Government House is mostly closed to the public but hosts a monthly English high tea for tourists and locals. If your cruise schedule coincides with the event, it's a charming way to spend an afternoon and make some new friends. Proper attire is required to enjoy the *veddy* proper repast of scones, clotted cream, cucumber sandwiches, and different types of tea. *(Held the last Friday of the month, January-November, at the Government House Ballroom, 4-5 p.m.; reservations: tinyurl.com/governmenthousetea.)*

STEP 9 Across Blue Hill Road from Government House is the **Graycliff Hotel** (8-12 W. Hill St.). Tour the grounds and check out the gardens and pools. There's a chocolate shop on-site.

STEP 10 Continue along West Hill Street to West Street. Here you'll find the **National Art Gallery of the Bahamas** and **St. Francis Xavier Cathedral,** the oldest Catholic church in the Bahamas. Beautiful in its simplicity, the church is a nice stop along the way for rest and reflection. *(National Art Gallery: open Tuesday-Saturday, 10 a.m.-5 p.m., Sunday noon-5 p.m.; admission prices vary; nagb.org.bs/visit. St. Francis Xavier Cathedral: open to visitors weekdays, 9 a.m.-4:30 p.m.; stfrancisxaviercathedral.org.)*

STEP 11 After touring the cathedral, head south (away from the water) on West Street to **John Watling's Distillery,** on your right at 17 Delancy St. The only distillery in the Bahamas, John Watling's makes rum in a fantastically restored colonial estate. Tour the distillery and try a generous sample at no charge. The gift shop sells liquor and offers tastings; lunch is also served in the on-site pub. *(Hours: daily, 10 a.m.-6 p.m., until 9 p.m. Friday; free admission; johnwatlings.com.)*

STEP 12 Return to West Bay Street and take a left, continuing west, away from the cruise terminal. Walk along the public beach. If you've packed a swimsuit, enjoy some time in the water.

STEP 13 (LUNCH) Instead of going to the Fish Fry, a cluster of tourist restaurants on Arawak Cay near the terminal, follow our advice and eat with the locals at the **food trucks** across the street—you'll know you're there when you see Bahamians buying food. Picnic tables are available. A large lunch plus drink runs about $10. The food is cooked to order, so relax and enjoy yourself. This is the freshest seafood we've ever eaten—don't be thrown off if your fish arrives with its head still attached.

STEP 14 Return to the ship via **Bay Street,** the center of duty-free shopping in Nassau. We don't find the goods worth haggling over, but it's always fun to browse. Jewelry and accessories are the big draws here, as is liquor. Two shops we like are **The Linen Shop,** which sells a nice selection of kitchen linens and Christmas decor, and **Cole's of Nassau** (Bay and Parliament Streets), for women's fashions.

Stop at Bay Street's **Straw Market** only if you feel you must in order to say you've been. Once upon a time, the market sold high-quality straw goods that were tasteful and well made; sadly, that's no longer the case. You may still find a few nice locally made pieces among the ones imported from China, but mostly it's the same old cheesy, overpriced T-shirts, beach towels, baseball caps, and fake designer bags you can get at any port.

Sint Maarten/Saint-Martin Walking Tour

Duration 4–7 hours. **Walking distance** About 1 mile not counting the time you'll spend in taxis. **Cost** About $35 per person for the Dutch side, plus an all-day taxi rental, which usually runs $250 (plus tip) for up to 6 people. The French side of the island uses the euro as its currency, so you should also bring about €40 per person for lunch and drinks. **Accessibility** Many taxi drivers are happy to accommodate passengers who use wheelchairs. Fort Louis, however, can be accessed only by climbing stairs. Shops and restaurants in Marigot and Philipsburg are at ground level, but many require navigating a step or two out front. Many public restrooms have doorways that are too narrow to accommodate a wheelchair. **Club Orient** resort, which isn't on our tour, has beach wheelchairs—the catch is naked people. An excellent resource is the tour operator **Accessible Caribbean Vacations;** for their St. Maarten advice, along with accessible port adventures, see accessiblecaribbeanvacations.com/st-maarten-disabled-access. **Kid-friendliness** Parents with young children should skip Maho Beach and start at Marigot. Also, the stairs at Fort Louis are too taxing for little ones. **Map** See tinyurl.com/stmaartenwalkingtour. **Special comments** Bring water, sunscreen, bathing suits, and a change of clothes.

Note: This is a walking tour only in the loosest sense. Because you'll be visiting a large swath of the island, you'll need to hire a taxi driver for the day. Typical rates are $200–$250 for four people, plus gratuity, for a safe, air-conditioned ride. Drivers are generally very friendly and occasionally hilarious, as this reader found:

> *My partner was champing at the bit to check out the clothing-optional section of Orient Beach. (Myself, not so much.) When he told our taxi driver where we wanted to go, she laughed, "Ah, so ya wanna go to the NEKKID beach!"*

Taxis are available at the port. You can negotiate with a driver on-site, or if you want to arrange day service in advance, start with taxistmaarten.com or dandataxiservice.com.

STEP 1 It's a 25-minute cab ride from the port in Philipsburg to the Dutch side's **Maho Beach,** a tiny strip of sand maybe 600 feet long and 50 feet wide, on the west side of the island. What makes Maho Beach unique is that it sits on the other side of a small two-lane road from the main landing strip of **Princess Juliana International Airport.** Most planes landing on the island pass directly over the beach at no more than a couple hundred feet of altitude and land at the edge of the runway directly across. Watching the approach of small planes is a thrill; watching the big jets land is terrifying. You'll love it! Check flightaware.com/live/airport/sxm for the airport's arrival and departure schedule.

Because of the island's prevailing winds, planes taking off start at the end of the runway closest to the beach, too. The propeller and jet wash from the engines are enough to push adults back on their heels and knock over small children, so be careful.

Sunset Bar & Grill (2 Beacon Hill Road), a small outdoor restaurant at the far end of the beach, serves burgers, sandwiches, and drinks of all kinds. Close by is the **Sonesta Maho Beach Resort** (1 Rhine Road). The Sonesta incurred significant damage during the 2017 hurricane season but is scheduled to reopen in early 2019; adjacent shopping and dining are likewise on their way to being rebuilt.

STEP 2 When you're ready for lunch, hop in your cab for the 20-minute ride to the middle of **Marigot,** on the French side. The main drag, the **Boulevard de France,** has some of the island's best dining and shopping. It's also home to the marina and to **Fort Louis,** built in 1767.

If you're looking for island cuisine, try **Rosemary's,** on Boulevard de France near the marina and Fort Louis. Rosemary's is a *lolo*—a grill that serves fresh seafood, stews, and other local favorites. The food is tasty, and the service is very friendly. While the menu is priced in euros, they'll usually accept a one-for-one exchange of US dollars, giving Americans a 30% discount.

If you're in the mood for a quick bite of French food, grab a croque monsieur or other sandwich at **Sarafina's,** a pâtisserie about a block from Rosemary's on Boulevard de France. Usually crowded, Sarafina's serves a surprisingly large selection of fresh French pastries, sandwiches, and desserts. We suggest grabbing a baguette sandwich to go and eating it while you window-shop.

The hike up to Fort Louis, northeast of Boulevard de France, is strenuous, especially in the sun, but it does offer the best views of this side of the island. *(Open daily, sunrise–sunset; free admission.)* To keep up your energy levels, pick up a quick something from Sarafina's after you return.

STEP 3 Here's your chance to work in some beach time. Skip **Orient Beach,** which is overcrowded and not a good choice if you're uncomfortable with toplessness or nudity. (On the upside, **Club Orient,** a naturist

resort, provides beach wheelchairs for visitors with disabilities.) We recommend one of the following beaches instead:

Baie de L'Embouchure is located off Rue du Coconut Grove, on the east side of the island, about 20 minutes from Marigot and a half-mile south of Orient Beach. A crescent-shaped bit of beach about half a mile long, the beach is protected by an offshore reef that dampens the incoming waves. This, along with its relatively small crowds, makes it great for families with young children.

Mullet Bay Beach, about a 15-minute taxi ride southwest of Marigot, has a wide, sandy shore. The south side of the beach sits across from Mullet Bay Golf Course, so there's no string of high-rise hotels to hamper your view.

Baie Longue is on the northwest side of the island, about a 15-minute taxi ride from downtown Marigot. Again, it's much less crowded than Orient Beach; the one downside is that the shoreline is filled with coral, making it unsafe for small children to play in. But it is pretty.

St. Thomas Walking Tour

Note: *As of press time, the interiors of Blackbeard's Castle are still being repaired following the 2017 hurricanes; the outside areas are open to tourists, however. Check blackbeardscastle.com for updates.*

Duration 3–5 hours. **Walking distance** About 6 miles on foot, 3 miles if you take a taxi back to the port, or less than a mile if you take a taxi both ways. **Cost** $22–$27/person, including lunch; add $5 each way if using a taxi. **Accessibility** The first two steps in the tour are out of the question for wheelchair users. **Kid-friendliness** Recommended for children age 6 and up; parents with small children should bring a stroller and use a taxi to get to Blackbeard's Castle and back to the ship. **Map** See tinyurl.com/stthomaswalkingtour. **Special comments** Bring water and sunscreen; swimsuits and towels are optional if you want to use the pools at Blackbeard's Castle.

STEP 1 It's a pleasant walk from the port to **Blackbeard's Castle,** on Blackbeard's Hill; if you take a taxi instead, the fare should be around $4 per person. Depart the ship at the West Indian Company Dock and walk northeast toward Edward Wilmot/Long Bay Road. Follow the road as it runs along the coast, and bear left toward the water when it becomes Veterans Drive. One block past the DeLugo Federal Building, turn right on Hospital Gade and walk north about four blocks; then turn left on Prindsens Gade. Turn right on Lille Taarne Gade and look for the signs.

There's no evidence that the British pirate whose real name was Edward Teach ever laid a boot upon "Blackbeard's Castle"—the reference is pure marketing. The "castle" is part of a hotel; what's more, it's a lookout tower, never meant for habitation—originally called Skystborg Tower, it was built far up on the hill by 17th-century Danish settlers for spotting incoming ships that wouldn't be seen from Fort Christian, farther down.

A climb to the top of the tower will get you a lovely panoramic view of the harbor and the town laid out in front of you, and of the mountains behind you. If you're a small group, the scenery alone is probably worth

the $10 admission. If the view isn't enough, your admission also includes access to the adjacent hotel's pools and tours of two restored Colonial-era homes nearby, and you can return later for those. *(Tour hours are usually 9 a.m.–2 p.m. Tuesdays and Wednesdays, but check at blackbeards castle.com before you go; you can also book your tour at the website.)*

Before you climb the tower's narrow stairs, you're asked to watch an almost certainly apocryphal, extremely corny, but mercifully brief retelling of Blackbeard's death. A good way not to dwell on the sad cringe you feel for the "actor" is to imagine he's wearing tights and holding a human skull, à la Hamlet.

STEP 2 Follow the signs from Blackbeard's Castle south, toward the harbor, to the **99 Steps.** These stone-and-concrete stairs built into the side of the mountain afford good views of the harbor and town. (For the fact-checkers among us, there are actually more than 100 steps.)

STEP 3 Turn left and walk one block east to the **Government House.** Built in the 1860s, it holds the offices of the island's governor (currently Kenneth Mapp), and tourists may visit the first two floors of the building. Besides Colonial architecture, on display are two small works by Camille Pissarro, a Danish-French Impressionist painter who was born on St. Thomas in 1830. *(Open 8 a.m.–5 p.m. weekdays; closed holidays; free admission.)*

STEP 4 From Government House, head south one block on Torvets State Road, then turn right on Norre Gade. About 100 feet ahead, on your right, is **Frederick Lutheran Church.** *(Open daily, 9 a.m.–5 p.m.; free admission).* Built in 1666, it's the oldest church in St. Thomas and one of the oldest Lutheran churches in the New World. The church's simple, elegant architecture features a vaulted ceiling. A narrow set of stairs leads to better views from the second floor's musician's area. *Note:* The church is well on its way to recovering from the impact of the 2017 hurricanes, but the interior may be closed to visitors as repairs continue. Please consider making a donation to assist with recovery efforts.

STEP 5 From the church entrance, turn right and walk to the corner of Norre Gade and Fort Pladsen. Turn left on Fort Pladsen, toward the harbor; about 75 feet down the road, on your left, is **Emancipation Park,** which commemorates the emancipation of slaves in the Danish West Indies following the Danish revolution of 1848. Inside the park are a memorial to the emancipation; a memorial to King Christian IX of Denmark, who brought parliamentary rule to the island; and a copy of the United States's Liberty Bell, which commemorates the temporary landing on St. Thomas, in April 1607, of British settlers bound for Virginia. (*Bonus fact:* Every US state and territory has a copy of the Liberty Bell. Find yours at tinyurl.com/statelibertybells.)

Jen's Island Café is across the street from the northeast corner of the park, at the intersection of Tolbod Pladsen and Forte Strade. The food is fresh and tasty, with friendly service. A full meal takes about an hour, so we recommend a quicker stop at the bar for a fast sandwich and drink.

Adjacent to Emancipation Park and Jen's Island Café is **Fort Christian,** the oldest building on St. Thomas. Completed around 1680, it served as a government building, church, and prison before being converted to

a museum in the 1970s; it reopened to the public in 2017 after being closed for more than a decade. Painted bright red, the fort is impressive to look at from the outside, and it makes for a striking photo op. And at more than 300 years old, it easily withstood the 2017 hurricanes. *(Hours: Monday–Friday, 9 a.m.–4 p.m.; guided tours at 10 a.m. and 1:45 p.m. daily; admission: $10 adults, $7 kids.)*

STEP 6 On the west side of the park, follow Fort Pladsen Street north, away from the harbor, to Tolbod Pladsen, which turns into Kongens Gade after about a block. Stay on Kongens Gade, which will change names to Main Street, then Dronningens Gade, then Curaçao Gade, then Kronprindsens Gade, all within the half-mile walk to **Saints Peter and Paul Cathedral.** You'll see the church's high school, on the corners of Kanal Gade and Kronprindsens, just before you get to the church. The church will be on your right. The oldest Catholic church on the island and the seat of the Diocese of St. Thomas, the present building was dedicated in 1848, although previous buildings on the site date back to 1802. Inside, columns support vaulted arches, giving the sanctuary a Gothic-inspired island feel; the stained-glass windows depict various scenes from the Old and New Testaments. *(See cathedralvi.com for hours; call ☎ 340-774-0201 to schedule a guided tour.)*

STEP 7 Upon exiting the church, walk down either Brond State Road or Stoners Alley one block toward the harbor. You'll end up on Veterans Drive; look for taxis heading east toward the port. Note that there are two ports in St. Thomas, so make sure that you're on the correct ship. The fare should be about $5 per person back to the port.

By foot, we recommend following Veterans Drive, which hugs the waterfront on your right, all the way back to the ship. You'll find plenty of spots for shopping, food, and drinks along the sidewalk on the left side of the street. With a bit of luck, you'll catch a seaplane landing or taking off at the nearby seaport. The walk is around 1.8 miles.

Europe

Copenhagen Walking Tour

Duration 4–6 hours, depending on how long you linger in the castle and museum. **Walking distance** About 2 miles. **Cost** About $30 US/person, plus food; about an extra $75 US/person if you dine at Geist. **Accessibility** The Round Tower does not accommodate wheelchairs; strollers are not allowed past the first ramp levels. Only the ground floor of Rosenborg Slot is wheelchair-accessible. **Kid-friendliness** There's nothing that's *not* kid-friendly on this tour, but honestly, if you have preteens or younger and you've got just one day in Copenhagen, you should bypass everything else and just head to **Tivoli Gardens** (tivoli.dk/en). Your kids will be over the moon if you spend the day at this center-city amusement park, which provided Walt Disney himself with inspiration about how to structure an amusement park. With rides, toy soldier–style marching bands, clouds of cotton candy bigger than your head, and free-roaming peacocks, you really can't go wrong. **Map** tinyurl .com/dcl-copenhagenwalkingtour.

STEP 1 Start at the **Rundetaarn (Round Tower),** at 52 Købmagergade. Wind your way up a spiral ramp to the observation deck for a bird's-eye view

of the city. Continue to the top of the tower for a look at Europe's oldest functioning astronomy observatory. If you're lucky, a docent will let you take a peek through the resident refracting telescope. *(Summer hours: daily, 10 a.m.–8 p.m.; admission: about $4 US adults, $1 US kids; rundetaarn.dk/en.)*

STEP 2 Your next stop is **Rosenborg Slot (Castle),** home of the Danish crown jewels and lovely manicured grounds and gardens. To get there, head northwest on Købmagergade toward Landemærket, and then continue straight onto Kultorvet; continue onto Frederiksborggade, turn right onto Nørre Voldgade, and continue onto Øster Voldgade. This walk takes about 10 minutes and passes many shops and restaurants in the city's Latin Quarter area. If you haven't had breakfast, grab a Danish on the way. (We mean a pastry. Grabbing a Danish person will probably get you in a mess of trouble.) In addition to holding the royal bling, the interior of the castle displays original decor from the Renaissance reign of King Christian IV, as well as ornate stucco ceilings and some of the eeriest royal busts we've ever seen. *(Summer hours: daily, 10 a.m.–5 p.m.; castle admission: about $16 US adults, free for kids 17 and under; information: kongernessamling.dk/en/rosenborg.)*

STEP 3 If the weather is good, continue on to the **University of Copenhagen Botanical Garden,** part of the Natural History Museum of Denmark. (If the weather is poor, skip to Step 4.) Exit the Rosenborg Slot at the Øster Voldgade gate. Turn left and then walk about 3 minutes to the corner of Gothersgade and the Botanical Garden entrance. The gardens feature more than 12,000 plant species situated in lush outdoor spaces as well as inside the publicly accessible glass conservatory. There are beautiful areas to explore and get lost in, but we must confess that we spend most of our time watching the many **Eurasian red squirrels** on the grounds. These rust-colored charmers with whimsically tufted ears are friendlier than their gray North American cousins. *(Summer hours: daily, 8:30 a.m.–6 p.m.; free admission; information: botanik.snm.ku.dk/english.)*

STEP 4 Exit the Botanical Garden via the Øster Farimagsgade gate, behind the Conservatory. Turn right and walk half a block to the corner of Sølvgade; turn right and continue one block to the **Danish National Gallery** (**Statens Museum for Kunst**), at 48–50 Sølvgade. The museum's collections showcase Danish art through the 20th century, as well as European art from 1300 to 1800, including works by Titian, Rubens, and Rembrandt; a large collection of French art from the early 1900s includes pieces by Matisse, Picasso, and Braque. Interactive children's exhibits are common. *(Hours: Tuesday and Thursday–Sunday, 10 a.m.–5 p.m.; Wednesday, 10 a.m.–8 p.m.; free general admission, fees charged for special exhibits; information: smk.dk/en.)*

STEP 5 Exit the museum grounds at Solvgade, turn left, and walk down Solvgade one long block to Kronprincessgade. Walk about 5 minutes to Gothersgade. Turn left and walk along Gothersgade (which becomes Kongens Nytorv) until you reach **Nyhavn** (KNEE-hah-vin), Copenhagen's picturesque canal area, with brightly painted houses and shops. Hans Christian Andersen lived at 6 Vingardssteaede as a young man. Enter via the **Magasin du Nord.**

STEP 6 If you have an hour, take a **canal tour** by boat. It's well worth the $12-per-person price to see the waterways of Copenhagen. (Information is available at stromma.dk, but there's no need to buy tickets in advance.) Nearly all canal tours pass the ***Little Mermaid*** statue. As you'll see, the statue really is little. Wave at her from the boat and you can feel like you've crossed her off your to-do list.

STEP 7 After your canal tour, a great spot for dinner is **Geist** (8 Kongens Nytorv), which you passed on the way to Nyhavn. Geist is a good example of contemporary Danish cuisine, which combines familiar foods with nontraditional ingredients and cooking techniques. It's pricey—expect to pay about $75 per person, plus alcohol—not to mention a little out there—we loved the grilled avocado with green almonds and curry, the heart of lamb with cherries and wood sorrel not so much—but it's neither as pricey nor as out there as Copenhagen's storied Noma, which is nearly impossible to get into. Consider this Noma-lite. *(Reservations: restaurantgeist.dk/en.)*

Oslo-Meets-Epcot Walking Tour

Duration 4–7 hours. **Walking distance** 1–5 miles, depending on how much public transportation is used. **Cost** About $50–$100/person. **Accessibility** The points of interest here have only limited wheelchair access. **Kid-friendliness** Recommended for kids age 8 and up; parents with young children should use the bus to get to and from the Folk Museum. **Map** See Step 2. **Special comments** Created with Walt Disney World fans in mind, this tour visits the inspirations for three of the most recognizable landmarks at Epcot's Norway Pavilion.

BEFORE YOU GO The **Oslo Pass** includes admission to all of the featured attractions, plus public transportation between them (subject to regular schedules). Cost is around $50 per adult and $27 per child (there are also slightly more expensive multiday passes); vouchers are available in advance at visitoslo.com. You'll need to exchange the vouchers for real passes at the **Oslo Central Station** (5 Fridtjof Nansens Pass), near City Hall about a mile north of the cruise terminal. You can also buy passes direct, with no need to pick up physical tickets, using the **Oslo Pass app** for iOS or Android. However you buy it, the pass saves you about $5–$20 per person for this tour. Norway's currency is the krone, one of which is worth about 12¢ US at current rates. If you need to convert a few dollars, pounds, or euros to kroner, ATMs are located around the port and at the Oslo Central Station hub.

STEP 1 Follow the signs from the port less than 0.5 mile to **Akershus Fortress,** parts of which date from the 1300s. The outer set of walls, known as the Outer Fortress, was built in the 17th and 18th centuries and holds government offices and the **Norwegian Armed Forces Museum.** The Inner Fortress holds **Akershus Castle,** featuring an impressive set of entertainment halls—still used by the Norwegian government for formal events, and the most likely inspiration for Epcot's Akershus Royal Banquet Hall—along with a chapel that is the resting place for several Norwegian kings and queens. Many other rooms are also accessible within the fortress; these display period furniture, paintings and artifacts. *(Summer hours: daily, 6 a.m.–9 p.m.; free admission; tinyurl.com/akershusfortress.)*

STEP 2 From the fortress, it's 3 miles to the **Norwegian Folk Museum** and the **Gol Stave Church**—a walk of a little more than an hour or a 25-minute bus ride. By foot, the route travels mostly along pretty, tree-lined streets such as Bygdøy Allé, past shops, restaurants, and apartments (see tinyurl.com/dcl-oslowalkingtour for a map of the route). The nearest bus stop is at Wessels Plass, about five blocks northeast of the fortress; pick up the #30 bus toward Bygdøy Allé via Bygdøynes. (Wessels Plass is one block southwest of Karl Johans Gate, the main shopping area in town—you'll be returning to this area later.)

The Norwegian Folk Museum comprises a massive collection of artifacts spanning Norway's cultural history, from A.D. 1300 to the present. Just as at a typical museum, this one has paintings, sculpture, clothing, and other examples of decorative arts, representing every period in the country's history. Unlike most museums, however, the Folk Museum's collection includes more than 160 buildings, most of which you can enter and which show the evolution of Norway's architecture (much of which apparently involves using grass for rooftops). Don't miss the apartment building representing life in the 18th, 19th, and 20th centuries.

The Gol Stave Church, built around 1200 in the city of Gol in central Norway, was relocated to the museum site in the early 20th century. It inspired the stave church at Epcot's Norway Pavilion (another replica stands in Minot, North Dakota). Made almost entirely of wood, the church is much larger than you'd expect inside, and remarkably detailed. The walls are covered with painted representations of various scenes from the Bible, including the Last Supper. A small wooden altar, supported by a floor of unfinished planks, gives the place a simple solemnity. We've visited many of Europe's most celebrated churches, and this tiny one ranks with the best of them. *(Summer hours: daily, usually 10 a.m.–6 p.m.; admission: about $18 US adults, $5 US kids, or $33 US per family; norskfolkemuseum.no/en.)*

STEP 3 (OPTIONAL) About 800 feet south of the Norwegian Folk Museum is the **Viking Ship Museum.** At the beginning of Epcot's no-longer-shown *Spirit of Norway* film, a small child runs up to a large black Viking ship on display in a museum. This is the museum, and the *Oseberg,* built sometime before A.D. 834 and one of three historic ships on display here, is the ship. (*The Spirit of Norway,* by way, can still be seen on YouTube.) Touring the museum probably won't take you more than 30 minutes. *(Summer hours, daily, 9 a.m.–6 p.m.; admission: about $12 US adults, free for kids; khm.uio.no/english.)*

STEP 4 By foot, follow the route you took in Step 2 in reverse, but when you're almost back to the fortress, turn left (northeast) onto Kongens Gate where it intersects Myntgata, and walk four blocks to **Karl Johans Gate.** Or take the #30 bus back to Wessels Plass—from here, it's about five blocks southwest back to the port or a couple of blocks northeast to Karl Johans Gate. (See the Google map referenced in Step 2.)

Karl Johans Gate is the thoroughfare where shopping, dining, and nightlife are concentrated in downtown Oslo. You'll find a wide selection of Norwegian clothing, accessories, and art on every street. (At the far end of the street sits Norway's Royal Palace, so you know the shopping is good.)

Disney/Epcot geeks will recognize Karl Johans Gate as the location of the parade that takes place in the *Spirit of Norway* movie—the parade was filmed in 1987 on Norway's Constitution Day (May 17).

Two More Easy Options

BARCELONA WALKING TOUR: CHURCHES, MEATS, AND CHEESES Several of DCL's Mediterranean cruises begin or end in **Barcelona, Spain.** If you've got a few hours to spare, here's a quick side trip into the heart of Barcelona. (See tinyurl.com/barcelonawalkingtour for a map and bus/subway options.) Beginning at the Port of Barcelona, walk to the Paral-lel L2 subway stop on Avinguda del Paral-lel. Take the L2 to the Monumental station and walk four blocks northwest to the **Sagrada Família** church (401 Carrer de Mallorca).

Construction on the church, designed by Catalonian architect Antoni Gaudí as a blend of Gothic and Art Nouveau themes, was begun in 1882 but remains unfinished—it's scheduled to be finished around 2026! Along with Paris's Notre Dame and London's Westminster Abbey, this is one of Europe's great churches; it's also the most airy and colorful. The church is open daily, 9 a.m.–8 p.m. Admission is around $35 US per person, giving you access to one of the towers, which affords spectacular views of the city. For more information, see sagradafamilia.org/en.

Next, pick up some supplies for a picnic lunch by heading for **Croissantería Forn de Pa** (34 Carrer de Sant Antoni Maria Claret), a 13-minute walk from the church. You'll find delicious French-quality croissants, baguettes, and pastries here. Next, make the 10-minute walk to **Charcutería Simón** (392 Carrer de València), a small neighborhood store stocked with delicious meats, cheeses, and olives. Pick up some drinks from any nearby grocer, head around the corner from Charcutería Simón to **Plaça de la Sagrada Família** park (12 Plaça de la Sagrada Família), find some shade, and enjoy your meal in the shadow of the church.

SAUNTER AROUND SAN JUAN In **San Juan, Puerto Rico,** DCL offers a popular guided tour of **Castillo de San Cristóbal;** built in 1783, it's the largest Spanish-built military structure in the New World. The tour costs around $55 for guests ages 10 and up and $36 for guests ages 3–9.

Note, however, that you can tour the fort on your own much more cheaply than you can through Disney. Castillo de San Cristóbal is part of the **San Juan National Historic Site,** administered by the National Park Service (NPS). Admission through the NPS is just $7 for guests ages 16 and up, with kids 15 and under admitted free. Admission is also free for holders of the **America the Beautiful National Parks & Federal Recreational Lands Annual Pass** ($80). Discounted versions of the pass are available for seniors and people with disabilities; active US military personnel and their families, along with people who volunteer

at national parks, national forests, and other federally owned recreational lands, are eligible for free passes. Visit store.usgs.gov/pass for more information.

Castillo de San Cristóbal also offers free guided tours; check nps.gov/saju for details. A cab ride between the fort and the port shouldn't run more than $25.

When you're done touring San Cristóbal, step out of the fort and into **Old San Juan.** Take a walk down Avenida Juan Ponce de León, heading west. Ponce de León becomes Calle Fortaleza, where you'll find lots of good restaurants for lunch, from all different cuisines. It's a nice walk, a little more than a mile one-way. Take a cab back to the port when you're done.

PART THIRTEEN

RIVER CRUISING

IN 2016 DISNEY BEGAN OFFERING RIVER CRUISES through **Adventures by Disney** (**AbD**), the world-travel arm of Disney Destinations (adventuresbydisney.com). Though these are Disney-branded experiences, they have nothing to do with Disney Cruise Line. And because AbD deemphasizes "all Disney, all the time" in favor of bringing Disney-caliber service and quality to world exploration, you won't be having Mickey moments on a river cruise.

unofficial **TIP**
When AbD is running a river cruise, it charters the entire ship: all guests follow an AbD group itinerary, booked through and organized by AbD. At other times of year, AmaWaterways books its own guests on its ships, but at no point are Disney and non-Disney guests on board at the same time.

Rather than starting its river-cruise operation from scratch, AbD worked in conjunction with river-cruise line **AmaWaterways** to construct two new ships: the ***AmaViola,*** which debuted in 2016, and the ***AmaKristina,*** which went into service in 2017. These new ships are similar to existing ships in the AmaWaterways fleet (notably the *AmaSerena*), but Disney requested many family-friendly touches in their construction, such as more cabins with connecting doors and cabins with pull-out sleeper chairs—rarities in the river-cruise market.

The deck plans of the ships can be viewed at amawaterways.com/ships/amaviola and amawaterways.com/ships/amakristina, and a full photo tour of the *AmaViola* is posted at tinyurl.com/amaviola. Each ship has a spacious sundeck, a walking track, a bar, a plush lounge and sitting areas, a small gift shop, a fitness room, a soaking pool, and two restaurants. Most staterooms are configured so that the main sleep surface can be converted from one queen-size bed to two twin-size beds, according to guests' needs.

Because Disney doesn't own these ships, there is no Disney theming in the decor or finishings, such as hidden Mickeys in the upholstery or ironwork. Further, there are no Disney characters on board, nor are there dozens of Disney-owned channels on your stateroom TV or Disney-themed items for sale in the gift shop. Rather than live-performance

variations of Disney films, the onboard evening entertainment is provided by local performers—a light-opera concert in Vienna or a Hungarian dance lesson in Budapest, for example.

In 2016, the initial series of AbD river cruises had five Danube River departures; demand was so high that AbD added two more sailings that year. Ports included Budapest in Hungary and Vienna in Austria. In 2017, Disney added seven sailings on the Rhine River, in addition to eight sailings on the Danube route. The 2018 offerings were further expanded, including four regular Danube sailings, one Oktoberfest-themed sailing, two winter holiday sailings, eight regular Rhine sailings, and three adults-only food-and-wine sailings.

Several nine-night Seine River cruises were added to the AbD roster for 2019, bringing the total number of river-cruise sailings offered by Disney to nearly two dozen, with several more AmaWaterways ships being worked into the rotation, including the ***AmaLea, AmaLyra, AmaMora, AmaSerena,*** and ***AmaStella,*** all with similar footprints and nearly identical amenities. While this is still a far cry from hundreds of sail dates listed by DCL, the steady growth over several years indicates that this is an area of interest for the Disney corporation. And for the right traveler, it can be a terrific alternative to ocean cruising.

Unlike DCL cruises, for which your booking price includes just your stateroom and nonpremium meals, AbD river cruises are all-inclusive: excursions; tips; airport and hotel transfers; adult dining; Wi-Fi; and free-flowing beer and wine during lunch, dinner, and various receptions. It can be much easier to anticipate your total costs on an AbD river cruise versus a DCL sailing. On the other hand, if you just want a bare-bones, budget-friendly trip, that's significantly easier to achieve with DCL (see Part Two, page 11).

RIVER CRUISING *for* FAMILIES

THE STEREOTYPICAL RIVER-CRUISE GUEST IS A RETIREE. (We've had 60-year-old friends returning from other river cruises tell us they were the youngest people on board.) Moreover, some river-cruise lines, notably Viking, prohibit guests under age 18. In contrast, Adventures by Disney is one of the first river-cruise operators to cater to families and offer primarily family-friendly activities. Kids will be occupied and entertained throughout their vacation.

Also expect adults on board to be younger than those on other river cruises. We've taken the Danube and Rhine AbD trips, and each sailing included two or three children ages 4–5, about 20 children ages 6–12, and about a dozen teens. Many of the adults, the parents of the children on the ship, were in their late 30s to late 50s. Also in the mix were a number of small groups of adults in their 20s to 50s, some vacationing couples, and some adult parent–child pairs. The number of senior citizens we saw on board was small, with most of those being grandparents.

While AbD river cruises welcome kids, there are three main differences between traveling with children on AbD versus DCL:

AGE TO TRAVEL On most DCL voyages, children may be as young as 6 months old (see page 220). Nurseries and other facilities are available to accommodate their needs. On AbD river cruises, children must be at least 4 years old, and age 8 is recommended. There are no cribs, high chairs, baby food, or the like.

DEDICATED CHILDREN'S SPACES For many families, the big draw of DCL is its kids' clubs (see page 223). In contrast, there are no corresponding spaces on the river-cruise ships—kids mix with adults virtually everywhere on the ship.

STATEROOM CAPACITY Most DCL staterooms sleep four guests, meaning that a family of four could stay together in one stateroom. The maximum number of guests allowed in any AbD river-cruise stateroom is three, meaning that a family of four would be obligated to book two staterooms. There are significant pros and cons to both situations.

What's more, AbD river cruises offer no drop-off childcare—you can't leave your child with a babysitter for a few hours while you and your spouse head into town to see a movie. There are, however, plenty of opportunities for kids and parents to get a break from each other. Every night, AbD guides invite "Junior Adventurers" (kids ages 4–12) to the lounge while their parents eat dinner in the dining room. In the lounge, kids watch movies, work on crafts, and play games. While they're welcome to dine with the grown-ups, the fun—and the piles of chicken nuggets and fries—makes this a rarity. Teens are typically invited to have their evening meal in their own space on the ship. Again, while they're welcome to join their families, most look forward to a break from their parents and enjoy meeting new friends.

Additionally, child-specific activities are offered during the "boring" excursions. For example, at many museum stops, kids are invited to play outdoor games with guides in the garden or participate in hands-on activities like baking a regional dessert. That said, if your child doesn't like being separated from you, you have a particularly rambunctious youngster, or your child doesn't enjoy group activities, an AbD river cruise may not be for you.

EXCURSIONS *on an* ABD RIVER CRUISE

A NUMBER OF DIFFERENCES EXIST between DCL port adventures (see Part Twelve) and AbD river-cruise excursions. On DCL, there is typically a menu of at least a dozen, usually many more, port activities at a range of price points for an additional fee; a penalty fee may be charged if you make a last-minute change or cancellation. Plus, DCL

contracts out its port adventures, which are run by outside companies once you're off the ship.

Many DCL cruisers elect to book excursions on their own or forgo them altogether. Guests have access to excursion booking at different points depending on their Castaway Club status (see page 65), and some port adventures may become fully booked many weeks prior to sailing.

In contrast, the price of all AbD port excursions is included in your cruise fee. Every morning or afternoon, one to four excursions are offered, and nearly every guest on board participates. Depending on your sailing, you may be asked to choose your excursions in advance, or you may work with an Adventure Guide on embarkation day to discuss your options. Check with AdD or your travel agent to see how port excursions are being handled for your trip.

On our 2018 Rhine River cruise, we prebooked our excursions, but after an onboard presentation about the various adventures, we, and nearly everyone else on the ship, made a few modifications. Even if you're told before a sailing that a particular excursion is overbooked and unavailable, chances are this can be sorted out on board. Changes can easily happen even during the middle of an excursion. For example, two families who were booked for the Van Gogh Museum's supplemental painting experience decided they'd rather explore Amsterdam on their own during the museum tour, so two other families stepped in to take their painting slots. Changes are easy, and there are no fees to cancel or modify plans, even at the last minute.

As with DCL, AbD contracts with local guides for some excursions; however, Disney guides, with access to Disney resources, accompany you at all times.

Also as with DCL, families on AbD river cruises are welcome to choose their port excursions together or separately according to their interests. If Dad wants to go on the *Sound of Music* tour (singing "Lonely Goatherd" all the way) and Mom wants to tour the Hallein Salt Mines, that's not a problem.

SAMPLE ABD RIVER-CRUISE EXCURSIONS

Note: *Excursions are subject to change.*

Danube Cruises

VILSHOFEN, GERMANY Oktoberfest party

PASSAU, GERMANY Visit to an aerial tree path and adventure playground; brewery tour and tasting; exploration on your own with recommendations from your guides

LINZ (SALZBURG), AUSTRIA Walking tour of Salzburg; visit to the **Basilica of Mondsee** (where Georg and Maria von Trapp's wedding was

filmed for the movie version of *The Sound of Music*); meal at **Stiftskeller St. Peter,** the world's oldest restaurant; tour of the **Hallein Salt Mines and Underground Slides**

MELK (KREMS), AUSTRIA Tour of **Melk Benedictine Abbey;** lesson in preparing local foods; hike to **Dürnstein Castle;** bike trip along the Danube; visit to a family-run apricot farm

VIENNA, AUSTRIA Coach tour of Vienna; tour of **Schönbrunn Palace;** marionette show and strudel-making class; bike trip to **Klosterneuburg Monastery;** visit to a traditional wine bar; concert featuring the music of Mozart and Strauss

BRATISLAVA, SLOVAKIA Walking tour of Bratislava, including a scavenger hunt; tours of the **Schloss Hof Palace,** along with lunch and a schnapps tasting

BUDAPEST, HUNGARY Tour of **Lazar Equestrian Park;** lesson in making Hungarian goulash; nighttime tour of Budapest

Rhine Cruises

BASEL, SWITZERLAND Wine-and-cheese party

STRASBOURG, FRANCE Tour of the **Black Forest,** with an alpine toboggan run or zip-line adventure; instruction in making whistles with wooden cuckoo-clock components; walk through the medieval town of **Riquewihr;** horseback ride on the scenic trails of **Champ du Feu;** private organ concert of Mozart music; canal boat trip to the **Strasbourg Cathedral de Notre Dame;** canoe through town; macaron-baking class; tour of the historic wine cellars of the **Cave Historique des Hospices de Strasbourg**

SPEYER, GERMANY Visits to the **Porsche** and **Mercedes-Benz Museums;** walking tour of **Heidelberg** and **Heidelberg Castle;** walking or biking tour of local villages

RÜDESHEIM, GERMANY Bike tour of wine country; gondola ride to **Niederwald Monument;** visit to **Siegfried's Mechanical Music Cabinet Museum;** coffee tasting at **Rüdesheim Schloss;** cruise through the **Rhine River Gorge**

KÖLN (COLOGNE), GERMANY Curling, zip lining, and snow biking in an indoor winter park; walking tour of Köln; fragrance-making and chocolate-making classes; chocolate tasting; pub tour

AMSTERDAM, THE NETHERLANDS Canal cruise; tours of the **Rijksmuseum** or **Van Gogh Museum;** visit to the fishing village of **Volendam;** visit to the community of **Zaanse Schans** to see an 18th-century village featuring active windmills, cheesemaking demonstrations, and wooden-clog decorating

Seine Cruises

PARIS, FRANCE **Louvre Museum** tour, with art detective game for children; **Notre Dame Cathedral** tour; tour of **Montmartre** with wine tasting; tour of fashion boutiques in **Le Marais;** visit to the **Eiffel Tower**

VERNON AND GIVERNY, FRANCE Visit to painter **Claude Monet's** house and gardens; painting class at the **Giverny Museum of Impressionisms;** bicycle ride through the town of Vernon; tour the **Chateau de Bizy**

LE HAVRE, FRANCE Visit to the **Normandy Beaches,** including **Omaha Beach,** site of the World War II D-Day Invasion and the **Normandy American Cemetery;** hike of the **Etretat Cliffs** overlooking the **English Channel;** visit to an apple orchard plus a Calvados tasting

ROUEN AND LES ANDELYS, FRANCE Walking tour of Rouen; visit to a tree-climbing park; horseback riding at **Rouen equestrian park;** canoeing in the Rouen countryside; French cheese-tasting seminar; hiking or biking around **Chateau Gaillard**

CONFLANS, FRANCE Visit to **Chateau Malmaison,** home to Napoléon and Joséphine Bonaparte; visit **Auvers-Sur-Oise,** a 19th-century artists' compound

SPECIALTY RIVER CRUISES

THESE CRUISES INCLUDE many of the same activities and excursions as standard AbD river cruises, but with some targeted tweaks:

- **Oktoberfest Danube Cruise** Explore the beer culture of Central Europe. (Adults only.)
- **Holiday Danube Cruise** Shop at the Christmas market in Passau, Germany; tour the parks and gardens of Salzburg, Austria; visit Schönbrunn Palace in Vienna; see the sights of Budapest.
- **Food & Wine Rhine Cruise** Enjoy a variety of wine, cheese, and coffee tastings; take a food tour of Riquewihr, France; explore the wine caves of Des Hospices in Strasbourg, France; learn to make "spaghetti" ice cream in an onboard cooking demo; take a pub tour and visit a chocolate museum in Köln, Germany; tour the Heineken Brewery in Amsterdam. (Adults only.)

MORE DIFFERENCES BETWEEN ABD RIVER CRUISING *and* DCL OCEAN CRUISING

SIZE OF THE SHIPS The *Disney Magic* and *Disney Wonder* are 964 feet long; the *Disney Dream* and *Disney Fantasy* are 1,114 feet long. The DCL ships are also tall: 11 and 14 decks high, respectively, for the *Magic/Wonder* and the *Dream/Fantasy.* Because of size constraints

related to rivers and river-lock systems, however, the river ships are necessarily much smaller—the *AmaViola* and her sister ships are just 443 feet long and three decks high. The river ships' petite footprint also allows them to maneuver quickly and dock in tight spaces.

PASSENGER CAPACITY While the *Magic* and *Wonder,* the smaller of the four DCL ships, have a maximum capacity of about 2,700 passengers, the river ships can carry a total of just 158 guests.

DISTANCES TRAVELED Some DCL voyages cover many thousands of miles. In contrast, the entire AbD Danube River cruise is just 650 miles, and the Rhine River cruise is an even shorter 460 miles. Some guests choose to bike between port stops. If you were to miss the all-aboard time on a DCL cruise, you might have to catch a plane to your next port; with an AbD river cruise, on the other hand, you could call an Uber. On our most recent Danube sailing, the ship took just 10 minutes to pull over at a dock to drop off a local entertainer near his home in town.

PRICING VARIABILITY DCL cruise prices may vary hundreds or even thousands of dollars depending on when you book (see "Saving Money," page 25, for pricing trends). AbD river-cruise pricing remains relatively steady, with minimal fluctuations. However, there are sometimes modest discounts for early booking or other promotions.

CABIN TYPES There are nearly 30 different stateroom configurations on the DCL ships. On the river-cruise ships, there are just 9, with only minor differences among them, making it easy to figure out which type of cabin is best for you.

BED CONFIGURATION Most DCL rooms have regular queen-sized beds. On AbD river cruises they're split twins, which can be set up as a queen bed or two twin beds. This may be useful for traveling companions who are fine sharing a room but don't want to sleep together.

RELATIONSHIPS The river ships' smaller scale means you'll see the same guests all the time, giving you an opportunity to really get to know them. The ship's officers and crew are also close at hand at all times. The AbD guides are extremely friendly and strive to foster personal relationships with all guests.

PRIVACY On DCL, how much you interact with other guests is largely up to you: you can request your own table in the dining rooms, skip group excursions, and just generally keep to yourself. On a river cruise, it's all but inevitable that you'll be interacting with other guests throughout the day. There are no private or assigned dining tables. Excursions are group affairs in which nearly everyone participates. And the AbD guides work to engage guests in conversation. A river cruise might not be the ideal way to spend, say, a honeymoon.

FLEXIBILITY DCL is a huge operation that must enforce strict rules to maintain order. On the other hand, AbD river ships are smaller, making it easier to focus on guests' needs and wants. For example, a child who

is nearly but not quite old enough for a particular kids' club on DCL will be denied admission, whereas kids on AbD cruises can participate in activities geared to them as they desire. For example, our well-behaved 16-year-olds were invited to dine at the Chef's Table on the river cruise, but there is a hard rule on DCL ships that guests must be 18 and up to dine in adult spaces.

MOTION OF THE SHIPS During even the calmest of ocean voyages, you'll feel the ship moving, and on open seas during turbulent weather, you may find yourself stricken by motion sickness (see page 53). On a river cruise, however, you may be entirely unaware that the ship is moving at all. Placid river waters and slower travel speeds make motion sickness extremely rare.

THE JOURNEY VS. THE DESTINATION Many DCL guests book a cruise without a particular destination in mind—they want someplace, *anyplace* warm on the right dates, at the right price. They care more about grazing at the buffet or getting pampered at the spa than experiencing the attractions in port. But on a river cruise, it's all about where you're going. Instead of playing bingo and watching shows on sea days, you'll be exploring historic sites, seeing magnificent artwork, and taking in lush landscapes. The draw is off the ship rather than on it.

WHERE THE SHIPS DOCK Depending on the DCL destination, your ship may dock at a forlorn industrial port several miles from town. This is less common with a river cruise, where much of the time the ship can dock right next to a city sidewalk. Hopping off for a walk around town can take less than a minute.

TIME IN PORT On DCL, most sailings leave port by dinnertime. On AbD river cruises, early all-aboard times are often around 8 p.m.—and sometimes well after midnight.

FOOD AVAILABILITY On DCL, there are two rotational dinner seatings, a full buffet that's open most of the day, a multitude of quick-bite windows, and 24-hour room service. While there's certainly plenty of food on board a river cruise, mealtimes are more condensed, with just one seating for the three main meals. Limited snacks are available at other times, but there's nothing comparable to full room service. On the other hand, you're likely to dock literally steps away from a quaint café with amazing food.

FOOD QUALITY Daily port stops and smaller guest loads make it easy for a river ship to acquire fresh (versus frozen and prepackaged) produce, meats, and dairy. Overall, we find AbD's food quality superior to DCL's. The AbD river cruises also take great care to accommodate guests with food allergies. At various points during our Rhine river cruise we dined with guests with gluten, tree-nut, and shellfish allergies, as well as a guest on a controlled-calorie diet. All were given many safe dining options. See tinyurl.com/abdrivercruisefood for a look at some of the food we got to try during a Danube AbD trip.

ALCOHOL Booze of all sorts is plentiful on both DCL and AbD cruises. The difference is that all alcohol costs extra on DCL, while beer and wine are included with both lunch and dinner on river cruises. Plus, many AbD river excursions offer wine, beer, and schnapps tastings—again included in the cost of your cruise.

INTERNET Wi-Fi generally costs extra on DCL (see page 110), and the connection quality can be spotty, particularly when you're at sea. In contrast, AbD river ships have free Wi-Fi, plus a full-size desktop computer in every stateroom (it doubles as your TV). The Wi-Fi quality is good enough for email and posting to social media, but, like DCL's, it's not quite up to the task of streaming video.

GUESTS WITH DISABILITIES Here, AbD lags behind DCL. For example, while a river ship has an elevator, it serves just part of the ship. This means that a guest who uses a wheelchair can't access the sundeck. Additionally, AbD river ships sometimes double-park at a dock, meaning that guests may have to walk through another ship, or possibly over its sundeck, to get to shore. Exiting this way is all but impossible for someone with restricted mobility.

TRAVELING *with* ADVENTURES BY DISNEY

ADVENTURES BY DISNEY TRIPS, including river cruises, are overseen by **Disney Adventure Guides.** Part tour guide, part cheerleader, part therapist, part PhotoPass photographer, part medic, part waiter, and part teacher, they're the best camp counselors you've ever had. Many Adventure Guides work for DCL or the Disney parks in the off-season; one of our recent river cruises, for example, was staffed by an Adventure Guide who had previously been a counselor at the Oceaneer Lab on the *Dream*. Other Adventure Guides are Disney-trained travel experts; they are fluent in the local languages and well versed in the history and customs of the regions visited. One guest writes:

> *Of all the Disney cast members I've encountered, the Disney Adventure Guides are my favorites. Every one of them is fabulous, fun, and incredibly competent. Their energy level is off the charts—which is impressive because they never seem to sleep!*

Typical land-based AbD trips have two guides for 30–40 guests, yielding a guide-to-guest ratio of about 1–20 or better. AbD river cruises are staffed by seven or eight Adventure Guides who attend to 135–150 guests, which comes out to more or less the same guide-to-guest ratio above.

On a standard AbD trip, including AbD supplements to DCL sailings (see page 33), you'll have the same 40 or so guests and the same

two guides for the entire trip. On river cruises, however, the guides rotate among the 140 or so guests as needed. You won't be assigned your own pair of guides.

You'll also be touring with different subsets of the guest pool, depending on which excursions you and they choose. All eight guides will be on the ship in the morning and the evening, so you'll see them all then. But you may have a different pair of guides on different excursions. For example, Guides A and B might lead a farm visit in the morning, with Guides C and D leading a museum visit in the afternoon. The next day, you could have Guides A and E for a wine tasting and Guides C and F for a city walk. If a particular excursion is especially popular, there might be two or three guide pairs at that stop—the Pink Guides, the Blue Guides, and the Orange Guides, for example. You might have the same guides leading your excursions many times; on the other hand, there might be a guide or two whom you never have leading your excursions.

Guest groups are similarly fluid on river cruises. You and the Smith family might both go to the Hallein Salt Mine on Day Three and to an apricot farm on Day Four. But if on Day Three you're randomly assigned to the Blue Group and the Smiths are assigned to the Pink Group and on Day Four you're in the Orange Group and the Smiths are in the Purple Group, you might have minimal contact with the Smiths off the ship.

If you're a veteran of AbD land-based trips, it may take you a day or two to get the hang of things. While river cruises certainly have a strong AbD feel, the shifting groups and guides make for slightly less continuity than on a land-based trip. If, however, your only cruising experience is on DCL, a river cruise will feel significantly more welcoming and personal than your previous experiences. Novice cruisers will also feel right at home on the AbD river ships.

COST CONSIDERATIONS

ABD VS. DCL

WHILE IT'S A BIT OF AN APPLES-TO-ORANGES COMPARISON, here's a look at potential costs for a DCL European sailing and an AbD European river-cruise sailing. All pricing is for two adults. We found the stated pricing for the DCL trip in mid-August 2018; DCL prices vary and may change depending on your search date.

Let's examine two cruises in summer 2019 with comparable travel dates: the June 21, 2019, 7-Night AbD Danube River Cruise on the *AmaLea,* sailing from Budapest, Hungary, and the June 22, 2019, 7-Night Mediterranean Cruise on the *Magic,* departing from Civitavecchia (Rome), Italy. Both trips include stops in major European cities, with similar opportunities for sightseeing. We'll assume that flight

prices to/from your home to Rome or Budapest will be similar, as will the price for a precruise hotel night near your point of embarkation.

The lowest listed price for the DCL trip for two adults is $5,346 for a bare-bones Category 11B Inside Stateroom. You'd have to add money for gratuities and transfers, but if you did absolutely nothing except sail, two adults could take that DCL Mediterranean cruise for slightly south of $6,000. But that experience would be quite different from an AbD river trip. To even things up, we have to look at different cabin selections.

Staterooms on DCL and AbD ships are not directly comparable. Going by square footage, the closest match would be a 214-square-foot Category 9D Oceanview Stateroom on Deck 2 for two adults on the *Magic* for $6,676, compared with a 210-square-foot Category BA Stateroom for two adults on the *AmaLea* for $13,398.

At first glance, this looks like a shocking difference: the river cruise appears to cost almost exactly double the price of the ocean cruise. But in terms of the feel of the room, it makes more sense to compare the river-cruise stateroom with a 268-square-foot Category 7A Verandah Stateroom, which costs $8,776 for an obstructed view or $10,806 for a full view. While the river-cruise stateroom has a slightly smaller footprint than the DCL 7A, the full wall of windows plus the balcony make it feel much more like a DCL Verandah room than a standard Category 9 Oceanview room. Also note that a smaller percentage of the river-cruise square footage is taken up by closet space than on DCL. In short, walking into a river-cruise room feels like walking into a basic Verandah room.

There are other considerations, however. Gratuities are included in AbD's price but not DCL's. The minimum suggested tip for two people on a seven-night DCL cruise is $168 (see page 114); we usually add a bit more, so we'll say $200. Let's also add $89 for a DCL internet package that would allow you similar access to the ship's onboard Wi-Fi. For DCL, you also have to add about $100 for a shared transfer from the Rome airport to Civitavecchia and about $120 for two people from the port of Barcelona to the Barcelona airport; again, similar transfers are included in your AbD price. These necessities raise the cost of the DCL trip to $9,285 for the Obstructed-View Verandah room and to $11,315 for the Full-View Verandah room.

Adding excursions on DCL also adds expense. In this example, let's look at full-day excursions that cover the highlights of a particular destination. The selected excursions are similar to those included in an AbD supplement to a DCL cruise (see page 33). For four of the Mediterranean ports on the DCL sailing, these might be Pompeii, Sorrento, and Capri ($279 per adult); Florence and Pisa ($182 per adult); Milan for Families—Through the Ages ($135 per adult); and Monaco, Monte Carlo, and Èze ($149 per adult). At press time, DCL hadn't released port-adventure prices for Toulon, France, so let's use $150 per adult

as an estimated price for an excursion there. This adds up to a total of $1,790 in excursion fees for two adults.

Adult dining at Palo on DCL costs $30 per person, plus tip, so we'll add $100 to the DCL price. Similar chef's-table dining is included on the river cruise. Add a $150 bar tab if two adults are going to have two beers each on the DCL cruise each evening; again, beer and wine are free with meals on the river cruise.

The real cost of the DCL trip has now risen to $11,325 for the Obstructed-View Verandah room and $13,355 for the Full-View Verandah room. You can see that the second price is nearly identical to the $13,398 for the river cruise, making them very similar propositions.

There also may be ways to bring down your AbD costs to add value to your vacation. For example, in 2017 and 2018, guests who booked river cruises in the first months they were offered received a $500-per-person discount.

Also consider that some of the pluses of AbD include intangibles such as greater flexibility, more personal attention, and more time in port. Others are perhaps quantifiable: additional port stops/excursions and higher-quality food, for example. To get the same level of personal attention on DCL that you'd get on the AbD river cruise, you'd have to upgrade to a Concierge-level stateroom, which would push DCL's price well above AbD's.

ABD VS. OTHER RIVER-CRUISE LINES

WHILE COMPARING ABD RIVER-CRUISE PRICES with DCL's is an apples-to-oranges proposition, you can compare apples to apples if you look at the cost of an AbD cruise versus one on a competing river-cruise line.

Because **AmaWaterways** uses the same ships for its non-Disney-branded river cruises on the same routes as for the AbD cruises, we can easily compare its regular pricing with its AbD pricing. Again, let's use the price for two adults for the June 21, 2019, seven-night AbD Danube River cruise on the *AmaLea:* $13,398. On June 9, 2019, the *AmaCerto* sails a seven-night cruise on a similar Danube route. The price for the latter sailing, in the same Category BA stateroom, is $10,760—a difference of about $2,638. The AmaWaterways price, however, doesn't include transfers to and from the pre- and postcruise hotel or airport, which can easily reach $400. Thus, the real difference in price between the AmaWaterways Danube sailing and the corresponding AbD sailing is about $2,200.

But what else is different? When AbD charters the ship, it includes more excursions, along with excursions that are geared to families. For example, on the Rhine River cruise to Cologne, Germany, AbD guests are offered a visit to an indoor ski hall in Neuss for sledding and tubing—a real treat for many children—but nothing similar is offered on AmaWaterways' Rhine River cruises that visit Cologne. On

most AbD stops, excursion options are available for both the morning and afternoon, but with Ama, it's usually just one or the other.

Another key difference with the AbD version of the cruise is that there are children on board. Standard AmaWaterways river cruises have children on board only rarely—typically just during the odd Christmas cruise—and almost never during the summer. The presence of kids also brings down the average age of adult guests on board considerably. Even if you don't have kids, if you're a preretirement adult you're likely to find many more contemporaries on your ship when sailing with AbD versus AmaWaterways.

The biggest difference, of course, is that when AbD charters the ship, you enjoy the services of the eight Disney Adventure Guides. They run activities for the kids both on the ship and during excursions. They make sure every birthday and anniversary is acknowledged. They crack jokes on boring bus rides. (Shout out to Adventure Guide Michaela. Her improvised comedy routine about our coach driver "Herman the German" was mentioned by many, many guests on our Rhine sailing as the highlight of their vacation.) They distribute special Disney collector pins acquirable only on the ship. One guide on our trip—an actor who's a veteran of several Broadway musicals—even sang show tunes on request. Generally, Adventure Guides make sure that everyone is engaged and having a good time.

Are extra excursions and extra attention worth about $1,200 more per person than an equivalent non-Disney river cruise? As with most things, that depends. If you're a retiree and you don't mind vacationing with your peers, then probably not. Many older adults won't need some of the Disney bells and whistles, and they'll likely appreciate the more serene atmosphere on board without kids around. On the other hand, if you have kids with you, or even if you don't and you're younger than 55–60, then the Disney version of the cruise will probably be more to your liking.

By way of additional comparison, **Tauck River Cruises** offers a similar seven-night Danube cruise on July 10 on the *msSavor.* The price for two adults in a Category 6 stateroom (similar to AmaWaterways' BA stateroom category) is $13,280—just $118 less than the AbD price. The May 8 and August 14 Tauck Danube sailings in a Category 6 stateroom on the *msJoy* are priced at $14,680, or $1,282 more than AbD. The Tauck trips include gratuities and transfers, as do Disney's. **Viking River Cruises** also offers a June 2019 Danube cruise with many of the same port stops as the Ama, AbD, and Tauck sailings, but with fewer excursions and amenities. For the June 12, 2019, sailing of the *Viking Longship Ingvi* in a Category A stateroom (again, similar to Ama's BA category), the price is $8,898. Add in transfers and other incidentals, and you're looking at a real price in the mid-$9,000s.

unofficial **TIP**
Comparing AbD's prices with Viking's makes sense only if your party consists solely of adults—Viking prohibits guests under age 18.

While the price for an AbD river cruise is about double the cost of the bare-minimum DCL European cruise, it's in the same ballpark as other river-cruise lines with the same itineraries. The extra service and children's activities may make the premium pricing worthwhile, particularly if you have kids who might not otherwise be interested in a river-cruise vacation.

The Bottom Line

AbD river cruises are a luxury product with a luxury feel. Everything is included, all the details are taken care of, and you get fantastic personal service and gourmet food. It's possible to pay about half the price of an AbD river cruise for a DCL Mediterranean cruise if you select the smallest inside stateroom, skip adult dining and alcohol, and don't go on any excursions. You'll have to stick with DCL if you have children younger than 4 years old or if you strongly prefer to be immersed in Disney-themed entertainment and decor.

WHAT'S NEXT FOR DISNEY *and* RIVER CRUISING?

AS OF PRESS TIME, Disney hadn't announced any river-cruise offerings past its 2019 AbD/AmaWaterways sailings on the Danube, Rhine, and Seine Rivers. But if we had to venture a guess, we'd say that Disney will be building on its river-cruise product in the future, possibly as it nears completion of the newly announced additions to the DCL fleet. When we asked a Disney executive who happened to be on a Danube sailing with us about expanded river-cruise offerings, he simply smiled and said, "There are a lot of rivers out there."

Disney-history buffs will remember that the very first Disney voyages weren't offered through a dedicated cruise line but rather in partnership with **Premier Cruise Line.** Founded in 1983, Premier was an upstart company that introduced the idea of family cruising out of Port Canaveral. An initial agreement to become the official cruise line of Walt Disney World later evolved into a paint job for Premier's *StarShip Oceanic,* which was marketed throughout the late 1980s as The Big Red Boat, with costumed Disney characters on board. Disney terminated its relationship with Premier in 1993 when it announced plans to launch its own cruise line; Premier disbanded in 2000.

While we're just speculation at this point, we wouldn't be surprised to see Disney follow a similar pattern with river cruising—testing the waters (literally) with a marketing partnership before launching its own branded fleet. Keep your (Mickey) ears peeled.

GLOSSARY

A CRUISE VACATION means you'll encounter a great deal of specialized lingo unique to the industry. That goes double for a Disney cruise, which has its own subjargon as well. Here are some general and Disney Cruise Line–specific terms that you may encounter both in your planning and on the ship.

ABD Adventures by Disney. This is the world-travel arm of Disney Destinations. They run the Disney river cruises as well as guided tours within some DCL sailings.

ADULT DISTRICT The area on each DCL ship that includes most of the bars and lounges. These areas are typically restricted to guests age 18 and up after 9 p.m.

ADULT DINING Describes the premium restaurants on the ship that require guests to be age 18 or older to attend and that carry an additional fee.

AFT The rear of the ship.

ADJACENT STATEROOMS Staterooms that are next to each other but aren't connected by an internal door. You must enter the hallway to travel between the rooms. (Also see **Connecting Staterooms.**)

ALL ABOARD The time at which you're required to be back on board the ship following a day in port. If you're not back at the ship by all-aboard time, you'll be left behind.

ALL ASHORE The time at which guests may disembark the ship for a day in port.

ASSISTANT SERVER This is the person on your serving team who is primarily responsible for your beverage orders and for making sure your plates are cleared between courses.

BACK TO BACK (B2B) Booking two consecutive cruises. This is most common on the *Disney Dream*, where guests with a fondness for Castaway

Cay can book a three-day and four-day cruise one after the other. You can sometimes keep the same stateroom for B2B sailings.

BACKSTAGE Behind the scenes. Refers to any area of the ship that is not normally accessible to guests. (Backstage has the same meaning at the Disney parks.)

BOW The front of the ship.

BLACKOUT DATES Specific sail dates for which onboard-booking (OBB) discounts (see page 418) are unavailable.

BRIDGE The area at the front of the ship where the captain and his staff navigate the vessel.

CAPTAIN The leader of the entire vessel. Responsibilities include navigating, operating the ship's equipment, overseeing personnel, and tending to miscellaneous business. Many longer cruises include an opportunity to meet the captain.

CAST MEMBER Disney-speak for "employee." Everyone who works for Disney is a cast member.

CASTAWAY CAY Disney's private island in the Bahamas. (*Cay* is pronounced "key.")

CASTAWAY CLUB Disney Cruise Line's "frequent flyer" program. See page 65.

CLOSED LOOP A cruise that starts and ends at the same port.

CONNECTING STATEROOMS These are staterooms that are next to each other and also have an internal door connecting them. (Compare with **Adjacent Staterooms.**)

COSTUME Anything worn by a DCL cast member.

CREW MEMBER Generally, the employees of a ship. On DCL, cruise staff (see below) are distinct from crew members.

CRUISE DIRECTOR Holds responsibility for onboard hospitality, entertainment, and social events; serves as the public face of the cruise line on his or her ship. (A good reference for Gen Xers is Julie McCoy on *The Love Boat.*) On the DCL ships, you'll hear the cruise director make most onboard loudspeaker announcements. He or she also will appear in the theater on most evenings, giving opening remarks.

CRUISE STAFF You'd think this would mean all of the crew who work on the ship. On DCL, however, "cruise staff" refers to the dozen or so attractive, personable, and hyperenergetic cast members who run the onboard family and adult entertainment activities: bingo, karaoke, dance parties, and so on. If they're not spiffed up for some themed event, you'll find them wearing a nautical look: white shoes and shorts with a red-and-navy-striped top.

DECK Nautical verbiage for "story," "floor," or "level." For example, your stateroom isn't on Floor 6 but Deck 6.

DCL Disney Cruise Line. (*Duh!*)

DOUBLE DIP Slang in the Disney-cruise community for an itinerary with two stops at Castaway Cay (see previous page). Each year there are just a handful of double-dip cruises, making them particularly coveted.

EXCURSION Known in Disney lingo as a **port adventure,** this is any organized land-based activity in the ship's port of call.

FISH EXTENDER (FE) A sort of "Secret Santa" gift exchange among Disney cruisers. Next to each stateroom door is a metal fish that serves as a hook/mail slot. Some guests hang fabric pockets from the fish (thus extending the fish), which they use to accept gifts from their Fish Extender group. To participate in an FE exchange, search Facebook for a group for your specific sailing. This is completely optional and not recommended during your first sailing.

FORWARD The front part of the ship.

GANGWAY The ramp or staircase that guests use to embark and disembark the ship. Depending on the specifics of a particular port, the location of the gangway may vary.

GTY Abbreviation for "Guarantee." Some guests book a stateroom without knowing the exact room number. Such bookings are known as guarantees because Disney guarantees that it will be in the category that the guest pays for or better. This is a nice way to book a room if you're not picky about its location.

HEAD SERVER The waiter in charge of the entire dining room in Disney's rotational restaurants. You may not see your head server much, but that's because he's extremely busy making sure the entire dining operation runs smoothly. If you're having any trouble with your primary serving team, speak with the head server.

IGT Abbreviation for "Inside Guarantee" (see **GTY**). This is a nonrefundable fare for an inside stateroom, typically booked at the last minute. You won't get to choose your exact stateroom, but you will get the category of room you want.

KEY TO THE WORLD (KTTW) CARD The card you receive upon check-in at the ship that functions as your room key, identification during onboard photo opportunities, and a charge card for merchandise and additional-cost food and beverage items on the ship. You will need your KTTW Card many times throughout your day on board, as well as to get on or off the ship. *Always* keep it with you during your cruise.

KNOT A unit of speed equal to 1 nautical mile (1.852 kilometers) per hour, or 1.151 miles per hour.

MDR Short for "main dining room," also known as a rotational dining room. Each DCL ship has three MDRs.

MUSTER The required first-day safety drill.

NAUTICAL MILE See **Knot.**

NAVIGATOR See ***Personal Navigator.***

OBB Abbreviation for "onboard booking," or booking your next Disney cruise while you're on your current cruise. All DCL ships have a dedicated Onboard Booking desk. If you book your next cruise while on board, you usually receive an onboard credit, a reduction in the required deposit, and a discount on the OBB sailing (typically 10%).

OFFICER A member of the leadership team of the ship. On Disney Cruise Line, officers typically wear white uniforms.

OGT Abbreviation for "Oceanview Guarantee" (see **GTY**). This is a nonrefundable fare for an Oceanview stateroom, typically booked at the last minute. You won't get to choose your exact stateroom, but you will get the category of room you want.

ONBOARD CREDIT "Gift" money that you can apply to your onboard account. Guests are often given onboard credit when they book their cruise through a travel agent. Guests also get an onboard credit when they've booked their current cruise on a previous cruise. You also can win onboard credit at bingo games on the ship and at promotional Disney Vacation Club, spa, and shopping presentations. Onboard credit can be used to pay for shore excursions, adult dining, shipboard merchandise purchases, and so on.

PERSONAL NAVIGATOR The daily publication detailing each ship's onboard activities. Available as a hard-copy brochure and a mobile app.

PFD Abbreviation for "personal flotation device," or life vest.

PLACEHOLDER A deposit for a future sailing, at a nonspecified date, made while you are on a DCL ship. Placeholders get the benefits of booking a future cruise, such onboard credit, reduced deposit, etc. but can choose their sail date later.

PORT (ADJ.) The left side of the ship, as you face the front of it.

PORT (N.) A town or city with a harbor. The ships makes stops in ports.

PORT ADVENTURE See **Excursion.**

ROTATIONAL DINING ROOM See **MDR.**

SERVER Your waiter. The server will guide you through the menu each night, take your order, and ensure that it's delivered to your table properly and promptly. If you have dietary issues or food idiosyncrasies, your server will be the one who makes sure your needs are met.

SHIP A large oceangoing vessel—*don't call it a boat*! With a few exceptions, the general rule of thumb is that a ship can carry a boat but a boat can't carry a ship.

STARBOARD The right side of the ship, as you face the front of it.

STATEROOM Your room on the ship. Most other cruise lines call them cabins; DCL calls them staterooms regardless of the size or location of the room.

STATEROOM HOST The person who cleans your room. Your stateroom host will also turn down your bed at night, deliver messages, and generally assist with any aspect of your room's functionality. Don't forget to tip!

STERN The back of the ship.

TENDER A small boat that transfers guests from the cruise ship to land. Tenders are used when a port's waters are too shallow for a large ship to dock next to a pier.

TRANSFER The Disney-arranged method of getting you to the ship prior to sailing or to another form of transportation after sailing. For example, you can purchase transfers from a hotel at Walt Disney World to Port Canaveral or from Port Canaveral to Orlando International Airport. Transfers are available at all home ports.

VGT Abbreviation for "Verandah Guarantee" (see **GTY**). This is a nonrefundable fare for a Verandah stateroom, typically booked at the last minute. You won't get to choose your exact stateroom, but you will get the type of room you want.

WAVE PHONE The mobile phone provided in your stateroom for communication with other guests while you're on board the ship.

ITINERARIES INDEX

DISNEY CRUISE LINE'S FOUR SHIPS serve seven main geographic areas: **Alaska, Atlantic Canada** (which DCL officially calls **Canadian Coastline** but is imprecise), the **Bahamas,** the **Caribbean** (with which we group DCL's **Bermuda** itineraries), the **Mediterranean,** the **Pacific Coast,** and **Northern Europe.**

DCL also offers **repositioning cruises** when it needs to move a ship between the United States and Europe, between the Atlantic and the Pacific, or from one base port to another within a geographic area (say, from San Juan to Port Canaveral). Any cruise that starts at one port and ends at another is a repositioning cruise, the most notable being DCL's **Transatlantic** and **Panama Canal** cruises.

To appeal to as wide an audience as possible, Disney cruises vary in length (and price) within each geographic area. Guests interested in visiting the Bahamas, for instance, can choose from cruises of three, four, or five nights.

There's even more variation, however, because Disney's ships visit the same ports as every other cruise line's ships and the destination ports can't dock every line's ship at the same time. (Disney's Castaway Cay is a good illustration—it can dock just one ship at a time.)

To help fit its ships into the ports' schedules, DCL offers multiple versions of most itineraries, each of which visits exactly the same ports, but in different order. As an example, consider a four-night Bahamian cruise out of Port Canaveral, which visits Nassau and Castaway Cay and usually includes a day at sea; Disney offers at least five separate variations on this itinerary.

Taking these variations into account, Disney's four ships sail more than 50 distinct itineraries, listed in the following section. We've also included maps of the ports for each geographic area. To keep things simple, the maps show only the ports visited along the ships' routes, not the order in which each port is visited.

See Part Eleven for detailed port information.

ONLINE FARE TRACKER

OUR WEBSITE HAS AN INTERACTIVE TOOL that demonstrates how Disney Cruise Line fares vary by date, stateroom type, and the size of your party. Access it here: touringplans.com/disney-cruise-line/tools/fare-tracker.

By viewing this data, you can get a sense of the best time(s) to book a cruise, and you can see which cruises are likely to have last-minute discounts. Full access to the Fare Tracker and other Disney Cruise Line content is available as an add-on to a TouringPlans.com subscription; the fees are nominal, and owners of the current edition of this book get a substantial subscription discount. If you aren't satisfied for any reason, we offer a 45-day money-back guarantee.

NEW ITINERARIES

DISNEY USUALLY ANNOUNCES its ships' schedules in seasonal blocks—spring, summer, and so on—13–15 months ahead of the first sailings of that season. For example, summer 2019 sailings (beginning in May 2019) were announced on March 1, 2018, and became available for booking to the general public on March 8, 2018. Summer 2018 sailings (beginning in May 2018) were announced on February 11, 2017, with general booking open on February 23, 2017. Summer 2017 sailings (beginning in May 2017) were announced on April 12, 2016, with general booking available on April 13, 2016. Following this pattern, you should expect to hear about DCL's summer 2020 itineraries in the late winter or early spring of 2019, with the fall 2020 itineraries announced a few months later.

Knowing when new itineraries are released is useful if you're trying to get the lowest possible price for a specific cruise. (See "Saving Money," page 25.) It's also helpful if you want to book a specific type of stateroom for a typically popular sailing (such as a Christmas cruise) or if you want a low price or specific stateroom type for a new route. For example, when Disney introduced its Northern European itineraries, several stateroom categories sold out almost immediately.

Also, our friend Scott Sanders posts notices about new sailings at his **Disney Cruise Line Blog** (disneycruiselineblog.com).

unofficial **TIP**
When DCL adds new itineraries, it sometimes also adds new ports of call. For example, as we were going to press with this edition, Disney announced first-time sailings out of New Orleans. As the DCL fleet expands (see page 3), keep an eye out for more new home ports and port stops.

ITINERARY CHANGES

BE AWARE THAT WHILE CHANGES to itineraries are infrequent, they're also not unheard of. We've seen port stops change months or just hours in advance due to issues in a foreign country; we've even seen itineraries change midtrip due to weather conditions.

For example, on one of our trips on the *Fantasy,* ocean conditions became too rough for tender travel; therefore, a scheduled stop in Grand Cayman was canceled and became a sea day instead. And in 2015, the *Magic* made substantial modifications to its eastbound transatlantic crossing a few days before sailing, skipping two major ports and substituting another, due to iceberg activity on the initially planned route. In situations like these, Disney will refund all fees for missed port excursions booked through them. DCL may also refund port docking fees and the like if an itinerary stop is omitted.

unofficial **TIP**
Anticipating potential cancellations isn't easy, but it can help you decide, say, whether to buy trip insurance or plan when to buy airfare.

Also in 2015, Disney announced a substantial itinerary change to a Mediterranean sailing on the *Magic* that was originally scheduled to make stops in Greece and Turkey. Due to concerns about political unrest, those port stops were replaced with visits to additional ports in Italy. Guests with prior reservations on this cruise were offered no-penalty cancellations or a $1,000 onboard credit if they elected to remain on the sailing with the altered itinerary.

Less common are cancellations or reschedulings of entire sailings. A few published sail dates for 2015 were canceled and rescheduled due to problems with a planned regular-maintenance dry dock of the *Dream.* Notice of the cancellations came nearly a year in advance, but some guests who were booked on these voyages had their plans affected by the change. Guests who had been booked on the canceled dates were offered assistance with rebooking and given a $250 onboard credit.

Cancellations can also happen much closer to the published sail date. In October 2016, one sailing of the *Dream* was canceled just before departure due to the impact of Hurricane Matthew. The storm also necessitated a minor rerouting of other *Dream* and *Fantasy* sailings, as well as a complete overhaul of one *Magic* voyage, which was originally scheduled as a trip to the Bahamas but ended up visiting Atlantic Canada instead.

The 2017 hurricane season was particularly troublesome for the cruise industry, with Hurricanes Franklin, Irma, and Maria all necessitating ship rerouting and the latter two storms causing substantial damage to popular ports. Some storm-related DCL itinerary changes in 2017 included a canceled port stop in Cozumel, some *Dream* and *Fantasy* sailings returning early to Port Canaveral, and other *Dream* and *Fantasy* sailings being scrapped completely; Eastern Caribbean sailings on the *Fantasy* were subject to itinerary changes well into 2018.

Even when wholesale itinerary changes can be avoided, changes may be necessary in parts of a sailing. For example, during the middle of a March 2018 sailing of the *Fantasy,* guests were informed that several planned port adventures in Cozumel—including a popular excursion to the Mayan ruins in Tulum—were being canceled due to travel-safety warnings issued by the U.S. Embassy in Mexico.

Also be aware that changes to port arrival and departure times aren't uncommon—we hear several stories each year about ships docking late due to bad weather or high seas. For example, heavy fog caused a 2017 *Fantasy* sailing to arrive at Port Canaveral several hours late, causing many passengers to miss their early-afternoon flights home. Consider whether such a possibility would affect your decision to book excursions through Disney or another vendor.

While weather-related itinerary changes can be impossible to predict when you're booking many months in advance, you should be particularly thoughtful about your postcruise travel plans if you're sailing immediately after a ship's scheduled dry dock. (In general, gaps in sail dates listed at the DCL website and the Disney Cruise Line Blog indicate major ship maintenance.) In mid-May of 2017, for example, the *Fantasy* was delayed by half a day in returning to Port Canaveral due to unexpected mechanical issues in the wake of a two-week-long dry dock earlier in the month. While such problems aren't commonplace, they can happen occasionally just after major rehabs, when mechanical and other systems are more likely to need tweaking.

unofficial **TIP**
If you're sailing just after a dry dock, it may be prudent to book a flight very late in the day or a postcruise stay at a hotel close to the port.

ALASKAN CRUISES *(see map on next page)*

Disney Wonder

- **5-NIGHT ALASKAN CRUISE FROM VANCOUVER**

ITINERARY **Day 1** Vancouver, British Columbia, Canada; **Day 2** at sea; **Day 3** Tracy Arm, Alaska; **Day 4** Ketchikan, Alaska; **Day 5** at sea; **Day 6** Vancouver, British Columbia, Canada.

2019 SAIL DATE July 17.

- **7-NIGHT ALASKAN CRUISE FROM VANCOUVER**

ITINERARY **Day 1** Vancouver, British Columbia, Canada; **Day 2** at sea; **Day 3** Tracy Arm, Alaska; **Day 4** Skagway, Alaska; **Day 5** Juneau, Alaska; **Day 6** Ketchikan, Alaska; **Day 7** at sea; **Day 8** Vancouver, British Columbia, Canada.

2019 SAIL DATES May 20, May 27, June 3, June 10, June 17, June 24, July 22, July 29, August 5, August 12, August 19, September 2.

- **7-NIGHT ALASKAN CRUISE FROM VANCOUVER**

ITINERARY **Day 1** Vancouver, British Columbia, Canada; **Day 2** at sea; **Day 3** Icy Strait Point, Alaska; **Day 4** Skagway, Alaska; **Day 5** Juneau, Alaska; **Day 6** Ketchikan, Alaska; **Day 7** at sea; **Day 8** Vancouver, British Columbia, Canada.

2019 SAIL DATES July 1, August 26, September 9.

- **9-NIGHT ALASKAN CRUISE FROM VANCOUVER**

ITINERARY **Day 1** Vancouver, British Columbia, Canada; **Day 2** at sea; **Day 3** Ketchikan, Alaska; **Day 4** Icy Strait Point, Alaska; **Day 5** Juneau, Alaska; **Day 6** Hubbard Glacier, Alaska; **Day 7** Sitka, Alaska; **Day 8** at

Alaskan Ports of Call (*Wonder*)

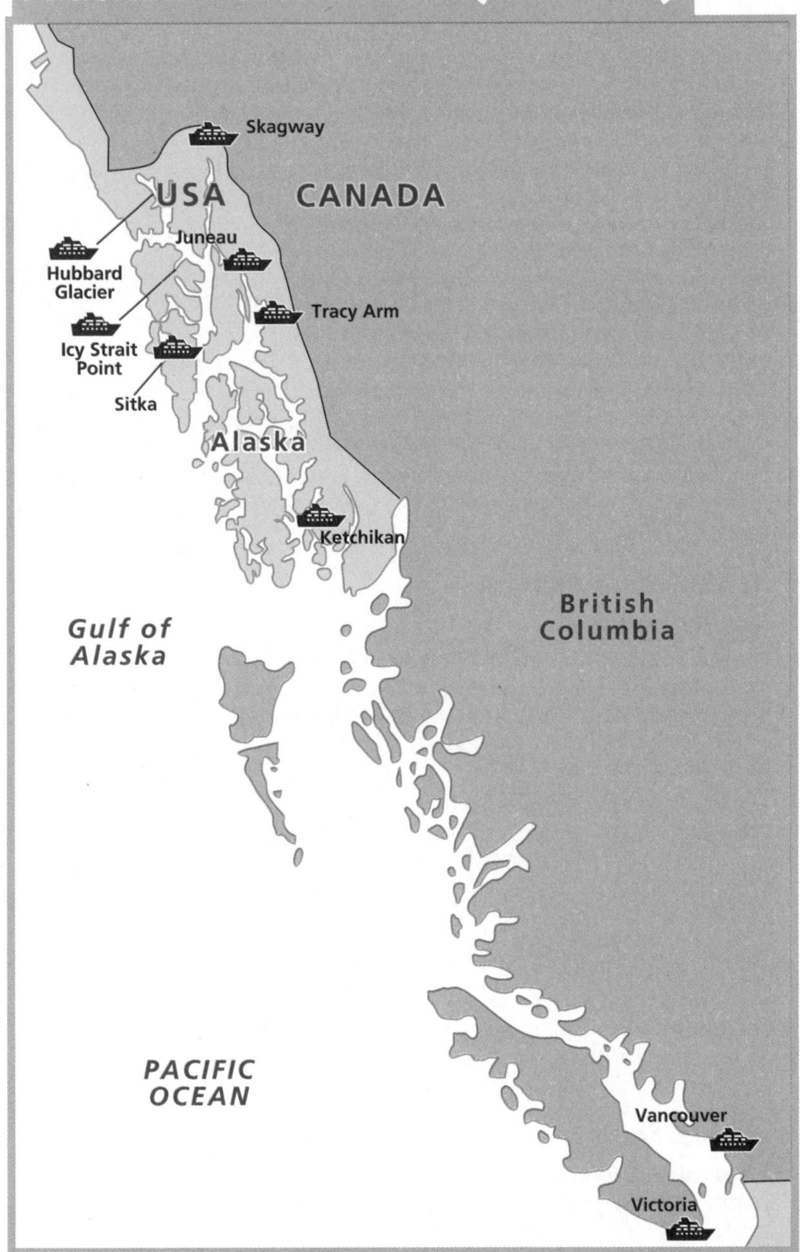

sea; **Day 9** Victoria, British Columbia, Canada; **Day 10** Vancouver, British Columbia, Canada.

2019 SAIL DATE July 8.

BAHAMIAN, BERMUDAN, AND CARIBBEAN CRUISES

(see map on following pages)

Note: *Please see our Mexico and Nassau travel advisories on pages 323 and 376, respectively.*

Disney Dream

• **3-NIGHT BAHAMIAN CRUISE FROM PORT CANAVERAL**

ITINERARY **Day 1** Port Canaveral, Florida; **Day 2** Nassau, Bahamas; **Day 3** Castaway Cay, Bahamas; **Day 4** Port Canaveral, Florida.

2018 SAIL DATE December 28.

2019 SAIL DATES January 4, January 11, January 18, January 25, February 1, February 8, February 15, February 22, March 1, March 8, March 15, March 22, March 29, April 5, April 12, April 19, April 26, May 3, May 10, May 17, May 24, May 31, June 7, July 26, August 2, August 9, August 16, August 23, August 30, September 6, November 1, December 27.

2020 SAIL DATES January 3, January 10, January 24, January 31, February 7, February 14, February 21, February 28, March 6, March 20, March 27, April 3, April 10, April 17, April 24, May 1, May 8, May 15, May 22, May 29.

• **3-NIGHT BAHAMIAN CRUISE FROM PORT CANAVERAL**

ITINERARY **Day 1** Port Canaveral, Florida; **Day 2** Castaway Cay, Bahamas; **Day 3** at sea; **Day 4** Port Canaveral, Florida.

2020 SAIL DATES January 17, March 13.

• **3-NIGHT HALLOWEEN ON THE HIGH SEAS BAHAMIAN CRUISE FROM PORT CANAVERAL**

ITINERARY **Day 1** Port Canaveral, Florida; **Day 2** Nassau, Bahamas; **Day 3** Castaway Cay, Bahamas; **Day 4** Port Canaveral, Florida.

2019 SAIL DATES September 13, September 20, September 27, October 4, October 11, October 18, October 25.

• **3-NIGHT VERY MERRYTIME BAHAMIAN CRUISE FROM PORT CANAVERAL**

ITINERARY **Day 1** Port Canaveral, Florida; **Day 2** Nassau, Bahamas; **Day 3** Castaway Cay, Bahamas; **Day 4** Port Canaveral, Florida.

2018 SAIL DATES November 23, November 30, December 7, December 14, December 21.

2019 SAIL DATES November 8, November 15, November 22, November 29, December 6, December 13.

• **3-NIGHT VERY MERRYTIME BAHAMIAN CRUISE FROM PORT CANAVERAL**

ITINERARY **Day 1** Port Canaveral, Florida; **Day 2** Castaway Cay, Bahamas; **Day 3** at sea; **Day 4** Port Canaveral, Florida.

2019 SAIL DATES December 20.

• **4-NIGHT BAHAMIAN CRUISE FROM PORT CANAVERAL**

ITINERARY **Day 1** Port Canaveral, Florida; **Day 2** Nassau, Bahamas; **Day 3** Castaway Cay, Bahamas; **Day 4** at sea; **Day 5** Port Canaveral, Florida.

continued on page 428

Bahamian, Bermudan, and Caribbean Ports of Call
USA
New Orleans
Galveston
Port Canaveral
Florida
Gulf of Mexico
Miami
Key West
Grand Cayman
Cozumel
Costa Maya
MEXICO
PACIFIC OCEAN

Not shown: Fort-de-France, Kings Wharf, New York, Tortola
ATLANTIC
OCEAN
Castaway Cay
BAHAMAS
Nassau
Falmouth
JAMAICA
San Juan
St John/
St Thomas
St John's
Philipsburg
Basseterre
Castries
Bridgetown
Caribbean
Sea
Kralendijk, Oranjestad, Willemstad

BAHAMIAN, BERMUDAN, AND CARIBBEAN CRUISES

(continued from page 425)

2019 SAIL DATES January 7, January 14, January 21, January 28, February 11, February 18, February 25, March 4, March 11, March 18, March 25, April 1, April 8, April 15, April 22, April 29, May 6, May 13, May 20, May 27, June 3, June 10, July 29, August 5, August 12, August 19, August 26, September 2, December 30.

2020 SAIL DATES January 13, January 20, January 27, February 10, February 24, March 9, March 16, March 23, April 6, April 20, May 4, May 11, May 18, May 25.

- **4-NIGHT BAHAMIAN CRUISE FROM PORT CANAVERAL**

ITINERARY **Day 1** Port Canaveral, Florida; **Day 2** Castaway Cay, Bahamas; **Day 3** Nassau, Bahamas; **Day 4** at sea; **Day 5** Port Canaveral, Florida.

2019 SAIL DATES February 4, November 4.

2020 SAIL DATES January 6, March 30, April 13, April 27.

- **4-NIGHT BAHAMIAN CRUISE FROM PORT CANAVERAL**

ITINERARY **Day 1** Port Canaveral, Florida; **Day 2** Nassau, Bahamas; **Day 3** at sea; **Day 4** Castaway Cay, Bahamas; **Day 5** Port Canaveral, Florida.

2020 SAIL DATES February 3, February 17, March 2.

- **4-NIGHT HALLOWEEN ON THE HIGH SEAS BAHAMIAN CRUISE FROM PORT CANAVERAL**

ITINERARY **Day 1** Port Canaveral, Florida; **Day 2** Nassau, Bahamas; **Day 3** Castaway Cay, Bahamas; **Day 4** at sea; **Day 5** Port Canaveral, Florida.

2019 SAIL DATES September 9, September 16, September 23, September 30, October 7, October 14, October 21.

- **4-NIGHT HALLOWEEN ON THE HIGH SEAS BAHAMIAN CRUISE FROM PORT CANAVERAL**

ITINERARY **Day 1** Port Canaveral, Florida; **Day 2** Castaway Cay, Bahamas; **Day 3** Nassau, Bahamas; **Day 4** at sea; **Day 5** Port Canaveral, Florida.

2019 SAIL DATE October 28.

- **4-NIGHT VERY MERRYTIME BAHAMIAN CRUISE FROM PORT CANAVERAL**

ITINERARY **Day 1** Port Canaveral, Florida; **Day 2** at sea; **Day 3** Nassau, Bahamas; **Day 4** Castaway Cay, Bahamas; **Day 5** Port Canaveral, Florida.

2018 SAIL DATE December 24.

- **4-NIGHT VERY MERRYTIME BAHAMIAN CRUISE FROM PORT CANAVERAL**

ITINERARY **Day 1** Port Canaveral, Florida; **Day 2** Nassau, Bahamas; **Day 3** Castaway Cay, Bahamas; **Day 4** at sea; **Day 5** Port Canaveral, Florida.

2018 SAIL DATES November 12, November 26, December 3, December 10, December 24.

2019 SAIL DATES November 11, November 18, November 25, December 2, December 9, December 16, December 23.

- **4-NIGHT VERY MERRYTIME BAHAMIAN CRUISE FROM PORT CANAVERAL**

ITINERARY **Day 1** Port Canaveral, Florida; **Day 2** Nassau, Bahamas; **Day 3** at sea; **Day 4** Castaway Cay, Bahamas; **Day 5** Port Canaveral, Florida.

2019 SAIL DATES December 2, December 9.

- **4-NIGHT BAHAMIAN CRUISE FROM PORT CANAVERAL WITH TWO STOPS AT CASTAWAY CAY**

ITINERARY **Day 1** Port Canaveral, Florida; **Day 2** Castaway Cay, Bahamas; **Day 3** Nassau, Bahamas; **Day 4** Castaway Cay, Bahamas; **Day 5** Port Canaveral, Florida.

2019 SAIL DATES June 19, July 3, July 17.

- **4-NIGHT BAHAMIAN CRUISE FROM PORT CANAVERAL WITH TWO STOPS AT CASTAWAY CAY**

ITINERARY **Day 1** Port Canaveral, Florida; **Day 2** at sea; **Day 3** Castaway Cay, Bahamas; **Day 4** Castaway Cay, Bahamas; **Day 5** Port Canaveral, Florida.

2018 SAIL DATE December 31.

- **4-NIGHT BAHAMIAN CRUISE FROM PORT CANAVERAL WITH TWO STOPS AT CASTAWAY CAY**

ITINERARY **Day 1** Port Canaveral, Florida; **Day 2** Castaway Cay, Bahamas; **Day 3** Nassau, Bahamas; **Day 4** Castaway Cay, Bahamas; **Day 5** at sea; **Day 6** Port Canaveral, Florida.

2019 SAIL DATES June 14, June 23, July 7, July 12, July 21.

- **5-NIGHT BAHAMIAN CRUISE FROM PORT CANAVERAL WITH TWO STOPS AT CASTAWAY CAY**

ITINERARY **Day 1** Port Canaveral, Florida; **Day 2** Nassau, Bahamas; **Day 3** Castaway Cay, Bahamas; **Day 4** Castaway Cay, Bahamas; **Day 5** at sea; **Day 6** Port Canaveral, Florida.

2019 SAIL DATE June 28.

Disney Fantasy

- **3-NIGHT BAHAMIAN CRUISE FROM PORT CANAVERAL**

ITINERARY **Day 1** Port Canaveral, Florida; **Day 2** Nassau, Bahamas; **Day 3** Castaway Cay, Bahamas; **Day 4** Port Canaveral, Florida.

2019 SAIL DATE August 7.

- **6-NIGHT WESTERN CARIBBEAN CRUISE FROM PORT CANAVERAL**

ITINERARY **Day 1** Port Canaveral, Florida; **Day 2** at sea; **Day 3** Cozumel, Mexico; **Day 4** Costa Maya, Mexico; **Day 5** at sea; **Day 6** Castaway Cay, Bahamas; **Day 7** Port Canaveral, Florida.

2019 SAIL DATE June 30.

- **6-NIGHT HALLOWEEN ON THE HIGH SEAS WESTERN CARIBBEAN CRUISE FROM PORT CANAVERAL**

ITINERARY **Day 1** Port Canaveral, Florida; **Day 2** at sea; **Day 3** Cozumel, Mexico; **Day 4** Costa Maya, Mexico; **Day 5** at sea; **Day 6** Castaway Cay, Bahamas; **Day 7** Port Canaveral, Florida.

2019 SAIL DATES October 27.

- **6-NIGHT WESTERN CARIBBEAN CRUISE FROM PORT CANAVERAL**

ITINERARY **Day 1** Port Canaveral, Florida; **Day 2** at sea; **Day 3** Costa Maya, Mexico; **Day 4** Grand Cayman, Cayman Islands; **Day 5** at sea; **Day 6** Castaway Cay, Bahamas; **Day 7** Port Canaveral, Florida.

2020 SAIL DATE March 29.

- **7-NIGHT EASTERN CARIBBEAN CRUISE FROM PORT CANAVERAL**

ITINERARY **Day 1** Port Canaveral, Florida; **Day 2** at sea; **Day 3** at sea; **Day 4** Tortola, British Virgin Islands; **Day 5** St. Thomas, US Virgin Islands; **Day 6** at sea; **Day 7** Castaway Cay, Bahamas; **Day 8** Port Canaveral, Florida.

2018 SAIL DATES November 3, December 29.

2019 SAIL DATES March 9, March 23, April 6, April 20, May 4, May 18, June 1, June 15, July 13, August 10, August 24, November 2, December 28.

2020 SAIL DATES January 11, January 25, February 22, March 7, April 4, April 18, May 2, May 16, May 30.

- **7-NIGHT EASTERN CARIBBEAN CRUISE FROM PORT CANAVERAL WITH STAR WARS DAY AT SEA**

ITINERARY **Day 1** Port Canaveral, Florida; **Day 2** at sea; **Day 3** at sea; **Day 4** Tortola, British Virgin Islands; **Day 5** St. Thomas, US Virgin Islands; **Day 6** at sea; **Day 7** Castaway Cay, Bahamas; **Day 8** Port Canaveral, Florida.

2019 SAIL DATES January 12, January 26, February 9, February 23.

- **7-NIGHT WESTERN CARIBBEAN CRUISE FROM PORT CANAVERAL**

ITINERARY **Day 1** Port Canaveral, Florida; **Day 2** at sea; **Day 3** Cozumel, Mexico; **Day 4** Georgetown, Grand Cayman; **Day 5** Falmouth, Jamaica; **Day 6** at sea; **Day 7** Castaway Cay, Bahamas; **Day 8** Port Canaveral, Florida.

2019 SAIL DATES March 16, March 30, April 13, April 27, May 11, May 25, June 8, July 6, July 20, August 17, August 31.

2020 SAIL DATES January 4, January 18, February 1, February 15, February 29, March 14, April 11, April 25, May 9, May 23.

- **7-NIGHT WESTERN CARIBBEAN CRUISE FROM PORT CANAVERAL WITH STAR WARS DAY AT SEA**

ITINERARY **Day 1** Port Canaveral, Florida; **Day 2** at sea; **Day 3** Cozumel, Mexico; **Day 4** Georgetown, Grand Cayman; **Day 5** Falmouth, Jamaica; **Day 6** at sea; **Day 7** Castaway Cay, Bahamas; **Day 8** Port Canaveral, Florida.

2019 SAIL DATES January 5, January 19, February 2, February 16, March 2.

- **7-NIGHT HALLOWEEN ON THE HIGH SEAS EASTERN CARIBBEAN CRUISE FROM PORT CANAVERAL**

ITINERARY **Day 1** Port Canaveral, Florida; **Day 2** at sea; **Day 3** at sea; **Day 4** Tortola, British Virgin Islands; **Day 5** St. Thomas, US Virgin Islands; **Day 6** at sea; **Day 7** Castaway Cay, Bahamas; **Day 8** Port Canaveral, Florida.

2019 SAIL DATES September 7, September 21, October 5.

- **7-NIGHT HALLOWEEN ON THE HIGH SEAS WESTERN CARIBBEAN CRUISE FROM PORT CANAVERAL**

ITINERARY **Day 1** Port Canaveral, Florida; **Day 2** at sea; **Day 3** Cozumel, Mexico; **Day 4** Georgetown, Grand Cayman; **Day 5** Falmouth, Jamaica; **Day 6** at sea; **Day 7** Castaway Cay, Bahamas; **Day 8** Port Canaveral, Florida.

2019 SAIL DATES September 14, September 28, October 12.

- **7-NIGHT VERY MERRYTIME EASTERN CARIBBEAN CRUISE FROM PORT CANAVERAL**

ITINERARY **Day 1** Port Canaveral, Florida; **Day 2** at sea; **Day 3** at sea; **Day 4** Tortola, British Virgin Islands; **Day 5** St. Thomas, US Virgin Islands; **Day 6** at sea; **Day 7** Castaway Cay, Bahamas; **Day 8** Port Canaveral, Florida.

2018 SAIL DATES November 17, December 1, December 15.

2019 SAIL DATES November 16, November 30.

- **7-NIGHT VERY MERRYTIME EASTERN CARIBBEAN CRUISE FROM PORT CANAVERAL**

ITINERARY **Day 1** Port Canaveral, Florida; **Day 2** at sea; **Day 3** at sea; **Day 4** Tortola, British Virgin Islands; **Day 5** San Juan, Puerto Rico; **Day 6** at sea; **Day 7** Castaway Cay, Bahamas; **Day 8** Port Canaveral, Florida.

2019 SAIL DATE December 14.

- **7-NIGHT VERY MERRYTIME WESTERN CARIBBEAN CRUISE FROM PORT CANAVERAL**

ITINERARY **Day 1** Port Canaveral, Florida; **Day 2** at sea; **Day 3** Cozumel, Mexico; **Day 4** Georgetown, Grand Cayman; **Day 5** Falmouth, Jamaica; **Day 6** at sea; **Day 7** Castaway Cay, Bahamas; **Day 8** Port Canaveral, Florida.

2018 SAIL DATES November 10, November 24, December 8, December 22.

2019 SAIL DATES November 9, November 23, December 7.

- **7-NIGHT VERY MERRYTIME WESTERN CARIBBEAN CRUISE FROM PORT CANAVERAL WITH TWO STOPS AT CASTAWAY CAY**

ITINERARY **Day 1** Port Canaveral, Florida; **Day 2** at sea; **Day 3** Cozumel, Mexico; **Day 4** Georgetown, Grand Cayman; **Day 5** at sea; **Day 6** Castaway Cay, Bahamas; **Day 7** Castaway Cay, Bahamas; **Day 8** Port Canaveral, Florida.

2019 SAIL DATE December 21.

- **8-NIGHT EASTERN CARIBBEAN CRUISE FROM PORT CANAVERAL**

ITINERARY **Day 1** Port Canaveral, Florida; **Day 2** at sea; **Day 3** at sea; **Day 4** Basseterre, St. Kitts; **Day 5** St. John's, Antigua; **Day 6** St. Thomas, US Virgin Islands; **Day 7** at sea; **Day 8** Castaway Cay, Bahamas; **Day 9** Port Canaveral, Florida.

2019 SAIL DATE June 22.

- **8-NIGHT HALLOWEEN ON THE HIGH SEAS EASTERN CARIBBEAN CRUISE FROM PORT CANAVERAL**

ITINERARY **Day 1** Port Canaveral, Florida; **Day 2** at sea; **Day 3** at sea; **Day 4** Basseterre, St. Kitts; **Day 5** St. John's, Antigua; **Day 6** San Juan, Puerto Rico; **Day 7** at sea; **Day 8** Castaway Cay, Bahamas; **Day 9** Port Canaveral, Florida.

2019 SAIL DATE October 19.

- **8-NIGHT EASTERN CARIBBEAN CRUISE FROM PORT CANAVERAL**

ITINERARY **Day 1** Port Canaveral, Florida; **Day 2** at sea; **Day 3** at sea; **Day 4** Basseterre, St. Kitts; **Day 5** St. John's, Antigua; **Day 6** San Juan, Puerto Rico; **Day 7** at sea; **Day 8** Castaway Cay, Bahamas; **Day 9** Port Canaveral, Florida.

2020 SAIL DATE March 21.

- **11-NIGHT SOUTHERN CARIBBEAN CRUISE FROM PORT CANAVERAL**

ITINERARY **Day 1** Port Canaveral, Florida; **Day 2** at sea; **Day 3** at sea; **Day 4** Oranjestad, Aruba; **Day 5** at sea; **Day 6** Bridgetown, Barbados; **Day 7** Fort-de-France, Martinique; **Day 8** Basseterre, St. Kitts and Nevis; **Day 9** San Juan, Puerto Rico; **Day 10** at sea; **Day 11** Castaway Cay, Bahamas; **Day 12** Port Canaveral, Florida.

2019 SAIL DATE July 27.

Disney Magic

• **3-NIGHT BAHAMIAN CRUISE FROM MIAMI**

ITINERARY **Day 1** Miami, Florida; **Day 2** Castaway Cay, Bahamas; **Day 3** Nassau, Bahamas; **Day 4** Miami, Florida.

2020 SAIL DATE May 8.

• **3-NIGHT VERY MERRYTIME BAHAMIAN CRUISE FROM MIAMI**

ITINERARY **Day 1** Miami, Florida; **Day 2** Castaway Cay, Bahamas; **Day 3** Nassau, Bahamas; **Day 4** Miami, Florida.

2019 SAIL DATES November 20, November 29.

• **4-NIGHT BAHAMIAN CRUISE FROM MIAMI**

ITINERARY **Day 1** Miami, Florida; **Day 2** Nassau, Bahamas; **Day 3** Castaway Cay, Bahamas; **Day 4** at sea; **Day 5** Miami, Florida.

2018 SAIL DATE December 26.

2020 SAIL DATES January 23, February 6, February 20, March 5, March 19, April 2, April 16, April 30.

• **4-NIGHT BAHAMIAN CRUISE FROM MIAMI**

ITINERARY **Day 1** Miami, Florida; **Day 2** Key West, Florida; **Day 3** Nassau, Bahamas; **Day 4** Castaway Cay, Bahamas; **Day 5** Miami, Florida.

2019 SAIL DATES February 27, March 13, March 27, April 10, April 24, May 8.

• **4-NIGHT BAHAMIAN CRUISE FROM MIAMI**

ITINERARY **Day 1** Miami, Florida; **Day 2** at sea; **Day 3** Key West, Florida; **Day 4** Castaway Cay, Bahamas; **Day 5** Miami, Florida.

2019 SAIL DATE January 2.

2020 SAIL DATE May 4.

• **4-NIGHT BAHAMIAN CRUISE FROM MIAMI**

ITINERARY **Day 1** Miami, Florida; **Day 2** Castaway Cay, Bahamas; **Day 3** at sea; **Day 4** Key West, Florida; **Day 5** Miami, Florida.

2019 SAIL DATE January 16.

• **4-NIGHT BAHAMIAN CRUISE FROM MIAMI**

ITINERARY **Day 1** Miami, Florida; **Day 2** Castaway Cay, Bahamas; **Day 3** Nassau, Bahamas; **Day 4** at sea; **Day 5** Miami, Florida.

2019 SAIL DATES January 30, February 13.

• **4-NIGHT BAHAMIAN CRUISE FROM MIAMI**

ITINERARY **Day 1** Miami, Florida; **Day 2** Castaway Cay, Bahamas; **Day 3** Nassau, Bahamas; **Day 4** at sea; **Day 5** Miami, Florida.

2020 SAIL DATE January 14.

• **4-NIGHT VERY MERRYTIME BAHAMIAN CRUISE FROM MIAMI**

ITINERARY **Day 1** Miami, Florida; **Day 2** Key West, Florida; **Day 3** Nassau, Bahamas; **Day 4** Castaway Cay, Bahamas; **Day 5** Miami, Florida.

2018 SAIL DATES December 5, December 19.

• **4-NIGHT VERY MERRYTIME BAHAMIAN CRUISE FROM MIAMI**

ITINERARY **Day 1** Miami, Florida; **Day 2** Nassau, Bahamas; **Day 3** Castaway Cay, Bahamas; **Day 4** at sea; **Day 5** Miami, Florida.

2018 SAIL DATE December 12.

• **5-NIGHT BAHAMIAN CRUISE FROM MIAMI**

ITINERARY **Day 1** Miami, Florida; **Day 2** Key West, Florida; **Day 3** Nassau, Bahamas; **Day 4** Castaway Cay, Bahamas; **Day 5** at sea; **Day 6** Miami, Florida.

2019 SAIL DATES January 12, January 26, February 9, March 9, March 23, April 20, May 4.

- **5-NIGHT BAHAMIAN CRUISE FROM MIAMI**

ITINERARY **Day 1** Miami, Florida; **Day 2** Key West, Florida; **Day 3** Nassau, Bahamas; **Day 4** Castaway, Cay, Bahamas; **Day 5** at sea; **Day 6** Miami, Florida.

2019 SAIL DATES March 22, April 5, April 19, May 3.

- **5-NIGHT BAHAMIAN CRUISE FROM MIAMI**

ITINERARY **Day 1** Miami, Florida; **Day 2** at sea; **Day 3** Key West, Florida; **Day 4** Castaway, Cay, Bahamas; **Day 5** Nassau, Bahamas; **Day 6** Miami, Florida.

2019 SAIL DATE December 30.

- **5-NIGHT BAHAMIAN CRUISE FROM MIAMI**

ITINERARY **Day 1** Miami, Florida; **Day 2** at sea; **Day 3** Key West, Florida; **Day 4** Nassau, Bahamas; **Day 5** Castaway Cay, Bahamas; **Day 6** Miami, Florida.

2020 SAIL DATE January 9.

- **5-NIGHT BAHAMIAN CRUISE FROM MIAMI WITH MARVEL DAY AT SEA**

ITINERARY **Day 1** Miami, Florida; **Day 2** Key West, Florida; **Day 3** Nassau, Bahamas; **Day 4** Castaway Cay, Bahamas; **Day 5** at sea; **Day 6** Miami, Florida.

2019 SAIL DATES January 11, January 25, February 8, February 22, March 8.

5-NIGHT VERY MERRYTIME BAHAMIAN CRUISE FROM MIAMI

ITINERARY **Day 1** Miami, Florida; **Day 2** Castaway Cay, Bahamas; **Day 3** Nassau, Bahamas; **Day 4** at sea; **Day 5** Key West, Florida; **Day 6** Miami, Florida.

2018 SAIL DATE December 14.

- **5-NIGHT VERY MERRYTIME BAHAMIAN CRUISE FROM MIAMI**

ITINERARY **Day 1** Miami, Florida; **Day 2** Nassau, Bahamas; **Day 3** Castaway Cay, Bahamas; **Day 4** at sea; **Day 5** Key West, Florida; **Day 6** Miami, Florida.

2019 SAIL DATE December 2.

- **5-NIGHT WESTERN CARIBBEAN CRUISE FROM MIAMI**

ITINERARY **Day 1** Miami, Florida; **Day 2** at sea; **Day 3** Grand Cayman, Cayman Islands; **Day 4** at sea; **Day 5** Castaway Cay, Bahamas; **Day 6** Miami, Florida.

2020 SAIL DATES January 4, February 1, February 15, February 29.

- **5-NIGHT WESTERN CARIBBEAN CRUISE FROM MIAMI**

ITINERARY **Day 1** Miami, Florida; **Day 2** Castaway Cay, Bahamas; **Day 3** at sea; **Day 4** Cozumel, Mexico; **Day 5** at sea; **Day 6** Miami, Florida.

2020 SAIL DATES January 18, March 14.

- **5-NIGHT WESTERN CARIBBEAN CRUISE FROM MIAMI WITH MARVEL DAY AT SEA**

ITINERARY **Day 1** Miami, Florida; **Day 2** at sea; **Day 3** Cozumel, Mexico; **Day 4** at sea; **Day 5** Castaway Cay, Bahamas; **Day 6** Miami, Florida.

2019 SAIL DATES February 3, February 17, March 3.

- **5-NIGHT VERY MERRYTIME BAHAMIAN CRUISE FROM MIAMI**

ITINERARY **Day 1** Miami, Florida; **Day 2** at sea; **Day 3** Key West, Florida; **Day 4** Castaway Cay, Bahamas; **Day 5** Nassau, Bahamas; **Day 6** Miami, Florida.

2019 SAIL DATE December 16.

2020 SAIL DATES January 27, February 10, February 24, March 9, March 23, April 6, April 20.

- **5-NIGHT HALLOWEEN ON THE HIGH SEAS BERMUDA CRUISE FROM NEW YORK**

ITINERARY **Day 1** New York, New York; **Day 2** at sea; **Day 3** King's Wharf, Bermuda; **Day 4** King's Wharf, Bermuda; **Day 5** at sea; **Day 6** New York, New York.

2019 SAIL DATES September 25, October 12, October 17.

- **7-NIGHT BAHAMIAN CRUISE FROM NEW YORK**

ITINERARY **Day 1** New York, New York; **Day 2** at sea; **Day 3** at sea; **Day 4** Castaway Cay, Bahamas; **Day 5** Port Canaveral, Florida; **Day 6** at sea; **Day 7** at sea; **Day 8** New York, New York.

2018 SAIL DATE November 3.

2019 SAIL DATE November 3.

- **7-NIGHT HALLOWEEN ON THE HIGH SEAS BAHAMIAN CRUISE FROM NEW YORK**

ITINERARY **Day 1** New York, New York; **Day 2** at sea; **Day 3** at sea; **Day 4** Castaway Cay, Bahamas; **Day 5** Port Canaveral, Florida; **Day 6** at sea; **Day 7** at sea; **Day 8** New York, New York.

2019 SAIL DATE October 27.

- **7-NIGHT VERY MERRYTIME BAHAMIAN CRUISE FROM NEW YORK**

ITINERARY **Day 1** New York, New York; **Day 2** at sea; **Day 3** at sea; **Day 4** Castaway Cay, Bahamas; **Day 5** Port Canaveral, Florida; **Day 6** at sea; **Day 7** at sea; **Day 8** New York, New York.

2018 SAIL DATES November 10, November 17.

Disney Wonder

- **3-NIGHT BAHAMIAN CRUISE FROM PORT CANAVERAL**

ITINERARY **Day 1** Port Canaveral, Florida; **Day 2** at sea; **Day 3** Castaway Cay, Bahamas; **Day 4** Port Canaveral, Florida.

2019 SAIL DATE February 7.

- **4-NIGHT BAHAMIAN CRUISE FROM PORT CANAVERAL**

ITINERARY **Day 1** Port Canaveral, Florida; **Day 2** Nassau, Bahamas; **Day 3** Castaway Cay, Bahamas; **Day 4** at sea; **Day 5** Port Canaveral, Florida.

2019 SAIL DATES February 10, February 17.

- **3-NIGHT BAHAMIAN CRUISE FROM PORT CANAVERAL**

ITINERARY **Day 1** Port Canaveral, Florida; **Day 2** Nassau, Bahamas; **Day 3** Castaway Cay, Bahamas; **Day 4** Port Canaveral, Florida.

2019 SAIL DATES February 14, February 21.

- **4-NIGHT WESTERN CARIBBEAN CRUISE FROM NEW ORLEANS**

ITINERARY **Day 1** New Orleans, Louisiana; **Day 2** at sea; **Day 3** Cozumel, Mexico; **Day 4** at sea; **Day 5** New Orleans, Louisiana.

2020 SAIL DATES February 27, March 2.

- **5-NIGHT BAHAMIAN CRUISE FROM SAN JUAN TO NEW ORLEANS**

ITINERARY **Day 1** San Juan, Puerto Rico; **Day 2** at sea; **Day 3** Castaway Cay, Bahamas; **Day 4** at sea; **Day 5** at sea; **Day 6** New Orleans, Louisiana.

2020 SAIL DATE February 2.

• **6-NIGHT SOUTHERN CARIBBEAN CRUISE FROM SAN JUAN**

ITINERARY **Day 1** San Juan, Puerto Rico; **Day 2** Philipsburg, Sint Maarten; **Day 3** St. John's, Antigua and Barbuda; **Day 4** Castries, St. Lucia; **Day 5** Bridgetown, Barbados; **Day 6** at sea; **Day 7** San Juan, Puerto Rico.

2019 SAIL DATE January 14.

• **6-NIGHT WESTERN CARIBBEAN CRUISE FROM GALVESTON TO SAN JUAN**

ITINERARY **Day 1** Galveston, Texas; **Day 2** at sea; **Day 3** Cozumel, Mexico; **Day 4** Grand Cayman, Cayman Islands; **Day 5** Falmouth, Jamaica; **Day 6** at sea; **Day 7** San Juan, Puerto Rico.

2020 SAIL DATE January 13.

• **6-NIGHT WESTERN CARIBBEAN CRUISE FROM NEW ORLEANS**

ITINERARY **Day 1** New Orleans, Louisiana; **Day 2** at sea; **Day 3** Cozumel, Mexico; **Day 4** Grand Cayman, Cayman Islands; **Day 5** at sea; **Day 6** at sea; **Day 7** New Orleans, Louisiana.

2020 SAIL DATE February 21.

• **7-NIGHT BAHAMIAN CRUISE FROM GALVESTON**

ITINERARY **Day 1** Galveston, Texas; **Day 2** at sea; **Day 3** Key West, Florida; **Day 4** Nassau, Bahamas; **Day 5** Castaway Cay, Bahamas; **Day 6** at sea; **Day 7** at sea; **Day 8** Galveston, Texas.

2018 SAIL DATE December 27.

• **7-NIGHT BAHAMIAN CRUISE FROM GALVESTON**

ITINERARY **Day 1** Galveston, Texas; **Day 2** at sea; **Day 3** at sea; **Day 4** Nassau, Bahamas; **Day 5** Castaway Cay, Bahamas; **Day 6** Key West, Florida; **Day 7** at sea; **Day 8** Galveston, Texas.

2019 SAIL DATE December 27.

• **7-NIGHT BAHAMIAN CRUISE FROM NEW ORLEANS**

ITINERARY **Day 1** New Orleans, Louisiana; **Day 2** at sea; **Day 3** at sea; **Day 4** Nassau, Bahamas; **Day 5** Castaway Cay, Bahamas; **Day 6** Key West, Florida; **Day 7** at sea; **Day 8** New Orleans, Louisiana.

2020 SAIL DATE February 7.

• **7-NIGHT VERY MERRYTIME BAHAMIAN CRUISE FROM GALVESTON**

ITINERARY **Day 1** Galveston, Texas; **Day 2** at sea; **Day 3** Key West, Florida; **Day 4** Castaway Cay, Bahamas; **Day 5** Nassau, Bahamas; **Day 6** at sea; **Day 7** at sea; **Day 8** Galveston, Texas.

2018 SAIL DATES November 16, December 7, December 14.

• **7-NIGHT VERY MERRYTIME BAHAMIAN CRUISE FROM GALVESTON**

ITINERARY **Day 1** Galveston, Texas; **Day 2** at sea; **Day 3** Key West, Florida; **Day 4** Nassau, Bahamas; **DAY 5** Castaway Cay, Bahamas; **Day 6** at sea; **Day 7** at sea; **Day 8** Galveston, Texas.

2018 SAIL DATE November 23.

• **7-NIGHT VERY MERRYTIME BAHAMIAN CRUISE FROM GALVESTON WITH TWO STOPS AT CASTAWAY CAY**

ITINERARY **Day 1** Galveston, Texas; **Day 2** at sea; **Day 3** at sea; **Day 4** Castaway Cay, Bahamas; **Day 5** Castaway Cay, Bahamas; **Day 6** Key West, Florida; **Day 7** at sea; **Day 8** Galveston, Texas.

2019 SAIL DATE November 29.

• **7-NIGHT SOUTHERN CARIBBEAN CRUISE FROM SAN JUAN**

ITINERARY **Day 1** San Juan, Puerto Rico; **Day 2** St. John's, Antigua and Barbuda; **Day 3** at sea; **Day 4** Kralendijk, Bonaire; **Day 5** Oranjestad, Aruba; **Day 6** Willemstad, Curaçao; **Day 7** at sea; **Day 8** San Juan, Puerto Rico.

2020 SAIL DATE January 19.

• **7-NIGHT SOUTHERN CARIBBEAN CRUISE FROM SAN JUAN**

ITINERARY **Day 1** San Juan, Puerto Rico; **Day 2** St. John's, Antigua and Barbuda; **Day 3** Philipsburg, Sint Maarten; **Day 4** Fort-de-France, Martinique; **Day 5** Bridgetown, Barbados; **Day 6** Castries, St. Lucia; **Day 7** at sea; **Day 8** San Juan, Puerto Rico.

2020 SAIL DATE January 26.

• **7-NIGHT WESTERN CARIBBEAN CRUISE FROM NEW ORLEANS**

ITINERARY **Day 1** New Orleans, Louisiana; **Day 2** at sea; **Day 3** Cozumel, Mexico; **Day 4** Grand Cayman, Cayman Islands; **Day 5** Falmouth, Jamaica; **Day 6** at sea; **Day 7** at sea; **Day 8** New Orleans, Louisiana.

2020 SAIL DATE February 14.

BRITISH ISLES CRUISES *(see map on pages 444–445)*

Disney Magic

• **7-NIGHT BRITISH ISLES CRUISE FROM DOVER**

ITINERARY **Day 1** Dover, England, United Kingdom; **Day 2** at sea; **Day 3** Cork, Ireland; **Day 4** Dublin, Ireland; **Day 5** Greenock, Scotland, United Kingdom; **Day 6** Liverpool, England, United Kingdom; **Day 7** at sea; **Day 8** Dover, England, United Kingdom.

2019 SAIL DATE September 8.

CANADIAN COASTLINE CRUISES *(see map on pages 450–451)*

Disney Magic

• **5-NIGHT HALLOWEEN ON THE HIGH SEAS CANADA CRUISE FROM NEW YORK**

ITINERARY **Day 1** New York, New York; **Day 2** at sea; **Day 3** Bar Harbor, Maine; **Day 4** Saint John, New Brunswick, Canada; **Day 5** at sea; **Day 6** New York, New York.

2019 SAIL DATE September 30.

HAWAIIAN CRUISES *(see map opposite)*

Disney Wonder

• **9-NIGHT HAWAIIAN CRUISE FROM VANCOUVER**

ITINERARY **Day 1** Vancouver, British Columbia, Canada; **Day 2** at sea; **Day 3** at sea; **Day 4** at sea; **Day 5** at sea; **Day 6** at sea; **Day 7** Nawiliwili, Hawaii; **Day 8** Kahului, Hawaii; **Day 9** Hilo, Hawaii; **Day 10** Honolulu, Hawaii.

2020 SAIL DATE April 29.

• **10-NIGHT HAWAIIAN CRUISE FROM HONOLULU**

ITINERARY **Day 1** Honolulu, Hawaii; **Day 2** Hilo, Hawaii; **Day 3** Nawiliwili, Hawaii; **Day 4** Nawiliwili, Hawaii; **Day 5** Kahului, Hawaii; **Day 6** at sea; **Day 7**

Hawaiian Ports of Call (*Wonder*)

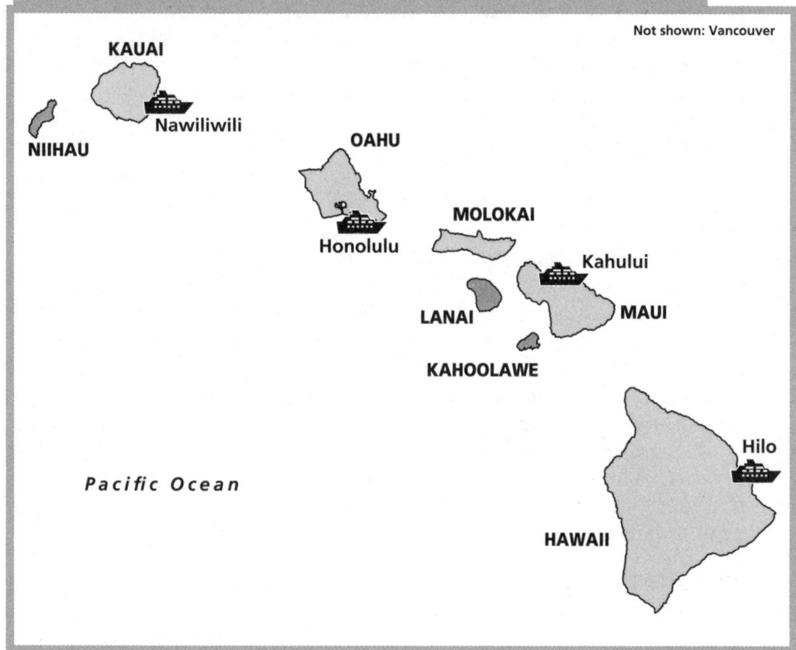

at sea; **Day 8** at sea; **Day 9** at sea; **Day 10** at sea; **Day 11** Vancouver, British Columbia, Canada.

2020 SAIL DATE May 8.

MEDITERRANEAN CRUISES *(see map on pages 440–441)*

Note: *Please see our European travel advisory on page 309 and our Barcelona travel advisory on page 311.*

Disney Magic

- **5-NIGHT MEDITERRANEAN CRUISE FROM BARCELONA**

ITINERARY **Day 1** Barcelona, Spain; **Day 2** Cannes, France; **Day 3** Livorno, Italy; **Day 4** Civitavecchia, Italy; **Day 5** at sea; **Day 6** Barcelona, Spain.

2019 SAIL DATE July 9.

- **6-NIGHT MEDITERRANEAN CRUISE FROM BARCELONA**

ITINERARY **Day 1** Barcelona, Spain; **Day 2** at sea; **Day 3** Naples, Italy; **Day 4** Civitavecchia, Italy; **Day 5** Livorno, Italy; **Day 6** Villefranche, France; **Day 7** at sea; **Day 8** Barcelona, Spain.

2019 SAIL DATE June 8.

• **7-NIGHT MEDITERRANEAN CRUISE FROM BARCELONA**

ITINERARY **Day 1** Barcelona, Spain; **Day 2** at sea; **Day 3** Naples, Italy; **Day 4** Civitavecchia, Italy; **Day 5** Livorno, Italy; **Day 6** Villefranche, France; **Day 7** at sea; **Day 8** Barcelona, Spain.

2019 SAIL DATES May 25, June 1.

• **7-NIGHT MEDITERRANEAN CRUISE FROM CIVITAVECCHIA TO BARCELONA**

ITINERARY **Day 1** Civitavecchia, Italy; **Day 2** Naples, Italy; **Day 3** at sea; **Day 4** Livorno, Italy; **Day 5** Genoa, Italy; **Day 6** Cannes, France; **Day 7** Toulon, France; **Day 8** Barcelona, Spain.

2019 SAIL DATE June 22.

• **8-NIGHT MEDITERRANEAN CRUISE FROM CIVITAVECCHIA**

ITINERARY **Day 1** Civitavecchia, Italy; **Day 2** Salerno, Italy; **Day 3** at sea; **Day 4** La Spezia, Italy; **Day 5** Villefranche, France; **Day 6** Marseilles, France; **Day 7** Barcelona, Spain; **Day 8** at sea; **Day 9** Civitavecchia, Italy.

2019 SAIL DATE June 14.

• **10-NIGHT MEDITERRANEAN CRUISE FROM BARCELONA**

ITINERARY **Day 1** Barcelona, Spain; **Day 2** at sea; **Day 3** Naples, Italy; **Day 4** Civitavecchia, Italy; **Day 5** Ajaccio, France; **Day 6** Livorno, Italy; **Day 7** at sea; **Day 8** Genoa, Italy; **Day 9** Villefranche, France; **Day 10** Marseilles, France; **Day 11** Barcelona, Spain.

2019 SAIL DATE June 29.

MEXICAN CRUISES *(see maps on pages 426–427 and 448–449)*

Note: *For more itineraries that visit Mexico, also see Bahamian, Bermudan, and Caribbean Cruises (page 425) and Panama Canal Cruises (page 443). Also see our Mexico travel advisory on page 323 and our Mazatlán advisory on page 326.*

Disney Wonder

• **2-NIGHT BAJA CRUISE FROM SAN DIEGO**

ITINERARY **Day 1** San Diego, California; **Day 2** Ensenada, Mexico; **Day 3** San Diego, California.

2019 SAIL DATES April 12, April 19.

2020 SAIL DATE April 10.

• **2-NIGHT HALLOWEEN ON THE HIGH SEAS BAJA CRUISE FROM SAN DIEGO**

ITINERARY **Day 1** San Diego, California; **Day 2** Ensenada, Mexico; **Day 3** San Diego, California.

2019 SAIL DATE October 18.

• **3-NIGHT BAJA CRUISE FROM SAN DIEGO**

ITINERARY **Day 1** San Diego, California; **Day 2** at sea; **Day 3** Cabo San Lucas, Mexico; **Day 4** at sea.

2019 SAIL DATE May 12.

• **4-NIGHT BAJA CRUISE FROM SAN DIEGO**

ITINERARY **Day 1** San Diego, California; **Day 2** at sea; **Day 3** Cabo San Lucas, Mexico; **Day 4** at sea; **Day 5** San Diego, California.

2019 SAIL DATES March 20, April 3.
2020 SAIL DATE March 25.

- **4-NIGHT HALLOWEEN ON THE HIGH SEAS BAJA CRUISE FROM SAN DIEGO**

ITINERARY **Day 1** San Diego, California; **Day 2** at sea; **Day 3** Cabo San Lucas, Mexico; **Day 4** at sea; **Day 5** San Diego, California.
2019 SAIL DATE October 14.

- **5-NIGHT HALLOWEEN ON THE HIGH SEAS BAJA CRUISE FROM SAN DIEGO**

ITINERARY **Day 1** San Diego, California; **Day 2** at sea; **Day 3** Cabo San Lucas, Mexico; **Day 4** at sea; **Day 5** Ensenada, Mexico; **Day 6** San Diego, California.
2019 SAIL DATES October 4, October 19.

- **5-NIGHT BAJA CRUISE FROM SAN DIEGO**

ITINERARY **Day 1** San Diego, California; **Day 2** at sea; **Day 3** Cabo San Lucas, Mexico; **Day 4** at sea; **Day 5** Ensenada, Mexico; **Day 6** San Diego, California.
2019 SAIL DATES March 10, March 15, March 24, March 29, April 7, April 14, November 3.
2020 SAIL DATES March 20, April 5, April 19.

- **7-NIGHT HALLOWEEN ON THE HIGH SEAS MEXICAN RIVIERA CRUISE FROM SAN DIEGO**

ITINERARY **Day 1** San Diego, California; **Day 2** at sea; **Day 3** Cabo San Lucas, Mexico; **Day 4** Mazatlán, Mexico; **Day 5** Puerto Vallarta, Mexico; **Day 6** at sea; **Day 7** at sea; **Day 8** San Diego, California.
2019 SAIL DATES October 20, October 27.

- **7-NIGHT MEXICAN RIVIERA CRUISE FROM SAN DIEGO**

ITINERARY **Day 1** San Diego, California; **Day 2** at sea; **Day 3** Cabo San Lucas, Mexico; **Day 4** Mazatlán, Mexico; **Day 5** Puerto Vallarta, Mexico; **Day 6** at sea; **Day 7** at sea; **Day 8** San Diego, California.
2019 SAIL DATES April 21, April 28, May 5.
2020 SAIL DATES March 29, April 12.

NORTHERN EUROPEAN CRUISES

(see map on pages 444–445)

Disney Magic

- **7-NIGHT NORWEGIAN CRUISE FROM DOVER**

ITINERARY **Day 1** Dover, England, United Kingdom; **Day 2** Amsterdam, Netherlands; **Day 3** at sea; **Day 4** Copenhagen, Denmark; **Day 5** Gothenburg, Sweden; **Day 6** Stavanger, Norway; **Day 7** at sea; **Day 8** Dover, England, United Kingdom.
2019 SAIL DATE August 18.

- **7-NIGHT NORWEGIAN CRUISE FROM DOVER**

ITINERARY **Day 1** Dover, England, United Kingdom; **Day 2** at sea; **Day 3** Copenhagen, Denmark; **Day 4** Oslo, Norway; **Day 5** Kristiansand, Norway; **Day 6** Bergen, Norway; **Day 7** at sea; **Day 8** Dover, England, United Kingdom.
2019 SAIL DATE September 1.

continued on page 442

Mediterranean Ports of Call (*Magic*)

ENGLAND
Dover
English Channel
FRANCE
ATLANTIC OCEAN
SPAIN
Barcelona
PORTUGAL
Lisbon
Cádiz

ITALY
La Spezia,
Pisa
Genoa
Livorno
Cannes,
Villefranche
Marseille,
Toulon
Ajaccio
Civitavecchia
Naples
Salerno
MEDITERRANEAN
SEA

NORTHERN EUROPEAN CRUISES *(continued from page 439)*

• **7-NIGHT NORWEGIAN CRUISE FROM DOVER**

ITINERARY **Day 1** Dover, England, United Kingdom; **Day 2** at sea; **Day 3** Ålesund, Norway; **Day 4** Geiranger, Norway; **Day 5** Olden, Norway; **Day 6** Stavanger, Norway; **Day 7** at sea; **Day 8** Dover, England, United Kingdom.

2019 SAIL DATE August 25.

• **7-NIGHT NORTHERN EUROPEAN CRUISE FROM COPENHAGEN**

ITINERARY **Day 1** Copenhagen, Denmark; **Day 2** at sea; **Day 3** Nynashämn, Sweden; **Day 4** Tallin, Estonia; **Day 5** St. Petersburg, Russia; **Day 6** Helsinki, Finland; **Day 7** at sea; **Day 8** Copenhagen, Denmark.

2019 SAIL DATE August 1.

• **10-NIGHT NORTHERN EUROPEAN CRUISE FROM COPENHAGEN TO DOVER**

ITINERARY **Day 1** Copenhagen, Denmark; **Day 2** at sea; **Day 3** Tallin, Estonia; **Day 4** St. Petersburg, Russian Federation; **Day 5** St. Petersburg, Russian Federation; **Day 6** Helsinki, Finland; **Day 7** Stockholm, Sweden; **Day 8** at sea; **Day 9** Fredericia, Denmark; **Day 10** at sea; **Day 11** Dover, England, United Kingdom.

2019 SAIL DATE August 8.

• **11-NIGHT NORWEGIAN FJORDS AND ICELAND CRUISE FROM DOVER TO COPENHAGEN**

ITINERARY **Day 1** Dover, England, United Kingdom; **Day 2** at sea; **Day 3** Kirkwall, Scotland, United Kingdom; **Day 4** at sea; **Day 5** Reykjavík, Iceland; **Day 6** Reykjavík, Iceland; **Day 7** Akureyri, Iceland; **Day 8** at sea; **Day 9** St. Petersburg, Russian Federation; **Day 10** Stavanger, Norway; **Day 11** Gothenburg, Sweden; **Day 12** Copenhagen, Denmark.

2019 SAIL DATE July 21.

WESTERN EUROPEAN CRUISES *(see map on pages 444–445)*

Disney Magic

• **7-NIGHT NORWEGIAN CRUISE FROM BARCELONA TO DOVER**

ITINERARY **Day 1** Barcelona, Spain; **Day 2** at sea; **Day 3** Cádiz, Spain; **Day 4** Lisbon, Portugal; **Day 5** at sea; **Day 6** Brest, France; **Day 7** Portland, England, United Kingdom; **Day 8** Dover, England, United Kingdom.

2019 SAIL DATE July 14.

PACIFIC COAST CRUISES *(see map on page 446)*

Disney Wonder

• **4-NIGHT PACIFIC COAST CRUISE FROM VANCOUVER TO SAN DIEGO**

ITINERARY **Day 1** Vancouver, British Columbia, Canada; **Day 2** Victoria, British Columbia, Canada; **Day 3** at sea; **Day 4** at sea; **Day 5** San Diego, California.

2019 SAIL DATE September 30.

• **5-NIGHT PACIFIC COAST CRUISE FROM SAN DIEGO TO VANCOUVER**

ITINERARY **Day 1** San Diego, California; **Day 2** at sea; **Day 3** San Francisco, California; **Day 4** at sea; **Day 5** Victoria, British Columbia, Canada; **Day 6** Vancouver, British Columbia, Canada.

2020 SAIL DATE April 24.

PANAMA CANAL CRUISES *(see map on pages 448–449)*

Note: *Please see our Mexico travel advisory on page 323.*

Disney Wonder

• **14-NIGHT WESTBOUND PANAMA CANAL CRUISE FROM PORT CANAVERAL TO SAN DIEGO**

ITINERARY **Day 1** Port Canaveral, Florida; **Day 2** Castaway Cay, Bahamas; **Day 3** at sea; **Day 4** Georgetown, Grand Cayman; **Day 5** at sea; **Day 6** Cartagena, Colombia; **Day 7** at sea; **Day 8** at sea; **Day 9** at sea; **Day 10** at sea; **Day 11** at sea; **Day 12** Puerto Vallarta, Mexico; **Day 13** Cabo San Lucas, Mexico; **Day 14** at sea; **Day 15** San Diego, California.

2019 SAIL DATE February 24.

• **14-NIGHT VERY MERRYTIME EASTBOUND PANAMA CANAL CRUISE FROM SAN DIEGO TO GALVESTON**

ITINERARY **Day 1** San Diego, California; **Day 2** at sea; **Day 3** Cabo San Lucas, Mexico; **Day 4** Puerto Vallarta, Mexico; **Day 5** at sea; **Day 6** at sea; **Day 7** at sea; **Day 8** at sea; **Day 9** Panama Canal, Panama; **Day 10** Cartagena, Colombia; **Day 11** at sea; **Day 12** Grand Cayman, Cayman Islands; **Day 13** Cozumel, Mexico; **Day 14** at sea; **Day 15** Galveston, Texas.

2019 SAIL DATE November 8.

• **14-NIGHT WESTBOUND PANAMA CANAL CRUISE FROM NEW ORLEANS TO SAN DIEGO**

ITINERARY **Day 1** New Orleans, Louisiana; **Day 2** at sea; **Day 3** Cozumel, Mexico; **Day 4** Grand Cayman, Cayman Islands; **Day 5** at sea; **Day 6** Cartagena, Colombia; **Day 7** Panama Canal, Panama; **Day 8** at sea; **Day 9** at sea; **Day 10** at sea; **Day 11** at sea; **Day 12** Puerto Vallarta, Mexico; **Day 13** Cabo San Lucas, Mexico; **Day 14** at sea; **Day 15** San Diego, California.

2020 SAIL DATE March 6.

TRANSATLANTIC CRUISES *(see map on following pages)*

Disney Magic

• **13-NIGHT EASTBOUND TRANSATLANTIC CRUISE FROM MIAMI TO BARCELONA**

ITINERARY **Day 1** Miami, Florida; **Day 2** at sea; **Day 3** at sea; **Day 4** at sea; **Day 5** at sea; **Day 6** at sea; **Day 7** at sea; **Day 8** Ponta Delgada, Azores Islands, Portugal; **Day 9** at sea; **Day 10** Lisbon, Portugal; **Day 11** Cádiz, Spain; **Day 12** Málaga, Spain; **Day 13** Cartagena, Spain; **Day 14** Barcelona, Spain.

2019 SAIL DATE May 12.

continued on page 447

British Isles and Northern European Ports of Call (*Magic*)

Norwegian Sea

North Atlantic Ocean

RUSSIA
NORWAY
SWEDEN
FINLAND
Geiranger
Olden
Helsinki
Gulf of
Finland
St. Petersburg
Oslo
Baltic
Sea
Tallinn
Nynashämn
ESTONIA
Gulf of
Riga
Gothenburg
RUSSIA
Fredericia
DENMARK
Copenhagen
erdam

Pacific Coast Ports of Call *(Wonder)*

TRANSATLANTIC CRUISES *(continued from page 443)*

- **10-NIGHT WESTBOUND TRANSATLANTIC CRUISE FROM DOVER TO NEW YORK**

ITINERARY **Day 1** Dover, England, United Kingdom; **Day 2** Portland, England, United Kingdom; **Day 3** Cork, Ireland; **Day 4** at sea; **Day 5** at sea; **Day 6** at sea; **Day 7** at sea; **Day 8** Sydney, Nova Scotia, Canada; **Day 9** Halifax, Nova Scotia, Canada; **Day 10** at sea; **Day 11** New York, New York.

2019 SAIL DATE September 15.

Panama Canal and Mexican Ports of Call *(Wonder)*

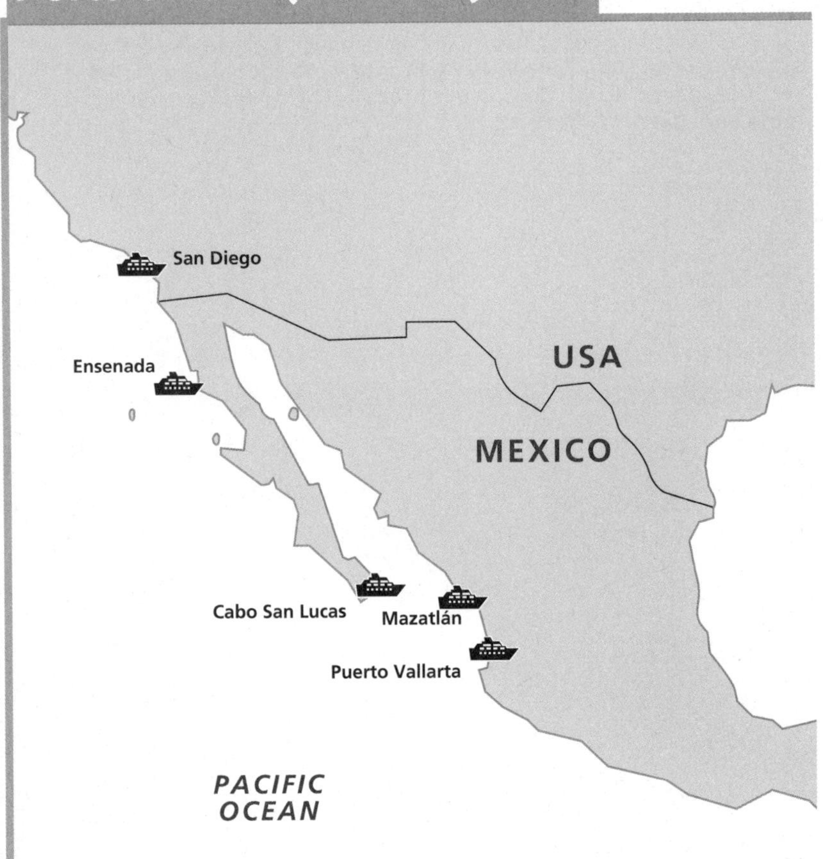

ATLANTIC OCEAN
New Orleans
Port Canaveral
Gulf of Mexico
Miami
Caribbean Sea
Cozumel
Cartagena
PANAMA
Panama Canal
COLOMBIA

Canadian Coastline and Transatlantic Ports of Call (*Magic*)

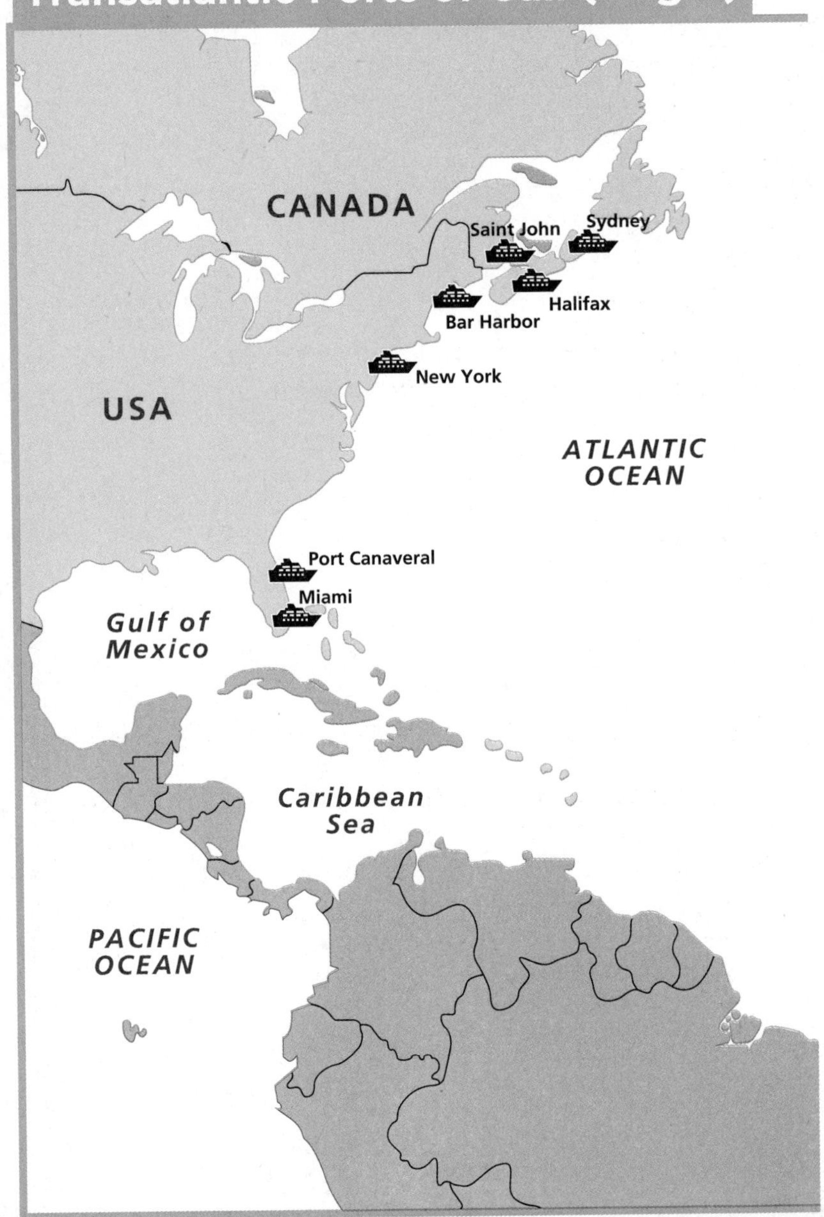

Cork
Dover
Portland
SPAIN
PORTUGAL
Barcelona
Ponta Delgada
Cádiz
Málaga
Cartagena
ATLANTIC
OCEAN

SUBJECT INDEX

The *Disney Dream* at Castaway Cay as seen from a parasail
(Photo: Erin Foster)

The *Disney Wonder* leaves Nassau in the twilight after a day in port.
(Photo: Laurel Stewart)

The *Disney Magic* heads toward the Manhattan Cruise Terminal in New York City.
(Photo: Erin Foster)

The *Dream* is decked out in holiday finery.
(Photo: Erin Foster)

Many Northern European sailings depart fro the charming city of Copenhagen, Denmark.
(Photo: Erin Foster)

the Unofficial Guide®

DISNEY Cruise Line 2019

Erin Foster and Len Testa with Ritchey Halphen